EZEKIEL

1–20

VOLUME 22

THE ANCHOR BIBLE is a fresh approach to the world's greatest classic. Its object is to make the Bible accessible to the modern reader; its method is to arrive at the meaning of biblical literature through exact translation and extended exposition, and to reconstruct the ancient setting of the biblical story, as well as the circumstances of its transcription and the characteristics of its transcribers.

THE ANCHOR BIBLE is a project of international and interfaith scope: Protestant, Catholic, and Jewish scholars from many countries contribute individual volumes. The project is not sponsored by any ecclesiastical organization and is not intended to reflect any particular theological doctrine. Prepared under our joint supervision, THE ANCHOR BIBLE is an effort to make available all the significant historical and linguistic knowledge which bears on the interpretation of the biblical record.

THE ANCHOR BIBLE is aimed at the general reader with no special formal training in biblical studies; yet, it is written with most exacting standards of scholarship, reflecting the highest technical accomplishment.

This project marks the beginning of a new era of cooperation among scholars in biblical research, thus forming a common body of knowledge to be shared by all.

William Foxwell Albright
David Noel Freedman
GENERAL EDITORS

THE ANCHOR BIBLE

Ezekiel
1–20

A NEW TRANSLATION
WITH INTRODUCTION
AND COMMENTARY
BY

Moshe Greenberg

DOUBLEDAY & COMPANY, INC.
GARDEN CITY, NEW YORK
1983

Library of Congress Cataloging in Publication Data

Bible. O.T. Ezekiel I–XX. English.
Greenberg. 1983.
Ezekiel 1–20.

(The Anchor Bible; v. 22)
Bibliography: p. 28.
1. Bible. O.T. Ezekiel I–XX—Commentaries.
I. Greenberg, Moshe. II. Title. III. Series.
BS192.2.A1 1964.G3 vol. 22 [BS1543] 224′.4077
ISBN: 0-385-00954-2
Library of Congress Catalog Card Number 77–12855

Printed in the United States of America
First Edition

To Evelyn

Genesis 2:24

ACKNOWLEDGMENTS

After rendering thanks to God, who has sustained me to this day, and to my parents, who trained me up in the love of Torah, I recall in gratitude the two men who most profoundly shaped my understanding of the task and method of biblical scholarship, and whose example has guided me in the ways of learning.

Yehezkel Kaufmann embodied a passionate commitment to grand ideas, combining the philosopher's power of analysis and generalization with the attention to detail of the philological exegete. His lifework is a demonstration that the study of ancient texts does not necessitate losing contact with the vital currents of the spirit and the intellect. What this work owes to him cannot be documented. Only one who is familiar with Kaufmann's *Toldot,* III, pp. 475–583 (Eng. 426–46), will be able to appreciate how much of his understanding of Ezekiel has been incorporated here.

E. A. Speiser was a master of language—as it appeared in ancient documents awaiting decipherment, as it flowed onto paper calling for parsimony, and as it was marshaled in a lecture spicing learning with wit. His pedagogy tempered rigorous discipline with unstinting consideration for his students, and set a standard for lifelong emulation.

I do not know whether these two men would be happy with my labor, but it gives me joy to acknowledge my sense that what worth it has stems from their teaching.

At the invitation of Chancellor Gerson D. Cohen, of the Jewish Theological Seminary of America, I spent the fall and winter of 1976–77 as scholar-in-residence at the seminary, with no task other than to hammer out the method of this commentary. To assist in the task, he arranged for a weekly seminar composed of selected participants on whom I could try out my ideas. After years of false starts, those months gave birth to the impetus behind the present form of this commentary. I am deeply obliged to Chancellor Cohen for his academic midwifery.

I owe an immeasurable debt to the University of Pennsylvania and, since 1970, to the Hebrew University of Jerusalem for providing me with a congenial academic berth and with colleagues and students whose challenge, stimulus, and curiosity helped keep me from intellectual torpor and complacency.

During the years of wrestling with this work, no person has done as much to sustain my faith in it and ease difficulties that cropped up along the way as the general editor of this series, D. N. Freedman. He provided a precious sounding board for the trial of my ideas; he criticized my writing section by section in a friendly, constructive way. I have incorporated some of his specific suggestions with the rubric "Freedman, privately," but my debt to him goes far beyond that, and I gladly acknowledge it.

CONTENTS

PRINCIPAL ABBREVIATIONS AND SIGNS

AB — Anchor Bible

*ANEP*² — *The Ancient Near East in Pictures,* 2d ed., by J. B. Pritchard, Princeton: Princeton University Press, 1969

*ANET*³ — *Ancient Near Eastern Texts Relating to the Old Testament,* 3d ed., ed. J. B. Pritchard, Princeton: Princeton University Press, 1969. When page numbers are followed by letters a–d, reference is to the top and bottom half of the first (a, b) or second (c, d) column.

BA — The Biblical Archaeologist

BASOR — *Bulletin of the American Schools of Oriental Research*

BDB — F. Brown, S. R. Driver, and C. Briggs, *A Hebrew and English Lexicon of the Old Testament,* Oxford: Clarendon Press, 1907 (corrected impression, 1952)

BHS — *Biblia Hebraica Stuttgartensia,* eds. K. Elliger and W. Rudolph, Stuttgart: Deutsche Bibelstiftung, 1977. See also MT

BKAT — Biblischer Kommentar Altes Testament

B-L — H. Bauer and P. Leander, *Historische Grammatik der hebräischen Sprache,* Halle, 1922 [rpt. Hildesheim: G. Olms, 1962]

BT — Babylonian Talmud

B-Y — E. Ben Yehuda, *A Complete Dictionary of Ancient and Modern Hebrew,* 17 vols., Jerusalem, 1910–59 [rpt. in 8 vols., New York/London: Thomas Yoseloff, 1960]

BZAW — Beihefte zur *ZAW*

CAD — *The Assyrian Dictionary,* The Oriental Institute, the University of Chicago, 1956–

EJ — *Encyclopaedia Judaica,* Jerusalem: Keter, 1971

EM — *Enṣiqlopedia miqra'it* [Encyclopaedia Biblica], Jerusalem: Bialik Institute, 1950–

G — Greek (Septuagint), according to J. Ziegler, ed., *Ezechiel,* Septuaginta . . . auctoritate Societatis Litterarum Göttingensis editum, XVI/I, Göttingen: Vandenhoeck und Ruprecht, 1952

GB — W. Gesenius, *Hebräisches und aramäisches Handwörterbuch über das alte Testament* . . . bearbeitet von F. Buhl, 17th Auflage, Neudruck, Berlin: Springer, 1949

GKC — *Gesenius' Hebrew Grammar,* as edited and enlarged by the late E. Kautzsch, revised . . . by A. E. Cowley, Oxford: Clarendon Press, 1910. Cited by section

GO	*Gottes Offenbarung: Gesammelte Aufsätze,* von W. Zimmerli, Theologische Bücherei 19. München: C. Kaiser, 1969
HAT	Handbuch zum Alten Testament
HSAT	*Die Heilige Schrift des Alten Testaments,* übersetzt von E. Kautzsch, hrsg. von A. Bertholet, 2 Bde., Tübingen: J. C. B. Mohr, 1922
HTR	*Harvard Theological Review*
HUCA	*Hebrew Union College Annual*
IB	The Interpreter's Bible
ICC	International Critical Commentary
IDB	*The Interpreter's Dictionary of the Bible,* 4 vols., New York and Nashville, Tenn.: Abingdon Press, 1962. Cited by entry (s.v.) and author
IDB Suppl.	*The Interpreter's Dictionary of the Bible,* Supplementary Volume (1976)
IEJ	*Israel Exploration Journal*
JANES	*Journal of the Near Eastern Society of Columbia University*
JAOS	*Journal of the American Oriental Society*
JBL	*Journal of Biblical Literature*
JNES	*Journal of Near Eastern Studies*
JPOS	*Journal of the Palestine Oriental Society*
JQR	*Jewish Quarterly Review*
JSS	*Journal of Semitic Studies*
JThS	*Journal of Theological Studies*
K	*K^{e}tib,* "written" consonantal form of a word in MT; contrast Q
KAI	*Kanaanäische und aramäische Inschriften,* von H. Donner und W. Röllig, 3 Bände, Wiesbaden: Harrassowitz, 1964
KAT	Kommentar zum Alten Testament
KB^{3}	L. Koehler und W. Baumgartner, *Hebräisches und aramäisches Lexicon zum alten Testament,* 3te Auflage . . . von W. Baumgartner, 2 Lieferungen, Leiden: E. J. Brill, 1967, 1974
MGWJ	*Monatschrift für Geschichte und Wissenschaft des Judentums*
MT	Masoretic Text, according to *Biblia Hebraica Stuttgartensia,* [fasc.] 9, Liber Ezechiel, K. Elliger praep. Stuttgart: Württembergische Bibelanstalt, 1971
NAB	*The New American Bible,* New York: P. J. Kenedy, 1970
NEB	*The New English Bible,* Oxford and Cambridge, 1970
N(= new)JPS	The new Jewish Publication Society of America translations of the Holy Scriptures: *The Torah,* 2d ed., Philadelphia, 1967; *The Prophets: Nevi'im,* Philadelphia, 1978; *The Writings: Kethubim,* Philadelphia, 1982
O(= old)JPS	*The Holy Scriptures, According to the Masoretic Text: A New Translation,* Philadelphia: The Jewish Publication Society of America, 1917
OTL	Old Testament Library

Q	*Q^{e}re*, "read" form of a word in MT (indicated by the vowel signs and the consonants in the margin); contrast K
RHPR	*Revue d'histoire et de philosophie religieuses*
RSV	*The Holy Bible, Revised Standard Version*, New York: T. Nelson, 1952
S	Syriac, i.e., Peshiṭta, according to S. Lee, *Vetus Testamentum Syriace*, Londoni: Impensis ejusdem societatis, 1823–26
SBANE	*Studies in Bible and the Ancient Near East, Presented to S. E. Loewenstamm.* 2 vols., Y. Avishur and J. Blau, eds., Jerusalem: E. Rubinstein, 1978
SVT	Supplements, Vetus Testamentum
T	Aramaic Targum (Jonathan), according to A. Sperber, ed., *The Bible in Aramaic*, vol. III, Leiden: E. J. Brill, 1962
THAT	*Theologisches Handwörterbuch zum alten Testament*, E. Jenni und C. Westermann, 2 Bände, München/Zürich: C. Kaiser, 1971
ThZ	*Theologische Zeitschrift*
TpJ	Targum pseudo-Jonathan, according to D. Reider, ed., *Targum Jonathan ben Uzziel on the Pentateuch*, Jerusalem: Salomon, 1974
V	Vulgate, as in *Biblia sacra vulgatae editionis* . . . Monachorum Abbatiae Pontificiae Sancti Hieronymi in Urbe, Ordinis Sancti Benedicti, Roma: 1959
VT	*Vetus Testamentum*
ZAW	*Zeitschrift für die alttestamentliche Wissenschaft*

SIGNS

in the translation:

[words]	words not in MT
(words)	words deemed an aside or "footnote"
/words/	words deemed glosses or a variant reading

in the commentary:

||	parallel to
*	an unattested, theoretically (re)constructed form

Introduction

I. The Book of Ezekiel: Its Parts and Arrangement

The Book of Ezekiel is the third large collection of ancient Israel's prophecies, alongside the other "major" (in size) prophetic books of Isaiah and Jeremiah. It is the account of receipt of a long series of oracles by an "I" who is identified in 1:2–3 as the priest, Ezekiel son of Buzi, who began to prophesy in Babylonia in the fifth year of Jehoiachin's exile (593 B.C.E.; for this and all subsequent dates see the next section of the Introduction). Now, since Isaiah is said to have begun in the time of King Uzziah (eighth century) and Jeremiah in the time of King Josiah (seventh century), the present canonical order of these books—Isaiah, Jeremiah, Ezekiel (so in mss. of the Ben-Asher tradition, e.g., Leningrad [*BHS*] and Aleppo, and in most printings)—accords with chronology. However, a tannaitic tradition recorded in the Babylonian Talmud (Baba Batra 14b) arranges the three differently:

> Since the book of Kings ends with doom and the book of Jeremiah is all doom, and the book of Ezekiel begins with doom but ends with consolation, while Isaiah is all consolation, you see that we place doom next to doom and consolation next to consolation.

This order—Jeremiah, Ezekiel, Isaiah—appears in some early Bible mss. (C. D. Ginsburg, *Introduction to a Massoretico-critical Edition of the Hebrew Bible*, 1894 [rpt. New York: Ktav, 1966], p. 5); it is of interest in that its principle is association of topics rather than chronology. As we shall see, this principle operated in some measure in the ordering of the Book of Ezekiel as well.

The tannaitic bipartition of the book into dooms and consolations has served to explain an otherwise enigmatic statement in Josephus (Antiq. 10.5.1 [79]) that Ezekiel "left behind him in writing two books." Since, in fact, the first half of the book (chs. 1–24) consists largely of prophecies of doom, while the last half (chs. 25–48) largely of consolations, it has been suggested that this underlies Josephus' remark (R. Marcus, ad loc., Loeb Classical Library edition). Be that as it may, it is convenient to begin a general review of the contents of the book with this ancient bipartition in mind.

As the following summary shows, all the dated prophecies from the prophet's call in July 593 (1:2f.) to the beginning of the siege of

Jerusalem in January 588 (24:1) are condemnatory; this, too, is the character of the bulk of the undated prophecies in this part of the book.

Chs. 1:1 – 3:21 (July 593), the call and commissioning of the prophet; 3:22 – 5:17, confinement, "dumbness," and symbolic acts representing the siege of Jerusalem and the exile of the population; 6:1 – 7:27, prophecies of doom against the mountains and the inhabitants of the land; 8:1 – 11:25 (Sept. 592), a visionary transportation to Jerusalem to witness the abominations in the temple and God's abandonment of the temple and the city to destruction; 12:1–20, dramatic representation of the exile and the dread of impending ruin; 12:21 – 14:11, denunciations concerning false prophets and prophecy; 14:12–23, an ironic exception, in the case of Jerusalem, to the principle that sinners cannot escape general dooms; ch. 15, the parable of the useless vinestock; ch. 16, the parable of the nymphomaniacal adulteress; ch. 17, the parable of the eagles and the treacherous vine; ch. 18, retort to an epigram impugning God's justice, a call to repentance; ch. 19, a parabolic dirge over the monarchy; ch. 20 (August 591), a compulsory new Exodus; ch. 21, three oracles on the punishing sword; ch. 22, three oracles on Jerusalem the polluted; ch. 23, the parable of the dissolute sisters; 24:1–14 (Jan. 588), the parable of the filthy pot (Jerusalem); 24:15–27, the death of the prophet's wife, a portent.

In chs. 26 – 32 prophecies dated during the siege (winter 588 to summer 586) and in the following twelvemonth (to March 585 [MT]) occur. These belong to a homogeneous section of prophecies (chs. 25 – 32) against the nations surrounding the land of Israel. Ch. 25, brief dooms against four neighbors; 26:1 – 28:26, against Phoenicia: four dooms against Tyre, one against Sidon; 29:1 – 32:32, seven oracles against Egypt.

Ch. 33 comprises a miscellany related to themes in the first part of the book, including notice of the arrival of the fugitive with word of Jerusalem's fall (Jan. 585). Consolatory prophecies and a blueprint for restoration follow.

Ch. 34, renovation of the leadership of Israel; 35:1 – 36:15, denunciation of Edom for encroaching upon God's land, prophecy of renewal of the mountain land of Israel; 36:16–38, renewal of Israel's heart; ch. 37, revival of Israel's dry bones and reunification of its kingdom under a new David; chs. 38 – 39, defeat of the rapacious horde of Gog, to the greater glory of God; chs. 40 – 48, a "messianic priestly code" (Kaufmann, *Religion,* p. 443): 40:1 – 46:24, a visionary tour of the future temple and ordinances of the cult and its personnel; 47:1–12, vision of the life-giving stream issuing from the temple; 47:13 – 48:35, the allocation of the land among the returned tribes and related matters.

The ancients seem to have regarded everything between chs. 25 and 48 as consolations, including the dooms against foreign nations, apparently on the general principle that the prospect of retribution upon Judah's treacherous neighbors was a comfort. While there is an occasional hint of such a concept (25:14; 28:24ff.; 29:6b–7, 16), it is more reasonable to treat these prophecies as a separate division and ascribe their position to the middle ground they occupy between the dooms against Israel culminating in the siege year (to which ch. 24 is dated) and the consolations, starting with ch. 34 after notice of the arrival of the bad news in ch. 33. Chronologically the dooms against the nations straddle these periods; thematically they partake of both doom and consolation.

Having allowed that the traditional bipartition is oversimplified, we proceed to note other irregularities in the grouping of the oracles. The first half of the book is not thematically homogeneous. Beside dooms, it contains calls to repentance (14:6; ch. 18) and some prophecies of restoration (e.g., 16:60–62; 17:22–24), of which 11:14–21 at least is clearly pre-fall. Similarly, condemnations appear in post-fall prophecies (e.g., 34:1–10; 36:31f.). Nor is the block of oracles against foreign nations exhaustive: preceding it, 21:33–37 may be a veiled anti-Babylon oracle; an explicit denunciation of Edom comes later in ch. 35. These "irregularities" are, for the most part, well integrated in their contexts from both a topical and literary viewpoint; nothing but hypercritical expectations of consistency and simplicity in ancient writings underlies the judgment of those critics who treat them as intrusions (see part III of this Introduction). Nor is the chronological order of the dated oracles consistently followed in the face of a countervailing reason. In the interest of gathering all the anti-Egypt oracles together, the latest-dated one (March 585 [MT]) got ahead of the notice of the arrival of the news of Jerusalem's fall (Jan. 585). Similarly, the latest-dated prophecy in the book is found in 29:17ff.—an appendix to an anti-Tyre oracle, substituting Egypt for Tyre as Nebuchadnezzar's prey. It was probably to give the background of this substitution that all the anti-Phoenicia prophecies have been placed ahead of those against Egypt, although the first prophecy against Egypt predates the first against Tyre.

The fact that, despite the chronological framework supplied by the dates, the desire to group similar matter prevailed in the arrangement of the oracles against the nations shows an editorial preference to be guided, in this case, by thematic considerations. Notwithstanding this evidence of editing, alongside the dooms of the first part of the book and the consolations of the last, occasional erratic oracles of another sort appear. This shows that the editor did not hold the view that Ezekiel prophesied in periods of exclusive themes. He was not troubled by an occasional oracle of comfort or hope appearing before the fall, or by words of denunciation insinuating themselves into a post-fall oracle of restoration. He did not share the modern critical allergy to variety in prophetic moods. Whether the original oracles as delivered or first arranged exhibited such a variety must be left moot; the literary integration of these "erratic" pieces in their present contexts shows, at the least, that before the book reached its present form someone (perhaps the prophet himself) saw no impropriety or grotesqueness in depicting a variety of moods not only within one of the periods of the prophet's career but within a single oracle.

Beside the gross thematic division of the book into dooms (chs. 1–24), prophecies against the nations (25 – 32), and consolations (33 – 48), and the general chronological arrangement of the prophecies, other principles of collocation may be seen. Between 12:21 and 14:11 not fewer than four distinct oracles about prophets and prophecy appear, part of one of which (13:1–16) may be much later than the rest. Clearly these have been grouped according to their common subject. Similarly, chs. 15 – 19 all have in common the term, or the fact of their being a, *mašal,* "parable, proverb." The collocation of topically heterogeneous material between the dated oracles has been explained by U. Cassuto by the principle of association of ideas and words (in his *Biblical and Oriental Studies, Vol. I: Bible,* Jerusalem: Magnes Press, 1974, pp. 227–40). While at times he seems to go too far—as when he invokes mere similarity in sound (e.g., *ptwty* || *ypth* in 13:19 and 14:9)—such concatenations as the following sets lend support to his proposal:

5:17 *wḥrb 'by' 'lyk;* 6:3 *mby' 'lykm ḥrb;* 6:12 *wklyty ḥmty bm;* 7:8 *ḥmty . . . wklyty 'py bk;* 7:20–22 temple abominations; chs. 8 – 11 temple abominations; 8:7 *ḥtr-n' bqyr;* 12:3ff. *ḥtr bqyr*

14:8 *whkrty m-;* 14:13 *whkrty m-;* 14:13 *lm'l m'l;* 15:8 *m'lw m'l;* 15:4 *hyṣlh lml'kh;* 16:13 *wtṣlḥy lmlwkh;* 16:8 *w'bw' bbryt;* 16:59 *bzyt 'lh lhpr bryt;* 17:13 *wykrt . . . bryt, wyb' . . . b'lh;* 17:16 *bzh 'ltw . . . hpr brytw*

Cassuto regards such chains as due to editorial juxtaposition; another possibility is that members of such chains belong to oracles that were, in fact, composed in temporal proximity and in the present sequence. At best, however, verbal association is subordinate to the primary principles of grouping by topics and chronological order.

A TABLE OF DATES

TABLE OF DATES IN THE BOOK OF EZEKIEL

Text	*Yr.*	*Mo.*	*Day*	*B.C.E.*[1]	*Occasion or Topic of Prophecy*	*Proximate Events*[2]
1:1	30	4	5	see note 3	heavenly vision	
1:2–3	5	—[4]	5	July 593	vision of divine vehicle and commission	anti-Babylon conclave in Jerusalem; Hananiah's prophecy of Jehoiachin's restoration "in two years"; Zedekiah's mission to Babylon[5]
3:16	a week later			July 593	appointment as lookout	
8:1	6	6	5	Sept. 592	vision of temple abominations	Egypt's Psammetichus II tours Kharu (Palestine-Phoenicia)[6]
20:1	7	5	10	Aug. 591	threat of new Exodus	end of the two-year term set by Hananiah for fulfillment of restoration prophecy[7]
24:1	9	10	10[8]	Jan. 588	beginning of Jerusalem's siege	beginning of Jerusalem's siege (II Kings 25:1)
26:1	11	—[9]	1	March/April 587–586	Tyre's destruction	beginning of Nebuchadnezzar's 13-year siege of Tyre[10]
29:1	10	10	12	Jan. 587	Egypt's destruction	Pharaoh Hophra's unsuccessful effort to relive Jerusalem's siege[11]
29:17	27	1	1	April 571	Tyre's doom amended; Egypt substituted	end of Nebuchadnezzar's siege of Tyre[10]
30:20	11	1	7	April 587	Egypt's destruction	see note 11
31:1	11	3	1	June 587	parable of Pharaoh as a fallen tree	see note 11
32:1	12[12]	12	1	March 585[12]	dirge for Pharaoh and Egypt	
32:17	12	—[13]	15	(March[13]) 585	lament over Pharaoh and his horde	
33:21	12	10	5	Jan. 585	fugitive from Jerusalem brings news of its fall	fall of Jerusalem and deportation of survivors[14]
40:1	25	1/7[15]	10	April/Oct. 573	vision of future temple	

NOTES TO THE TABLE OF DATES

1. The year count in the dates starts from the exile of King Jehoiachin of Judah (1:2; cf. "[year X] of our exile" in 33:21 and 40:1; on the date in 1:1 see note 3), which put an end to the revolt against Babylonian domination begun a few years earlier by his father, King Jehoiakim. II Kings 24:8–17 (more briefly II Chron 36:9f.) reports how Nebuchadnezzar arrived on the scene to receive Jerusalem's surrender and order the deportation of the king with his aristocracy and military elite. The Babylonian then raised to Judah's throne Mattaniah (Jehoiachin's uncle), whom he renamed Zedekiah. These biblical data are seconded by a Babylonian chronicle that assigns them to Nebuchadnezzar's seventh year—spring 598 to spring 597 B.C.E.:

> Year 7, month Kislimu (Nov.–Dec.): The king of Akkad (Nebuchadnezzar) moved his army into Hatti land (Syria-Palestine), laid siege to the city of Judah, and the king took the city on the 2nd day of the month Addaru (16 March 597). He appointed in it a (new) king of his liking, took heavy booty from it and brought it into Babylon (*ANET*³, p. 564).

While the exact date of the city's fall is given, and its conversion into our calendrical terms fairly sure (Parker-Dubberstein, pp. 27f.), that of the deportation is not given (indeed, the deportation is not even mentioned) in the Babylonian source. II Kings 24:12 places it in Nebuchadnezzar's eighth year, which would have set in the following month (Nisan). That seems to be the meaning of II Chron 36:10 dating the transportation to Babylon of Jehoiachin and the booty "at the (re)turn of the year"—that is, the Judahite civil year, which, like the Babylonian regnal one, began in the spring (Exod 12:2; Esther 3:7, "the first month, namely, Nisan"). The era of Jehoiachin's exile thus began in or around Nisan 597 with the deportation; the anniversary of the deportation, Nisan 596, would have begun year 2 of "our exile" and Nisan 593 year 5.

Recent discussions of the resources for and the problems of establishing the chronology of the Book of Ezekiel are: K. S. Freedy and D. B. Redford, "The Dates in Ezekiel in Relation to Biblical, Babylonian and Egyptian Sources," *JAOS* 90 (1970), 462–85; and the two historical syntheses of A. Malamat, "The Last Kings of Judah and the Fall of Jerusalem," *IEJ* 18 (1968), 137–56; "The Twilight of Judah: In the Egyptian-Babylonian Maelstrom," SVT 28 (1975), 123–45 (with a valuable chronological table, pp. 144f.).

2. Such events are listed as are known from biblical or extrabiblical sources to have occurred close to the date in question; they are either reflected in, or may somehow underlie, the oracle of that date. Several more speculative combinations are proposed by Freedy-Redford and Malamat.

3. If this date belongs to the era of "our exile" like all the others, then it is equivalent to July 568, and though it stands at the head of the book it is the latest (the next latest being in 29:17). However, it is commonly taken as an equivalent of the date in vss. 2f., and thus belongs to a different era; see next note and comment to 1:1–3.

4. Understanding the initial "on the fifth of the month" to be a catchword drawn from the end of the date formula of vs. 1 and introducing a gloss on it

—a plausible assumption whatever be the authentic meaning of the date in vs. 1—supply here "the fourth month."

5. These events occurred in Zedekiah's fourth regnal year—Tishri (Sept./Oct.) 594–Elul (Aug./Sept.) 593, for so the data of Jer 27:1, vague ("at the start of the reign") and erroneous ("of Jehoiakim") are specified and corrected in 28:1 (cf. 27:3, 12). On the Tishri-Elul regnal year in Judah, see Freedy-Redford, pp. 464ff. Hananiah's prophecy occurred in the fifth month—Ab (July/Aug.) 593 (Jer 28:1), while Jeremiah was still bearing the yoke he was ordered to display before the emissaries of Judah's neighbors meeting conspiratorially in Jerusalem (28:10; cf. 27:2ff.). Just when in that year the royal mission to Babylon alluded to in Jer 51:59 took place is not known, but its connection with the anti-Babylonian agitation seems likely (M. Greenberg, *JBL* 76 [1957], 304ff.). The significance of the juxtaposition of Ezekiel's call to these events was pointed out by G. Hölscher, *Hesekiel, der Dichter und das Buch,* BZAW 39 (Giessen: A. Töpelmann, 1924), pp. 12–14.

6. This trip was undertaken in the fourth regnal year of Psammetichus II (see the translation of the relevant passage from the Rylands IX papyrus in Freedy-Redford, p. 479)—that is, 592; on this date see Malamat, 1975, p. 141, fn. 40. (The date in Greenberg, cited above, and in Freedy-Redford must be corrected accordingly.) While it is not described as a military campaign, even a nonmilitary assertion of the Egyptian royal presence in territory claimed by Babylonia to be within its orbit was calculated to promote anti-Babylonian forces in Palestine and Phoenicia.

7. The coincidence of this construed "event" with the date of 20:1 was remarked by Malamat, 1975, pp. 138f. Disillusion with Hananiah's sanguine prediction might have improved the credit of Jeremiah's somber one (in his letter to the exiles, Jer 29) that the exile would be long and must therefore be adjusted to. Undue accommodation to exilic exigencies appears to be the issue of ch. 20; see commentary.

8. The expression *bḥdš h'śyry* diverges from all other month-formulas, in which *b* is attached to the ordinal—e.g., *b'śyry* in 29:1—with no intervening *ḥdš*. (Even in 32:1, where *ḥdš* appears in order to set off "the twelfth month" from "the twelfth year," it comes at the end: *bšny 'śr ḥdš*.) The breakup of the revelation formula by insertion of the date formula before *l'mr* is also anomalous. Since a virtually identical date formula appears in II Kings 25:1, it is generally assumed that the Kings formula was copied here. By a fortunate coincidence the date is the same whether one follows the Tishri-Elul regnal year of Kings or the Nisan-Adar year of "our exile" in Ezekiel.

9. G (Alexandrinus) supplies "the first month"—of dubious worth; cf. at 32:17.

10. No exact year is given in our sole source, Josephus (Apion, I.20 [143f.]; Antiq. 10.11.1 [228]); conjectured to have begun after the fall of Jerusalem, i.e., 586–585, the siege ended in 573–572. See H. J. Katzenstein, *The History of Tyre* (Jerusalem: Schocken Institute, 1973), pp. 328, 330.

11. Jer 37:7, 11. The futile Egyptian campaign is reflected again in the oracles dated in 30:20 and 31:1. Malamat, 1968, p. 152, and Freedy-Redford, pp. 470ff., diverge in their efforts to correlate these dates with the unknown time and course of the campaign.

12. This date in MT is out of chronological order in relation to that of

33:21. G (Alexandrinus) reads here "eleventh year" (i.e., 586), according to which—and for the sake of restoring order—some critics emend MT *šty 'śrh* "twelve" to *'šty 'śrh* "eleven" (e.g., Freedy-Redford, p. 468, fn. 30). But this is a dubious measure, since G may well reflect a similar harmonizing motive. Grouping the oracles against Egypt probably caused the overlap.

13. One naturally supplies the missing month from vs. 1, namely, "twelfth," making this oracle two weeks later than its predecessor. G supplies "the first month"—viz. April 586; this date is in proper chronological order with respect to 33:21, and for that reason is preferred by some critics (e.g., Freedy-Redford, p. 468, fn. 31)—again, a dubious ground.

14. II Kings 25:8 = Jer 52:12 place these events in the nineteenth year of Nebuchadnezzar (Nisan 586–Adar 585), which overlaps the eleventh year of Zedekiah (Tishri 587–Elul 586) in the crucial spring and summer. In the fourth month (July) the city fell (Jer 39:2; 52:6f.), and in the fifth the survivors were deported (II Kings 25:8–11). The fugitive arrived, probably with the deportees, in January 585—just under five months later. With this, compare the four months that Ezra's immigrant train took to cover the same distance in the opposite direction (Ezra 7:9).

15. Heb. *r'š hšnh* "the head (beginning) of the year"; G's "the first month" may merely interpret that as an allusion to Nisan, called *r'š ḥdšym* "the head (beginning) of months" in Exod 12:2. Tradition, and some moderns, prefer to connect this formula with Lev 25:9, where the tenth of the seventh month is the beginning of the jubilee year. (This supplies tradition with an ingenious explanation for the thirtieth year of 1:1 and its equivalence to year 5 of Jechoiachin's exile [1:2f.]: for if year 25 of "our exile" was a jubilee year [year 50 of a cycle], then year 5—twenty years earlier—was year 30 of the same jubilee cycle.)

II. The Dates and the Historical Setting

Contemporary and other ancient records, biblical and extrabiblical, tend to corroborate the testimony of the dates in Ezekiel that its contents fall between 593 and 571 B.C.E. Events of those years are reflected in the prophecies, no event after 571 is reflected in them, and any that precedes 593 is clearly past.

By the beginning of the sixth century, Babylonia under Nebuchadnezzar II (605–562) had gained the upper hand over Egypt in the struggle for control of the states of the Mediterranean coast that served as a buffer between them. But the Saitic Pharaohs who succeeded Psammetichus I (d. 610) did not abandon his policy of intervening in west-Asiatic affairs in order to secure Egypt's east flank. Pharaoh Necho (610–595) tried unsuccessfully to shore up the remnant of Assyria, which was collapsing under the attacks of the Babylonians and Medes. Defeated at Carchemish on the Euphrates in 605, he fell back, leaving his former domains and dependents in Syria-Palestine to fend for themselves in the face of the incursions of Nebuchadnezzar in the years 604, 603 and 602 (apparently in order to establish his presence and collect tribute). But Necho was not a negligible quantity. Receiving word (from friends on the coast?) of the advance of a Babylonian army upon Egypt in 601, he met and checked it, inflicting such heavy losses that decades passed before Nebuchadnezzar ventured another campaign against Egypt.

It was probably this setback to Babylonian arms that encouraged King Jehoiakim of Judah—Necho's protégé (II Kings 23:34)—to rebel against Nebuchadnezzar shortly thereafter. The terse notice in II Kings 24:7 that the king of Egypt came forth no more from his land may indicate that hope of Egyptian help had also figured in the rebellion. After sending his vassals—Judah's neighbors—to harass the rebel, Nebuchadnezzar himself arrived in 598 (see note 1 to Table of Dates) in time to receive the surrender of Jerusalem and the entire royal establishment, now headed by King Jehoiachin, the deceased rebel's young son. He appointed Jehoiachin's uncle, Zedekiah, to be king, and imposed on him an oath of loyalty which Josephus aptly summarizes: ". . . that he would keep the kingdom for him, and make no innovation, nor have any league of friendship with the Egyptians" (Antiq. 10.7.1 [102]). (Since Josephus probably had no source other than Ezek 17:13f. and II Chron 36:13, the last clause, which has no biblical correspondent, bespeaks his own political sagacity.)

Under Psammetichus II (595–589) no change occurred in Egypt's

Asiatic policy. Possibly in order to prevent continued restiveness, Nebuchadnezzar appeared in Hatti both in January and in December of 594, first in order to collect tribute, then with his army (Wiseman, *Chronicles,* pp. 72–74). Was it during that time, and to show submission, that Zedekiah went to Babylon in his fourth regnal year? (See note 5 to Table of Dates.) But restiveness continued, and in that year Zedekiah called a conclave of west-Asiatic states in Jerusalem with a view to throwing off the Babylonian yoke—to judge from Jeremiah's symbolic behavior (Jer 27). It is significant of the political basis of Zedekiah's initiative that just at this time evidence exists for military cooperation between Judah and Israel. Psammetichus II won a victory in Nubia in 593 with the help of Judean troops (Letter of Aristeas, 3; Freedy-Redford, p. 476). Following up this victory, Psammetichus organized a triumphal visit to Phoenicia-Palestine in 592, which cannot but have strengthened the hands of the anti-Babylonian forces in that region (W. Helck, *Geschichte des alten Ägypten,* Leiden: E. J. Brill, 1968, p. 254; Freedy-Redford, p. 471). Whether Zedekiah's revolt is to be connected with that visit (Freedy-Redford, p. 480, fn. 100), or only with the accession of Pharaoh Hophra in early 589 (A. Malamat, *The World History of the Jewish People, The Age of the Monarchies,* IV/1 [Jerusalem: Massada, 1981], p. 215), preparations for the revolt, especially the acquisition of chariotry and auxiliaries from Egypt (cf. Ezek 17:15) must have antedated it considerably.

Pharaoh Hophra continued his predecessors' interventionist policy in Asia in the face of the Babylonian response to the revolt. By January 588, Judah, abandoned in the field by its neighbors, had been reduced, and the siege of Jerusalem began. Precisely when Lachish letter 3 was written, in which reference is made to the descent of "commander of the army Coniah ben Elnathan, in order to go to Egypt," is not known, but it is another testimony to the undying hope of Judah for Egyptian help. Hophra did send his army against the Babylonians, but the relief of besieged Jerusalem was ephemeral (see note 11 in Table of Dates). After two and a half years, famine brought the city to its knees; it was razed and again depopulated. The Babylonian-appointed governor, one Gedaliah, was soon assassinated by a Davidide client of Ammon; many remaining survivors then fled to Egypt, where they were stationed in the fortress of Daphne—probably as a border garrison (see note 14 in Table of Dates; Jer 40–43).

Judah gone, Nebuchadnezzar still had to deal with its restive neighbors, who, though they exploited Judah's fall, did not willingly bear the Babylonian yoke. According to Josephus, five years after Jerusalem's fall, in Nebuchadnezzar's twenty-third year (582–581), the Babylonian made yet another campaign in the west, "against Coele-Syria . . . against the Ammonites and the Moabites" (Antiq. 10.9.7 [181]). This was but preliminary to another last effort against Egypt. Josephus there tells of a subsequent successful campaign against Pharaoh Amasis (570–526), but external sources do not back this up. An obscure, fragmentary Babylonian text refers to a campaign against Egypt undertaken by Nebuchadnezzar in his thirty-seventh year (568–567; see *ANET*[3], p. 308d). We know that Amasis was not dethroned, but the very effort shows that to his last years the Babylonian regarded Egypt as a threat to his western flank.

The data in the Book of Ezekiel dovetail with this course of events.

The major concern of Ezekiel's doom prophecies is to convince his audience that their hope of independence and well-being—fanned by prophecies of Ezekiel's rivals—was false. Underpinning this hope was the constant encouragement Egypt gave anti-Babylonian forces throughout this period. A flurry of rebellious activity coincided with the time of Ezekiel's call and commissioning (see note 5 in Table of Dates); a connection between the two seems plausible. The next dated prophecy, depicting the abandonment and destruction of the temple and Jerusalem, approximates Psammetichus II's state visit in Palestine-Phoenicia, a gesture calculated to promote resistance to Babylonia. Ch. 17 denounces Zedekiah's alliance with Egypt. The oracles against foreign nations follow the course of Nebuchadnezzar's campaigns in the west, and the involvement of Egypt, Tyre, and other neighboring states in Judah's fall and subsequent partial dismemberment. The date of the oracle in 29:17—571—is particularly notable, reflecting, on the one hand, the end of the Babylonian siege of Tyre (see note 10 in Table of Dates) and predicting, on the other, an invasion of Egypt (undertaken, in fact, in 568).

Confirmation of the appropriateness of Ezekiel's prophecies to the period and place to which they are ascribed comes from Jeremiah. The description of the mood and expectations of the exiles given in Jer 29—his letter to them—could not better illustrate the setting assumed in Ezekiel's prophecies. Jeremiah's concern is to disabuse the exiles of their hope of a speedy restoration to their homeland; "it is to be long" he says of the exile (vs. 28a). The refusal of the exiles to accept such a message was reinforced by prophets among them who proclaimed to them what they wished to hear (vss. 8f.); Jeremiah denounces them as liars without divine authorization. The deleterious effects of such prophets of comfort are portrayed in almost identical terms in Ezek 13. Jeremiah advises the exiles to settle down in Babylonia, build their families there, and pray to God for forgiveness and the welfare of the country in which they live (vss. 5–7, 12–13). The assimilation to the nations decried by Ezekiel in ch. 20 may reflect a popular acquiescence—misguided and exaggerated in Ezekiel's estimate—in this call for accommodation to exilic circumstances (see note 7 in Table of Dates).

That many of Ezekiel's prophecies failed to materialize is weighty attestation to the time limits of his purview. The dates in the book all fall within the reign of Nebuchadnezzar II, and no subsequent ruler or cosmocrat is foreseen. Ezekiel himself lived to see the failure of his prophecy that Nebuchadnezzar would destroy Tyre and amended it (29:17ff.); but his amendment also proved wrong. Egypt remained independent until the Persian Cambyses conquered it in 525, and then it did not suffer a forty-year desolation and exile, as Ezekiel had predicted in 29:8–12. If 21:36f. is a veiled allusion to Babylon's bloody end, it too failed to materialize, since the political collapse of Babylon was bloodless (539). Persia is mentioned in passing as an auxiliary of Tyre (27:10) and of Gog (38:5); the author of these allusions plainly had no knowledge of the Persia created by Cyrus after unification with Media in 550—the dynamic center of an empire greater than Babylon's. The detailed program of restoration in chs. 34–48 is entirely out of line with events after 538, when Cyrus allowed the exiles to return home. The Davidic kingdom was not reestablished over the combined territories of Israel and Judah; the temple was not built and the Zadokite priests were not installed in it, as prescribed in the blueprints and ordinances of Ezekiel; nor was his sacred calendar and its sacrifices ever put into effect.

Nothing in the book, then, supposes a historical setting later than its latest date; whatever is represented as contemporary agrees precisely with what we know of events during the two decades embraced by its extreme dates—593–571.

The prophet is located in the Babylonian exile, specifically at the Chebar canal (near Nippur) in a town called Tel Abib (3:15). Nonetheless, from early times arguments have been advanced to remove at least part of the prophecies to a Judean setting. Rashi (following the Mechilta and the Targum) combines a theological scruple against the fitness of prophecy on foreign unclean soil with the observation that "the exile is not apparent" in some prophecies (e.g., ch. 17), concluding that not only did Ezekiel begin his career in the land of Israel but that some of the prophecies in his book must belong to the time he still lived there (at 1:2). Modern critical advocates of this view reason that the focus on Jerusalem's doom and the passionate addresses to her—with hardly a message for the exiles—would have been grotesque in a prophet situated hundreds of miles away from the city. Some have been impressed with the apparently intimate familiarity of the prophet with activities in Jerusalem (e.g., in chs. 8 and 11); unwilling to credit him with clairvoyance, these critics simply transfer him there bodily. (These alternatives, however, do not exhaust the possibilities for explaining the facts; they can be accounted for without physical transference. See comment at 11:13 and pp. 201f.)

Advocates of this view must somehow nullify the passages in which the Babylonian locale is explicit or implicit, and these are not few: "I was among the exiles" (1:1); "come, go to the exiles" (3:11); "I came to the exiles" (3:15; cf. vs. 23); visionary transportation from home to Jerusalem and back "to Chaldea" (8:3; 11:24f.); and the era of "our exile" (33:21; 40:1). Ezekiel's audience has been alienated from the land of Israel by the Jerusalemites (11:15); Jerusalemites are "they," over against "you," who are the audience (e.g., 12:11; 14:22f.). The prophets threatened with exclusion from the company of those returning to the soil of Israel (13:9) must be in exile; the same must be true of the persons addressed in 20:34–38. If Ezekiel were in Jerusalem he could hardly "set his face toward it" and "toward the soil of Israel" (21:7f.). Only exiles could be said to have left sons and daughters in Jerusalem (24:21). In the face of such evidence, critics have maintained a Jerusalem locale for Ezekiel either by attributing these passages to an editor or admitting that in these cases, at any rate, a Babylonian situation obtained. What these critics have not succeeded in explaining is why oracles delivered all, or in part, in Jerusalem should ever have been falsely given a Babylonian setting.

Is the reason for positing a Jerusalem setting for the prophecies cogent? We set aside the later theological scruple concerning prophesying on unclean land; it is unknown to the Bible (see below, p. 59). It is true that in most of his dooms Ezekiel appears to have no distinctive message for the exiles; and that he fails to discriminate exiles from homelanders in his blanket epithets "house of Israel" and "rebellious house." But that can be accounted for by the circumstances. We know from Jer 27 – 28 that in the year of Ezekiel's call a conspiracy, initiated by King Zedekiah, was afoot, with a view to rebelling against Nebuchadnezzar—an act that Jeremiah represented as flouting the will and decree of God. Hananiah's prophecy of restoration concurred in the self-estimate of his audience that God was with them, that they were untainted by any deep-dyed guilt. From Jeremiah's letter to the exiles we gather that precisely the same self-estimate and hopes animated the exiles. Jeremiah desired to separate the exiles from the homelanders with regard to their expectations for the immediate future. His call for reconciliation with the fate of exile, together with his predictions of doom for Jerusalem, were designed to wean the exiles from the hopes to which they clung, exactly like their kin in the homeland. The moral position of the exiles, their stance before God, was at that time indistinguishable from that of the homelanders; Jeremiah strove to change their hearts by his letter, but there can be little doubt that he failed.

It must be remembered that the exiles were, surely in the main, from Jerusalem, its royalty and its elite (II Kings 24:14ff.); the fate of the city from which they had been cruelly torn just a few years before was no less their concern than that of its remaining inhabitants. Had Jeremiah lived in Tel Abib, he could have found no topic of more absorbing interest to his compatriots than the future of the city. And his letter to the exiles, no less than his addresses to the homelanders (e.g., ch. 24), indicates that the tenor of his message to them would have been "laments, and moaning, and woe" (Ezek 2:10).

That Ezekiel in exile should be preoccupied with Jerusalem's fate is not astonishing. But what of his appearance of addressing an audience (Jerusalem) hundreds of miles away? Here appearances can mislead. Prophecies against foreign nations—an established prophetic genre—always involve an incongruity between the ostensible audience (the foreign nation, addressed as "you") and the real audience (the Israelites, for whose ears the prophecy is intended, and for whom it bears an important message). In the same way we may suppose that an exiled prophet's address to Jerusalem would really have been aimed at the ears of his proximate audience. In Ezekiel's case, little contrast would be felt between the ostensible and the real audience, since the hearers of the prophet were, in fact, Jerusalemites who identified themselves with their fellow citizens in the homeland in every way. If there is any anomaly in Ezekiel's addressing Jerusalem from the exile, it is no greater than the anomalous contemporaneity of two Jerusalemite communities hundreds of miles apart at this juncture of history.

Further, detailed treatment of Ezekiel's message and its relation to the situation of the exiles will appear in the Introduction to the second volume of this commentary.

We conclude that the dates of the book are in line with the contents of its oracles; that nothing in the book requires transgressing its explicit chronological boundaries—though, to be sure, there are violations of chronological order, and a likelihood that other principles (such as topical grouping and association of ideas) operated in the collocation of the material. The speculation that some part of the book was originally located in Jerusalem has little to commend it; it cannot account for the present attribution of the oracles to the Babylonian exile setting.

It now remains to discuss the method of this commentary, describing its parts and the policy that guided the writing of each of them.

III. The Method of This Commentary: Holistic Interpretation

A translation of and commentary on a biblical text should bridge the gap that separates the present-day reader—with his culture and tradition-bound range of knowledge, assumptions, and conventions—from the ancient Israelite, who encountered the text with different knowledge, assumptions, and conventions conditioned by his circumstances. There is no direct way of ascertaining how the ancient Israelite was informed, but since biblical literature in general, and prophecy in particular, aimed at edifying the people, there is every reason to assert that it was composed in accord with the understanding of the people. Idioms, figures, and forms of expression and composition familiar to his audience must be reflected in, must indeed have determined, the formulation of a biblical author's creations. Knowledge of these elements of communication, never articulated in antiquity but implicitly shared by author and audience, has now to be gathered from the texts themselves. It is a precondition for a correct translation and a proper commentary.

The linguistic gap between the ancient Israelite and the modern reader is obvious and suffices to justify and, to a large extent, define the task of translation. Present-day ignorance of ancient persons, places, and things likewise defines an aspect of the work of a commentator. Less obvious, and less understood, is the gap in assumptions and conventions governing audience expectations that separates the modern man from the ancient Israelite. Even a cursory perusal of modern scholarly Bible commentaries will attest to this gap in the amount of rewriting, reshaping, and reordering of text that every commentator feels is necessary for bringing the biblical writing up to his standards. Since this commentary on Ezekiel takes a different tack, it is fitting here to describe and account for the difference.

Modern scholarly commentaries on Ezekiel all take it as their primary task to reconstitute the closest approximation to the very words of the prophet. Identifying the authentic oracles is fundamental and precedes, in time and importance, every other operation. Their translations (where they do not simply adopt a church version) reflect not only text-critical but historical decisions regarding what is authentic; their interpretation of any given passage depends not only on how they reconstruct it but on systematic alteration or elimination of related passages throughout the book. For example, the interpretation of a given oracle of doom that ends with a reference to future restoration is much altered if the end is considered inauthentic—an opinion usually bolstered by the systematic deletion of all restoration elements from other doom prophecies. Now this priority seems legitimate. Must not a Homer scholar sift the mss. and early editions to determine the best readings—those most likely to represent the lost original? What point is there in commenting upon a text whose authenticity has not been established?

Yet the case of Ezekiel, like that of most of Hebrew Scriptures, is fundamentally different. For Homer, many Greek manuscripts and fragments with variant readings are extant, among which scholars must decide. For Ezekiel there is but one complete text, the so-called Masoretic Text [MT], whose consonantal form has come down to us since about the second century C.E. in a single standardized edition—with hundreds of trivial differences in mss. and fragments, reflecting human inability to copy infallibly, but also perhaps some stubborn relics of pre-standard texts. Since the Ezekiel scroll found at Qumran cannot be opened (see W. H. Brownlee, *Revue de Qumran* 4 [1963], 11–28), we have no record of Ezekiel's oracles in Hebrew—the language in which they were certainly delivered—nearer than eight centuries removed from the time when the prophet lived. There is the highest probability that during these centuries changes, inadvertent and deliberate, occurred in the transmission of these oracles by the prophet and by transcribers and later copyists; we thus can hardly suppose that the standard text represents a verbatim record of what Ezekiel published to his audience of exiles. But the received Hebrew is the only Hebrew version of his words extant; it must ultimately go back to him and therefore must serve as the main—often the sole—primary source for the study of his message—until proved unreliable by anachronism (linguistic, historical, or ideational), or indubitable corruption, or intolerable variations in style or texture. But here we reach the slippery ground of assumptions and conventions on which so much biblical scholarship has come to grief.

Have we no resources for getting behind the standard text? It would seem that we do, in the translations from Hebrew that were made either before the standard swept the field—namely, the Greek, from the last centuries B.C.E., or at about the time of its promulgation or shortly thereafter, and thus perhaps showing nonstandard readings—namely, the Vulgate, the Syriac, and the Aramaic Targum. Divergences in these translations from MT must always raise the possibility of a different *Vorlage* (the text in the original language that lay before the translators), and thus serve as the poor man's equivalent of divergent Hebrew mss., giving biblicists a taste of what a classicist faces in his divergent Greek and Latin mss. But it is a misleading taste for the following reasons:

1. The texts of the translations are not finally established; this is particularly unfortunate in cases where only some of their extant copies show divergence from MT while others do not.

2. The task of retroverting the translation to a possibly divergent *Vorlage* is full of pitfalls. The habits of a given translator must be ascertained more thoroughly and systematically than has been done for any book of the Bible. In particular, the measure of his literality must be taken in order to evaluate properly any divergence from MT. Devices to measure literality are just being developed, and their application to Ezekiel is still in the future. (See E. Tov, "Septuagint: Contribution to OT Scholarship," *IDB Suppl.*, pp. 807–11; *The Text-critical Use of the Septuagint in Biblical Research,* Jerusalem Biblical Studies, 3 [Jerusalem: Simor, 1981]; on literality, see esp. J. Barr, *The Typology of Literalism in Ancient Biblical Translations,* Mitteilungen des Septuaginta Unternehmens, XV [Göttingen: Vandenhoeck und Reprecht, 1979].)

3. Even if a given retroversion appears highly probable, and thus establishes a good probability of a variant Hebrew reading, its evaluation is a separate task. For one thing, it may not be subject to evaluation in isolation; a pattern of divergences may appear in a given passage, affecting judgment of any single divergence (see the example in my SVT article). But in judging patterns of divergence, the habits and style of Ezekiel are at issue, and we have moved from "simple" text-criticism to the study of style and literary conventions, where other criteria come into play.

Once again we are thrown back on MT, with all its dubiousness, as the least shaky foundation for the study of the prophecy of Ezekiel. Now we must address the literary and ideational criteria by which scholars have impugned the authenticity of large tracts of the book.

In judging questions of composition and style, the unexamined assumptions and conventions of modernity have deeply affected scholars. Hölscher, *Hesekiel,* operated with the romantic prejudice that the authentic prophecies of Ezekiel were poetic, thus denying the prophet most of the book that goes by his name. W. Irwin (*The Problem of Ezekiel* [Chicago: University of Chicago Press, 1943]) held the prophet to a kind of logic that broke down in Irwin's analysis of ch. 15, thus providing a clue for isolating the original prophecy from later accretions. A universal prejudice of modern biblical criticism is the assumption of original simplicity. A passage of complex structure, or one containing repetition, or skewing a previously used figure is, on these grounds, suspect of being inauthentic. Another widespread prejudice equates authenticity with topical or thematic uniformity. A temporal vista that progresses from present, to penultimate, to ultimate time is considered an artificial result of successive additions to a single-time original oracle. Doom oracles that end with a glimpse of a better future are declared composites on the ground of psychological improbability. Such prejudices are simply a prioris, an array of unproved (and unprovable) modern assumptions and conventions that confirm themselves through the results obtained by forcing them on the text and altering, reducing, and reordering it accordingly. (A good survey of the range of modern scholarly opinion on the extent of inauthentic material in Ezekiel, from "conservative" [e.g., Fohrer, who discounts about one third of the verses of the book] to "radical" [e.g., Hölscher, who discounts about nine tenths], is found in B. Lang, *Ezechiel,* pp. 2–18. Identical criteria have been used in general literary criticism of ancient narrative—what T. Todorov calls the "laws" of the "esthetic of primitive narrative," which he lists and rejects out of hand; see his *The Poetics of Prose,* trans. R. Howard [Ithaca: Cornell University Press, 1977], pp. 53–55.)

There is only one way that gives any hope of eliciting the innate conventions and literary formations of a piece of ancient literature, and that is by listening to it patiently and humbly. The critic must curb all temptations to impose his antecedent judgments on the text; he must immerse himself in it again and again, with all his sensors alert to catch every possible stimulus—mental-ideational, aural, aesthetic, linguistic, visual—until its features begin to stand out and their native shape and patterning emerge. If such features are seen to pervade poetry and prose alike, then the a priori separation of the two is rash. If they appear only when doom and restoration are combined in a whole, to lop off the latter will seem unjustified. If skewing of figures not only recurs but constitutes a dominant pattern of oracles, its authenticity will be hard to impugn. If repetition of a special kind can be shown to be a structural principle of a given piece, its elimination on the basis of versional minuses will appear unpersuasive.

How this conception of the task of the commentator has been embodied in the present work will now be described.

The book has been divided into sections according to its own highly formalized openings and closings. These often disagree with the chapter division; e.g., § VII = 8:1 – 11:25, while ch. 12 = §§ VIII, IX, and X. Each section is subjected to four operations: translation; textual annotation; comment clarifying questions of lexicon, grammar, relation to immediate context, parallels; and, finally, discussion of its structure and themes.

The translation aims at maximum fidelity to the received Hebrew (MT). To the grounds given above for making MT the foundation of the commentary may now be added another: no reader of the Hebrew can fail to observe how greatly the wording of the oracles is governed by internal associations among the parts, and between one oracle and another; and, further, how many and how significant for interpretation are the evocations of traditional Israelite and contemporary literature (e.g., Jeremiah). This profusion of verbal signifiers cannot survive translation; indeed, the ancient versions do not preserve key words (see in the description of the comments)—often derivatives of the same root that in translation lose their similarity—or reflect the many echoes of passages outside the book. Moreover, they are inconsistent in rendering a given word (thus effacing connections present in the Hebrew), and at times render literally, at times paraphrase. The literary riches of MT are distinctly superior to the possible alternative readings suggested from time to time in the versions; effort has therefore been focused on describing and interpreting them.

Fidelity to MT means a sacrifice in elegance (e.g., repetition of terms where English prefers variation). Grammatical consistency and propriety are at times violated—as when an address vacillates between second- and third-person addressees, or syntactically faulty Hebrew is put into similar English. Where MT appears unsound, reference to the textual notes appears, yet an effort is made to construe MT (explained in the comments). Fidelity has been abandoned a few times where adding a word, transposing a phrase, or paraphrasing would avoid stilted language or promote clarity without obliterating some value of the Hebrew. Though the translation approaches a "one-to-one" rendering, the nuances of single words or elements are not ignored (e.g., the meanings of the connective *waw* cannot be conveyed by "and" repeating itself ad nauseam). Conflation—the incorporation of alternative readings—is indicated by slashes, asides or "footnotes" by parentheses. Square brackets indicate a word supplied for understanding.

MT contains several auxiliaries to interpretation. Its vocalization has been followed regularly; the accentuation (*ṭeʿamim*) within the verse—joining and disjoining words and phrases—has been more honored than the verse division since the English notion of a sentence diverges more from the Hebrew verse than its phrasing does from that of Hebrew. The element of MT least respected in our translation is its paragraphing (*parašiyyot*). We paragraph more liberally, but beyond that MT's paragraphing reflects a different conception of the function of a break in a speech sequence—one that is not always clear to us.

Textual notes follow the translation. These offer variant readings from the Greek, Syriac, Vulgate, Targum, medieval Hebrew mss., and early printings. The basis of annotation is some difficulty or disorder in MT that the versional reading illuminates: it may offer a basis for conjecturing a reading in which the difficulty in MT is obviated; it may offer a stimulus to further inquiry, leading to a better understanding of the Hebrew. On rare occasions a conjectural emendation of MT appears without versional basis. All the textual notes are explained in the following department of the commentary, called Comment.

Where MT offers no difficulty, divergences from it in the ancient versions are not, as a rule, recorded—even where some critics have pronounced the divergence superior. There are thousands of such divergences, many quite substantial, and numerous factors must be weighed in assessing them. To name a few: some divergences derive from translator's exigency (i.e., requirements of the language into which the translation is made, or its literary canons); some from his technique or his license; some from changes that occurred in the transmission of the version; some from a divergent *Vorlage*. To sort out which of these factors is present in a given case is not simple; when it appears due to a divergent *Vorlage,* to correctly retrovert the underlying Hebrew is, as was pointed out earlier, a delicate and uncertain operation. Further to decide, after one has retroverted a *Vorlage,* between it and MT is yet another formidable task. Our present state of knowledge and art in these tasks is very imperfect, with opinion and whim dominating decisions in the absence of a body of systematically developed knowledge. The true measure of the complexity and difficulty of deciding such matters is obscured by the simplified apparatus of *BHS;* it can be glimpsed in *The Hebrew University Bible: The Book of Isaiah,* Parts I–II, edited by M. Goshen-Gottstein (Jerusalem: Magnes Press, 1975)—for the theoretical basis of which see his exposition in *The Book of Isaiah—Sample Edition with Introduction* (Jerusalem: Magnes Press, 1965). Hence the textual notes of this commentary are restricted to such as throw direct light on the constitution and meaning of MT, more often than not by stimulating inquiry into it (see the description of the comments). Little or no attention is paid to possible alternative text forms that may lurk in this or that versional alternative to a perfectly sound and intelligible MT.

The section called Comment follows. It consists of comments both retrospective—in that they explain the translation and the textual notes—and prospective, in that they prepare the reader for the final stage of inquiry, titled Structure and Themes.

For aid in solving the lexical and grammatical problems of translation, every modern Bible commentary resorts to the standard helps—BDB, GB, GKC, and so forth—yet their resources have sometimes been neglected; *waw* serving as a relative or a conjunction is recorded in these works, but it has not been utilized in explaining, e.g., 12:25 or 13:11; similarly, a documented use of the infinitive has not saved *lqls* in 16:31 from violence. The effort to exhaust the already documented usages of biblical Hebrew, as well as to identify hitherto unrecognized ones, accounts for the greater conservation of MT in this translation.

But biblical Hebrew is a limited resource, and the Book of Ezekiel contains many hapax legomena and unusual formations; commentators have therefore always stepped into adjacent fields for aid. Following the lead of medieval commentators, we have laid the lexicon of early postbiblical Hebrew under contribution when it can be argued that a given expression continued in living use, not merely as a biblical citation; see, e.g., comments to *ḥyṣ* (13:10), *mspḥt* (13:18), and *msrt* (20:37). Comparative Semitic evidence (from Akkadian, Ugaritic, Phoenician, Syriac, etc.) has been adduced only for defining or illustrating an otherwise unknown or rare idiom (e.g., *nḥšṭk* 16:36; *qpdh* 7:24), never merely to supply a parallel for an otherwise clear expression, as though a Bible commentary were an anthology of ancient Near East parallels.

For the thought and the connection of sentences, extensive use has been made of premodern commentators to the Hebrew—such as are found in rabbinic Bibles (*Mikra'ot Gedolot*), namely, Rashi, Kimḥi, Joseph Kara, and such as are not, namely Eliezer of Beaugency, Menahem bar Shim'on of Posquières, Moshe ben Sheshet, Isaac Abarbanel, as well as the early modern S. D. Luzzatto. As manifestly utilizing the Hebrew, Calvin's commentary on Ezekiel—extant only to ch. 20—has also been consulted. One is impressed with the modesty of advances made since their time in linguistic matters and contextual interpretation, compared to the gravity of the losses sustained by modern commentators in these areas as a result of ignoring medieval scholarship. For obscure passages medieval commentators have been cited, even when admittedly unconvincing, because of their suggestiveness; a reader might be stimulated to a new insight through them (e.g., Abarbanel on 9:4; Kara on 20:39). The debt I owe to modern critical Ezekiel scholarship, for guidance and insight as well as for provocation, is attested on every page of the commentary—and not only where named citations occur. Cornill's text-criticism, the important commentaries of Smend, Herrmann, Cooke, and Zimmerli, and the useful and stimulating works of Fohrer, Eichrodt, and Wevers have been my constant study. Many comments incorporate their wisdom; many others are implicit reactions and responses to positions taken by one or more of them.

The versions are frequently cited in the comments more than in the textual notes. Their divergence from MT is utilized for focusing attention on the peculiarities of MT (e.g., the simplified reading of the versions at 18:2 invites study of the unusual idiom of the longer received Hebrew). Where the versions seem to improve on MT, investigation may lead to a better understanding of Hebrew idiom generally or that of Ezekiel in particular (see, e.g., at 7:2). While our results indicate that MT deserves far more credit than modern critics have tended to give it, its soundness cannot always be maintained; versional evidence and good judgment indicate that passages in it have been corrupted (e.g., 16:32), conflated (e.g., 1:3, 8), glossed (e.g., 12:13b), and misplaced (e.g., 17:13b). Yet our policy of translating MT necessitates explaining it even where our express preference is for a versional reading (e.g., 16:32, 53). Such regard for MT will appear to some, perhaps to many, undue, but it arises from observing how many critical judgments of predecessors have been overthrown by new or reactivated knowledge.

The comments also call attention to literary aspects of the text. This serves two purposes: to help create awareness and appreciation of the art and distinctive style of these prophecies; and, through that, to assist judgment of what is and is not authentic in them. There are many, and many types of, repetition in the book; the comments point them out and seek their significance (e.g., at 3:5f.; 11:17; 20:22). "Genius with words is often a matter of being original with the minimum of alteration" (T. S. Eliot, quoted in L. Michaels and C. Ricks, eds., *The State of the Language*

[Berkeley: University of California Press, 1980], p. 63); Ezekiel's renovation of clichés and realization of stereotypical figures belong to that sort of genius and are described in comments to, e.g., 2:4; 6:13; 7:2. The intrusion of the referent is a feature of allegorical passages, noted at 16:39f. and 17:9. The Aramaisms of the book and its late language are pointed out (e.g., *lqym* 13:6; *hṭ'w* 13:10); these are clues for dating and justify the appeal to postbiblical Hebrew for linguistic illustrations.

The connections of Ezekiel with other biblical writings is a regular concern of all commentaries to the book; its usual aim is the determination of the genetic-historic relation of this book to others—a topic to be treated in the Introduction to the second volume of this commentary. Beside remarking such connections, the comments endeavor to describe the peculiar adaptation of the common element to its context in Ezekiel—the concretization of the razor figure of Isa 7:20 in Ezek 5:1f.; the exaltation of the sabbath in the citation of Exod 31:13 in Ezek 20:12.

Finally, the comments take note of inconsequence, inconsistency, skewing, and other sources of tension within the piece as preparation for the discussion in the following section, Structure and Themes.

The comments aim at exhibiting the reasoning behind all decisions, the operation of the critical faculty. Where decision is difficult, alternatives are weighed (e.g., at 3:19; 17:5); sometimes a position is adduced without comment, signifying that I regard it as noteworthy but inconclusive (e.g., at 10:12, 14). Irremediably obscure passages, conjectures, and guesses are identified as such (e.g., 13:20; 19:2, 10; 20:39).

The final section of commentary on each literary unit is devoted to the general topics of its Structure and Themes. As a rule, what pertains to structure precedes the treatment of themes, but it has proven impracticable to separate the two absolutely. The discussion of structure reviews all the formal characteristics of the piece, its opening and closing formulas, its articulation—looking for design and for integrating elements. Are there expressions or figures that run through the piece, compacting its parts together? (see, e.g., 1:28–3:15; 12:17–28.) Are there distinctive homogeneous linguistic or poetic textures (chs. 7, 16)? Large patterns emerge, and as they recur they serve to determine the conventions of composition in this book. The most important of these are the "halving" pattern and repetition. The "halving" pattern consists of the following: a theme, A, is propounded in the first, usually longest, part of an oracle; it is followed by a second theme, B, which is somehow related to the first theme (by skewing or development of an aspect of it); B characteristically ends, or is followed by a coda, with elements of A and B intermingled. (A Berkeley student, Roy Gane, suggested partial comparisons with the rounded binary and sonata forms in musical composition; indeed the express comparison of Ezekiel's delivery of his oracles to song accompanied by instrument [in 33:32] virtually invites musical analogies.) This pattern appears clearly as the organizing principle in the oracles of chs. 6,

7, 13, 16, 18, and 20, and is discussed there. Since much matter judged inauthentic by critics is organized and integrated in this pattern, the strength of the ideational and psychological arguments for this judgment ought to be reconsidered.

Repetition with variation features prominently in the book; variety is an irreducible concomitant of Ezekiel's repetition and pleads against the critical tendency to assimilate repeated elements to each other. Parade examples of the style of repetition in Ezekiel are found in chs. 14 and 18.

Other structural features are the "afterwave" effect in oracle-closure (see, e.g., chs. 6 and 15) and graduated utterances of several kinds, including perception in stages (ch. 1), spiraling (i.e., return to stage one on a higher plane, ch. 17), and progress in passionateness (ch. 18).

The synthesis of the main theme(s) of the oracle entails comparison and contrast with other related formulations in the book. Thus, a proper view of the remnant theme in ch. 6 requires surveying its changes as it recurs further on; the stages of the prophet's withdrawal from public activity is a recurrent topic in chs. 3–4 and 6. When a theme is reused or recombined in a new context, it is necessary to ask whether significant changes, suitable to the new context, have been introduced, so that one cannot speak simply of "doublets" (e.g., repentance in 3:16–21; 18; 33:1–20). Such discrimination is even more necessary in discussing the reuse of themes in Ezekiel that have close connections with passages in other prophets (e.g., the marital metaphor; the depraved sisters—in chs. 16 and 23). Only by close examination of differences, not only of resemblances, can the ground be prepared for an eventual decision respecting the genetic relation of Ezekiel's themes to those of the Pentateuch (see, e.g., chs. 4–5; 20).

Criteria for determining the integrity of complex oracles are discussed in connection with themes: the juncture of dooms and prophecies of restoration (chs. 16; 17); post-event prophecy (ch. 12); simplicity as a sign of originality (ch. 12). Signs of artificial combination of disparate matter are discerned in oracles of chs. 8–11 and 13.

The possibility that thematic links among oracles determined their juxtaposition is suggested in the discussion of, e.g., ch. 6 and its connection with 4–5; ch. 19 and its connection with 17, 18.

The various operations undertaken in this commentary test the working assumption that the present Book of Ezekiel is the product of art and intelligent design. Results so far obtained tend to indicate that details of this art and immanent patterning revelatory of this design disclose themselves to the patient and receptive reader who divests himself of preconceptions regarding what an ancient prophet should have said and how he should have said it. A consistent trend of thought expressed in a distinctive style has emerged, giving the impression of an individual mind of powerful and passionate proclivities. The chronology of the oracles and the historical circumstances reflected in them assign them to a narrow temporal range well within the span of a single life. The persuasion grows on one as piece after piece falls into the established patterns and ideas that a coherent world of vision is emerging, contemporary with the sixth-century prophet and decisively shaped by him, if not the very words of Ezekiel himself.

(Further theoretical observations and arguments for the approach taken here to biblical interpretation are found in the introduction to my article "The Vision of Jerusalem in Ezekiel 8–11: A Holistic Interpretation," in J. L. Crenshaw and S. Sandmel, eds., *The Divine Helmsman: Studies on God's Control of Human Events, Presented to Lou H. Silberman* [New York: Ktav, 1980], pp. 146ff.)

BIBLIOGRAPHY

Commentaries and Other Works Cited by Author
or by Author and Short Title

Abarbanel, Don Isaac. *Peruš ʿal neviʾim ʾaḥaronim.* Jerusalem: Torah va-Daʿat, 1957.

Albright, W. F. "The Seal of Eliakim and the Latest Preëxilic History of Judah, with Some Observations on Ezekiel." *JBL* 51 (1932), 77–106.

Avishur, Y. *The Construct State of Synonyms in Biblical Rhetoric* [Hebrew]. Jerusalem: Kiryat Sepher, 1977.

Bar Hebraeus, Gregorius Abulfaragius. *Die Scholien des . . . zum Buche Ezechiel,* hrsg. R. Gugenheimer. Berlin: H. Itzkowski, 1894.

Bergsträsser, G. *Hebräische Grammatik* (W. Gesenius' Heb. gram. 29 Auflage) I–II. Leipzig: F. C. W. Vogel, 1918–29.

Bewer, J. "The Text of Ezekiel 1:1–3." *American Journal of Semitic Languages and Literatures* 50 (1933–34), 96–101.

———. "Textual and Exegetical Notes on the Book of Ezekiel." *JBL* 72 (1953), 158–68.

Blau, J. "Zum angeblichen Gebrauch von *'t* vor dem Nominativ." *VT* 4 (1954), 7–19.

Brin, G. *Studies in the Book of Ezekiel* [Hebrew]. Haifa: Hakibutz Hameuhad, 1975.

Brockelmann, C. *Lexicon Syriacum,* 2d ed. Halle: M. Niemeyer, 1928.

———. *Hebräische Syntax.* Neukirchen, Kreis Moers: Verlag der Buchhandlung des Erziehungsvereins, 1956.

Brownlee, W. H. "The Scroll of Ezekiel from the Eleventh Qumran Cave." *Revue de Qumran* 4 (1963), 11–28.

Buber, M. "Zu Jecheskel 3:12." *MGWJ* 78 (1934), 471–74.

Calvin, John. *Commentaries on the First Twenty Chapters of the Book of the Prophet Ezekiel,* trans. T. Myers. Grand Rapids, Mich.: Wm. B. Eerdmans, 1948.

Caquot, A. "Le Messianisme d'Ézéchiel." *Semitica* 14 (1964), 13–23.

Carley, K. W. *The Book of the Prophet Ezekiel.* The Cambridge Bible Commentary. Cambridge: Cambridge University Press, 1974.

Casanowicz, I. *Paronomasia in the Old Testament.* Boston: Norwood Press, 1894.

Cassuto, U. "The Arrangement of the Book of Ezekiel." In *Biblical and Oriental Studies, Vol. I: Bible.* Jerusalem: Magnes Press, 1974, pp. 227–40.

Cogan, M. *Imperialism and Religion: Assyria, Judah and Israel in the Eighth and Seventh Centuries B.C.E.* Missoula, Mont.: Scholars Press, 1974.

Cooke, G. A. *The Book of Ezekiel.* International Critical Commentary. 2 vols. New York: Scribners, 1937.

Cornill, C. H. *Das Buch des Propheten Ezechiel.* Leipzig: J. C. Hinrichs, 1886.

Dahood, M. "Ezekiel 19, 10 and Relative kî." *Biblica* 56 (1975), 96–99.

Dalman, G. *Arbeit und Sitte in Palästina.* 7 Bände. Gütersloh: Bertelsmann, 1928 (rpt. Hildesheim: Georg Olms, 1964); abbreviated *AuS.*

Davidson, A. B., and A. W. Streane. *Ezekiel.* The Cambridge Bible for Schools and Colleges. Cambridge: Cambridge University Press, 1916.

Driver, G. R. "Difficult Words in the Hebrew Prophets." In *Studies in Old Testament Prophecy, Presented to . . . T. H. Robinson,* ed. H. H. Rowley. Edinburgh: T. & T. Clark, 1950, pp. 52–72.

———. "Ezekiel's Inaugural Vision." *VT* 1 (1951), 60–62.

———. "Ezechiel: Linguistic and Textual Problems." *Biblica* 35 (1954), 145–59, 299–312.

Driver, S. R. *A Treatise on the Use of the Tenses in Hebrew.* 3d ed. Oxford: Clarendon Press, 1892.

Ehrlich, A. B. *Randglossen zur hebräischen Bibel,* 7 vols. Leipzig: J. C. Hinrichs, 1908–14; reference by name only to ad loc. comments in vol. 5. [Hebrew] refers to ad loc. comments in *Mikra ki-Pheschuto* III, Berlin: M. Poppelauer, 1901.

Eichrodt, W. "Der Sabbat bei Hesekiel." In *Lex tua veritas. Festschrift für H. Junker,* ed. H. Gross et al. Trier: Paulinus Verlag, 1961, pp. 65–74.

———. *Ezekiel,* trans. C. Quinn. Old Testament Library. Philadelphia: Westminster Press, 1970.

Eissfeldt, O. "Ezechiel als Zeuge für Sanherib's Eingriff in Palästina." *Palästina-Jahrbuch* 27 (1931), 58–66 (= *Kleine Schriften* I [Tübingen: J. C. B. Mohr, 1962], pp. 239–46).

———. "Hesekiel Kap. 16 als Geschichtsquelle." *JPOS* 16 (1939), 286–92 (= *Kleine Schriften* II [Tübingen: J. C. B. Mohr, 1963], pp. 101–6).

Eliezer of Beaugency. *Kommentar zu Ezechiel und den XII kleinen Propheten von Eliezer aus Beaugency . . . ,* hrsg. S. Poznański. Lief. I: *Ezechiel.* Warschau: Mekize Nirdamim, 1909.

Field, F. *Origenis hexaplorum quae supersunt . . .* 2 vols. Oxford, 1875; rpt. Hildesheim: Olms, 1964.

Fohrer, G. *Ezechiel,* mit einem Beitrag von K. Galling. HAT 13. Tübingen: J. C. B. Mohr, 1955.

Freedy, K. S., and D. B. Redford. "The Dates in Ezekiel in Relation to Biblical, Babylonian and Egyptian Sources." *JAOS* 90 (1970), 462–85.

Friedmann, M. *Ha-ṣiyyun, hu be'ur li-nvu'at yeḥezqel siman 20.* Vienna: n.p., 1888.

Gaster, T. H. *Myth, Legend, and Custom in the Old Testament.* New York/Evanston: Harper & Row, 1969.

Greenberg, M. "Ezekiel 17 and the Policy of Psammetichus II." *JBL* 76 (1957), 304–9.

———. "On Ezekiel's Dumbness." *JBL* 77 (1958), 101–5.

———. "Ezek 20 and the Spiritual Exile" [Hebrew]. In *Oz le-David* [Ben Gurion volume]. Jerusalem: Israel Society for Biblical Research, 1964, pp. 433–42.

———. "Prolegomenon." In C. C. Torrey, *Pseudo-Ezekiel and the Original Prophecy, and Critical Articles.* New York: Ktav, 1970, pp. xi–xxix.
———. "The Sabbath Passage in Jeremiah" [Hebrew]. In *'Iyyunim be-sefer yirmeyahu* [Jerusalem?]: Israel Society for Biblical Research, 1971, II, pp. 27–37.
———. "The Citations in the Book of Ezekiel as a Background for the Prophecies" [Hebrew]. *Beth Mikra* 50 (5732/1972), 273–78.
———. "NḤŠTK (Ezek. 16:36): Another Hebrew Cognate of Akkadian *naḫāšu.*" In *Essays on the Ancient Near East in Memory of Jacob Joel Finkelstein,* ed. Maria de Jong Ellis. Memoirs of the Connecticut Academy of Arts and Sciences, XIX. Hamden: Archon Books, 1977, pp. 85–86.
———. "The Use of the Ancient Versions for Understanding the Hebrew Text: A Sampling from Ezek II,1–III,11." *Congress Volume, Göttingen 1977,* SVT 29. Leiden: E. J. Brill, 1978, pp. 131–48.
———. "The Vision of Jerusalem in Ezekiel 8–11: A Holistic Interpretation." In *The Divine Helmsman: Studies on God's Control of Human Events, Presented to Lou H. Silberman,* ed. J. L. Crenshaw and S. Sandmel. New York: Ktav, 1980, pp. 146–64.
Greenfield, J. C. "Two Biblical Passages in the Light of Their Near Eastern Background—Ezekiel 16:30 and Malachi 3:17." In *Eretz-Israel* 16 (*Harry M. Orlinsky Volume*), ed. B. A. Levine and A. Malamat. Jerusalem: Israel Exploration Society, 1982, pp. 56–61; English summary, p. 253*.
Halperin, D. J. "The Exegetical Character of Ezek. X:9–17." *VT* 26 (1976), 129–41.
Held, M. "Pits and Pitfalls in Akkadian and Biblical Hebrew." *JANES* 5 (1973), 173–90.
Herntrich, V. *Ezechielprobleme.* BZAW 61. Giessen: A. Töpelmann, 1933.
Herrmann, J. *Ezechiel,* Kommentar zum alten Testament XI. Leipzig/Erlangen: A. Deichert, 1924.
Heschel, A. J. *The Prophets.* New York: Harper & Row, 1962.
Hitzig, F. *Der Prophet Ezechiel.* Kurzgefasstes exegetisches Handbuch zum alten Testament, VIII. Leipzig: Weidmann, 1874.
Hoffmann, Y. "On the Question of the Structure and Meaning of Ezek 20" [Hebrew]. *Beth Mikra* 63 (1975), 473–89.
Hölscher, G. *Hesekiel, der Dichter und das Buch,* BZAW 39. Giessen: Töpelmann, 1924.
Houk, C. B. "The Final Redaction of Ezekiel 10." *JBL* 90 (1971), 42–54.
Howie, C. G. *The Date and Composition of Ezekiel. JBL* Monograph Series, IV. Philadelphia: Society of Biblical Literature, 1950.
Ibn Caspi, Joseph. *Adne Keseph,* pt. 2, ed. I. Last. London: privately printed, 1912. Commentary to Ezekiel, pp. 25–48.
Ibn Janaḥ, Jonah. *Sefer ha-riqma . . . be-targumo ha-'ivri šel R. Yehuda ibn Tibbon,* ed. M. Wilensky. Berlin, 1929; rpt. and enlarged ed. by D. Tené et al. 2 vols. Jerusalem: Hebrew Language Academy, 1964.
———. *Sepher Haschoraschim* (Wurzelwörterbuch der hebräischen Sprache) von Abulwalid Merwan Ibn Ganah, aus dem Arabischen ins Hebräische ubersetzt von Jehuda Ibn Tibbon, hrsg. W. Bacher. Berlin: H. Itzkowski, 1896.

Irwin, W. A. *The Problem of Ezekiel: An Inductive Study*. Chicago: University of Chicago Press, 1943.

Joüon, P. *Grammaire de l'Hébreu biblique*. Rome: Pontifical Biblical Institute, 1947. Cited by section.

Kara, Joseph. Commentary in *Mikra'ot Gedolot*.

Katzenstein, H. J. *The History of Tyre*. Jerusalem: Schocken Institute for Jewish Research, 1973.

Kaufmann, Y. *Toldot ha-'emuna ha-yiśre'elit*. 4 vols. Tel Aviv: Mosad Bialik and Dvir, 1937–56; *The Religion of Israel*, abridged and trans. M. Greenberg. Chicago: University of Chicago Press, 1963 (only includes vols. I–III).

Keller, B. "La Terre dans le livre d'Ezechiel." *RHPR* 55 (1975), 481–90.

Kimḥi, David. Commentary in *Mikra'ot Gedolot*.

———. *Mikhlol* = *David Ḳimḥi's Hebrew Grammar* (*Mikhlol*), ed. W. Chomsky. New York: Bloch, 1952.

———. *Sefer ha-šorašim* [dictionary], ed. J. Biesenthal and F. Lebrecht. Berlin: G. Bethge, 1847.

Kohut, A. *Aruch Completum* [Hebrew title: *'Aruk ha-šalem*], 8 vols. Vienna: Menorah, 1878–92; *Additamenta ad librum Aruch Completum* [Hebrew title: *Tosefot ha-'aruk ha-šalem*], ed. S. Krauss et al. Vienna: Kohut Memorial Foundation, 1937.

Komlosh, Y. "Ezekiel's Silence at the Start of His Prophecy" [Hebrew]. *Zer ligevurot. Shazar Jubilee Volume*. Jerusalem: Israel Society for Biblical Research, 1973, pp. 279–83.

König, E. *Historisch-kritisches Lehrgebäude der hebräischen Sprache*, 2te hälfte, 1 Theil, cited as II; 2 (Schluss-)Theil, cited as III. Leipzig: J. C. Hinrichs, 1895–97.

Landersdorfer, S. *Der βααλ τετραμορφος und die Kerube des Ezechiel*. Paderborn: F. Schöningh, 1918.

Lang, Bernhard. *Kein Aufstand in Jerusalem*. Stuttgarter Biblische Beiträge. Stuttgart: K. B. W. Verlag, 1978.

———. *Ezechiel: Der Prophet und das Buch*. Erträge der Forschung, 153. Darmstadt: Wissentschaftliche Buchgesellschaft, 1981.

Levenson, J. D. *Theology of the Program of Restoration of Ezekiel 40–48*. Missoula, Mont.: Scholars Press, 1976.

Lindars, B. "Ezekiel and Individual Responsibility." *VT* 15 (1965), 452–67.

Lindblom, J. *Prophecy in Ancient Israel*. Philadelphia: Fortress Press, 1962.

Löw, I. *Die Flora der Juden*. 4 vols. Wien und Leipzig: R. Löwit Verlag, 1924–34.

Luckenbill, D. D. *Ancient Records of Assyria and Babylonia*. 2 vols. Chicago: University of Chicago Press, 1926; abbreviated *ARAB*.

Lust, J. " 'Mon Seigneur Jahweh' dans le texte hébreu d'Ézéchiel." *De Mari à Qumran: Hommage à J. Coppens*, ed. H. Cazelles. Bibliotheca Ephemeridum Theologicarum Lovaniensium, 24. Gembloux: Duculot, 1969, pp. 167–73.

———. "Ez. XX, 4–26 une parodie de l'histoire religieuse d'Israel." *De Mari à Qumran: Hommage à J. Coppens*, Bibliotheca Ephemeridum Theologicarum Lovaniensium, 24. Gembloux: Duculot, 1969, pp. 127–66.

Luz[z]atto, S. L. *Erläuterungen über einen Theil der Propheten und Hagiographen* [Hebrew]. Lemberg: A. I. Menkes, 1876.

Malamat, A. "The Last Kings of Judah and the Fall of Jerusalem." *IEJ* 18 (1968), 137–56.

———. "The Twilight of Judah: In the Egyptian-Babylonian Maelstrom." *Congress Volume, Edinburgh, 1974,* SVT 28. Leiden: E. J. Brill, 1975, pp. 123–45.

———. "The Last Years of the Kingdom of Judah." In *The World History of the Jewish People, The Age of the Monarchies: Political History,* IV/1, ed. A. Malamat. Jerusalem: Massada, 1981, pp. 205–21.

Mandelkern, S. *Concordance = Veteris Testamenti Concordantiae Hebraicae atque Chaldaicae,* post F. Margolinii et M. Gottsteinii editiones: editio septa aucta atque emendata. Hierosolymis-Tel Aviv: Schocken, 1967.

May, H. G. "The Book of Ezekiel: Introduction and Exegesis." In *The Interpreter's Bible.* New York/Nashville: Abingdon, 1956, VI, pp. 39–338.

Mechilta. *Mekilta de-Rabbi Ishmael,* ed. J. Z. Lauterbach. 3 vols. Philadelphia: Jewish Publication Society of America, 1949.

Menahem bar Shim'on of Posquières. Cited from Paris ms. 192, photocopy in National Library, Hebrew University of Jerusalem.

Meṣudot. Meṣudat, David; Meṣudat ṣiyyon. Name of a two-tiered commentary by Jehiel ben David Altschul, in *Mikra'ot Gedolot.*

Mikra'ot Gedolot [Rabbinic Bible]. Lublin: Schneidmesser and Herschenhorn, 1911. Contains commentaries of Rashi, Joseph Kara, David Kimḥi, and Jehiel ben David Altschul (*Meṣudot*).

Milgrom, J. "The Concept of *ma'al* in the Bible and the Ancient Near East." *JAOS* 96 (1976), 236–47.

———. *Cult and Conscience: The Asham and the Priestly Doctrine of Repentance.* Leiden: E. J. Brill, 1976.

Minḥat Shay. Critical notes on MT by Shelomo Yedidiah Norzi (1st ed. Mantua 1732–44), in *Mikra'ot Gedolot.*

Moffatt, J. *A New Translation of the Bible, Containing the Old and New Testaments.* New York: Harper & Row, 1954.

Moshe ben Sheshet. *A Commentary upon the Books of Jeremiah and Ezeqiel by Mosheh ben Shesheth,* ed. S. R. Driver. London: Williams and Norgate, 1871.

Muffs, Y. "Studies in Biblical Law, IV: The Antiquity of P." Lectures at the Jewish Theological Seminary of America, New York, 1965. Mimeographed.

Müller, D. H. *Ezechiel-Studien.* Israelitish-theologische Lehranstalt, Jahresbericht, 1. Wien, 1894.

Noth, M. "Noah, Daniel und Hiob in Ezechiel XIV." *VT* 1 (1951), 251–60.

Oppenheim, A. L. *The Interpretation of Dreams in the Ancient Near East.* Transactions of the American Philosophical Society, n.s. 46/3. Philadelphia: American Philosophical Society, 1956.

Parker, R. A., and W. H. Dubberstein. *Babylonian Chronology, 626 B.C.–A.D. 45.* Brown University Studies 19. Providence: Brown University Press, 1956.

Parunak, H. van Dyke. "Structural Studies in Ezekiel." Ph.D. diss., Harvard University, 1978.

———. "The Literary Architecture of Ezekiel's Mar'ôt 'Elohîm." *JBL* 99 (1980), 61–74.

von Rad, G. *Old Testament Theology,* trans. D. M. G. Stalker. Edinburgh/London: Oliver and Boyd, vol. I, 1962; vol. II, 1965.

Rashi [acronym of Rabbi Solomon ben Isaac]. Commentary in *Mikra'ot Gedolot.*

Rivlin, A. "The Parable of the Eagles, the Cedar and the Vine" [Hebrew]. *Beth Mikra* 54 (1973), 342–59.

Rothstein, D. "Das Buch Ezechiel." In *HSAT,* 1 Band, pp. 868–1000.

Saggs, H. W. F. "The Branch to the Nose." *JThS* 11 (1960), 318–29.

Sarna, N. "Ezekiel 8:17: A Fresh Approach." *HTR* 57 (1964) 347–52.

Schmidt, H. "Kerubenthron und Lade." In *Eucharisterion. Studien zur Religion und Literatur des Alten und Neuen Testaments* (H. Gunkel Festschrift). Göttingen: Vandenhoeck & Ruprecht, 1923, pp. 120–44.

Schmidt, M. A. "Zur Komposition des Buches Hesekiel." *ThZ* 6 (1950), 81–98.

Schoneveld, J. "Ezekiel XIV, 1–8." *Oudtestamentische Studiën* 15 (1969), 193–204.

Segal, M. H. "Prophet, Lookout, Reprover" [Hebrew]. In M. H. Segal, *Masoret u-Biqqoret.* Jerusalem: Kiryat Sepher, 1957, pp. 150–59.

Seidel, M. "Parallels Between the Book of Isaiah and the Book of Psalms" [Hebrew]. *Sinai* 38 (5616 [1956]), 149–72, 229–40, 272–80, 333–54 ("Seidel's law," p. 150).

Smend, R. *Der Prophet Ezechiel.* Kurzgefasstes exegetisches Handbuch zum alten Testament, VIII. 2te Auflage. Leipzig: S. Hirzel, 1880.

Smit, E. J. "The Concepts of Obliteration in Ez. 5:1–4." *Journal of Northwest Semitic Languages* I (1971), 46–50.

Smith, M. "The Veracity of Ezekiel, the Sins of Manasseh, and Jeremiah 44:18." *ZAW* 87 (1975), 11–16.

Spiegel, S. "Ezekiel or Pseudo-Ezekiel." *HTR* 24 (1931), 245–321; rpt. in Torrey, *Pseudo-Ezekiel,* pp. 123–99.

———. "Noah, Daniel and Job: Touching on Canaanite Relics in the Legends of the Jews." *Louis Ginzberg Jubilee Volume* (English part). New York: American Academy for Jewish Research, 1945, pp. 305–55.

Stalker, D. M. G. *Ezekiel.* Torch Bible Commentary. London: SCM Press, 1968.

Stummer, F. "*'ᵃmulla* (Ez xvi 30a)." *VT* 4 (1954), 34–40.

Talmon, S. "Tabûr Ha'aretz and the Comparative Method" [Hebrew]. *Tarbiz* 45 (1976), 163–77.

Torrey, C. C. *Pseudo-Ezekiel and the Original Prophecy,* with critical articles by S. Spiegel and C. C. Torrey and a prolegomenon by M. Greenberg. New York: Ktav, 1970.

Tsevat, M. "The Neo-Assyrian and Neo-Babylonian Vassal Oaths and the Prophet Ezekiel." *JBL* 78 (1959), 199–204.

Tur-Sinai, N. H. *Pešuṭo šel miqra III/b.* Jerusalem: Kiryat Sepher, 1967.

Uffenheimer, B. "Ezekiel 12:1–16." In *SBANE,* Hebrew part, pp. 17–44; English summary in English part, pp. 213ff.

de Vaux, R. *Ancient Israel: Its Life and Institutions,* trans. J. McHugh. New York: McGraw-Hill, 1961.

Vogt, E. "Der Nehar Kebar: Ez 1." *Biblica* 39 (1958), 211–16.

———. "Der Sinn des Wortes 'Augen' in Ez 1, 18 und 10, 12." *Biblica* 59 (1978), 93–96.

Wagner, M. *Die lexikalischen und grammatikalischen Aramaismen im alttestamentlichen Hebräisch.* BZAW 96. Berlin: Töpelmann, 1966.

Weinfeld, M. *Deuteronomy and the Deuteronomic School.* Oxford: Clarendon Press, 1972.

Weiss, R. "The Double-Duty of *l': On* the Use of the Negative Word *l'* in Parallelism" [Hebrew]. *Shnaton* 2 (1977), 82–92.

Wevers, J. *Ezekiel.* The Century Bible, n.s. London: Nelson, 1969.

Wilson, R. R. "An Interpretation of Ezekiel's Dumbness." *VT* 22 (1972), 91–104.

Wiseman, D. J. *Chronicles of Chaldean Kings (626–556 B.C.) in the British Museum.* London: Trustees of the British Museum, 1956.

Yellin, D. *Ketavim nivḥarim* II. Jerusalem: Kiryat Sepher, 1939.

Zadok, R. "The Nippur Region During the Late Assyrian, Chaldean and Achaemenian Periods, Chiefly According to Written Sources." *Israel Oriental Studies* 8 (1978), 266–332.

Zimmerli, W. "Die Eigenart der prophetischen Rede des Ezechiel. Ein Beitrag zum Problem an Hand von Ez 14, 1–11." *ZAW* 66 (1954), 1–26 (= *GO*, pp. 148–77).

———. *Erkenntnis Gottes nach dem Buche Ezechiel: Eine theologische Studie.* Abhandlungen zur Theologie des Alten und Neuen Testaments, 27. Zürich: Zwingli-Verlag, 1954 (= *GO*, pp. 41–119).

———. "'Leben' und 'Tod' im Buche des Propheten Ezechiel." *ThZ* 13 (1957), 494–508 (= *GO*, pp. 178–91).

———. "The Special Form- and Traditio-Historical Character of Ezekiel's Prophecy." *VT* 15 (1965), 515–27.

———. *Ezechiel.* Biblischer Kommentar altes Testament 13. Neukirchen/Vluyn: Neukirchener Verlag des Erziehungsvereins, 1969 (Vol. I [chs. 1 – 24], trans. R. Clements, Philadelphia: Fortress Press, 1979).

Translation and Commentary

I. Ezekiel's Call: The Vision
(1:1–28b[a])

1 1 It was in the thirtieth year in the fourth month on the fifth of the
month, as I was among the exiles by the Chebar canal, that the
heavens opened and I saw a divine vision. 2 (On the fifth of the
month—that was the fifth year of King Jehoiachin's exile— 3 it happened that the word of YHWH came to the priest Ezekiel son of Buzi
in the land of the Chaldeans by the Chebar canal, and the hand of
YHWH came upon him[a] there.)
4 As I looked, a stormy wind came from the north, with a large
cloud and a mass of fire, surrounded by a radiance; out of it—out of
the fire—appeared something that looked like *ḥashmal*. 5 Out of it the
figures of four creatures emerged and this was their appearance: they
had a human shape, 6 but they each had four faces and each four wings.
7 For legs, they had a straight leg, and their feet were like a calf's foot.
They gleamed like burnished bronze. 8 Human hands were under their
wings on their four sides. As for the faces [b]and the wings[b] of the four
of them, 9 [b]their wings were joined one to another[b]; they did not
change position as they went, but each went straight ahead. 10 The
shape of their face was human; but on the right the four of them
had a lion's face, and on the left the four of them had a bull's face;
and the four of them had an eagle's face. 11 [b]And their faces[b] and
their wings were separated above; each had two joining each, and two
covering their bodies. 12 Each went straight ahead; wherever the
spirit would go they went, without changing position as they went.
13 [c]And the shape of the creatures, their appearance, was like[c] burning
coals of fire; something with the appearance of torches it was, moving
around amidst the creatures. The fire had a radiance and from it
lightning flashed. 14 [d]/And the creatures darting to and fro with the
appearance of sparks./

[a] G S "me" (as from *'ly*).
[b–b] Not in G.
[c–c] G "And amidst (as from *wbynwt*) the creatures (was) an apparition like" (as from *mr'h k-*); S "And the shape of the creatures (was) like the appearance of" (as from *kmr'h*).
[d] This verse is not in G.

15 As I looked at the creatures I saw one wheel on the ground
alongside the creatures, [e]with its four faces. 16 And[e] the appearance
of the wheels [b]and their design[b] were like chrysolite and all four had
the same shape; [b]their appearance[b] and their design were as if one
wheel were inside the other wheel. 17 When those went these went on
their four sides, without changing position as they went. 18 As for
their rims, they had height and [f]they had dread[f]; and their brows were
inlaid all around with eyes for the four of them. 19 When the creatures
went the wheels went beside them; when the creatures rose off the
ground the wheels rose too. 20 Wherever the spirit would go they
went [g]/wherever the spirit go/[g] and the wheels rose alongside them,
for the spirit of the creature was in the wheels: 21 when these went
those went and when these halted those halted and when these rose
off the ground the wheels rose alongside them, for the spirit of the
creature was in the wheels.

22 There was a shape over the heads of the creature, of an expanse
that looked like dreadful ice, stretched over their heads above them.
23 Below the expanse their wings were extended one toward the
other; each had two giving cover, [b]each had two giving cover[b] to his
body. 24 I heard the sound of their wings as they went like the sound
of the deep sea like the voice of the Almighty, a sound of tumult like
the sound of an army; when they halted their wings slackened.
25 [h]There was a sound from above the expanse that was over their
heads; [b]when they halted their wings slackened.[b]

26 [b]Above the expanse that was over their heads[b] was [i]the figure of
a throne with the appearance of sapphire-stone[i], and above, on the
figure of a throne was a figure with the appearance of a human being.
27 From the appearance of his loins upward I saw the like of *ḥashmal,*
[b]having something with the appearance of fire surrounding it[b]; and
from the appearance of his loins downward I saw something with the
appearance of fire; and he was surrounded by a radiance. 28 Like the
appearance of the bow that is in a cloud on a rainy day such was the
appearance of the surrounding radiance. That was the appearance of
the figure of the Majesty of YHWH; when I saw it, I fell on my face—

e–e G "for the four of them. 16 And" (as from *l'rb'tm w-*).

f–f G "and I saw them" (as from *w'r'h lhm?*); S "and they were seeing."

g–g Not in G and S.

h Vs. 25 is missing from some medieval Heb. mss.

i–i G "like the appearance of sapphire-stone (S "and like") the image of a throne upon it" (= *'lyw;* G does not reflect *'lyw* at the end of the verse where MT has it).

COMMENT

1:1–3. Ezekiel's custom of opening accounts of his prophetic experiences with their date and sometimes their circumstances (see the Table of Dates in the Introduction) caused a departure here from the usual beginnings of prophetic books. Whereas books usually open with a superscription giving details of identification and setting (as, e.g., Isa 1:1; Jer 1:1–3; Hosea 1:1; Amos 1:1), here these appear in vss. 2–3 as an explanatory interruption of the first-person narrative of vs. 1. The date in vs. 1 is explained in vs. 2 in terms of the era of Jehoiachin's exile, in accord with the rest of the dates in the book; then the "I" of vs. 1 and his location are identified. Since vss. 2–3 are in the third person, they are generally supposed to be, like the superscriptions of other prophetic books, from an editorial hand, not the prophet's. If so, however, and if the equation of "the thirtieth year" with the fifth of Jehoiachin's exile is accepted as correct, then the prophet will have jumped from one era in 1:1 to another throughout the rest of his book, taking no account of the change. One can avoid this embarrassment by supposing the prophet to have been his own editor and the author of the explanation in vss. 2–3—an extraordinary but not impossible procedure.

The era to which "the thirtieth year" belongs is unknown. If it is Jehoiachin's exile, like all the other dates in the book, then the equation of the "thirtieth year" of vs. 1 with the "fifth year" of vs. 2 is wrong, and this first date will be the latest in the book (after year 27 of 29:17); some modern scholars have felt that this is so and regard the verse as a fragment—the start of the latest dated prophecy. For example, S. Spiegel (*HTR* 24 [1931], 282ff.), W. F. Albright (*JBL* 51 [1932], 96f.) and C. Howie (*Date and Composition,* pp. 41, 49f.) take the "thirtieth year" as the date when Ezekiel first published his book; Freedman privately adds that it may have been the occasion of a closing vision essentially the same as that of "the fifth year." This proposal reads a great deal into the text. The vision that follows is later repeatedly referred to as having been "by the Chebar canal" (3:23; 10:15, 22; 43:3); since nowhere in the book but in our vss. 1 and 3 is any vision located there, to separate the referents of these verses from each other and from the following vision seems unreasonable. The editorial explanation (vss. 2–3) takes "the thirtieth year" as another era's equivalent of year 5 of Jehoiachin's exile. What that other era might be has been guessed at several times. T reads: "In the thirtieth year from the time when Hilkiah the high priest found the book of Torah in the Temple" (cf. II Kings 22:8ff.); and, indeed, if one counts back from the fifth year of the exile thirty years according to the regnal years given in the Book of Kings one arrives at year 18 of Josiah, in which the Torah book was found and the great reform undertaken. While that event might plausibly have begun an era for the priesthood (and Ezekiel was a priest), and while Ezekiel is, of all the prophets, the most closely identified with the language and content of the Torah, the fact is that nowhere else does he or anyone hint that the event marked the start of a year count. No more convincing are other ancient and modern guesses—e.g., the Jubilee era, or the prophet's age (see J. Bewer, "The Text of Ezekiel 1:1–3," pp. 96–101, for a summary of opinions).

the fourth month. Counting from the spring (cf. 45:21 with Deut 16:1), that is, the summer month later called by the Babylonian name Tammuz (= June–July).

among the exiles . . . That is, living among the exiles but not at that moment actually among them. For although the vision occurred at the Chebar canal (cf. 3:23, etc.), it was only when it was over that the prophet went (returned?) to the exile settlement Tel Abib, on the Chebar, to be actually among his fellow exiles (3:15).

the Chebar canal. Hebrew *nᵉhar kᵉbar* corresponds to Akkadian *nār kabari/u* "the Kabaru canal," an obscure body of water mentioned twice in the archives of the Murashu family, bankers in the Babylonian city of Nippur in the fifth century B.C.E. In one document this canal is said to lie near Nippur; it cannot, therefore, be identical with the "Euphrates of Nippur" (the modern, dry Shaṭṭ en-Nil), which anciently ran through the middle of Nippur, and with which some have identified it (E. Vogt, "Der Nehar Kebar: Ez 1," pp. 211–16; R. Zadok, "The Nippur Region," p. 287).

That Ezekiel was standing by a stream on the occasion of his inaugural vision may have significance; note that one of Daniel's visions, also seen in exile, was "by the great river, the Tigris" (Dan 10:4; in 8:2ff., however, the scene in the vision is at the Ulai stream, while Daniel is in Susa). Foreign lands were considered unclean (Amos 7:17; Ezek 4:13); Israelite exiles would therefore seek communion with God most suitably at running water, whose purifying quality was traditional (Lev 14:5, 50; 15:13; Num 19:17); a later reflection of this practice is in Acts 16:13 (with all the above cf. *Mechilta, Pisḥa,* 1, ed. Lauterbach, vol. 1, p. 6).

A fourth–fifth-century C.E. mystical midrash on Ezek 1 called *Re'uyot Yeḥezqel* "Visions of Ezekiel" (ed. I. Gruenwald, *Ṭemirin* 1 [1972], 101–39) gives a striking interpretation of the connection between vision and bodies of water: Ezekiel was gazing at the water when he saw reflected in it the celestial vision.

> The matter may be compared to a man who was taking a haircut and was handed a mirror by the barber. As he looked in the mirror, the king and his entourage passed by the doorway [of the shop]. When the barber saw them, he said [to his customer], "Turn around and look at the king!" The man replied, "I have already (*kᵉbar*) seen him in the mirror (*mar'a*)."

Gruenwald has remarked that this procedure could be a means of avoiding the immediate sight of divine beings (*Apocalyptic and Merkavah Mysticism* [Leiden/Köln: E. J. Brill, 1980], p. 135), and M. Idel has shown that such a technique was practiced by mystical visionaries down through the Middle Ages (*Sinai* [Hebrew] 86 [5640/1980], 1–7).

the heavens opened. A unique expression; elsewhere God is said to "incline" or "rend" the heaven in order to descend and reveal himself (II Sam 22:10; Isa 63:19).

a divine vision. Others, "visions of God," but *mar'ot* is not a true plural but what Joüon calls "a plural of generalization" (§ 136 j) often to be rendered as a singular (cf. Gen 46:2 and *ḥ^{a}lomot* in Gen 37:8; Dan 2:1, and GKC § 124 e), and *'^{e}lohim* is in Ezekiel usually an appellative, "divinity," not the proper noun "God." Here and in 8:3 and 40:2 the sense is "a supernatural vision," one no mortal eye could see without divine help.

The epithet "divine vision" marks vs. 1 as the retrospective title of the entire passage, vss. 4–28, from the vantage point of full knowledge of its character.

2. *On the fifth of the month.* The last element of the date in vs. 1 serves as a catchword for the explanatory note; a similar procedure appears in 23:4, which see. The explanatory note (running through vs. 3) is an alternative sequel to the date formula in vs. 1; the combination of two verbs in the resulting sentences—"[1]It was . . .[3] it happened, etc." (*way^{e}hi . . . hayo haya*)—is normal Ezekelian style; cf. the date formulas of 20:1; 29:17; 30:20, etc. (*way^{e}hi . . . haya*).

3. *it happened . . . came.* An attempt to render the force of the combination of infinitive and finite verb, *hayo haya.* This construction is usual at absolute beginnings of narrative, favored for "possessing a certain fulness of sound" (GKC § 113 o; Joüon § 123 k, with reference, e.g., to Gen 43:7, 20; Judg 9:8; II Sam 1:6). Hereafter only the finite verb (*haya*) recurs in the formula "the word of YHWH came [lit. was] to me" (as in the examples cited at the end of the previous note). This formula regularly introduces divine messages to the prophet and here must refer to the speech that starts in 2:1. The formula is discussed at 3:16.

the land of the Chaldeans (Kaśdim). The Chaldeans were an Aramean group (cf. the affiliation of Kesed, Gen 22:22) who entered southern Babylonia in the early part of the first millennium and succeeded in winning independence from Assyria in 625 with the founding of the neo-Babylonian dynasty by Nabopolassar, the father of Nebuchadnezzar. Chaldean interchanges with Babylonian in 12:13; 23:15, 23.

the hand of YHWH came upon me. Cf. 8:1 "fell upon me." Thus the prophet describes "the urgency, pressure, and compulsion by which he is stunned and overwhelmed" (Heschel, *The Prophets,* p. 444). God's "hand" is a manifestation of his power (Exod 9:3; Deut 2:15; I Sam 5:9; Isa 41:20). When it lights upon a prophet he may be charged with uncanny strength (I Kings 18:46, Elijah), or with that supreme tension outwardly manifest as a trance brought on by consciousness of being addressed by God (II Kings 2:15, Elisha). Ezekiel uses the phrase in the latter sense, but in connection with some sensory or physical effect other than mere audition: here the vision of ch. 1 and the extraordinary sensory experiences of chs. 2–3. Elsewhere the hand controls his movement (3:22), detaches him from his surroundings and transports him in spirit to faraway places (8:1; 37:1; 40:1), or rivets his attention to a psychophysical change that is to occur in him (33:22). Susceptibility to seizure is characteristic of Ezekiel, distinguishing him from other literary prophets who never employ this expression in describing the onset of their prophecy. The phrase does occur, however, in connection with earlier prophets, as mentioned previously. (Isa 8:11 and Jer 15:17 are related expressions, but they denote no more than the prophets' sense of being under a divine compulsion; they are not descriptions of the onset of prophecy in a trance.) J. J. M. Roberts ("The Hand of Yahweh," *VT* 21 [1971], 244–51) notes the connection of the expression with pathological phenomena in the Bible and outside it in the ancient Near East.

upon him. In MT the last clause of vs. 3 belongs to the explanatory note, thus overloading the verse with two descriptions of the onset of prophecy, an otherwise unattested manner of expression. G S read "upon me" and thus shift the clause into the following first-person narrative of the visionary experience, where, on the analogy of 8:1, we expect it to lead directly into the relation of the start of the vision.

4. *from the north.* It is suggested on the basis of a mythical belief alluded to in Isa 14:13 and known outside Israel that the divine apparatus came from the north because there the abode of the gods was situated. But aside from the unlikelihood of the prophet adopting literally such a mythic belief for Israel's God (even the poet of Ps 48:3 must skew it to make it palatable ["north" = Zion]), the title verse (1) expressly has the heavens open (not the north) in order to release the apparition of the divine Majesty. A more mundane line of interpretation combines the observation that prophetic visions sometimes arise out of an everyday occurrence suddenly transformed (the burning bush [Exod 3]; the boiling pot [Jer 1]) with the peculiarity of Iraq's summer climate, presumably the same in Babylonian times. "From May onward the predominating element is the existence of a . . . zone of extremely low . . . pressure . . . at the seaward end of the Persian Gulf . . . This . . . produces a very persistent and regular northwesterly wind (*shamāl*) over the whole of Iraq . . . Strong winds produce blowing dust or sandstorms; July is the worst month, with an average of five storms at Baghdad [central Iraq] and eight at ash-Shu'aybah [far south]" (W. B. Fisher, "Iraq," in Encyclopaedia Britannica, 15th ed. [1974]; Macropaedia, vol. 9, p. 874). Since our prophet was near Nippur, about halfway between Baghdad and the Gulf, and the month was July, it may well be that on that fateful day the

shamāl ("north [wind]") blew up a storm that bore into the prophet's view, not the usual dust or sand cloud, but the strangely incandescent cloud he proceeds to describe.

a mass of fire ('eš mitlaqqaḥat). Of uncertain meaning, this phrase recurs only in Exod 9:24 in the story of the plague of hail. Both here and there a supernatural fire is denoted—perhaps "fire caught onto itself," that is, not having an object onto which it has caught but merely burning there "in the air" as a fiery mass. G. R. Driver's comparison of Syriac *'ettawḥad* "be kindled" as a semantic parallel (base *'ḥd* "hold" || Hebrew *lqḥ; VT* 1 [1951], 60) is clever but yields a flat meaning; neither T nor S uses derivates of *'ḥd* here but rather verbs meaning "blazing."

surrounded by a radiance. Radiance (*nogah*) attaches to fire in vss. 13 and 27 (see comment there), and in other theophanies (II Sam 22:13 [Ps 18:13]; Isa 4:5). By transposition, G attaches the radiance to the cloud, perhaps to avoid the anomaly of a masculine pronoun (*lo*) referring to normally feminine *'eš* "fire"; there are, however, other passages in which *'eš* is referred to both as feminine and masculine (in that order, as here) in the same verse (Jer 20:9; Job 20:26).

something that looked like. Hebrew *keʿen,* lit. "like the color, appearance of," from *ʿayin* "color," as in Lev 13:5, 55; Num 11:7; Prov 23:31. In Mishnaic Hebrew it means "dye" (Shabbat 1:6), while the form *keʿen* is simply "like" (parallel to the semantic development of Mishnaic Hebrew *kegon* "like," from Persian *gūn* "color").

ḥashmal. Used only here and in vs. 27, and in 8:2, for describing the divine Majesty. The context indicates a bright substance, with a color like that of fire; G, agreeably, *ēlektron;* V *electrum* "amber" (a yellow, translucent resin). As it belongs to the heart of the vision of the Majesty (vs. 27), *ḥashmal* later came to be regarded as endowed with holy and dangerous properties (cf. the anecdote of the child burned up by fire from *ḥashmal* [*Ḥagigah* 13a]); S consistently avoids rendering it. The etymology of the word is unknown, but Akkadian has in *elmešu* what may well be a cognate. An undefined precious stone, *elmešu* often occurs in mythical contexts; e.g., "[Nergal's] upper cheeks are *elmešu,* his lower cheeks flash constantly like lightning" (*CAD* 4, p. 107b). *elmešu* is also listed among dyes of mineral origin. ". . . the word must be taken as referring to a quasi-mythical precious stone of great brilliancy and with a color which one tried to imitate with dyes" (*CAD* 4, p. 108a; cf. B. Landsberger, "Akkadisch-hebräische Wortgleichungen," SVT 16 [1967], 190–94, arguing that the Akkadian word = amber).

5. *Out of it.* Out of the fire and below it, as the apparition approached, emerged the figures of four—

creatures. Hebrew *ḥayyot* "animals" seems here to be employed in its basic, vaguer sense of "living things" (so G *zōa*) to denote the strange beings about to be described.

In the description the gender of the verbal and pronominal references to the creatures vacillates. Out of forty-five, only twelve are the grammatically proper feminine plural (e.g., the *n* pronoun suffix); the others are masculine plural (e.g., the *m* suffix), which is substantially correct since the creatures are not gynecomorphous. The vacillation is extreme in vss. 9–11 and 23–25, where it occurs in one and the same clause; it flows over into the description of the wheels as well (vss. 16, 18).

a human shape. In that they stood erect; Dan 7:4. The face they presented to the onlooker (cf. vs. 10) and their limbs (vss. 7–8) were also like those of a human.

7. *a straight leg.* "Straight" has generally been interpreted "unjointed," i.e., without a break in the vertical line at the knee; this would be part of the creatures' lack of orientation, along with their four-facedness. (They need no joint since their motion is through flight, not walking.) But the same word (*y^{e}šarot*) in vs. 23 means "extended" (used of wings), and may mean that here too; the creatures were not in a couching position, with legs bent under them, but were standing with legs straight.

Whether the singular "leg" means each of two legs or is used deliberately to say that each creature had but one leg is unclear. If their design expressed a lack of orientation, the latter interpretation is more likely.

a calf's foot. That is, round (T, in fact, renders "round") and so lacking orientation.

They gleamed. The legs did (cf. Dan 10:6), though the masculine form of the verb is inappropriate since "legs" in Hebrew is feminine.

8. *on their four sides.* Here, as in vs. 17, the meaning seems to be "on the four sides of the square (or whatever four-sided figure) they formed"; as there was but one wheel per creature (vs. 15; 10:9), so there was but one set of hands for each. It cannot be denied, however, that the Hebrew permits an interpretation giving each creature four (sets of?) hands, one for each face; earlier exegetes held this view.

As for the faces and the wings. In MT faces and wings continue to be treated together (vs. 6), with vs. 9a taking up the last-mentioned "wings" and vs. 9b the first-mentioned "faces" (since "straight ahead" in Hebrew is literally "in the direction of his face"). G offers a shorter version of vss. 8b–9, dealing only with "faces." Vss. 11–12 contain what seem to be doublets of vss. 8b–9, each supplying some lack in the other: e.g., vs. 9's *'išša 'el '^{a}hotah* complements *ḥob^{e}rot* better than vs. 11's *'iš;* on the other hand, vs. 11's distinction between the two sets of wings and vs. 12's mention of the motive force of the "spirit" supplement the data of vs. 9.

9. *wings were joined.* Cf. vss. 11, 23; the (upper set of) wings of each creature were joined at their tips to those of its fellows on either side. The outspread wings of the cherub statues in the holy of holies are said to have "touched" one another (I Kings 6:27); the verb used here occurs in Exod 26:3 and elsewhere for the interlinking of cloth strips that made up the curtains of the desert tabernacle, and thus expresses a strong juncture.

The impression that the wings were actually joined, linked to one another, may imply that they moved in perfect unison.

straight ahead. Lit. "to the region-opposite (*'eber*) his face." The general sense is: in order to change direction, the creatures did not have to wheel around, for (and this seems to be the meaning of our phrase) whichever direction they wished to take was straight ahead for one of the four. Change of direction was therefore effortless; all directions were "straight ahead." The nif'al of *sbb,* like the qal (e.g., Num 36:7), can mean "change (position, status)" as well as "turn"; what clinches this sense is 10:16 below. An aspect of omnipotence is symbolized here, and it must not be pressed to mean that the creatures could move only at right angles, not diagonally.

10. The peculiar formulation of this verse is explicable on the supposition that it reflects the sequence of observation. The onlooker (on any side) was confronted by a human face; it was one of these human faces that looked "ahead" (vs. 9) in whatever direction the group of creatures moved. But one immediately noticed that two animal faces flanked the human one to its right and left. Finally, from what could be seen on the heads of the rest of the creatures, the onlooker inferred that in back of the human face confronting him was an eagle's face.

11. *And their faces and their wings.* MT's coupling of faces and wings here is even more difficult than in vs. 8 (see comment), for while wings may be said to be "separated," that is, outspread, what can this mean when predicated of faces? Calvin thought that the faces "are not united together so that a fourfold form could be seen on one head . . . Here the prophet points out a diversity of heads"; but this goes against the tenor of all that is said about the faces. G's shorter text here seems the only sensible one, and is virtually confirmed by the syntactically implausible disjunctive accent on *upᵉnehem* "and their faces," which OJPS (following traditional exegesis) renders "Thus were their faces"—a desperate shift. The troublesome word is either a misplaced variant of *udᵉmut pᵉnehem* at the beginning of vs. 10 or the result of mechanically following the pattern "faces + wings" found in vss. 6 and 8 (for an analogous situation, see vs. 16).

joining each. Supply mentally "to his fellow creature"; but the transitive use of the verb is otherwise unattested and the object *'iš* is unusually brief. G renders "coupled to each other" and S translates here and the beginning of vs. 9 identically, but these may reflect translators' exigency rather than a Hebrew text differing from MT, since traditional interpreters (Rashi, Meṣudot) construe MT in the very same way (cf. MT-true OJPS "joined to one another").

covering their bodies. Out of modesty; cf. Isa 6:2, where T renders Hebrew "legs" by Aramaic "bodies."

12. *the spirit.* Hebrew *ruᵃḥ;* T "the will"—the animating impulse that moved and directed the creatures, originating in him who sat enthroned

above them. That this and not "wind" (as in vs. 4) is meant emerges from comparison with *ruaḥ haḥayya* "the spirit of the creatures" in vs. 21.

13. MT is hard. The topic of the shape of the creatures is broached once again, only to be immediately altered into their "appearance," which is likened to "coals of fire." A torchlike apparition in the space bounded by the creatures is then mentioned, followed by a description of "the fire" (which?). Now, from the notice in 10:2 that "coals of fire" (afterward in vss. 6, 7 called merely "fire") were located "amidst the creatures," G's reading of the beginning of our verse gains support; MT appears to be a corruption of it, originating in a miscopying of *b(y)nwt* "among" as *dmwt* "shape"—the latter being far more common in this chapter. S's rendering of the next phrase can be retroverted into idiomatic Hebrew, while that of G presupposes an unexampled *mr'h k-* (with the sense "an apparition like"). The proposed reconstruction of vs. 13a is: *wbynwt hḥywt kmr'h gḥly 's b'rwt* "And amidst the creatures was something like burning coals of fire." The verse is thus devoted to a description of the fiery, torchlike apparition that blazed in the space enclosed by the creatures; the fire mentioned at the end of the verse belongs, naturally, to this apparition.

it was. Hebrew *hi'* "it" (fem.)—apparently a general reference to the burning coals of fire. For such a neutral use of the feminine, see also Josh 10:13; Ps 118:23.

14. The verse hardly accords with Hebrew idiom. Infinitives (*rṣw' wšwb*) serving as finite verbs at the beginning of sentences regularly precede the subject—here their putative subject (*hḥywt*) comes first (cf. OJPS: "And the living creatures ran and returned"; for the rule, see GKC § 113 aa–gg; Joüon § 123 *u–y*—especially the examples in the last sections of each). Nor does the excited motion ascribed to the creatures ("like flame issuing from the mouth of a kiln," R. Judah, BT *Ḥagigah* 13b) suit their description up to this point. Missing in G, the verse seems to be merely a variant of the ending of vs. 13: connected by the catchword "the creatures" (to which the copula "and" was later erroneously prefixed) to the last occurrence of the word in vs. 13, it is an alternative description of the scintillations of the fiery apparition (thus: ". . . moving around admist the creatures, darting to and fro," etc.). This mere variant was mistaken for an independent sentence, at which time the copula "and" was attached to the catchword.

darting . . . sparks. *rṣw'* is taken as a by-form of *rwṣ* "run" and its sense illuminated by Nahum 2:5, where chariots have "the appearance of torches, darting (*y^eroṣeṣu*) like lightning-flashes." The meaning "sparks" is ascribed to *bazaq,* otherwise unattested in biblical Hebrew, on the basis of context and the later Hebrew verb *bazaq* "scatter." T renders it "lightning," S "shooting-star."

15. *on the ground* (b'rṣ). This seems to anticipate the situation of the vehicle in vss. 24f., at rest; then the wheels, as its lowest part, would be

"on the ground." T renders by *mlr'* "below" (so Kimḥi), while Kaufmann (*Religion,* p. 437) takes *b'rṣ* as "on the earth," which he interprets, together with the "firmament" of vs. 23, as endowing the vehicle with self-contained cosmic symbolism.

with its four faces. The four faces of the wheels may be detailed in 10:14 (see comment there); no further mention of them occurs in this chapter. G's reading is simpler and MT's is graphically derivable (by copyist's error) from it (conversion of *-m w-* into *pn[y]w*); it is therefore plausible to suppose the priority of G's reading. Whether the erroneous conversion into MT was facilitated by speculation on the nature of the wheels (see comment on 10:9–13) is a nice question.

16. The pair "appearance + design" occurs twice in this verse and each time only one of the two is, strictly speaking, appropriate (cf. the analogous situation with "faces + wings" above, vss. 9, 11); in each case G omits the unsuitable member.

chrysolite (taršiš). By so rendering here (and in Exod 28:20), G takes the word to refer to a bright yellow precious stone, probably topaz; however, in 10:9; 28:13 it translates by *anthrax*—a precious stone of dark red color, such as the carbuncle or ruby; on the other hand, T Onkelos in Exod renders *krwm ym',* lit. "sea-color"—perhaps aquamarine (bluish green beryl).

one wheel . . . inside the other. The view of older commentators that a wheel made of two wheels intersecting at right angles is meant by this phrase has in its favor the four-directional aspect thereby gained for the wheels. Mechanically simpler is the interpretation that concentric circles are meant. Two possibilities come to mind: (a) an archaic type of disk wheel with a protuberance around its axle that looked like an inner wheel (*ANEP*² ※689, from a third-millennium cylinder seal); later, when spokes were introduced, it may have been preserved for religious purposes; (b) alternatively, the concentric rims of the spoked wheel on Sargon's throne chariot (referred to in Structure and Themes) may be compared.

18. *rims . . . brows.* Hebrew *gabbehem* (so, too, I Kings 7:33), *gabbotam* (Lev 14:9, *gabbot 'enaw* "his eyebrows"); the signification of both words here seems the same, namely, the rim of the wheel, which, as extending on either side of a center disk or spokes, might be regarded as a "brow," especially in association with the "eyes."

and they had dread. Hebrew *wyr'h lhm,* a strange phrase taken (e.g., by T; cf. vs. 22) to mean "they were dreadful." Perhaps this and the previous phrase amount to "dreadfully high" (Freedman, privately). G and S render as though from the root *r'h* "see," but it is not clear that they had before them a Hebrew text differing from MT. Critics assume that MT is in disorder and postulate a simpler text out of which it arose through copyists' errors (e.g., *wᵉgabbehem wa'er'e wᵉhinne gabbotam* "As for their rims, I saw that lo! their brows"; D. J. Halperin, "The Exegetical

Character of Ezek. X:9–17," p. 137, fn. 22, excises our phrase and regards the three words with the consonants *gb* as variants).

19–21. Creatures and wheels moved in perfect unison and kept their relative positions (despite the absence of any physical bond between them) because both were animated by the same controlling impulse. To further emphasize the unity of the ensemble the singular *ḥayya* "creature" is employed in vss. 20, 21, and 22 (cf. 10:15, 17, 20).

20. The matter between slashes, absent in G and S, is a doublet of words at the start of the verse (with *šamma* instead of *šam*).

22. *an expanse.* Hebrew *raqi^{a}'*, used in Gen 1:6ff. for the "firmament"—the hard plane dividing the upper from the lower waters—here refers to the platform on which the divine throne stood. Those who take *ba'areṣ* in vs. 15 to refer to the ground, or earth-plane of the vision understand *raqi^{a}'* here to mean its sky, with the vehicle representing the cosmos.

dreadful. That is, dazzling.

23. Right below the expanse each creature had its upper wings outstretched toward those of its fellows (vss. 9, 11); in addition, nether wings covered its body. The better to contrast the clauses, S adds "above" to the end of the first one and "and below" to the beginning of the second.

extended . . . toward. Hebrew *y^{e}šarot 'el,* lit. "straight toward"; a pregnant construction, with a verbal idea (e.g., "outstretched") implicit and governing the preposition; cf. GKC § 119 gg.

giving cover. An attempt to suggest the ethical dative construction of *m^{e}kassot lahenna* (fem., agreeing with "wings"; in vss. 22–23 all references to the creatures are masc.); for the range of meaning of this idiom, see the excellent treatment in BDB, p. 515, col. b, def. i. For the distributive force of the repetition, cf. 10:9 (GKC § 134 q; Joüon § 142 p); both here and there G shows only one of the repeated clauses; is this translator's simplification?

24. *the deep sea.* Lit. "many waters." The possible mythical overtones of this expression (e.g., in Hab 3:3ff.) were delineated by H. Mays, "Some Cosmic Connections of *Mayim Rabbîm,*" *JBL* 74 (1955), 9–21. If they exist at all in Ezekiel, they are muted; in most occurrences (17:5, 8; 19:10; 26:19; 27:26; 31:7; 32:13f.), reference is to the real ocean—visible and awesome or subterranean and fecund. Here the roar of its billows and breakers is alluded to, as in Ps 93:4.

of the Almighty. English versions render *šadday* (in 10:5 *'el šadday*) by "(God) Almighty," following V *omnipotens* (its almost consistent translation in its many occurrences in Job, where it most often = G *pantokrator*). Exod 6:3 interprets it (schematically) as the name of the God of the patriarchs, who later revealed himself to Moses as YHWH. The origin and meaning of this archaic epithet are obscure; see the good survey by M. Weippert in *THAT* II, pp. 873–81. To the comparison, 10:5 adds "when he speaks"; cf. Ps 18:14; 29:3ff.

army. This is a recognized meaning of *maḥ*^{a}*ne* (e.g., II Kings 3:9), properly "(en)camp(ment)"; see BDB, p. 334, col. a, def. 3c.

slackened. "Wings" must be the subject of the verb (so in G), since the creatures have been referred to as masculine up to now; but in the following word the possessive suffix is feminine. The pi'el (*t*^{e}*rapenna*) must be equivalent to qal (*tirpena*) as happens in Mishnaic Hebrew.

25. The resemblance of elements of this verse to elements of its immediate neighbors (vs. 25a is like vs. 26a$^{\alpha}$; vs. 25b = 24b), unclarity about the motive of the repetition of vs. 24b in vs. 25b, and the absence of the whole, or parts, of the verse in mss. and versions have led critics to regard it as secondary. But vs. 25a is attested by the early versions, and the argument (first advanced by Merx and cited by Cornill) discounting G's evidential value by asserting that "voice" in G is secondary (Merx would have G attest vs. 26a only) is both arbitrary and leaves unexplained the presence of *qol* ("sound/voice") in MT. Why a "sound" from above the expanse should later have been inserted at this point, when it is only at the end of vs. 28 that the prophet hears speech emanating from there, is hard to explain. On the other hand, in this context replete with sounds it is not strange to find the first allusion to "a sound from above the expanse," only now become audible due to the stilling of the creatures' wings. The prophet first perceived only another, different kind of sound (*qol*) that he did not yet identify as speech. This notice does not mark a new stage in the narration (and G's "And lo!" is therefore not preferable to Hebrew "[And] there was") but rather ends the account of nonverbal sounds. As yet mere sound, it did, however, draw the prophet's attention to what was above the expanse—which he proceeds to describe.

G's omissions, resulting in the unintelligible join of vs. 25a to 26aβ, are, in fact, best explicable on the basis of MT: one need only suppose that the eye of a copyist (probably of the Greek) skipped from the end of 25a to the identical words at the end of 26a$^{\alpha}$. The omission of the entire verse from some medieval Hebrew mss. can be similarly accounted for: the copyist's eye skipped from vs. 24b to the end of vs. 25b (identical words). Such omissions are readily explicable on the assumption of the originality of MT; to try to account for MT—especially vs. 25a—on the assumption that the omissions are original is harder. Fohrer is not persuasive when he calls vs. 25 "a supplementary gloss to 22f."

The omission in (some texts of) S of vs. 25b probably has more to do with exegetical difficulty than with text history since S often simplifies hard passages by omission. The disconnected repetition of vs. 25b is awkward and suspicious, and the attempts to relate it to the context are not convincing (T renders vs. 25 thus: "And when it was his will to declare a word to his servants, the prophets of Israel, there was a voice and it was heard from above the expanse that was over their heads; when they stood, they stilled their wings on account of the word"; OJPS: "For, when there was a voice above the firmament . . . , as they stood, they let down their wings"). As it stands, the repetition emphasizes the stillness of the apparition as the prophet focused on its apex.

26. While MT evidently represents the throne itself to be of sapphire, G takes the sapphire to be a pavement on which the throne stood—a conception influenced, it seems, by Exod 24:10 (". . . the God of Israel with something like a pavement of sapphire under his feet"). Ezek 10:1 supports MT here; both lack *'lyw* "on it" after "throne."

27. This verse is characterized by an intricate quasi-balance. Its main burden is the difference between the upper, most holy, part of the enthroned human figure and his lower part, to underline which it enlists the effect of chiasm:

I saw X / from his loins up
From his loins down / I saw Y

X consists of an object ("the like of *ḥašmal*") followed by a circumstantial clause that reads literally "[with] something with the appearance of fire [being] a house for it (fem.) round about" (with the unusual *bet* [for *bayit*] *lah*—cf. *ḥamat lamo,* Ps 58:5; the feminine pronoun *lah* must refer to *k'yn hḥšml,* of which pair *'yn* is surely feminine while *ḥšml* is of unknown gender). The upper part of the human figure was *ḥšml*-like and encased in fire; the relation of the two elements recalls the end of vs. 4: out of the midst of the fire something like *ḥšml* could be seen.

Y consists entirely of what at first seems a parallel to X's circumstantial clause (*kmr'h 'š . . . lh/w sbyb*) but is, in fact, syntactically much different. Y's *kmr'h 'š* is the object of "I saw," and thus its equivalent in X is *k'yn hḥšml;* Y's *wngh lw sbyb* (lit. "with radiance to it round about") is a circumstantial phrase, and thus its equivalent in X is the whole *kmr'h . . . sbyb* sequence. To ignore this difference and assimilate the two is to court trouble; *RSV,* for example, reads *wngh lw sbyb* in Y as a descriptive complement to what precedes it—as *byt lh sbyb* in its clause —with this result: "(like the appearance of fire) enclosed (= [with] a house for it) round about." This is grammatically possible but meaningless.

Since the circumstantial clause in X qualifies the object of "I saw" that precedes it (namely, *k'yn hḥšml*), one tends to refer the circumstantial phrase in Y (*wngh lw sbyb*) to the object of "I saw" that precedes it (namely, *kmr'h 'š*); the resulting message is that the radiance surrounded the firelike lower part of the figure. (Accordingly, the masculine *lw* refers to [*wm*]*mr'h* [*mtnyw*] or, alternatively, to either element of *kmr'h 'š*—on the gender of *'š* see comment to vs. 4.) However, since the radiance of vs. 4—spoken of in terms identical to those of our passage—evidently surrounds all the fire, it seems better so to interpret here as well. Accordingly, one should apply the phrase *wngh lw sbyb* not to its immediately preceding context (the fiery lower part of the figure) but to the entire human figure, both of whose parts were fiery (the upper part was encased in fire). *lw* will then refer to *'dm* of vs. 27, and the radiance will then surround the entire figure, like the nimbus surrounding the god Asshur described in Structure and Themes.

G lacks the circumstantial clause of X and is therefore simpler—and less related to the end of vs. 4:

> I saw . . . amber . . . from / his loins upward
> And from . . . his loins downward I saw . . . fire
> And its radiance round about

The radiance clause, here outside the chiasm, is the more readily associated not with its immediate context but with the figure as a whole. MT impresses one as literarily more elaborated.

28. *That,* namely, the human figure of vss. 26ff., with the elements of *ḥašmal,* fire and radiance, *was the . . . Majesty of YHWH;* that the Majesty did not include the creatures is inferable from 9:3; 10:4, 18f.; 11:22, where it is distinguished from its vehicle (the cherubs). For a more inclusive use of the term, see comment at 3:22.

"Majesty" is Hebrew *kabod* (usually rendered "glory"), used for the visible manifestation of God in Exod 16:7; 24:16f.; 40:34f., etc.; see the detail in BDB, p. 458, def. 2c. The only other indication outside of this passage that the *kabod* may appear as a figure is Exod 33:18, 22, where Moses is denied a view of the face but is granted a view of the back of God's *kabod.* Since *kabod* may also serve poetically for the person of a man (Gen 49:6; Ps 16:9), it is fitly rendered by English "majesty," among whose usages is not only "the person of a sovereign" but also "a representation in . . . art of God . . . or . . . the Trinity enthroned in glory" (Webster's Third New International Dictionary).

when I saw it, I fell. "The order of narration follows the order of perception in strict sequence; although he saw *ḥashmal* right at the beginning, he did not perceive the humanlike figure at that time. Therefore, only now did he fall on his face from dread of this overwhelming apparition" (Eliezer of Beaugency).

STRUCTURE AND THEMES

Reduced to its essentials, this is the narrative of the vision of the divine Majesty: While the prophet stood beside the Chebar canal one summer day, a tempestuous north wind (not unusual for the season) bore toward him an incandescent cloud, encircled by a radiance (vs. 4). As the cloud neared, four glowing creatures became visible in its lower part, like humans in their erect posture, their leg(s) and hands, but unlike them in having four faces and four wings (vss. 5–8a). The creatures, disposed perhaps in a square, were joined at their wing tips to one another. They gave the impression of a unity as they moved, and, facing in every direction, always went in the direction they faced, without needing to turn (vss. 8b–12). Amidst them was a flashing, torchlike apparition (vs. 13). The prophet noted that below and alongside each creature was a high, complex wheel, rimmed with eyes, that moved in unison with the creatures (vss. 14–21).

The prophet's gaze moved from the creatures upward, to take in a dazzling, icelike expanse borne above their heads and outspread wings. As they neared, he grew aware of the terrific noise made by their wings in motion (vss. 22–24).

Then the wings slackened and the apparition came to a halt; the prophet heard a sound from above the expanse that drew his gaze further upward. He saw a sapphire throne standing upon the expanse, upon which an effulgent human figure sat, all brilliant and fiery, and encased by a rainbowlike radiance. Only then did the prophet realize that what he beheld was the Majesty of God; at that, he fell awestruck to the ground (vss. 25–28).

The order of the narrative represents the order of the prophet's perception: first sights, then (as the apparition drew near) sounds; first the lower part of the vision (that nearer the earth), then the upper; first the motion of the apparition, then its halting. Vss. 4 and 27f. form an envelope for the entire narration: the undifferentiated, uncomprehended pyrotechnics in the cloud of vs. 4 are by stages put in their proper place and finally deciphered in vss. 27f. There is an evident aim to reconstitute for the reader the movement of the prophet's senses and the course of his understanding of the experience. However, in places the good order of the narrative breaks down (e.g., vss. 8b–12); this is most likely due to the accumulation of doublets in our text, from which G is freer. Moreover, the depiction of the various motions and situations of the apparition—the ability of the creatures to change direction without changing their stance, the unity of wheels and creatures in ascending and traveling, the wheels' location on the ground—seems to be based on a combination of observations more complex and varied than the mere approach of the apparition involved in this vision; it would seem, therefore, that at least here later information gotten otherwise and from elsewhere has been incorporated in ch. 1 (cf. 3:12f.; 10:15, 19; 11:22). Recent commentators (e.g., Fohrer, Zimmerli) go far in reducing the narrative to a hypothetical original terseness, but their criteria for originality are arbitrary (e.g., the assumption of a system in the present vacillation of gender in reference to the creatures), and the resultant creativity ascribed to copyists or the (assumed) circle of the prophet's disciples is excessive. There is little reason to suppose that the original conformed exactly and consistently to any single norm.

The frequent use of comparison in the description is an aspect of the desire to be faithful and exact while indicating consciousness of the visionary nature of the event. The most frequent expression of comparison is *k*^{e}*mar'e,* lit. "like the appearance of"; this does not signify a reservation with respect to looks but with respect to substance. When Manoah's wife describes the man of God who appeared to her as one "whose appearance was like the appearance of an angel, very dreadful" (Judg 13:6), she means to convey exactly the looks of the man, though in substance he was no angel. Similarly, "something with [lit. like] the appearance of torches" (vs. 13), "of sapphire-stone" (vs. 26), "of a human being" (vs. 26) mean that what was seen looked just like that with which it is compared; the use of *k*^{e}*mar'e* (and of *k*$^{e'}$*en* and *d*^{e}*mut* also) signifies unwillingness to commit oneself to the substantial identity of the seen with the compared. It looked like torches, sapphire, a human being, but that is not to say that torches, sapphire, and a human being were actually there. The use of these buffer terms indicates that the prophet wished to have his audience bear in mind always that this was *mar'ot* "vision"; there is no ground for supposing he had any reservations respecting the visual likeness in these comparisons. For exact parallels, note the dream report of a Hittite queen: "In a dream something like my father has risen again alive" (Oppenheim, *Dreams,* p. 204a); and of Egypt's King Merneptah: "Then his majesty saw in a dream as if it were the image of Ptah standing in the presence of the Pharaoh" (ibid., p. 251 § 16).

To such a vision as the first element in the account of a prophet's call few analogies exist. Moses was prepared for his commissioning by a simple, fiery theophany in a burning bush (Exod 3). Isa 6 describes a vision of the celestial court that has points in common with Ezek 1—winged attendants on God, who is seated on his throne—and is generally taken to be an account of Isaiah's call. (Kaufmann, *Religion,* p. 388, fn. 5, demurs, comparing the similar scene in Micaiah's vision, I Kings 22:19ff., not part of the prophet's call.) But in these visions God is not seen (or said) to have come to the prophet from heaven or from afar; he is statically present throughout the vision. On the other hand, God is commonly pictured as riding in heaven (Ps 68:5, 34; 104:3) and coming as judge or king to save his faithful or punish the wicked (Deut 33:26; Isa 19:1). The characteristics of the divine manifestation in Ezekiel—the storm, the cloud, lightning, fire, and radiance—are regularly associated with awesome public theophanies; cf. Exod 19; Deut 33:2f.; Judg 5:4f.; Nahum 1:3ff.; Hab 3:8–15. The closest analogue to Ezekiel's private vision occurs in Ps 18 (II Sam 22), vss. 8–14. In answer to the psalmist's cry for help,

The earth quaked and trembled . . .
[God] tilted the sky and came down
Thick clouds were under his feet
He rode on a cherub and flew
He appeared [var. soared] on wings of wind
He put darkness about him as his pavilion . . .
In the radiance before him fiery coals burned
YHWH thundered from heaven
The Most High gave forth his voice

One may also compare Isa 63:19b. The image of God as a rider in the sky with the clouds as his chariot is common to the Bible, Ugaritic texts (Baal's stock epithet is "Rider of the clouds" [e.g., *ANET*[3], pp. 130b, 131a]), and Mesopotamia (see below); in itself it is not remarkable.

The closest approach to an ancient illustration of the divine figure seen by Ezekiel is *ANEP*[2] ⁂536, a colored ceramic from Ashur depicting the god Ashur floating amidst rain clouds, accompanying his army, and shooting with a bow. "The flying god . . . is . . . unusually beautiful . . . The head and uppermost part of the body seem to have been white, and the wing feathers yellow and blue . . . a double yellow ring [is] in his flaming nimbus. Great flaming streamers fly back from him . . ." (W. Andrae, *Colored Ceramics from Ashur* [London: K. Paul, Trench, Trubner & Co., 1925], pl. 8, p. 27; reproduced in color in A. Parrot, *Nineveh and Babylon* [London: Thames and Hudson, 1961], fig. 282).

The appearance of the Majesty of YHWH in cloud and fire (but without visible shape) is a feature of the wilderness narratives of the Pentateuch. The Majesty appears in order to support the leader(s) of Israel set upon by the people in the episodes of the manna (Exod 16:10), the spies (Num 14:10), and Korah's rebellion (Num 16:19). On Mount Sinai (Exod 24:17), on the tabernacle on the day of its inauguration (40:34f.), at the inauguration of the priests (Lev 9:23), as later at the inauguration of Solomon's temple (I Kings 8:11), the Majesty appeared to signify God's proximity to and presence amidst his people. Moses' plea to see God's Majesty (Exod 33:18) indicates that its revelation to an individual is the highest token of divine favor.

The combination of features in the divine appearance to Ezekiel thus expressed powerfully, and in concentrated form, God's support of and intimate presence with the prophet.

The search for analogues to the structure of the apparition and, particularly, to its creatures gives the same result: individual elements are found in the tradition, but the ensemble is unique. God is said to ride "on the wings of the wind" (Ps 18:11)—of which the "cherub" (ibid.) is a personification; elsewhere God is said to be the "enthroned-one of the cherubs" (i.e., upon them; I Sam 4:4; II Sam 6:2; Ps 99:1). The shape of the cherubs is not indicated by the sources; they were winged—and their two wings covered the ark in the holy of holies (I Kings 6:27); between the outspread wings of the small cherubs on the desert ark God "met" Moses to speak to him (Exod 25:22). Combining these data, it seems that the cherubs were celestial winged bearers of God upon which he was imagined as sitting enthroned; the sanctuary images were but representations of them. Modern scholars have compared the winged sphinxes and other composite quadrupeds that are pictured as supporting (or constituting) the throne of ancient Near Eastern kings (e.g., Ahiram, *ANEP*[2] ⁂458; cf. ⁂332) or serving as pedestals of gods (*ANEP*[2] ⁂534). On the other hand, the cherub of Ezek 28:14ff.—a denizen of

God's garden, Eden—appears to have a human form; moreover, the "creatures" of ch. 1 are, in Ezek 10, named cherubs—and they are here said to have a human shape. That Ezekiel did not immediately identify the creatures as cherubs indicates that some difference set them apart from the sanctuary images, but it was not so great as to exclude his later identifying them as such. What the difference was is not specified.

Like the seraphs seen by Isaiah, Ezekiel's creatures had several sets of wings; the seraphs had one additional set in order to cover their faces, since they hovered above the divine throne and might otherwise gaze upon God, while Ezekiel's creatures were positioned below and looked straight ahead.

The compositeness of Ezekiel's creatures accords entirely with Mesopotamian and Syrian iconography. Composite deities and mythical beings are common in Egypt and Mesopotamia; an Egyptologist explains the symbolism as follows: ". . . whenever possible they combined [the zoomorphic and anthropomorphic] ideas in a composite whole. Thus the anthropomorphized gods were given a human body, but only seldom a human head, this being mostly replaced by that of the animal in whose form the god originally used to appear." "Also for the purposes of art . . . some material personification of deities was indispensable, and if human bodies of gods kept the heads of various animals, this was certainly largely because it was a convenient means of distinguishing their various personalities. That the head of the animal should in some way recall the qualities attributed to the god is only natural" (J. Černý, *Ancient Egyptian Religion* [London/New York: Hutchinson's University Library, 1957], pp. 29–40). In Mesopotamia it is the lesser divinities (e.g., guardian genii) and demons that are portrayed in composite form, including winged quadrupeds with human faces (*ANEP*[2] ⁂644–66); here, too, we are to understand the combination to express attributes conjoined in these celestial attendants, the bearers of the divine throne. Multiplication of faces in the manner of Ezekiel's creatures is, however, extremely rare. Two tiny bronzes from Old Babylonian times show a god and a goddess, each with four identical human faces; the impression is of all-observing potency (A. Parrot, *Sumer* [London: Thames and Hudson, 1960], p. 349). Janus (=two)-faced gods are more common (not usually great gods; e.g., an attendant upon Ea, *ANEP*[2] ⁂685, 687, 693), a variation of which is the following late description of the Phoenician El (=Kronos) by Sanchuniathon: "[The god Tauthos] devised for Kronos as insignia of royalty four eyes, before and behind [of which two were waking] and two quietly closed; and on his shoulders four wings, of which two were as flying and two as folded. And the symbol meant that Kronos could see when asleep and sleep while waking: and similarly in the case of the wings, that he flew while at rest and was at rest when flying" (Eusebius, Praeparatio Evangelica I, 10. 36–37). However, the symbolism of four distinct faces must be different, and for that we have no analogues. (The evidence collected by Landersdorfer, *βααλ τετραμορφος* [Paderborn: Schöningh, 1918], contrary to his intent, all bears on four-faced deities whose faces are the same; cf. the rationale given by Basil of Caesaria [fourth century] for the four-faced idol ascribed to Manasseh [J. Migne, *Patrologia Graeca,* CXXI, p. 228; cited by Landersdorfer, p. 7], "so that one might pray to the images from whatever side one approached" [= *Deuteronomy Rabba* 2.20]—necessarily based on the idol's showing the same aspect every way. Cf. also Pesikta de-Rav Kahana's depiction of God's revelation at Sinai as "like a statue with faces on every side so that though a thousand people looked at it, it would look back at each one" [12.25, ed. B. Mandelbaum, 2 vols. (New York: Jewish Theological Seminary of America), I, pp. 223f.].) To get at its meaning we must note the figurative use of each of the animals whose faces are on the head of Ezekiel's creatures.

The lion is proverbially the fiercest of beasts (Num 23:24; 24:9; Judg 14:18; II Sam 1:23; 17:10, etc.); the eagle the most imposing (swift, high-flying) of birds (Deut 28:49; II Sam 1:23; Jer 48:40; Lam 4:19; Job 39:27; Akkadian *ašarid iṣṣurē* "foremost among birds" [D. Luckenbill, ed., *The Annals of Sennacherib* (Chicago: University of Chicago Press, 1924), p. 36]); the swiftness of eagles and the might of lions are both alluded to in David's lament in II Sam 1:23. The bull is the most valued of domestic animals (for plowing and breeding: Prov 14:4; Job 21:10; cf. Exod 21:37). Men, of course, ruled them all (Gen 1:28; Ps 8:7). In ancient Near Eastern art these animals, or combinations of them, served as bearers or pedestals of images of gods (*ANEP*[2] #472–74, 486, 830 [lion]; 500, 501, 531, 835 [bull]; 534 [winged lion with bull's head]; 537 [a number of gods mounted on different animals]). An eagle-headed human figure with two sets of wings supports overhead a symbol of a god (#855); horned bull-men hold a "stool" on which the divine symbol sits (#653; cf. 645, probably the same). In Ezekiel's vision the traditional bearers of God are portrayed as combining the attributes of the "lords" of animate creation in their faces, the dominant shape of their bodies being human. The following midrash to Exod 15:1 gives as fine an interpretation of the creatures as can be found: "Four kinds of proud beings were created in the world: the proudest of all—man; of birds—the eagle; of domestic animals—the ox; of wild animals—the lion; and all of them are stationed beneath the chariot of the Holy One . . ." (*Exodus Rabba* 23.13). That is to say, the most lordly of creatures are merely the bearers of the Lord of lords.

Two concepts appear to be fused in the apparition taken as a whole: that of a deity borne by mythical beings and that of a throne-chariot. For the two-level image of a deity enthroned and riding on an animal or a mythical being (cf. YHWH's epithet: "the enthroned-one of the cherubs") good Mesopotamian and west-Asiatic representations exist to help us envisage the general aspect of this apparition. A goddess enthroned and borne by a lion is a commonplace (M. Jastrow, *Bilder-*

mappe zur Religion Babyloniens und Assyriens [Giessen: A. Töpelmann, 1912], pl. 204; C. L. Woolley, *Carchemish*, II [London: Trustees of the British Museum, 1921], pl. B 19a; E. Strommenger, *5000 Years of the Art of Mesopotamia* [New York: H. N. Abrams, 1964], pl. 179, 2nd row, right); particularly suited for comparison owing to its complexity is the depiction in the Maltaï procession scene (*ANEP*² ⋇537). The second divine figure from the left is a goddess seated on a throne, resting on a high pedestal, whose side shows a griffin, a scorpion man with upraised wings, and a (worshiping?) human figure. Between the pedestal and the seat of the throne appear three views of a king, between which are two composite creatures (upper half human, lower animal) whose upraised hands support the seat of the throne. The whole rides on the back of a walking lion.

Related to this image is *ANEP*² ⋇653, in which "bull-men" support a "stool" on which the symbol of a god rests; or ⋇855, in which a four-winged "eagle-man" with upraised arms supports a divine symbol over his head.

This straightforward concept is complicated by the wheels in Ezekiel's apparition. Four wheels belong to a cart (cf. the bases of the temple lavers, I Kings 7:27–37, with four wheels and decorated by figures of cherubs, lions, and cattle!) or a primitive type of chariot (*ANEP*² ⋇303); comparable is the early disk-wheeled divine chariot with a god standing in it, shown in *ANEP*² ⋇689 (the chariot is drawn by a winged lion on whose back a goddess rides). Now, YHWH is said to ride in a chariot too (Hab 3:8; Isa 66:15), and it appears that Ezekiel's vision combined the two modes of locomotion. In the vision of divine judgment in Dan 7:9 God's throne is also equipped with wheels. What facilitated the combination was the actuality of throne-chariots in Near Eastern antiquity. A scene from an eighth-century Assyrian palace relief depicts servants carrying an empty wheeled throne: the visible wheel is quite large and, interestingly, though spoked it has a thick rim made up of three concentric bands; above and alongside the wheel, beside and below the seat of the throne, is the image of a harnessed, striding horse. This vehicle has a yoke shaft for draft animals (G. Perrot and C. Chipiez, *Histoire de l'art dans l'antiquité*, II [Paris: Hachette, 1884], fig. 23, p. 100). Perhaps even more apt is the high-backed, wheeled sedan chair of Assurnaṣirpal II depicted on the as yet unpublished bronze gates found at Balawat (E. Sollberger, "The White Obelisk [of Aššurnaṣirpal II]," *Iraq* 36 [1974], 232; I owe this reference to the courtesy of Dr. Irene Winter); a device normally borne by bearers may thus be furnished with wheels.

The dominance of four in the apparition must be connected with the division of the world into four parts (Isa 11:12, "the four corners [*kanpot*] of the earth") or the circle of the horizon into four directions ("seaward [west] and forward [east] and north and south," Gen 13:14; 28:14). It symbolizes the divine capacity to control the whole world—to see all, to be everywhere effortlessly. These traditional Israelite notions can only have been enforced by contact with the Babylonians, whose literature was full of "the four regions of the world" (*kibrāt arba'i* or *erbetti*) and *šār erbetti* "the four winds"—a notion that occurs in the Bible from the Babylonian period onward (Jer 49:36; Ezek 37:9, etc.).

The eyes with which the rims of the wheels were inlaid may be supposed to signify the constant divine watchfulness. Compare what was adduced earlier concerning the many eyes of Kronos and the many "eyestones" that adorned the tiaras of the Assyrian gods' statues (S. Parpola, *Letters from Assyrian Scholars to the Kings Esarhaddon and Assurbanipal,* Pt. I: Texts [Neukirchen-Vluyn: Neukirchener Verlag des Erziehungsvereins, 1970], no. 276, obv. 11; "26 'eyestones' [*aban* *īnu*] for the tiara of the god Nabu"; cf. E. Vogt, *Biblica* 59 [1978], 93–96).

If a basis in some earthly reality exists for the fiery appearance moving about among the creatures, it escapes us. As a sign of divine fierceness—the fire will figure in the punishment of Jerusalem in 10:2—it recalls the poetic allusions to fire "going" or "consuming" before God (Ps 50:3; 97:3) and the "coals of fire" that "burned out of the radiance that was in front of him" (Ps 18:13f.). Here the position of the fire has changed in accord with the disposition of the entire apparition vertically (throne, beneath which are the ministers-bearers) instead of horizontally (chariot, ahead of which are draft animals and outrunners).

Virtually every component of Ezekiel's vision can thus be derived from Israelite tradition supplemented by neighboring iconography—none of the above-cited elements of which need have been outside the range of the ordinary Israelite. Indeed, the divine imagery of the Bible resembles closely that of the surrounding (esp. west Asiatic) cultures; it was not in imagery but in divine attributes and manner of worship that Israel's religion differed. The specific combinations, such as the four distinct faces, and the ensemble remain unprecedented for us—and for the prophet. There is no ground for asserting that he saw an earthly equivalent anywhere, or that he followed a Babylonian prototype. As a captive domiciled away from the great centers of culture, Ezekiel had little opportunity to study the artwork of Babylonian temples or witness the grand processions of the gods. Even in the event that he had, he was too concerned over the purity of Israel's worship (see esp. chs. 8–11) to have imported into it images drawn directly from the pagan sphere (H. Schmidt, "Kerubenthron," *Eucharisterion,* p. 124, fn. 2). Indeed, the whole tenor of the description bespeaks wonder at the unfamiliar. Here was a new revelation of the suite of Israel's God, displaying, to be sure, enough of the known to be identifiable in the end, yet so new as to exclude for the prophet the possibility that he was merely drawing out of the stock of memory a sight that his heart craved.

The meaning of this vision for the prophet can best be discussed with the auditory event that followed it. Here, however, it is convenient to question the widespread view that the vision showed "God's ability to work as he wishes. He is not bound to the holy land. This was an almost revolutionary idea" (Stalker, p. 49, epitomizing many others, among them

Fohrer and Zimmerli). In these general terms the view is untenable; YHWH is nowhere in Scripture anything less than a god of universal dominion; however, his special favor, the manifestation of his sanctity and, consequently, the sites at which he may be worshiped are usually limited to the people and the land of Israel, respectively (the gentiles' lands are "impure" [Amos 7:17], hence YHWH may not be worshiped on them [cf. II Kings 5:17]; Ezekiel rebuts a Jerusalemite claim that the exiles are removed from God, i.e., from his gift of possession of the land [11:15f.]; see the discriminating discussion in Kaufmann, *Religion,* pp. 127ff.). At most, then, it might be supposed that Ezekiel's vision "revolutionized" a notion that YHWH's revelation could not occur outside the land of Israel. The later discussion of Ezek 1:3 in the Mechilta (*Pisḥa,* 1, pp. 6ff.) starts precisely from the proposition that the Shekinah (the indwelling presence of God) does not rest on prophets outside the Holy Land. But is that a biblical doctrine? The Mechilta's proof text is Jonah 1:3 ("Jonah rose up to flee to Tarshish from the presence of YHWH"); which says only that Jonah sought to shirk his duty by taking a course diametrically opposite to that commanded by God; with *brḥ mlpny YHWH,* S. D. Goitein ("Some Observations on Jonah," *JPOS* 17 [1937], 67) aptly contrasts *'md lpny YHWH* "attend upon, serve YHWH" said of the prophet's duty (I Kings 17:1; 18:15, etc.) and compares I Sam 25:10. On the other hand, there is clear evidence of the exiles' situation and state of mind on this topic, and it runs counter to the assumed significance of this vision. The exiles of that time were confident of God's attention and believed themselves abundantly endowed with his prophets and his words. Thus Ezek 13 denounces "base prophets" who prophesy out of their own invention; that they are among the exiles is shown by the threat that "they shall not be entered in the register of the Israelites and shall not come to the soil of Israel" (vs. 9). As we hear in Jer 29:15, such prophets were the pride of the exiles ("YHWH has raised up prophets for us in Babylonia!"). They encouraged the hope of a speedy restoration, confidently asserted God's care for his scattered ones—and posed the most serious challenge to both Ezekiel and Jeremiah. The two labored (in vain, before the fall) to persuade the exiles that God's intentions toward Israel were utterly opposed to what these prophets proclaimed; that God had not, in fact, "raised up" these prophets, and that God, in fact, was not "with them" in their sense. Later Jeremiah prophesied in Egypt without the ado one might expect to have been made about a "revolutionary idea" (Jer 43:8).

So it could hardly have been to prove God's presence with the exiles that Ezekiel needed this vision, or to persuade them that there could be prophecy in "impure land." An alternative view will be proposed after consideration of the message the prophet received along with the vision.

Out of this description of the divine suite early Judaism developed a body of mystical speculation on the structure and personnel of the divine realm (see note appended to ch. 10).

II. Ezekiel's Call: The Commissioning (1:28bβ–3:15)

1 28bβ Then I heard the voice of one speaking 2 1 and he said to
me: Man, get on your feet and I shall speak to you. 2 Spirit entered
me as he spoke to me and got me on my feet, and I heard the one
speaking to me.
3 He said to me: Man, I am sending you to the sons of Israel, to
the rebellious nations who have rebelled against me; they and their
fathers have transgressed against me to this very day. 4 The sons—
brazen-faced and tough-hearted—I am sending you to them, and you
shall say to them, "Thus said Lord YHWH." 5 And they—whether
they listen or not, for they are a rebellious house—shall [yet] realize
that a prophet was among them.

6 You, man, do not be afraid of them,
  and of their words do not be afraid;
For nettles and thorns are with you,
  and you sit on scorpions.
Of their words do not be afraid,
  and by their faces do not be daunted,
  for they are a rebellious house.

7 But speak my words to them, whether they listen or not (for they
are rebellious).
8 You, man, listen to whatever I speak to you: do not be rebellious like that rebellious house; open your mouth and eat whatever
I give you. 9 I looked and saw a hand sent forth toward me, and in it
was a written scroll. 10 He unrolled it before me, and its front and
back were covered with writing. On it was written, "Laments and
moaning and woe."
3 1 He said to me: Man, whatever you find there, eat! Eat this
scroll and go, speak to the house of Israel. 2 I opened my mouth and
he gave me this scroll to eat, 3 saying to me: Man, feed your belly
and fill your stomach with this scroll that I give you. So I ate it, and
in my mouth it turned sweet as honey.
4 He said to me: Man, come! Go to the house of Israel and speak
to them in my words. 5 For you are not being sent to a people whose

speech is obscure and whose language is difficult, [but] to the house of
Israel; 6 not to one of the many peoples whose speech is obscure and
whose language is difficult, whose words you cannot understand—
surely if I sent you to them they would listen to you. 7 But the house
of Israel will refuse to listen to you because they refuse to listen to
me; for the whole house of Israel are tough-browed and hard-hearted.

8 See, I make your face tough to match their faces,
and your brow tough to match their brows;
9 like diamond tougher than flint I make your brow.
You shall not be afraid of them
or be daunted by their faces,
for they are a rebellious house.

10 He said to me: Man, all my words that I speak to you take into
your heart and hear with your ears, 11 and come, go to the exiles, to
the sons of your people, and speak to them and say to them, "Thus
said Lord YHWH"—whether they listen or not.

12 A wind lifted me and I heard behind me a great rumbling
noise[a]—[b]"Blessed be[b] the Majesty of YHWH from its place!"—
13 the noise of the creatures' wings beating against one another, and
the noise of the wheels alongside them, a great rumbling noise. 14 A
wind lifted me and took me, and I went, bitter, my spirit raging,
overpowered by the hand of YHWH. 15 I came to the exiles at Tel
Abib, who were living by the Chebar canal and[c], [d]where they were
living[d], there I sat seven days, desolate among them.

[a] S adds here "of one saying"; T "of ones praising and saying."
[b–b] Hebrew *baruk;* conjecture *b*^{e}*rum* "at the rising of."
[c] Not in G.
[d–d] Not in S.

COMMENT

1:28 *the voice of one speaking.* So rendered by G; or translate "a voice speaking (2:1 and *it* said . . .)"; either way the expression avoids ascribing the speech directly to the human figure visible on the throne in the apparition, as though reserving the source of the speech for the unseen God.

2:1 *Man.* Hebrew *ben 'adam* "son of mankind"; *ben* + generic noun is a common manner of expressing a male member of a class; e.g., *ben baqar* "a (male) head of cattle." *ben 'adam* is almost entirely limited to poetic or prophetic literature; Ezekiel is called this in order to single him out from the divine beings that fill this scene. He continues to be addressed thus throughout the book (over eighty times) rather than by name (contrast Amos 7:8; 8:2; Jer 1:11; 24:3), underlining his mortal nature among the divine beings he sees and has contact with (chs. 8–11; 40ff.).

get on your feet. As Dan 8:17f.; 10:9–11 show, the biblical visionary must be in possession of himself in order to receive the divine word. The ecstasy of biblical prophecy consists in a Godward concentration of consciousness that obliterates circumstances, in contrast to the ecstasy of pagan prophets, in which consciousness itself was obliterated; see Kaufmann, *Religion,* pp. 94–100.

2. *Spirit.* Hebrew *ruaḥ,* here in the sense of vigor or even courage (BDB, p. 925a, 3.a.b.) infused into the prophet by the address of God.

as he spoke to me. The phrase connects his invigoration with the preceding speech without explicitly ascribing it to God.

the one speaking. Hebrew *'et middabber* is peculiar in having *'et* before an indefinite substantive, and in the vocalization of the participle as reflexive (hitpa'el) "speaking to himself" (T *mtmll*). Both appear to express reservations: the former—defining yet leaving indefinite "the one speaking"; the latter—redirecting the divine speech back onto the speaker. The reflexive vocalization of *mdbr* recurs in 43:6, in the vision of the future temple, when from the interior, just reoccupied by the divine Majesty, Ezekiel hears "one-speaking-to-himself" (*middabber*) to him; the speech can only emanate from the Majesty, but that is not said explicitly. Both passages must be related to Num 7:19, the only other passage in which the hitpa'el of *dbr* occurs—the archetypical description of Moses' regular oracular hearing "the voice"—it is not said "God's voice"—speaking to him from the holy of holies. In these three passages, where the consonantal text was oddly vague about the source of speech—though it was obviously divine—a peculiar vocalization of the pertinent verb reinforces the impression of a reverential reservation respecting the directness of God's speech: "The Shekinah [the immanent divine presence] speaks in its majesty to itself; its messengers only overhear it" (Rashi). The same reflexive form appears in the common Mishnaic *niddabber* (*-bar*), specialized for God's speech to prophets (its nominal analogue is *dibber* "God's utterance," plural *dibberot* as in *'aśeret haddibberot* "the Decalogue," based on the hapax legomenon in Jer 5:13). The rare MT vocalization seems to be artificial—an exploitation of a textual opening for introducing a later reverential linguistic conceit.

3. *sons of Israel.* This rendering of *bene yisra'el,* otherwise "Israelites," brings out its relation to "the sons" of vs. 4a, both expressions of the father-sons subtheme of this passage—the theme of hereditary sinfulness (see Structure and Themes). For the purpose of this subtheme *bene yisra'el* was employed here instead of *bet yisra'el,* which is far more common in Ezekiel (and, indeed, is read here by G—which, however, lacks 4a!).

The prophet's mission is to "Israel" at large, no distinction being made here between exiles and those in the homeland (after the fall of the northern kingdom, "Israel" came to designate the remaining kingdom of Judah as well as the ideal whole nation; see BDB, p. 975, 2.a.[3]). This vague entity is described as "the rebellious nations," an unclear epithet. (The absence of the article, as here with *goyim,* often occurs when a following attribute consists of a participle; the article attached to the attribute alone (*hammorᵉdim*) approaches the relative in meaning; GKC § 126 w–x; Joüon § 138 b–c.) Perhaps the simplest explanation of "nations" is found in God's promise to the patriarch Israel that "a nation, indeed an assembly of nations, shall stem from you" (Gen 35:11), in which "nations" must mean "tribes" (cf. Deut 33:19, where "peoples" [*'ammim*] must refer to Israelite tribes); "the rebellious nations" will then refer either to the remaining kingdom of Judah, consisting of Judah, Benjamin, and Simeon, or—if by "Israel" the ideal whole is meant, as seems more likely—to the ideal twelve-tribe entity. Alternatively "nations" may mean the two kingdoms of Judah and Israel, called "two nations" by the prophet in 35:10; 36:13ff.; and 37:22.

Note that in the peroration of this speech, God defines the audience of the prophet more narrowly and realistically as the community of exiles (3:11).

rebellious nations. The participle (*morᵉdim*) expresses a characteristic attribute; cf. the string in Isa 1:4 ("sinful nation," etc.). The following verb clauses (*'šer marᵉdu,* etc.) refer to repeated acts exhibiting the attribute.

who have rebelled (marᵉdu) . . . *revolted* (pašᵉ'u). The essence of Israel's offense is political or, better, theopolitical: rebellion against their divine Lord and King (on this concept consult index in M. Buber, *Moses* [Oxford and London: East and West Library, 1946] s.v. Theopolitical idea). The primary sense of *marad* is "refuse allegiance to, rise up against, a sovereign"; its antonym is *'abad* "serve, be subject to" (Gen 14:4; II Kings 18:7). This is also the sense in the context of Israel's relation to God, as here. *paša',* too, has this sense (I Kings 12:19; II Kings 8:20; "violation of vassal duties . . . breach of covenant relations," J. Pederson, *Israel* I–II [London: Oxford University Press, 1926], p. 417), but more commonly it has a religious or ethical meaning, "transgress, commit an offense" (e.g., Ezek 18:31); the latter predominates in the noun *peša'* "transgression, offense" (Ezek 14:11; 18:22ff.; 21:29, etc.). The combination of the two verbs points to the dual aspect of Israel's offense, denoted by the coinage "theopolitical"; it recurs only in Ezek 20:38—an eminently theopolitical context (cf. 20:33: ". . . I will be king over you").

4. *brazen* (lit. *hard*)*-faced.* Impassive, with a face that shows no emotion or disconcertion when it should—as when confronting divine Majesty or displeasure (Isa 50:7 ". . . I have made my face like flint and I know I shall not be shamed"; cf. Exod 20:20; Jer 5:3). This unique phrase is

an adaptation of the common *qᵉše 'orep* "stiff-necked (lit. naped)"—cf. the contrast "nape–face" in Jer 2:27; 18:17; 32:33—with "face" giving the nuance of impudence and *qᵉše* shifting its weight from "stiff, unbending" to "hard, unimpressionable," as in *qᵉše leb* "hard-hearted" of 3:7; see next comment. The substitution of "face" here adds a dimension to the commonplace *'al teḥat mippeᵉnehem* of vss. 6 and 3:9; ordinarily it would be rendered "do not be daunted by them," but in this context it must be more literally "daunted by their faces"; see comment to 3:9.

tough-hearted. Obdurate, having a "heart of stone" (36:26) incapable of receiving impressions; this and the related "hard-hearted" of 3:7 recall the cognate verbal terminology used of Pharaoh's obstinacy in Exod 7:3, 13, and elsewhere.

In "brazen-faced and tough-hearted" the moral fault of the people is expressed in an exterior and an interior figure, each with a different nuance (impudence-obstinacy). This may be contrasted with the language of II Chron 36:13, "he stiffened his neck and toughened his heart," which, while using closely related exterior and interior images, expresses the same idea—obstinacy—twice.

"Thus said . . ." This is the prophetic adaptation of the formula with which messengers began their verbatim delivery of messages (Gen 32:5; 45:9; Exod 5:10; Num 20:14; Judg 11:15; for extrabiblical examples, see *ANET*³, pp. 480, 482f., 484ff., 623ff.). The frequency with which it is found in Ezekiel (129 times according to Müller, *Ezechiel-Studien,* p. 33) is matched only in Jeremiah. Precisely these two contemporaries explicitly challenged, and were challenged by, other prophets of their time who claimed divine authority for messages diametrically opposed to theirs (e.g., Jer 23; Ezek 13; cf. esp. Ezek 22:28; on the formula, see Y. Hoffmann, "Two Opening Formulae in Biblical Style" [Hebrew], *Tarbiz* 46 [1977], 157–80).

With respect to the double appellation of the deity *'ᵃdonay YHWH* "(my) Lord YHWH," it is to be noted that often in the messenger formula the sender's name is accompanied (preceded in biblical usage) by a qualifier—"your servant," "your brother"; in this context *'ᵃdonay YHWH* may well have been interpreted thus, *'ᵃdonay* meaning something between "my lord" (its literal, vocative sense) and a divine name (see the perplexed treatment in BDB, p. 11, defs. 3 and 4) but in any case clearly conveying the notion "Lord" (cf. the archaic formula *ha'adon YHWH,* Exod 23:17; 34:23). The double appellation occurs 217 times in this book, overwhelmingly (208 times) in the opening formulas of oracles (as here) and in their closings (or internal pauses) in the phrase *nᵉ'um 'ᵃdonay YHWH* "the speech of Lord YHWH"; in these phrases the tetragram alone does not occur. This preference appears to be rhetorical, a verbal signature to the oracle. In our passage the mere message formula, without any specific content to be delivered, is dictated to the prophet. Now, since an alternative wording for the charge to speak to the people was available (see vss. 7; 3:4), this choice of the empty messenger formula must have its own significance. It may be suggested that the meaning of the mere formula, with its double divine appellation, is given by the context of vss. 3–5. Israel's rebelliousness is emphasized; it is the prophet's duty to take them to task in the name of their Lord, against whom they have rebelled. The very pairing of YHWH with "Lord" aims to force upon them awareness of their true state—subjection to a Lord whom they refuse to acknowledge. The imprint of this initial experience of a messenger formula with a double appellative (chosen here for its specific contextual value) became normative for the rest of Ezekiel's experience. He continued to use the double appellative virtually without variation in the openings of all his messages, and in a common closing formula (see at 5:11) as a kind of divine signature. (This suggestion resembles that made earlier with regard to the consistent use of *ben 'adam* as the prophet's appellative, from the call narrative onward.) J. Lust has proposed that since only in the prophet's speech does this double appellation appear, it must be understood personally, "my Lord YHWH" (Lust revocalizes *'ᵃdoni*), and is intended to deny the people's servantship to YHWH in the present, as opposed to the future (in *De Mari à Qumran: Hommage à J. Coppens,* ed. H. Cazelles [Gembloux: Duculot, 1969], pp. 167–73).

In the witnesses to G, the occurrences of a double appellative are far fewer than in MT, and without pattern. Zimmerli (pp. 1250–58, 1265) has marshaled arguments indicating the likelihood that this is a result of the transmission of G and without relevance for Hebrew usage. Preserved Jewish relics of translation into Greek keep the tetragram in Hebrew letters; Christian copyists replaced this, to them meaningless, graph by *kyrios* "lord" or *theos* "God," and in the case of the double appellative—since the result was repetition (*kyrios kyrios*)—might simply omit it (see also G. Howard, "The Tetragram and the New Testament," JBL 96 [1977], 63–83). The nearly systematic, limited use of the double appellation in MT itself argues strongly against the widespread older assumption (still maintained by Elliger in *BHS*) that it is a secondary development.

5. *or not.* Lit. "or forbear (from listening)"; for this use of *ḥadal* as asserting the nonperformance of the act denoted by the previous verb, cf. I Kings 22:6; Jer 40:4.

a rebellious house (bet mᵉri). *mᵉri*—in I Sam 15:23 an antonym of obedience and in Deut 31:27 a synonym of recalcitrance (*'orep qaše*)—is the noun of *mara* "be defiant, contumacious, disobedient" (synonymous with "not [be willing] to listen to" in Josh 1:18; I Sam 12:15; I Kings 13:21; Ezek 20:8). In Num 17:25 Israel are called *bᵉne meri* "sons of *meri*" (cf. Num 20:10, *hammorim* "You rebels!") and in Isa 30:9, *'am mᵉri* "a people of *meri*" (parallel to "disloyal [*keḥašim*] sons"). *bet mᵉri* is Ezekiel's coinage; in the light of vss. 3–4 above, it is to be understood as "a line (*bayit* = dynasty) of *meri*" with reference to the generations-long persistence of the trait. The conventional rendering "rebellious house" has been retained here, although the root *mr(y)* must be distinguished from *mrd,* whose derivatives in vs. 3 were also rendered "rebel." (To be sure, in exilic and later texts, as well as in theological contexts, *mr(y)* is combined both with *mrd* [Neh 9:26] and *pšʿ* [Lam 3:42].)

As a recurring closing formula in this commissioning speech, "for they are (a) rebellious (house)" justifies gloomy expectations of Israel; from a people of such ingrained contumacy little can be hoped for.

shall [*yet*] *realize.* When the doom you foretell comes (cf. 33:33).

6. Ezekiel's prose occasionally passes into a style characterized by short clauses, with repetition, parallelism, rhyme, or chiastic inversion; formally this style is poetic. The shift does not correlate with thematic changes, but slowing down the argument and dwelling on a matter conveys heightened feeling. Such a stylistic shift may be a brief flash (e.g., the chiasm in 3:10b), or it may extend, within a prose context, over several clauses or verses (as here). Often it is arguable whether the style of a given passage is poetic or merely repetitious, parallelistic, or otherwise structured prose. The decisions made here and expressed graphically in the translation do not reflect a scholarly consensus; they are based on the presence of short clauses with at least some of the accompanying above-mentioned features over a considerable stretch of text.

For nettles . . . scorpions. And so, to be sure, an ordinary person would be justified in being afraid. Hebrew *sarab* here rendered "nettle" is a hapax whose meaning is conjectured from its association with *sallon,* apparently = *sillon* in 28:24, parallel to *qoṣ* "thorn" (for an etymology Mandelkern, *Concordance,* s.v., compares *ṣarab* "burn" and German *Brennessel* "stinging [lit. burning] nettle"). G S T render these two words as participles (e.g., S: *dsrbyn wmslyn* "for they reject and despise"), but in view of the "scorpions" in the next clause, one prefers to take them as analogous stinging things.

7. *they are rebellious.* The usual *bet* "house" is missing here in order to assimilate this clause with the contrasting one in vs. 8, where the prophet is admonished not to be rebellious (*'al tᵉhi meri*). For the adjectival use of the abstract *meri* in these two verses, cf. GKC § 141 c and fns. 2 and 3 (where there is no reason to treat *šalom* as an adjective); Driver, *Tenses,* pp. 251f.

8. *whatever.* Hebrew *'et 'ᵃšer,* which occurs in three consecutive commands (here, vss. 8b; 3:1), not uncommonly has a vague inclusive connotation roughly equivalent to "all or any/everything that, whatever"; cf. NEB at Gen 18:19; 34:28; Exod 34:34; Deut 29:14 and TpJ at Num 32:31; Deut 29:14. In these three commands the object is left vague in order to stress the unconditional submission of the prophet to the divine will, whatever it should entail—in starkest contrast to the "rebellious house."

eat whatever I give you. The prophet had, of course, no idea what was to be proffered him; he (and the reader) might well imagine it was some kind of food.

10. "Writing on both sides was usual on papyrus scrolls both in ancient Egypt and in the Greco-Roman period . . . but . . . on . . . a scroll of skin [it] is inconceivable before the beginning of the common era, when the quality of skins greatly improved" (M. Haran, "Scribal Workmanship in Biblical Times," *Tarbiz* 50 (1981), v [English summary]). The content of this scroll, too much to be taken in at a glance, was evidently summarized as "Laments, etc." by its endorsement, located, as on Egyptian Aramaic papyri, on the outside of the rolled document (R. Yaron, *The Law of the Aramaic Papyri,* Oxford: Clarendon Press, 1961, pp. 24f.). The "Manual of Discipline" of the Dead Sea Scrolls had precisely such a title written on the outside (only a few letters remain; see D. Barthelemy and J. T. Milik, *Qumran Cave I,* Discoveries in the Judaean Desert, I [London: Oxford University Press, 1955], p. 107 and pl. xxii); Greek and Roman scribes likewise inscribed a title on the outside of scrolls (*EM,* v, pp. 1084f.).

and woe (why). G *kai ouai,* V *et vae* take the Hebrew word as an interjection expressing grief, and so it is in Mishnaic Hebrew: e.g., "When [Hillel] died they said of him, *hy ḥsyd hy ʿnw* 'Alas, O pious one; alas, O meek one'" (BT Sanhedrin 11a). For the quasi-substantive use of *hy*—here synonymous with "lament" (Rashi and Kimḥi gloss it with the assonant *nhy* "lament," Jer 9:9, 17ff., etc.)—compare English "woe" and the common *'oy l-* "woe to" discussed at 13:3.

T *tynḥt'* "sigh" cannot be adduced, as some have done, in support of emending to *nhy,* for that Hebrew word is regularly rendered in T by *'ly'*. On the other hand, S *'wlt'* here does render *nhy* elsewhere but may simply reflect not a different *Vorlage* but an interpretation in line with that of Rashi and Kimḥi aforementioned.

3:1. *whatever you find there.* For this meaning of *maṣa,* see BDB, p. 593, d: "*find* a condition, *find* one in a situation." This third command in the idiom of unqualified submission, preceding as it does the specific command to "eat this scroll," implies the prophet's hesitation to follow the order of 2:8b and eat the inedible object he saw in front of him. It answers the unspoken, incredulous question, "Am I supposed to eat *that?*" underlying which is revulsion. The check in the movement is indicated by the traditional paragraphing (reflected in the translation).

go, speak. I.e., its contents to the Israelites.

3. *feed your belly* . . . Although the prophet showed his readiness to obey by opening his mouth to the scroll (vs. 2), this third command to eat is couched in terms indicating his apprehension that he would never be able to down the indigestible mass of papyrus. Answering that, he is now ordered to fill his belly with that which God gives him (an echo of the demand for unconditional obedience in 2:8). The unique phrase "feed your belly" ("fill stomach" again in 7:19) is aptly glossed by

Kimḥi: "so as not to vomit it out"—for that is precisely the issue, namely, the ability to keep down the scroll.

So I ate it. That is, took it into my mouth and began to chew it, when, marvelous to say—

in my mouth it turned sweet (construing *lᵉmatoq* with *wattᵉhi*) *as honey.* And so was easily swallowed. Kimḥi: "thus I fed my belly, for I did not vomit it." The sense is literal, materially different from the metaphors in Ps 19:11; 119:103.

4. *speak . . . in my words.* Hebrew *dibber b-* can mean "speak in a particular form"; e.g., in Deut 6:2 it means "recite" the commands of God to keep them alive in memory; in Dan 9:21 *dibber bitᵉpilla* is to "utter prayer." Here the nuance (absent in the commonplace *dibber 'et* of 2:7) seems to be verbatim repetition of the message—an aspect of absolute obedience. Focus on the form of speech leads, through a transition (vs. 5) to the next thought (vss. 6–7): the common language of prophet and people aggravates the people's guilt.

5. *For . . .* The transition: you can speak my message verbatim since you are not addressing a foreign people but one whose language is yours (and that of my messages to you).

[*but*] *to the house of Israel.* "But" is supplied. The abruptness of the Hebrew "to the house of Israel" is somewhat mitigated by its following immediately upon *'atta šaluᵃḥ* "you are sent" of the previous clause; by an echo effect—as though these two words faced backward and forward and did double-duty—a complete clause is suggested ("you are sent to the house of Israel"). This suggestion in the Hebrew cannot be conveyed in translation except through supplying "but."

6. The new thought: had I sent you to any of the innumerable foreign peoples with whom you cannot communicate, you would have been listened to. The plural is used here as an indefinite singular (see Gen 8:4, "on [one of] the mountains of Ararat"; cf. GKC § 124 o) and is significant: the pertinent part of vs. 5a could have been repeated in place of vs. 6a (with "people" [sing.] instead of the present "many peoples") and vs. 6b attached to it; but Israel's guilt-by-contrast is dyed deeper by the emphatic pluralization: any one of the many foreign nations to whom the prophet would have spoken God's message would have submitted to it across the language barrier (the quick response of Nineveh to Jonah's prophecy of doom comes to mind), but not the house of Israel (vs. 7).

speech is obscure, language is difficult ('imqe śapa, kibde lašon). Comparison with Isa 33:19 ("A people whose speech is too obscure [*'imqe śapa*] to understand / Whose language is inarticulate [*nil'ag lašon*] beyond comprehension") shows that *śapa* and *lašon* are used here not as organs but in their extended sense of speech and language. The second phrase is therefore different in meaning from (*kᵉbad pe u*)*kᵉbad lašon* of Exod 4:10—"(clumsy-mouthed and) clumsy-tongued" (i.e., with a speech impediment; see J. Tigay, "Moses' Speech Difficulty," *Gratz College Annual* III [Philadelphia: Gratz College, 1974], pp. 29–42).

whose words you cannot understand. Although the context demands "who cannot understand your words," the subjective viewpoint of the prophet is maintained: he is among people whose speech is to him obscure, "whose words he cannot understand." The main point is unaffected: no communication is possible between him and them.

surely if I sent . . . Originating as an introduction to affirmative oaths (Isa 5:9; 14:24), *'im lo,* lit. "if not," appears in Ezekiel both in that function (17:16, 19; 20:33; 33:27) and as a mere emphatic expletive with the sense "surely, truly" (e.g., 34:8; 36:5; 38:19). The rest of the verse is a conditional clause (for the perfect in protasis and the imperfect in apodosis, see Job 23:10b and GKC § 159 h) with emphatically placed pronouns: "(if) to them I sent you, they (for sure! GKC § 135 a; Joüon § 146 a) would listen to you,"

7. *because they refuse . . . me.* "Lest it should be vexatious to the prophet to see his labour profitless [God says this to him] . . . because he ought to bear it patiently if he should suffer the same obloquy which they did not hesitate to display against the Almighty himself" (Calvin). Cf. the closely related consolation of Samuel in I Sam 8:7.

tough-browed = brazen (hard)-faced of 2:4; cf. English "effrontery" going back to Latin *ex* ("out") + *front-* ("forehead"). The figure appears in Jer 3:3 ("You have the forehead of a harlot; you refuse to feel shame") and again in Isa 48:4 ("your brow is brazen [*n^e^ḥuša*]"). It is noteworthy that monotony is avoided by replacing "face" of 2:4 with "brow" and by reversing the adjectives of 2:4 so that *ḥizqe* ("tough") now goes with the external figure and *q^e^še* ("hard") with the internal.

8–9. These verses focus on the counter-adamancy with which the prophet is equipped. The topic "heart" is not pursued; instead "face" and "brow" dominate a threefold, almost spell-like, declaration of God's outfitting the prophet to outface his opponents. "Diamond" renders the sense in context of Hebrew *šamir,* an adamantine substance (cf. Jer 17:1, where it is parallel to iron) said here to be harder than flint—the "faces" of the Israelites presumably being "flintlike" (cf. their "heart of stone," 36:26). The prior alternation between *ḥzq* and *qšy* (2:4; 3:7) is replaced here by a monotonous threefold repetition of *ḥzq,* perhaps a play on the prophet's name *y^e^ḥezqel* = *y^e^ḥazzeq 'el* "God toughens."

10. *take into your heart . . .* This unique combination compacts what is said more fully in Job 22:22, "take from his mouth . . . and put into your heart (*qaḥ mippiw . . . w^e^śim . . . bil^e^bab^e^ka*)"; with the next clause it constitutes a *hysteron proteron* ("last first"), a mode of speech in which what (chrono)logically is last in a series is placed first owing to its importance (cf. the English expression "put on your shoes and socks"). An ancillary reason for the illogical sequence may be the desire to resume the

topic *leb(ab)* "heart," which has been suspended since vs. 7 in favor of concentration on "face/brow" in vss. 8–9.

11. *the exiles, the sons of your people.* At once more specific and more intimate appellations than in 2:3. The second appears again only in the collection of prophecies in ch. 33 (vss. 2, 12, 17, 30), most of which are thematically related to the following oracle in this chapter!

12. *A wind.* This mode of locomotion recurs in 8:3; 11:1, 24; 43:5—all visionary experiences. Only here does it combine with normal motion ([14] "I went . . . [15] I came"—contrast "it brought me" in the other passages), suggesting a passage from visionary (vss. 12–14a) to real experience (vss. 14b–15). As opposed to "the wind from YHWH" that was believed to transport Elijah (I Kings 18:12; II Kings 2:16—*ruaḥ YHWH* is construed with masc. verbs), the "wind" that transported Ezekiel (construed with fem. verbs) is, to be sure, supernatural in origin, but unattributed—another sign of reserve.

"Blessed be . . . place!" All the ancient versions take this to be a doxology, a salute to the departing Majesty from unspecified heavenly beings; cf. the explicit additions in S T (note a). As a doxology, its meaning is not altogether clear, the closest analogy being Ps 135:21, "Blessed be YHWH from Zion" (apparently = blessed by those who are in Zion). Starting from there, M. Buber (in *MGWJ* 78 [1934], 471–74; in Hebrew, *Darko šel Miqra* [Jerusalem: Bialik Institute, 1964], pp. 334–36) explained our passage as an exclamation of the prophet, to this effect: not only Zion is a "place of God, but here too he has a place, and from it he is to be praised as once he was from Zion." One of the difficulties of this explanation, the cargo it loads onto "from his place," is obviated by an ingenious construction of Eliezer: "from its place" is to be connected with "I heard behind me," and the doxology consists only of "Blessed . . . YHWH": "for the place quaked in anticipation of its [the Majesty's] departure from it, and bade it farewell with a blessing. It is like a king who, when he departs from a city, is attended by all the citizens who do obeisance to him and salute him at his departure." But not even these exegetic acrobatics can mitigate the awkwardness of a contextless, abrupt doxology at this point in the narration, or the strain put on "a great rumbling noise" by interpreting it as the noise of speech, when it is clear from the end of vs. 14 (where the phrase is resumed) that the commotion was caused by various movements of the components of the divine vehicle (and cf. 1:24). Scholars have therefore embraced the conjecture (arrived at independently by Hitzig and Luzzatto) that *baruk* of MT is corrupted from *berum* (the distinction between the letters *k* and *m* in the old Hebrew alphabet being slight), and the end of the verse will therefore be: "when the Majesty of YHWH rose from its place." For this use of *rum* 10:4, 15–19 have been compared. In view of the scholarly consensus with regard to this solution to the problem of the verse, it may seem captious to point out (with Müller, *Ezechiel-Studien,* p. 16, fn. 2) that *rum* is pe-

culiar to the vision of the vehicle in ch. 10, while in the initial vision of the divine vehicle (ch. 1) *hinnaśe* alone occurs; moreover, "the Majesty of YHWH" in both visions refers to the figure on the throne rather than to the entire apparatus, which one would expect to be the subject of a verb meaning "to rise (from its place)"; cf. the above-cited passages in ch. 10. Perhaps the phrase originated as a later interpolated explanation of "a great rumbling noise," giving its occasion in the idiom of 10:4 (for focus on the Majesty even where the entire apparatus was involved, see also 11:23).

13. The *waw* of the first and last *wᵉqol* is explicative (BDB, p. 252, def. 1.a–b; GKC § 154, fn. 1 [b]) and is indicated in translation by the long dash. The "great rumbling noise" emanated from two sources that the prophet could identify even without seeing them (for they were behind him); it consisted of the din of the creatures' wings, with which he was familiar from the incoming flight of the vehicle (see 1:24, in which the din is described by several similes), and the rumble of the (presumably turning) wheels (which would have run along the ground a bit at takeoff [see note to 1:14], or revolved even in the air)—a sound distinctive enough to be recognized from hearing alone.

14. *I went, bitter.* The vision ended (see earlier comment to vs. 12, "A wind"), the prophet describes his mood on his way to the nearby settlement of exiles. It is not clear whether his bitterness (answering to the "laments and moaning and woe" he must proclaim, as 27:31–32 show) and his rage are reflections of God's feelings toward Israel (cf. the thesis of Heschel, *The Prophets,* ch. 18), or his own distress over the dismal, thankless, and perhaps dangerous task imposed on him. The sense of being "overpowered (another use of *ḥzq*) by the hand of YHWH" is compatible with both possibilities; for a similar ambiguity see Jer 15:17.

15. *Tel Abib.* Akkadian *til abūbi* "mound of the flood"; that is, a mound long deserted and believed to have been the site of a town destroyed by the primeval Flood (*CAD* 1, pt. 1, p. 78). The Akkadian was Hebraized as though "mound of spring fruit."

who were living . . . where they were living. The repetitive overloading, together with the evidence of the versions, suggest that our text is conflate and contains doublets:

"... to the exiles at Tel Abib { who were living . . . canal / where they were living };

there I sat . . ." When the two were copied into the text, "and" (missing in G) was inserted to connect them. If we suppose a text containing only the lower clause, it is understandable why the upper was added to it, since it defines the location of Tel Abib; S will then repesent the type of text from which the upper clause developed.

desolate (mašmim). The sense is illuminated by Jer 15:17, "Because of your hand I lived isolate [*badad*], for you filled me with indignation." *mašmim* adds to aloneness the notion of numbing wretchedness, unnerving shock; T "silent" renders a single aspect of the word. Its full range, and the connection between the physical and emotional meanings, are discussed by N. Lohfink, "Enthielten die im Alten Testament bezeugten Klageriten eine Phase des Schweigens?" *VT* 12 (1962), 267f.

STRUCTURE AND THEMES

Although at first glance the commissioning of the prophet appears prolix and repetitive, upon careful consideration a finely crafted structure is revealed in which scarcely a word is without significance.

1:28b–2:2 The disposition of the prophet to receive God's message: having been prostrated by the awesome vision of the Majesty, he is invigorated by a command and an infusion of spirit to rise and listen.

2:3–5 The program of the mission: the prophet is to confront the brazen-faced, obstinate "nations" of Israel, whose recalcitrance is hereditary, with the word of their divine Lord; whether or not they listen now, ultimately the prophecy will be vindicated. Thus the task, its dubious issue, and its justification in spite of that are set out compactly.

Two figures are used to characterize the people: an exterior ("brazen-*faced*") and an interior ("tough-*hearted*"); both play a formative part in the sequel.

The passage opens with "He said to me" and closes with "whether they listen or not" and "for they are a rebellious house," closing refrains of the commissioning speeches (see 2:7; 3:9, 11) and what may be called the recognition formula ("they shall know/realize . . ."), a characteristic ending of divine speeches in Ezekiel.

2:6–7 Countering the prophet's implied fear of his audience's hostility and defiance (here and subsequently there is a kind of hidden dialogue—God's speeches are responses to unspoken reactions of the prophet): truculent as the people admittedly are, the prophet must not be afraid of them, but is to counter their stinging words with God's. Three times God repeats the oracular encouragement "Do not be afraid" (cf., e.g., Gen 15:1; 26:24; 46:3; Num 21:34; Josh 10:8; II Kings 19:6), three times the people's truculence is characterized, and three times "words" appears (twice the people's, once God's), providing keys to the heart of the message (and reflecting the prophet's anxiety).

In this passage the exterior figure is taken up in the clause "do not be dismayed by their *faces*"; the interior is represented here not by *leb* ("heart") but by the iterated "words," for it is to be noted that *leb* also means "source of speech," i.e., chest (H. L. Ginsberg, "Heart," *EJ*, vol. 8, pp. 7–8; to the passages there cited he now adds Prov 23:33).

The passage opens with "You, man," a formula marking a new stage in a discourse, and ends with the closing refrain (vs. 5). In vs. 7 the peculiar *m^eri,* instead of *bet m^eri* (which is found in some Hebrew mss. and in the versions), provides a link with the following section, for in vs. 8 the prophet is exhorted not to be *m^eri.*

The prophet is equipped for his task interiorly and exteriorly:

2:8–3:3 Interiorly: the prophet must obey God unconditionally and eat whatever God proffers him; he is handed a scroll filled with laments and, dutifully responding to orders, is miraculously enabled to down it. The passage is an implicit dialogue in which the iterations of God's command to eat answer precisely to stages in the prophet's apprehensiveness and incredulity.

The passage is intricately linked with the preceding one: the eating of the scroll is as much a test of the prophet's obedience, in contrast to the people (cf. the contrastive recurrence of "listen to," "rebelliousness," in vss. 7, 8), as a stocking of the prophet with a content by which to counter the defiant words of the people (cf. 3:1 with 2:7).

The passage begins with "You, man" and ends with the eating of the scroll. The absence of the closing formulas gives the following passage the character of a continuation rather than an entirely new beginning.

3:4–9 Exteriorly: a renewed charge (cf. 2:7; 3:1; the present charge fuses elements of both) to speak God's message (verbatim—apparently the consequence of ingesting it with the scroll) leads to reflection upon the extreme defiance of the people, unparalleled among the nations. The prophet is enabled to outface his impudent audience, so he must not be in fear of them.

This passage resumes themes of the preceding, in every case heightening them. The faithful agency of the prophet (cf. 2:7) is underscored by the charge to repeat God's words verbatim. The inveterate rebelliousness of Israel (cf. 2:3b–4a) is emphasized by contrast with the compliance of the gentiles, notwithstanding their incomprehension of God's message. The doubt about Israel's listening to that message (cf. 2:5, 7) turns into certainty that they will refuse to listen. The exhortation (*'al*) not to fear the hostile audience (2:6) turns into a categorical assertion that he shall not (*lo*) fear them. The negative substance of the exhortations of 2:6 is adapted to the context of this passage: the categorical assertions of 3:9b are attached to the toughening of the prophet's exterior to match his audience's "face," hence the topic "words," so prominent in 2:6, disappears in 3:9b.

The passage closes with the "rebellious house" refrain alone, the clause expressing doubt whether Israel will listen or not omitted in view of the affirmation of vs. 7 that they would refuse (contrast 2:5, 7).

3:10–11 Final summary charge: the prophet is to absorb God's messages and convey them to his fellow exiles, who may or may not listen. The mild, nonfigurative language of this passage, together with its realistic definition of the prophet's audience, set it off from the preceding. Gone are references to the people's defiant hostility and the corresponding fears of the prophet—as though these were purged by the foregoing oracles. The residue—the essential charge of the prior passages—is here soberly and moderately expressed.

Comparison with the initial, programmatic statement of God's commission in 2:3–5 (minus the depreciatory references to Israel) reveals the effect of the intervening passages. Multiple occurrences of "words" and "speak" (derivatives of *dbr*) distinguish the final summary from the initial statement, in which there is not a single occurrence. The most telling case is in vs. 11, where vss. 2:4b–5a are virtually repeated, with an apparently redundant "and speak to them" placed at the head; but the iteration of derivatives of *dbr* stems from the intervening matter. The possibility that the *hysteron proteron* in vs. 10b resulted from the resumption of the item "heart" from vs. 7b, left without continuance in the following vss. 8–9, has been mentioned in the comments.

The closing consists only of "whether they listen or not," the "rebellious house" clause omitted in accord with the mild tone of the whole passage, and in contrast to the closing of the previous passage, in which the more drastic term of derogation alone appears.

3:12–15 End of the call scene; the prophet takes up with the exiles in Tel Abib: the skeleton of the narrative is carried by the verbs "(A wind) lifted me . . . and took me, and I went . . . I came . . . I sat . . ." This is filled out by what may be a gloss (vs. 12b), an explicative chain of phrases (vs. 13), and a precise statement of the location of the exile settlement. The whole passage, repeating elements of the vision of ch. 1 (wind, sound/noise, wings, creatures, wheels, the hand of YHWH, the exiles, the Chebar canal), acts with ch. 1 as an envelope for the entire call scene.

The contrast between the stunned silence of the prophet and his commission, so full of orders to speak, is remarkable.

The passages comprising the commission of the prophet are permeated by key expressions: the most pervasive are derivatives of *dbr* "speak," "word," and the corresponding verb *šamaʿ* (in several meanings: hear, listen to, understand—subtly alternating); next in frequency and pervasiveness are the alliterating *marad* and *mᵉri* "rebel(lious)." The exterior and interior figures of 2:4a recur with variations (e.g., the allusion to *leb* as an organ of speech) and are echoed throughout.

Noteworthy stylistic features are (1) the variety of double expressions —apposition ("to the children of Israel, to the rebellious nations"; "to the exiles, to the children of your people"), synonymy and parallelism ("rebelled/transgressed"—cf. 20:38) "brazen-faced/tough-hearted"; "do not be afraid of them/of their words do not be afraid"; "feed your belly/fill your stomach"; "speech obscure/language difficult"; "tough-browed/hard-hearted"; "do not be afraid of them/do not be dismayed by their faces"; "take into your heart/hear with your ears"). Double expressions may be augmented into triplets ("nettles/thorns + scorpions"; "obscure language/difficult speech + not understand"; "face match face/brow match brow + adamant"). (2) chiastic alternation of parts—often indicating resumption: *šole^{a}ḥ '^{a}ni/'^{a}ni šole^{a}ḥ* "I am sending," 2:3, 4; *'al tira me-X / mi-Y 'al tira* "do not be afraid of X / of Y do not be afraid," 2:6; object + *'^{e}kol / '^{e}kol* + object "eat X!," 3:1; *q^{e}še* X *ḥizqe* Y / *ḥizqe* X^1 *q^{e}še* Y "hard-X tough-Y" / "tough-X^1 hard-Y," 2:4, 3:7; *'el b^{e}ne* X *'el goyim / 'el haggola 'el b^{e}ne* Y "to the children of X to nations / to the exiles to the children of Y," 2:3, 3:11; "take into (*bi-*) your heart / with (*b^e*) your ears hear," 3:10; *wattiśa'eni ru^{a}ḥ / w^{e}ru^{a}ḥ n^{e}śa'atni* "A wind lifted me," 3:12, 14. (3) innovative combinations in one member of a double expression: *q^{e}še panim,* 2:4; *ḥizqe meṣaḥ,* 3:7; *kibde lašon,* 3:5, 6; *qaḥ bil^{e}bab^{e}ka,* 3:10—see comments on each. (4) the use of opening and closing formulas.

Together with the careful structure of the commission scene, these pervasive stylistic features, giving it a consistency of texture, indicate its general integrity, apart from a possible gloss (3:12) and a doublet (3:15).

The basic theme of the commissioning narratives—as of all such narratives—is the appointment of the prophet as a messenger of God: God sends (*šalaḥ*) the prophet on a mission to his people (2:3f.; 3:5f.; cf. "go, speak" in 3:1 and 3:4, 11). God's opening addresses to Moses (Exod 3:10), Gideon (Judg 6:14), Isaiah (6:8f., taking this to be the inaugural vision of the prophet), and Jeremiah (1:4f.) are comparable. At bottom this is a revelation of God's concern for his people, even when, as here, the content of his message is wrath and doom. In his wrath over their evildoing he does not abandon them but sends them repeated warnings of the misfortune that must overtake them; this constant theme of Jeremiah (7:25; 25:4; 26:5; 35:15; 44:4) is elaborated in II Chron 36:15—"YHWH God of their fathers sent word to them by his messengers, sending every day anew, because he had compassion for his people and his house." Even when there is little hope of averting the misfortune, a prophet is still sent, so that afterward the people will realize that a prophet had been among them, that is, God had given them warning in due time; it was no lack of consideration on his part but their own heedlessness that caused their downfall.

The resistance of the intended audience is usually mentioned in the commissioning speech by way of steeling the prophet for his task and forestalling his despair at its failure. Moses is forewarned that Pharaoh will not listen to him (Exod 3:19); Isaiah is called for no other reason than to increase the spiritual obtuseness of a corrupted people (Isa 6:9f.); Jeremiah is told that the people would "fight against" him (1:19), and Ezekiel hears the Israelites stigmatized as impudent and obstinate, defiant, prickly, and stinging. Their reproach is intensified in two ways. Their evil character is hereditary, ingrained, and therefore hopeless. "He does not extenuate their crime when he says they imitated the example of their fathers, but he rather increases their own impiety when he says they were not the beginners of it but were born of impious parents, as if he should say, according to the vulgar proverb, 'a chip of the old block'" (Calvin). The theme dominates ch. 16, where the genetic and family taint of Jerusalem is dwelt upon ("Quipsters will quip about you, 'Like mother like daughter'" vs. 44). The theme appears in Jeremiah with a nuance: the sinfulness of children of sinners is progressive, "But you have done worse than your fathers . . ." (16:12; cf. 7:26). Both prophets share the view that their contemporaries climax a generations-long line of sinners; this justifies their harsh presages of doom.

A second intensification of Israel's reproach is through comparison with the gentiles: had he preached to gentiles, Ezekiel would have brought them to repentance! This is a recurrent theme; Israel is more wicked than the gentiles (5:6f.; 16:47ff.), who are shocked at its depravity (16:27). Jeremiah likewise uses this mode of denunciation (e.g., 2:10f.), whose ultimate purpose is to justify the severity of Israel's punishment, with which nothing that befell the gentiles can compare (Ezek 5:8; cf. Lam 2:13).

Facing so hard a task, some of those called by God resist his commission: Moses raises one difficulty after another; Gideon protests his weakness; Jeremiah pleads his youthful inexperience (Isaiah stands out for his alacrity to serve as God's messenger). In the divine responses to this resistance a certain similarity is evident. To Moses' protestations God answers, "I will be with you," and "I will be with your mouth and teach you what to speak"; to Gideon he answers, "I will be with you." Jeremiah is reassured with the words ". . . all that I command you, you shall speak. Do not be afraid of them, for I am with you to save you . . . Do not be dismayed by them . . . For I am with you . . . to save you." In Jer 1:9 we read, "YHWH put out his hand and touched it to my mouth [saying] 'See, I have put my words in your mouth.'" This verse fuses elements of Isa 6:7 (the prophet is separated from the unclean people by a seraph who takes a glowing coal from the altar "and touched it to my mouth") and Deut 18:18 (of the future prophet God says, "I will put my words in his mouth"). Jeremiah is further strengthened by God: "See I have now turned you into a fortified city, an iron pillar, and bronze walls . . . They will fight against you but will not prevail against you . . ."

In Ezekiel's commissioning most of these motifs appear, often with some kind of adaptation. The implicit fears of the prophet are answered by the repeated formulas, "Do not be afraid/daunted"; his exterior is toughened to match his audience's truculence. The divine promise to be with the prophet does not occur, but its assurance of a shared responsibility has a counterpart in the several expressions minimizing Ezekiel's responsibility. It is no matter whether the people listen to him or not; he is not to be anxious about their unrepentance; in 3:7 the brunt of their defiance is explicitly shifted from the prophet to God. God's purpose in sending Ezekiel will have been fulfilled simply by the establishment of a record that "a prophet had been among them" who foretold the impending doom. Isa 30:8f. anticipates this prophetic role in words echoed here by Ezekiel: "Now go write down on a tablet, / And inscribe it in a record, / That it may be with them for future days, / A witness forever. / For they are a rebellious people [*'am m^eri*], / Faithless sons, / sons who refuse to listen / To the instruction of YHWH." (Note how in Isaiah *banim* refers to Israel as disobedient sons of God, while in Ezekiel's context it means sons having the same sinful nature as their fathers.) Such a restrictive definition of the prophet's task averted the danger of his demoralization in the face of his audience's obduracy. It has a direct continuation in the "lookout" passage and in the redefinition of the task in 3:16–27.

Corresponding to God's assurance elsewhere that he will supply the speech deficiency of his messenger is his feeding Ezekiel the scroll of laments. It has been observed that 3:1, 3 evokes the language of Jer 15:16—"When your words were offered [*nimṣ^e'u*], I devoured them; your words brought me delight and joy of my heart, in that your name was attached to me, O YHWH God of hosts." But whereas in Jeremiah the motif of eating words is figurative and its meaning simple—an expression of the prophet's willing acceptance of his role—in Ezekiel it is literal and its meaning complex. It concretizes the idea that God "puts his words into his prophet's mouth." Here is the ultimate alleviation of the anxiety felt by the prophets that they would be inadequate to their calling. The central part played by the scroll reflects the common use of writing in Ezekiel's time and, particularly since the eighth century, its service to prophecy (Isa 30:8; Hab 2:2; Jer 29:1; 30:2; 36:2; 51:60ff.; cf. Kaufmann, *Religion*, pp. 359ff.). "The combination of the written scroll and ingestion by the mouth evidently underscores the duality of speech and writing that in general characterized the mission of the classical prophets" (A. Demsky, "Literacy in Israel" [Hebrew], Ph.D. diss., Hebrew University, 1976, p. 136). His inner parts suffused with the scroll (cf. the metaphors in Ps 40:9; Prov 22:18), the prophet must henceforth speak "in God's words." This is a far-reaching limitation of the prophet's spontaneity and responsibility. Zimmerli noted, with respect to 14:1–11, that "the individuality of Ezekiel's prophetic style is recognizable by the fact that the sin of the audience is not set forth as, say, by Amos (4:1f., cf. 5:1–3), in a reproving discourse formulated by the prophet himself, but is wholly included in the divine address [to the prophet]" (*ZAW* 66 [1954], 6). Such, indeed, is the case throughout the book: Ezekiel's denunciations are exclusively reports of what God said. The prophet's task is reduced to the conveyance of God's message; he has no further responsibility toward his audience and is answerable only to God for delivering his message and thus establishing a record that "a prophet had been among them."

The context, the circumstances, and the reality of the scroll event make it signify the absolute subjection of the prophet to the will of God. The particular command to eat the scroll is preceded by general exhortations to behave in a way diametrically opposed to that of the people: to listen to God's words; not to be rebellious. (The concern to separate the prophet from his surroundings recalls the purgation of Isaiah's lips in order to set him apart from the people of unclean lips among whom he lived; Isa 6:5–7.) What follows is something of an ordeal intended to try the prophet's obedience, as is suggested by the graduated series of commands overriding the prophet's hesitation about his capacity to perform the monstrous feat he has been commanded to carry out. How monstrous it is may be gauged by comparison with the imbibing of the curse-filled potion by the suspected adulteress (Num 5) and the ingesting of magical formulas known from Greco-Egyptian magical papyri (R. Olsson, "Die verschlungene Buchrolle," *Zeitschrift für die neutestamentliche Wissenschaft* 32 [1933], 90f.). In these, words alone are washed or licked off and drunk down; "the main thing . . . was not to ingest . . . the writing material but what was written on it" (ibid.). Here an intractable and indigestible mass had to be swallowed, as is emphasized by the threefold iteration of the key phrase "this scroll" (not "these words" or "laments") as the object of the verb "eat" in 3:1–3. (Olsson compares practices of "ancient and modern folk-medicine" in which "paper, leaves, bread, fruit, and the like" are written upon and sometimes eaten—without considering the fact that all these are quite edible, in contrast with a scroll.) The point of the whole procedure comes out in the vagueness of the opening command to the prophet: "Open your mouth and eat whatever I give you" (2:8). The prophet is required to be unconditionally submissive to God, to dissociate himself from "the rebellious house" by readiness to swallow anything offered by God, be it ever so unswallowable. This is only the first of a series of acrobatic symbols the prophet was summoned to perform, and its complexity is typical of the rest. Most of them entailed, like this act, harsh inflictions on the prophet (to be sure, miraculously alleviated in this case), and thus conveyed, along with whatever specific cargo, his total subjection to the divine will.

Ezekiel's adherence to traditional themes and phrases drawn from the stories of Moses in Egypt, the prophecy of Isaiah and Jeremiah (chiefly but not exclusively from their commissioning scenes), psalmody, and wisdom goes hand in hand with distinctive modifications. Commonplaces and figures of speech are vivified, literalized, or skewed in a dramatic manner. God's feeding a scroll to the prophet is the most complex combination of traditional elements ("I put my words in your mouth," "He touched it to my mouth," "Your words were offered and I devoured them," "Your teaching is in my belly," "Sweet as honey," etc.). The commonplace "sons [*b*ᵉ*ne*] of Israel" is peculiarly literalized in the context of the theme of hereditary sinfulness. The iterated variations on the conventional notion "brazen-faced [*panim*]" injects life into the nominal complement of the stock phrase "do not be dismayed by them [*p*ᵉ*nehem*]"—lit. "by their faces." This, in turn, generates the image of a counter-toughening of the prophet's face and brow, in place of the pure metaphors in the comparable passages in Jeremiah (1:18; 6:27; 15:20). Such abundant utilization of tradition, together with a highly individual penchant for concretization and dramatization, is characteristic of Ezekiel.

An outcome of the prophet's extravagant mode of expression is inconsistency or tension between parts of his message. It is predicted as a certainty in 3:4–9 that the people will refuse to listen to the prophet, but the rest of the commissioning speech leaves the matter in doubt; in the event, the reception of the prophecy was far milder than the apprehensions reflected here. The mode of inspiration suggested by the ingestion of the scroll of laments—as though from the outset the entire content of the prophecy was instilled in the prophet—is inconsistent with the piecemeal conveyance of oracles envisioned in the final admonition (3:10) and prevalent throughout the book. Nor do all the prophecies of Ezekiel—even in the pre-fall period—fall under the rubric "laments and moaning and woe." Just as it would be misguided to find in the ingestion scene a unique doctrine of prophetic inspiration (rather than an innovative brew of ingredients drawn from and determined by the tradition of prophetic commissionings), so it would be wrong to make such inconsistencies the basis for disintegrating this closely interwoven commissioning scene.

Perhaps the greatest inconsistency is that between the behavior of the prophet subsequent to his commissioning and the task he was called to perform. After having been exhorted and fortified to speak out to the exiles, when he arrived among them he immediately withdrew into a morose silence. That his "desolateness" was linked with the bitterness and rage he felt on his way from the revelation site to the exiles' settlement is indicated by the closely analogous passage in Jer 15:17; the prophet there gives poignant expression to the effects upon him of the divine wrath:

I have not sat in the company of revelers
And made merry;
I have sat lonely because of your hand upon me,
For you have filled me with indignation.

(The ban on family life in Jer 16:2 may also be compared.) There is a striking similarity, both verbal and ideational, between the passages in Jeremiah and Ezekiel; both evidently draw upon a common fund of experience and expression. In the case of Ezekiel, the tension between the task of the prophet and the retreat into himself induced by exposure to the divine wrath led immediately to a week-long lonely muteness; in modified form the prophet's withdrawal continued for many years afterward, as will be elaborated at the end of ch. 3.

The arrival and departure of the divine vehicle mark off the event of the prophet's call. Having earlier rejected the view that the theophany signified a general theological teaching (Israel's God is active and present in the exile), we may now, in conclusion, consider some other more particular signification.

Besides summoning Ezekiel to serve as a prophet, the commissioning speech seeks to allay the prophet's fears and fortify him against a hostile reception of his messages. The exiles had strong grounds for rejecting Ezekiel's baleful predictions: the good tidings proclaimed to them by other prophets in Jerusalem and among themselves. To run counter to the popular trend required certainty that one had divine backing, that one truly knew the will of God. Perhaps the prophet's great need for assurance that he ran with God offers a key to the meaning of the theophany.

In the wilderness narratives of the Pentateuch the divine Majesty appears in order to demonstrate the presence of God with the people or his agents on critical occasions—in support of Moses and Aaron when the people rise against them (in the episodes of the manna, the spies, and Korah's rebellion), and amidst the people in moments of favor (the Sinai lawgiving, the inauguration of the tabernacle and the altar). Moses asks for a view of the divine Majesty in the context of pleading for a sign of divine favor (Exod 33:18). Elsewhere, too, the private theophany is a divine response to a needy caller (e.g., Ps 18); the case of Ezekiel seems to fit this category.

The Majesty appears to Ezekiel on two kinds of occasions: in chs. 1 and 3 to commission him and further instruct him concerning his task, and in chs. 8–11 and 43 as an integral part of visions of the temple (its abandonment and its future rehabilitation). The appearances of the first kind are private events unrelated to any public pronouncements of the prophet; they have a meaning for the prophet alone. Appearances of the second kind are of the essence of visions the prophet must communicate to the public. Consistent with the privacy of the first kind is their location, on a canal-bank (ch. 1), in the valley-plain (ch. 3)—both deserted places, apart from the exiles' settlements. Such places are suitable for seeking communion with God.

Taken together, these considerations suggest the following interpretation of the theophany. Distressed by his people's fate, convinced of impending doom, Ezekiel was cast out by his community, which clung to the hopeful oracles of the prophets promising the exiles a speedy restoration to their homeland. Disconsolate, he repaired to a lonely spot by the Chebar canal, there to seek divine solace and support. By way of response, and in accord with traditional imagery, the heavens opened and the Majesty of God appeared, vindicating the nonconformist and proving that right and divine favor were with him, not with the many. The detail of the theophany and its dramatic elements accord with the individual predilections of the visionary. (Rava [BT *Ḥagigah* 13b] remarked Ezekiel's impressibility: "All that Ezekiel saw Isaiah saw, but Ezekiel was like a rustic who got a look at the king, while Isaiah was like a townsman who got a look at the king.")

The event was such overwhelming evidence of divine favor and support that the tyro in prophecy neither asked for a sign to confirm his mission (in the manner of Moses or Gideon) nor had to be told "I am with you" (like Moses, Gideon, and Jeremiah). Without such evidence it is scarcely credible that Ezekiel would have braved the terrors of his new role. Even with it he confined himself to acts and speeches made only under direct divine impulse, being incapable of taking any initiative on his own.

In the end the prophet did record and publish his private vision, as he did God's commissioning speech, meant originally for him alone (whether we have Ezekiel's very words is irrelevant; our text descends at least from an account most plausibly attributable to the prophet himself). His purpose in so doing must have been to confirm his vocation—the sheer weight of detail in itself convincing of the reality of the experience. Calvin expounded the public purpose of these private revelations as follows:

> Since . . . God alone is to be heard, every mortal . . . must be rejected, unless he comes in the name of God, and can prove his calling, and really convince men that he does not speak except by God's command. Therefore, that Ezekiel may not labour in vain, he ought to prove himself divinely inspired, and this was done by the vision. Now [in ch. 2–3] he more clearly explains that object of the vision. Here it may be remarked that figures are illusory without an explanation. If the vision only had been offered to the eye of the Prophet, and no voice of God had followed, what would have been the advantage? But when God confirmed the vision by his word, the Prophet was enabled to say with advantage, I have seen the glory of God (comment to 2:3).

III. The Lookout
(3:16–21)

3 16 After seven days, [a] the word of YHWH came to me: 17 Man, I
have appointed you a lookout for the house of Israel; when you hear
a word from my mouth, you must warn them against me.
18 When I say to a wicked man, "You shall die," and you do not
warn him—you do not speak up to warn the wicked man against his
wicked course so as to keep him alive, he, wicked man, shall die
because of his iniquity, but I will hold you responsible for his death.
19 But if you warn the wicked man and he does not turn away from his
wickedness and his wicked course, he shall die because of his iniquity,
but you will have saved your life.
20 Or when a righteous man turns back from his righteousness, and
he does evil, and then I put a stumbling block before him—he shall
die; since you did not warn him he shall die because of his sin, no
regard being paid to the righteous acts he did, but I will hold you
responsible for his death. 21 But if you warn [b]him, the righteous man,
that he, righteous man, should not sin, and he does not sin, he[b] shall
live since he took warning, while you will have saved your life.

[a] In MT a "break in the middle of the verse" occurs here, followed by a space marking an interval between paragraphs.
[b–b] G S: "the righteous man not to sin and he does not sin, the righteous man."

COMMENT

3:16. The "harsh" (Zimmerli) sequence of *wayhi . . . wayhi*—lit. "It was (after seven days) was (the word of YHWH to me . . .)"—taken together with the "break in the middle of the verse" have given rise to speculations concerning the irrelation of the clauses of this verse. Cooke, for example, held vs. 16a to be the date of the symbolic acts in chs. 4 and 5, with the intervening matter secondary insertions. Zimmerli, on the other hand, argued for the connection of vs. 16a with vss. 22ff. Now, it is true that the verbal sequence in question does not recur in Ezekiel, but it appears in Exod 19:16; Judg 19:1; Ruth 1:1; II Sam 7:4 and I Kings 13:20—in the last two with a "break in the middle of the verse" separating the two verbs, just as in our verse. The sequence can therefore not be regarded as outlandish and a sign of "a disturbance of the original narrative" (Cooke). What the significance of the break in the mid-verse is, not just here but in the scores of verses in which it occurs, has still not been determined (remarkably, in two other passages the break occurs, as here, before "the word of YHWH came to X": II Sam 7:4 and I Kings 13:20). No scholarly theory commands a consensus, but an attractive idea that seems to fit a number of cases (and there is no reason to think that all cases are embraceable in one category) was put forward by S. Talmon ("Pisqa Be'emṣa Pasuq and 11 Q Ps[a]," *Textus* 5 [1966], 11–21): the break often occurs where supplementary information—from elsewhere in the Bible (e.g., parallel texts) or from extrabiblical writings (Talmon adduces material from extracanonical Psalms)—is available on the event in question; for example, the break in II Sam 7:4 may be intended to invite reflection on Ps 132, which adds significant data to the event in question. To Talmon's examples our passage may be added, for (if his idea is correct) the break after vs. 16a comes just at the point where a parallel version of vss. 16b ff. sets in, namely, 33:1–9, in which there is much supplementary material of interpretative value.

The formal features of vs. 16 do not, then, give grounds for supposing some disturbance or dislocation in the text at this point.

the word of YHWH came to me. This clause occurs close to fifty times in the Book of Ezekiel, reporting a revelation-experience by way of introducing a prophecy. "The word of YHWH came to [some prophet]" occurs in the prophetic narratives of the monarchy, being said of Samuel (I Sam 15:10), Nathan (II Sam 7:4), Gad (24:11), the Bethel prophet (I Kings 13:20), Jehu (16:1), Elijah (17:2, 8; 18:1; 21:17, 28), and Isaiah (II Kings 20:4; cf. Isa 38:4). Elsewhere in biblical narrative it is uncommon; it is absent in the writings of the literary prophets, excepting Jeremiah (where it is moderately frequent) and Ezekiel (where it appears regularly), and the postexilic Haggai and Zechariah. Its use in superscriptions of some pre-exilic prophetic books is editorial and reflects late usage. The uneven distribution may indicate an archaizing tendency of the later prophets; alternatively, the phrase may have originated in the seventh century and its usage in stories of the monarchy may be "modernizing." The origin of the expression must be prophetic since it has no secular parallel (unlike the message formula "thus said so-and-so"). The phrase "word of YHWH" follows the pattern "word of the king" = a royal command, edict, message, or commission (II Sam 24:4; II Kings 18:28; Esther 1:13, 19; 2:8; 4:3; 8:17; Qoh 8:4) and may belong to the (self-)image of the prophet as a messenger of the divine king. It does not imply any distance between prophet and God (as though the word were a hypostatization, a medium between God and the prophet), since in the narratives in Jeremiah and in Ezekiel direct dialogue and address ("YHWH said to me/him") often appear as well. "Came" renders *haya* in the sense of "come into being, arise, appear"; see BDB, p. 225, col. b. For the phenomenon of such auditory revelation, see the remarks of Lindblom, *Prophecy,* pp. 108ff.; a theological treatment may be found in von Rad, *Theology,* II, pp. 80ff. (the sentence running from pp. 87–88 is a gross error).

17. *a lookout.* In order to give timely warning of approaching danger, lookouts were posted on high places (roofs of gatehouses, II Sam 18:24; towers, II Kings 9:17) that they might see afar. The prophet's closeness to the divine author of dooms puts him in an analogous position.

when you hear . . . you must warn. For this use of the double perfect consecutive in hypotheticals, see Driver, *Tenses,* § 149; Joüon § 167 b.

a word. An edict, a decree of doom—as indicated by the next verse. This sense is often inherent in the phrase "the word of YHWH" in Ezekiel (e.g., 6:3; 13:2; 16:35; 21:3).

against me. hizhir "admonish" is found with *min* only in our passage (and the parallel 33:7–8); an appropriate sense for all its occurrences is "advise of the danger or evil consequences coming from someone or something"—in other words, "warn against." In this verse God is the danger as an executioner; in the next verse it is the wicked man's fatal course. G renders the first occurrence "threaten them from me (i.e., in my name)" and the second "separate (i.e., turn him away) from his evil way"; but it seems unnecessary to posit different meanings for the same expression.

18. *to a wicked man* (laraša') . . . *the wicked man* (raša'). In Hebrew the determination is reversed; the translation follows the requirements of English. In Hebrew, when nouns serve as types they may be determined or not—and no rule is apparent; compare I Kings 8:32 with Deut 25:1; for a mixture in one and the same verse, as here, see Ps 58:11f. and Hab 1:4. Translators' license is illustrated by the renderings of *h'šh* in Qoh 7:26: *RSV* "the woman," NJPS "woman," *NEB* "a woman." Cf. Joüon § 135 c with § 137 i.

"You shall die." The form of a royal death sentence delivered as direct address (I Sam 14:44; 22:16; I Kings 2:37, 42; cf. the judicial verdict in Jer 26:8), spoken by God as well (Gen 2:17; 20:7; II Kings 1:4, 6, 16). Here, too, God's sentences are in the form of addresses, but the wicked, who are not privy to God's counsel, depend on the prophet, who is to convey these sentences to them.

The nature of God's death sentence (cf. also 18:4ff.) is not explained anywhere in these prophecies, but evidently it was commonly understood to mean untimely death, often in unusual circumstances; see Ps 37:35f.; 55:24; Prov 10:27, and the rich discussion of M. Tsevat, "Studies in the Book of Samuel. I," *HUCA* 32 (1961), 191–216.

and you do (lit. *did*) *not warn him.* w^e- "and" here is nearly *ki* "if" as in vss. 19, 21a, and the following verb is, in effect, the protasis of a hypothetical (conditional) sentence. The perfect form of the verb in the protasis conveys the supposition that the event has occurred and the situation after its occurrence is being contemplated (expressed here by the imperfect, e.g., in vs. 19 *yamut, 'ᵃbaqqeš*). Such use of the perfect is common in priestly legislation, as in Num 5:27 ("if she defiled herself"), 30:6 ("if her father heard her"), and 35:16 ("if he struck him"); see Driver, *Tenses,* § 138 (pp. 177f.). Brockelmann, *Syntax,* § 164bβ, calls this perfect "timeless"; indeed, it is up to the translator to decide whether to render it by past or present in English; cf. below, 18:10–17.

he, wicked man . . . Hebrew *hu raša',* and so, too, in the parallel 33:8; it might also be rendered "he being wicked." G "that wicked man" appears to interpret the construction in an Aramaic manner, where the demonstrative *hu* can precede or follow the noun (which noun, however, is determined in Aramaic); cf. Dan 2:32 *hu ṣalma* "that image" (and Montgomery's note to vs. 31 in *Daniel,* ICC, p. 166). Wilson's idea that this is a declaration, "he is (a) wicked (man)," (*VT* 22 [1972], 95) is not supported by the word order, e.g., *ṣaddiq hu,* Ezek 18:9.

but I will hold you . . . Lit. "but I will require (an accounting for) his blood from your hand"; that the death penalty is intended is clear from the sense of this idiom in II Sam 4:12–13.

20. *a stumbling block.* Though this is the conventional rendering of *mikšol,* its meaning here is closer to "calamity"—not an occasion for sin but a cause of downfall and ruin. Cf. Jer 6:21: "I shall put before this people stumbling blocks over which they shall stumble (= calamities by which they shall be destroyed)—fathers and children alike; neighbor and friend shall perish." Also comparable is Ezek 33:12: "The righteousness of the righteous man shall not save him . . . and the wickedness of the wicked man—*lo yikkašel bah* he shall not be felled (= destroyed) by it."

Vs. 20 describes the stages leading up to the doom of the backsliding righteous man: he "turns back" (mentally? see comment to vs. 21); he does evil; then, unbeknown to him, God places a "stumbling block" in his path—this is the equivalent of the death sentence at the beginning of vs. 18—by which he must die.

The Israelite is forbidden to "put a stumbling block before" a blind man in Lev 19:14 (this expression is found only there and here). That God's judgment is described in terms of an act prohibited to men bespeaks a scandalous situation that the prophet is empowered to avert.

he shall die. This marks the end of the backslider's career, as does "he shall die," said of the wicked in vs. 18; a misused life has been snuffed out. But whereas in vs. 18 the prophet's failure to warn ("and you do not warn him") precedes the report of the wicked man's death in correct sequence, here it follows the report of the backslider's death as its cause hitherto unmentioned ("since you did not warn him"). This peculiar change is discussed in Structure and Themes.

no regard being paid. So 18:24; 33:13; the latter verse adds the idea that the backslider "trusts in his righteousness," that is, banks on the credit of his righteous past. Such a calculation will misfire, since "all the righteous acts he did will be disregarded" when he backslides. This consideration belongs to the argument of 18:21ff. (33:12ff.) that God judges persons as they are, not holding against them a sinful past of which they have repented or crediting them with the good deeds of a past from which they have lapsed. It seems out of place here, where the focus is the prophet's responsibility, and may have been interpolated from the later passages to aggravate the consequences of the prophet's failure to warn. Note that the feminine *ṣidqotaw* "righteous acts" belongs to the vocabulary of chs. 18 and 33; here the masculine *ṣedeq* "righteousness" is used; similarly, the masculine *reša'* is used here (vs. 19), while the feminine *riš'a* is found in chs. 18 and 33.

21. By iterating (to the point of awkwardness) the righteousness of the warned man, the present text emphasizes the point that the prophet's warning reached him when he was still righteous, that is, before he actually sinned. In terms of vs. 20, this suggests that an interval lies between the righteous man's "turning back" (mentally) from his righteousness and his actively "doing evil"; during this interval the prophet's warning can take effect, "and he does not sin."

Some of the awkwardness of the Hebrew is alleviated in G and S, where the object suffix on *hizharto* "warned him" is not represented, and the second *ṣaddiq* "righteous man" is made the subject of "shall live." But the assumed *Vorlage—ṣaddiq ḥayo yiḥye*—is ungainly Hebrew, and the subject (*ṣaddiq*²) remains extra baggage in the sentence. Hebrew idiomatic usage can, at a stretch, accommodate the first *ṣaddiq* by subsuming the object suffix of *hizharto* under the category of anticipatory object suffixes (GKC § 131 m). But the verse looks overloaded, and this is probably due to conflation of its middle with explicatory or variant elements. Thus, first the suffix of *hizharto* was glossed by *ṣaddiq,* taken from an alternative version *hizharta ṣaddiq* (cf. vs. 19; so, apparently, G S). Then *lᵉbilti ḥᵃṭo,* which seems originally to have meant "so that he does not sin" (cf. 13:22, "encouraging him so that he does not [others: not to] turn away from his evil course"), was glossed by the equivalent (and unambiguous) alternative reading *wᵉhu lo ḥaṭa* "and he does not sin," whose function as a gloss was indicated by the prefix catchword *ṣaddiq.* The full gloss *ṣaddiq wᵉhu lo ḥaṭa,* at first interlinear, was subsequently copied into place, after *lᵉbilti ḥaṭo* (whose sense was consequently changed).

he does not sin . . . Cornill observed: "Sense and parallelism urgently require the opposite: 'If the righteous man, despite your warning, sins, he must die, but you will have saved your life.'" So, indeed, the text should have run had the intent been to repeat exactly the pattern of vss. 18–19; the fact that it does not undercuts the contrast between the fate of the warned and that of the prophet connoted by the final clause "but [here rendered "while"] you will have saved your life." This surprising turn of the argument is discussed in Structure and Themes. Cornill abated the surprise by emending the text; others, such as Fohrer, followed suit.

STRUCTURE AND THEMES

The section is opened by a date notice connecting it with the preceding one and the standard report of a revelation experience that opens most prophecies in the book; its ending is delimited by the start of a new prophetic experience in vs. 22.

Vs. 17 defines the task of the prophet as a lookout to warn the people of the danger threatening them from God. There follows a detailing of the prophet's responsibility toward two endangered classes: the doomed wicked and the backsliding righteous.

3:18–19 Responsibility toward the doomed wicked: the prophet's task is underlined by three verbal expressions; he must *warn, speak up to warn, so as to keep alive* the doomed. Failing to do so, he forfeits his own life, but by doing so he saves it even though the wicked die.

3:20–21 Responsibility toward the backsliding righteous: three steps leading to the doom of the unchecked backslider are given and the alternative courses of the prophet are stated: if the prophet fails to warn the backslider, he forfeits his own life with that of the backslider, but if he warns the man and keeps him from sinning, he saves his own life with that of the righteous.

Formally these two paragraphs are similar in that each comprises one case in which the prophet forfeits his life for neglecting his task and a second in which he saves his life by fulfilling it. In content, however, they differ; for while the doomed wicked man is depicted as incorrigible and must die in any event (thus giving meaning to the adversative "but you will have saved your life"), the backsliding righteous man reverts to his goodness under the influence of the prophet and so lives (thus blunting the point of the adversative final clause). The structural identity of the paragraphs heightens the effect of the divergence in content. What is the meaning of the shift in the consequences of the prophetic warning?

The first paragraph contemplates the extreme case of the incorrigibly wicked; here the sole concern of the prophet must be to acquit himself before God. Whether or not his warning is heeded matters not; as soon as he has performed his appointed task he is in the clear. Now, this definition and limitation of responsibility is in line with the task assigned to the prophet in the commissioning speech and addresses the same issue: what is the point of speaking to this people if they will not listen? The answer: God is concerned to establish beyond a doubt his fair dealing with the refractory people; the prophet as a lookout embodies this concern. How seriously God views the matter appears in the death penalty he imposes for failure to do the job. A similar note was sounded in the commissioning speech (2:5), save that there only the desire to establish a record against the people was expressed, while here the fateful (even fatal) consequences to the prophet of his role are in the forefront. The intent of this shift in focus is to provide motivation for Ezekiel to take up his hard task.

The second paragraph contemplates a more disturbing case: the backsliding righteous man. Uncurbed, he marches to his doom, God cutting his hitherto blessed life short by an unlooked-for calamity (stern necessity of "putting a stumbling block before him"). The alternatives before the prophet are these: for having failed to warn, his life is forfeit, along with that of the backslider (whose lapse cancels out his whole record of good deeds—an apparently later reflection upon the tragedy), but if he warns the backslider and thus keeps him righteous, both will live. In contrast to the wicked man, who is portrayed as incorrigible, the righteous man depicted here reverts to his goodness immediately upon being warned, before sullying himself in actual sin.

Now, if despite the requirement of the closing formula of each paragraph that the fates of warned and warner be distinct ("but you will have saved your life") the outcome of the second paragraph is life for both, an intention to skew the argument must be assumed. Its reason may be inferred from its effect: to endow the prophet's work with a social value that could not appear in the first paragraph. The house of Israel is made up not only of incorrigibly wicked men on whom his message of doom can have no effect; there are others of a more impressionable nature for whom it may mean the difference between life and death. The righteous man, who, at the critical moment of decision upon a career of sin, hears the alarm, reconsiders, and saves himself from disaster, is a character calculated to engage the sympathy of the prophet. (What man, righteous as he may be, is proof against such momentary lapses?) For him, too, the lookout's warning is intended, and for him it is the indispensable prod to salvation. Let Ezekiel bear in mind that this, too, is part of his task—a positive, socially beneficial aspect to add to the somber, essentially negative motive supplied by the preceding paragraph. Nor is it also without adumbration in the commissioning speech; the summary exhortation (3:10–11) does, after all, leave the matter of "whether they will listen or not" open.

The odd location of *ki lo hizharto* "since you did not warn him" in vs. 20 can now be discussed. Wilson (*VT* 22 [1972], 95f.) described well the asymmetry of vs. 20 vis-à-vis its apparent parallel, vs. 18.

> To be truly parallel to v. 18, v. 20 should contain the condition . . . "if you do not warn him." . . . Such a statement of the case is missing, however. The effect . . . is to make v. 20 dependent on vv. 18–19 for its

> proper interpretation. . . . it is necessary for the reader to know that in vv. 18–19 the first case considered is that of the prophet not exercising his office and that the second case . . . is that of the prophet exercising his office. The reader . . . must then assume that vv. 20–21 are to give two cases parallel to the ones found in iii 18–19. This assumption is confirmed only after the reader reaches the phrase "because you have not warned him he shall die in his sin" in v. 20b.

Why is the lookout's omission ("you did not warn him") absent in vs. 20a and present only in the retrospective ground clause ("since . . .") in vs. 20b? In vss. 18–19 references to warning appear in parallel positions at the start of the chain of fatal events; could not the same structure have been maintained in vss. 20–21? The answer is no. Omission of warning in the case of the doomed backslider (vs. 20a) and the timely warning in that of the redeemed one (vs. 21) cannot be temporally parallel. The first case is parceled out in stages, at any of which the prophet's warning might have saved the backslider. In the second case, in order to rescue the backslider from sinful action the warning had to occur at the very start of the evil process—in the interval between evil intent and evil action. There was thus no way of placing the omission of warning in vs. 20 in such a way as to provide a temporal parallel for the commission in vs. 21. The only way the lookout's omission could be alluded to in vs. 20 was after the backslider's passage through all the stages of his fall unto death, and then only as its retrospective cause.

Wilson showed the dependence of the second paragraph (vs. 20) on the first and rebutted the idea that it might once have circulated as a separate piece (p. 96, fn. 1). We argued earlier that the second paragraph is a fitting conclusion to the commission because by asserting the potential benefit to the righteous from the lookout's warning it supplied a positive motivation for accepting a desperate task. We conclude this structural discussion by adducing one more literary testimony to the integrity of the entire passage and the connection of its parts. The following sequence crosses the border between the two paragraphs: "his wicked course" (vs. 18), "his wickedness and his wicked course" (vs. 19), and "his righteousness" (vs. 20). The middle term of the sequence combines, by way of a bridge, the concrete first term and the abstract antonym (*reša'*) of the third term (*ṣedeq*). Since both abstracts are of the identical noun-formation, a pleasing alternation results, a, ba, b¹. (This sequence pleads against some critics' deletion of *meriš'o* in vs. 19 on the ground of its absence in 33:9, indeed, against their general tendency to adjust parallel texts to each other; the same must be said of their "correction" of *miṣṣidqo* in vs. 20 to *miṣṣidqato* comparing 18:24 and 33:18. The two masculine antonyms verify each other in our passage; the feminine *ṣidqato* goes with its antonym *riš'ato* in chs. 18 and 33, and both have to do with the phrase *mišpaṭ uṣedaqa,* recurrent in those chapters, in which the second element seems to have determined the gender of the antonyms there.)

The theme of this passage is the responsibility of the prophet as a lookout. The image, drawn from the war situation known only too well to the Judahites of the time, first appears in Jer 6:17 in a denunciation of Judah's ungrateful obstinacy: "And I raised up lookouts for you: 'Heed the sound of the horn!' But they said, 'We will not.'" While in Jeremiah the focus is on God's benevolence, here, with the consequences to the prophet spelled out in detail, the point is the definition of the prophet's responsibility—a new application of the image. Hitherto stated only in terms of message-bearing, the prophet's task is here delineated as a matter of life and death—for himself no less than for his audience. At the same time it is rigidly limited to admonition: the prophet is relieved of what would have been the intolerable burden of answerability for the anticipated indifference of the people. Comparable are the repeated releases of Muhammad (in the Koran) from responsibility for unbelief; e.g., ". . . if they surrender themselves, they have let themselves be guided, but if they turn away—thou art only responsible for the proclamation" (3.19: Bell translation; cf. variations on this idea in 6.68 and 13.8). Like the commissioning speech, our passage is addressed to the prophet; he is not commanded to relay it to the people. This accords with its content, which aims at making a grim and thankless task palatable by narrowing its scope and supplying the prophet with negative and positive motivation for undertaking it. There is merit, then, in the attempts made by early commentators to link our passage with what precedes it; here, for example, is Eliezer on vs. 17: ". . . Inasmuch as you are a lookout, you are not to wait . . . until I tell you to speak, but as soon as you hear a word issuing from me, tell it to them and warn them. Why, then, have you kept silent these seven days and not told them that I am vexed with them!" However, it is not reproach but motivation and encouragement that is the aim of our passage, for which the dispirited silence of vs. 15 serves as a fitting background.

The themes of the lookout and the backsliding righteous recur separately in chs. 18 and 33, in each embodied in fully developed arguments. Many critics (Cooke, Zimmerli, Wevers, Fohrer [in modified form]) regard our passage as artificially abstracted and built up from them and secondarily inserted here, with the role of lookout belonging to the second phase of Ezekiel's career. Included in this view is the interpretation of the lookout's activity as "aimed entirely at individuals" and hence "while not altogether impossible at the beginning of the prophet's career, [it is] more probable after all the hopes of the exiles had collapsed than during their period of proud inaccessibility" (Eichrodt, p. 75). Since this position has survived Schmidt's brief rebuttal (*ThZ* 6 [1950], 91–93), it must now be reexamined.

Ch. 33 contains an exposition of the lookout motif in vss. 1–9 that, because of its elaborateness, has been adjudged the primary version. Its salient features are as follows: it is part of a message to be conveyed to the Israelites (vs. 2); it begins with an object lesson on the usefulness and responsibility of a lookout to the townsmen who appoint him to forewarn them of a menacing enemy. Emphasis is laid upon the responsibility of a townsman for his own death if he fails to heed the alarm sounded by the lookout. The lesson is then applied to the prophet only in terms of our first paragraph—the prophet's responsibility of warning the wicked man against his evil course "that he should turn back from it" (vs. 9, a stress on the wicked man's share of responsibility that is absent in the parallel 3:19; contrarily, the stress on the lookout's share expressed in 3:18 by "so as to keep him alive" is missing in the parallel 33:8). In the following verses the cry of the people, asking how they can live under their crushing burden of sin (33:10), is answered by an assurance that what God seeks is not the death of the sinner but his conversion; the repentant are always accepted, and past states are no basis for the judgment of those who have broken with them (vss. 11–20).

The occasion of this entire discourse is the people's hopeless cry, and all its parts form an integrated response to it. To affirm the good will of God toward the people and the efficacy of their repentance, the prophet is ordered to expound to them his role under the image of the lookout. In good homiletic style he is to set out the familiar facts: the prudential appointment of a lookout by the men of an imperiled town, his solemn responsibility, the responsibility of a townsman for his own death if he ignored the lookout's alarm. He is then to repeat to them God's appointment of him as a lookout for them in order to give the wicked timely warning to abandon their evil course, failing which they shall die. This provides the background for God's impassioned appeal to the people to turn away from their evil, since he does not seek the death of the wicked man but rather that he should convert and live.

The elaboration of the lookout theme in the object lesson of ch. 33 belongs to the public nature of the discourse; it is a rhetorical device to illuminate the situation at hand for an audience. Hence its presence in ch. 33 is not in itself an argument for the origin of the theme there; the rhetorical needs of a public message do not exist in a private one, and 3:17–21 is, after all, a private communication (cf. Schmidt, p. 92). Moreover, the fitness of the object lesson for the purpose of ch. 33 is, in one essential, so much greater than that of its application to the prophet in vss. 7–9 as to raise a doubt whether the application was originally formulated for that context. The purpose of revealing to the people the prophet's role as a lookout is to motivate their repentance. By paralleling the townspeople's appointment of a lookout with God's sending his prophet, God's solicitude for his people is brought out: the self-interest of the townsmen has its analogue in God's care to save his people by timely warning. This is calculated to persuade the people of God's desire that they live. Furthermore, since the aim of the discourse is to move the hearers to action, particular stress is laid on the unheeding townsman's share in responsibility for his fate: "he alone is to blame for his death" (vss. 4, 5); "had he taken warning he would have saved his life" (vs. 5). Now, just this case of the doomed man's taking warning and thereby saving his life fails to appear explicitly in the divine charge to the prophet either in 3:17f. or 33:7f. (The only hints of this contingency are, in 3:17, "so as to keep him alive"—in terms of the prophet's responsibility, consonant with the context—and, more vaguely, "so that he should turn away from it [his evil course]" in 33:9—in terms of the wicked man's responsibility, consonant with *its* context.) That it should fail to appear in the earlier passage (ch. 3) is not remarkable, since the whole tenor of the passage is of the prophet's accountability to God. That it should be absent from ch. 33 is remarkable. It suggests that while the object lesson was composed for the encouraging purpose of ch. 33, the application, although well integrated, was originally formulated for another context (perhaps that of ch. 3?).

The theme of the backsliding righteous is also treated elsewhere—in chs. 18 and 33. In both it belongs to an argument denying any carryover of retribution from a past moral state to the new man: the repentant evildoer will not be punished for his past, nor will the backsliding righteous man be saved from punishment by his past. Only in ch. 3 does the theme serve to illustrate the responsibility and opportunity of the prophet; only here are the stumbling block by which God fells the backslider and the eventuality of his reversion to good mentioned. Clearly, then, while the theme is common to both contexts, it has not been mechanically copied from one to the other.

Are there grounds for supposing that the theme originated in the later chapters and insinuated itself here only secondarily? Substantive and stylistic arguments have been adduced in the comments for considering the clause about the cancellation of past merits a secondary interpolation here from chs. 18 and 33. Once that has been bracketed, only the bare theme remains—a backsliding righteous man will be punished for evildoing. At bottom this is but the obverse of the theme of the repentant wicked man who will be rewarded for his conversion. In itself the conception is banal (though admittedly never formulated before Ezekiel); whether its mere formulation had to wait on its connection with the novel doctrine of "atomized retribution" (chs. 18, 33) or appeared here first (without the interpolation)—as a variation of the foregoing case (the inveterately wicked)—is a question to which no definite answer can be given.

The specific use to which themes common to chs. 3, 18, and 33 are put in our passage argues against the contention that it is a secondary concoction. The lookout metaphor for prophets (to judge from Jeremiah, a commonplace of the times) is here adapted for the original purpose of defining for the reluctant (or dismayed) prophet a role he should be ready to undertake. The theme of retribution for the wicked and the backsliding righteous, central in chs. 18 and 33, is here subordinated to and integrated with this purpose. In ch. 33 the lookout metaphor serves the entirely different purpose of persuading the despairing exiles of God's concern for their survival, while its parallel to our passage lacks specific adaptation to that purpose (the case of the wicked man taking warning and saving himself is missing). Accordingly, there is no ground for supposing the occurrence of the metaphor in ch. 33 to be more original than here; but there is some ground for regarding its application to the prophet in 33:7–9 as an imperfect adaptation to that context of a formulation original to our passage. To be sure, our version of the backsliding righteous does seem to be interpolated with an element from chs. 18 and 33 (an editorial alerting of the reader to something that will be taken up elsewhere [Freedman]?). But once that is removed, there is no reason to say that the residue as well is derived from those later chapters.

As mentioned earlier, the location of our passage has been considered unsuitable to the first stage of the prophet's career. As charging him with a "cure of souls" (von Rad, *Theology*, II, p. 231)—the care of individual sinners—it is regarded as appropriate only after the dissolution of the national body politic; moreover, the role is said to contradict that described in the commissioning speech "where no repentance is envisaged" (May, p. 49), and therefore to belong rather to a later period of the prophet's activity.

With respect to its suitability to the later phase of Ezekiel's activity, it must be said at once that all the prophecies expressly dated after the fall of Jerusalem, or whose presupposition is the political collapse, and all prophecies placed in the book after the notice of the fall (33:21ff.) are, without exception, consolatory. So far from warning against calamity and calling for repentance, they contain only promises of restoration and the assurance of redemption even without prior repentance (God will himself remake the hard heart of Israel as part of the redemption; ch. 36). Even the presence of the lookout metaphor as late in the book as ch. 33 is not enough to justify the view that it heralds the later phase of Ezekiel's activity when weighed against the massive evidence for the consolatory character of his post-fall prophecies.

But suppose that other prophecies scattered through the first part of the book, in the same style as the lookout one and dealing with the theme of retribution (in chs. 14 and 18), are falsely embedded among pre-fall prophecies; do not the address to the individual and the call to repentance found in such passages in themselves justify collecting them and placing them, along with both lookout passages, at some remove from the ambiance of the commissioning speech and the predictions of Jerusalem's destruction that follow it? Is the plausibility of this picture not ground enough for postulating that after the fall Ezekiel exercised a cure of individual souls in addition to his role as consoler?

The issue turns upon the understanding of the peculiar style of the prophecies in question—the address to the individual in chs. 14, 18, and the two lookout passages. Does the address to the individual really signify a contrast with the collective, so that one may speak of a fundamentally new office of the prophet, a "cure of souls"? Some observations on the style of our passage (and its congeners) are necessary before an answer can be given.

The style of our passage is quasi-legal, stating cases and consequences in closely reasoned order ("When/if . . . then"); the opening formula of vss. 19 and 21—subject + *ki* + verb (*w^{e}atta ki hizhart-*)—is modeled upon that typical of torah legislation in priestly matters (noted by Zimmerli, *VT* 15 [1965], 524). To "put a stumbling block before" someone is cited from the law of Lev 19:14. Clothed in this quasi-legal language are propositions concerning life and death—of the righteous, of the wicked, and of the prophet himself. Such matters are everywhere in the Bible the domain of prophecy; God's decisions regarding the life and death of individuals or collectives are communicated to the persons involved exclusively through prophets. Examples are: the decision regarding the Israelites, through Moses (Num 14:35; 26:65); the Elides, through Samuel (I Sam 2:33f.); David, through Nathan (II Sam 12:13f.); Ahaziah, through Elijah (II Kings 1:4ff.); Hezekiah, through Isaiah (II Kings 20:1); and Zedekiah, through Jeremiah (Jer 38:17). Declaratory formulas close to those of our passage are found in Elisha's sentence to Hazael (regarding King Ben-Hadad): "Go say to him, 'You shall live' (*ḥayo tiḥye*), but YHWH has shown me that he shall die (*mot yamut*)" (II Kings 8:10; cf. also I Kings 14:1ff.).

Zimmerli has argued that the sentencing to life or death had its setting in alleged sanctuary-entry rites, supposedly performed by priests, and that thus both the form and the content of such passages as ours are priestly (the argument was first developed by Zimmerli in *ThZ* 13 [1957], 494–508 = *GO*, pp. 178–91, briefly stated in *VT* 15 [1965], 523f., and accepted by Lindars, *VT* 15 [1965], 459ff.). The sanctuary-entry rite will be discussed at ch. 18; here it must be observed that not a single verse associating the sentencing to life or death with the priesthood can be opposed to the many associating it with the prophets. It is true that the traditional law, which punished certain offenses with death, was studied, transmitted, and in part administered by priests (see discussion at 44:24). But the conveyance of ad hoc divine decisions to persons in specific circumstances as sentences of life and death ([*ḥayo*] *t/yiḥye,* [*mot*] *t/yamut*) was never, in our evidence, a priestly function. Accordingly, when Ezekiel denounces certain women for fraudulently promising life and death to their clients (13:19) he styles them "those who play the prophet (*mitnabb^e'ot*)" not "those who play the priest."

Clothing the content of prophetic oracles in the form of case law is an invention of Ezekiel designed as a vehicle for stating principles of God's dealing with men, or, in other words, theological doctrines. Case law was the only available literary form of discourse about particulars on an abstract, generalized level. Ezekiel, whose priestly provenience familiarized him with torah literature (as his idiom shows at every turn), made innovative use of this form for teachings which, though given for an occasion, he wished to present in the guise of general theological principles. Such are 14:4–11—on the denial of oracles to the idolatrous-minded; 14:12–20—the inability of the righteous to save their (unrighteous) sons from a general doom; ch. 18—the "atomization" of retribution; and 33:1–20—the possibility of repentance. Our passage is a private message, defining for the prophet the limits of his responsibility, couched in the same abstract terms.

The model for Ezekiel's quasi-legal style—biblical case law—is generally framed in the singular, in accord with universal ancient practice (see the various law collections in *ANET*[3], pp. 159–98, 523–28). Even though the ideal audience of the lawgiver is the people at large (cf. the standard opening of law-clusters in the priestly legislation, "YHWH spoke to Moses, saying, 'Speak to the Israelites and say to them . . .'"), the bulk of the laws is framed with the subject in the singular (this holds true for the priestly laws as well). Sometimes the ideal setting influences the draftsman and he breaks into the plural, but that this overlies a singular substratum is betrayed by frequent lapses into the singular even amidst runs of the plural; see, e.g., Lev 19 and 25. The effect of this linguistic habit of the draftsman is to obliterate distinctions between the individual and the collective; all "singulars" (individuals) at once are addressed or spoken of in sentences framed in the singular—which is precisely what is asserted in the narrative setting of the laws.

The Torah laws, whose style Ezekiel imitates, use the singular in particular cases without intent to oppose the individual to the collective; the signification of the singular is, rather, each and every individual in the collective. The same appears true of Ezekiel's usage.

For whom, in our passage (and the parallel in ch. 33) is the prophet a lookout? "For the house of Israel," says God (3:17; 33:7); "You must warn *them* against me." Agreeably, in the object lesson of 33:2ff. it is the townsmen as a collective that the lookout is set up to warn. When God proceeds to describe the prophet's responsibility in terms of a single wicked or righteous man, has he changed the terms of reference? Is the prophet no longer sent to the collective but to the individual as a "shepherd of souls"? The object lesson provides a clear answer. The lookout sounds his alarm for the entire town; the consequences, however, are described in terms of an individual townsman who ignored it (vss. 4f.). The lookout fails to sound the alarm, and again the misfortune is described as being borne by an individual, although clearly the ensuing disaster would be a general one. It is a manner of speaking: the division of responsibility between the lookout and his clients is discussed in terms of a single client; such simplified abstraction is useful for clarifying the principle. But no one would infer from this that the lookout was charged with warning each and every townsman individually. The same holds for the application to the prophet: "wicked man" and "righteous man" are abstractions for classes within "the house of Israel." There is no intent to oppose individuals to the collective. The prophet is a lookout and gives his warnings to all; their various responses, however, are conveniently discussed in terms of single persons.

This interpretation is supported by the easy transfer from plural to singular in our passage(s), and even more by the transfer from plural to singular and back to plural again in chs. 14 and 18 (composed in the same legal style). At the start and finish, where the real setting of the address—to the whole "house of Israel"—is depicted, the plural is used (14:5, 6, 11; 18:2, 3, 30); in between the abstract cases are couched in the singular (see, esp., the juxtaposition of plural in the address and singular in the doctrinal teaching in 18:31f. [33:11]). Lindars (*VT* 15 [1965], 462ff.) observes well that the individuals in the cases set forth in ch. 18 (father, son, grandson) must be "allegorical" in the sense that they correspond to the sequence of generations (collectives), about whose treatment by God the people complain. "Even though Ezekiel's real concern is the fate of the nation as a whole, the way in which he uses this legal language as if he were speaking about the fate of individuals is . . . a striking feature of his teaching" (ibid., p. 261).

That Ezekiel's call for individual repentance is not peculiar to him and does not suppose a "disintegrated" or "individualized" exilic society is shown, finally, by its frequency in Jeremiah's prophecy, made in a pre-exilic setting and as a condition for national salvation: Jer 18:11; 25:5 (an epitome of all pre-exilic prophecy! so, too, 35:15); 26:3ff. One may also compare the individualized appeal of the king of Nineveh, designed to save the collective from destruction (Jonah 3:8).

But does not the distinction between the doomed wicked and the backsliding righteous suppose separate and individual treatment of these very different cases? It has already been pointed out that the statement of the case of the backsliding righteous man supposes, in its first alternative, the situation obtaining in the first alternative presented in the case of the doomed wicked—namely, that the prophet failed to warn. This is a literary hint of the simultaneity of the cases that deeper consideration of the object lesson in ch. 33 bears out. The lookout on the wall has no message tailored to the needs of each townsman; he sounds a general alarm—but the general alarm is perceived by each hearer in personal as well as collective terms. Not only "The town is imperiled!" but also "My home, my wife, my children are in danger!" The same would appear to be true of the prophet. Warning the wicked man that God has sentenced him to death means to announce to the house of Israel that God's doom is in store for them because of their evildoing. To this general announcement the incorrigibly wicked will be impervious; the righteous, tending to backslide, will take warning and be saved; whatever the effect, the prophet will have discharged his task. (Taken thus, a minor puzzle is solved: how does the prophet know the inclination of the righteous man to backslide so that he can catch him in time to keep him from sinning? Answer: the announcements of doom fall on diverse ears with diverse effects; among the hearers will also be persons on the verge of backsliding who, when they hear the prophet, will be saved.)

When did the prophet assume the role of a lookout and where in his prophecies is this role expressed? Against the view that this figure represents the later phase of Ezekiel's activity Herntrich (*Ezechielprobleme,* p. 111) argued: "The ideas in [33:]10–20 are already present in the prophecies of woe . . . [In chs. 1–24] Ezekiel had blown the horn and warned incessantly, 'Disaster is coming to Jerusalem, to the land.' So we see that the insertion 3:16b–21 is by no means so senseless as has for the most part been believed, but that the ideas expressed there are altogether in their right place. Ezekiel 33:1–9 too would fit far better there than in its present late context." It is certainly true that "warning of doom" is a title generally apt for chs. 1 – 24 but entirely inappropriate for chs. 34 – 48. With regard to the nature of his task, the prophet is told nothing here beyond what he heard at his commissioning. New is the angle from which the task is viewed—the focus on the prophet's responsibility and opportunity. But Herntrich overshoots the mark when he judges 33:1–20 more fitting here than in its present late context. For the main point of ch. 33 is the appeal to conversion, the insistence on the possibility and efficacy of repentance; the lookout theme subserves the exposition of God's readiness to take the people back. That is absent from our passage and belongs (as Eichrodt recognized) to a state of despair from which the exiles were remote at the start of Ezekiel's career. Repentance and conversion is a minor theme of Ezekiel's prophecy, merely adumbrated in the commissioning speech ("whether they listen . . ."), glimpsed as a missed opportunity in our passage ("he does not turn away from his wickedness . . ."), and developed only in chs. 18 and 33 (but cf. 13:22; 14:6). The socially beneficial aspect of the lookout role, indicated (without reference to repentance) in the second paragraph of our passage, appears to have developed over time into the call for repentance, especially in response to the exiles' growing hopelessness. But that is beyond the concern of our passage, whose main burden is to supply the prophet with a rationale and a motivation for his thankless task. Understood so, its location directly following upon the prophet's week of desolation is unexceptionable.

(A sidelight is thrown on the continuity of the lookout passage with the account of the commissioning that precedes it by the verse from the Koran [3.19] cited earlier. The verse nicely fuses themes found separately in the two Ezekiel passages: the Koran's "if they surrender themselves . . . but if they turn away . . ." = "whether they listen or not" of Ezekiel's commissioning; the Koran's "thou art only responsible for the proclamation" = the main burden of the lookout passage.)

IV. Confinement and Symbolic Acts (3:22–5:17)

3 22 The hand of YHWH came upon me there, and he said to me:
Get up and go out to the plain and there I shall speak to you. 23 So I
got up and went out to the plain, and there was the Majesty of YHWH
waiting—like the Majesty that I saw by the Chebar canal; and I fell
on my face. 24 Then spirit entered me and stood me up on my feet,
and he spoke to me and said to me: Go, shut yourself in your house.
25 You, man, see, they put ropes on you and bound you with them so
that you must not go out among them. 26 I shall make your tongue
stick to your palate so that you will be dumb and not be a reprover
for them, for they are a rebellious house. 27 But when I speak to you
I shall open your mouth, and you will say to them, "Thus said Lord
YHWH": whoever listens will listen, whoever will not will not; for
they are a rebellious house.
4 1 You, man, take a brick and set it before you, and engrave on
it a city, Jerusalem. 2 Lay siege to it—build a siege-wall against it,
throw up a ramp against it, set army camps against it; place rams
against it on all sides. 3 You, take an iron griddle and set it as an iron
wall between you and the city. Direct your face toward it; let it be
under siege with you besieging it. It is a sign for the house of Israel.
4 You, lie down on your left side and place the iniquity of the house
of Israel on it; for the number of days[a] that you lie on it you shall bear
their iniquity. 5 I am converting for you [b]the years of their iniquity[b]
into a number of days—390[c] days; thus you shall bear the iniquity of
the house of Israel. 6 When you finish these, you shall lie down a
second time, on your right side, and bear the iniquity of the house of
Judah for forty days; I am converting each year of it into a day for
you, each year into a day. 7 Direct your face toward the siege of
Jerusalem and with your arm bared prophesy against it. 8 See, I am

[a] G inserts here "150."
[b–b] S "two (G "their two") iniquities," as though Hebrew *š^{e}ne* were derived from *š^{e}naim* "two" rather than *šanim* "years"; impossible, inasmuch as *^{ʿa}wonam* is "their iniquity" (singular).
[c] G "190."

putting ropes on you so that you will not turn from one side to another until you finish the days of your siege.

9 You, take some wheat, barley, beans, lentils, millet and emmer and put them into a single dish and make them into bread for yourself; during the number of days that you lie on your side, 390[c] days, you shall eat it.

10 Your food that you eat shall be by weight—
twenty shekels a day;
You shall eat that from one day to the next.
11 Water you shall drink by measure—
one sixth of a hin;
You shall drink it from one day to the next.
12 A barley-cake you shall eat;
And it—on pellets of human excrement you shall bake it
in their sight.

13 YHWH said: So shall the Israelites eat their bread unclean among
the nations to which I will banish them. 14 Then I said: Ah, Lord
YHWH! My throat is undefiled; from my youth till now I have not eaten the flesh of a carcass or of an animal torn by wild beasts, nor has fouled meat ever entered my mouth.
15 He answered me: See, I allow you to use cattle dung instead of human pellets; make your bread on that.

16 He said to me: Man, I am going to break the staff of bread in Jerusalem;

They shall eat bread by weight and in anxiety,
and water by measure and in desolation drink;
17 thus they shall lack bread and water.
Each with his fellow shall be desolate,
and they shall pine away in their iniquity.

5 1 You, man, take a sharp blade,
a barber's razor take in hand,
and pass it over [the hair of] your head and beard.
Take a balance and divide it up:
2 One third you shall set on fire amidst the city
when the days of the siege are over.
[d]You shall take another third,
shall strike it[d] with the blade around her;

d–d G "And you will take the third and will burn it in her midst, and the third you will cut down; S "and you will take another portion and will cut (it)."

And another third you shall scatter to the wind,
And [e]I will unsheathe the sword[e] after them.

3 From there you shall take a small amount and wrap it in the ends
of your garment. 4 Of it take some again and throw it into the fire,
and burn it up in the fire; from it fire shall spread to the whole house
of Israel.

5 Thus said Lord YHWH: This is Jerusalem:
I set her amidst the nations,
with lands around her.
6 She rebelled
against my judgments
becoming more wicked
than the nations;
against my laws,
than the lands that are around her.
For they rejected my judgments;
my laws—they would not follow them.

7 So then, thus said Lord YHWH: Because you have been more
tumultuous than the nations that are around you,

You have not followed my laws,
You have not executed my judgments,
Even in accord with the judgments of the nations
that are around you you have not[f] acted!—

8 So then, thus said Lord YHWH:
I am coming at you, I, for my part;
I will execute judgments in your midst
in the sight of the nations,
9 Doing in you what I never did,
and the like of which I shall not do again
because of all your abominations.
10 Surely parents will eat children in your midst,
and children shall eat their parents,
I will work judgments in you
and scatter your survivors to every wind.

11 Surely, by my life, declares Lord YHWH, I swear: Because you
defiled my sanctuary with all your loathsome and abominable things,

I too will shear[g], my eye not sparing,
nor will I have pity.
12 One third of you shall die in the plague
and perish by famine in your midst;

[e–e] S "the sword shall lay waste"; so too in vs. 12.
[f] Not in S, and in some Hebrew mss.
[g] T "will cut off," as though *'gd'*; so read in some Hebrew mss. (*Minḥat Shay*).

Another third shall fall by the sword around you;
Another third I will scatter to every wind,
And unsheathe the sword after them.

13 My anger will be spent; I will assuage my fury against them, and get satisfaction. And they shall know that I YHWH have spoken in my passion, when I spend my fury against them. 14 I will turn you into a ruin and a reproach among the nations that are around you, in the sight of every passerby. 15 It[h] will be a reproach and a revilement, a warning and a horror for the nations that are around you, when I execute judgments against you in anger and in fury and by chastisements of fury; I YHWH have spoken; 16 when I let loose against them my deadly arrows of famine, which are for destroying, [i]which I will let loose to destroy you; and more famine will I inflict upon you,[i] breaking your staff of bread. 17 I will let loose upon you famine and wild beasts—they shall bereave you; plague and bloody death shall pass through you; and I will bring upon you the sword: I YHWH have spoken.

[h] G S T "You."
[i–i] Not in G.

COMMENT

3:22. *hand*. See comment to 1:3.

plain (biqʿa). Lit. "cleft, opening"; a geographic term for a valley surrounded by hills, it is extended to broad vales like that of the Jordan at Jericho (Deut 34:3), and even, as here, to the wide plain of Euphrates in Babylonia (Gen 11:2; as such it serves as a synonym of *mišor* "flatland" in Isa 40:4); see G. A. Smith, *Historical Geography of the Holy Land,* 25th ed. (London: Hodder and Stoughton, 1931), pp. 385, 684f. G regularly translates it *pedion* "plain." At this site the prophet later had the vision of the dry bones (37:1ff.); evidently uninhabited, the plain was suitable for a private divine vision.

23. *the Majesty . . . like the Majesty.* Is the comparison being made with the luminous human figure alone (called *kᵉbod YHWH* in 1:28) or with the combination of the enthroned human figure and its bearers, as is the sense of *kabod* in 43:2 ("the Majesty . . . its sound was like that of the deep sea"—an allusion to the din made by the flying bearers; cf. 1:24)? D. H. Müller, *Ezechiel-Studien,* pp. 27f., argued that our passage with its specification of "like the Majesty . . . at the Chebar canal" refers only to the human figure, for when, as in ch. 43, the whole complex is intended, comparison is made with "the apparition (*marʾe*) . . . at the Chebar canal" (43:3). Cf. the discussion on the ambiguity of the similar expression in 8:4, where the distinction is crucial.

24. *shut.* T renders "hide," evoking Isa 26:20 ("Go, my people, enter your chambers, / And lock your doors behind you. / Hide but a little moment, / Until the indignation passes.") and suggesting the prophet's retreat from a hostile environment. S employs a derivative of the root *ḥbš,* from which its rendering of "siege" in 4:3, 8; 5:2 is also derived, thus relating the sequestration of the prophet to the symbolic acts that follow.

25. *they put.* The third-person plural suffix of *b^etokam* "among them" requires the verbs to be taken as third-person plural actives, not as expressions of the passive (e.g., "ropes have been put," etc.). While the literal meaning cannot be excluded (cf. Jer 20:2; 29:26; 37:21), the more likely sense seems to be: the public repulsion toward you is so great, it has as good as driven you off the streets and confined you to your quarters.

26. Answering to the people's repulse of the prophet, God now binds (*ne'^elamta* "you shall be dumb" from *'lm* "bind") Ezekiel's tongue and forbids him to fill the role of a reprover—one who reproaches wrongdoers with their wickedness and calls on them to mend their ways. A public censor—"the reprover in the gate"—is mentioned in Amos 5:10 and Isa 29:20f.; nothing more is known of him, and it is not clear that he had official standing (so M. H. Segal, "Prophet, Lookout, Reprover," in *Masoret u-Biqqoret,* pp. 150ff.). He evidently fulfilled, on a communal scale, the religious injunction of Lev 19:17, "You must reprove your neighbor and not incur guilt on his account" (for this interpretation of the last clause, see G S T). Prudence admonishes the zeal of the reprover in Prov 9:7f.: "To correct a scoffer, or reprove a wicked man for his blemish, is to invite abuse on oneself." Here reproof is checked by a moral motive: the people do not deserve it, for they are a rebellious house.

The tension between this check on public reproof and the prophet's commission to warn the people led Wilson (*VT* 22 [1972], 91ff.) to posit the meaning "intercessor" for *moki^aḥ;* the term never carries that sense, however, but only reprover, arbitrator, or judge.

27. Only when God addresses the prophet with a message for the people, may he speak, and then only to deliver the message; a new twist to 2:4 and 3:4.

In 24:27, the prophet is told that with the arrival of the news of Jerusalem's fall his mouth would be opened, he would speak (freely) and be dumb no longer; in 33:22 the report of this happening is given, "and I was dumb no longer." Zimmerli understands this passage in the light of those, and so takes "when I speak to you" not in a repetitive ("whenever") but in a momentary sense ("at the time when"); the contradiction between the command to be dumb—lasting, on this reading, from the start of Ezekiel's career to the fall of Jerusalem—and all the intervening prophesying (cf., e.g., the explicit 11:25) is removed by the assumption that our passage is secondary and not to be taken entirely seriously.

Some connection of our passage with 24:27; 33:22 is certain, but Zimmerli's exegetical conclusions are not inevitable. Here it is said that when God speaks to the prophet, his mouth will be opened and he will say "Thus said YHWH"; in chs. 24 and 33 it is said that upon receiving news of the fall, the prophet's mouth will be/was opened and he will be/was dumb no longer—that is, his dumbness never returned afterward. These are not the same. Here God's speech refers to oracles generally, as is clear from the subsequent "Thus said YHWH," referring to the prophet's transmission of God's speech to the people; there God's speech (in ch. 24) is a private message to the prophet concerning the end of his "dumbness," and its fulfilment (in ch. 33) is not communicated (there is no "Thus said YHWH"). Moreover, no termination of the "dumbness" is mentioned here (no equivalent to "being dumb no longer" of chs. 24 and 33). Finally, the intended content of "Thus said YHWH" must be here a message of doom—which is why the audience's acceptance is in doubt ("he who listens will listen," etc.); but such a message would have been meaningless after the fall. The conclusion must be that while indeed 24:27 and 33:22 are related to our passage, our passage does not allude to them. "When I speak to you" means "whenever"; in the intervals between God's addresses and the consequent empowerment of the prophet to transmit them onward, he remained dumb. These lapses into dumbness ceased once for all when news of the fall arrived. There is thus no contradiction between our passage and the rest of the book. On the meaning of the "dumbness" see Structure and Themes.

4:1. *brick.* Hebrew *l^{e}bena,* Akkadian *libittu* "sun-dried brick," a commonly used building material throughout Mesopotamia, Palestine and Egypt (*IDB,* s.v. "Brick"). The prophet was to incise a drawing, or perhaps a map (cf. *ANEP*² #260), of Jerusalem on the brick before hardening it, much as kings' names were inscribed on building bricks before they were baked (*ANEP*² #253).

2. *Lay siege.* The distinctive verbs that follow, particularizing the stages of the siege, suggest that the prophet was to construct models of the siege-works rather than draw them on the brick. *dayeq* is a cognate of Akkadian *dāiqu* "siege-wall" (*CAD* s.v.; cf. II Kings 25:1 [= Jer 52:4] *dayeq sabib* "a *d.* all around"). G. R. Driver (*Biblica* 35 [1954], 147f.) takes both to mean "observation tower" (Syriac *daq* "watch")—the upper part of the ram-machine (see, e.g., Y. Yadin, *The Art of Warfare in Biblical Lands,* 2 vols. [New York: McGraw-Hill, 1963], II, pp. 390f.)—but then he must correct (or render) it as plural, conforming to *karim* "rams," at the verse-end, and has no explanation for its being separated from *karim. sol^{e}la* is the mound or ramp up which rams were pushed; for its verb *šapak* "pour out" compare Akkadian *a[ra]mmu ina šipik epri iṣṣe u abne . . .* [*ušakbis*] "[I had (my men) pack down] a ramp with earth, wood, and stones (Esarhaddon, cited in *CAD* 4, p. 188, col. a, end). For *maḥ^{a}ne* see comment at 1:24. *karim* "rams" (Latin *aries*) are frequently pictured in Assyrian reliefs (*ANEP*² #367, 369);

see the discussion by Y. Yadin in *EM* 5, s.v. *"nešeq,"* cols. 967–72, with illustration.

3. *iron griddle.* An impenetrable barrier, representing the total severance of relation between the city and God (cf. Lam 3:44, "You have screened yourself off with a cloud, that prayer may not pass through"); cf. also "R. Eleazar said: From the time the temple was destroyed an iron wall has cut Israel off from its Father in heaven, as it is said, 'You, take an iron griddle'" (BT *Berakot* 32b). Others have seen in it a symbol of sin, on the basis of Isa 59:2, "But your iniquities have been a barrier between you and your God."

Direct (haken) *your face toward.* This is an intensified form of "Set (*śim*) your face toward" (6:2; 13:7; 21:2, 7, etc.), a command that often precedes the text of a prophetic harangue. By glaring at (or in the direction of) some object, the prophet represents God's angry purpose regarding it; this appears more clearly in vs. 7, in which the prophet is ordered not only to "direct his face" toward the besieged city but to "prophesy against it." (Such physical symbolization of intention occurs in Israel's worship: Daniel in exile faces windows open to Jerusalem when he prays [Dan 6:11].)

a sign. The siege played by Ezekiel is a portent of Israel's fate.

4. *left side.* The inauspicious quality of left (cf. Gen 48:17; Qoh 10:2) suffices to explain the choice of the left side for "bearing iniquity"; see comment, however, on vs. 6.

place . . . bear iniquity. Cf. Lev 16:21f., "[The priest] shall set them [the iniquities of Israel] on the head of the goat . . . and the goat will bear all their iniquity on him to an inaccessible region." Ezekiel's adaptations of other traditional idioms warn against the simple equation of traditional senses with his, though the earlier uses of *naśa ʿawon*—particularly the priestly—are instructive. In addition to the above-cited passage, it is to be noted that priests "bear (i.e., take on themselves) the iniquity" of Israel, thus atoning for them (Exod 28:38; Lev 10:17); moreover, God "bears (i.e., tolerates) iniquity" (Exod 34:7), meaning that he forbears to punish. But *ʿawon* also means "punishment" (consequence of iniquity), and the phrase occurs, accordingly, with the meaning "undergo punishment," notably in Num 14:33f., where Israel must "undergo their punishment for forty years, according to the number of days—forty days—that they scouted the land: "a year for a day, a year for a day"; in the light of the next verse this passage is highly significant for the present context. The decision among the various possibilities must be deferred to Structure and Themes.

house of Israel. The scope of this term heretofore (3:1, 7, 17; 4:3) has included all Israel; only the contrast with "house of Judah" in vs. 6 indicates, indeed demands, its restriction here to the northern kingdom (so again only in 9:9 and perhaps 37:16).

5. *I am converting . . . years . . . into . . . days.* A striking reversal of

Num 14:33f. where days (of iniquity) are converted into years (of punishment).

For the number 390, see the comment to vs. 6.

6. *a second time.* As Josh 5:2 shows ("again circumcise the Israelites a second time"), *šenit* may be used to signify nonidentical repetition: in Joshua, the sense is, see that the new generation is circumcised as was the old; here, start up a new period of lying down on your right side (with, perhaps, a new set of symbols) after completing the period on your left. The particular sense of *šenit* (the word does not appear in G) seems to be: resume from the beginning. There is a slight suggestion of a different sequel to "lie down"—and indeed it is borne out, for now the prophet must lie on his—

right side. Taken with the unexpected "house of Judah" (which requires a revision of one's understanding of "house of Israel" in vs. 4), right indicates south, as in 16:46: Sodom is to the right (south) of Jerusalem. This entails in turn a reinterpretation of left in vs. 4 as north —again as in 16:46: Samaria is on Jerusalem's left (north).

forty days . . . This is an adaptation of Num 14:34 that hews closer to it than vs. 6, yet with the same reversal of years and days.

Ancient and medieval attempts to interpret the numbers in vss. 5 and 6, and the phrase *naśa ʿᵃwon* in both, within a single frame of reference have not succeeded. Thus, taking *ʿᵃwon* as "(past) iniquity" works tolerably in vs. 5: counting back from Ezekiel's time 390 years brings one to the beginning of the tenth century B.C.E., roughly when the temple was built—perhaps the start of an era for Ezekiel; this era, then, was (on this interpretation) all sin. But this interpretation meets an insuperable difficulty in the 40 years of Judah; for where does one start to work out 40 years (only!) of iniquity for the southern kingdom? No suggestion persuades; and when, in the light of "house of Judah," "house of Israel" is made out to be the northern kingdom alone, the number 390 defies all explanation.

Taking *ʿᵃwon* as "punishment" (i.e., exile) works tolerably well for Judah (cf. 29:11–13, a 40-year exile imposed on Egypt)—the prophet may well have envisaged such a "wilderness" age of punishment for his wicked compatriots. But no effort has succeeded in making a 390-year exile for the northern kingdom plausible (even counting the last 40 years as running concurrent with that of Judah, and so reducing it to 350 years).

In addition to the gross discrepancies between these numbers and any historical reality (on a single interpretation), vs. 9 seems to take account only of a single period of lying on the side, that of 390 days; what of the 40 days of Judah?

G has a set of numbers significantly differing from MT, and capable of being given a single interpretation: the prophet lies on his left side 150 days, on his right, 40—a total of 190 days for "their two (!) iniquities" (an impossible construction of *šᵉne ʿᵃwonam*). Taking *ʿᵃwon* as "punishment," this means that Judah's exile will last 40 years, Israel's 150: 110 years before that of Judah (e.g., 590 B.C.E. + 110 = 700 B.C.E.), then running concurrently with Judah's, both terminating together (e.g., till around 550 B.C.E.). In vs. 9, "the number of days you lie on your side (= sides)" is, rightly, 190. G has undoubtedly a neat system, but its very neatness, and in particular its forced interpretation of *šᵉne ʿᵃwonam* on which much is based, raises the suspicion of artifice.

(As Freedman observes privately, the figures in G bear a "curious relationship" to similar numbers in the Flood story: there are 40 days of rain [Gen 7:12, 17] and 150 days during which the water "prevailed over" the land [7:24]. The similarity is even more striking if Cassuto is right in calculating that the 150 include the 40, so that the period of "prevailing" was 110 days after the rain [*From Noah to Abraham* (Hebrew) (Jerusalem: Magnes Press, 1959), p. 67 (at 7:24)].)

The difficulties in MT of vss. 4–6 correlate with difficulties in interpreting all the symbolic acts of ch. 4 under a single heading; resolution must await the larger discussion in Structure and Themes.

7. *with your arm bared.* "Because one who wants to deal a blow or to fight energetically strips his arm of clothing; cf. 'YHWH has bared his holy arm' (Isa 52:10)" (Kimḥi). In this gesture, the prophet's representation of God as the enemy reaches maximum clarity. Cf. Jer 21:5: "I [YHWH] myself will battle against you, with outstretched hand and mighty arm, with anger and fury and great wrath."

Verses 7–8 show that the siege of Jerusalem, the lying on the side (so! note the singular and the apparent ignorance of a command to change sides), and the prophesying went on simultaneously. The usual view that these acts were a "dumb show" is therefore mistaken.

8. *I am putting ropes.* A metaphor for divinely imposed restraint—or restraint felt imposed by outside force—echoing 3:25.

9. All these products were found in Mesopotamia: Hebrew *ḥiṭṭa* is Akkadian *kibtu,* "wheat"; *śᵉʿora—šeu,* "barley"; *pol—pulilu,* "bean"; *ʿᵃdašim—kakkū,* "lentils"; *doḥan—duḫnu,* "millet"; *kusmim—kunāšu,* "emmer." Dough composed of such a mixture represents siege food—no one kind being available in amounts sufficient to bake a loaf of it. The Babylonian Talmud (*Erubin* 81a) relates an experiment made in the third century C.E. proving that Ezekiel's bread would not be touched even by a dog.

on your side 390 days. The plain sense is that siege food was to be eaten only during the time the prophet lay on his left side; vss. 4–5.

10. *by weight.* Cf. Lev 26:26, where there is added, "so you shall eat and not be satisfied"; twenty shekels is about eight ounces (shekel = four tenths of an ounce).

from one day to the next. meʿet ʿad ʿet is lit. "from time to time," but cf. Mishnaic *meʿet lᵉʿet* "a twenty-four-hour period."

one sixth of a hin. Two thirds of a quart (hin = gallon = four quarts).

12. The Hebrew of the first clause is literally "And a barley-cake (fem.) you shall eat it" (fem.), commonly taken to mean "you shall eat it"—namely, the bread loaf of vs. 9—"as a barley-cake,"—that is, perhaps, without relish. Besides the obscurity of the injunction when taken this way, the interposition of the passages on doling and the incongruence of the feminine suffix with the masculine *leḥem* "bread" (cf. vs. 9) (or *ma'ᵃkal* "food," vs. 11) argue against connecting vs. 12 with vs. 9. It is more natural to understand vs. 12, on the analogy of vss. 10–11, as starting a new topic, with the noun ("barley-cake") the logical object—though grammatically the subject—as it were, suspended and resumed in the object suffix of the verb (*t'kl-nh*). Similarly, in the next clause *hy'* is the logical object—though grammatically the subject—and is taken up in the suffix of *t'g-nh* (the absence of *dageš* in the *n* is irregular; GKC § 58 k). For similar constructions see 32:7b and 30:18b, respectively, and the discussion of *casus pendens* in Joüon § 156 and Driver, *Tenses,* § 197, (1), (4). Note the variations, so typical of Ezekiel's style, on the sequence object—verb—adverb in the contiguous vss. 10–12.

Barley bread was the staple of lower income groups, wheat products the food of the privileged (H. Lewy, "Some Old-Assyrian Cereal Names," *JAOS* 76 [1956], 203). The mode of baking (verb *'wg* "make/bake a cake") referred to is described by E. Robinson, *Biblical Researches* II (London: J. Murray, 1841), p. 76: "The men were baking a large round flat cake of bread in the embers of a fire of camel's and cow-dung [cf. *'ugat reṣapim* "ember-cake," I Kings 19:6]. Taking it out when done, they brushed off the ashes and divided it among the party . . . I tasted it, and found it quite as good as the common bread of the country . . . this is the common fare of persons travelling in this manner [a camel caravan from Nablus to Bethlehem]." However, the use of human excrement is irregular (Dalman, *AuS* IV, p. 20) and defiling: cf. Deut 23:15 on the desecration of the army camp by unsanitary conditions.

in their sight. The people must see how it is baked on excrement to realize that it is unclean (see next verse).

13. *unclean.* Lands outside the land of Israel were "unclean" (*ṭame;* cf. Josh 22:19; Amos 7:17), probably on account of the idolatrous practices that went on in them (cf. Ezek 36:18b). Exiles were therefore necessarily in a state of uncleanness, and the food they prepared and ate, unclean—comparable to "the bread of mourners" (Hos 9:3f.; cf. Deut 26:14).

14. *throat.* Unclean food *ṭimme nepeš* "defiles the gullet," according to Lev 11:44; for *nepeš* in this sense, see, e.g., Isa 5:14 (|| *pe* "mouth").

carcass . . . torn. Lev 22:8 and Ezek 44:31 forbid such flesh to priests as causing a defilement that disqualifies them from divine service.

fouled meat. Hebrew *piggul* refers to sacrificial flesh that was kept beyond the term prescribed for its consumption on penalty of excision (Lev 7:18; 19:7f.). Isa 65:4 juxtaposes "broth of *piggulim*" to "swine's flesh."

15. If even after God's allowance, the prophet's act was to carry its original meaning, it must be supposed that—for ritual reasons?—priests were known not to use animal dung as fuel.

16–17. These verses contain phrases found in Lev 26:26 ("break the staff of bread") and vs. 39 ("pine away in iniquity"); the former recurs in Ezek 5:16; 14:13, the latter in 24:23; 33:10. The second half of vs. 16 evokes Ezek 12:18f. The language of these verses is thus stereotypical.

The use of *lᵉma'an* (properly "in order that") in vs. 17 in the sense "so [= with the result] that" occurs elsewhere in Ezekiel, especially in conclusions (6:6; 12:19; 14:5; 16:63).

5:1. *blade.* Hebrew *ḥereb* "sword" serves for "sharp tool" (26:9; Exod 20:25) and "knife" (Josh 5:2f.); the specific sense here is determined by the next clause.

a barber's razor take in hand. Lit. "take it" (fem.)—another *casus pendens* construction. The feminine suffix of the verb refers to *ta'ar* "razor" which is feminine only here and in Isa 7:20—the apparent inspiration of our passage: "In that day, my Lord will cut away with the razor that is hired [*ta'ar haśśᵉkira*] beyond the Euphrates—with the king of Assyria—the hair of the head and the hair of the feet, and it shall clip off the beard as well."

The ambiguous word *ḥereb* is used here in order to prepare the way for interpreting the blade as God's sword (vss. 2, 12). G S (and apparently T) heavy-handedly render: "as a barber's razor take it"—namely, the "sword" which, as they understand it, the prophet was supposed to use.

The word for barber, *gallab,* is a hapax, probably a loan from Akkadian *gallābu.*

2. *set on fire amidst the city.* Hebrew *ba'ur tab'ir bᵉtok ha'ir*—a rhyme with consonantal alliteration and stress-vowel alternation (*u-i, o-i*) evidently determining the choice of the rare *'ur* "fire" here; in vs. 4 the common *'eš* occurs (congenial to the environing sibilants—*hišlakta, śarapta, teṣe*). *'ur* and *'eš* occur in a construct pair in Isa 50:11 (on this phenomenon cf. Y. Avishur, *The Construct State of Synonyms in Biblical Rhetoric.*

The hair is to be burnt *amidst the city,* i.e., in the fire kindled on the brick of vs. 1.

The fire is interpreted in vs. 12 as representing death by famine and plague (cf. 7:15 "he who is in the city—famine and plague shall consume him"). Famine appears as a fiery figure in Lam 5:10, "Our skin glows like an oven with the burning blasts of famine" (cf. Rashi); that the same is true of plague may be inferred from its connection with *rešep* (e.g., Hab 3:5), ultimately a Canaanite plague-god whose name came to mean "flame, spark" in Hebrew (Song of Songs 8:6 [see Pope, in AB]; Job 5:7). Cf. also the comment to vs. 16.

strike it. Hebrew has no object—not in itself unusual; GKC § 117 f; Joüon § 146 i; but taken with the asyndeton (relieved in S by the copula), a question arises whether MT is not an awkward fusion of two alternatives:

a. *wlqḥt 't*	*hšlšyt*	[*whkyt*]	*bḥrb*
b. [*w*]		*tkh*	

a. and you shall take	a third	and you shall strike (it) (cf. S)	with the blade
b. and		you shall strike (cf. G end)	

you shall scatter . . . I will unsheathe. "I (will unsheathe)" is an awkward intrusion of the referent (God) into the directions for the symbolic act; indeed, it is the language of the interpretation of the symbol in vs. 12b. S smooths by rendering "shall lay waste," but MT is not a mere lapse, but the influence of Lev 26:33, upon which these clauses are modeled. Indeed, Lev 26:33–40 offer the key to a deeper understanding of the interrelation of vss. 2–5 here. First, although "I will unsheathe" belongs properly only below, in vs. 12b, it appears here under the influence of the juxtaposed sequence "I will scatter . . . I will unsheath" in Lev 26:33. Secondly, Lev 26:36–38 go on to speak of one "remnant" among the exiles that will perish, and vss. 39f. speak of another that will survive to confess their sins. Following this model our vss. 3–4 also distinguish two groups among the dispersed, the first of which will be preserved, the second, destroyed in the fire kindled in the city. The similarity is striking, but equally so is the difference. In Lev 26 the former remnant perish in an inherent process, unconnected with the "sword unsheathed after them" at the time of their dispersion. Here, through the identity of the object of the actions—the hair—and of the symbol of calamity—fire—the continuity of the process of destruction is underlined (though it is somewhat encumbered by the introduction of the "sword" alongside the fire—the effect of concretizing several figures of speech); see comment to vs. 5. Our passage thus gives the impression of an interpretation of Lev 26:33–40, interrelating what is there depicted as discrete events. (Note, however, that Lev 26:36b "as though fleeing from the sword" does offer a verbal link between the perishing exiles and the "unsheathed sword" pursuing the dispersed in vs. 33.)

Once all this complex representation of the extension of calamity to the exiles has been symbolized in detail and interpreted in vss. 3–5, the subsequent reference to it in vs. 12 can do with "I will unsheath the sword after them" alone. That suffices to evoke the whole complex of events described in vss. 3–5 in the wake of the identical clause.

3. From the last third of hair consigned to dispersion, Ezekiel is to take and bind some in the edge of his garment as a token of the survival of part of the exiles. In the loose, flowing end (*kanap* "wing") of a garment objects could be carried (Hag 2:12; cf. Akkadian *rakāsu ina qanniša*

"bind into her hem"—said of the delivery of a bride-price into the bride's safekeeping); in a midrash God warns Moses that he will "wrap into the edge of his garment (*ṣrr bknfk*)" (=hold against him) his resistance to being commissioned (*Canticles Rabba* to Song of Songs 1:7). By protectively extending it over a woman, a man showed his intent to marry her (Ezek 16:8; Ruth 3:9). Overtones are audible: *w^eṣarta* "you shall wrap" is a strikingly antonymous homophone of the word rendered "you shall besiege" in 4:3—there a hostile act, here a friendly act. More remarkable is the evocation of the regrettably obscure Hos 4:19; "the wind wrapped her/it up in its wings" (*knpyh,* plural—an apparent echo of which is the otherwise strange plural form of the word in our verse).

4. Of those wrapped in his garment the prophet must again take a bit and burn it in the fire kindled in the city, indicating that destruction shall reach even to those scattered in exile. Vs. 3 is not a self-contained symbol, but merely a background for vs. 4: there will be survivors of the dispersion (vs. 3), but they will survive only that some might fall victim to a punishment whose long arm will reach out to them from the doomed city. This spells out the meaning of "I will unsheathe a sword after them" (vs. 3 end).

from it (mimmennu). The suffix is masculine; G "from her"; S "from them"—the expression is vague; perhaps the most apt interpretation is Kimḥi's: "From the fire I commanded you to kindle, a fire will spread to the entire house of Israel, be they in Jerusalem or in exile. For what I have commanded you is a sign of the destruction of Israel." The meaning is, then: the symbolic act you perform presages a general destruction. The masculine suffix of MT is most likely to be taken as a neuter, a reference to the whole symbolism that preceded (on masculine for neuter, see Joüon § 152).

5. *This is Jerusalem.* Here starts the interpretation of all the foregoing.

amidst the nations, with lands around her. In vss. 5–8, 14–15 the nations surrounding Jerusalem serve as a foil for her depravity and as astonished onlookers at her exemplary fate. Her geographic location "amidst the nations" is exploited rhetorically in this way. Originally a nation among nations (the sense of "being on an equal footing with" attaches to *b^etok* "amidst," cf. 19:2, 6; 31:14, 18), she exceeded them all in wickedness (vss. 5–7). Not hidden in some obscure corner, her misconduct was the more scandalous; correspondingly her punishment in the sight of her surrounding neighbors aggravates her disgrace (vss. 8, 14–15; cf. similar motifs in 16:27, 57). More remote is Palache's view (cited by I. Seeligmann in "Jerusalem in Hellenistic-Jewish Thought," *Judah and Jerusalem* [Hebrew] [Jerusalem: Israel Exploration Society, 1957], p. 204, fn. 37) that the intent of the sentence is: set amidst the gentiles, Jerusalem learned from them, but surpassed them in corruption (Deut 17:14; II Kings 17:15). The words cannot be made to bear the later Jewish cosmogonic doctrine (derived probably from Greek thought) that

Jerusalem was "the navel of the earth"—i.e., the place from which the earth was formed; see further at 38:12 (see Seeligmann, loc. cit., and S. Talmon, *Tarbiz* 45 [1976], 163–77).

6. *judgments* (mišpatim), *laws* (ḥuqqot). In Ezekiel as in Deuteronomy and cognate literature and as in the priestly writings, the terms of this pair have lost any distinctiveness they once might have had (e.g., *mišpaṭ* "a decision, a sentence in a case; a precedent"; *ḥoq/ḥuqqa* "regulation, ordinance"); cf. *THAT* I, p. 629. In this passage the semantic range of *mišpat* is brought into play; here it means "rule," in vs. 7 "custom," while in vs. 8 "punishment."

becoming more wicked than the nations. See next verse and the similar thought in 16:27, 52, 54; cf. also II Chron 33:9, whose reformulation of II Kings 21:11 may have been influenced by this verse. Cornill deleted *lᵉriš'a* "becoming wicked" and translated, "she rebelled against my judgments more than the gentiles"; but since God did not give laws to the nations (Ps 147:20), Israel cannot be said to have outdone them in rebellion against those laws. However, having received God's laws and rebelled against them, Israel can be said to be more wicked than the nations whose mores (however base) kept them on a higher level than the depravity to which Israel sank in her rebellion.

For they rejected. The change into the plural, makes this almost a citation of Lev 26:43—the ground given there of the exile.

7. *So then.* In Ezekiel, the particle *laken* introduces the message formula ("thus said Lord YHWH") twenty-four times, and occurs otherwise thirty-seven times; it is thus a characteristic of this prophet's style (and is almost as common in Jeremiah). In the bulk of its occurrences it connects the depiction of an evil or unwanted situation with the divine response to it—punishment or remedy. W. E. March has described its effect in these terms: "here comes the response [to the foregoing]; get ready!" ("*Lākēn:* Its Functions and Meanings," in *Rhetorical Criticism: Essays in Honor of J. Muilenburg,* ed. J. Jackson and M. Kessler [Pittsburgh: Pickwick Press, 1974], pp. 256–86, citation on p. 274). Often in Ezekiel the statement of the bad situation is introduced by *ya'an* "because," in which case the complementary *laken* means "correspondingly"—normally rendered "therefore," "so (then)." Equally often, though *ya'an* is missing, the relation of the *laken* sentence to what precedes it is the same—a conclusion or a consequence; but that does not exhaust the possibilities. "As a rule, the best rendering of the word would be: under these circumstances . . . When Ezekiel threatens an awful judgment and then continues: *lākhēn* fathers shall eat their children . . . (Ez. 5, 10), then the connecting word clearly indicates that in the following he will further elaborate the description given in the preceding [passage]. It indicates what is going to happen under present conditions" (J. Pedersen, *Israel: Its Life and Culture,* I–II [London: Oxford University Press, 1926–40], pp. 116f.). Here, in vss. 7–11 *laken* appears four times imparting urgency and a climactic assur-

ance of consequences. To such cases Kimḥi's observation seems applicable that "some occurrences, especially at the opening of statements, are to be understood as 'in truth'" (*Ha-šorašim,* s.v. *"kwn"*); NJPS translates all *lakens* in vss. 7–11 "assuredly," and so regularly. Some have gone so far as to see in *laken* an assurance of (con)sequentiality equivalent to an oath (*Exodus Rabba* at Exod 6:6; F. J. Goldbaum, "Two Hebrew Quasi-Adverbs: *lkn* and *'kn," JNES* 23 [1964], 132ff.; cf. NJPS at Gen 4:15, "I promise"); but this is denied by March, *Rhetorical Criticism,* p. 271.

more tumultuous than. Hebrew *hamonkem min* is a crux. The first word looks like an infinitive construct, normal after *ya'an* "because" (13:8, 22; 21:29, etc.; for the vocalization cf. *'akolkem,* Gen 3:5; Num 15:19), but the root *hmn* is otherwise unknown. Alternatively it may be a slightly irregular form of the noun *hamon* "tumult, crowd, abundance, wealth"—but a noun after *ya'an* is uncommon (in spite of vs. 9). Our consonantal text is presupposed by the early versions, though they diverge in its interpretation. Some construe the sentence as stating a cause and an effect: G, Symmachus: "Because your capital/magnitude was of [from] the nations, you followed their heathen ways . . ."; V: "Because you surpassed . . . ," seconded by Kimḥi: "Because I made you more numerous and wealthy than the gentiles, you rebelled; compare 'Jeshurun grew fat and kicked'" (Deut 32:15). Others construe it as a statement of sin followed by an elaboration: T: "Because you sinned [guessing at the crux] more than the nations . . . [in that] you did not follow my rules," etc. *hamon-* is taken by most to be a verb; Menahem (cf. Rashi) and König (II, § 64.3, pp. 128–29) compare *hama* "be turbulent, wild" in Ps 46:7; BDB, p. 243a, suppose a denominative *haman* "rage, be turbulent." Since analogy requires the *ya'an* clause (*ya'an . . . sebibotekem*) to have as its complement the *laken* clause in the next verse, the contiguous clause (*beḥuqqotay . . . 'aśitem*) is most naturally taken (with T) as an elaboration of the sin referred to in the *ya'an* clause, and has so been rendered here. Moreover, since *ya'an* normally precedes a verbal form BDB's shift has also been adopted, with all due reservations. The meaning will be that Israel has been wilder than the nations—a reproach repeated at the end of the verse where Israel is said not to have conducted itself even in accord with the heathens' standards.

A commonly accepted emendation of *hmnkm* to *hamrotkem* "your rebelling [more than the nations]" fails to reckon with the difficulty that the nations cannot be said to have rebelled against a God whom they did not know (see comment above to "becoming more wicked than the nations").

not acted. The talmudic sage Joshua ben Levi pointed to the contradiction between this passage—"not acting"—and 11:12—"acting [like the nations]," and solved it as follows: "not acting" like the civilized nations; "acting" like the uncivilized ones (BT *Sanhedrin* 39b). We should rather say that here (according to MT) Ezekiel accuses Israel of being worse than the nations (as in 16:27; cf. II Kings 21:11; Jer 2:11)—a hyperbolic aggravation of the commonplace that it is as bad as the nations (e.g., II Kings 17:8ff.). Alternative readings without "not" (see textual note f) adjust this passage to the commonplace, but Kara astutely observed that the punitive *lo 'aśiti* and *lo 'e'eśe* in vs. 9 mirror a double *lo 'aśitem* in describing the sin in our verse. God will work unprecedented punishments because Israel has done unprecedented evil; this supports MT. (Freedman suggests privately that *l'* here is asseverative; but the few passages in which this usage of *l'* have been posited [see, e.g., KB³, p. 486, col. 2, top] are too shaky a foundation for confidently assuming its existence.)

8. *I am coming at you.* The first example of a divine *hineni 'al-* (*'el-* in 13:8; 21:8; 29:10) announcing imminent retribution is Nahum 2:14, against Nineveh; a phrase originally used of a divine judgment on the nations is here turned against Israel. S. T. Byington ("Hebrew Marginalia," *JBL* 60 [1941], 282) aptly rendered our phrase "Have at you!" citing with approval Sellin's suggestion (at Nahum 2:14) that it was originally the challenging cry of a man-to-man fight. Cf. the analogous *pelištim 'aleka* "The Philistines are upon you, Samson!" (Judg 16:9). For a full study see P. Humbert, "Die Herausforderungsformel 'hinnenî êlêka,'" *ZAW* n.s. 10 (1933), 101–7.

I, for my part. Hebrew *gam 'ani*—the correlative *gam*, expressing correspondence (BDB), is frequent in threats. Here and in vs. 11 it is unclear whether correspondence of divine act to one of the symbolic acts of the prophet is meant, or, more vaguely, to the outrageous conduct of Israel.

judgments. This unique use of *mišpaṭim* in the sense of *šepaṭim* (vs. 10) "punishment" matches crime (see vss. 6–7) and punishment by employing identical terms in their depiction.

9. *abominations.* Hebrew *to'eba* belongs to the vocabulary of the Deuteronomic polemic against idolatry (e.g., Deut 7:25f.; 13:15; 17:4). M. Weinfeld's suggestion (*Deuteronomy,* p. 323) that the usage originated in the poem of Deut 32:16 is noteworthy, since other echoes of that poem occur here in vss. 16f. The idolatry alluded to is more specifically described in vs. 11.

10. Here is a gem of literary adaptation and combination. Lev 26:29 phrases filicidal cannibalism, a standard punishment of covenant-violators (D. Hillers, *Treaty-Curses and the Old Testament Prophets* [Rome: Pontifical Biblical Institute, 1964], pp. 62f.; cf. Deut 28:53–57; Jer 19:9), in climactic chiastic parallelism:

> You shall eat the flesh of your sons
> And the flesh of your daughters you shall eat.

In accord with God's threat of unprecedented retribution in vs. 9, Ezekiel caps this by inventing a hitherto unheard of patricidal cannibalism. Vs. 10

is framed in climactic chiastic parallelism, but its terms derive from Deut 24:16:

Parents shall not be put to death for children,
Nor children put to death for parents

The punishment rejected by Deut 24:16 is unnatural and grotesque (the first sentence in particular highlights this aspect); these very attributes prompted the prophet to refashion the Leviticus curse in his uniquely horrible manner.

11. *by my life.* Hebrew *ḥay 'ani,* an oath formula, for whose interpretation see my article, "The Hebrew Oath Particle *Ḥay/Ḥē,*" *JBL* 76 (1957), 34–39.

"I swear" renders the oath-derived *'im lo* discussed above at 3:6; the present usage is midway between that of its original oath context (cf. the preceding "by my life") and its merely emphatic use outside of oaths, as in 34:8. Note its separation from the asseveration by other words ("Because you . . . I too"), unobjectionable in the merely emphatic usage, but not acceptable in the oath.

declares Lord YHWH. Lit. "utterance [*n*e*'um*] of Lord YHWH." This phrase, a verbal signature, calls attention to the divine author of the prophet's speech. It is used by many of the Hebrew prophets but clusters in great numbers in Jeremiah and Ezekiel. Following R. Rendtorff ("Zum Gebrauch der Formel *n*e*'um jahwe* im Jeremiabuch," *ZAW* 66 [1954], 27–37), my student Susan Rattray (Berkeley) studied the usage in Ezekiel; the following remarks draw on her seminar paper. Ezekiel uses the phrase regularly (fourteen times) after the oath formula "by my life" taken by God, evidently to heighten its intrinsic solemnity by identifying the swearer unmistakably as God (speaking through the mouth of the prophet). The two occurrences of the oath formula not so qualified (17:19; 33:27) are directly preceded by "Thus said Lord YHWH," which serves this function. The phrase appears twenty times at the end of an oracle, as a signature usually corresponding to the opening "Thus said Lord YHWH" (e.g., 11:21; 12:25; 14:23). In fact, Ezekiel uses the two formulas interchangeably in 13:6f. and 22:28 to represent the oracles of false prophets. Some twenty-seven times the *n*e*'um* phrase appears at the end of a verse, often marking a "paragraph"—i.e., a change of topic within an oracle (e.g., 13:16; 14:14; 18:9). At times it constitutes an anticipatory, false ending (e.g., 30:6; 32:31). The remaining thirteen occurrences are in mid-verse, where, owing to its heightening effect, it serves to draw attention to what is being said (e.g., 36:32). The grossly disproportionate use of this phrase in Jeremiah and Ezekiel correlates with the bitter polemics of these two prophets of doom against rival prophets of weal who insisted that it was they who spoke for God (Jer 23; Ezek 13).

On the distinctive double appellation "Lord YHWH" characteristic of

Ezekiel, see comment at 2:4. In Jeremiah simple *n*ᵉ*'um YHWH* is vastly preponderant (it occurs in Ezekiel only twice, at 16:58 and 37:14).

defiled my sanctuary. The details are given in chs. 8 and 11.

shear. Hebrew *gara'* means this in Isa 15:2 = Jer 48:37, where, unlike some printings, the Aleppo and Leningrad mss. read "every beard *g*ᵉ*ru'a* shorn" (lit. "a sheared spot" || *qorḥa* "a bald spot"); T to Judg 16:19; II Sam 10:4 uses *gr'* for Hebrew *gillaḥ* "shave" (see Sperber's edition of T, *The Bible in Aramaic,* and apparatus; A. Kohut, *Aruch Completum* s.v. "*gr'* "). God's threat corresponds ("I too") to the prophet's shaving off the hair of his head.

my eye . . . pity. Outside of Ezekiel, the doubled phrase occurs only in Deut 13:9, where the Israelite is enjoined to suppress his tender feeling toward an apostate relative and deliver him up to death. In Ezekiel it is a characteristic expression of God's grim resolve to punish renegade Israel (7:4, 9; 8:18; 9:5, 10). "It shows clearly (what merits repeated emphasis) that the normal, basic attitude of God toward Israel is not determined merely by law, but by love. It is his proper manner to spare and pity, but there is a level of human guilt at which this mode is set aside, and the standard of his judicial righteousness comes into force" (Herrmann at 9:10, pp. 65f.).

12. The double-death of famine and plague in the besieged city is a theme of Lev 26:25f.

13. A similar string of (four) expressions of spending fury occurs in 16:42; in third place there is "I will be quiet" (*šqṭ*), paralleling "I will get satisfaction" (*hinneḥamti*) here. This latter is an unusual form of hitpa'el, with the meaning that nif'al has in Isa 1:24; 57:6 ("Should I quiet myself in spite of these things?" [T. K. Cheyne, *The Prophecies of Isaiah* (London: K. Paul, Trench and Co., 1884), II, ad loc.]). A formal analogue is *hinnabe* in 37:10 in the sense of *nibbe* (37:7).

in my passion. Reference to God's passion (*qin'a*) is common in Ezekiel (8:3, 5; 16:38, 42; 23:25); he speaks in passion again in 36:6; 38:19. By *qin'a* is meant the resentful rage of one whose prerogatives have been usurped by, or given to, another. Among humans, it seizes the husband who suspects his wife of adultery (Num 5:14ff.) or knows her to have been faithless (Prov 6:34). Since YHWH's relation to Israel is figured as a marriage (see discussion below, ch. 16), *qin'a* is appropriate for his rage at Israel's breach of faith with him. Precursors are the Decalogal epithet of YHWH *'el qanna* "a passionate [traditionally, "jealous"] God"; the account in Num 25:11 of Phineas' act of zeal (*qin'a*) by which he averted YHWH's fury (*ḥema*) and imminent wiping out (*kallot*) of Israel in his passion (*qin'a*); and the dooms pronounced by Zephaniah (Zeph 1:18; 3:8) in which, as here, terms of rage are heaped (see the summary of G. Sauer in *THAT* II, pp. 647–50).

14. These expressions recall Lev 26:31 and a Jeremianic commonplace (Jer 24:9; 29:18; cf. Joel 2:19); the amazement of every passerby is

mentioned in I Kings 9:8; Jer 18:16; 19:8. But the combination "in the sight of [*l^{e}'ene*] every passerby" is unique to Ezekiel (again at 36:34) and reflects his peculiar sensibility to the public, international humiliation inflicted on Israel.

15. The fourfold (two pairs of) invective is Jeremiah's style (see in preceding note), but the items are only partly so (*ḥerpa, musar*). The third-person singular feminine verb (*w^{e}hay^{e}ta*) is unexpected; Luzzatto supplies an impersonal subject: what befalls you will give occasion for reproaching and reviling you, will be an event from which one will take a lesson and at which one will be horrified. The versions ("You will be [an object of] . . .") reflect a more normal reading (*w^{e}hayit*). *g^{e}dupa* "revilement" is often revocalized *giddupa* (so Isa 51:7), but the two forms are related as *r^{e}tuqa* is to *rattuqa* "chain." The first of each pair is a simpler noun form, usually linked with qal verbs, but not invariably; cf. *y^{e}šu'a* which goes with *hoši^{a}'*. *m^{e}šamma* "horror" derives from *šmm,* a base denoting devastation and desolation, spiritual as well as physical; cf. I Kings 9:8, "every passerby will be dismayed *yiššom*" and 3:15 above *mašmim* "desolated" (dismayed, disconcerted). It recurs in 6:14 and elsewhere.

chastisements of fury. Kara contrasts chastisements of love, Prov 3:12.

16. This and the next verse are variations on classical threats of doom in Deuteronomy and Leviticus.

Ezekiel	Deut 32:23f.
ḥiṣṣe hara'ab hara'im	*'aspe 'alemo ra'ot*
"deadly (lit. evil) arrows of famine"	"I will sweep evils upon them"
w^{e}ra'ab 'osep '^{a}lekem	*ḥiṣṣay '^{a}kale bam*
"And more famine will I inflict upon you"	"I will use up my arrows on them"
	m^{e}ze ra'ab etc.
	"Wasting famine," etc.

In Deuteronomy "wasting famine" is the first of God's "arrows" (plagues), whence here the unique phrase "arrows of famine." Ezekiel's *'osep* is an indicative qal imperfect of *yasap* (Joüon § 75 f, 114 g); for the whole clause, cf. Lev 26:21: *w^{e}yasapti '^{a}ḷekem makka* "I will inflict on you more blows." But it unmistakably echoes Deuteronomy as well: G S V render *'aspe* in Deut 32:23a by "I will gather"—that is, *'os^{e}pa;* in this light, Ezekiel's *'osep* might be construed as the imperfect of *'asap* "gather" (cf. *'oḥez* "I shall seize" from *'aḥaz*), though "I will gather famine against you" seems an inferior rendering. However that may be, Ezekiel's *ra'ab 'osep '^{a}lekem* cannot be separated from Deuteronomy's *'aspe 'alemo ra'ot*.

The repeated verb *šillaḥ* "let loose" (also in vs. 17a) echoes Lev 26:25b; "breaking the staff of bread" cites Lev 26:26. The phrase *haya l^{e}mašḥit* recalls language used in the tale of the Egyptians' firstborn plague (Exod 12:13).

G omits the second qualifying clause in vs. 16a ("which I will let loose," etc.); since it duplicates in meaning the preceding clause, it may well have been a variant of it that was missing in G's *Vorlage*. On the other hand, G's further omission of the following clause (*w^e^ra'ab 'osep ^a^lekem*), whose perplexities, discussed two paragraphs above, speak for its originality, may be due to the translator's inability to render it.

17. The terms of this verse, too, echo Deut 32:24f. ("Let loose . . . beasts . . . the sword bereaves") and Lev 26:22 ("let loose among you wild beasts who will bereave you") and vs. 25 ("I will bring a sword upon you . . . plague"). Ezekiel's fusion of elements from the threats of Deuteronomy and Leviticus was echoed by the tannaitic commentator to Lev 26:22 in the *Sifra* (third century C.E.).

STRUCTURE AND THEMES

The section opens in 3:22 with a notice of "seizure" (cf. 1:3 end) and runs on without formal interruptions to 6:1, where a revelation formula (cf. 1:3a) marks a new prophecy. It contains two unequal parts, I (3:22–5:4)—a complex series of commands to perform certain actions, and II (5:5–17)—a prophecy of doom loosely related to those actions. Each part is articulated: I—in a second theophany, the prophet is consigned to his home and given new orders; these appear in three sections, each beginning with the formula "You, man"; II—the prophecy of doom has six subsections, marked by opening and closing formulas.

Part I: Commands to perform certain actions (3:22–5:4)

- A. Theophany and consignment to home (3:22–24)
- B. Command to be shut indoors and be dumb (3:25–27)
- C. Command to enact a siege (4:1–17)
  This is a complex section, with subsections beginning "And you"
  1. The griddle (4:3)
  2. Lying on sides (4:4–8)
  3. Preparing foods (4:9–17)
- D. Command to dispose of hair (5:1–4)

In general, the structure is intelligible. After being told to shut himself up in his home and remain silent except for prophesying, the prophet is ordered to perform various acts symbolizing Jerusalem's imminent doom. These involve domestic objects (e.g., brick, griddle, scales, razor) and can be done at home. After enacting the siege of the city (C), he must represent the annihilation and dispersion of the population (D)—a suitable order of events.

But there are questions. Why should 3:25, which elaborates on the brief command at the end of vs. 24, begin with a section formula? Does it mean that "You, man," may introduce what is no more than a supplement to what precedes it? The section cannot, at any rate, be considered secondary, since it supplies essential details of the terse command at the end of vs. 24.

C1 is a close adjunct to the preceding siege command, adding a second level (the divine hostility) to the siege play (the human attackers). The connection of the two is recognized by the paragraphing, which breaks only after vs. 3 (in spite of the subsection formula that opens vs. 3).

C2 and C3 prescribe actions that are to go on during the enactment of the siege. Their complexity has already been remarked in the comments. C3 is heterogeneous. Vss. 9–11 prescribe the rations to be doled out during 390 days of siege. Vss. 12–15, without a formal break, detail the preparation of a barley-cake and interpret it as the unclean food of the exile. Vss. 16–17 return to the siege theme with a prophecy of famine, introduced—unusually for this passage—by "man." The verses on exile-food thus appear as interpolated amidst the section dealing with siege rations (vss. 9–11, 16–17). However, the threatening prophecy of vss. 16–17 also stands out amidst the series of prescriptions; its originality is made more dubious by its anticipation of 5:16 and its likeness to 12:9. As an interpretation of the scant rations, it corresponds to vs. 13 (the interpretation of the unclean food) and may have been added here as its complement.

C2 is only slightly less heterogeneous. Vss. 4–5, 7–8 prescribe lying on one (the left) side, bearing the iniquity of the house of Israel for 390 days, while prophesying against the besieged city. As though this were not sufficiently complicated, vs. 6 prescribes lying on the right side to "bear the iniquity of the house of Judah" for 40 days. We have argued that these two "iniquities" cannot be the same, but that the first is best taken as the sin of all Israel during the period of the First Temple (or the monarchy) and the second, as the punishment—the exile—of Judah, supposed to last forty years.

Here again, then, a reference to exile interrupts a complex of siege symbols. Its extraneousness to its context is confirmed by the subsequent allusion (in vs. 9) only to the 390-day "lying on your side" (one side only!) during which siege rations are to be eaten.

It seems that prescriptions for two different sets of symbols have been artificially fused. Vss. 4–5, 7–8 (in C2) order the prophet to "bear the iniquity" of all Israel as he lays siege to Jerusalem for 390 days, and to prophesy against the city (signifying God's wrath over its sin). Vss. 9–11, 16–17 (in C3) prescribe the scant food and drink to be consumed during this period—representing the siege again. Thus the theme set at the beginning of C—the city's siege and God's anger toward it (C1)—is appropriately continued. Engrafted onto this is a parallel symbolism of exile—lying on the right side for 40 days (vs. 6) and eating unclean food—presumably during that time (vss. 12–15). Further indication that the exile symbols are out of place is that they mar the natural sequence of siege, depopulation, and dispersion symbolized in C and D. Moreover, the prophecy of doom in part II of our passage ignores the spiritual suffering of the exiles (the unclean food), since it is devoted wholly to the doom of the people—to which spiritual suffering would be anticlimactic indeed! (G supplies the lack of a prophecy of exilic spiritual suffering in part II by reading, in 4:13, "And say, 'Thus said the Lord God of Israel: So shall the Israelites eat,'" etc.)

The exile symbolism (4:6, 12–15) is a self-contained little unit; its introduction—"When you finish these (days)"—connects it with the series of siege symbols, placing it after them, as is chronologically fitting. In the present text, the prescriptions for exile symbolism have been separated and attached to their corresponding siege prescriptions, making it possible for the prophecy of doom in 5:5ff. to follow directly on the siege series, which it interprets.

Part II. Prophecy of Jerusalem's doom (5:5–17)

- A. Indictment (vss. 5–6): opening formula, "Thus said the Lord YHWH"; Jerusalem worse than the nations
- B. Sentencing (vss. 7–17): subdivided into two main statements, each with an opening formula containing the ground ("So then/ Surely . . . because . . .")
  1. Statement 1 (vss. 7–10): three parts, each beginning *laken*
     - a. Ground (vs. 7): Israel's unprecedented evildoing
     - b. General sentence (vss. 8–9): God's unprecedented punishment
     - c. Specification (vs. 10): cannibalism and dispersion
  2. Statement 2 (vss. 11–17): an interpretation of the symbolic action with the hair, with three codas, each ending ". . . I, YHWH, have spoken . . ."
     - a. Interpretation of the symbolic act with the hair (vss. 11–12): ground (defilement of temple), general sentence (ruthless shearing), specification (dealing in thirds)
       1. Coda 1 (vs. 13): God vents his fury
       2. Coda 2 (vss. 14–15): Jerusalem's desolation and public humiliation
       3. Coda 3 (vss. 16–17): reiteration of afflictions let loose against Jerusalem (cf. the afflictions listed in vs. 12)

The skeletal form of prophetic sentences of doom can be seen in 25:8–17:

> Thus said Lord YHWH: Because . . . surely [thus said Lord YHWH]: [Behold] . . . And they shall know that I am YHWH, when . . . [alternative conclusion: declares Lord YHWH].

The skeleton may be expanded by repetition of any of its elements (note how even in the skeleton "Thus said Lord YHWH" may be repeated); here the expansion is unusually great, especially in B2, giving the effect of wave upon wave of fury; but cf. similar effects in 23:22–35; 29:1–16; ch. 34; ch. 36. Such accumulations are a literary feature of the book.

It is remarkable that the prophecy lacks an opening formula (e.g., "Man, set your face toward . . . and prophesy to . . ." [6:2; 25:2]). But such is the case too of all the prophecies after the first in ch. 25. There the reason is plain: the opening formula appears in the first prophecy of the series (25:2–3) and so may be dispensed with in the rest. Here something similar may be suggested. In 4:3, among the directions for enacting a siege, the prophet was told to "direct his face toward the city"; to this vs. 7 adds, "and with bared arm prophesy against it." This amounts to a formula for opening a prophecy—and taken with the abrupt commencement of the prophecy in 5:5 one might suppose that the prophecy which the prophet is ordered to speak in 4:7 is in fact spelled out in 5:5–17. (Indeed it would have been strange not to have found the content of the prophecy commanded in 4:7 spelled out nearby, after the prophet has been repeatedly exhorted to speak only that which God puts in his mouth.) The setting of 4:3, 7—the prophet glaring at the model of the besieged city with his arm outstretched toward it—accords with the opening words of the prophecy, "This is Jerusalem" (namely, the model); moreover, the topics of the prophecy—starvation, wrath of God, the sin of the people—not to speak of the dealing in "thirds" and the dispersion—agree in general with what the prophet symbolized in actions. If 5:5–17 was intended as the verbal accompaniment of the actions (which were to go on day after day), its repetitive, spiraling quality would be very appropriate.

We turn now to the themes of the passage, reserving to the end discussion of the relation of the new commission of the prophet to the preceding one(s).

The "dumbness" of the prophet has been variously explained. Some have thought it pathological ("alalia"), and connected it with what they took to be catatonic immobility (his lying on his side for long periods of time). More recent commentators (e.g., Fohrer, Zimmerli, Wevers) connect this passage with the constraint on mourning imposed on the prophet (24:17), the dumbness commanded in that context (24:27), and the release from it upon receipt of the news of Jerusalem's fall in 33:22. This passage is taken either as a misplaced or invented adjunct of that later, and supposedly brief, interval of silence. In this way the embarrassment of seven years of "dumbness" which are in fact filled with prophesying is eliminated. But these devices misconceive our passage. The "dumbness" must be understood in the context of the command to be shut indoors and the ban on reproving as reflections of and responses to the (prophet's sense of his) rejection by the people: as they rejected the prophet, so God withdraws from their midst the healing presence of the prophet.

Confinement to home is reflected in all the locations of prophesying mentioned in the book (8:1; 14:1; 20:1; 33:30). The "dumbness" of the prophet lasts, as above-said, until the arrival of news of Jerusalem's fall.

This supports its connection with the prophet's experience of rejection and suggests that dumbness and confinement had both the same cause and extent of time. In 24:27 and 33:22 the end of the dumbness is described as the prophet's mouth "being opened" (*niptaḥ pe*); light is shed on this expression by the phrase *pitḥon pe,* lit. "opening of the mouth"—a phrase peculiar to Ezekiel. In 16:63 it is said that the redeemed Israel of the future, recalling their past sin, will have no *pitḥon pe* because of their deep humiliation. Again, in 29:21 it is said that the eventual fulfilment of certain delayed prophecies will give *pitḥon pe* to Ezekiel. In both cases the phrase may be rendered "a claim to be heard"; this is agreeable to its later meaning in Mishnaic Hebrew, "an occasion for complaint, a pretext for accusation." The context of 29:21 is especially suggestive: if fulfilment of long-delayed prophecies will afford Ezekiel an "opening of the mouth" ("a claim to be heard"), it is inferable that during the previous period of waiting the prophet felt deprived of such a claim; the incredulous, hostile attitude of the people "closed his mouth." Our passage may be interpreted in this light: the prophet's extreme despondency ("desolateness") estranged him from and opposed him to his neighbors. He lost the capacity for normal human contact (cf. the striking parallels in Jer 15:17; 16:1), and felt particularly powerless to express himself to them concerning their misdeeds—to act as a reprover. Agreeably, God commands him to withdraw to his home and be silent—except for speaking forth divine oracles, the indispensable core of his calling.

At the time of this redefinition of his task, no limit was set on his withdrawal. That Ezekiel felt released by the news of the fall tends to confirm our interpretation: this terrible concurrence of events with his reiterated prophecies of doom vindicated him, gave him at once the credit he had lacked for seven years—gave him "a claim to be heard," "an opening of the mouth." And the restoration of the prophet to normal intercourse with his neighbors reflected and expressed the great turn of God toward his people, now that they were broken by the punishment; for concurrent with Ezekiel's release from "dumbness" is the second period of his prophecy—the predictions of Israel's restoration. (Wilson's effort to interpret this passage without the radical rearrangements mentioned above has been criticized in the comments; my earlier effort [*JBL* 77 (1958), 101–5] is superseded by this one. For criticisms of my earlier view, see Brin, *Iyyunim,* pp. 70–76, and Y. Komlosh, "Ezekiel's Silence," in *Zer ligevurot,* pp. 279–83; they, too, keep the present order and interpret the prophet's dumbness in a somewhat similar fashion.)

The series of actions now prescribed conforms to the situation of the prophet. Under a kind of house arrest, he must lay siege to "Jerusalem." Various inflictions follow: he must lie on his side a very long time, during which he is to eat siege rations; afterward he must disfigure himself by shaving off all his head-hair. Another set of commands has him preparing food in a repulsive way and lying on his other side for a long time. On the one hand, these inflictions share in the nature of the prophet's enforced confinement (note the unmistakable echo of 3:25 in 4:8); on the other hand, he is relieved thereby from abrasive confrontation with a hostile public.

The explicit aim of the first symbolic act, the siege of the city, is to be "a sign for the house of Israel" (4:3). Like other similar acts (which make the prophet a *mopet* "portent" for the people, 12:6, 11; 24:24, 27), this one represents as a present reality a future but impending event. More such acts are laid upon Ezekiel than on any other prophet—for the most part related to doom prophecy (by G. Fohrer's count in his *Die symbolischen Handlungen der Propheten* [Zürich: Zwingli-Verlag, 1953], Ezekiel was ordered to perform twelve symbolic acts; his nearest rival, Jeremiah, had to perform ten). While elsewhere such symbolic acts at times partake of a magical quality, and hence need not be witnessed (e.g., Jer 51:63f., the sinking of a written curse against Babylon in the Euphrates), for the most part, and always with Ezekiel, they are intended to impress a public—and are often accompanied by verbal explication to the witnesses (the phrase *'ot le* "a sign for" implies onlookers; Isa 7:14; I Sam 2:34; Num 17:3, 25). Late antiquity shows sign of embarrassment with these actions—"A heretic said to Rabbi Abbahu [Palestine, third century C.E.], 'Your God is a joker; first he commands to lie on the left side, then on the right side!'" (BT *Sanhedrin* 39a; the rabbi goes on to interpret these inflictions as vicarious atonement for Israel's sin—the heretic was probably a Christian.) Medieval rationalists were scandalized; Maimonides exclaims "God is too exalted than that He should turn His prophets into a laughingstock and a mockery for fools by ordering them to carry out crazy actions" (*Guide of the Perplexed,* II 46); he goes on to explain such actions as merely visionary, and in this he was followed by medieval and some early modern commentators. But the explicit anticipation of public reaction to such actions (e.g., Ezek 12:9) excludes taking them as visionary. The current consensus is given in Lindblom's assessment of the prophetic symbolic act (*Prophecy,* p. 172):

> It is a *verbum visibile,* a visible word . . . As a divine word, the word uttered by a prophet had an effective power. The same is true of the visible word . . . Such an action served not only to represent and make evident a particular fact, but also to make this fact a reality . . . The effect . . . upon the onlookers was consequently not only to present visibly what the prophet had to say, but also to convince them that the events . . . would really take place. They were also intended to arouse the emotions of fear or hope . . . what was done powerfully reinforced what was said.

This assessment, grounded on the formal similarity between many of the prophetic actions and sympathetic magic, may hold true for the effect of these acts on simpleminded onlookers. For the prophet, as Lindblom admits, the acts were always divine orders, and (it must be added) whatever power may have been thought to reside in them—and there is no evidence that the prophets did ascribe power to them—would have derived from their divine provenience. (See the lengthy but discriminating treatment by Fohrer, *Die symbolischen Handlungen,* esp. chs. 3–5.)

This series of acts was to be accompanied by prophesying against the model of the city. It has been suggested above that 5:5–17 was in fact the "script" of this prophesying. The address in those verses is mostly to Jerusalem or about it, with only occasional lapses into "you" (plural)—meaning the inhabitants of the city. A similar ignoring of actual surroundings occurs in the next chapter—an address to "the mountains of Israel" (6:1), and the next—addressed to Israel's land (7:1). The elders of the exiles sit before the prophet during the great temple vision in chs. 8–11, but only afterward does he speak to them directly. Ch. 12 is the first oracle in which, from the outset, he is directed to act "in the sight" of his neighbors, as he moves away from his home, and to respond to their query (on "in their sight" of 4:12, see below, p. 126). Thereafter he is regularly ordered to "speak to them." There seems to be a record here of Ezekiel's gradual return to his environment, after an initial period of extreme withdrawal from it. The prophet's shrinking from the public's hostility is not only legitimated by the second theophany ("come shut yourself in your home"), but the very messages of God are adjusted to his reluctance to confront the people directly. As Moses' hesitation to execute his commission at the burning bush caused a modification of the charge (e.g., Aaron was co-opted), so the new theophany in 3:22ff. and the initial acts and speeches of Ezekiel bear the marks of modification caused by his "desolation." The essential aim of the first commission—"that they may know that a prophet was among them" (2:5), as well as of the lookout passage—"you must give them warning of me" (3:17)—remained in principle unchanged and unaffected. But the withdrawal of the prophet to his home and his cutting off normal communication with his surroundings are events which, though authorized by divine orders, betray the interposition of his own intimidated personality. May it not be that the unusual accumulation of self-afflictions in this passage is at bottom a kind of compensation for withdrawal from the public fray, a turning upon oneself of stoppled anger and resentment?

The symbolic acts raise two questions: How are the enactments of the siege and the "bearing iniquity" interrelated? What are the exile symbols doing here?

The first question requires a preliminary clarification. Fohrer laid down the rule (*Die symbolischen Handlungen,* pp. 87f.) that "no double symbolism exists in the prophetic acts—say, of the present or past and of the future besides, but always a simple, single symbolism as in magical acts. An impending event is always meant." Though this is generally valid, it cannot be so for the 390 (or the 190, as in G) days of "bearing the iniquity of the house of Israel"; on either reading, the greater part of this number of days represents past years (either of sin—of all Israel, or of punishment—the exile of North Israel). If the concurrence of acts is significant, then the years of the people's sins (following the 390 of MT) and the wrathful siege of Jerusalem by God went on simultaneously; that would be the meaning conveyed by the prophet's prophesying against the besieged city as he lies on his side "bearing iniquity." From the prophet's angle, this means that the sin and God's siege had been going on together for centuries, were still going on, and would continue until the allotted term was filled (a total of 390 years), at which time the city would be destroyed, its population annihilated or dispersed. Since the fulfilment of the term was still in the future (the near future must have been intended), it is impossible to say precisely when its beginning was, but clearly it was in the distant past.

The only model upon which this picture could have been based is Lev 26:14–39. That passage, which offers so many parallels to the language and ideas of Ezek chs. 4–5 is one of the pentateuchal lists of "covenant curses" (*'alot habbᵉrit,* Deut 29:20) with which collections of laws (= terms of God's covenant with Israel) are terminated. The similarity of these to the sanctions enforcing law collections and international treaties in the ancient Near East has been observed (D. R. Hillers, *Treaty-Curses and the Old Testament Prophets* [Rome: Pontifical Biblical Institute, 1964]; M. Weinfeld, *Deuteronomy,* pp. 116–57). How these sanctions determined the actual course of events in the mind of the ancients is strikingly set out in a passage from the Annals of Ashurbanipal. Describing the havoc he wrought on rebellious Arabs, he writes:

> Irra, the Warrior (i.e., pestilence) struck down Uate' [the Arab king], as well as his army, who had not kept the oaths sworn to me . . . Famine broke out among them and they ate the flesh of their children against their hunger. Ashur, Sin Shamash, [etc.] . . . inflicted quickly upon them all the curses written down in their sworn agreements . . . Whenever the inhabitants of Arabia asked each other: "On what account have these calamities befallen Arabia?" (they answered themselves) "Because we did not keep the solemn oaths (sworn by) Ashur, because we offended the friendliness of Ashurbanipal . . ." (*ANET*³, pp. 299–300).

It is an identical mentality that permeates Ezek 4–5; we note how in particular the threat of Lev 26:25, "I will bring upon you a sword exacting retribution for [breach of] the covenant" is repeatedly picked up in ch. 5: what is in Lev 26 a hypothetical threat ("If you reject my judgments . . .") is here a sure prediction of coming doom.

Now, what singles out Lev 26 from other lists of covenant curses (e.g., Deut 28) is the portrayal of continuing sin, punctuated by staged, escalated punishments (the resemblance to Amos 4:4–12 has been pointed out by H. G. von Reventlow, *Das Amt des Propheten bei Amos* [Göttingen: Vandenhoeck & Ruprecht, 1962], pp. 75ff.; developed by W. Brueggemann, "Amos IV 4–13 and Israel's Covenant Worship," *VT* 15 [1965], 1–15, from which Reventlow is cited). Lev 26:14–17 foresee plagues, harassment, and defeats; vss. 18–20—drought and crop failure; vss. 21–22—infestation by wild beasts; vss. 23–26—siege and famine; vss. 27–33—cannibalism, devastation, occupation, dispersion of survivors and their pursuit by the sword (a theme continued in vss. 36ff.). Interlaced and contemporaneous sin and punishment are depicted as going on for a long time, ending only with the devastation of the land and exile of the survivors. It would have been simple for anyone acquainted with the history of Israel as described, say, in the Book of Kings to have perceived it according to this scheme. Not only the literary prophets but Elijah and Elisha lived through droughts, plagues, and invasions; the first invasion on record during the monarchy was by Shishak of Egypt (c. 925 B.C.E.)—like all subsequent calamities, understood as punishment for sin. By the standard of the Book of Kings, Israel's age of sin began with the erection of the temple (c. 970 B.C.E.) and the failure to stop forthwith the worship carried on at the high places (cf., e.g., I Kings 14:23, and see Ezek 20:27–29 and comments thereto). This brings us close to 390 years of sin, if the terminus (the dispersions) is placed some years ahead of the moment of Ezekiel's enactment of it (970 minus 390 = 580; the traditional talmudic datum for the length of time the First Temple stood is 410 years [*Leviticus Rabba* 21.9, on Lev 16:3 *b^{e}zot*]). The interlacing in Ezekiel's symbolic acts of siege and "bearing iniquity," if modeled on Lev 26, will represent the First Temple period as one long age of wrath, in which sin and punishment went on simultaneously. In principle, though not in detail, Ezekiel's subsequent depiction of Israel's history in ch. 16 and, to some extent, in chs. 20 and 23 agree.

In this setting, what can "bearing iniquity" while lying on one's side mean? Among the earliest recorded interpretations is the polemical one adduced in the Talmud (see above)—that by submitting himself to such affliction, the prophet expiated some of Israel's sin (an analogy with the scapegoat is perceived). According to another early view, the prophet represented God's suffering the burden of Israel's effrontery through the centuries (Rashi). That a prophet should represent God in a symbolic act is unusual, but Hosea's marriage appears to have cast him in a similar role. (In prophesying with outstretched arm against the city, Ezekiel acts as a representative of God, but that is no more than his normal role; he is God's messenger.) Perhaps the simplest view is that he represents Israel suffering for its iniquity during the period of sin; by lying down, he represents a battered, beset, enfeebled object of wrath.

The two exile symbols that appear in this passage seem to have been worked into it secondarily. Lying on the right side 40 days "bearing the iniquity of the house of Judah," while formally similar to what precedes it, defies integration from the aspect of its content. It seems to be an afterthought, an imitation of the preceding action; yet we have no indication of a more appropriate setting for this symbol. The command to eat unclean food, the ensuing dialogue, and the divine interpretation of the act are foreign to the siege-sin context both in form and in content. "In their sight" of vs. 12 has no parallel here (for that matter, "their" has no proper antecedent either); it does recall the symbolic actions of ch. 12, whose directions are filled with the phrase (12:2, 3 [twice], 4 [twice], 5, 6, 7). Nonetheless, it cannot be said that the symbol of unclean food belongs to the actions of ch. 12, for the latter represent dynamically the exile of the king and his entourage, whereas the former represents the static exilic situation of the whole community. Lying on the side (representing the paralysis of the exiles) and eating unclean food (during the period of lying?) combine into an intelligible symbol, but there is no assurance that from the first the two were indeed combined. Nor is there any indication as to their original location and context. Their present situation appears to result from an editorial decision and be based on the external similarities to the main body of symbolic acts.

The last symbolic act—shaving the head-hair—is, like eating the scroll (2:8ff.), a concretization of a figure of speech—this time taken from Isa 7:20. Like grass (Job 5:25), hair is a figure of multitude (Matt 10:30; *Mishnah Nazir* 1.4 [|| dust, sand]) but also, by virtue of its growth, of vitality (R. Dentan, *IDB,* s.v. "hair"). Ritual shaving signified surrender of power or personality (Gaster, *Myth,* pp. 437–38); hence it is an easy step to make hair represent human beings, as here. The notion of a threefold sifting first occurs in the charge to Elijah (I Kings 19:17), where emphasis is on the survival of a remnant. Here the point is that even some of the survivors will be reached by the calamity that will pursue them into exile. The special treatment of the last third seems to have inspired Deutero-Zechariah 13:8f., which serves, therefore, as its earliest attestation and interpretation:

> Of the whole country—declares YHWH—
> Two thirds shall be cut off and perish;
> Only a third shall survive in it.
> And I shall make that third pass through fire,
> Refining it as one refines silver . . .

In Zechariah, the purge of the last third (=Ezekiel) results in a refined remnant (=Elijah [Isaiah]). For Ezekiel's peculiar adaptation of the remnant idea see Structure and Themes section to 6:8–10. (E. J. Smit's comparison of Ezek 5:1–4 with Moses' threefold activity in destroying the Golden Calf [in turn supposedly an echo of Ugaritic Anath's killing of Mot and disposing of his remains] in the *Journal of Northwest Semitic Languages* I [1971], 46–50, is not enlightening.)

Maimonides was perhaps the first to point to the contradiction between the command to shave the head-hair and the priestly prohibition on so doing (Lev 21:5 and Ezek 44:20). There is an analogy here with the requirement that the prophet defile himself with unclean food. It is perhaps significant of the earliness of the shaving passage that the prophet does not protest, as it is of the later provenience of the unclean food passage that he is so self-possessed as to protest. The common feature of all these symbolic acts is the affliction of the prophet—by scant food, by prolonged immobility, by the degradation of shaving off all the head-hair (cf. II Sam 10:4f.). In view of the ambiguous role of the prophet in these acts—now he seems to be the people, now God, now himself—one is inclined to see in the symbols a mixture of identification with the impending suffering of the people (we can imagine the prophet wasting away as the months wore on), of sympathy with God's passion, and a deflection upon himself of anger at the hostile people for having driven him into withdrawal.

In the prophecy of 5:5–17, which, as has been suggested above, may be the "script" of the prophesying alluded to in 4:7, the affinities with Lev 26 are most pronounced (with embellishments, toward the end, from Deut 32). No better example of the relation of covenant curses to prophetic dooms can be found: what in the former is a threat contingent upon breach of covenant appears in the latter as a certain prediction for accomplished wrongdoing. All indications are of Ezekiel's dependence upon Lev 26. Lev 26:29 threatens the people with being reduced to filicidal cannibalism; Ezek 5:10 caps this with a unique prediction of patricidal cannibalism (cf. comment to vs. 10). Lev 26:15 describes Israel's wickedness as "not executing the laws and judgments" of God; Ezekiel adopts this phraseology (5:7) but climaxes it with "not even acting according to the judgments of the gentiles" (ibid.). It is more plausible to regard Ezekiel's notions as hyperbolic extensions of Lev 26 than to assume that Lev 26 toned Ezekiel down (why should it have done that?).

In 5:5–10 there is an emphasis on balance, on "measure for measure," which, though not altogether lacking in Lev 26 (see esp. vss. 15–35), is more thoroughly developed here. Israel has been worse than the nations, so God's punishment will be worse than any he ever inflicted; Israel did not execute God's judgments, so God will execute judgments in it; even the innovation of patricidal cannibalism is an outcome of "balancing" the standard form of the curse. The repeated use of "I, on my part" (once in Lev 26; namely, in vs. 24) underscores God's aim to make his acts correspond to the people's.

The second part of the prophecy opens (vs. 11) with a reference to defiling the sanctuary—unmentioned in Lev 26 and conditioned by specific events—as the ground of the final punishment, annihilation, and dispersion. God's inexorable anger is signaled by his double repudiation of pity. The interpretation of the handling of the hair, described as a venting and an easing of God's rage, is followed by two passages in which calamities and expressions of wrath come in heaps. In the first, the theme of Israel's public disgrace resumes the motif of the nations found in the first part of the prophecy; hereafter it will recur throughout the book, reflecting the prophet's sense of a deep wound to national pride inflicted by the fall. The last passage is a scarcely coherent agglomerate of threats (found in Lev 26 and Deut 32) now turned into predictions. The effect is of a transport of fury—set off, it must be remembered, by the mention of the defilement of the sanctuary at the beginning of this section. Thus "all your abominations" of vs. 9 gains specification, though the full picture of the offense is not portrayed until chs. 8 – 11.

In the very first address to Jerusalem, emphatic expression is thus given to the unfathomable guilt of the people and the relentless fury it has evoked in God.

V. Doom upon the Highland of Israel (6:1–14)

6 1 The word of YHWH came to me: 2 Man, set your face toward
the mountains of Israel and prophesy to them, 3 and say: Mountains
of Israel, hear the word of Lord YHWH! Thus said Lord YHWH
to the mountains and to the hills, to the gullies and to the valleys:

I am going to bring a sword upon you
  and destroy your shrines.
4 Your altars shall be desolate,
  and your incense braziers shall be broken.
I will make your slain lie fallen in front of your idols,
5 [a]and I will set the corpses of the Israelites in front of
  their idols[a],
  and I will scatter your bones around your altars.
6 Wherever you live,
  cities shall be ruined
  and shrines desolated;
So that your altars shall be ruined and desolate,
  your idols shall be broken and banished,
Your incense braziers shall be hewn down
  and what you have made wiped out.
7 Slain men shall lie fallen in your midst,
  and you shall know that I am YHWH.

8 [b]I will leave you[b] / when you have / survivors of the sword among
the nations, when you are scattered among the lands. 9 Your survivors
will think of me among the nations where they are held captive, [c]how
I was grieved[c] at their whoring heart that turned away from me, and
at their eyes that whored after their idols; they will loathe themselves
for the evil things they did, their abominations of every sort. 10 And
they shall realize that not for nothing did I, YHWH, declare that I
would do this evil to them.

a–a Not in G.
b–b Not in G; MT is conflate; see comments.
c–c G "I swore" (as though *nšb'ti*); S "when I broke."

11 Thus said Lord YHWH:

Clap your hand and stamp your foot and say "Ah!" over all the evil abominations of the house of Israel, who shall fall by the sword by famine and by plague!

12 He who is far off shall die by the plague,
he who is nearby shall fall by the sword,
and he who remains under siege shall die by famine;
Thus will I spend my fury on them,

13 And you shall know that I am YHWH, when their[d] slain lie amidst their[d] idols around their[d] altars
On every high hill,
on every mountaintop;
And under every luxuriant tree,
and under every leafy oak—
the place where they offered soothing savors to all their idols. 14 I will
stretch out my arm against them and turn the land into an utter waste wherever they live, from the desert to Diblah, and they[e] shall know that I am YHWH.

[d] G "your."
[e] G "you."

COMMENT

6:2. *set your face toward.* A command phrased thus to direct himself toward the object addressed is a common opening of Ezekiel's prophecies: 21:2, 7 (Jerusalem, etc.); 25:2 (Ammonites); 28:21 (Sidon); 29:2 (Pharaoh); 35:2 (Mt. Seir); 38:2 (Gog). As here, the object is usually not nearby; once it is so vague (13:17 "women prophets"), it cannot be supposed that the object of address was in any specific location. Hence one cannot infer from this passage that the prophet must have been in the land of Israel (else how could he have "set his face" toward its mountains). All the same, it is likely that, for the most part, a gesture in some direction was called for (see comment at 4:3).

the mountains of Israel. Since gullies and valleys too are addressed (vs. 3), the sense must be "the mountainous land of Israel"; this and similar terminology (20:40; 35:12) reflect not only the confinement of Israelite settlement to the highlands (D. Baly, *Geographical Companion to the Bible* [London: Lutterworth Press, 1963], pp. 70–77) but, in all likelihood, the contrast felt by the exiles with the river-valley environment in Babylonia.

Everything on the surface of the land is to be swept away, starting with the offending cult-installations, and ending with towns and their populations. Kimḥi notes that *ḥereb* ("sword," vs. 3) also denotes a tool of destruction (e.g., 26:9 "he shall demolish your towers by the *ḥereb*"), hence may be wielded against buildings as well as human beings; the image is of an attacking army that falls indiscriminately upon animate and inanimate objects in its way. Compare the fate of Jerusalem described in II Kings 25:8–10, or Sennacherib's account of the sack of Babylon that did not spare its people or its sanctuaries (Bavian inscription, Luckenbill, *ARAB* II, p. 152). Accordingly, the reference of the pronoun "your" shifts from the mountains in vs. 3 to the population at the end of vs. 4; see comment at vs. 5.

3. *Mountains of Israel, hear the word of Lord YHWH!* The auspicious counterpart to this prophecy of doom in 36:1 opens similarly. "Hear the word of [Lord] YHWH" is a prophetic adaptation of the usage of royal heralds (cf. "Hear the word of the great king, the king of Assyria! Thus said the king . . ." [II Kings 18:28]); it is a fixed form of introducing oracles. In narratives about early times there is some variation (Josh 3:9; I Sam 15:1), but this form is found in stories about Micaiah (I Kings 22:19), Elisha (II Kings 7:1), and Isaiah (II Kings 20:5), and in prophecies of Amos (7:16), Isaiah (1:10; 28:14, 16) and, most frequently, in Jeremiah (2:4; 7:2; 17:20; 19:3; 22:2, 29; 29:20; 31:10; 34:4; 44:24, 26). In almost all of these passages, the summons to listen is delivered in a confrontation, explicit or implicit; accordingly, if the one summoned is named, his name follows the summons (e.g., "Hear . . . , O house of Jacob," Jer 2:4; cf., outside the message context, Num 16:8; Judg 5:3; I Sam 22:12). In the one Jeremiah passage where the summoned is only imagined as present, her name comes first: "Land, Land, Land, hear . . ." 22:29. In Ezekiel, however, not a single case involves a real confrontation; hence, whenever the formula includes the name of the summoned, it comes first—as here and in the starred passages: 13:2; 21:3; 25:3; *34:7, 9; *36:1, 4; *37:4. The formula in Ezekiel is thus consistent with his sequestration in his home.

Thus said . . . to the mountains. Properly, the message formula is part of the proclaimed message (e.g., 13:2f.; 16:35f.; 21:3; 36:1f.) but here where the message is for a party other than the real audience (the prophet's neighbors) the formula is completed by naming the ostensible addressee (the mountains of Israel). The message formula is thereby transformed into a vehicle for imparting information to the real audience on the identity of the ostensible addressee of the oracle; contrast the normal usage in 36:1f. and vs. 6 with the skewed in 36:4. The skewed recurs in 7:2; 16:3; 26:15; 37:5.

shrines. bamot, usually rendered "high places," were raised platforms, usually on a natural height outside towns, on which sacrifice was performed (one of the earliest datable occurrences of the term, Amos 7:9

[mid-eighth century B.C.E.] parallels it with *miqdašim* "sanctuaries"). Valley shrines included the *bama* in the Valley of Ben Hinnom outside Jerusalem (Jer 32:35). See the comprehensive and balanced account of the present state of knowledge on such shrines in P. H. Vaughan, *The Meaning of 'BĀMĀ' in the Old Testament* (London and New York: Cambridge University Press, 1974); their funerary origin, advocated by Albright, is deprecated by Vaughan and strongly contested by W. B. Barrick, "The Funerary Character of 'High Places' in Ancient Palestine: A Reassessment," *VT* 25 (1975), 565–94.

4. *incense braziers.* Some such meaning of *ḥammanim* is suggested by Nabatean and Palmyrene *ḥmn'* in contexts indicating "incense altar." A Palmyrene altar inscription tells of the dedication of an altar and a *ḥmn'*, the latter apparently represented on a relief (on another side of the altar) as an incense stand or brazier (*Views of the Biblical World* [Hebrew], ed. B. Mazar et al., III [Jerusalem: International Publishing Co., 1960], p. 164; W. F. Albright, *Archaeology and the Religion of Israel* [Baltimore: Johns Hopkins Press, 1946], p. 215, fn. 58; *KAI* II, p. 77).

idols. Baudissin (reference at BDB, p. 1122a) compared our *gillulim* with a bilingual Palmyrene inscription (G. A. Cooke, *A Text Book of North–Semitic Inscriptions* [Oxford: Clarendon Press, 1903], p. 334 [Greek, p. 314, l. 11; Aramaic, p. 321, l. (9) 22]) in which *gll'* is rendered "stela" in Greek, and conjectured that at bottom the term designated a menhir-*maṣṣeba;* in Hebrew, the constant pairing with opprobrious terms for idols (e.g., Deut 29:16; Jer 50:2; Ezek 30:13) defines the term adequately. Very frequent in Ezekiel (thirty-nine times), the term clusters in literature inspired by Deuteronomy (Kings, Jeremiah, Ezekiel; once only in Deut 29:16, and once in Lev 26:30), justifying Zimmerli's question whether it was not a favorite of the cult-reformers. Older etymologies connected the word with *galal* (*gell-*) "dung pellet" (see 4:12, 15), supposedly a pejorative styling of idols (Ibn Janaḥ, Kimḥi, in their dictionaries). The vocalization has been assimilated to that of *šiqquṣim* "detestable objects," with which it is occasionally paired (Deut 29:16; II Kings 23:24; Ezek 37:23).

5. The first half of the verse, with its third-person formulation breaking the connection between vs. 4b and vs. 5b, its absence in G, and its similarity to Lev 26:30, may have originated as an explanation of a difficulty in vs. 4b: since it is a strain to understand the pronoun of "your slain" in vs. 4b as still referring to the mountains, vs. 5a refers the pronoun to the inhabitants of the (mountainous) land in language inspired by Lev 26:30—a verse which doubtless is echoed in vs. 4b.

6. *Wherever you live.* Lit. "in all your settlements," a stock phrase of the priestly laws (e.g., Exod 12:20; Lev 3:17; 7:26; 23:3, 14; Num 35:29); here (and below, vs. 14) ironic in a context of depopulation and ruin.

desolated (tišamna), *desolate* (ye'ešmu). *yšm* and *'šm* are rare alternative by-forms of *šmm* (the usual root), all going back to a biconsonantal base *šm* (G. R. Driver, *Problems of the Hebrew Verbal System* [Edinburgh: T. & T. Clark, 1936], pp. 6–7). *yšm* appears in *yešimon* "wasteland"; *'šm* occurs in Hosea (5:15; 10:2; 14:1; G renders all by an equivalent of *šmm*) and also in Isa 24:6; Joel 1:18.

So that. See the end of the comment to 4:16–17 (on *lema'an*).

what you have made wiped out. The Hebrew *wenimḥu ma'ašekem* is evocative: verbal forms of *mḥ(y)* "wipe out" recur throughout the Flood story (Gen 6:7; 7:4, 23); verb and noun forms of *'ś(y)* are frequent (esp. in Isaiah) in descriptions of men's perverse cultic inventions, in defiance of God. Of especial relevance here is Isa 17:7ff. "In that day, a man shall turn to his Maker [*'osehu*], his eyes look to the Holy One of Israel; he shall not turn to the altars his own hands made [*ma'aśe yadaw*], or look to the cult poles and incense braziers his own fingers made [*'aśu*]." Cf. also the emphatic repetition of *'aśa* "he made" throughout the account of Jeroboam's cultic inventions in I Kings 12:28, 31–33. This climactic clause refers to the illicit forms and installations of worship mentioned above, but no less to civilization at large (vs. 6a, "cities").

7. *you shall know that I am YHWH.* The name YHWH is properly synonymous with power (to punish and to rescue), sovereignty, holiness, and authorship and control of events. Presently it is not recognized as such either in Israel, who are apostate or faithless, or among the nations, who are idolatrous. But when disaster strikes them or they experience a miraculous deliverance, the God who announced the event through the prophet will be acknowledged as possessing the attributes properly attached to his name. For roughly contemporary variations of this idea, cf. Jer 16:21:

> So now I am going to show them,
> Once for all I will show them
> My power and my might,
> And they shall know that YHWH is my name.

And again Isa 52:6:

> Assuredly my people shall know my name;
> Assuredly, on that day, that it is I who have spoken,
> Here I am!

In Ezekiel this clause is a characteristic close of oracles or sections within oracles (some sixty occurrences), and it expresses the intended effect of the event predicted in the oracle. Outside Ezekiel it figures in the priestly narrative of the events of the Exodus (e.g., Exod 7:5; 14:4, 18) and in the story about the anonymous prophets who encouraged Ahab (I Kings 20:13, 28). Zimmerli has dealt with the expression at great length in *Erkenntnis Gottes . . .*

8. The strange initial sequence, lit. "I will leave, in their being to you"

(*w^{e}hotarti bihyot lakem*), is best resolved as a conflation of two alternative sequels to vs. 7. The first, *w^{e}hotarti* (*lakem*) "I will leave [you]" starts a new sentence, after the manner of 12:16; it is not found in G. The second *bihyot* (*lakem*) "when you have" is a trailing infinitive clause after the closing "and they/you shall know . . ."—characteristic of Ezekiel's style (e.g., vs. 13 and 12:15; 20:42); it attaches onto the end of vs. 7.

when you are scattered. The Hebrew *b^{e}hizzarotekem* bears a plural suffix *-ekem* (instead of the regular *-kem*), not an error but an interpretation of the *ot* ending of the infinitive as though it were that of the feminine plural; this happens again in 16:31 (*bibnotayik*). See GKC § 91 l.

9. *How I was grieved* (nišbarti, lit. *broken*) *at* ('et, lit. *with, in the presence of*). This singular expression, the meaning of which Kimḥi compares with "[God] was vexed to his heart" (Gen 6:6), is rendered according to the analogy with Syriac *tbr* "break," in the passive "be brokenhearted" (proposed by G. R. Driver in his review of *CAD* 7 in *JSS* 7 [1962], 96). Note also Jer 8:21 *hošbarti* "I was broken [in spirit]." S's active rendering (see text footnote) is followed by some, who explain the *n* of *'šr nšbrty* as an inadvertent copyist's error induced by the immediately preceding *'šr nšbw*. G's "I swore," impossible contextually, attests that a word beginning with *n* (*nšb'ty*) lay before the translators. Favoring MT, and our rendering of it, is the preceding notion, equally singular for Ezekiel, that the minds of the exiled survivors will turn to God (see Structure and Themes); how God was grieved at them is a fitting penitential thought.

whoring heart . . . The rest of vs. 7 exhibits a mosaic of literary echoes: *zana me'al,* lit. "to play the whore on [one's husband]," elsewhere only in Hosea 9:1; *sar me'al* "turn away from," elsewhere only in Jer 32:40—both theological metaphors; "do not follow your heart and your eyes after which you go whoring" (Num 15:39). (For a noun qualified by a participle and followed by a relative clause, cf. 2:3: "rebellious nations who rebelled against me.") In Ezekiel's new combination, the heart and eye become the agents of sin, endowed with the autonomous impulse later ascribed to them in a midrash to the cited Numbers passage: "The heart and the eye are the two brokers of sin" (*Numbers Rabba* 10.6). Ezekiel often refers to this evil brokerage; cf. 11:21, and the "new heart" passages 11:19; 36:26; on "eyes," see 18:6, 12, 15; 20:7, 8, 24; 23:27.

loathe themselves. Idiom and idea are peculiar to Ezekiel; again in 20:43; 36:31.

10. *not for nothing.* The meaning of this phrase in 14:23, where it is followed by "did I do all that I did to them," must be, "for just cause." That is probably its sense here too; but its present sequel, "did I . . . declare that I would do this evil," etc., allows it to be understood alternatively as, "not as a vain threat." It will then (like 13:21ff.) answer to the skeptical reception of the prophet's threats (so Kimḥi). This alternative

cannot be ruled out in view of Ezekiel's propensity for varying the meaning of familiar phrases. Note, for example, how *hara'ah* "[this] evil" (=harm)—God's punishment—in vs. 10 corresponds to "the evil" (=wicked) things (*hara'ot*) they did of vs. 9. The expression *dibber la'aśot ra'a le-* "[God] declared he would do an evil to" occurs, outside of this passage, only in the story of the Golden Calf (Exod 32:14: God's decision to destroy Israel) and in the echo of that passage in Jonah 3:10. Both passages lend some support to the alternative understanding of "not for nothing" since in both, God's declaration to "do an evil" was, in fact, rescinded ("in vain").

11. *Thus said Lord YHWH.* Here the message formula introduces a new oracle (vss. 11–44) related to what came before (as, e.g., 7:5; 17:22; 23:32). Since it is normally followed by a message to be conveyed verbatim (2:4; 3:11), the present sequel, a set of instructions for certain gestures, is surprising. (Instructions are normally introduced by the regular revelation formula, as above, vs. 1, or simply by "he said to me" as in 2:1; 3:1, 3, 4, 10, 22; 4:15, etc.) This irregular usage may be an editorial makeshift solution to the problem of identifying precisely which words of God are to be conveyed to the people. Starting from vs. 12 there would seem to be little question: God is speaking ("I will spend my fury"), and in the poetic style associated with delivered oracles. But what of vs. 11? After the order to perform gestures, the prophet is told to say "Ah!"; are the following words too included in the saying, or are they an aside to the prophet? What is the status of "Ah!"; is it a citation of God's exclamation or purely the prophet's? The perplexities are "solved" by placing the message formula, which correctly identifies some part of vss. 11–12 as God's speech to the people, at the very start of the passage. After all, by stretching the formula to include anything God said to the prophet, it can apply as well to the instructions Ezekiel received from God. Such a loose employment of the message formula is to be ascribed to the final editorial stage of the material, at a considerable remove from the revelation-experience, when, presumably, the questions mooted above might have been answered clearly.

Clap your hand. In 25:3, 6, the gestures and a similar exclamation (*he'aḥ*) recur as expressions of malicious glee. (For *aḥ,* cf. Galilean Aramaic *waḥ,* signifying pleasure [S. Lieberman, *Hayerushalmi Kiphshuto* (Jerusalem: Darom, 1934), p. 83].) The prophet is to represent God's satisfaction at venting his rage upon Israel; cf. "And as YHWH once delighted in making you prosperous and numerous, so YHWH will now delight in making you perish and destroying you" (Deut 28:63).

the evil abominations of the house of Israel. This rendering hides an untranslatable Hebrew combination of synonyms (*tw'bwt* and *r'wt,* see vs. 9 and the related 20:43 and 36:31) in a construct chain with a third noun (*byt ysr'l*)—as it were "the abominations of the evils of the house of Israel." Cf. *qb't kws htr'lh* (Isa 51:17) as it were "the bowl of the cup of reeling"; *nhy bky tmrwrym* (Jer 31:14) as it were "the lament of the weeping of bitterness." See GKC § 130 e, and the monograph of Y. Avishur, *The Construct State of Synonyms in Biblical Rhetoric*. S solves the problem of translating by inserting "and" between the synonyms; in G the second does not appear.

sword, famine, and plague. The three are included in Lev 26:25f., II Sam 24:13 [enemy = sword; cf. Lev 26:6f.], and Amos 4:6–10, but the triad as it appears here occurs (repeatedly) only in Jeremiah (e.g., 14:12; 21:9; 27:8, 13; 29:18).

12. The allocation of three scourges among two groups—those outside the city and those inside it—is accomplished by dividing the outsiders into "those nearby" and "those far off"—a merism (an expression of a whole by halving it into two inclusive groupings, "young and old" = everybody; "man and beast" = all living things) (see also 22:5; Deut 13:8; I Kings 8:46; Isa 57:19; Dan 9:7; in general, cf. J. Krašovec, *Der Merismus im Biblisch-Hebräischen und Nordwestsemitischen,* Biblica et Orientalia 33 [Rome: Pontifical Biblical Institute, 1977]). Comparison with 5:12 and 7:15 shows that only famine is consistently located—inside the city; sword and plague are free elements.

remains under siege. Expressed by the hendiadys "he who remains and he who is blockaded"; on this figure of speech, see E. Z. Melamed, *Tarbiz* 16 (5605/1945), 173–89, 242. The second term, *naṣur,* is the passive of *naṣar* "set watch over, blockade" (Jer 4:16); were it from *ṣwr* "besiege" the vocalization would have been **naṣor;* Joüon, § 80 l.

13. *you shall know . . . their slain.* The pronouns are inconsistent (see further vs. 14 "they shall know") because the focus shifts from those in the land, about whom the prophet speaks, to the exiles, to whom in reality the words are addressed. The pronouns in G diverge (see text note) but the result is just a different inconsistency: vs. 13 becomes consistent, but vs. 14—which in MT is internally consistent—is inconsistent in G. The shifting focus is evidently inherent and existed in ancient variant versions as well.

On every high hill . . . The terms for the idolatrous cult sites are arrayed in two parallelistic bicolons—a combination of familiar elements innovatively adapted. The late-monarchic commonplace "on every high hill and under every luxuriant tree" ([Deut 12:2] I Kings 14:23; Jer 2:20, etc.) is expanded by giving each noun a synonymous mate. The first adjective is slightly altered, *rama* replacing the usual *g^{e}boha* "high" (so too in 20:28; 34:6—only in Ezekiel); to create a parallel, Hos 4:13 is drawn upon: "[they sacrifice] on the tops of the mountains." For the parallel of the second noun ("tree"), "oak" is drawn from the same Hosea verse ("under oak, poplar and terebinth . . ."), and "leafy" from the "leafy tree" of Lev 23:40. The invention "leafy oak" is treated as identical with "luxuriant tree" and indeed takes its place in 20:28.

14. *an utter waste* (š^{e}mama um^{e}šamma). Cf. 33:28f.; 35:3. "Some-

times the completeness of an action or state is expressed by placing together two or even three substantives of the same stem and of similar sound" (GKC § 133 l, comparing among others Nahum 2:11; Zeph 1:5).

from the desert to Diblah. midbar is indefinite in accord with poetic style (cf. Isa 16:8; 42:11; Ps 29:8a); it seems to have been mistaken however for a construct form and vocalized accordingly with short *a,* as though "from the desert of Dibla[thah]." The desert in question is the southern wilderness (as in the boundary list of Exod 23:31). Diblah was understood already in medieval times to be the same as Riblah (Kimḥi, who compares the interchange of Reuel-Deuel in Num 1:14; 2:14); indeed G renders Riblah (*rblh, rblth*) in II Kings 25 and Jer 52 mostly by *Deblatha*—going back, it would seem to a variant *dbl*(*t*)*h* in G's *Vorlage* and preserved in MT only here. R/Diblah was a town in the land of Hamath (II Kings 23:33), that land being the north boundary of Ezekiel's land of Israel (47:17; in Num 34:8 Lebo Hamath). However, nowhere else is R/Diblah the northern limit of the land of Israel (*hrblh* in Num 34:11 is a different place on the eastern border); is alliteration a factor in the choice here? (See Structure and Themes.)

STRUCTURE AND THEMES

This section begins with the report of a revelation and continues with the message(s) to the end of the chapter; 7:1 marks the start of a new unit with its report of the next revelation.

The oracle opens with an order to address the countryside (vs. 2), the message begins in vs. 3 ("Mountains . . . hear . . .") and is articulated as follows:

a. Main oracle (vss. 3–7): devastation of the country and death of its inhabitants; conclusion, "and you shall know . . ."

b. Afterwave (vss. 8–10; variant openings—a perfect or an infinitive with *b*-): the remorse of the dispersed survivors; conclusion: "And they shall know . . ."

c. Second oracle ("Thus said Lord YHWH," vss. 11–13aα): glee over the annihilation of the population; conclusion, "And you shall know . . ."

d. Afterwave (vss. 13aβ–14; opened by an infinitive with *b*- [cf. vs. 8]): corpses strewn on the illicit cult sites on the mountains, the whole land a waste; conclusion, "and they shall know . . ."

The overall structure is of a main oracle (*a–b*) followed by a shorter second one related to it (*c–d*) and resuming, at its end, the themes of the main oracle (with some heightening; see below). Such "halving" of a prophecy—a main oracle followed by a shorter echoing one—is a literary feature of the book. Here the "halves" are structurally alike—an oracle (*a, c*) and an afterwave attached to "And they shall know" (*b, d;* see

12:15ff. and 20:42ff. for such afterwaves); note the regular alternation "you"-"they" in the concluding formulas in each "half."

The section is tightly bound together by repetitions and resumptions within each division and across the divisions. Within the main oracle, *a,* vs. 6b is a climactic summary of the foregoing, with heaps of synonyms and parallelisms, and an "objective" (passive), dispassionate formulation throughout. Division *b* is knit together by repetitions of *p^{e}liṭim baggoyim* (vss. 8, 9), *zana* (twice in vs. 9), *‘aśa ra‘a* (vss. 9–10); it is connected with *a* through *ḥereb* (vs. 8 [3]), *zr(y)* (vs. 8 [5]), *nišbar* (vs. 9 [4]), and *gillulim* (vs. 9 [4, 6]). Division *c* is knit together by the triad *ḥereb, ra‘ab, deber* and is connected with what precedes it by *to‘^{a}bot ra‘ot* (vs. 11 [9, 10]), *ḥereb,* and *napal* (vs. 12 [4, 7]). Division *d* is marked not only by its own repetitions (*kol*—5 times; *gillulim*—twice), but by an echoing and augmenting relationship to division *a.* Echoes are *ḥalal b^{e}tok* (vs. 13 [7]), *gillulim* (vs. 13 [4]), *s^{e}bibot mizb^{e}ḥot-* (vs. 13 [5]), *gib‘a—harim* (chiastic to *harim-g^{e}ba‘ot* of vs. 3), derivatives of *šmm* (vs. 14 [4, 6]), *b^{e}kol moš^{e}botekem* (vs. 14 [6]). Augmentation and supplementation are achieved by the repeated *kol,* by the explicit connection between the topographical features of the land and the illicit cults (vs. 13b), and by the depiction of "the land [as] an utter waste," a generalized summary of all the detail of *a.*

Stylistically the passage is marked by a uniform repetitiveness, involving alliteration, rhyme, parallelism, and synonymy. Examples of alliteration and rhyme are: *harim-g^{e}ba‘ot / ’^{a}piqim—ge’ayot* (vs. 3); *-kem* suffixes in vss. 4–5; *-hem* in vs. 13; *napal ḥalal* (vs. 7); *’^{a}šer nišbu . . . ’^{a}ser nišbarti* (vs. 9); *ḥammanekem w^{e}nimḥu* (vs. 6); *hakke b^{e}kapp^{e}ka, r^{e}qa‘ b^{e}ragl^{e}ka* (vs. 11); *š^{e}mama um^{e}šamma, mimmidbar diblata* (vs. 14). Examples of parallelism and synonymy (often with rhyming and alliteration): *teḥ^{e}rabna . . . tišamna, yeḥerbu w^{e}ye’š^{e}mu, nišb^{e}ru w^{e}nišb^{e}tu* (vs. 6); *raḥoq . . . qarob, yamut . . . yippol . . . yamut, hanniš’ar w^{e}hannaṣur* (vs. 12); *gib‘a rama . . . raše harim . . . ‘eṣ ra‘anan . . . ’ela ‘^{a}butta* (vs. 13).

G is markedly less full than MT. Not only does it lack the conflations of MT (see comments at vss. 5, 8), but much of the peculiar literary character of MT effected by the above-listed elements is absent in G. In vs. 4a, only the verb "will be broken" appears and serves both subjects; in vs. 6b, "will be destroyed" stands for the first pair of verbs, "will be broken" for the second, and the whole last clause is absent. In vss. 9–11 "for the evil things they did," "not for nothing," "that I would do this evil thing to them," "evils" (*ra‘ot*) are missing. In vss. 12–13, the synonyms "he who remains" (see comment), "at every mountaintop," "under every leafy oak" are absent. The conflations show that MT here, as in previous chapters, is a maximizing text, into which variants have been incorporated. On the other hand, G's trimmer text sometimes suggests it has been contracted; there seems no better explanation for its giving two subjects to one verb in vs. 4a (unique in the chapter), or its simplification of the two alliterating verb pairs in vs. 6. Cooke explained G's simplification of the two synonymous noun-phrase pairs in vs. 13 thus: two variant readings existed, "on every high hill and under every luxuriant tree" (G), and a unique (and more "original") "at every mountaintop and under every leafy oak," these have been combined in a conflate MT. This explanation would be more persuasive had not the entire chapter so consistently exhibited repetition and synonymy. G's minuses in vss. 9–11 actually alter the message, eliminating the "measure for measure" of MT and the lesson of the calamity. In sum: MT exhibits a maximizing occasionally conflate text, consistent in texture and rich in literary devices; G, a sparser text, occasionally contracted, otherwise plainer and literarily poorer. On the question of "originality," see Greenberg, SVT 29 (1977), 131–48.

Thematically, ch. 6 continues chs. 4 – 5 with its prediction of the devastation of the land and the death and dispersal of its inhabitants. Points of linguistic contact are "I am bringing the sword against you" (vs. 3 [5:17]), derivatives of *šmm* (vss. 4, 6, 14 [4:17; 5:15]), "spend my fury against" (vs. 12 [5:13]), "sword, famine and plague" (vs. 11 [cf. 5:17]). The indirect contact of prophet and audience also continues; at the start, the address is to the countryside, later (vs. 4b) to the inhabitants of the land. There is as yet no direct address to the exiles. Calvin remarks on this: "Thus God obliquely signifies, first, that the Israelites were deaf, and then unworthy of the trouble which Ezekiel would spend in teaching them." He compares Ezekiel's address to the countryside with the anonymous prophet's address to the altar in I Kings 13:20: "That was no common reproof, to pass by the king as if he had been only the shadow of a man, and to admonish the dead altar." This is an interesting analogy, though in the case of Ezekiel, the obliqueness had more to do with shy withdrawal. Ultimately, however, rejection and alienation are at the bottom of both phenomena.

The passage is a rich blend of motifs. First, the curse against illegal cult-installations and the threat against cities found in Lev 26:30f. is evoked. Then Deteronomic-Hoseanic idiom is heard locating the illicit cults on the mountains (cf. also Jer 16:16–18). Thence emerges a third motif: mountain slopes strewn with corpses. The earliest biblical occurrence is in the lament of David over Saul and Jonathan (II Sam 1:18ff.), which exhibits at its beginning the cluster of key words: *bamoteka* "your slopes" (same word as *bamot* "high places"), *ḥalal* "slain," and *nap^{e}lu* "lie fallen." Isa 14:25 speaks of Assyria trampled on the mountains of Israel, and in chs. 38 – 39 of Ezekiel, the carnage of Gog's army on the same mountains is depicted. D. H. Müller (*Ezechiel-Studien*) was the first to refer to Akkadian descriptions of battle scenes illustrating this motif; e.g., "With their blood I dyed the mountains and with their corpses I filled the ravines and the mountain slopes" (Assurnasirpal, Annals, ii, 114 [*ARAB* I, p. 157]); "[the corpses of the army of Akkad] will fill the mouths of the ravines of Tupliash, lowlands and highlands" (*CAD,* s.v. "*ḫarru* B," pp. 114f.).

In the welter of destruction, one image stands out, "I will make your slain lie fallen in front of your idols, and I will scatter your bones around your altars" (vss. 4b, 5b, omitting the gloss, vs. 5a). The gloss of vs. 5a, linking the image to Lev 26:30 is only a partial clue to the meaning. Jer 8:1f. depicts the disinterment of the sinful Judahites, and the exposure of their bones to the heavenly bodies they worshiped; they will, as it were, lie at the feet of their false gods, who proved helpless to save them. To complete the picture, we must add the scene in Jer 7:32f.—the slain lying unburied in the former cult site of Tophet, the Valley of Hinnom. Ezekiel foresees the corpses of the Israelites strewn unburied among their impotent idols on the sites of their illicit worship on mountains and in valleys, their bones around their altars, thus polluting them; cf. II Kings 23:16, 20. The slain will be denied their final rest and the cult sites defiled by their former devotees (see M. Cogan, "A Note on Disinterment in Jeremiah," *Gratz College Anniversary Volume* [Philadelphia: Gratz College, 1971], pp. 29–34).

The afterwave (vss. 8–10) introduces Ezekiel's version of the remnant idea. (In 5:3 it is foreshadowed in the command to symbolize survivors, but nothing positive is said of them there.) That those who survive God's punishment will undergo a conversion to him is predicted by many prophets (see E. Jenni, *IDB,* s.v. "Remnant"); with our passage Isa 17:7ff. is especially to be compared:

> In that day, men shall turn to their Maker,
> Their eyes look to the Holy One of Israel;
> They shall not turn to the altars that their own hands made,
> Or look to the cult-poles and incense braziers that their own fingers wrought.
> In that day, their fortress cities shall be like the deserted sites
> Which the Horesh and the Amir (G: the Amorites and the Hivites) abandoned because of the Israelites;
> And there shall be desolation.

As there, so here the survivors will remember God, turning to him after the collapse of their idolatrous faith, filled with remorse over their sinful past (cf. Lev 26:40–41: those who survive in exile will confess their guilt; their uncircumcised hearts will be humbled). The prophet's expectation centers upon those now in the land; of that corrupt lot some will escape, and in their captivity will come to realize the justice of what befell them and turn back in contrition to God. This lies within the orbit of the ideas of pre-exilic prophecy and Lev 26.

The theme recurs in Ezekiel, each time with significant variation. In 12:16 the remnant survives "in order that they may relate all their abominations among the nations into which they have come, that they may know that I am YHWH" (it is not clear who is to be convinced of YHWH's godhead, the remnant or the nations). A didactic role is envisaged for the remnant: to teach, by the tale of their wicked conduct, the justice of God's punishment. The center of concern has shifted somewhat from the remnant to their environment, which must be taught God's justice.

The next occurrence of the theme, in 14:22f., shows marked progress. A remnant will be extricated from the ruin of Jerusalem for the sake of the exiles (for the first time explicitly brought into the picture), so that the exiles may see their depraved state at first hand. "When you see their conduct and their [mis]deeds you will be consoled over the evils that I brought upon Jerusalem . . . and you shall realize that not for nothing did I do all that I did to it." The center of concern has definitely shifted from the survivors to their environment. The purpose of preserving them is to vindicate God's evil decree: the manifest depravity of the survivors will convince the exiles that the fall of Jerusalem was deserved, and that will be their consolation.

The motif of remembrance of past wickedness and self-loathing underwent a parallel development. Here it is the survivors who in exile remember their misdeeds and loathe themselves; subsequently we never again hear of their remorse. In ch. 12 the survivors serve as informants; not they but their audience evaluate their story; in ch. 14 they constitute living, mute evidence of depravity from which others must learn a lesson in theodicy. As the action shifts to the exiles, one might expect the motif of remembrance and remorse to be transferred to them. In fact, its next occurrence, in 16:61ff., is timed only after the restoration of Israel to their land; only after experiencing the loyalty of God to his ancient covenant, despite their own faithlessness, will the restored people recall their evil past and be thoroughly ashamed of themselves. The sequence of events in 20:33–44 is even clearer: there will be a forced repatriation (vss. 33ff.); only those who survive the purge of sinners in "the wilderness of the nations" will arrive in the homeland; they shall then (vs. 43) remember their wicked past and loathe themselves for it. It is the same sequence in 36:31—an extension of the thought of ch. 20 and a counterpart of our chapter. The development of the remnant theme and that of the remembrance and self-loathing motif are thus intertwined; in relation to the subsequent stages, ours is primary. Here Ezekiel still adheres to the pre-exilic notion that punishment would humble the survivors and turn their hearts to God. The later passages reveal the prophet's growing realization that the anticipated consequences of the catastrophe were beside the mark.

VI. The End of the Civil Order
(7:1–27)

7 1 The word of YHWH came to me: 2 You, man[a]—thus said Lord
YHWH to the soil of Israel:

An end!
    Comes the end upon the four corners of the earth!
3 The end is now upon you!
I will let loose my anger against you,
    and punish you according to your ways,
    and lay upon you all your abominations.
4 My eye shall not spare you,
    nor will I have pity;
But I will lay upon you all your ways,
    and your abominations shall fester within you;
    and you shall know that I am YHWH.
5 Thus said Lord YHWH:
[b]An evil!
    A singular evil[b];
    see, it is coming.
6 Comes an end;
    the end is coming;
    it is ripe for you!
See, it is coming:
7 Doom has come upon you,
    O inhabitant of the land!
The time is coming,
    the day is near—
    of tumult, not harvest-cries upon the hills.
8 Soon now I will pour out my fury on you,
    and spend my anger on you.
I will punish you according to your ways,
    and lay upon you all your abominations.

[a] G S add "say."

[b–b] Hebrew mss., editions, "evil after (*'aḥar* = T *batar*) evil"; S "evil for (*ḥlp* = Heb. *taḥat*) evil."

9 My eye shall not spare,
nor will I have pity;
[c]According to your ways[c] I will requite you,
and your abominations shall fester within you,
And you shall know that I, YHWH, strike.

10 The day is here!
See, it has gone forth;
doom has gone forth,
the rod has sprouted,
insolence has put forth flowers;
11 lawlessness has grown into a rod of wickedness.
[d]Nothing of them and nothing of their masses
and nothing of their tumult and no lament among them.[d]
12 The time has come;
the day has arrived!
The buyer—let him not rejoice;
the seller—let him not mourn;
for wrath is upon all her masses.
13 For the seller shall not return to what he has sold,
though both parties still be alive;
for the vision concerning all her masses shall not be revoked;
and each, living in his iniquity, shall not hold firm.
14 [e]They have blown[e] the horn
and made everything ready,
but no one goes out to battle,
for my wrath is upon all her masses.
15 The sword without,
plague and famine within:
He who is in the country
shall die by the sword,
And he who is in the city—
famine and plague shall consume him.
16 Those of them who escape
shall haunt the mountains
like doves of the valleys,
all of them moaning[f] each in his iniquity.

c–c G reflects *ky drkyk* as in vs 4.
d–d G "and not with tumult (as from *mhwmh*) nor with speed (as from *mhrh*)."
e–e G "Blow!"
f G "I will kill" (as from *'myt*); S "will die."

17 Every hand shall hang limp,
all knees shall run with water.
18 They shall gird sackcloth,
and shuddering shall cover them;
Confusion on every face,
hair plucked from every head.
19 They shall fling their silver into the streets;
their gold shall be as an unclean thing.
Their silver and gold shall be powerless to save them
on the day of YHWH's rage.
They shall not satisfy their hunger,
nor fill their bellies [with it],
For it was their stumbling-block of iniquity.

20 Their[g] beautiful adornment in which they[g] took pride—out of it they made images of [h]their abominable, loathsome[h] things; therefore I will turn it into an unclean thing for them.

21 I will hand it over to strangers as booty,
to the wicked of the earth as spoil,
and they shall desecrate it.
22 I will avert my face from them
and they shall desecrate my treasure;
Violent men shall enter it
and desecrate it.

23 Forge the chain!
For the land is full of bloody judgments
and the city is full of lawlessness.
24 So I will bring the worst of the nations
and they shall take possession of their houses;
And I will put an end to the pride of [i]the fierce[i],
and their sanctuaries shall be desecrated.
25 Terror is coming!
They shall seek peace, but there'll be none.
26 Disaster shall come after disaster,
bad news on the heels of bad news.
They shall seek [in vain] for the prophet's vision,
instruction shall fail the priest,
and counsel, the elders.

[g] MT "his" (S "their"); "he" (G S "they").
[h–h] G reflects only one of these, but which one cannot be determined.
[i–i] G "their strength" (as from *'zm*).

27 The king shall be in mourning,
the chief wear desolation,
and the hands of the citizenry shall be paralyzed.
I will give them a taste of their own ways,
and by their own judgments I will judge them;
And they shall know that I am YHWH.

COMMENT

7:2. *You, man.* Although commonly marking subdivisions of an oracle, this formula occasionally stands, as here, at its beginning; see also 21:24; 22:2; 27:2; 37:16 (not in G).

The message formula ("thus said . . .") is most often preceded by a command to speak (e.g., "say [to them] . . ."—12:10, 23, 28), but often too it is not (e.g., 26:3). Hence it is not surprising that in several passages the text witnesses diverge on this matter; here MT lacks "say" but G S show it; in 11:5 MT has "say" and G lacks it. When, as here, the message formula is not part of the proclamation (see comment at 6:3), it is more logical not to have "say." A passage very like ours is 39:17: in MT the message formula precedes and stands outside the prescribed proclamation, but in G, again, "say" precedes it, converting it (in accord with customary usage) into a part of the proclaimed speech, while at the same time creating a fresh difficulty (cf. comment there).

the soil of (admat-) *Israel.* A phrase peculiar to Ezekiel. More than *'ereṣ yiśra'el* "the land of Israel," *admat-* "soil of" evokes the earth of the cultivated homeland lived on by Israel; it is particularly poignant in the mouth of an exile. B. Keller's attempt to attach a theological evaluation to the phrase—"the land without YHWH and without a united people" (*RHPR* 55 [1975], 481–90)—breaks down in the face of the usage in the Gog chapters (chs. 38–39) and 36:17 (of the past when YHWH was amidst the people united in their land).

An end! For a similar abrupt exclamation, see vs. 5, "An evil!" Elliger (*BHS*), reflecting most moderns, recommends inserting *b'* "comes" after "an end" (*qṣ*) "with 2 [medieval Hebrew] mss., T (V), as in vs. 6; cf. G S." The chiasm of vs. 6 (*qṣ b' / b' hqṣ*) is certainly pleasing (Freedman, privately, considers it "too striking to be dropped," and explains MT as having dropped it by haplography); its importation into vs. 2 is supported by the modern tendency to regard vss. 2b–4 and 6–9 as containing doublets (variants of a single original which may be reconstructed by judicious selection of data from both; cf. Herrmann, Wevers)—a counterpart of the ancient leveling of differences between like texts in order to assimilate them as completely as possible. This ancient tendency reached its height in T, whose invocation by Elliger in favor of his emendation is surprising. Here is T's rendering of the relevant passages:

vss. 2b–3: The end has arrived;
Has arrived the punishment of the end, to come upon the four winds of the earth
Now has arrived the punishment of the end, to come upon you.
vs. 6: The end has arrived;
Has arrived the punishment of the end, to come upon you.

To invoke such a free version to attest to conjectural restoration of an original Hebrew seems questionable. S exhibits translator's license in another manner: the two clauses in which *qṣ* appears in vs. 2 are filled out and assimilated through the creation of synonymous parallelism.

Has arrived the end (*qṣ'*) on the land of Israel
Has arrived the end (*swp'*) on the four wings of the land

Aside from the fact that no chiasm appears here, we may again doubt the value of such a version in reconstructing any *Vorlage* at all, let alone one superior to MT. We cannot be sure that V's reading in vs. 2: "End comes; comes an end" (= V at vs. 6) is not translator's license as well. But even if it is based on a Hebrew reading—say, like that of the "2 [medieval] mss." cited in *BHS*—it does not exempt one from weighing the evidence to judge whether the assimilated reading is superior.

As to G, its evidence is extremely problematic. "G gives a different arrangement from M[T] in the opening verses . . . The general effect in G is to bring the parallel passages together" (Cooke). G's reading of the relevant portion of vs. 2 is:

End comes (= *qṣ b'*)

The end comes upon the four wings of the land

followed by a short version of MT vss. 6–7:

Comes the end upon you, the inhabitant of the land

We note that G does not exhibit the chiasm (cf. MT vs. 6) that *BHS*, comparing it, wishes to restore to vs. 2. To be sure, G seems to be based on a *Vorlage* very different in wording and arrangement from MT (Zimmerli attempts a detailed reconstruction of its development, alongside a conjectured evolution of the "original" Hebrew into the present MT; contrast H. Parunak, *Structural Studies*, pp. 194–98, who argues for the priority of MT to G); yet, difference, even in so early a witness to the text, is not in itself a mark of superiority. In the end (as in the case of V), we shall still have to judge between alternatives—MT (*qṣ*) and the conjectured *Vorlage* of G (*qṣ b'*). Cooke judged the brevity of MT to be "impressive," while Fohrer pointed out that the repetitiveness of MT vss.

2–4, 5–9 was typical of Ezekiel's style. Indeed the argument from style decisively pleads against the assimilation of vs. 2 to vs. 6; for throughout this oracle varied repetition prevails; see, e.g., the variations on "day/time" in vss. 7, 12, or on *ḥaron/ḥazon* in vss. 12–14.

Comes the end. A standard announcement of doom, cf. Gen 6:13 (of the Flood); Amos 8:2 (see Structure and Themes); Lam 4:18. Hebrew *qeṣ* means properly "term, measure of time" (Mishnaic *qaṣaṣ* means "measure out, fix terms"), whence evolves the sense "time's end"; cf. Ps 39:5 "Let me know my *qeṣ*, the measure of my days." In late biblical Hebrew it serves for the eschatological "end-time" (Dan 8:17; cf. H. L. Ginsberg, *Koheleth* [Hebrew] [Tel Aviv and Jerusalem: M. Newman, 1961], p. 81).

four corners (lit. "wings"; see comment to 5:3) *of the earth!* As Isa 11:12 shows, the phrase means the whole earth (cf. Job 37:3); for this scope, see Structure and Themes. The earth is conceived as an outspread surface which, sheetlike, has four corners; cf. "The four corners of your garment" in Deut 22:12, and the image in Job 38:13 of taking the earth by its corners to shake the wicked out of it. Our phrase is thus different from Akkadian *kippat erbette* "circle [circumference] of the four [quarters of the world]" with which it has been compared.

3. *The end is now upon you!* See comment to *hnny ʿlyk* at 5:8.

let loose my anger. Closest analogues to this unusual phrase are Exod 15:7 (Song of the Sea) and Ps 78:49. God's anger is here given a personality apart from him; cf. 5:15–17; 14:19–21; 28:23, in which the objects of the verb *šillaḥ* are baleful agents and appurtenances of God.

punish. This sense of *šapaṭ* (BDB, p. 1047, def. 3) is required by the context. The following parallel phrase *natan ʿalayik* "lay upon you" does not mean "charge you with" as it is usually rendered but "impose on you [the penalty for]." This is seen in Jonah 1:14, where the desperate sailors, about to throw Jonah into the sea, pray to God, "Do not lay upon us [the penalty for shedding] the blood of an innocent man." What they fear is not a divine indictment but a divine punishment. Similarly, in Ezek 23:49, "[Your executioners] shall lay upon you [the penalty of] your depravity, and you shall bear the guilt (= suffer the punishment [see comment to 4:4 above]) of your idolatry." Again, since the subjects are not judges (or plaintiffs) but executioners, their acts are not a mere proffering of charges, but a carrying out of a penal verdict.

4. *your abominations shall fester* (lit. *be*) *within you.* Compare 24:7 "Her blood [= the blood of those slain in her] festers [lit. was] within her; she put it on glaring rock; she did not pour it out on the ground to cover it with dirt." The guilty evidence will not be obliterated, but, ever-present, will call down retribution on the culprits.

5. *An evil! A singular evil . . .* This word division—*rʿh / ʾḥt rʿh*—follows the accents. The alternative *rʿh ʾḥt / rʿh hnh bʾh* "a singular evil, an evil, surely is about to come" (Freedman, privately), while theoret-

ically possible, is less likely in view of the exclusively deictic function of *hnh* in the phrase *hnh b'(h)* throughout Ezekiel (7:6, 10; 17:12; 21:12; 33:33). (And when it is not deictic, *hnh* never links subject and predicate —a rarity even outside Ezekiel [e.g., Gen 34:21].) *'ḥt r'h* is an irregular sequence; for similar precedence of the number "one" to its noun, see Num 31:28 (*'ḥd 'ḥwz*); Dan 8:13 (*'ḥd qdwš*); Neh 4:11 (*b'ḥt ydw*). The translation "a singular evil" follows Rashi and Kimḥi, who explain the expression in the light of God's threat in 5:9 to inflict an unprecedented punishment on Israel. Some Hebrew mss. and T render "evil after [Hebrew *'ḥr*] evil" (implied also in Kara's litany of evils), but this idea is expressed otherwise in vs. 26 (and in Jer 4:20; the preposition is *'el/ 'al*). S's rendering "evil for [Hebrew *tḥt*] evil" is attractive precisely because its legal analogies ("an eye for an eye") accord with the notion of measure for measure that permeates these verses (cf. Jer 14:16 "I will pour out their evil upon them"). The versional readings involve each the change of a single letter of MT; it is almost as though MT were a combination of them (MT *'ḥt* = a fusion of *'ḥr* plus *tḥt*)!

6. *it is ripe for you.* This rendering of *heqiṣ* as from *qayiṣ* "ripe summer fruit" takes its cue from the agricultural imagery of vss. 10–11 and its provenience in Amos 8:2, where the connection of *qeṣ* and *qayiṣ* (it is argued below) is more than mere assonance. Others render more conventionally, "it has awakened" (BDB, p. 884).

7. *Doom has come.* This conventional translation of *ṣp(y)rh* is a guess based on the context (here and in vs. 10), where it is associated with "time" and "day" of reckoning; "doom" (a fatal sentence) may also be construed with "come" and "go out" (usually opposites!), much as is *dabar* in the related sense of "promise" or "decree"; cf. Josh 23:15; Esther 7:8. Ibn Janaḥ connected our word with *ṣpyrt tp'rh* "diadem of glory" (Isa 28:5) and Mishnaic *ṣpyrh* "plaited circling band" (in basketwork; *Kelim* 16.3). He defined the basic sense as Arabic *dawr*^{un} "turn" (cf. *dur* "circling band" in the very same mishnah), whose range includes "change of fortune"; Maimonides (in his commentary to the Mishnah, ad loc.) used the same Arabic term to explain our passage: "the turn of that (other) kingdom (to rule) arrived." Moderns have accordingly connected *ṣp(y)rh* with Arabic *ḍafara* "to plait." In view of the association with imagery drawn from plant life—ripening, flowering, and (by implication) harvest-time—Luzzatto's conjecture that *ṣp(y)rh* means "season" (a "round" of the year) is noteworthy. G omits in both verses; S "kid" (Bar Hebraeus: "the Babylonians who skip like a kid"; cf. Hebrew *ṣ*^{e}*pir* "goat").

harvest-cries upon the hills. This conjecture is based on the assumed equivalence of *hed* = *hedad,* the shouting of harvesters and grape-treaders, Isa 16:9f.; Jer 48:33. Not the cheerful work cries of harvest-time, but the sounds of rout and confusion will reverberate through the hills.

9. *according to your ways.* Evidently under the influence of the previ-

ous verse, MT slightly alters the text and meaning of vs. 4b, *ky drkyk* to *kdrkyk;* G characteristically presents the identical text in both cases. For the authenticity of such variations in repeated passages, see comment above to "An end!" vs. 2.

that I, YHWH, strike. A predicate participle in the recognition formula is rare, but recurs in 20:12 and 37:28. It is another variation in the repetition of vs. 4.

10. The botanical expressions in this verse evoke Num 17:23: the proof that God chose Aaron was that ". . . the rod of Aaron . . . had flowered; it had brought forth flowers, and produced sprouts . . ." (the relation of these passages was pointed out by D. Yellin, *Ketavim nivḥarim,* II, pp. 118f.). The use of these terms here appears as a grim parody of election. The verse is pervaded with ambiguity: on the one hand, enigmatic *maṭṭe* "rod" evokes rulership and discipline (19:11ff.)—combined in the Isaianic figure of the heathen kingdom used as a chastising rod by God (Isa 19:5); but on the other hand, its combination here with *zadon* "insolence" (and its proximity to *ḥamas* "lawlessness" in the next line) evokes *muṭṭe* "perversion of law" (9:9 || *damim* "bloodshed"; cf. *damim* || *ḥamas* in vs. 23 below). Indeed on the ground of parallelism, Ibn Janaḥ expressly defined *maṭṭe* here as injustice.

"Insolence" too is ambiguous: is it Israel's insolence that is now "bearing fruit," or is it Insolence, the epithet of the enemy (in Jer 50:31f., Babylon), that has now reached its flowering?

11. The first half-verse continues the ambiguity: it could mean "the lawlessness of Israel has now turned into a scourge of their wickedness" (evil recoiling upon its doers), or, "lawlessness incarnate (the enemy, cf. vss. 21, 24 below) has now risen up as an evil scourge"—or any combination of these elements. At any rate, the sense is: the time is ripe for punishment.

The rendering of *qam* l^e by "grown into" is conjectured on the basis of *qama* "standing grain" (N. H. Tur-Sinai, in B-Y, p. 5842b top).

The rest of the verse is obscure, with its crazy variations on *h* and *m/n* sounds (note that in the sequel laryngeals [h, ḥ] and liquids [m, n, r] continue prominent in the refrain of vss. 12–14). Kimḥi's guess as to the sense is as good as any: nothing of them will remain after the day of doom. For "no lament" (taking $no^ah = n^ehi$ [Jer 9:9]) cf. Jer 16:6 and Ezek 24:23.

12. "It is customary that a buyer rejoices in his purchase and a seller is sorry that out of need he had to part with his property; compare the talmudic adage, 'People say, If you've bought you've gained, if you've sold, you've lost' [BT *Baba Meṣi'a,* p. 51a]. Here, however, it is said that whoever sells an estate in the land of Israel has nothing to mourn over, for even if he will not sell it, it will not be his for long, since he will soon go into exile and have to abandon it. Nor has the buyer reason for rejoicing, for he will retain possession only briefly" (Kimḥi). Cf. further, "Usually

when a man sells something to his fellows the seller is sad and the buyer is happy" (*Berakot* 5a), on which, see Y. Muffs, "Joy and Love as Metaphorical Expressions . . ." *Festschrift Morton Smith,* III (Leiden: E. J. Brill, 1975), pp. 26f. Eliezer of Beaugency adds: " 'The seller—let him not mourn,' for had he not sold it, the property would have devolved upon foreigners; better, then, that he take its equivalent in money."

for wrath . . . Standing alone without its complement *'ap* (*ḥ^{a}ron 'ap* lit. "burning anger"), *ḥaron* is rare and poetic (Exod 15:7; Ps 2:5; 58:10; also Neh 13:18); its isolation (also in vs. 14) facilitates replacement in vs. 13 by the assonant *ḥazon* "(prophetic) vision, oracle."

her masses. "Her" refers to the land (fem. in Hebrew) heretofore addressed. "Masses" renders *hamon* (cf. vs. 14; 32:12, 16, 24, etc.), but since the sense "wealth, abundance" also attaches to this word (see comment at 29:19), it must be considered ambiguous—"wealth" being a suitable sense (and certainly an inevitable overtone) in the present context.

13. *the seller . . . sold.* The idiom is borrowed directly from the jubilee laws (cf. Lev 25:28) from which fact an unwarranted deduction has been drawn that the law was practiced in Ezekiel's time; all that may be deduced is that Ezekiel knew the idiom of the law. No more is said here than that the seller will never again see his property, even if he and the buyer remain alive (for they will both be refugees or in exile). The noun **ḥyh* "life" is a rare, poetic word || *npš* "life" in Ps 78:50; 143:3; Job 33:18, 22, 28; the phrase *w'wd bḥym ḥytm,* lit. "while still in life is their life," sounds as strange in Hebrew as in English. The corresponding language at the end of the verse is even stranger (though each word in itself is clear) and raises the suspicion that we are missing the true sense of the combination (on the omission in G of this phrase and more, see the end of this comment).

But, the verse goes on to say, the prophetic *vision* (= oracle, as in vs. 26, and 12:22ff.; 13:16)—here the doom proclaimed in the foregoing verses—*shall not be revoked* (*l' yšwb,* the same words that were rendered "shall not return" in the first part of the verse, an instance of antanaclasis [repetition of the same word in a different meaning], see I. Casanowicz, *Paronomasia,* p. 34; D. Yellin, *Ketavim,* pp. 107ff.; C. C. Torrey, *The Second Isaiah* [New York: Charles Scribner's Sons, 1928], pp. 199ff.); hence each man shall languish because of his sin (lit. "each in his iniquity his life [they] shall not hold firm"—unusual and unclear language, but the wording is confirmed by G).

G does not represent all that lies between *yšwb* "shall return" in vs. 13a$^\alpha$ and *yšwb* "shall be revoked" in 13b$^\alpha$. Despite the critical consensus in G's favor (*BHS;* see the detailed argument in Zimmerli), the striking balance of the two halves of MT (with a break at the *atnaḥ*) argues for its integrity. The translation can only partly reflect the formal parallelism (pointed out by Freedman, privately):

aα *ky* noun *'l . . . l' yšwb*
aβ *w*-monosyllable . . . *ḥyt-*
bα *ky* noun *'l . . . l' yšwb*
bβ *w*-monosyllable . . . *ḥyt-* . . . (extended for closure)

From such a text, G will have arisen by the error of homoioteleuton ("similar endings").

14. *They have blown the horn* (taqᵉʿu battaqoᵃʿ). Hebrew *taqoᵃʿ*, translated in G as "horn," is otherwise unknown; the pattern of the word is common in adjectives (e.g., *gadol* "big") and agent-nouns (*ʿašoq* "extortioner")—hence *taqoᵃʿ* "blower"? The past tense of the verb accords with the usage in vss. 10–12. However, the phrase is very similar to Jer 6:1 *ubitᵉqoᵃʿ tiqʿu šopar* "And in Tekoa [a town southeast of Bethlehem] blow the horn!"—a similarity increased by G's reading the verb here as imperative. Brushing aside the Jeremianic phrase as senseless here, Cornill emended our phrase *tiqʿu taqoᵃʿ*, with postpositive infinitive on the pattern of the verbs in Isa 6:9; it must be admitted, however, that such a play on what was perhaps a familiar phrase would accord with Ezekiel's manner (see esp. vs. 10), and the hapax *taqoᵃʿ* is not so strange in this this chapter, containing as it does an unusual number of unique and rare expressions.

made . . . ready. In later biblical Hebrew, the infinitive construct is used (as here) to continue a finite verb; e.g., Esther 1:7; I Chron 21:24b; II Chron 7:3 (disregard GKC, p. 345, note).

15. The three scourges of 5:12; 6:12 are divided between "the city" and "the country," on which cf. Jer 14:18.

16. *shall haunt*. Lit. "shall be on"; *haya 'el* = *haya ʿal* "be located on" for which sense cf. Exod 10:6; 28:28; Isa 30:25; Jonah 4:2. In Ezekiel *'el* often = *ʿal* (e.g., 2:6, 10; 3:15; 6:11, 13; 7:18, 26; 11:11; 12:12, 19; 13:2, 9 [*haya 'el* = *haya ʿal;* see comment at 13:9]).

The simile of birds on heights for refugees seeking safety is found elsewhere. Thus: "Abandon the towns! Make your home in the cliffs, O inhabitants of Moab! Be like the dove that nests on high on the sides of the gorge" (Jer 48:28; cf. the parallel in Isa 16:2, alluding to "fugitive birds, like nestlings driven away"); or again, Ps 11:1, "Flee to the mountain like a bird" (reading *km*[*w*] *ṣpr*). On "doves of the valley" Bodenheimer writes (*EM* III, col. 606, s.v. *"yona"*): "One finds the rock dove (*Columba livia*) especially in the northern and southern parts of the land of Israel; it nests in the mountain regions, in caves, in valleys and in rocky crags." The epithet "of the valleys" (*hagge'ayot*) affords a double wordplay: the surface contrast of "mountains—valleys," as in 6:3, and the subtler evocation of moaning (**hogiyyot*) doves—cf. Isa 38:14, but especially 59:11, where *hgh* is in parallel to *hmh* as here.

The conflict between the masculine suffix of *kullam* "all of them" and the feminine participle *homot* "moaning" indicates vacillation between doves and men as the subject (*hmh,* though not attested with doves, can, like *hgh,* refer to delicate as well as rough sounds [Isa 16:11 (harp); Jer 48:36 (flutes)]). For men repining in iniquity both *hgh* and *hmh* are suitable verbs, as Isa 59:11f. shows. The grammatical tension is absent in G S, where *hmwt* is rendered as though derived from *mwt* "die"; elsewhere in Ezekiel, however, survivors are allowed to live on in self-disgust (see 6:9), as is the sense of MT.

17. *knees shall run with water.* G "thighs shall be defiled with moisture," that is, from urine passed in fright. Cf. "One who hears the blare of horns and recoils in fright, the clash of shields and recoils in fright, the flashing of swords and water flows (*šwttyn*) upon his knees" (BT *Sotah* 44b). With this and the preceding image compare this Assyrian description of enemies in flight: "Their hearts beat like that of a fledgling dove chased away, they passed hot urine" (Luckenbill, *ARAB* II, p. 128 and fn. 1, corrected by *CAD* s.v. *"ṣarāpu"*). For the Hebrew idiom, cf. "our eyes flow (*trdnh,* lit. run down) with tears" (Jer 9:17; Lam 1:16); "hills shall flow (*tlknh,* lit. go) with milk" (Joel 4:18). Our phrase locates the urine on the knees perhaps because it would appear there on infantry wearing knee-length skirts (the common dress of Egyptian and Assyrian soldiers; see, e.g., *ANEP*² #311, #369, #370). On the other hand, Ehrlich aptly adduces the variant ending to the talmudic passage cited above: "water runs down between (*byn*) his knees" in *Sifre* to Deuteronomy, § 192, while G. R. Driver, ("Some Hebrew Medical Expressions," *ZAW* 65 [1953], 260) suggests that *birkayim* here serves as a euphemism for penis, like Akkadian *birku.* The phrase appears again only in 21:12; owing to its connection there with "melting" heart (cf. Josh 7:5, "heart turned into water") and "fainting" spirit, and the further combination of limp hands and collapsing knees in Isa 35:3 (see the heaping up of such phrases in Qumran Hodayot iv 33f.; viii 34), it has been rendered "knees turn to (or: weak as) water" (*RSV,* NJPS). But this seems to be a euphemistic skewing of the primary sense (Freedman, privately).

18. Such mortifications were customary on occasions of public calamity as well as in mourning (Amos 8:10; Isa 22:12; Ezek 27:31; cf. de Vaux, *Ancient Israel,* pp. 59–61). Note the interweave of ordinary parallelism—in the *a*-colon *ḥagᵉru* ‖ *kissᵉta,* in the *b*-colon *kol panim* ‖ *bᵉkol rašehem*—with chiasm: a^{α} and $b\beta$ mourning rites, $a\beta$ and b^{α} discomfiture.

19. *an unclean thing. nidda* refers specifically to menstrual impurity—of a high degree according to the system of impurity; cf. Lev 15:19ff.; 18:19 (excision the penalty for disregarding it cf. too Ezek 22:10). It serves as an image for that which is shunned in abhorrence: Lam 1:17; a synonymous term is used in Isa 30:22, a passage very similar to ours (see Structure and Themes).

The line on the futility of silver and gold seems to be quoted from Zeph 1:18; on its altered sense here, see Structure and Themes.

their stumbling-block of iniquity (mikšol ʿawon). This expression is peculiar to Ezekiel; it recurs in 14:3, 4, 7 applied to idols; in 18:30 to unrepented transgression; in 44:12 to Levites who served at the illegal shrines. The usage in chs. 14 and 44 shows that the two nouns are bound together, precluding the theoretically possible construction here, "their iniquity was a stumbling-block" (see comment at 18:30). In accord with Ezekiel's use of "stumbling-block" (see note at 3:20), the phrase means "cause of downfall (consisting) of iniquity"; or "the iniquitous cause of their downfall." For this usage of the genetive construction, cf. *ṣon 'adam* (36:38) "flocks (consisting) of human beings"—human flocks; *'ᵃḥuzzat qeber* "property (consisting) of a tomb"—a hereditary burial site (GKC § 128 k–m; Joüon § 129 f [3]–[4]). The suffix on *'ᵃwonam* belongs to the entire phrase; cf. Weingreen, "The Construct-Genetive Relation in Hebrew Syntax," *VT* 4 (1954), 50–59. The phrase derives from the verb clause *kašal ba'awon* "fall because of iniquity" (Hos 5:5; 14:2; Ps 31:11). In this verse, the people are referred to consistently in the plural (*yšlyku, yśb'u, yml'w,* the suffix *-m*), while the gold and silver are construed as a unitary concept, in the singular (*ywkl, hyh*).

How their gold and silver became an iniquitous cause of their downfall is told in the next verse.

20–21. There are two views on the interpretation of these verses: one takes the proud ornament as an allusion to the temple (as in 24:21; see ahead on "the pride of the fierce" in 7:24); "in it they made" (*'św bw*) idols—evidently a reference to Manasseh (II Kings 21:7), hence it will become unclean, desecrated by invaders (cf. Rashi, Kimḥi, Abarbanel). The other (cf. Kara, Ehrlich [Hebrew]) takes the source of pride (sinful pride according to Eliezer of Beaugency, Luzzatto) to be ornaments made of the aforementioned silver and gold; "out of it [*'dy* being a collective] they made" (*'św bw*) idols—on which see Structure and Themes. The end of vs. 20 repeats vs. 19aα—the future repulsion toward the useless precious metals—while vs. 21 predicts their "desecration" (violation through spoliation and violent expropriation, cf. Isa 23:9; 47:6) at the hands of invaders. The second view is preferable: (1) because the first would have been better expressed by *śmw bw* "they set in it" (Ehrlich; cf. I Kings 21:7); (2) only the second allows the "unclean thing" of vss. 19 and 20 to refer to the same thing—the precious metals. In either case, *w-* of *wṣlmy* introduces the predicate (BDB, p. 254, def. 5), and the singular pronominal elements of *'dyw* "his ornaments" and *sam-* "he took (pride)" must be collective (hence "their" and "they"). Since they are so taken by most medievals, the plural pronominals in G S cannot for certain be considered as evidence for a different *Vorlage;* they may be simply the result of translators' exigency.

On any interpretation, at least vs. 20aβ must speak of cultic offenses ("abominable . . . things"). Thus between vs. 19, which speaks solely of silver and gold, and vs. 24, which speaks clearly of sanctuaries, vss. 20–22 form a bridge whose terms are sufficiently ambiguous they can be understood as applying to either, or (and perhaps this is intended) to both.

the wicked of the earth. Otherwise only in the Psalms, this term combines here with "strangers," in vs. 22 with "violent men" (*pariṣim*) and in vs. 24 with "the worst of the nations" to characterize the foreign invader destined to destroy Israel for its sins. In 30:11f. Nebuchadnezzar's hordes are similarly styled, and it is a reasonable supposition that they are meant here. Such depictions of the enemy as ruthless and barbarous augment the terror of the prophecy; cf. Deut 28:50 and Jer 6:23.

22. *my treasure.* Judging from the feminine suffixes in the next clause ("it") this is an epithet of the city or land of vs. 23 (both fem. in Hebrew); so T ("the land in which my Presence dwells").

23. *Forge the chain!* The hapax *rattoq* is understood as equivalent to *rattuqa/rᵉtuqqa* "chain" (I Kings 6:21; Isa 40:19). On the basis of Nahum 3:10 "bound (*ruttᵉqu*) in fetters"—said of exiles—this may be interpreted as a call to an undefined hearer (like the call of 24:3) to make preparations for an exile train; however, the context does not speak of exile but of the city's fall. The versions guess desperately and we can do little better.

bloody judgments. A unique phrase whose meaning "judicial murder" is spelled out in the parallelism of 9:9 "the land is full of bloodshed, and the city full of perverted judgments"; cf. the accusations of 11:6; 22:6, 12a, 25, 27. That "judgment, verdict" is the sense of *mišpat* here, rather than "case, crime" (*RSV:* "bloody crimes"), seems to be required by the context of vs. 27 where the noun is resumed; see comment there. From 9:9 it is inferable that "lawlessness" in the sequel refers likewise to that of officials, not of the general population.

24. *take possession of their houses.* The occupation of the land by invaders is not a common theme of covenant curses, but it does occur in Lev 26:32: "Your enemies who dwell in it will be appalled over it[s desolation]." The take-over of parts of the land after the fall was indeed a burning issue in later prophecies; see 35:10ff.; 36:2ff.

The exact quantitative equivalence of the a and b clauses of this verse, the assonance of the first half of the a clause with the first half of the b clause—

WHB'TY	rA'e GOyIM	(note partial chiastic assonance
WHšBTY	Gᵉ'On 'AzzIM	in the last two words)

and the pseudo-parallelism of the two b clauses (*nḥlw* in the second clause, nif'al from *ḥll* "desecrate" [as in 25:3] has overtones of a derivative of *nḥl* "take possession" because of its "parallel" in the a clause, *yršw;* indeed S actually takes it to mean "inherit," though as a pi'el of *nḥl* it could only mean "allot as a possession"!) are all formal similarities which contrast (strikingly and pleasingly) with the dissimilar content of the two clauses.

the pride of the fierce (g^{e}'on [cf. vs. 20] 'azzim). "The fierce" is an unusual expression, recurring in Ps 59:4 as an epithet for the wicked, who in the previous verse are called "men of blood (*damim*)"—cf. our vs. 23. The combination *g^{e}'on 'azzim* is unique; G renders the phrase in accord with the commonplace *g^{e}'on 'uzzam* "their proud strength" (or the like)—as in 24:21; 30:6, 18; 32:12; 33:28, often combined with derivates of *šbt* "be ended," as here. But our clause has a close analogue in Isa 13:11 "I will put an end to the pride of the arrogant [*zedim*]," of which, indeed, it seems a variation based on the commonplace *g^{e}'on 'uzzam* which it playfully skews. The denseness of artifices in vs. 24 inclines one to prefer the unusual MT to the commonplace G.

their sanctuaries (m^{e}qad^{e}šehem). Except for lack of lengthening of *d* (GKC § 93 oo, fn.), the word is vocalized as the active pi'el participle, "those sanctifying them." In order to justify the stative sense inherent in "sanctuaries" (=hallowed place), Kimḥi (*Sefer ha-šorašim,* s.v. *qdš*) compares *m^{e}ta'eb* "abhorrent" in Isa 49:7, which, in turn, he compares to *m^{e}malle* "full" (=*male*) in I Chron 12:15. The ancient versions translate and later interpreters explain the word as equivalent to *miqd^{e}šehem* "their sanctuaries"—the plural (so in 21:7; also in Jer 51:51; Ps 73:17) of the many sacred places in and about the Jerusalem temple (BDB, p. 874, col. a). The vocalization appears to be a later deliberate distortion, perhaps intended to convey the sense "those [places] they [not God!] sanctify"; compare Kimḥi's first explanation of *m^{e}ta'eb goy* at Isa 49:7: "he whom every nation abhors."

25. *Terror.* Hebrew **q^{e}pad* (with archaic, unstressed *-a* ending, not feminine; in poetry, perhaps for rhythmic reasons [here to avoid the sequence of two main stresses?] GKC § 90 f; Joüon § 93 i), a hapax, is explained by Syriac *q^{e}fada* "bristling, stiffening (from terror)," derived from the verb *q^{e}fad* "bristle, shrink, creep (from fear—said of the skin)."

26. *Disaster . . . howa* recurs only in Isa 47:11 || *ra'a* "misfortune"; for the phrase pattern, cf. the synonymous *šeber 'al šeber* in Jer 4:20. The structure and terms of vs. 26 look backward and forward. As vs. 26a develops the thought of vs. 25a (note the resumption of *bw'* "come"), so vs. 26b develops that of vs. 25b (note the resumption of *wbqšw* "and they shall seek"). Moreover, as in vs. 25a, "and they shall seek" is answered by "there'll be none" (*w'yn*), so "and they shall seek" of vs. 26b must be complemented in thought by an implicit *w'yn,* carried over from vs. 25a and expressed in the translation by "[in vain]."

Now the first line of vs. 26b "They shall seek vision from the prophet" —designed as an echo of vs. 25b so as to evoke *w'yn,* necessary for completing its thought—is at the same time the first member of a tricolon based on the three associated and formally identical pairs *ḥazon mnby'* "vision from prophet," *twrh mkhn* "instruction from priest," and *'ṣh mzkn* "counsel from elder." The last two form in turn a subunit, a bicolon in which the verb *t'bd* "will perish" of the first member is carried over in thought to complete the verbless second. The unity of the tricolon, based primarily on the three noun pairs, is enhanced by the shadow of *wbqšw* "and they shall seek" of its first member cast ahead on the two subsequent cola as their implicit preliminary. (One cannot speak of *wbqšw* as carried over to complete the following lines since, unlike *w'yn* and *t'bd* which are carried over, it cannot be syntactically worked into those lines.) The artful fashioning of the line "they shall seek vision from prophet" so that it calls for a complement from what precedes it, as it starts off its own tricolon, is a capital device for bonding vss. 25–26; this device is missed (indeed obliterated) by the proposal to supply that line with a "fitting" conclusion of its own (*BHS: *wl' ymṣ'* "and it shall not be found").

The counselors of the realm are three classes (cf. 22:26–28: priests, officers [= elders, Isa 3:4; Lam 5:12], prophets; the same in Jer 4:9), a triad almost identical with that of Jer 18:18: "shall not perish instruction from priest, and counsel from sage, and word from prophet" (cf. Micah 3:11 for an earlier age: heads, priests, prophets). The unusual grouping in our passage of the two sacral institutions (prophet and priest) before elder places first what pertains to the preceding (vss. 13, 24) and last what pertains to the following topic (in vs. 27)—the civil order.

As for the substance of vs. 26: cessation of oracles ("vision") was a sign of God's displeasure (I Sam 14:37f.; 28:6) held over the people as a threat (see esp. Amos 8:4); at the time of the fall it seems to have materialized (Lam 2:9). The paralysis of the other two classes of counselors is caused by the terror of the enemy; for the priests' torah as embracing both morality and religion, see the balanced discussion of de Vaux, *Ancient Israel,* pp. 353–55.

27. Here the civil hierarchy is divided into three. The extremes—king and "people of the land" (= the whole body of citizens; de Vaux, *Ancient Israel,* p. 71)—offer no difficulty. In Ezekiel, however, the usual contrast is between *naśi* "chief, prince" and "people of the land" (45:16, 22; 46:2f., 8f.) where *naśi* stands for the king. That makes the *naśi* here, standing after the king, problematic. (In G the whole first clause about the king is absent; in MT it makes vs. 27a correspond to the threefold division of vs. 26b.) We know of a threefold civil division of contemporary Judah from Jer 44:21 (37:2): king, officers (*śarim*), people of the land; since *śarim* were in all likelihood heads of families (de Vaux, *Ancient Israel,* p. 69), one wonders whether *naśi* here has (unusually for Ezekiel) its common sense of "clan chiefs"; this is the likely explanation in 32:29, where Edom's *m^{e}lakim* "kings" and *n^{e}śi'im* "chiefs" are mentioned as two different groups. If *naśi* here means "chief," its not having the article may indicate a class-noun; cf. the indeterminate class-nouns ("priest," "prophet," etc.) in vs. 26 and in Isa 3:2f. Alternatively (cf. Kimḥi) *melek* and *naśi* may simply be synonymous, in what Levenson (*Theology*, pp. 64ff.) calls "synthetic" or "impressionistic parallelism, the same unit of meaning expressed completely in each of two clauses"; the

contrast will then be between king/chief on the one hand and people on the other (Freedman, privately).

I will give them a taste of their own ways. Lit. "out of (the repertoire of) their way (conduct) *middarkam,* I will do to them" (for this use of *mi-* see BDB, p. 579, col. a bottom; G reflects the more common *kdrkm*). The people's way—resuming the terms of vss. 3f., 8f.—has been to turn their backs on God; he, on his part, will turn his face from them (vs. 22a). Thus too the next clause: their judgments have been bloody (vs. 23); his judgments of them will be of the same sort.

STRUCTURE AND THEMES

The boundaries of this difficult oracle are the revelation formula of vs. 1 and the recognition formula of vs. 27, followed in 8:1 by a new revelation formula. What lies between is unified by poetic style (see below) and intertwined topics. According to topics and formulas the oracle falls into two main parts: A alarms of doom (vss. 2–9), and B aspects of the dissolution of communal life on doomsday (vss. 10–27). The two are interwoven at the beginning and end of the second part: vs. 10 opens the second part with an alarm passage (cf. also vss. 12 and 25) while vs. 27 closes it with a line fusing elements of both parts ("their way," "judgment") forming a conclusion to the entire prophecy. Such halving of oracles, with a conclusion resuming elements of the first half at the end of the second, is a literary feature of the book. (The following analysis is indebted to Parunak, *Structural Studies,* pp. 192–205, even though it differs from it.)

A. Alarms of doom.

1. Vss. 2–4, beginning with an address and message formula and ending with a recognition formula: the threat of imminent doom as the divine requital for evildoing.

2. Vss. 5–9, beginning with a message formula and ending with a recognition formula: almost a repetition of the foregoing, with some elaboration consisting in the main of obscure allusions to harvest.

B. The dissolution of communal life on doomsday.

This part opens abruptly, with no introductory formula (indicating a close connection with the preceding section), and with a variation on the alarms of vss. 6–7, bonding the two parts (vss. 10–11). From the alarm of vs. 12 the texture changes into comments upon and scenes of the end, in sequences of different length without clear demarcation.

1. Vss. 10–11 first announce the arrival of doomsday with a chiastic inversion (with elaboration) of the elements "comes the doom" and "day" of vs. 6; there follows in vs. 11 a figure of ripeness in which terms that

appear in the sequel occur: "lawlessness" (cf. vs. 23), "wickedness" (cf. vs. 21), and "masses" (cf. vss. 12–14). The final burst of *m-h-m* sounds in vs. 11 carries on *m^{e}huma* "tumult" of vs. 7.

2. Vss. 12–18, the first round of scenes of the end: (a) the futility of commerce (vss. 12–13); (b) impending war, disasters and refugees (vss. 14–16); (c) interspersed references to divine anger and the people's sin (vss. 12b, 13b, 14b, 16b); (d) the general appalment (vss. 17–18).

3. Vss. 19–27, the second round of scenes of the end: (a) the futility of wealth (vs. 19); (b) invasion, desecration, spoliation (vss. 21–24); (c) interspersed references to sins and God's anger (vss. 19b, 20, 22a, 23); (d) all classes paralyzed (vss. 25–27).

It is evident that the second round not only corresponds to the first, but heightens and specifies it; this is especially clear in the particularization of sin—cultic and civil, of the cruel punishments, and of the detail of institutional collapse.

The episodic disjunctiveness of the oracle is counteracted by repetitions and anticipations. The large-scale repetition in A and the continuation of the alarms of A in B have been noted above. The threefold refrainlike sequence "for (my) wrath/vision is upon/about all her masses" crosses a scene boundary (vss. 12–14, B1. [a] and [b]). "Each in his iniquity" appears in separate scenes (vss. 13b [c], 16b [d]). The comment on the futility of gold and silver (vs. 19a) anticipates at its close (vs. 19b) the idolatry described in the next scene.

A peculiar pattern of anticipation and elaboration recurs in B: a segmented line of which segment *a* forms the subject of the next line(s) and segment *b* forms the subject of the line(s) after that. Thus vs. 15: "sword" of a^{α} is taken up as the subject of b^{α}, while "plague and famine" of a^{β} is taken up at length in b^{β}. Similarly in vss. 25–26: "terror is coming" of vs. 25a is taken up in detail in vs. 26a (enumerating the coming terrors), while the futile search for peace in vs. 25b is elaborated on in vs. 26b (the failure of all counselors). Again (though more loosely) vs. $19a^{\alpha}$ (the throwing-away of silver and gold) is explained in $19a^{\gamma\delta}$ while $19a^{\beta}$ (treating them as unclean things) turns out to be an anticipation of vss. 19b, 20a (the sin of idol-making) as 20b makes clear ("therefore I will turn it into an unclean thing for them").

These repeated patterns and parallel structure show that the oracle is not simply an amorphous agglomerate of lines and glosses, as may seem at first, though it cannot be said to be a tight construction. But what in Ezekiel is?

This impressionistic, episodic oracle is couched in poetry. While short lines, repetitions, and parallel cola sometimes appear in previous chapters, here they predominate (in the translation, indented lines are usually in parallelism to the preceding). Repetition may serve as a refrain (with slight, typical variations, as in vss. 12b, 14b; see also vss. 6, 22) or it may develop into the elaboration-pattern described in the previous paragraph, and the even more extensive expansion of vss. 2–4 in 5–9. Parallelism may be synonymous (e.g., in vss. 4 [9], 8, 12a$^{\alpha}$, 19a$^{\alpha\gamma\delta}$, 21, 23) or antonymous (vss. 12a$^{\beta}$, 15a, 16a), with intricate chiasm (see comment to vs. 18) and paronomasia (see at vs. 24). The variety of figures and ambiguous expressions is evocative but at the same time it cumbers interpretation (e.g., in vss. 7, 10, 20). Alliteration also occurs frequently (e.g., in vss. 6, 10, 11, 13, 14, 24—see comments).

In the vocabulary of the oracle, familiar elements appear (e.g., "loose against," "spend upon," "judge/punish," "abominations, loathsome things," "stumbling-block"), but interspersed among them are sequences of lines with expressions that never recur in the book, including hapax legomena (*ṣᵉpira* [as used here], *qᵉpada, hed, taqoaʿ*). Many such expressions appear in (mostly poetic) texts outside of Ezekiel:

four corners of the earth (Isa)
inhabitant of the land (Isa, Jer, Pentateuch)
sprouted, put forth flowers (Num, Isa)
rod of wickedness (cf. Isa 14:5)
what has been sold (Lev)
wrath (*ḥaron*) (Exod 15, Jer, Isa)
shuddering (Isa, Ps, Job)
confusion (*buša*) (Micah, Obad, Ps)
wicked of the earth (Ps)
seek peace (Ps)
calamity (*howa*) (Jer)

Such evidence points to borrowing in our chapter from poetic and prophetic sources. Direct loans from texts presently in hand are hardly demonstrable (though vs. 19 seems to be taken from Zeph 1:10; see below), but at the least the treasury of language and imagery common to poets and prophets was heavily drawn upon here. Perhaps the closest analogue is Isa 13, usually dated later than our chapter; this tends to confirm the notion of a common treasury upon which the authors of both drew. Like our chapter, Isa 13 dwells upon an imminent doom (of Babylon)—and clothes it in a description of "the day of YHWH" and its various terrors: God's wrath, the victim's helplessness, and the enemies' barbarousness. The more remarkable linguistic parallels are (numerals refer to verses in Isa 13):

the sound of masses/tumult on the mountains (4)
the day of YHWH is near (6)
every hand will be limp (7)
nibhalu (be terrified) (8)
rage (*'ebra*), wrath (*ḥaron 'ap*) (9)
evil . . . iniquity . . . put an end to the pride of the insolent (11)
houses will be plundered (16)

silver . . . gold (powerless to save) (17)
their eye will not spare (18)
splendor (*ṣ^ebi*) . . . pride (*ga'on*) (19)
time (*'et*) about to come (*qarob labo*) (22)

The fountainhead of all "day of YHWH" doom prophecies appears to be Amos (5:18–20; 8, cf. M. Weiss, "The Origin of the 'Day of the Lord' —Reconsidered," *HUCA* 37 [1966], 29–60). In the collection of dooms in Amos 8, several elements of our chapter appear for the first time. The beginning of our oracle contains an elaboration of Amos 8:1–3—the vision of the basket of ripe summer fruit (*qayiṣ*), interpreted as a signal that "the end (*qeṣ*) is coming" (the interrelation of Amos and Ezekiel here was noted by W. Rudolph, *Amos,* KAT, ad loc.). Amos 8:10 predicts universal mourning on "that day," while vss. 11f. describe it as a time when prophecy would fail and people would "seek the word of YHWH but not find it." The Amos passage is mostly "subjective": God speaks in the first person of what he will do.

A related passage in Zeph 1:7–18 (see Weiss, cited above) opens with an alarm, "the day of YHWH is near!", repeated in vs. 14, then proceeds to describe its victims. The wealthy are singled out, who "fill the house of their Lord with lawlessness [*ḥamas*] and deceit." Their silver and gold will not save them; terror will seize the entire population. The passage alternates between subjective and objective expressions.

An even closer antecedent to the second part of our chapter is Jer 4:5–9: Sound the horn throughout the land, "for I am bringing evil!" The destroyer of nations is on his way to ravage the land. All shall go into mourning, for YHWH's rage is unappeased. "On that day the intelligence of the king and officers will be gone, the priests will be desolated, and the prophets struck dumb." Subjective and objective expressions are interwoven.

Viewed in the context of such prophecies, two difficulties of our chapter are obviated: first, the repeated shift from subjective to objective language —from statements by God speaking for himself to descriptions of aspects of the calamity—appears normal; it should not serve as a basis of critical dissection (although a variety of sources for the materials here combined is not improbable). The many threads of style and language that bind the parts of our chapter together indicate its general integrity. The second difficulty is the scale of events suggested by vs. 2b "the four corners of the land/earth." The last word *ha'areṣ* occurs in related passages, and there as here commentators wonder whether to render it "the land" (of Israel, Judah) or "the earth" (see, e.g., Fosbroke, IB, on Amos 8:8, 11; Taylor, IB, on Zeph 1:2, 11 [Lindblom, *Prophecy,* pp. 369f. regards these verses as announcing a universal judgment that "serves as a background" for judgment on Judah—this in the light of Isa 2:10ff., their presumed model]). But this genre of prophecies is fundamentally ambivalent, since the enemies of God who are the victims of his judgment are now the heathen, now Israel; hence its idiom shares at once universalistic and particularistic elements (on this ambivalence, see briefly Jenni in *THAT* I, p. 726). Moreover, from the prophet's viewpoint, the doom of his people is tantamount to the end of the world (see the striking expression of this feeling in Ezek 21:8f.).

The theme of maturation, ripening, and harvest that glimmers through the first part of the chapter develops from the wordplay of Amos 8 on *qayiṣ* "ripe summer fruit (usually harvested figs)" and *qeṣ* "end." That play is not merely aural; *qayiṣ*, naturally linked to harvest-time, calls up associations of cutting down and sweeping clean that may serve as metaphors for the ravages of an invader. "The proud crowns of the drunkards of Ephraim," warns Isaiah, ". . . shall be like an early fig before the fruit harvest (*qayiṣ*); whoever sees it devours it while it is still in his hand" (28:3f.). The link of *qyṣ* (the root of *hqyṣ*) and *hydd* (of which *hd* seems an abbreviation) in Isa 16:9–10 also occurs in a doom context:

Therefore I weep for Jazer,
For Sibmah's vine . . .
Ended are the shouts (*hydd*)
Of your fig and grain harvests (*qyṣk wqṣyrk*)
No more does the treader
Tread wine in the presses;
To shouts I have put an end (*hydd hšbty*)

"One inevitably wonders," writes Kaiser (*Isaiah 13–39*, OTL, p. 73), "whether the vines and grapes are not meant here as a symbol of the Moabite population." Justifiably so, in the light of other passages utilizing such imagery; here, for example, is a passage in a prophecy against a gentile nation (Isa 18:5):

For before the harvest, when the blossom is gone
When the flower has ripened into berries
He will trim away the twigs with pruning hooks
And lop off the trailing branches . . .
The kites shall summer (*qṣ*) on them,
And all the beasts of the field shall winter on them.

While Isaiah is rich in such passages (see 17:5ff.; 24:13), he is by no means alone. Micah 7:1 puts this complaint into Israel's mouth: "Woe is me! I have become like leavings of the fig harvest [*qyṣ*], like gleanings when the vintage is over." Both Zeph 1:2 and Jer 8:13 play on the assonance of *'asap* "gather [in harvest]" and *swp* "put an end to" in harvest images of destruction. Joel 3:13 represents the time of punishment as a ripe harvest, overflowing vats. In part A of our chapter, the echo of Amos 8 in vss. 2f. ("the end [*qṣ*] is coming") is taken up in vss. 6f. ("it has ripened," "harvest-shouts") and culminates in the image of the rod in flower in vs. 10 (adapting the language of Num 17:23). The allusions are glancing and border on the enigmatic, but their references seem certain.

In vss. 19–24 the theme of wealth as a stumbling-block appears. In its early statements, silver and gold are tainted as being the stuff out of which idols are made (Exod 20:23; 32:2ff.) or plated (Deut 7:25; cf. Isa 30:22). Then the notion arises that ungrateful Israel has made over to "no-gods" the wealth bestowed upon it by its solicitous God (adumbrated in Deut 32:15f.; explicit in Hos 2:10, 16; elaborated in Ezek 16:17). Accordingly, the wealth of Israel too will perish on doomsday; in Isa 2:2f. increase of wealth and of idols are closely associated, while in vss. 20f. the two are fused in the first expression of their futility on doomsday:

> On that day, humankind shall cast away
> To the flying foxes and the bats
> The idols of silver and the idols of gold
> Which it made for itself to worship
> As it enters the clefts of the rocks
> And the crevices of the cliffs
> On account of the terror of YHWH . . .

A recurrence of the theme in Isa 30:22 adds the element of pollution and revulsion:

> You will treat as unclean the silver overlay of your images and the gold plating of your idols. You will cast them away as something defiled, you will call them filth.

Zeph 1:18 treats the theme in the context of the complacent indifference toward God of the wealthy merchants of Judah (vss. 11ff.); on doomsday they will discover that their wealth cannot shield them from the divine rage (= our vs. 19a).

In Ezek 7, all the aspects of the theme are resumed and interwoven. The futility of commerce (vss. 12f.) is punctuated by a refrain making ambiguous reference to God's anger at the people's wealth (*hamonah,* vs. 12; see comment). The futility of wealth is forcefully expressed in vss. 19f. in language evocative of Isaiah and Zephaniah (is the citation of Zephaniah original or editorial?), but manifestly adjusted (in vs. 19aγ) to the present context: no wealth will assuage the hunger-pangs of the starving (cf. "famine" of vs. 15). That the wealth will be regarded as unclean is explained in characteristically Ezekielian terms as the outcome of the impure use to which it was put in worship (vs. 20), harking back to the earliest use of the theme. The climax is the dual threat of desecration and dispossession (vs. 24).

A new ground of judgment is mentioned for the first time in vs. 23 (and perhaps in vs. 11; see comment): bloody crimes (*mišpaṭ damim*) and lawlessness (*ḥamas*) fill the land. Heretofore Ezekiel arraigned the people for cultic "abominations" and "loathsome things," in line with the priestly covenant threats of Lev 26 (see ch. 5). Now social wrongs are added, in the idiom of the Flood story ("the earth was filled with lawlessness," Gen 6:11, 13) and earlier prophecy (e.g., Isa 1:15, "Your hands are full of bloodguilt"). *ḥamas* and *damim* are crimes against the divinely established order for which God punishes all men; cf. Hab 2:8, 11, 17, where Babylon is condemned for these very crimes. Ezekiel's contemporary Jeremiah also accused his age of such crimes (2:34; 6:7), and both prophets directed their accusations particularly at the leaders (Jer 22:17; Ezek 19:3, 6; 22:6, 27). II Kings 21:16 asserts that Manesseh filled Jerusalem with "innocent blood," an expression identical with Jer 19:4, in which the human sacrifice practiced in the Valley of Hinnom is denounced. This association of bloodshed with cultic crimes is explicit in Ezek 16 (cf. Ps 106:37f.), and may underlie our passage too, though *ḥamas* "lawlessness" shows that a wider range of civic wrongdoing is included; cf. 8:17; 9:9; 11:6.

Language and ideas characteristic of Ezekiel are combined in our chapter with an unusually rich array of poetic elements echoing passages from elsewhere in the Bible. Abrupt changes in perspective, obscurity, even incoherence (vs. 11b), bespeak a passion and excitement that could not be contained in the prophet's usual prosaic framework, and that sought release in language and figures drawn from the reservoir of Hebrew poetry evidently known to him. As in the few other instances in which he demonstrated his poetic range (e.g., chs. 21; 28:11–19), the modern interpreter encounters insuperable difficulties in following him.

VII. The Defiled Temple and Its Abandonment (8:1–11:25)

(*Note:* Translation and comments are by chapter. Structure and Themes of the whole follows.)

(8:1–18)

8 1 In the sixth year, in the sixth[a] month, on the fifth of the month,
as I was sitting in my house with the elders of Judah seated before
me, the hand of Lord YHWH fell upon me there.

2 I looked, and there was a figure having the appearance of fire[b]:
from the appearance of his loins down was fire, and from his loins
up was something with a brilliant appearance, like *ḥashmal*. 3 He
reached out the likeness of a hand and seized me by a lock of my
hair. A wind bore me between earth and heaven and brought me to
Jerusalem in a divine vision, to the entrance of the gate of the inner
court that faces north, where the statue of outrage that outrages was
situated. 4 There I saw the Majesty of the God of Israel, like the
apparition I had seen in the plain. 5 He said to me, "Man, look north!"
I looked north, and there, north of the altar gate, was this statue of
outrage in the approachway. 6 He said to me, "Man, do you see what
they are doing, the great abominations that the house of Israel are
committing here, removing themselves from my sanctuary? You
will yet see other great abominations."

7 He brought me to the entrance of the court, [c]and there I saw a
hole in the wall[c]. 8 He said to me, "Man, burrow [c]through the wall!"[c]

[a] G "fifth."
[b] G "a man" (*'iš* for MT *'eš*).
[c–c] Not in G.

I burrowed [c]through the wall[c], and there was an entrance. 9 He said
to me, "Go in and see the evil abominations that they are committing
here." 10 I went in and saw that there were [c]figures of all sorts of
creeping things and beasts[c], detestations and all the idols of the
house of Israel engraved on the wall all around, 11 and seventy men
of the elders of the house of Israel were standing before them—with
Jaazaniah son of Shaphan standing among them—each with his
censer, and the smoke-cloud of incense ascending! 12 He said to me,
"Do you see, man, what the elders of the house of Israel are doing
in the dark, each in his image-chambers, for they say, 'YHWH does
not see us. YHWH has forsaken the land.'" 13 He said to me, "You
will yet see other great abominations that they are committing."

14 He brought me to the entrance of the gate of the house of
YHWH that is on the north, and there sat the women who were
wailing for Tammuz. 15 He said to me, "Do you see, man? You will
yet see abominations even greater than these."

16 Then he brought me to the inner court of the house of YHWH,
and there at the entrance of YHWH's temple, between the porch and
the altar, were about twenty-five men whose backs were to YHWH's
temple and whose faces were turned east and they were prostrating
themselves[d] eastward to the sun. 17 He said to me, "Do you see, man?
As if the abominations they commit here are too slight a thing for
the house of Judah, they fill the land with lawlessness and vex me all
the more; indeed they reach the vine-branch to [e]their noses![e] 18 For
my part, I will react in fury, my eye shall not spare nor will I have
pity; they shall cry loudly for me to hear, but I will not listen to
them."

[d] MT *mštḥwytm,* generally taken as a scribal error for *mštḥwym* (GKC § 75 kk); medieval grammarians regarded it as a "mixed form"; for details, see W. Chomsky, ed., *David Kimḥi's Hebrew Grammar* (*Mikhlol*) (New York: Bloch Publishing Co., 1952), § 40 h′ (e), and note 339.

[e–e] "It should have read 'to my nose' but the text resorts to euphemism" (*Minḥat Shay,* citing, among others, *Mechilta, Shirta* 4 [J. Goldin, *The Song at the Sea* (New Haven: Yale University Press, 1971), p. 155]).

COMMENT

8:1. *sixth year . . . sixth month.* About 18 September 592. The last date (3:15) was about 7 August 593; the subsequent prescribed period of siege-symbolism lasted (in MT) 390 days, thus ending about 31 August 592—some three weeks before our date. The critical preference for G's "the fifth month" (about 18 August) as original, on the ground that MT postponed it so as to clear the period of the symbolic action (Smend and most others), ignores the real total of 430 days (390 of siege-symbols plus 40 of exile) that MT assigns to that period (Wevers). If the 40-day exile-symbolism followed directly on the siege-symbolism, this visionary experience would have interrupted it even by MT's reckoning; this offers no insuperable strain, however, for why should the prophet not have experienced a vision during his long immobility? But there is in fact no way of knowing whether indeed the two symbolic actions were consecutive, and thus whether the second overlapped this oracle. G dates the vision a month earlier "probably under the influence of 'the fifth day'" (Wevers), but since G reduces by 200 days the period of the symbolic acts (see at 4:5, 9), this earlier date is by G's reckoning still well after the conclusion of those acts.

elders . . . seated before me. Evidently awaiting an oracle; see 14:1, 3; 20:1. In 33:30f. there is a vivid report of the assemblage at the prophet's home in order to hear an oracle of YHWH.

fell upon me. napal 'al is used of the sudden onset of overpowering forces, often bad (Exod 15:16; Isa 47:11; Ps 105:38; Dan 10:7) but also neutral or supernatural (Gen 15:12; I Sam 11:7; 26:12; Job 4:12f.). Here it is worn down to the equivalence of *haya 'al* (see comment to 1:3, "hand . . . came upon him")—which G actually represents here; MT *napal* is supported by its later recurrence in 11:5 ("spirit fell upon")—a usage peculiar to this vision.

2. Only the human figure, the last item perceived in the vision of ch. 1 (vss. 26b–28), appeared. G's reflection of *'iš* "man" (for MT *'eš* "fire") makes this clearer, provides an antecedent for the possessives ("his") that follow, and restricts "fire" to the bottom half of the figure, where alone it should be (note, however, that in 1:26 the word for "man" is *'adam;* another instance of variation). MT *'eš* may have arisen under the influence of the second *'eš* (the two words standing each in a pause), as the strange form *ḥašmala* at the end of the verse seems to have arisen by assimilation to *lᵉma'la* (both standing in pause in the second half of the verse).

a brilliant appearance. In Hebrew "like the appearance of *zohar";* the word recurs only in Dan 12:3, where it is said that "those who are wise shall shine with the brightness of the firmament" (*yazhiru k^ezohar haraqi^a'*). Association with the divine apparition here, and with heaven in Daniel, made the term fitting for the title of the "bible" of Jewish mystics, the Zohar.

3. *the likeness of* (tabnit) *a hand.* Nowhere in Ezekiel but in this vision does *tabnit,* lit. "construction, model," occur—here, in vs. 10, and in 10:8, a clue to the unity of the vision. G translates uniformly *homoiōma* "'that which is made like,' a likeness, an image" (the same word translates Hebrew *d^emut* "likeness, image" in 1:5, 16, 22, etc.); S *dmwt'* "likeness." In descriptions of heavenly beings, *tabnit* is employed, like *d^emut* (cf. 10:21 *d^emut yad 'adam*) and *mar'e,* to distinguish between the real thing and something that looked like it but which the author wishes to keep apart from it. Thus, *yad* = human hand (in 10:8 and 21 expressly, *yad 'adam*); but what the prophet saw here and in 10:8 was not a human hand but a likeness of it that belonged to no human. In 8:10 the prophet saw not creeping things but the figures of them on the wall (cf. Deut 4:17f.; Ps 106:20). Outside Ezekiel, the architectural use of *tabnit* in descriptions of the sanctuary and its parts is typical, e.g., in Exod 25:8f. "model" and in I Chron 28:11ff. "drawing, plan" (cf. vs. 19, "all in writing"; G *paradeigma,* which has a similar range). In Josh 22:28 *tabnit* conveys the essential point: the transjordanian tribes intended to build, not a real altar of YHWH, but merely a model or likeness (G *homoiōma*) of one.

"Hand" and "loins" go with the description of the apparition here as like a man; from vs. 4 onward, however, it is referred to as "the Majesty of [*kbwd*] God."

by a lock of my hair. Lit. "tuft of my head." *ṣiṣit* "tuft"—in Num 15:38 "tassle"—was suggestively associated by Ibn Janaḥ with the verb *ṣyṣ* "sprout" (cf. Ezek 7:10), for which he also compared the talmudic definition "*ṣiṣit* means *'anap* ["offshoot, branch"]" (*Menahot* 42b), and T's *ṣiṣin* which translates "fins" (Lev 11:9); this in turn sheds light on the traditional interpretation of Jer 48:9, "Give *ṣiṣ* ["wings"] to Moab." Accordingly, our phrase will be literally "outgrowth of my head." Kimḥi regards the seizure of the prophet by his hair as a sign of anger. Compare the description in the Akkadian "Vision of the Nether World" of an audience with the underworld god Nergal: ". . . valiant Nergal was seated on a royal throne . . . *from* [. . .] of his *arms* lightning was flashing [. . .] took me by the locks of my forehead and dre[w me] before him" (*ANET*[3], p. 110a). Note that the fiery figure reaches out and seizes Ezekiel, but it is the wind that transports him to Jerusalem. It is not said that the human figure accompanied him; in fact nothing is said of the location of the figure during the journey (on this point see Structure and Themes). Similarly, and probably inspired by our passage, in the apocryphal story of Bel and the Dragon the prophet Habakkuk is carried to Babylon both by an angel who seized a lock of his hair and by "a rush of his wind/breath" (vs. 36, Theodotian version).

between earth and heaven. That is, through the air.

in a divine vision. On the meaning of this phrase see comment to 1:1. What follows is thus not to be taken as an account by an eyewitness in the flesh; in a vision Ezekiel "went" to Jerusalem, and in the same vision he "returned" to Babylonia (11:24), "like one who sees in a night-dream that he is in Jerusalem but when he wakens he finds himself sitting in Babylonia" (Kara). So too the transportation in 40:2.

gate of the inner court. The inner court is mentioned again in vs. 16 and 10:3; 10:5 mentions an outer court. The visionary temple of the future also had two courts (40:17ff., 23ff.), and so did the Jerusalem temple of late monarchic times, II Kings 21:5; 23:12. The north gate of the inner court is probably the same as the "altar gate" mentioned below in vs. 5, so called because it was opposite the great altar of sacrifice in the inner court. Ezekiel was set down, it would seem, at the outside entrance of this gate—which means, in the outer court just north of the entrance.

the statue (semel) *of outrage that outrages.* Phoenician *sml* denotes the statue of a divine or human being (C. F. Jean and J. Hoftijzer, *Dictionnaire des inscriptions sémitiques de l'ouest* [Leiden: E. J. Brill, 1965], s.v. *"sml"*). II Kings 21:7 tells of the "sculptured image" (*pesel*) of Asherah that King Manasseh set up in the Jerusalem temple; this very image is called (*pesel has*) *semel* in II Chron 33:7, 15—apparently reflecting our Ezekiel passage, and identifying "the statue of outrage" with Manasseh's image of the Canaanite goddess, Asherah. (It is fitting that this goddess's image should be referred to by the Phoenician/Canaanite *sml.*) The term occurs in the anti-idolatry warning of Deut 4:16–18, linked again to our passage by vs. 10 below. *qin'a,* here rendered "outrage," is the passionate resentment one feels at seeing what is his being given to another (it is therefore often rendered "jealousy"). For the form of *maqne* (=*maqni*[']), cf. GKC § 75 qq, and Deut 32:16, 21. Virolleaud's suggestion that *qin'a* is cognate with Akkadian *uqnu,* Ugaritic *'iqn'u* "lapis lazuli," is an ingenious curiosity; adopting it, Driver (*Biblica,* p. 149) invents a Hebrew *qunna'a* after Syriac, *qūnā'a* "sky-blue"—disregarding the Greek provenience of the Syriac word (*kuaneos;* C. Brockelmann, *Lexicon Syriacum,* p. 674). The possible ultimate connection between the early Semitic and the Greek words (see Brockelmann) does not justify treating the Syriac form as native.

4. *in the plain.* See 3:23. Whether the reference is to the human figure alone (so D. H. Müller, *Ezechiel-Studien;* see at 3:23), or to it and its throne-vehicle is unclear; see Structure and Themes.

5. Since in Ugaritic mythology Mount *Ṣpn* is the abode of Baal, with whom Asherah is associated as mother (in the Bible, apparently as consort; *THAT* II, p. 577; *IDB,* s.v. "Asherah," p. 251), the location of the statue in the north (*ṣapon*) area of the temple may be significant.

6. *removing themselves from. raḥaq me'al* implies more than a physical

distancing; it includes sentiments of indifference or hostility where attachment formerly existed—i.e., alienation (Jer 2:5; Ezek 44:10; Job 19:13); here the bestowal of worship on objects outside the sanctuary, in disregard of the divine presence inside it (cf. vss. 15–16). Alternatively, there may be an allusion here to a compulsory alienation from the sanctuary in the form of exile—the inevitable effect of the people's misdeeds. These interpretations take the subject of the verb to be the people (as always with the idiom *raḥaq me'al* when men and God are involved). Some medieval and modern exegetes, however, make God the subject: "so that I must alienate myself from my sanctuary"; the phrase thus anticipates the description given later of the departure of the Majesty from the temple.

7. *entrance of the court*. Perhaps the south opening of the north gate, that gave onto the inner court.

The sequence in vss. 7–8 is strange: in the wall of the entrance to the gate the prophet sees a hole ("a certain [lit. one] hole," no more definite than colloquial English "this [here] hole"; BDB, p. 25, col. b, defs. 3, 4), which he is commanded to enlarge; on doing so he discovers (inside?) an (lit. "one," colloquial "this") entrance (to a chamber of the gatehouse?), through which he is bidden to enter (vs. 9). G shortens by eliminating the hole and the wall, but the result is still the strange discovery of a (blocked up?) entrance by burrowing. Vs. 7b, missing in G, may have been merely a variant of the last clause of 8 ("and there was an entrance"); originally the text will have said that on burrowing through the wall, Ezekiel found a recess—*ḥor* = "hiding place," as in I Sam 14:11; Job 30:6. The present text resulted from understanding *ḥor* as "hole" and trying to accommodate both clauses in a remotely plausible sequence. A secret meeting place is meant; our puzzlement in making out precise details is somewhat mitigated by bearing in mind the visionary character of the experience.

10. *figures of . . . creeping things and beasts*. Not in G, this combination of phrases from Deut 4:17–18 interrupts the expected sequence *kol šeqeṣ* "every detestation," as though to guarantee the reading *šeqeṣ* for the graph, which when elsewhere combined with *gillul-* (as here) is read *šiqquṣ* "loathsome thing"—always an idol. Here, on the contrary, the sense is "detestable animals," as in Lev 11:10–42 where *šeqeṣ* is the term for creatures (e.g., vermin) forbidden as food. The point here is that these "idols" were engravings of animal figures on the wall. It is difficult to identify this cult with any known outside the Bible. The figures on the wall recall the "Ishtar Gate" of Babylon, with its lions and serpent-dragons inlaid all over it, or the rock carving at Maltaya of gods in procession on the backs of all sorts of real and imaginary creatures (*ANEP*² ※760, ※537); coming from Mesopotamia and Asia Minor, the combination with Tammuz, mentioned in vs. 14, is at least fitting. Egyptian theriomorphic deities (*ANEP*² ※573) and even totem animals (as a regression to primitivism) have also been invoked as possible sources of

this scene (S. A. Cooke, in additional notes to W. R. Smith, *Lectures on the Religion of the Semites,* 3d ed. [London: A. & C. Black, 1927], pp. 625ff.). See Structure and Themes.

Our passage is similar to 23:14—Judah-Oholibah lusts after the Babylonians on seeing their pictures engraved in red; a Mesopotamian background appears here again, but its exact connection with the prophecy is unknown.

11. *seventy . . . elders.* See 7:26; for the number, see the etiological story of Num 11:16, 24 (cf. Exod 24:1, 9). Without actually saying so, "seventy elders" implies that the corruption of Judah's religion involved even the national council (on which see M. Weinfeld, *EJ,* s.v. "Elders"). Jaazaniah must have been a familiar notable, perhaps of the family of the royal scribe Shaphan (II Kings 22:3; cf. other members of the family mentioned in Jer 29:3; 36:12).

the smoke-cloud of incense. Here is an ironic echo of the awesome moment in the ceremonies of the Day of Atonement when the high priest confronts the divine presence in the holy of holies, screened by "the cloud of incense" (Lev 16:2, 13). The phrase is preceded here by the hapax *'tr,* evidently related to Syriac *'eṭra* "vapor, fume," especially of anything offered in sacrifice (Payne-Smith)—a word that may have had pagan overtones.

Incense was part of idolatrous private cults (Jer 19:13 "on rooftops"; Isa 65:3 "on bricks"); in Israel's cult it was regarded as a very powerful propitiator (Num 17:12), and therefore comparable in weight to whole offerings (Deut 33:10).

12. *each in his image-chambers.* The vision of the seventy elders all together seems to have been replaced by another of each in his private rooms (G actually renders "secret room"). These are called "chambers of *maśkit,*" a term found in idolatrous contexts in priestly writings (Lev 26:1; Num 33:52) and, in the form *mśky* "image, statue," in the eighth-century B.C.E. Aramaic inscription of Panammuwa II (*KAI* ※215.18).

The plural *ḥadre* "chambers" seems to have been entailed by the ambiguous numerical reference of distributive *'iš* "each/every = all," resulting in vacillating constructions (e.g., verb in sing., Gen 44:13; Lev 25:46; in plural, Gen 44:11; Lev 25:17), even within a single phrase: Neh 4:12, "each [with] his sword were girded on his lions"; so here "his (image)" and "(their) chambers" have been fused. The ancient versions represent *ḥadre* simply by the singular "room."

YHWH does not see us. Cf. the disdainful thoughts of the wicked man in Ps 10:11: "God is not mindful; he hides his face; he never looks (*ra'a*)"; cf. 94:7 and Job 22:13f. for more of the same. God no longer pays attention to what men are doing; he has left the land. A similar mood is described by Zephaniah (before Josiah's reform): "YHWH will do nothing, good or bad" (1:12). Why, then, do these idolaters work in the dark? Perhaps because of the requirements of their cult—of which we know nothing, or perhaps because they are paradoxically ashamed of what they are doing.

14. This gate-entrance is hardly identifiable; some have supposed it was an entrance to the side-structure of the temple (and so further into the heart of the sacred zone).

women. Heb *hnšym* (so again in II Kings 23:7); Joüon (§ 137 m–n) calls this idiomatic usage of the article (*ha-*) "imperfect determination." Compare English "a certain person"; see also GKC § 126 q–s.

wailing for Tammuz. Hebrew "the *tammuz,*" as though it were a common, not a proper noun, a thing rather than deity; cf. "the *baals* and the *ashtoreths*" (Judg 10:6, etc.), reducing them to fetishes. The rite alluded to here can be traced back to ancient Sumer (S. Kramer, *The Sacred Marriage Rite* [Bloomington: Indiana University Press, 1969], ch. 4), where it marked the annual death and descent into the netherworld of the minor god Dumuzi, a symbol of plenty. "In the cult drama of the death of the god and lament for him, celebrated at the end of spring, the loss of the god, the waning of the power for new life in nature, is counteracted by mourning and lament" (T. Jacobsen, *Toward the Image of Tammuz and Other Essays* . . . [Cambridge: Harvard University Press, 1970], p. 100). Wailing for Tammuz (in his several forms) was a women's rite practiced widely over the Near East through centuries. A seventh-century B.C.E. Assyrian daybook ordains *bikitu* "weeping" on the second of the month of Tammuz. As late as the tenth century C.E., the pagan Sabaeans of north-Syrian Haran kept a wailing (*al-Bukat*) for Tammuz in his month (S. Langdon, *Babylonian Menologies and the Semitic Calendars* [London: Oxford University Press, 1935], p. 120). The complex of Dumuzi/Tammuz myths and rites has been somewhat clarified by the recent recoveries of extensive parts of the Sumerian myth; still the life-setting of the later laments remains obscure. Our passage, much too brief to shed any light on the question, fits the knowledge we have of the rite, which presumably was imported into Judah—ultimately from Mesopotamia. (See Gurney, "Tammuz Reconsidered: Some Recent Developments," *JSS* 7 [1962], 147ff.) For the unreality suggested by the fact that Ezekiel sees this weeping not in the fourth month of Tammuz, where it belongs, but in the sixth month (vs. 1), see Structure and Themes.

15. The activity described in the next verse is expressly qualified as the worst abomination of all, perhaps because of its location; see next comment.

16. *between the porch and the altar.* In Joel 2:17, this area is where priests pray to God on a fast day; it appears to have had a special sanctity within the inner court. (*Mishnah Kelim* 1.9 ranks it only less than that of the sanctuary proper, the eighth of ten degrees of sanctity.) This sacred space is taken by men who give the sanctuary their backs and bow toward the sun; such contempt for YHWH is counted as the climactic abomination.

Sun worship existed in Judah in late neo-Assyrian times (see N. Sarna, "Psalm XIX and the Near Eastern Sun-god Literature," *Fourth World Congress of Jewish Studies Papers* I [Jerusalem: World Union of Jewish Studies, 1967], pp. 171–75). Josiah's purge did away with horses and chariots dedicated to the sun and used in a temple rite (II Kings 23:11), and with priests who made offerings to the sun and other astral bodies (vs. 5). Like so many other pagan practices, these evidently were introduced by Manasseh, who is blamed for building altars for the entire "host of heaven" in the two courts of the temple (II Kings 21:5). Generally regarded as evidence of Mesopotamian influence, a good case can be made for its western (e.g., Aramaic) provenience (see M. Cogan, *Imperialism and Religion* [Missoula, Mont.: Scholars Press, 1974], pp. 84–87). This weakens somewhat the appeal of the G reading "twenty men" (for MT "twenty-five") based on the association of Mesopotamian Shamash with the "sacred" number twenty. Twenty-five men appear again in this vision (11:1), and the number is a favorite of Ezekiel's, who uses it more frequently than any other biblical author (cf. 40:1, 13, 29; and, with "thousand," throughout the boundary descriptions of ch. 45). The construction with *k^{e}*- "about" treats it as a round number, which suits Ezekiel's penchant for it.

17. At this point in previous scenes, God promised to show the prophet still more (vss. 6, 13; "greater" in vs. 15) abominations. But here, after the refrain "Do you see, man?", he unexpectedly lumps all the temple abominations as evils outweighed by an even more outrageous provocation: the lawlessness rampant in the land (an evocation of the Flood story, Gen 6:11, 13; cf. 7:23). The sequence *h^{a}naqel l^{e} . . . me'^{a}śot . . . ki* verb . . . *wayyiqtol* combines two separate constructions: *h^{a}naqel . . . wayyiqtol* (e.g., I Kings 16:31, "as if it had been a slight thing [for him to follow the sins of Jeroboam . . .] he married Jezebel . . ."), and *ham^{e}'aṭ . . . ki* verb (e.g., Isa 7:13, "Is it too little [for you to treat men as helpless] that you treat my God as helpless?"). This unexpected shift to denunciation of social wrongdoing (for Elliger [*BHS*] and others the words in question are "probably an addition") is confirmed in the next episode—the scene of punishment; for in 9:9, God affirms his ruthless verdict upon the people on the ground of their social wrongdoing—in the very terms of our passage. Accordingly, the obscure expression at the end of the verse ("reach the vine-branch to their noses") is not connected with the temple abominations, which are superseded in vs. 17a, but with the social wrongdoing of vs. 17b. Its general sense (as rendered in a note in NJPS) is "goad me to fury" (G "sneering, turning up their noses"); the specific sense is beyond us, but it is noteworthy that Jewish tradition regards the suffix of *'appam* "their nose" as a euphemism (*tiqqun sop^{e}rim*) for *'appi* "my nose." This suggests some provocative gesture. Sarna has interpreted the phrase as "they despatch bands of toughs (*z^{e}mora* as from

ḏmr "be strong") to execute their anger" (*HTR* 57 [1964], 347–52), which has the virtue of taking account of the context (social wrongdoing).

Ignoring the context, exegetes old and new have looked for some idolatrous rite in this clause—with or without relation to one or another of the previously mentioned abominations. A scatological interpretation of vs. 16 found in the Talmud (*Yoma* 77a) led some medievals to take *z*ᵉ*mora* as the sound of breaking wind, and, either literally or figuratively (i.e., an allusion to the odor of idolatrous offerings), a contemptuous flouting of God. Another interpretation, equally old, takes *z*ᵉ*mora* as phallus (lit. rod), and the phrase as alluding to some phallic rite (summary in A. Kohut, *Aruch Completum,* vol. III, p. 300). Modern interpreters seek a pagan cultic gesture; since an earlier suggestion that it is Iranian has been generally discredited (see the debate between Torrey and Spiegel, in Torrey, *Pseudo-Ezekiel and the Original Prophecy,* pp. 84, 177–79, 216–20, 242–49), recent attention has been focused on Assyro-Babylonian customs. H. Saggs (*JThS* 11 [1960], 318–29) argued for the identity of our gesture with what is called in Akkadian *labān appi* (*CAD* 9, p. 12a: ". . . a gesture involving both nose and hand, meant to express humility toward gods, kings and human beings"), particularly when the hand held before the face holds a branch, as, e.g., Sennacherib is portrayed in the Bavian relief (A. Parrot, *Nineveh and Babylon* [London: Thames and Hudson, 1961], pl. 81, p. 73; cf. idem, *Babylon and the Old Testament* [New York: Philosophical Library, 1958], p. 141). (For a comprehensive recent discussion of the Akkadian phrase, see M. Gruber, "Akkadian *labān appi* in the Light of Art and Literature," *JANES* 7 [1975], 73–83, with a drawing of the Bavian relief.) But these efforts to link pagan cultic gestures with our Hebrew phrase seem misplaced, in view of the dissociation of "reaching the branch to their noses" from the idolatrous rites.

(9:1–11)

9 1 Then he cried loudly in my hearing, "Bring on the executioners
of the city, each with his weapon of destruction!" 2 Six men appeared,
coming by way of the upper gate which faces north, each with his
weapon for clubbing; among them was one dressed in linen, with a
scribe's kit at his waist. They came and stood beside the bronze altar.
3 Now the Majesty of the God of Israel had moved off the cherub,
on which it had been, to the threshold of the house.

He called to the man dressed in linen with the scribe's kit at his
waist, 4 and YHWH[a] said to him, "Pass through the city, through
Jerusalem, and put a mark on the foreheads of those who moan and
groan over all the abominations being committed in it." 5 To the
others he said in my hearing, "Pass through the city after him and
kill; let your eyes not spare and have no pity; 6 slay and destroy old
men, youths and maidens, little ones and women, but stay away from
any who bear the mark; and start from my sanctuary!" So they
started with the elders[b] who were before[c] the house. 7 He said to
them, "Defile the house and fill its courts with corpses; [d]go forth!"
So they went forth and killed[d] in the city.
8 As they were killing, I alone was left[e]; throwing myself down on
my face, I cried, "O Lord YHWH, will you destroy the entire remnant of Israel, as you pour out your fury upon Jerusalem?" 9 He
said to me, "The iniquity of the house of Israel and Judah is very very
great. The land is full of bloodshed[f] and the city full of injustice, for
they say, 'YHWH has left the land; YHWH does not see.' 10 For
my part, my eye shall not spare nor will I have pity; I will bring
their ways down on their heads!"
11 Then the man dressed in linen with the scribe's kit at his waist
appeared and reported: "I have done as you commanded me."

[a] Not in G.
[b] G "the men" (not reflecting MT *hzqnym*).
[c] G "inside."
[d–d] G S reflect *ṣ'w (w)hkw* "go forth and kill."
[e] The anomalous form has been explained as a fusion of *w'š'r* and *wnš'r* (GKC § 64 i).
[f] Some mss. read *ḥamas* "lawlessness" (*Minḥat Shay*).

COMMENT

9:1. *in my hearing*. The phrase *qara bᵉʾozne,* lit. "call/cry in the ears of," means different things in 8:18 and here. There, the ears are those of him who is addressed, hence the translation "cry . . . for me to hear" (as Exod 24:7 "read it out for the people to hear"; cf. Jer 36:15 and Judg 7:3, "proclaim for [all] the people to hear"). Here the ears merely overhear what is addressed to others, hence the rendering "in my hearing" (as in II Sam 18:12; II Kings 18:26). The use of identical words with different meaning is characteristic of Ezekiel; the play is lost in G, which lacks our phrase in 8:18 (perhaps through *homoioarkton* "similar beginnings").

Bring on . . . ! The authoritative (royal) imperative (piʿel), addressed to implicit attendants; with humans, in Gen 43:31; 45:1; I Kings 3:24f.; with God, Isa 40:1f.; Jer 46:3; Joel 4:9f. S (and possibly T) renders as an intransitive imperative, "come near!" which would normally be *qirbu* (qal). Least satisfactory is G's rendering it a past qal, "drew near."

executioners. This rendering (Cooke's) seeks to convey the ambiguity of *pᵉqudda,* meaning both "visitation, punishment" (Num 16:29) and "functionary" (II Kings 11:18). These figures were rightly regarded by the third-century C.E. sage R. Ḥisda as personifications of divine wrath; accordingly he named them *qeṣep* "wrath," *ʾap* "anger," *ḥema* "fury," *mašḥit* "destroyer," *mᵉšabber* "shatterer," *mᵉkalle* "annihilator" (BT *Shabbat* 55a), following Ps 78:49, in which similarly named personified attributes of God, let loose against the Egyptians, are collectively called "a mission of baneful angels."

weapon of destruction. In the next verse, the same weapons are for "clubbing." The cognate verbs *hišḥit* "destroy" and *nippeṣ* "club" occur in parallelism in Jer 51:20 with the only other recurrence of the noun *mappaṣ* "clubbing." G lacks the parallel here, since vs. 2b does not appear in it.

2. *Six men*. Plus the heavenly scribe makes seven, a number symbolizing completion (*IDB,* s.v. "Seven"). These have been regarded as a reflex of the seven planetary deities of the Babylonians, among whom was Nabu, a scribe-god as well (e.g., H. Zimmern, H. Winckler, *Die Keilinschriften und das Alte Testament,* 3ᵗᵉ Aufl. [Berlin: Reuther & Reichard, 1903], p. 404). If this is so, the transformation into six destroyers has quite effaced their original character. There is a clearer line of descent from the Babylonian deities to the later Jewish conception of seven archangels (Rev 8:2, 6; Enoch 20:1–8). It is noteworthy that the third-

century C.E. R. Ḥisda did not equate the destroyers of Ezekiel's vision with any named and known (arch)angels, even though the scribal figure was in talmudic times identified with Gabriel (*Yoma* 77a).

upper gate. In the wall of the exterior court, called in Jer 20:2 "the upper gate of Benjamin in the house of YHWH," because through it one gained access to the Benjamin Gate of the city wall (Jer 37:13); it is perhaps the same as "the upper gate of the temple" built by Jotham (II Kings 15:35; see B. Mazar, *EM* III, p. 814).

dressed in linen. Like ordinary priests (Exod 28:29–42); henceforth angels are portrayed so dressed (Dan 10:5; 12:6f.). Priests and angels have their ministry to God in common, and, since ordinarily linen was bleached (*IDB*, s.v. "Linen"), their garments signified their purity.

scribe's kit. "A palette with a slot in which the pens were kept, and hollowed places in which the ink was put, generally two—for black and red ink . . . the Hebrew word [*qeset*] was an Egyptian loan word *gst*(*y*) 'writing outfit'" (G. R. Driver, *Semitic Writing,* rev. ed. [London: Oxford University Press, 1954], p. 86, pl. 31.1). An Egyptian scribe with his kit tucked into his waistband is portrayed in *Views of the Biblical World* [Hebrew], ed. B. Mazar et al. (Jerusalem: International Publishing Co., 1958–61), III, p. 166 (to our verse).

bronze altar. The Solomonic altar (I Kings 8:64), which Ahaz had removed and placed to the north of his new-style Damascus altar (II Kings 16:14).

3. *moved off the cherub, on which it had been.* T adds "in the holy of holies" by way of explanation, showing that it understood the passage, in connection with I Kings 8:10f., to mark the first stage of the Majesty's abandonment of the temple, where it had dwelt since Solomon's time (see Rashi). This and related verses are discussed below in Structure and Themes.

4. *and YHWH said to him.* The tetragram seems as out of place as it is in Lev 1:1; not surprisingly G omits it here. In both passages it would have been more fitting (if at all) after the preceding verb *wyqr'* (here in vs. 3b). Critics have regarded such awkwardness as a result of combining disparate elements. That may be so, but the product has its own logic: Lev 1:1 continues the narrative of Exod 40:35 (interrupted by vss. 36–38); the *kabod* of the Exodus verse is the implicit subject of *wyqr'* in Lev 1:1. Similarly, the *kabod* of vs. 3b in our passage is the implicit subject of *wyqr'* of vs. 4, and both here and in Lev 1:1 the implicit *kabod* is then identified with the express subject of the following coordinate verb, namely, YHWH. That the subsequent weighty commands (in both books) originated in YHWH himself is evidently an important point for the narrator. Now, had YHWH appeared as the subject of the verb immediately following mention of the *kabod,* it would have impressed on the reader a contrast between the two that was, in its turn, unwanted; in the

present text, the identification comes upon one gradually through means of coordinate verbs, only the second of which has YHWH as its subject.

put a mark (taw). *Taw,* the last letter of the alphabet, had in the old Hebrew script the shape of an X, the simplest of marks (Driver, *Semitic Writing,* pp. 88f. [esp. p. 89, fn. 3], p. 162; it was used as a builders' mark: *EM* II, p. 187, fig. 8, bot.). As Bar Hebraeus observes, its purpose here was merely to discriminate the good people from the rest of the population. Exegetes, however, have connected this mark with other saving marks—for example, the blood sign placed on the lintels and doorposts of the Israelites to ward off the "destroyer" who struck Egypt's firstborn (Exod 12:23) or devices set on the forehead (the protective priestly rosette, which expiated for Israel's sins [Exod 28:38]; the "frontlets" [*ṭoṭapot*] or "memorials" regarded by some early Jews as *phylakteria* "guardians" [Matt 23:5; for mitigation of such magical notions, see L. Blau, *Altjüdische Zauberwesen,* Jahresbericht der Landes-Rabbinerschule in Budapest (Budapest, 1898), p. 152]; these identified the bearer to onlookers [or evil forces] as devoted to God).

The implication of vs. 11 is that the linen-clothed man found some people worthy of being marked, but since this is not said explicitly, Abarbanel inferred from the prophet's intercessory expostulation in vs. 8 that none were to be spared. It is true that Ezekiel's doctrine of a remnant does not suppose any righteous Jerusalemites (see 6:9; 7:16; 12:16; 14:22f.), yet it would be forcing his words here to follow Abarbanel (note that 21:8 refers to righteous Jerusalemites). Some later Jews, apparently stung by Christian delight over the anticipation here of the saving power of the cross (X), arrived at the same result as Abarbanel by interpreting the effect of the sign as a quick and easy death, untouched by the destroyers who were set loose in the city by God (S. Lieberman, *Greek in Jewish Palestine* [New York: Jewish Theological Seminary of America, 1942], p. 190). This agrees with the talmudic view that even those marked were killed, since their (assumed) silence in the face of the wicked implicated them in their guilt (Rashi, citing BT *Shabbat* 55a).

6. *and destroy*. Lit. "to destruction"—*l^emašḥit* echoing *mašḥet* of vs. 2 and anticipating *h^amašḥit* of vs. 8.

and start. Hebrew *taḥellu* evokes *ḥallel* "profane, desecrate," from a homonymous, if not identical, root—an evocation reenforced by the express command of vs. 7 to defile the temple (note *ḥ^alalim* "corpses").

the elders who were before. The *elders* of 8:11f. who were inside some structure, and to whom 8:12 ascribes the saying below in vs. 9, are here (con)fused with the twenty-five men of 8:16 who were *before* the house, giving it their backs. G, in turn, produces a similar (con)fusion with its phrase "the *men* who were *inside*."

7. Contrast II Kings 11:15: Athaliah is deliberately dragged out of the temple before being executed; here, since these men had already defiled the house with their idolatry, it is no matter if they are killed there

(Kimḥi). God's shocking command expresses the total unfitness of the temple for his presence; while strictly speaking it is out of sequence (since the slaughter has already begun) it is no mere parallel to vs. 6, but an explicit divine license to commit an unthinkable desecration.

In vs. 7b *wyṣ'w whkw* can only be perfects, as in MT; but normally, in the sequel to a command narrating its fulfilment, the verb is in imperfect consecutive (Exod 2:8b; Jer 36:14b; Neh 8:15f.). Yet *w-* plus perfect in positions normally served by imperfect consecutive does occur in Ezekiel; see, e.g., 13:6 and the comment to 20:22 (*whšbty*). G S translate as though their *Vorlage* had imperatives *ṣ'w whkw* "go forth and kill!"; in view of the unity of place maintained throughout the vision (see vs. 11; 10:7 and below, Structure and Themes), this reading seems preferable to MT (or to an expanded reading *ṣ'w* [*whkw*] *wyṣ'w whkw*—Freedman, privately). MT's intrusive *wyṣ'w* will have arisen from this primary reading by dittography.

8. *the entire remnant of Israel.* The Judahite population that survived the deportation of 597 B.C.E. The prophet's cry is evoked by the sight of the slain in the temple courts; if the sanctuary gave no asylum, what hope was there for those outside?

9. *house of Israel and Judah.* A strange combination (previously either "of Israel" [8:6, 10–12] or "of Judah" [8:1, 17]), calculated to express the wide diffusion of the sin, answering to the prophet's "the *entire* remnant."

The land is full of bloodshed. The third echo of Flood story language (even stronger according to the alternative reading "lawlessness" cf. 7:23; 8:17), to which the derivatives of *šḥt* earlier in the chapter also belong (see Structure and Themes).

for they say. The reversal of the elements of the saying of 8:12 indicates a purposeful reference to it. It is noteworthy that the setting of the saying here is social wrongdoing, while above it was cultic.

10. In ironic answer to their assertion that God does not see, God's eye will not spare. He will forsake his compassion and make the wicked suffer the consequences of their conduct ("to set one's way on one's head" recurs in 11:21; 16:43; 22:31; cf. I Kings 8:32).

(10:1–22)

10 1 I saw that on the expanse above the heads of the cherubs was
something as of sapphire; what appeared to be the figure of a throne
was visible above them. 2 He addressed the man clothed in linen and
he said, "Go in among the wheelwork beneath the cherub[a], fill both
your hands with burning coals from among the cherubs and strew
them over the city"; he went in before my eyes.
3 The cherubs were standing to the south of the house when the
man came, and the cloud filled the inner court. 4 The Majesty of
YHWH rose off the cherub onto the threshold of the house, and the
house was filled with the cloud and the court was filled with the
radiance of the Majesty of YHWH. 5 The sound of the cherubs'
wings could be heard as far as the outer court, like the sound of
God Almighty when he speaks.
6 When he commanded the man clothed in linen, "Take some fire
from among the wheelwork, from among the cherubs," the man went
and stood beside the wheel. 7 One of the cherubs reached his hand
among the cherubs to the fire that was among the cherubs, and taking
some, he put it into the hands of the one clothed in linen, who
received it and departed.
8 The likeness of a human hand was visible under the wings of
the cherubs. 9 I saw that there were four wheels beside the cherubs,
one wheel beside one cherub, and one beside every other cherub; the
appearance of the wheels was like chrysolite. 10 As for their appearance, the four had the same shape, as though one wheel were inside
the other. 11 When those went, these went at their four sides; they
did not change position as they went. All went in the direction in
which the head faced, without changing position as they went. 12 [b]All
their flesh[b] and their backs and their hands and their wings and the
wheels were filled with eyes—[c]the four of them /their wheels/[c]. 13 It
was those wheels I heard referred to as wheelwork. 14 Each had four

[a] G S V T^ms. "cherubs" (plural).
[b–b] Not in G.
[c–c] G "to the four wheels" (as from *l'rb't h'pnym*). The last word in MT may originally have been *[w]'pnyhm* "[and] their wheels"—a superior variant of the mid-verse *wh'pnym* "and the wheels."

faces: [d]the faces of one were[d] the face of a cherub, [e]the faces of the
second[e] the face of a human, the third[e] the face of a lion, and the
fourth[e] the face of an eagle.

15 The cherubs rose; they were the creatures I saw at the Chebar
canal! 16 When the cherubs went the wheels went alongside them;
when the cherubs raised their wings to rise off the ground the wheels
did not change their position beside them. 17 When those halted
these halted, and when those rose these rose with them; for the
spirit of the creatures was in them.

18 The Majesty of YHWH came forth [f]off the threshold of[f] the
house and halted upon the cherubs. 19 The cherubs raised their wings
and rose off the ground; I watched them depart, with the wheels
alongside them. They halted at the entrance of the east gate of the
house of YHWH, the Majesty of YHWH above and upon them.
20 They were the creatures I saw beneath the God of Israel at the
Chebar canal; I realized now that they were cherubs. 21 Each had four
faces and each had four wings, and the likeness of human hands under
their wings. 22 As for the shape of their faces, they were the faces I
saw at the Chebar canal, with the selfsame appearance. Each went
straight ahead.

d–d S "one."
e–e S "another" and so for each of the following ordinal numbers.
f–f G "from."

COMMENT

10:1. This verse differs from 1:26 chiefly in substituting "cherubs" for the "living creatures" mentioned in ch. 1 (cf. 10:15, 20). The purpose of this verse, which interrupts the narrative, may be to call attention to the presence on the scene of the (empty) throne, in anticipation of the Majesty's mounting it shortly (vs. 18).

2. *He addressed* (wayyomer) . . . *and he said* (wayyomer). The repeated *wayyomer,* whose effect is to slow and thus lend solemnity to the narration, occurs elsewhere: Gen 22:7; 46:2; II Sam 24:17; Esther 7:5; Neh 3:34.

It is the priestly aspect of the man clothed in linen that qualifies him to enter among the cherubs and handle the heavenly fire blazing among them (on which, see 1:13).

beneath the cherub. As 1:15 suggests, the wheels extended lower than the creatures, hence the space "among the wheelwork" (*galgal,* see at vs.

13 below) was "beneath" as well as "among them" (as in the sequel). Since in subsequent allusions to this event only *krwbym* in the plural occur (vss. 2b, 3a, 6, 7), the versional evidence for a plural here (in vs. 2a) is convincing: MT *krwb* is an error by haplography—the ending *ym* omitted due to its similarity to the beginning of the next word *wml'*.

strew them over the city. For the immolation of the wicked in a rain of heavenly fire cf. Ps 11:6; 140:11 and the fate of Sodom and Gomorrah (Gen 19:24). *zaraq* "strew," mostly in priestly lustrations, is also occasionally used in nonsacramental contexts (Exod 9:8 [most like our passage], 10; Job 2:12); Houk's view of this act as a purification (*JBL* 90 [1971], 53f.) is thus not necessarily confirmed by the language. This vision meant that the doom of the city had been sealed. Earthly events were merely the working out of this antecedent decree.

3–4. Vs. 3a places the cherub vehicle to the south of the house, at a remove from the abominations in the northern area; all the rest is obscure. Is "the man" = the man clothed in linen, or he of 8:2 (= the fiery human figure), in which case these verses take us back to the start of the vision, in order to follow the movements of the divine apparition. Vs. 4a repeats vs. 9:3a in different terms, but the concern here is with the locations of the cloud and the radiance accompanying the Majesty. It has been supposed (by Kaufmann, *Toldot* III, p. 490, fn. 15) that these verses intend to account for the visibility of the scene to the prophet; if that is so, the account is no longer intelligible.

5. The purpose of this verse is obscure. If the noise of the wings means that the cherubs are taking off, the notice comes too soon (cf. vs. 19). Is the allusion to the arrival of the cherubs—when and whence? The implication of the passage is that the external court was quite a distance from the southern part of the internal one; if the external court extended far to the north, that might well have been true of its northernmost limits.

6–7. "[The man clothed in linen] did not obey the order . . . but acted as one who feared entering a place too holy and sublime for him. He halted beside the wheel to see what would happen; the cherub then took some fire from among the cherubs and filled his hands with it" (Kimḥi). The detail into which the action is broken down in vs. 7 has a retarding effect heightened by the abrupt end of the scene. The vision does not include a vista of the burning city; cf. the unity of the scene in ch. 9, in which the divine agents do their work out of sight of the visionary.

8–17. Mention of the cherub's hand triggers a description of their entire appearance, starting from their hands and the wheels—the latter, as the locale of the previous action, being the initial focus of the prophet's gaze. Changes from the parallel passage 1:8–21 are noted below.

9. For the distributive force of the repetition cf. 1:23b.

11. *in which the head faced*. Perhaps this means that the human face gave orientation to the head, so that the head "faced" in the direction toward which the human face looked. If it is further assumed that the

human face of each cherub was the one that looked outward, in whatever direction the ensemble moved, they always were following the lead of one of the heads. (This supposes that each of the cherubs, like the creatures of ch. 1, had a human face; but see vs. 14.)

12. This verse resembles 1:18, which ascribes eyes to the wheels; it differs from it in including flesh, hands and wings—attributes more befitting the cherubs than the wheels! Rashi and Kimḥi applied all these terms to the wheels (Kimḥi gives "flesh" a mystic sense); D. J. Halperin (*VT* 26 [1976], 137) agrees, taking this verse as an early (post-Ezekiel) testimony of the conversion of the wheels into what was later a class of angels (*ofannim;* see G. F. Moore, *Judaism,* 3 vols. [Cambridge: Harvard University Press, 1927], I, p. 409). However, the wording (an admittedly shaky basis, in view of the divergences of G) separates "the wheels" from "their flesh," which evidently refers to the cherubs (though flesh is surprising in a cherub too; is that why G lacks it?). Taken so, the cherubs, unlike the creatures of ch. 1, will be studded all about with eyes—cf. some Egyptian Bes figures (apotropaic daemons) whose bodies are "superstrewn with *udjat*-eyes [eyes of Horus]" (H. Bonnet, *Reallexikon der ägyptischen Religionsgeschichte* [Berlin: W. de Gruyter & Co., 1971], p. 107—note esp. fig. 37, a multiheaded, four-winged figure).

13. *It was those wheels* (wᵉha'opannim) *I heard referred to as wheelwork* (galgal). The prophet identifies the wheels, called *'opannim* in his description (vss. 9–19), with the *galgal* he heard in the divine speech above, vss. 2, 6. *galgal* is used as a collective for chariot wheels (below, 23:24; 26:10; in Isa 28:28, of a sledge; cf. Ps 77:19) and in the plural with the same meaning (Isa 5:28; Jer 47:3). *'opan* is used similarly for chariot wheels (Exod 14:25; I Kings 7:33; Nahum 3:2; in Isa 28:27, of a sledge) and for the wheels of the laver-stand of the temple, which are explicitly compared to chariot wheels, I Kings 7:30–33. It is impossible to establish a semantic distinction between these words: both are equally appropriate for the divine vehicle. Our rendering, *galgal* by "wheelwork," reflects only its collective use here. (In Ps 83:14; Isa 17:13 *galgal* is some wheel-shaped plant, perhaps a thistle, blown by the wind.)

Since there is no reason for the visionary (or anyone else) to have invented the replacement of one term by another (since the two are identical in meaning), vs. 13 appears to be an authentic record of an experience: this is what the prophet heard.

14. The wording of this verse differs, perhaps significantly, from its parallel 1:10. (a) The plain sense of MT is that each cherub, or wheel (see below), had four of the same faces, but the form of the faces differed for each cherub. This diverges from 1:10, which gives each creature a set of four different faces. (b) Instead of a bull's face (1:10) a cherub's face appears; cf. the Akkadian "Vision of the Nether World" in which Namtartu "was provided with the head of a *kuribu* [a sphinxlike demon

cognate with cherub], her hands and her feet were human" (*ANET*³, p. 109c).

To harmonize our verse with 1:10, Kimḥi stretched the meaning of *pᵉne ha'eḥad* to "the aspect of one (face)" = "one face" (cf. S), with the result that each cherub had four different faces. Some modern commentators achieve the same result by eliminating *pᵉne*. As to the substitution of the cherub's face for that of the bull, the Talmud explains "Ezekiel prayed concerning the bull's face, and it was turned into that of a cherub; he said, 'Lord of the universe, how can an accuser [for the bull recalled the golden calf] be an intercessor [the function of these angelic creatures in rabbinic theology]!'" The Talmud distinguished the cherub's face from the human face—both of which belonged to these creatures—in that the former was small (wordplay, Aramaic *kᵉrabya* = "like a child"), the latter large (BT *Ḥagigah* 13b). A less fanciful explanation is suggested by the above-cited Akkadian passage, in which "the head of a *kuribu*" is evidently not human (though what exactly it is cannot be said). The alternative to these attempts at harmonizing 10:14 with 1:10 is to accept the discrepancy as an unexplained divergence from 1:10, or to apply our verse to the wheels—the immediate antecedent of "each," since according to MT of 1:15 they too had four faces (Eliezer of Beaugency, Halperin). The latter recourse, obviating the need to harmonize 10:14 with 1:10, is shaky in view of the allusion in vs. 21 below to "the four faces of the *cherubs*."

All vs. 14 is not in G. Does that mean that it was not in its *Vorlage*, or perhaps that it was, but the translators found it too hard to handle? Halperin regards the absence in G as a sign of the verse's lateness, according to his theory that MT here reflects the later tendency to transform the wheels into a category of angels.

15. An awkward anticipation of vss. 19a, 20a below; apparently fragments copied in at the wrong place.

18. After *wayyeṣe* "he came forth" one expects *min* "from" (as G) the house; MT *me'al* "from off" is naturally preceded by *wayyarom* "he rose" (as in 10:4). Is MT a fusion of a single-step departure of the Majesty from the temple (the basic text having been *wayyeṣe min*) with the depiction in 10:4 (9:3) of an exit in stages?

20. *I realized.* "'Since I heard them called cherubs [vss. 2, 6] I knew them to be cherubs'; similarly the prophet is careful to note how other parts of the vehicle were named in heaven [vs. 13]" (Kara). But perhaps the temple setting was what impressed the true identity of the creatures onto the prophet's consciousness. Why did Ezekiel not identify the creatures of the inaugural vision with cherubs at once? It must be borne in mind that Ezekiel is the only person who claims to have seen the heavenly cherubs; the only cherubs previously seen by humans were the statues in the inner sanctum, which were only approximations. That the ancients were aware of a gap between their iconography and the real appearance

of divinities is suggested by the Sumerian Gudea's ignorance of the glorious divine apparitions that came to him in his dream; a goddess identified them to him as Ningirsu—a common Sumerian god who surely was represented in art, and yet not so as to enable the visionary to identify his true apparition (for the Gudea text, see A. L. Oppenheim, *The Interpretation of Dreams in the Ancient Near East* [Philadelphia: American Philosophical Society, 1956], pp. 245f.).

21–22. What identified the cherubs with those creatures were these peculiar features: four faces, four wings (contrast the six wings of Isaiah's seraphs [Isa 6:2] and the single set of wings of the statue cherubs [I Kings 6:27]), hands under their wings, and their way of moving. Hence these features are repeated.

with the selfsame appearance. Lit. "their appearance and them [selves]." The wording is strange, but attested in the versions. (Cf. P. P. Saydon, "Meanings and Uses of the Particle *'t*," *VT* 14 [1964], 202f.)

(11:1–25)

11 1 A wind lifted me and brought me to the east gate of the house
of YHWH, which faces eastward. There at the entrance of the gate
were twenty-five men, and among them I saw Jaazaniah son of Azzur
and Pelatiah son of Benaiah, public officials. 2 He[a] said to me: Man,
these are the men who are planning trouble and hatching evil plots
in this city, 3 who think, "No need now to build houses; it is the pot
and we are the flesh." 4 So prophesy against them; prophesy, man!
5 The spirit of YHWH fell upon me, and he said to me: Say, thus
said YHWH: Yes that is what you are thinking, O house of Israel;
I know what has come into your minds! 6 You have piled up corpses
in this city and have filled its streets with slain. 7 So then, thus said
Lord YHWH: The corpses you have set in it—they are the flesh, for
which it is the pot; as for you—you [b]shall be led out[b] of it. 8 You
feared the sword, and I will bring the sword upon you, says Lord
YHWH. 9 I will lead you out of it and deliver you into the hands of
foreigners and execute judgments against you. 10 You shall fall by the
sword; I will judge you on the border of Israel, and you shall know
that I am YHWH. 11 Neither shall it be a pot for you nor you flesh
in it. I will judge you on the border of Israel, 12 and you shall know
that I am YHWH, whose laws you did not follow and whose judgments you did not execute, but you acted according to the judgments
of the nations around you!
13 As I was prophesying, Pelatiah son of Benaiah fell dead. I
threw myself on my face and cried out in a loud voice, saying,
"Alas, Lord YHWH, you are putting an end to the remnant of
Israel!"
14 The word of YHWH came to me: 15 Man! Your brothers, your
brothers, your [c]next of kin[c], and all of the house of Israel entire, of
whom the inhabitants of Jerusalem say, "Remove yourselves from
YHWH; the land has been given to us as a heritage!"—16 Assuredly,
say: Thus said Lord YHWH: Though I have removed them into the

[a] G S "the Lord."
[b–b] MT *hwṣy'* active infinitive construed as passive? (König, III, § 215 a); Hebrew editions, G S T "I will lead out" (*'wṣy'*).
[c–c] G S "fellow exiles" (as from *glwtk*).

midst of the nations and scattered them through the lands, and am but a small sanctuary for them in the lands into which they have come—17 Assuredly, say: Thus said Lord YHWH: I will gather you[d] from the peoples and collect you[d] out of the lands into which [e]you have been scattered[e], and I will give you[d] the soil of Israel. 18 When they arrive there, they will remove all its loathsome and abominable things from it. 19 I will give them a single[f] heart and put a new spirit into you[g]; I will remove the heart of stone from their flesh and give them a heart of flesh, 20 so that they follow my laws and carefully execute my judgments. They shall be my people and I will be their God. 21 But [h]those whose hearts go after their heart-of-loathsome[h]-and-abominable things—I will bring their conduct down on their heads, declares Lord YHWH.

22 Then the cherubs raised their wings, with the wheels alongside them and, above, the Majesty of the God of Israel upon them. 23 The Majesty of YHWH rose above the city and stopped on the mountain east of the city.

24 Then a wind lifted me and brought me to Chaldea, to the exiles, in vision by the spirit of God. The vision I had seen disappeared from my sight, 25 and I related to the exiles all the acts of YHWH which he had shown me.

[d] G "them."
[e–e] G "I scattered them."
[f] G "another," S "new"; T renders this and the next phrase with the same adjective (*dḥyl* "fearing") it uses in 18:31, 36:26, where both phrases have *ḥdš*.
[g] G S and Hebrew mss. "them."
[h–h] MT strained; read perhaps *w'lh bšqwṣyhm,* see comment.

COMMENT

11:1. The scene sufficiently resembles that of ch. 8 for Rashi, Kara, and Kimḥi to identify the twenty-five men here with those of 8:16. The named men are unknown, but their names recur in monarchy texts: Jaazaniah, II Kings 25:23; Jer 35:3; seals from seventh century B.C.E. (R. Hestrin, M. Mendeles, *Ḥotamot mime bayit rišon* [Jerusalem: Israel Museum, 1978], p. 19); Azzur, Jer 28:1; Pelatiah, I Chron 3:21; Neh 10:23; Benaiah, common throughout the monarchy.

2. *He said.* As repeatedly in 8:5–17 (9:1–9); hence the versional "the Lord" seems secondary.

3. *who think.* Taking *'amar* as think in the light of vs. 5b. Ezekiel else-

where also exposes the innermost thoughts of his audience (14:3; 20:32).

No need now. Lit. "not close." The translation of the first clause follows Fohrer, who explains: "For the time being the building of more houses seems unnecessary to the new rich [the second rank who moved up to fill the positions evacuated by the exiles with Jehoiachin], because they not only took over the property of the deportees (vss. 14–21), but appropriated the estates of the defenseless—their 'slain' (vs. 6)." An alternative is suggested by vs. 8, "You feared the sword": "No time now for building houses"—since all resources must go into fortifying the city in preparation for the planned rebellion; cf. the Isa 9:9 reference to demolition that accompanied preparation for war. Either interpretation fits the context better than the medieval view that gives *qarob* the sense it has in 7:7 and paraphrases: "The doom predicted by the prophets is not close at hand [cf. 12:22f.], so let us build houses and settle in them!" (Rashi, Kimḥi).

it is the pot. Cf. 24:3ff. where Jerusalem is figured as a pot being filled with the choicest morsels. Here the contents of the pot, the choice pieces, are equated by the speakers with themselves; to this God responds that in fact they are offal, to be cast out of the pot (vs. 7), while their victims are the choice morsels.

This seems to exhaust the meaning of the figure here. In ch. 24 it is given an ominous turn by including the fire beneath the pot; the charring of the contents of the pot and the incineration of its impurities serve as a parable of Jerusalem's destruction. Jer 1:13 uses the image of a steaming pot somewhat similarly, to represent a troubled country.

5. *The spirit of YHWH*. Preparing the prophet for the vision (so, too, in vs. 24). In early prophecy the spirit empowers one to prophesy (I Sam 10:6; I Kings 22:24; in pre-exilic classical prophecy, only Micah 3:8; later Isa 61:1; cf. Joel 3:1); it is said to "leap upon" (*ṣalaḥ* I Sam 10:6 [S. Lieberman, *JBL* 65 (1946), 67ff.]) a person—for which "fall" (*napal*) is here a pale variant. Or *napal 'al* "fall upon" may be equivalent to *haya 'al*—cf. 8:1 and comment thereupon; *haya* (*ru^{a}ḥ YHWH*) *'al* alternates with *ṣalaḥ* (I Sam 18:10 || 19:9). On the action of the spirit see the incisive distinctions made by Kaufmann, *Religion*, pp. 98–100.

6. The leaders are here specifically accused of bloodshed; so too 19:3, 6; 22:6, 25. Contemporary literature echoes the accusation: the kings Manasseh (II Kings 21:6; cf. Jer 2:30) and Jehoiakim (Jer 22:17; 26:20–24) are singled out for denunciation on this count. Lam 4:13 (on which see D. Hillers, AB) accuses prophets and priests of bloodshed. Few details are given; we can only surmise that under Manasseh the chief ground of oppression was religious, under Jehoiakim, political, and under Zedekiah, political and social.

7. By including the slain victims in the figure, the prophet skews it in the direction of Micah 3:3f.: "You have devoured my people's flesh; you

have flayed the skin off them, and their flesh off their bones. And breaking their bones to bits, you have cut it up as into a pot, like meat in a cauldron."

8. *You feared the sword.* Because of your bad conscience. Or, if vs. 3 alludes in its first part to preparations for war, that is alluded to here.

10–11. They will not be left in Jerusalem, their imagined bastion, but shall be led out far away from it, to the very border of Israel, where they shall be cut down by the strangers' (*zarim* as 7:21) sword. "The border of Israel" is at the utmost distance from the "pot" and expresses the extremity of the expulsion (vs. 7b) or the frustration of escape on the threshold of success (cf. Lam 1:3b: "all her pursuers overtook her between the boundaries [*mᵉṣarim* = T *tḥwmy'*; see B-Y, s.v. *"meṣar"*]). In the light of later events, this was taken by medieval commentators as a prediction of Nebuchadnezzar's punishment and execution of the royalty and nobility of Judah at Riblah in the land of Hamath (Jer 39:6f.), and as such, by moderns as "prophecy" on the basis of events (*vaticinium ex eventu*) penned by a later hand. But if the interpretation offered here is correct, this is not the case, although the wording of the original vague prophecy ("the border of Israel") lent itself readily to being taken later as an allusion to the Riblah executions. (On the relation of Riblah to Israel's border, see comment to 6:14.)

11. *Neither.* So those G mss. that contain our verse (Vaticanus omits it and 12a[a]—perhaps through homoioteleuton with vs. 10) and S V, making the negative at the beginning of the verse govern the second clause as well (Isa 38:18 is another example of this common phenomenon; GKC § 152 z; Joüon § 160 q; esp. R. Weiss, *Shnaton* 2 [1977], 82–92).

12. *whose laws.* Virtually identical with the end of 5:7, except for the absence here of the negative in the last clause (on which see the comment at 5:7). The two contexts have in common a clustering of derivatives of *špṭ* "judge" in a variety of senses (11:9–12 || 5:6–10). For the range of *mšpṭ* see comment at 5:6; the "judgments of the nations" are in fact their customs and manners, but the translation (wooden as it is) seeks to retain the connection between derivatives of *špṭ* here.

The recognition-clause ("you shall know that I am YHWH") has, as it occasionally does, an "afterwave" ("whose laws you did not follow . . ."; cf. 6:13, "when their corpses . . ."; 12:15, "when I scatter . . ."). But this one is unique in its reference to Israel's sin rather than to God's action, which will bring about recognition of his authority. This singular turnabout, emphasizing the ground of punishment rather than the punishment itself, inverts the order of the elements of 5:7–10 (where ground [vs. 7] precedes consequence) and thus calls attention to its echoing character.

13. We know no more about Pelatiah than we do about Jaazaniah of 8:11. Kara's supposition that his death was connected with the visionary slaughter by the executioners of 9:6f. is valid insofar as both occur in

vision and both inspire the prophet's intervention (9:8 and here), yet clearly they are separate episodes. Nothing suggests that there was more reality to Pelatiah's death than to the mass execution of ch. 9, yet several moderns distinguish between them, ascribing facticity to the former (e.g., Cooke, Carley). Stalker's sober judgment commends itself: "The death of Pelatiah is often taken as meaning that Ezekiel possessed powers of clairvoyance. This may be so, but on the other hand the incident is set in the context of a vision. Nor is it said that the death was the result of the prophet's words [against Kaufmann, *Religion,* p. 431]. It is much more naturally to be ascribed to the divine judgment [cf. Kara]. If Ezekiel had foreseen or foretold it, his reaction would not have been the dismay and horror that it was" (cf., also, Lindblom, *Prophecy,* p. 134). We cannot say why his death was so portentous. Was there something particularly ominous in the sudden death of one whose name meant "Yah delivers [a remnant], son of Yah builds up"? (Note the descending expectations.)

14. *your next of kin.* Lit. "your redemption-men," i.e., the kinsmen duty-bound to redeem you and your property if you are reduced to alienating them; Lev 25:25–55. The term fits the context in which rights in an inheritance are at issue. The threefold repetition of kinship expressions at the beginning of the statement, followed by the elaboration "all . . . Israel entire," underlines the extent of the diaspora, as if answering the prophet's concern (vs. 13) over Israel's extinction: the destruction of Jerusalem and Judah can hardly be complete when the diaspora is taken into consideration (Smend). "All the house of Israel entire" (recurs only in restoration prophecies 20:40; 36:10), as opposed to those in the homeland, must include all Israelites in exile, the northern deportees as well as the exiles of Judah. So Kimḥi interprets the opening threefold repetitions: "The Gadite and Reubenite [transjordanian] exile [I Chron 5:26, identified with the first exile mentioned in II Kings 15:29, in 732 B.C.E.], the exile of Samaria [II Kings 17:6, in 722], and the exile of Jehoiachin; then he recapitulates the three in 'all the house of Israel entire'" (cf. Rashi). *kullo* "all of it" (entire) echoes *kala* (vs. 13) "end, extinction" effecting a contrast between the two populations mentioned—the one destined to extinction, the other for a fate about to be described.

Remove yourselves from YHWH. Joined to the claim of exclusive possession of the land, the imperative carries a demand to renounce the privileges of YHWH worship; the issue recalls Josh 22:24–27 where territory and worship are combined. Here expulsion from YHWH's land is equated with a severance of ties with YHWH and hence of title to his land. By this reasoning, the homelanders claimed all the property left by the exiles.

While G reflects MT's vocalization, some medievals (Kara, Eliezer of Beaugency) take the verb as a past ("they have become alienated from YHWH"), which does read more smoothly.

The entire verse is an incomplete sentence (*casus pendens*), whose subject is taken up in the object pronouns of the following verse.

16. God has indeed driven them away, and his presence among the exiles is but a shadow of what it was formerly; again the sentence is incomplete and waits for its resolution in the next verses. Since the divine presence is fully manifest only in the Jerusalem sanctuary (cf. 37:26–28), the reduced presence among the exiles is boldly figured as "a small sanctuary": *m*ᵉ*'aṭ* is in apposition to *miqdaš,* as in *'ezer m*ᵉ*'aṭ* "little help" (Dan 11:34). In this statement of deprivation, it is obliquely conceded that the exiles enjoy a measure of divine nearness even in the exile (contrary to the Jerusalemites' view). Jewish interpreters turned the concessive clause in vs. 16b into a consoling asseveration: "Yet I have given them synagogues, second [in rank] to my sanctuary" (T); on the theory of the origin of the synagogue in the Babylonian exile, see I. Sonne, *IDB,* s.v. "Synagogue," and L. I. Rabinowitz, *EJ,* s.v. "Synagogue."

17. God's response to the Jerusalemites: not to them, but to the ingathered exiles will the land be given. The sudden change to object pronouns of the second person reflects awareness of the exile audience, the real addressees of the prophet (G remains with third person). It accords with the pattern of these formulaic clauses in 20:34, 41 and 36:24. Peculiar to this passage is "I will give you the soil of Israel"—pointedly contradicting the confident claim of the Jerusalemites.

18. The homelanders will perish, leaving their idols as evidence of their wickedness; it will fall to the ingathered exiles to purge the land of those abominations.

19–20. In turn, the ingathered will be purged by God (*hesiru* [vs. 18] || *h*ᵃ*siroti* [vs. 19]). Vss. 19–20 foreshadow the doctrine of the future compulsory obedience of the Israelites worked out later in 36:26–27 (whence the misfit "into you" of MT; cf. *Minḥat Shay*). Note how the terms used in God's foreclosure of future sinning echo those used above in vs. 12 to describe the sin.

a single heart. In Jer 32:39 "one heart" is complemented and explained by "one way"—singleness of mind and constancy of conduct. The contrasting expression is *b*ᵉ*leb waleb* (Ps 12:3) "with two hearts," i.e., insincerely (in I Chron 12:34 *b*ᵉ*lo leb waleb* || *b*ᵉ*lebab šalem* in vs. 39 ["wholeheartedly"]). This idiom is present in the prayer *yaḥḥed l*ᵉ*babi* (Ps 86:11) "let my heart be undivided," i.e., concentrate its affections (BDB) in the fear of you. Elsewhere, Ezekiel uses "new (*ḥdš*) heart" (18:31; 36:26). G renders all MT's *'eḥad* "one" here and in Jer 32:39 by *heteros* "another" as though from Hebrew *'aḥer* (though in I Sam 10:9 it renders *leb aḥer* by *allos!*); this is a possible Hebrew reading, but it lacks the rich overtones of the reading *'eḥad* as set out above. S goes in another direction, assimilating "one" here and in Jer 32 to "new" in Ezek 18 and 36, reading *ḥdt'* in all cases: this seems to be a deliberate attempt to assimilate all these closely allied passages. T assimilates the various terms in another way—see textual footnote.

21. The first half of the verse is hardly intelligible. The translation assumes the following line of thought: in contrast to the ingathered who will be given "one heart," the Jerusalemites have a divided heart, or "two" hearts, one of which is fixed on the abominations ("their heart-of-abominations"), the other, still free (and therefore responsible) which wickedly goes after that fixated one (but *halak 'el* does not otherwise mean "follow"). G reflects MT; S "But in thought of their idols and their abominations their hearts go" (no rendering of the initial *w*^{e}*'el*). The proposed emendation (see textual footnote [h–h]) yields: "But these, their hearts follow (*hlk b-* as in vss. 12, 20) their loathsome . . ." Smoother but farther from our text would be *wa'*^{a}*šer b*^{e}*šiqquṣehem . . . libbam holek* "But as for those whose hearts follow their loathsome . . ." In any case, *halak b*^{e}*huqqotay* "follow my laws" (vss. 12, 20) and *leb* (vs. 19) supplied the ingredients from which this contrasting image was fashioned; the present MT of vs. 21a cannot then be far from its original form.

22–23. The east gate of the temple where the cherubs had previously halted (10:19) was situated in a continuation of the city wall; hence soaring above it might be said to be soaring "over the city." The Majesty, leaving the city, takes the direction of King David's flight from Absalom —east to the Mount of Olives (II Sam 15:23ff.). It halts again on the mountain east of the city, as though loath to abandon the city altogether. A midrash ascribed to the third-century C.E. R. Johanan expresses this as follows: "For three and a half years the Presence [*hašš*^{e}*kina*] tarried on the Mount of Olives, proclaiming thrice daily, 'Return, wayward sons' (Jer 3:22). When it saw they would not repent, it flew away, saying, 'I will go back to my [heavenly] abode till they realize their guilt; in their distress they will seek me and beg for my favor'" (Hos 5:15) (*Pesikta de-Rav Kahana* 13.11; see Structure and Themes). Aside from its poignancy, this midrash has the merit of underlining the difference between the situation supposed in ch. 11 and what precedes it. Although chs. 9 – 10 tell of the city annihilated and razed, nothing in ch. 11 even hints at that; it is perfectly consistent with the picture of ch. 11 that God should wait for a change of heart in the city's inhabitants, and contradictory to all that we learn from chs. 9 – 10 (see Structure and Themes).

Fohrer's idea that the Majesty moved from the Mount of Olives to Babylonia to appear in the opening vision (ch. 1) goes beyond the text both here and there. The concluding stage of the Majesty's departure, as fancied by R. Johanan, was "my abode," namely, heaven; indeed it is from there (or from the north) that the apparition of ch. 1 appears—in any case, not from Jerusalem.

24. *disappeared from my sight.* Lit. "lifted up from me," as in Gen 17:22; 35:13 to mark the end of theophanies. The vision terminates only after the prophet is "back" in Chaldea, a clear indication that the entire trip is visionary.

STRUCTURE AND THEMES

The diverse material of chs. 8–11 is organized into a single visionary experience whose complexity indicates a considerable literary effort.

The opening and closing verses of the vision correspond, and form a frame for the whole:

(a) 8:1a date, location, audience of exile elders
(b) 8:1b God's hand falls upon the prophet (start of vision)
(c) 8:2–3 a luminous human figure seizes the prophet; a wind transports him to Jerusalem in vision
(c′) 11:22–24a the Majesty is borne off eastward; the wind transports the prophet back to Chaldea in vision
(b′) 11:24b the vision "lifts off" the prophet (ends)
(a′) 11:25 the prophet tells what he saw to the exiles

The double agency in (c)—the luminous figure (the Majesty) and the wind both involved in transporting the prophet—is confirmed in (c′) where both recur, each going its own way. A hint of the troublesomeness of the Majesty, as well as its integration in this vision, is thus given in the very framework.

In the course of the vision, the prophet is carried by a wind not only to and from Jerusalem (8:3b; 11:24), but within the temple precinct from the northern area where the first scene occurs to the east gate where the second takes place (11:1). This internal movement marks a major break in the continuity of the vision. The narrative elements grouped before it in the first scene (8:4–10:7) are—with the exceptions noted below—in an intelligible sequence; so too are those that follow in the second scene. But the latter scene itself seems out of sequence; after the general slaughter depicted in 9:6–8, how did twenty-five men come to be at the east gate of the temple?

Allusions to the divine Majesty and its bearers interrupt the flow of narrative in 8:2; 9:3 and 10:1, 3–5; the detailed description of the cherub vehicle in 10:8ff. supplants it entirely. The narrative is resumed in 10:18–19 with the flight of the cherubs, but halts again in vss. 20–22 for repeated assertions of the identity of the cherubs with the creatures of ch. 1. If up to 10:7 these allusions are disconnected, in 10:18–19 (linked to 9:3; 10:4) and 11:22–23, they cohere, being a description of the gradual departure of the Majesty from the doomed temple and city. Perplexing though they are, these allusions are too considerable a part of this vision to be disregarded in its interpretation; they are not merely an intrusive element.

But let us for the moment leave them aside and study the rest of the vision. It falls into two parts: A, 8:5–10:7: the abominations and their consequences; and B, 11:1–21: the cabal and related matters.

A in the main is reasonably well knit. It consists of 1, a climactic account of four (three plus one) abominations in the temple area (8:5–18), and 2, the slaughter of the sinners and the orders to burn the city (9:1–10:7). The particulars are in sequence; generally speaking, the prophet moves along a north-south axis. Many features link 1 and 2. Not only is the border between them marked by an echo (8:18's *qara b^{e}oznay qol gadol* in 9:1), but they share the expression of God's ruthlessness (8:18; 9:5, 10). The lawlessness mentioned in 8:17 at the end of 1 is enlarged upon in 9:9 at the end of 2. Indeed, 8:17, where "filling the land [n.b. the extension of the horizon beyond the temple area] with lawlessness" caps the cultic abomination, forms a bridge to 2, in which social wrongdoing prevails, the doomed include the entire population of the city, and their offense is both city- and country-wide. The saying of the lawless at the end of 2, "YHWH has left the land; YHWH does not see" (9:9), virtually repeats in inverted form what the idolatrous elders said in 8:12.

The effect of the appearance of the man clothed in linen to report on his action in 9:11 is to suggest an unseen periphery to this vision, in which crucial events are occurring. Unity of place is thus preserved, owing to which the massacre of the city's inhabitants is not described.

The order to burn the city (10:2) is linked to what precedes through the man clothed in linen. It is linked to the Majesty and the cherubs through the fiery coals drawn from among the cherubs. The theme of burning is abruptly broken off with the man's departure, nothing being said of how the order was executed. This has been needlessly thought to indicate that the original continuation has been lost; it may in fact be due to the desire to maintain unity of place throughout the vision. Notice of the cherub's handing over the fire to the man clothed in linen provides the point of linkage to the following long description of the cherub vehicle, which begins with the cherubs' hands (10:8).

B, 11:1–21, consists of 1, a scene of the cabal at the east gate (vss. 1–13) and 2, an assurance to the exiles that they will be restored to their land (14–21). At first glance 2 seems unrelated to 1. (However the revelation formula in vs. 14 is no proof of that; cf. 21:5 where similarly God's response to a protest starting "Alas, Lord YHWH" begins with the formula.) On reflection, it appears that in fact 2 serves as a reply to the prophet's cry, "Alas Lord YHWH are you putting an end to the remnant of Israel" with which 1 ends (vs. 13). The exiles, says 2, shall be spared and regathered to their land; only the Jerusalemites (Judahites) will be annihilated. It is true that the responsive character of 2 is not explicit, and thus its relation to 1 less organic than that of A2 (punishment) to A1 (sin). Indeed it is likely that originally independent entities have been juxtaposed in B in accord with the pattern of A. In both A and B the prophet is first shown wickedness, followed by punishment of death; he expostulates and receives a reply—in A, a justification of the punishment, in B an assurance of survivors (a happy ending to a dreadful vision). B appears to be a construct based on A with the aim of setting forth civil aspects of Jerusalem's guilt.

Other features promoted the connection of the two parts of B. Both open with a self-serving assertion of the Jerusalemites (vss. 3, 15b), followed by a command to prophesy God's angry reply. There is, moreover, a noteworthy assonance of *(h)syr . . . bśr* in vss. 3, 7, 11 (of 1) with *hsyr . . . bśr* in vss. 18f. (of 2).

As noted above, B1 seems out of sequence; the general slaughter and burning reported in A2 hardly leaves room for a cabal of twenty-five men at the east gate of the temple. One might suppose that, in a vision, temporal sequence need not be observed. But other features of B mark it as an echo or an inverted correspondent rather than a sequel to A. (To be sure, B1's location at the east gate links it to the eastward movement of the Majesty in 10:19 [A2], but that is a merely external connection; it facilitated the juncture of B to A, if it was not made for it.) Only here and in 8:16 (A1) are groups of "[about] twenty-five men." In 11:6 *milletem ḥuṣoteha ḥalal* "you have filled its streets with slain" evokes *maleʾu haḥaṣerot ḥalalim* "fill the courts with corpses" of 9:7. The accusation in B1 is virtually identical with the ground given for God's irrevocable decree in 9:9 (A2)—bloodshed and perversion of justice. Even more noteworthy are the connections between B2 and A1—the two extremes of the vision. Both refer to the abominable and loathsome practices of the Jerusalemites (*toʿebot, šeqeṣ/šiqquṣim*). The ambiguous *leroḥoqa meʿal miqdaši* (8:6) has an echo divided among 11:14–15: *raḥaqu meʿal YHWH* and *miqdaš meʿaṭ;* these expressions illuminate one another. In the opening scene God charges the Jerusalemites with being removed (alienated) from his sanctuary. It is therefore ironic that in the closing scene Jerusalemites should taunt the exiles with being removed from YHWH, and more so that God asserts he is a "small sanctuary" for the exiles while the Jerusalemites (amidst whom the sanctuary building stands) are destined for destruction. B2 thus exhibits that resumption of opening themes or language which is characteristic in Ezekiel of closing passages. Whether its message of consolation is not out of place in a doom vision has been asked (but cf. chs. 14, 16, 17 and 20, each with some variety of consolation after dooms); due weight must be given, however, to the incidental nature of the consolation: what consoles the exiles is the prediction of Jerusalem's destruction. Whether this would have been regarded by the audience as a happy ending is itself a question.

The following overall pattern of thematic alternation appears in this vision:

A1 cultic abominations, capped by social wrongdoing
A2 punishment grounded on social wrongdoing
B1 a cabal charged with social wrongdoing
B2 preferment of exiles over Jerusalemites sunk in cultic abominations

Such chiastic alternation, foreshadowed within A1, suggests a deliberate design.

Between parts A and B, that is, in center position, appears the description of the cherub vehicle, onto which the Majesty mounts when it exits from the temple.

The Majesty and its cherub vehicle have a prominent but not always clear role in this vision. From 10:18 on, the sequence is clear: the Majesty moves off the threshold of the house onto the cherubs; these take off, pausing at the east gate (vs. 19), then bear the Majesty away from the city to the Mount of Olives (11:22f.). Thus the Majesty exits eastward in stages from temple and city.

Going backward from 10:18, through the description (vss. 8–17), we arrive at the obscure 10:1, 3–5. The cherubs are located to the right (south) of the house while the Majesty is on the threshold. Ch. 10:4a repeats the movement of the Majesty off the cherub (singular) to the threshold already related in 9:3a (there the terms are *na'ᵃla, 'ᵉlohe yiśra'el,* here *wayyarom, YHWH*). The hardest passage is 9:3a where suddenly and in no context "the cherub [singular] on which [the Majesty] had been" is introduced only to say that the Majesty left it for the threshold. Where was this cherub and what was the Majesty's relation to it up to now? Why did it move off it to the threshold?

Let us trace the allusions to the Majesty and cherub(s) from the start of the vision. The brilliant human figure in 8:2—evidently the Majesty—is not expressly located (note that not it but the wind carries the prophet to and from Jerusalem), but it is plausible to say that it was in Babylonia. If it is identified with the Majesty (*kᵉbod 'elohe yiśra'el*) waiting for the prophet somewhere in the temple area (vaguely "there") in vs. 4, a certain leap must be postulated—tolerable perhaps in a vision—to bring the Majesty from Babylonia to Jerusalem. Are the bearers of the Majesty present in either verse? The language of 8:2 seems to exclude them; the phrase of 8:4 ("the Majesty of the God of Israel") may (so in 1:28 and perhaps 3:23—see comments there) or may not.

Is the Majesty of ch. 8 inside the sanctuary or outside; does it move about with the prophet? "There" in 8:4 is too vague for defining where the Majesty was when Ezekiel arrived at the temple. That it is the subject of "he said to me" and "he brought me" in the following narrative does not prove it to be outside, since in 43:7; 44:2 the Majesty speaks from inside the visionary temple of the future to the prophet. In 40:1–3 God "brings" the prophet in vision to "a high mountain" without actually accompanying him (throughout the book, God "brings" objects everywhere without being "there" himself).

If we suppose the Majesty of ch. 8 to be outside the sanctuary and to include its bearers, the presence and exterior location of the cherubs in 10:1, 3, 18, etc., is accounted for. On the other hand, the subsequent movements of the Majesty off the cherub onto the threshold and back again onto the cherubs (9:3a [10:4a]; 10:18) will be inane. If, on the contrary, we suppose that the Majesty of ch. 8 is inside the sanctuary, the external cherubs of 10:3, etc., are not accounted for, but the movement of 9:3a outward to the threshold (for so it will then be) will be of a piece with its continuation in 10:18, and have significance: the divine presence is departing from the temple. The cherub (singular) from which the Majesty moved to the threshold (9:3a [10:4a]) will be the statuary in the holy of holies "where [the Majesty] had been" ever since the temple was inaugurated (cf. I Kings 8:10f. and Weinfeld, *Deuteronomy,* pp. 204f.).

Neither supposition, then, accommodates all the data or resolves the ambiguities. Is the text, therefore, to be judged in disarray, the result of inorganic layering? Some disarray must be allowed, especially in ch. 10; but the allusions to the Majesty and its bearers are too rooted in the vision to be explained away. If they are excised, much that does make sense is lost (e.g., the counterpoint between God's departure and human "removal" from the sanctuary [or from him] referred to in 8:6 and 11:15).

The difficulty seems related to the paradoxical notion shared by all ancient religions that the deity is at once localized in its temple and "in heaven" (or ubiquitous). The image in the pagan temple is literally the seat and residence of the deity; through their images, Marduk dwells in his temple in Babylon and Sin in Haran. Analogously, the cherub statues in Jerusalem's holy of holies (like their antecedents in the tabernacle) were the throne on which YHWH sat, shrouded in darkness. At the same time the pagan god dwells in heaven or on the mountain of the gods (the two may not be sharply differentiated), and moves freely about the universe. (For the paradoxical notions concerning the ancient Near Eastern gods, see "The Significance of the Temple in the Ancient Near East," *Biblical Archaeologist Reader* I, ed. G. E. Wright and D. N. Freedman [Garden City, N.Y.: Doubleday & Company, 1961], pp. 152–54, 159, 164, 169–71.) Similarly YHWH dwells in heaven, his majesty covers the heavens and fills the earth, and he rides the clouds or a cherub on his travels. M. Haran puts it well:

> We must emphasize the fact that although the cherubs of the ark-cover and the ark symbolize a throne and a footstool respectively, the Bible *does not* bind the deity to them or for a moment suppose that he is located (as it were) only there . . . God's chief place is conceived to be in heaven and there too is the place of his throne. His heavenly throne is supported by living cherubs; as a reflection of those heavenly cherubs the Israelites fashion cherub statues in the holy of holies of the tabernacle. The throne behind its curtain is only a miniature and a replica of the celestial throne: the heavenly cherubs are "living creatures" as Ezekiel calls them . . . real creatures who have will; the cherubs on the ark are metal figures. The heavenly cherubs are huge, those of P occupy a space on the two ends of a plate two-and-a-half cubits square. Yet P's metal cherubs serve also as a seat—God appears upon them and talks from between them to Moses

(Exod 25:22); upon them he manifests himself in a cloud (Lev 16:2) ("Ark and Cherubs" [Hebrew], *Eretz Israel* 5 [1958], 88f.; cf. his *Temples and Temple Service in Ancient Israel* [Oxford: Clarendon Press, 1978], pp. 256ff.).

(See also M. Metzger, "Himmlische und irdische Wohnstatt Jahwes," *Ugarit-Forschungen* 2 [1970], 139–58.) All this applies equally to the cherubs of the Jerusalem temple; in its light, the contradictions of our vision, while not resolved, are at least understandable.

The luminous figure—the Majesty—appears at the start of the vision, not because otherwise the prophet cannot be transported (for it is the wind that actually bears him to and fro), but to focus attention on its presence: this vision will convey something about the Majesty. When the prophet arrives at the temple area, "the Majesty of the God of Israel" is "there" waiting for him; it is free to appear anywhere at any time. The narrative has to establish its presence in the temple area; whether with or without its bearers, inside the temple or outside, are matters of no consequence and so not noted. Only the 9:3 notice of the movement of the Majesty off the cherub forces upon us the awareness that it had previously been located on it; and since the only meaningful direction of motion to the threshold is from inside outward, we gather that the cherub here refers to the statuary in the inner sanctum, and the Majesty—to the permanent divine presence within it. This outward movement occurs just before the order to slay the population of Jerusalem is given, suggesting that it signals God's withdrawal of his protecting presence from the city.

Next, just before the order to burn the city is given, mention is made of the (apparently empty) throne above the cherubs (10:1); this awkwardly placed notice seems to anticipate and be related to the departure of the Majesty from the threshold and its alighting upon the cherubs in vs. 18. If so, these cherubs must be outside the temple; these must be real celestial cherubs (among which alone fiery coals [vs. 2] are to be found), and indeed 10:3 expressly places them to the south (away from the abomination-side) of the temple. How and when they came to be in the court south of the temple is less important to the narrator than following the movements of the cloud that screened the Majesty (in an obscure passage, 10:3b–4, in part related to I Kings 8:10f.). However 10:5 gains some point if the noise of the cherubs' wings alludes to their arrival in flight on the scene coincidentally with the movement of the Majesty to the threshold, mentioned in vs. 4; as the inner Majesty began its departure, the celestial throne vehicle of the real cherubs arrived to receive it.

The vision's unity of location dictated that the theme of the burning of the city be broken off with the exit of the man dressed in linen to execute his orders (vs. 7). A detailed description of the cherubs follows, beginning (vs. 8) with their just-mentioned hands (vs. 7), and ending with their movement in unison—to which the account of their taking off is juxtaposed (vss. 17–19). The placement of this static interruption of the flow of events is at a juncture—the incendiary has gone off to his terrible business; the Majesty must now start on the next stage of its departure; there is a breathing-space in which to focus on the cherubs—objects of intense interest to the priest-prophet. The structure of their description must now be examined.

The items of this description are similar to but not identical with those of the creatures of ch. 1; the similarity increases when the isolated notices of 8:2, 10:1, 5 are taken into account. The reference to ch. 1 is underlined by inverse order of the items listed in our vision—excepting the hands and the motion in unison whose location here is determined by their links with the adjacent narrative.

	our vision	*verse in ch. 1*
8:2	luminous human figure	27
10:1	throne	26
10:5	sound of wings	24
(10:8	hands	8)
10:9–13	wheels	15–18
10:14	faces	10
(10:16–17	motion in unison	19–21)

The use of inversion to signal literary reference was observed by M. Seidel: "When the prophet uses the language of some verse he has in mind, he reverses the order of its elements . . . This always occurs in verses consisting of bicola, with a verb in each colon, when the same verbs recur in the parallel verse" ("Parallels Between the Book of Isaiah and the Book of Psalms" [Hebrew], *Sinai* 38 [1956], 150). This usage was further elaborated by R. Weiss, who adduced these examples from within Ezekiel: 8:12; 9:9; 11:3, 7, 11 ("On Chiasm in the Bible" [Hebrew], *Beth Mikra* 7 [1962], 46ff.); but neither Seidel nor Weiss alludes to this striking example—which was observed by Abarbanel.

The reason for the detailed description, so far as is hinted in the text, is the realization expressed in 10:20, when the prophet saw the entire apparatus rise in flight: "They were the creatures I saw beneath the God of Israel at the Chebar canal; I now realized they were cherubs." The creatures at Chebar were so different from the traditional portrayal of cherubs—viz. from the cherub statues in the temple—that the prophet could not at that time identify them; hence the use of the neutral *ḥayyot* "living beings" throughout ch. 1. (For one thing, the statues were two, the creatures four.) In the temple vision, the bearers of the Majesty appeared again, this time in propinquity to the cherub statues. For the three-way identification the prophet repeats the gist of the description in ch. 1, replacing *ḥayyot* by *k*ᵉ*rubim;* at the sight of the apparatus in flight—the very circumstance in which he first beheld it—he notes his realization of its identity. (The artificial distinction between the singular "cherub" for the statues [9:3; 10:4] and plural "cherubs" for the real ones [on *k*ᵉ*rub* in 10:2, see comments] may be due to the difference in their number; singular is a pair [statues], plural is two pair [real].)

The marked disorder in the gender of pronominal elements referring to the *ḥayyot* gives way to regularity in the case of the cherubs, for unlike the former, the grammatical and real gender of the latter agree. That differences exist between the two descriptions is probably essential to the repetition: the use in 10 of *rum* (qal and nif'al) for *hinnaśe* "rise" of ch. 1 may be deliberate variation, common in Ezekiel's repetitions (cf. 9:3a with 10:4a); the face of a cherub replacing that of a bull perhaps, the reference to the wheels as *galgal* certainly, offers new facts. If there are other substantial changes (see comments to vss. 12, 14), the repetition of the entire description is easier to account for; that of ch. 10 will be the record of a variation in detail on the experience of ch. 1, conditioned by the "natural" setting of the vehicle on the temple grounds and the greater ease and leisure of the prophet to observe, distinguished from it in terminology, despite its essential identity. Most recent critics regard the description of ch. 10 as secondary, some conjecturing a tendentious reason for it (Halperin—see reference in comment to vs. 12; Houk, *JBL* 90 [1971], 42–54, includes the description in the supposed reworking of the entire chapter from a purification to a punishment scene). This touches on a larger issue concerning the interpretation of the entire vision.

Complex, in some parts disjointed and not sequential, the vision is treated by recent commentators either as a patchwork of additions laid upon an original kernel, or as a compilation of separate entities. Fohrer finds four pieces (temple abominations, burning and abandonment, evil leaders, promise to exiles); the description of the cherubs is an "elaborating gloss to 1:1–28a." Zimmerli retains an essence of 8:1–10:7; the allusions to the cherubs are secondary (through the Majesty's coming in full panoply to Jerusalem as it came to Babylon in ch. 1, Ezekiel's "school" rationalized the paradox of its being in Jerusalem as well as in heaven); so too is all of 11:1–21. Such analyses aim at "restoring" a form of text free of the tensions of the present one; their diversity—reflecting different tolerances of tension—does not inspire confidence in the criteria underlying them.

The working assumption underlying our attempt to interpret the text without eliminating the tensions is that the present composition is an intentional product. That assumption has to an extent been justified by the evidences of design and interconnection of parts that have been found (cf. the schematic description of this vision, stressing [without much interpreting] chiastic features, by H. Parunak in *JBL* 99 [1980], 66–69). Enough tensions remain to render plausible the guess that not all the elements of this vision were from the first united (e.g., one might conjecture that the evil cabal at the start of ch. 11 belonged to a different, parallel vision). But they have been put together with some art; he who did so must be supposed to have recognized the incompatibility of those elements upon which the modern critic bases his analysis, yet what was conveyed by the composition as a whole overrode considerations of consistency and total coherence. Since this is a report of a visionary, not a real, experience, perhaps a bit of incoherence was not felt as a fatal objection to the combination of these parts.

What is the message conveyed by this complex vision?

After receiving the announcement of "the end" in ch. 7, due to the social and religious wrongdoing of the people, and with occasional echoes of the Flood story ("the end is coming," "the land is filled . . . with lawlessness" vss. 6, 23; cf. Gen 6:13), the prophet is made witness in a vision to the corrupt practices of the Judahites (described again in Flood story terms, 8:17; 9:9) and is shown their destruction (with *šḥt* used in 9:1, 6, 8; cf. Gen 6:13, 17). In earlier prophecy, visions occur (e.g., I Kings 22:17–22; Amos 7:1–9; 8:13; 9:1; Isa 6) and at least in the case of Elijah, transportation by the wind (I Kings 18:12; II Kings 2:1ff., 16); Ezekiel is the only prophet to have experienced visionary transportation, here and twice again (chs. 37, 43). Eye-witnessing, so agreeable to the vivid realism of this prophet's imagery, here serves theodicy: the prophet sees with his own eyes the depravity of the people and hears judgment pronounced with the culprits in his presence (Parunak sees certain analogies to the "prophetic *rîb* pattern").

The motive of the two constitutive elements of the vision is provided by the repeated, twofold assertion of the culprits, "YHWH does not see us; YHWH has left the land" (8:12; 9:9). By way of confuting the first part, God takes the prophet on a tour of the temple area, showing him the various abominations practiced there, and checking on the prophet's observation by asking him at each site, "Do you see, man?" The prophet knows that God has seen all, including the clandestine rites of the elders who believe him blind to them. As for the second part of their assertion, it turns out to be ironically prophetic: God had in fact not left the land when the people believed he had, but now their behavior brought it about; the prophet witnesses the divine presence departing from temple and city. This is the first example in the book of oracles built upon, perhaps occasioned by, sayings of the people that had reached the prophet. The second part of our passage consists primarily of oracular responses to two popular sayings (11:3, 15); see M. Greenberg, *Beth Mikra* 50 (5732/1972), 273–78.

No temple was destroyed—so was the common belief in the ancient Near East—unless its god had abandoned it, whether reluctantly under coercion of a higher decree ("Lamentation over the destruction of Ur," *ANET*[3], pp. 455ff., ". . . over the destruction of Ur and Sumer," p. 617d), or in anger because of the offenses of the worshipers (the Cyrus inscription, *ANET*[3], p. 315c). The mother of Nabonidus accounts for the desolation of Haran and its temple by the Manda-hordes (*ANET*[3], p. 311b) thus: ". . . Sin, the king of all gods, became angry with his city and his temple, and went up to heaven, and the city and the people in it became desolate" (*ANET*[3], p. 560d). In our vision, this commonplace is expressed by the interwining of the stages of the Majesty's departure with scenes of the people's wrongdoing. When, on the other hand, the gods were reconciled and their temples rebuilt, they returned and took up their abode among their worshipers again (see the above-cited texts). Accordingly when the prophet is shown a vision of the future rebuilt temple, he sees also the return of the Majesty to the holy of holies, expressly corresponding to our vision of its departure (43:2–4).

The midrash perceived the gradual nature of God's exit from temple and city in this vision as bespeaking his patient hope that the disaster might be avoided. It augments the few stages of our text into ten by a mosaic of other prophetic passages, and draws out the last stage for years: (1) from one of the Ark cherubs to the other (Ezek 9:3, hence the singular "cherub"); (2) from that to the temple's threshold (10:4); (3) from there to the cherubs (vs. 18); (4) from there to the east gate (vs. 19); (5) thence to the court (vs. 4[!]); (6) thence to the altar (Amos 9:1); (7) thence to the roof (of the temple, Prov 21:9[!]); (8) thence to the (temple) wall (Amos 7:7); (9) thence to the city (Micah 6:9[!]); (10) thence to the Mount of Olives (Ezek 11:23). R. Jonathan said: "For three and a half years the Presence tarried on the Mount of Olives, proclaiming thrice daily, 'Return, wayward sons' (Jer 3:22). Seeing they would not repent, it flew away, saying, 'I will go back to my [heavenly] abode till they realize their guilt; in their distress they will seek me and beg for my favor'" (Hos 5:15) (*Pesikta de-Rav Kahana* 13.11). Note the accord between the last sentence and the citation from the mother of Nabonidus adduced above.

The prophet is guided through the northern area of the temple from one cultic abomination to the next. The stress on north (8:3, 5 [twice], 14) may have a symbolic meaning: we recall the Ugaritic notion that the seat of the gods was in the north. The coming of the executioners from the north may be connected with the location of the temple sins there, or is it also a reflection of the common notion (Jer 1:14, etc.) that misfortune comes from the north (see Sarna, *EM*, s.v. "*ṣpwn*")? The concentration of pagan rites and their simultaneous performance by groups oblivious of each other lends a certain unreality to the scene. It appears as a montage of whatever pagan rites ever were conducted at the Jerusalem temple rather than a representation of what occurred there in the summer of the sixth year of Jehoiachin's exile. (T. H. Gaster, with bold invention, reconstructed an elaborate pagan harvest rite out of elements in chs. 7–9 ["Ezekiel and the Mysteries," *JBL* 60 (1941), 289–310, summarized in his *Myth, Legend, and Custom in the Old Testament*, pp. 607–15; Albright, *Archaeology and the Religion of Israel* (Baltimore: Johns Hopkins Press, 1946), pp. 165–68, largely rejected Gaster's suggestions]). The data of ch. 8 are generally thought to give a true picture of the state of Judahite religion contemporary with Ezekiel, but their contrast with the data of Jeremiah and Lamentations, whose authors were actually in Jerusalem at the time of the fall, points to an opposite conclusion. Only a visionary and an audience at a remove from the reality of Jerusalem, and suffering the exile threatened for breach of covenant might have accepted and understood at once the point of such a fantasy: to collect and display vividly the notorious instances of cultic pollution of the sanctuary, so as to bring home the awful realization that its sanctity had been hopelessly injured, and its doom irrevocably sealed. The public pagan rites of ch. 8 belong historically to the age of Manasseh; the secret cults of vss. 10–12 are another story and may have been practiced in Ezekiel's time (Greenberg, "Prolegomenon," pp. xviii–xxix; cf. the critique of M. Smith in *ZAW* 87 [1975], 11–16). A certain veracity is given to the account by the naming of Jaazaniah—evidently a prominent man of the times; report of his practice might have reached Ezekiel through letter—a form of communication between Judah and the exiles testified to by Jer 29.

While the pagan rites are never referred to again, the social wrongs denounced here—especially in 11:2–8—recur in the parable of Judah's rapacious kings (ch. 19) and the scathing rebuke of its evil leaders in ch. 22. Both Jeremiah and Lamentations give concurring testimony: the former blames Jehoiakim for having spilled innocent blood and pursuing illegal gain (Jer 22:17; cf. 2:34); the latter denounce priest and prophet for having shed innocent blood (Lam 4:13). The Book of Kings says nothing of the kind about the last kings of Judah; however, since it does not allude as a rule to social wrongs (Manasseh's "filling Jerusalem with innocent blood from one end to the other" [II Kings 21:16] is a notable exception), its silence is inconclusive. The sociopolitical turmoil of Judah's last years is likely to have generated violence; the notorious case of the royal murder of the prophet Uriah (Jer 26:20f.) may have sufficed for the blanket accusation of Jer 2:30. We do not have the data to say what the state of civic morality was in Judah at this time, and whether the biblical accusations are sober or exaggerated for the sake of theodicy.

Six years before the fall of Jerusalem, the prophet wrote the city off—he "saw" its population massacred and its buildings condemned to flames. Some years after the fall, with the same assurance, he saw a vision of his nation's resurrection and the restoration of its temple (chs. 37, 40ff.). Prophetic vision represented future events as accomplished; when they occurred, they appeared as but the fulfilment of prophecy—the effect intended (2:5). God's management of history was thus demonstrated.

The visionary destruction is a glimpse, rare in prophecy, of the "upper story" of events (cf., e.g., I Kings 22:19–23). Human agents would eventually execute judgment on Jerusalem and Judah, but they would only be translating a prior heavenly reality into an earthly one. Basically, the enemy was God; the Babylonian army was but a later projection of his celestial executioners. The latter, incidentally, further enhance Ezekiel's picture of the divine realm as containing a variety of supramundane beings.

This anticipation in vision of the destruction of Jerusalem had an afterlife. Lam 4:6 avers that Sodom's destruction at the hand of God was preferable to Jerusalem's at the hand of men; Sodom was spared vengeance, rapine and pillage, and the humiliation of being vaunted over by a conqueror. From that standpoint, the visionary destruction depicted here, of a temple and a city forsaken by their God, snatches triumph away from the Babylonians. This is spelled out in postbiblical literature. According to the Apocalypse of Baruch (II [Syriac] Baruch), the invading Babylonians were preceded by angels who destroyed Jerusalem's walls and temple "lest the enemy should boast and say, 'We have overthrown the wall of Zion, and we have burnt the place of the mighty God' . . . . A voice was heard from the interior of the temple, after the wall had fallen, saying: 'Enter ye enemies and come ye adversaries; for he who kept the house has forsaken it'" (chs. 6–8). The midrashic version conditions Jerusalem's fall upon the (unbiblical) departure of its resident prophet: "As soon as Jeremiah left Jerusalem, an angel descended from heaven and, placing his feet on Jerusalem's walls, breached them. He cried, 'Let the foes come and enter a house whose owner has abandoned it . . . a vineyard . . . whose watchman has deserted it—so you may not boast and say that you conquered it! A conquered city you have conquered, a slain people you have slain'" (*Pesikta Rabbati* 26 [ed. Buber, p. 131]).

As he beholds the sentence of death being executed in this vision, the prophet twice cries out on behalf of the condemned people (9:8; 11:13). These are the only instances of Ezekiel's attempt to intercede for his people, and they may have to do with his (visionary) presence amidst the slain. The otherwise striking omission of intercession from the book is perhaps connected with its unconditional message of doom; compare how God repeatedly thwarts Jeremiah's attempts at intercession (Jer 7:16; 14:7–15:4; on the prophetic duty of intercession, see the insightful studies of Y. Muffs: "Tefillatam šel nevi'im," *Molad* 35/36 [5735/1975], 204–10; and "Reflections on Prophetic Prayer in the Bible" [Hebrew], *Eretz Israel* 14 [1978], 48–54).

The Jerusalemites' arrogation to themselves of all the exiles' property (11:14f.) on the ground that the latter had been removed from YHWH belongs to this vision as another aspect of the central issue of YHWH's nearness and distance. It appears that after the deportation of King Jehoiachin and Judah's aristocracy, a question arose as to their rights in the land and in YHWH (the interconnection of these two comes out in the incident recorded in Josh 22). Only the homelanders could carry on the traditional temple worship of YHWH, just as only they actually possessed the land. A claim followed that they alone constituted henceforth "the people of YHWH" and the heirs to the covenant promises. To the general claim, Jer 24 addresses itself: the homelanders are likened to a basket of bad figs, destined for destruction; the exiles are good figs, destined for replanting in the land. They shall be given a heart to know YHWH, and through them the ideal relationship with him will be reestablished: "They shall be my people and I will be their God."

Ezekiel addresses himself to the specific claim. God's answer to the Jerusalemites' exclusive claim to the land is that though his presence is diminished among the exiles ("a small sanctuary [= sanctity]"), yet it is they who will return and purge the land of the abominations set up in it by its present, doomed occupants. Afterward, they will be given a new heart, and in consequence of their obedience "they shall be my people and I will be their God" (on this expression, see section XII, Structure and Themes, end).

Doubts have been raised about the location of this passage; its message of consolation is deemed out of place, and its similarity to post-fall oracles—33:23–29; 36:24–28—is remarked. Now it is true that in the former oracle the Jerusalemite claim is adverted to after the fall, but the circumstances of our passage differ from those of 33:23ff. Here the claimants are "the inhabitants of Jerusalem," there they are "the inhabitants of these ruins . . . those who are in the open country . . . in fastnesses and caves"; this passage is from before the fall, that one from after it. Furthermore, here the claimants haughtily thrust the exiles away from YHWH, while there they pathetically base their claim on their being more than one—more than Abraham, who, though alone, yet inherited the land. The argument bespeaks the small number of claimants, the decimated remnant of post-fall Judah; our passage, on the other hand, reflects the time before Jerusalem's plight.

There is indeed an element of consolation in the divine answer, but its main burden is the rejection of the Jerusalemites' claim. Promise of restoration is necessary to show that the present homelanders will be supplanted; promise of the new heart is incidental to the angry assertion that the returnees will remove the abominations left behind by the doomed present occupants. Jer 24 shows that a consolatory message to the exiles might attach itself to a condemnation of the Judahites well before the fall; its thematic identity with our passage (preference of the exiles, their restoration and change of heart, "I their God, they my people") adds to its evidential value. Particularly telling is the embryonic state of the "new heart" doctrine here and in Jer 24, as contrasted with its developed form in the later prophecies of Jer 31 and Ezek 36.

All this is not to say that vss. 14–21 are integral to the vision; they appear, on the contrary, to have been an originally independent oracle. But the oracle has been integrated into the vision, and its dating to before the fall is defensible, even likely.

These four chapters offer a panorama of the crimes of the Jerusalemites and the divine intervention to punish them, featuring the two planes of events, the awful preview of the execution of God's wrath prior to his abandoning temple and city, and, finally, the rejection of the Jerusalemites' claims to the land in favor of the exiles. In course, three popular sayings are exposed as wrath-provoking delusions. The various materials that have been fitted into the framework of the vision have been so disposed that the statement of the main theme (sin and punishment) is followed by an echo (not necessarily sequential or contemporaneous) analogous in structure and content. An auxiliary theme, the Majesty's abandonment of the temple, runs through the whole from beginning to end yet concentrating in the center of the panorama. Material within the vision as well as its narrative framework is arranged in successive "envelopes" so that first corresponds to last, second to next-to-last, and so forth. An integrating design is clearly evidenced.

Note on the afterlife of the divine chariot (*merkaba*)

The description of the Majesty enthroned upon its bearers, here and in ch. 1, had extensive repercussions in later literature. The Chronicler's calling the cherub statues of Solomon's temple "the likeness of the chariot" (*tabnit hammerkaba,* I Chron 28:18) is probably based on these passages, since nowhere else can an association of the statues with the wheeled-throne bearers (= a form of chariot) be found. The term *merkaba* served thereafter to designate the God-bearing creatures. Ben Sira (early second century B.C.E.) writes: "Ezekiel saw a vision (*mr'h*) and described (*wygd*) the species [or: details] of [the] chariot [*zny mrkbh;* 49:8]." Whether Ben Sira refers to diverse kinds of chariot (viz. in chs. 1 and 10) or the various parts of a single one is unclear. Influenced by Ezekiel, later visions of the divine throne provided it with fiery wheels (Dan 7:9; contrast the simple throne of I Kings 22:19; Isa 6:1). To the Jewish and early Christian liturgist, the scene of the angelic praise of God in Isa 6:3 (the Trisagion) was augmented by items from Ezekiel's vision. The sectaries of Qumran describe an angelic liturgy involving cherubs, blessing "the figure of the chariot-throne, wheels (both *galgallim* and *'opannim*), and *ḥašmal*" (Strugnell, "The Angelic Liturgy at Qumran—4Q Serek Šîrôt 'Ôlat Haššabbāt," SVT 7 [1960], 335ff.; Dupont-Sommer, *Essene Writings from Qumran* [Oxford: Blackwells, 1961], pp. 333ff.). The Book of Revelation, ch. 4 (dated to pre-Gospel times; see AB ad loc.), blends elements from Dan 7, Isa 6 and Ezek 1 and 10: from ch. 1 comes the bow around the throne (Rev 4:3); from ch. 1 the four living creatures, but from 10:12 their being full of eyes (4:6). Especially noteworthy is the distribution, in 4:7 of the animal features—one to each creature, as is the plain sense of Ezek 10:14, against 1:6.

The metamorphosis of the wheels into a class of angels (*Ofannim,* in the Talmud, see *Ḥagigah* 13a, and in the early Jewish liturgy) has been ingeniously rooted in Ezek 10:9–17. D. J. Halperin argues for the secondary, exegetical character of that passage, with the attributes of vss. 12 and 14 (flesh, back, hands, wings, eyes, faces) to be applied to the wheels, not, as is usually understood, to the creatures (as indeed the author of Rev 4:7 understood them). Whether or not this suggestion can stand as the best interpretation of these obscure verses, it may surely serve to explain how later readers came to ascribe independent angel-status to the wheels—the earliest attestation of which is the angelic triad Seraphim, Cherubim and Ophannim in I Enoch 61:10; 71:7 (D. J. Halperin, *VT* 26 [1976], 129–41).

The vision of the *merkaba,* including the stages of ascent to the divine throne, is the earliest type of mystical experience recorded for rabbinic Judaism (Yohanan ben Zakkai, first century C.E., R. Akiba and his colleagues, second century C.E.; BT *Ḥagigah* 14b). Since the journey of the ecstatic through the celestial stages was mortally dangerous, the lore regarding it was taught only to a rigorously selected few: "One may not expound the *merkaba* (i.e., the relevant passages in Ezekiel) even to a single student unless he is wise enough to fill in the clues by himself" (*Mishnah, Ḥagigah* 2.1). Moreover, it is the anonymous dictum of *Mishnah Megillah* 4.10 that Ezekiel's description of the *merkaba* may not be recited publicly in the synagogue (as a prophetic lection complementing the Torah reading); this, lest its recitation arouse curiosity about so dangerous a matter. (The dictum is contradicted in the sequel [cf. *Tosefta Megillah* 4.33]; in fact Ezek 1 is the prescribed lection accompanying the account of the Sinaitic theophany, read by Jews on Pentecost.) From the third to fourth centuries C.E., a ramified literature has survived describing, and prescribing rites for, the mystical ascent to the *merkaba,* the *Hekalot* "palaces" literature, on which one may consult G. Scholem, *Major Trends in Jewish Mysticism* (New York: Schocken Books, 1946), pp. 40–79, and *Jewish Gnosticism, Merkabah Mysticism, and Talmudic Tradition* (New York: Jewish Theological Seminary of America, 1960); I. Gruenwald, *Apocalyptic and Merkavah Mysticism* (Leiden/Köln: E. J. Brill, 1980). An outline of an important specimen of this genre, a characterization of the genre and a suggestion of its Hellenistic congeners is given by M. Smith in "Observations on *Hekhalot Rabbati,*" in A. Altmann, ed., *Biblical and Other Studies* (Cambridge: Harvard University Press, 1963), pp. 142–60. D. J. Halperin traces the early exegesis of the *merkaba* passages in *The Merkabah in Rabbinic Literature,* American Oriental Series 62 (New Haven: American Oriental Society, 1980).

VIII. Symbolizing the Exile
(12:1–16)

12 1 The word of YHWH came to me:
2 Man, you dwell amidst the rebellious house
who have eyes to see but would not see,
ears to hear but would not hear,
for they are a rebellious house.
3 Now you, man, put together an exile's pack
[a]and go into exile[a] during the day in their sight;
[b]go into exile[b] from your place to another place [b]in their sight[b],
perhaps they will see—
for they are a rebellious house.
4 You shall take out your things, as an exile's pack, during the day, in their sight,
but you yourself shall set out at evening [ab]in their sight[ab],
as a setting-out for exile.
5 In their sight, burrow a passage through the wall
and [c]take [your things][c] out through it;
6 [b]In their sight[b], you shall shoulder your burden,
[c]you shall bring it[c] out in the dark;
you shall cover your face so you shall not see the land;
for I am making you a sign for the house of Israel.
7 I did just as I was commanded:
My things I took out as an exile's pack during the day,
and at evening I burrowed through the wall [a]with my hand[a];
I [d]brought it[d] out in the dark;
I shouldered my burden in their sight.

8 The word of YHWH came to me in the morning: 9 Man, see, the
house of Israel, the rebellious house, have said to you, What are you
doing? Say to them: Thus said Lord YHWH:

[a–a] Not in G.
[b–b] Not in S.
[c–c] G S T "go."
[d–d] G S T "went."

10 The chief is this burden, in Jerusalem, and the whole house of
Israel who are in their midst.

11 Say: I am your sign;
as I did so it shall be done to them:
they shall go into exile in captivity
12 And the chief who is among them
shall shoulder his burden [e]in the dark and[e] set out;
they[f] shall burrow through the wall to [c]take him[c] out
through it;
he shall cover his face
[g]since he shall not see by eye the land[g]
13 I will spread my net for him
and he shall be caught in my trap;
I will bring him to Babylon, the land of the Chaldeans,
and he shall not see it,
and there he shall die.
14 All who are around him,
his auxiliaries and his divisions
I will scatter in every direction,
and I will unsheathe my sword after them.
15 And they shall know that I am YHWH,
when I disperse them among the nations
and scatter them among the lands.

16 But I will let a small number of them survive the sword, famine
and plague, so that they may tell of all their abominations among
the nations whither they come, and they shall know that I am YHWH.

e–e G S T "[and] in the dark he shall."
f G S "and he."
g–g G "in order that he not be seen to an eye (and he shall not see the land"—not in the Chester Beatty papyrus, B967); S "so that he shall not see the land."

COMMENT

12:2. One may compare Jer 5:21 "that have eyes but can not see, that have ears but can not hear," and Isa 6:9 "Hear indeed, but do not understand; see indeed but do not grasp." In those passages, however, it is the stupidity and mindlessness of the people that is denounced (see the contexts), while here it is their willfulness. Having eyes "to see" (that can see) and ears "to hear" (that can hear) they have refused to use them, "for they are a rebellious house." The nuance conveyed by the perfect verbs (*ra'u, šame'u;* in Jer 5:21 these are imperfect verbs) is of "general truths known to have actually occurred and so proved from experience" (Driver, *Tenses,* § 12). For more than a year in act and word, Ezekiel had exhibited his message to their eyes and ears, but they had disregarded him and held fast to their hope in Jerusalem's survival and their speedy return to it.

3. The instruction of vs. 3 is general and uses the proper terms of the reference: *gala* "go into exile," *k*ᵉ*le gola,* lit. "vessels of exile"; in vss. 4–6, on the other hand, the instructions are particular and use similes (*kkly gwlh, kmwṣ'y gwlh*) and the common term *yaṣa* "go forth, depart." The distinction between the two is somewhat blurred by the presence of *yomam* "during the day" in vs. 3; it is a detail more suitable to the specific division of activity between day and night set out in vs. 4 (*yomam* is almost always balanced by a counterpart time-term [e.g., *layla* "at night"]; that this is not the case in vs. 3 is remarkable). Moreover, the command in vs. 3 "go into exile during the day" conflicts with the particularization in vs. 4 consigning the daytime for the preparation and exhibition of the pack only, and the evening for the movement of the prophet. Hence moderns, on the basis of G, delete *wglh* "go into exile" as a dittograph of the preceding *gwlh; yomam* will then define the time for preparing the pack, in agreement with vs. 4a. This removes the conflict between vss. 3 and 4, but it effaces even more the generality of vs. 3 (over against vss. 4–6), while leaving *yomam* in vs. 3 without a balancing counterpart. The difficulties are removed by deleting *yomam* also. Supposing vs. 3a to have read originally *'śh lk kly gwlh l'nyhm* "Put together an exile's pack in their sight," G, with its implied sequence *gwlh ywmm l'nyhm,* will have arisen by assimilation to the identical sequence in vs. 4a. MT will have developed from that by dittography (*gwlh wglh*). (The present MT of vs. 3a lay before S, which typically abridges repetitive passages; here vs. 3b was trimmed so as not to repeat elements of vs. 3a.)

an exile's pack is represented in Egyptian and Assyrian pictures of victories (*ANEP*² ⋇10 [lower right], ⋇366, ⋇373). It must have contained the barest necessities; R. Ḥiyya bar Abba (third-century C.E. Palestinian tanna) said: a skin, a mat, and a bowl, each doing double-duty—the skin for holding flour (another version: water) and for use as a pillow; the mat for sitting and lying; the bowl for eating and drinking (*Lamentations Rabba* 1.23; another listing in BT *Nedarim* 40b replaces the skin by a lamp).

in their sight, perhaps they will see. "In their sight" (lit. "to their eyes") is repeated seven times in vss. 3–7, emphasizing that the prophet must force himself on their attention. (Note how the versions, especially S, blur this feature by their omissions.) Even so, they may refuse to take notice ("see") since they are rebellious.

4. During the day the prophet was to bring his things out of his house

and prepare his exile's pack (perhaps several times) to put the community on notice that a dumb show was in progress; the actual departure, however, was only at dark. Medievals interpreted the darkness as a cover for the shame of the exiles; moderns regard the coolness of night as suitable for setting out on the trek to exile (but, apart from the fact that modern trekkers set out at, or just before, dawn for the best results, the notion of such rational consideration and orderliness seems out of keeping with the rest of the symbolism). Taken with some elements of the next verse, furtiveness cannot be ruled out—e.g., out of a desire to escape captivity. There is, finally, the symbolization of calamity and termination through darkness or evening; cf. Jer 13:16 "Give honor to YHWH your God, before he brings darkness, before your feet stumble on the mountains in shadow—when you hope for light, and it is turned to darkness, and becomes deep gloom"; even more pertinent to our passage is Isa 24:11 "The sun has set (*'rbh*) on all joy, the gladness of the earth has gone into exile (*glh*)."

as a setting-out. For an exact parallel (and antonym) to the plural abstract noun *moṣa'e-* see 26:10 *m^ebo'e-* (for the form, see Joüon § 88 L d–e and 136 g–i).

5–6. These verses particularize "a setting-out for exile." Burrowing through the wall (*qir*) of the house (Amos 5:19) may be "a sign of ruined houses and desperate efforts to escape" (Cooke), or represent attempts to escape furtively, circumventing the besiegers. (To allow burrowing, the wall must have been of mud/clay, the most common building material in Mesopotamia [G. Contenau, *Everyday Life in Babylon and Assyria* (London: E. Arnold, 1954), pp. 26ff.].) Medievals applied this action (influenced by vs. 12) to Zedekiah's effort to escape Jerusalem by night after the city walls had been breached (II Kings 25:4ff.; Jer 39:4ff.; 52:7ff.). However, nothing is said there about burrowing, but rather of leaving through "the gate between the double walls"; this is more than a "trifling inconsistency" (Cooke) and argues against identification of the burrowing with Zedekiah's escape attempt.

and take [your things] out through it. w^ehoṣeta resumes the same verb at the start of vs. 4, and its unexpressed object is the exile pack specified there. Forms of this verb appear again without object in vss. 6, 7, and 12; this is entirely regular (GKC § 117 f) and occurs repeatedly in these same verses with the verb *naśa* "bear" (supply: the pack or burden). Attention is thus focused on the exile pack—the main prop of the dumb show. The versions level all verbs with *yaṣa* "go out" of vss. 4, 12, evidently a secondary simplification.

you shall cover your face so you shall not see the land. A difficult clause. Fohrer takes it as purely symbolic: it corresponds to the night departure and to the exiles' ignorance (darkness, blindness) concerning the foreign land to which they were to go. Medievals conform the item to its predecessors, all predictive, and interpret it as bespeaking the shame felt by the exiles over their disgrace (Rashi; Kimḥi compares Jer 9:18, "We are covered with shame because we have had to leave our land, to give up our dwellings"); not seeing the land is equated with not being seen by others (Eliezer of Beaugency). Covering the face was, however, also a sign of grief (II Sam 19:5—with a different verb); was it, then, to keep the exile from seeing the dear land he was so painfully leaving (Zimmerli)? J. Licht suggests, privately, that a symbol is superadded to a predictive act: the furtive fugitive who covers his face so as not to be recognized thereby impedes his sight of the ground—a symbol and omen of his never again seeing his native land; cf. Jer 22:12, the exiled King Jehoahaz *'t h'rṣ hz't l' yr'h 'wd* "shall never again see this land." That a standard doom underlies this wording is made probable by the following curse in the treaty between Ashurnirari V of Assyria (eighth century B.C.E.) and Mati'ilu of Arpad (in Syria):

> [If M. breaks the treaty] then, just as this spring lamb, brought forth from its fold, will not return to its fold, will not behold its fold again, alas, M. together with his sons, daughters, officials, and the people of his land [will be ousted] from his country, will not return to his country, and not behold his country again (*ANET*³, p. 532; reference courtesy of M. Weinfeld).

On this interpretation "shall not see," whose primary meaning is simply inability to discern through the face cover, evokes the second, broader sense, which would entail *'wd* "again" for its explicit expression. The view of some commentators (e.g., Herrmann, Cooke, Wevers) that the line is secondarily added from vs. 12b, after that passage had been doctored to allude to Zedekiah's blindness, depends on one's understanding of vs. 12b, on which see below.

I am making you a sign (mopet). That is, a portentous example of what is to befall the Israelites; see vs. 11 and 24:24; this sense is found elsewhere only in Isa 8:18.

7. *with my hand.* Not with a tool, betokening the improvisation of those who have been surprised by catastrophe. The medievals see here a sign of furtiveness (so that efforts to escape not be heard) and apply it to Zedekiah, disregarding the discrepancy in situations.

Vs. 7 combines the instructions of vss. 4–6 in its account of their execution, eliminating whatever is unconnected with the exile's pack. This focus on the essential prop may be sufficient reason for omitting the matter of "covering the face," etc., undercutting the argument that the omission indicates its secondary character.

8. *see. hᵃlo,* lit. "is not?" often serves as no more than an affirmative particle, nearly = *hinne,* G *idou* "behold," which at times translates *hᵃlo,* as in I Sam 26:1.

10. *The chief is this burden.* Hebrew *hannaśi hammaśśa hazze;* this alliterative phrase is patterned after Jer 23:33 (read in accord with G S) *attem hammaśśa* "you are the burden [and I will cast you away, declares

YHWH]." The meaning of the sentence is: this burden—the exile's pack—represents the chief and the Israelites of Jerusalem; they will be taken out of the city into exile. Two things are unexpected: the reference to two subjects, the chief (king) and the people, and the symbolic character of the exile's pack (*maśśa* is linked to *naśa 'al katef* "carry [the pack] on the shoulder" in vss. 6f.); but as we shall see, the double aspect of the prophet's actions (predictive and symbolic) carries into the rest of the interpretation as well. S simplifies, retaining the merely predictive sense: "The chief will carry this burden in Jerusalem and all the house of Israel with him." T follows the other sense of *maśśa* (that is punned upon in Jer 23:32f.) and renders: "Concerning the chief is the burden of this prophecy in Jerusalem," etc.

The last three words of vs. 10, *'ašer hemma betokam,* cannot be construed intelligibly; alternative readings seem to have been fused, namely, "[Israel] who are in its [Jerusalem's] midst (**betokah*)"; or "[the chief] who is (**hu*) in their [Israel's] midst."

The analysis of the inhabitants of Jerusalem into "chief [king] and house of Israel" follows a common practice of pairing king and city/people as equal partners in a unit of destiny. Often in the Book of Joshua the defeated are recorded as (the populace of) a certain city and its king (6:2; 10:28ff., etc.); Amaziah's summary of Amos' seditious prophesying mentions only king and people (Amos 7:11); cf. Hos 10:7 ("Samariah is destroyed, its king is like foam" [the verse is to be so divided]). The particular humiliation of the king, on account of which he is singled out, arises from the popular conception of him as a talisman. Striking testimony to this estimate of Zedekiah is Lam 4:20, in which the king is called "our breath of life" (a notion known in Egypt; cf. *ANET*3, p. 376d of Merneptah), and his shadow is a guarantee of life among the nations (cf. the comparable use of Akkadian *ṣillu* with reference to the king, *CAD* s.v., vol. 16, pp. 191ff.); see Hillers' comment in *Lamentations,* AB, p. 92.

11. *Say.* This introduces a speech whose "I" is the prophet. Since vs. 10 was spoken in God's name—it was introduced by "Thus said Lord YHWH"—it was necessary to mark the shift to a new "I" in vs. 11 by breaking the flow of speech with this "Say" at its start.

as I did so it shall be done to them. Viz. the chief and the people. Comparison with 24:22, 24 is instructive: there the expression runs "As I/he did so shall you do"—meaning unequivocably that Ezekiel's actions will be copied by the people. The passive ending of our sentence suggests it is at least ambiguous; not merely "as I acted so it shall fall to them to act" but "as I did [to my pack, taking it out of my home and out through a breach in the wall] so shall it be done to them: they shall [be forcibly expelled from their homes and] go into exile in captivity." The switch into the passive at the end of the sentence thus gives the prophet's action with his pack a symbolic color, which justifies the repeated use of *hoṣi* "bring/take out" in vss. 5–7 calling attention to what is done to the pack: the exile's pack is a symbol of the remnant that will be led out of the homeland as captives. This symbolic sense overlays the merely predictive, which is expressed through *yaṣa* "go out" (vs. 4), referring to the departure of the exiles, carrying their packs on their backs.

12. *the chief who is among them* . . . Since *naśi* "chief" is a passive form of *naśa* "raise, carry" the effect is ironic: "The uplifted one (*naśi*) among them shall on [his] shoulders lift [*yiśśa* his burden]." As a predictive sign, the prophet stood for the representative of the nation, the king; the king would try desperately to escape at night carrying his bundle, his attendants would dig through the ruined walls to get him through unnoticed (*hoṣi* alludes to the symbolic use of the pack, vs. 5b), and he would cover his face—

since (ya'an) *he shall not see by eye the land.* Here the covering of the face is expressly given an explanation which seems to point to a second meaning: he will hide his face from view, and in so doing block his view of the land, since in fact he will not see the land (ever again[?]). The redundant *hu* has an analogue in 11:15, but *l'yn* "by the eye" is awkwardly intrusive. T dealt with it by paraphrase: "since he incurred the penalty of an eye [i.e., of being blinded] he will not see the land"; T thus found an allusion here to Zedekiah's later fate (so too Kara), but such allusion would be premature in this sentence, which refers to actions connected with the king's attempt to escape from the city.

G S V and the medievals interpret *ya'an* as "so that," to arrive at which meaning moderns emend the text to *lᵉma'an.* The resulting sentence is virtually equivalent to vs. 6aβ ("you shall cover your face so you shall not see the land"); indeed S renders both passages the same way. The divergent reading of this whole clause in G is notable. Critics reconstruct the *Vorlage* of its first half as *lᵉma'an 'ᵃšer lo yera'e la'ayin* "so that he not be visible to the eye." This is regarded as the original reading, and is an allusion to a disguise for eluding recognition (e.g., Cooke). The second half of the clause in G (absent in the Chester Beatty papyrus B967) is "and he the land shall not see"; it is regarded as a makeshift rendering of MT *hu 'et ha'areṣ,* and its very awkwardness, together with B967's omission, shows these words to be an addition, entailed by misreading the preceding *yr'h* as active *yir'e* "he shall see," and applying it after the event to Zedekiah's blindness.

This interpretation of G's data is plausible, but not inevitable. For interestingly enough, Abarbanel arrived at G's very understanding on the basis of MT: "He will cover his face in order that his flight not be visible to the eyes of the populace (*h'rṣ* = the inhabitants of the land, as in Gen 11:1; cf. Ezek 14:13ff.), as a man ashamed of his flight; hence he will try to flee secretly so that no one of the land see him" (= G's "original" reading in the first half of the clause). Might not the *Vorlage* of G have been the equivalent of MT and been rendered by G like Abarbanel? The convenience of the rendering of G and Abarbanel, and its superiority to T, is that it does not import blindness prematurely into the context of escape. As was said above, by this interpretation the prediction of vs. 12b is aligned fully with the representation of the prophet ordered in vs. 6a.

We have endeavored thus far to interpret MT as is; to do so, we have supposed a complex meaning for vss. 6a and 12b—a predictive action at the same time symbolic; we have made the symbolic sense explicit, at least in vs. 12b; we have admitted the intrusiveness of *l'yn* and excused the redundancy of *hu* at the end of that verse. All this adds up to a strain; we shall consider an explanation of this strain in our comment to the next verse.

13. *spread my net for him* ('alaw). The image is of a fowler (see Hos 7:12) or hunter (Ezek 19:8), hence the net is spread along the ground (Dalman, *AuS* VI, pp. 335ff.). Prov 29:5 "he spreads a net *'al pe'amaw* for his feet" shows that *'al* in this context means "for, so as to trap" not "over" (Ehrlich). The Judahite king's future capture by Babylonian forces is translated into divine terms; the deity as a hunter seizing his (worshipers') enemies in a net is an ancient Near Eastern motif (*ANEP*² ※298, a giant, probably a god, holds a net containing captives; cf. ※307; in *ANET*³, p. 625, i, the god Dagan threatens, "O Babylon . . . I am going to gather you into a net"; ibid., p. 632, x, "I am going to gather [your enemy] into a net which holds fast"). In our passage, God's enemy is the Judahite king who rebelled at once against him and the Babylonian suzerain (see Ezek 17). The prediction that he would be captured and deported to Babylon need not be *ex eventu* (based on the event, and therefore after it); it reflects a policy of deporting rebel kings to the capital, where they were held in captivity or killed, that was followed by neo-Assyrian (eighth–seventh centuries) and neo-Babylonian kings: for the former see *ANET*³, pp. 295a (Egyptian), 300b (Arab), 301d (Babylonian); for the latter, cf. the fate of Jehoiachin, but especially *ANET*³, p. 308c—a list of seven kings, including those of Tyre, Gaza, Sidon, Arvad and Ashdod, captives at Nebuchadnezzar's court. II Kings 25:28 refers to fellow royal captives of Jehoiachin, above whom he was raised; these "were presumably political prisoners or hostages for the good conduct of their subjects" (Gray, *Kings*² [OTL], p. 774).

and he shall not see it. Is this, as most medievals and moderns opine, a reference to the blinding of Zedekiah before his deportation (II Kings 25:7; Jer 39:7; 52:11), and, if so, a skewing of the motif of unseeing (vss. 6, 12) on the basis of later events? P. E. Deist compared the events (capture and burning of the city, massacre of courtiers, blinding) with the curses preceding blindness in the Aramaic Sefire treaty (from about 750 B.C.E.) I A 35–40 (*ANET*³, p. 660); he supposed that the treaty that bound Zedekiah to vassaldom to Babylon had similar provisions, and hence that these penalties were "an inevitable consequence of breaching the oath of loyalty" ("The Punishment of the Disobedient Zedekiah,"

Journal of Northwest Semitic Languages I [1971], 71f.). Accordingly, there is no need to regard this prediction as "prophecy after the event." The argument might be strengthened by noting that what in Sefire is a curse (to be enforced by the gods, not men) was occasionally practiced by Assyrian kings on defeated enemies; a Nineveh relief shows Sargon II (eighth century) putting out the eyes of an enemy held on a leash (A. Parrot, *Samaria: The Capital of . . . Israel* [New York: Philosophical Library, 1958], fig. xxiii, p. 82). Yet doubts remain, chiefly because of the precision with which the combination of penalties inflicted on King Zedekiah is described—both blinding and exile to Babylon. If the prediction of the fugitive's "not seeing the land" (vss. 6aβ, 12b) is susceptible to being understood without reference to the king's blindness, it is because the land in question may be taken as his homeland. But when it is said in this verse that the king "shall not see it," the reference can only be to Chaldea (unless one is ready, with Ibn Janaḥ [*Ha-riqma* I, ch. 34 (33), pp. 363f.] to refer "it" to Jerusalem—as a distant antecedent; see Wilensky's reservations in fn. 5). Such precise prediction of interlocked details is not characteristic of biblical prophecy and looks, therefore, to be after the event. Since the similar oracle in 17:16b, 20 does not contain this detail, we conclude that the theme of sight/unseeing, so dominant in this oracle, facilitated the subsequent glossing of its message with an ironical reinterpretation of unseeing applied to the king after his blinding at Riblah.

This instance of later revision having been admitted, the accumulated strains on interpreting vss. 6aβ, 12b listed in the comment to the previous verse may now be reconsidered. The critical view that these passages in their entirety are after-the-event glosses goes too far. The strains may be relieved by the more modest assumption that only their chief cause, (*hw' 't*) *h'rṣ,* is a gloss—of a piece with *w'wth l' yr'h* of vs. 13—designed to alter the originally passive sense of the clause *l' t/yr'h* "you/he shall not be seen." For, as some medievals saw (and as G translated in vs. 12b), the clause explains the covering of the face as intended to avoid recognition. Only after Zedekiah's blinding (we surmise) was this primary text (written only consonantally) subtly altered by reading the verbs as actives, supplying their objects in vss. 6aβ and 12b ("[he] the land"), and adding the new clause ("but he shall not see it") in vs. 13, all required to express clearly the new understanding of the oracle as applying to that blinding. This may be regarded as a prototype of a homiletic device known in talmudic times as "read not [X but Y]" (see *EJ,* s.v. *"Al tikre"*), save that here, unlike there, the alteration was embedded in the wording of the text. The glossator—perhaps the prophet himself, who only later came to see the "deeper" reference of his actions—was not deterred from this coup by the incongruity of representing the king's blindness at the earliest stage of his flight; this should not occasion surprise in view of the fact that T and Kara were likewise oblivious to the difficulty. Harmonistic interpreters, from Rashi onward, strained to tease out the original sense, required by the context, or something like it, from the new wording.

and there he shall die. So again in 17:16. This prediction is of a piece with that of Amos 7:17 concerning the death of another enemy of God, the priest Amaziah, "on unclean [i.e., foreign] soil," or Isa 22:18, that the miscreant Shebna would be hurled away and die in exile, or Jer 20:6, that Pashhur would be exiled and die in Babylon. That in fact Zedekiah eventually did die in Babylonian captivity (Jer 52:11) no more makes this a prophecy after the event than the "fulfilment" of Jeremiah's prophecy (Jer 22:10f.) that Jehoahaz would die in Egypt (II Kings 23:34) makes that such a prophecy (on the contrary, Rudolph, *Jeremia,* HAT, 3te Auflage [Tübingen: J. C. B. Mohr, 1968], p. 139, dates the latter precisely to the moment of the king's deportation to Egypt).

14. *his auxiliaries* ('zrh). The versions translate as a plural "his helpers." Since elsewhere Ezekiel uses the plural participle *'(w)zryw* (32:21; 30:8), critics have substituted that word for *'zrh.* But *'ezer* can mean "one who helps" (though this would be the only example of a collective usage), and the old *h* form of the third-person masculine singular suffix occurs in Ezekiel (e.g., in 11:15 *klh* and ten other instances listed in R. Gordis, *The Biblical Text in the Making* [Philadelphia: Dropsie College, 1937], pp. 93ff.). Since the sentence would be smoother without *'zrh,* Ehrlich proposed to read *'zrh* "I will scatter" instead (as in the next clause). The first two lines might then be alternative variants (or, keeping *'zrh,* perhaps it and *'ᵃšer sᵉbibotaw* are variants).

his divisions. Akkadian *agappu* and later Hebrew (*'a*)*gap* mean "wing," whence the suggestion that Ezekiel's *'agap-* (never found elsewhere) has a military sense like Latin *ala* "wing" (". . . *squadron* originally Roman cavalry disposed on both sides of the legions like wings; later allied troops, especially cavalry," *Cassel's New Latin Dictionary*); others compare Arabic *ja/uff* "numerous company" (perhaps ultimately the same word?).

With the first half of this verse cf. the similar 17:21 (also of Zedekiah); with the second half cf. 5:2 (12)—applied only here to Zedekiah's forces.

16. That some would escape the disaster and survive among the nations was foreshadowed in 5:3 and foretold in 6:8ff. "They shall say, 'We have been punished for our sins, for we committed such and such deeds'; thus I shall make it known that not for nothing did I wipe them out" (Rashi, echoing 6:10). Whether it is the remnant or the gentiles who are to "know that I am YHWH" is not immediately clear. Since the gentiles' blasphemous reaction to the fall later troubled Ezekiel (36:20ff.), this may express an earlier expectation (which events disappointed) that the Jerusalemite remnant would vindicate God to the gentiles.

STRUCTURE AND THEMES

The account of the symbolic action falls into three parts and has temporal unity: A., the command, vss. 3–6; B., the performance during a day and a night, vs. 7; and C., the interpretation given the next morning, vss. 8–15. A sweeping indictment of the people as willfully blind and deaf sets the theme (vs. 2) and is counterbalanced by a closing notice of the confession of guilt by survivors of the predicted catastrophe (vs. 16).

A. "You, man" (vs. 3) opens the command concerning the symbolic action, couched in terms of exile (*gala*). Its first part (vs. 3a–bα) is a generality which the following verses detail; its last part (vs. 3bβ) resumes the terms of the indictment (vs. 2: "see," "rebellious house") and thus rounds off the general statements of this oracle. Details of the prophet's movement, and especially of his handling of the exile pack, comprise vss. 4–6a, followed by the conclusion (vs. 6b) that the prophet is a sign.

B. Vs. 7 recounts the prophet's performance of those actions that touched directly on the exile pack; this signals the focus of what follows.

C. The people having asked about the meaning of the action, on the following morning God reveals it to the prophet (vss. 8–9): the burden (= the exile pack) stands for the king in Jerusalem and the Israelites (vs. 10); the prophet is a sign for his audience—as he did (to the pack) so it shall be done to those in Jerusalem: they would go into exile in captivity (vs. 11). However, the commanded actions of vss. 5–6 have a particular application to the king, whose behavior at the collapse of the city they foretell (vs. 12). But the king's flight would end in his capture and the dispersal of his forces (vss. 13–15); a remnant of the dispersed would confess the guilt of the Jerusalemites throughout the lands of their exile (vs. 16).

As the passage proceeds it becomes more and more complex. The opening command (vs. 3) does not divide the prophet's activity into day and night (even according to MT). When this division is made in vs. 4, there is no hint of the complexity of the night activity that emerges only in vss. 5–6. When in vs. 6 the prophet is declared to be a sign, no hint is given to the double reference of the sign as it later unfolds.

In the interpretation, the full complexity of the sign emerges. The prophet's actions and props are at once symbolic and predictive: as symbolic, "this burden" which was removed by stages "to another place" stands for the king and people of Jerusalem—a double reference. The surprise ending of vs. 11—"so it shall be done to them"—focuses again on objects, not on subjects, that is, on the transportation of the pack as symbolizing the deportation of the Jerusalemites. (The thought crosses one's mind that in "as I did" of vs. 11a glimmers a suggestion that the prophet symbolizes the enemy—as in 4:3.)

Vs. 12 gives another interpretation to the night activity of the prophet; it acts out in advance what the king would be reduced to in Jerusalem's collapse (in vs. 12's interpretation of vs. 5 there is a momentary reversion to the symbolic; as *hoṣi* shows, the king is identified with the pack of vs. 5—others would burrow through the wall to bring him out). In order to fulfil the program of vs. 3 ("from your place to another place"), the interpretation runs on to the king's capture and exile to Babylonia ("another place"); to this the dispersal of his forces is attached (the same sequence recurs in 17:20–21), ending with the recognition formula (vss. 13–15).

A small mirror of the process of complexification is the career of the detail concerning the covering of the face and the nonseeing of the land (whose meaning never emerges into full clarity). Conforming to the context of its first occurrence (vs. 6), the prophet represents the exiles as an undifferentiated mass. Later, when the interpretation divides the mass into king and people (vs. 12), this detail is attached specifically to the king; now, however, later events cast their shadow backward to add overtones to this image. Not only did the blinding of Zedekiah enter the text in the (secondary) allusion to it of vs. 13 ("and he shall not see it [the land of Chaldea]"), but the covering of the face of vs. 12 was so understood subsequently (e.g., T)—enforcing puzzlement respecting its proper meaning there and in vs. 6. In this way, the covering of the face came to have a symbolic meaning—a sign of blindness.

The history of interpretation of this oracle as a whole shows a trend toward assimilation and simplification. The ancient versions, by rendering "go out" wherever MT has "bring out," avoid the double focus on the prophet and on his pack in vss. 5–7 (12); we regard this as a secondary feature in the versions, not as a reflection of different (let alone better) readings. Similarly, in vs. 12, G levels all the activities, making the king the subject of all the verbs, against MT's shift in the "burrowing" clause to a plural subject—the king's attendants, with the king becoming the implicit object.

Modern commentators adopt simplicity as the criterion for isolating the hypothetical original kernel of this passage from its later additions: it is axiomatic with moderns that the primary creation was free of tension and ambiguity. For Herrmann, the original kernel consisted of the representation of the exile of the populace; allusions to the flight and fate of the king are secondary—including all references to covering the face (which he takes as allusions to Zedekiah's blindness). Cooke's treatment of the covering of the face is noteworthy: its appearance in vs. 6 is derived from vs. 12, where its original sense (given in G's reading of vs. 12bα) was "so that he shall not be seen to the eye"—a reference to the king's disguise, itself a post-event addition to the oracle. Further glossing made it allude to blindness ("so he shall not see the land"). Zimmerli assumes more stages: the first had the prophet represent the exile of the people in daytime actions; burrowing was added to reflect the breaching of Jerusalem's walls by the Babylonians; nighttime actions reflect Zedekiah's flight by night; later still are the allusions to blindness. This sampling of critical opinion does not exhaust the variety of expedients resorted to for the elimination of the complexity of our passage.

Judgment of what in the Book of Ezekiel constitutes an internal tension great enough to justify literary surgery for its relief should be based on evidence drawn from the book rather than on the critic's tolerances, and the assumption of stratification should rest on unmistakable anachronism. On both these counts something can be said in favor of less extensive strictures on the integrity of our passage. It is undeniable that the action of the prophet in our passage is overcharged, but it is more than the symbolism of the actions in chs. 4–5? There the prophet is at once under siege, "bearing iniquity," and besieging and haranguing—that is, both victim and aggressor; the fire in which he burns a third of his hair stands for the famine and plague in Jerusalem and, at a later moment, for the sword pursuing the dispersed. It is true that there, too, the tendency of modern critics is to break up the text into kernels and accretions in order to sort out the symbolism into simpler forms, but our passage and chs. 4–5 support each other in testifying that Ezekiel's symbols may be complicated and multivalent. As his visions outdo those of other prophets in their intricacy, so his symbolic actions are not to be tailored and trimmed along the simple lines of theirs. The possibility must be allowed that Ezekiel, the authentic Ezekiel, was baroque.

Are there anachronisms that justify the supposition that the passage has been touched up and layered? As recent victims of neo-Assyrian and neo-Babylonian aggression, neither the prophet nor his audience had to wait until 586 B.C.E. to imagine the mood and manner of fugitives and deportees, or to foresee the king's fate after his rebellious designs were discovered in his fourth year (cf. the prophecy of Jer 34:3 that Zedekiah would be captured and deported to Babylon; omission of the blinding shows it to have preceded the events). The mingling of the fates of king and nation is a natural outcome of the biblical conception of the solidarity of the two (cf. the discussion of communal vs. ruler responsibility in D. Daube, *Studies in Biblical Law* [Cambridge (England): The University Press, 1947]; rpt. New York: Ktav, 1969, pp. 160ff.). Some take the "burrowing through the wall" as an anachronistic reflection of Zedekiah's flight through the city gate—but this makes too light of the discrepancy between these two modes of flight (against Cooke). Nor can the fugitives' burrowing (*ḥtr*) readily be identified with the Babylonians' breaching (*bq'*) of the city walls (Zimmerli). The details of the prophet's actions and their interpretation too obviously diverge at crucial points from the later events to be judged as anachronisms. It is true that these same details are hard to interpret, but the difficulty is not eased by disintegrating the passage; indeed it is all the more reason for hesitating to resort to literary surgery, since we are in any case on dubious ground. On the other hand, the allusion to the king's blindness in vs. 13 does appear to be a later reinterpretative touch (perhaps by the prophet himself) in the light of events. We have surmised (comment to vs. 13) that further doctoring in the same spirit resulted in the obscurity shrouding the sense of "covering the face and not seeing the land" in vss. 6 and 12. In no case, however, is the altering and additional matter extensive; given Ezekiel's penchant for the baroque, it may be affirmed, then, that the oracle shows a reasonable literary and temporal integrity. (For an appreciation of its general integrity, its ambiguity, and its reinterpretation, one may profitably consult B. Lang, *Kein Aufstand in Jerusalem,* pp. 17ff.; see also B. Uffenheimer, "Ezekiel 12:1–16.")

The passage resumes the theme of exile, announced for the first time through two of the symbolic acts of chs. 4–5—eating unclean food and scattering hair in every direction. Whereas those actions were conformed to the prophet's confinement, the present ones gain vividness from his freedom to move about. The purpose is the same, to convince his audience that the destruction of Jerusalem and the exile of its inhabitants are inevitable. It is not meant to enable the Jerusalemites to avert their fate, for their repentance is not called for or considered; no room is made for mitigating the doom. The message was to the exiles, whose sympathy with Jerusalem and hopes of speedy repatriation justified their stigmatization as "the rebellious house." Only if they abandon their illusions ("perhaps they will see," vs. 3) could they come to realize their deep guilt and comprehend their exile as a means of paying off the debt of sin they owed God and thus be reconciled with him. (The weakness of B. Lang's affirmation in *Kein Aufstand,* p. 24, that this oracle "contains the (inexplicit) demand upon the exiles and the king to take last-minute measures to avert the dreaded fate" is betrayed by the parenthesis.)

Echoes of earlier prophecies occur at the beginning and at the end of our passage. Vs. 14 recalls 5:2 (12) as it applies the terms of dispersion and persecution by the sword to the fate of the king's troops. The remnant, who in 6:8ff. will realize their guilt, here (vs. 16) become confessors in heathen lands. There is a notable development in the description of "the rebellious house." When God commissioned Ezekiel, he doubted whether they would, or foresaw they would not, listen to the prophet (e.g., 2:5, 7; 3:7, 27). Now having displayed their obtuseness toward his words and deeds for over a year, they are denounced as a people who "having eyes to see, would not see . . . ears to hear, would not hear." (One notes the associative link between the mention of these senses in 12:2 and their involvement in the immediately preceding 11:24f.—the prophet's report to the exiles of the vision he had seen.) The phrasing of the instructions to the prophet takes into account the people's demonstrated fault—willful unseeing; each and every action is to be performed "in their sight" (*l'nyhm*—repeated six times). And when he relates his performance, he does not fail to say (for a seventh time) that he did all "in their sight."

Verbal artifices and allusions abound. The dominant theme of unseeing, stated in vs. 2, evokes from the derivatives of the immediately adjacent *glh* ("exile") in vs. 3 overtones of the homonym "disclose, uncover"—enforced by association with "eyes" (cf. *g*ᵉ*luy ʿenayim* "open-eyed" [Num 24:4, 16]; *gilla l*ᵉ*ʿene* "disclose to sight of" [Ps 98:2]); the evocation is particularly strong in MT with its added (dittographed?) *ug*ᵉ*le* . . . (*l*ᵉ*ʿenehem*) in vs. 3a. The theme is given a twist in the sequel, where (*"not being seen") "not seeing the land" figures prominently. "Burrowing through the wall" connects this oracle with the previous vision of the temple abominations, in which the only other occurrence of the expression appears (8:8). The most intricate combination of wordplay and allusion is with the root *nś'* "carry [a burden]." Ezekiel carries out ("carries and takes out") his pack as a sign of the exile of the king (*naśi*) and the Jerusalemites, who together are symbolized by "this burden" (*maśśa*). Jeremiah's acerbic pun on *maśśa* ("divine pronouncement"/"burden on God, to be cast away") may well have been known to Ezekiel, but we need not go that far; Jeremiah's witness to the vogue the word enjoyed in his time is enough to clarify Ezekiel's similar use of it.

These verbal artifices are of a piece with the complex symbolism of our passage and tend to confirm its authenticity.

IX. The Coming Terror (12:17–20)

17 The word of YHWH came to me:
18 Man! Eat your bread in quaking
and drink your water trembling with anxiety,
19 And say to the people of the land: thus said Lord YHWH concerning the inhabitants of Jerusalem on the soil of Israel:
They shall eat their bread in anxiety,
and drink their water in desolation;
So its[a] land shall be desolate because of what fills it,
because of the lawlessness of all its inhabitants.
20 The inhabited towns shall be ruined,
and the land shall be a desolation;
and you shall know that I am YHWH!

[a] G S T "the"; a few Hebrew mss. and editions read "their" (*'rṣm*).

COMMENT

12:18. *quaking* (r'š), *trembling* (rgzh), *anxiety* (d'gh). *r'š* (noun and verbs), previously in 3:12, 13, again in 37:7; 38:19, is mostly associated with earthquake. Once, however, a war-horse is described as *br'š wbrgz* (the masculine form of *rgzh*) "quivering with excitement" (Job 39:24); that suggests why in the second colon of our verse "in anxiety" has been added to "in trembling." Since *rgz* denotes many sorts of agitation—including eagerness (Job 39:24), jubilation (Jer 33:9), grief (II Sam 19:1), and rage (Hab 3:2)—the order to quake and tremble had to specify the emotion to be conveyed, e.g., by facial expression. Since "in anxiety" mars the balance of the colon and indicates emotion, it has been taken by moderns as a secondary intrusion from the next verse, but it is a necessary part of the instructions to the prophet on how he must playact. Contrast 4:10f., where the actions of doling out are enough to convey the message of scarcity; the mental distress mentioned in the interpretation (4:16) adds nothing to them.

19. *say to the people of the land.* That is, to the community of exiles. Some moderns render "say of" (*'el* = *'al,* II Kings 19:32; Jer 22:18), referring to the homelanders (since a population element of the land of Israel is the usual referent of the phrase), and declare the following "concerning the inhabitants of Jerusalem," etc., to be a secondary explanation. But this is not necessary. Ezekiel uses "the people of the land" variously: in 33:2 it means the populace of a hypothetical country, in 39:13 of the future land of Israel, and in 7:27; 22:29; 45:16, 22; 46:3, 9, contrasting with king or other higher classes, it means the common folk of the present or future land of Israel. While it usually refers to inhabitants of the land of Israel, Ezekiel customarily includes, or alludes to, the exiles in such general phrases (like "the house of Israel, the rebellious house"). Hence medievals and other moderns are justified in taking "people of the land" here as the exiles, the normal audience of the prophet. In the sequel, and especially in vs. 20, "the land" is the entire land of Judah; hence the exiled "people of the land" must have included provincials in addition to Jerusalemites—as is hinted at by Jer 52:28, in which the deportees (of Jehoiakim's time?) are called "Judahites" (Malamat, *Congress Volume,* p. 134). Eichrodt detects irony: they are a "people of the land" without a land.

the inhabitants of Jerusalem on the soil of Israel. As opposed to Jerusalemites among the exiles. S, Kimḥi, *NEB* take the prepositional phrase to refer to another, broader group: "and concerning (those dwelling on) the soil of Israel," influenced perhaps by the scope of vs. 20. But the later parallel "the inhabitants of these ruins on the soil of Israel" (33:24) speaks against treating the *'al* phrase as alluding to a separate grouping.

in desolation (šmmwn). Paired with *d'gh* "anxiety" (as in 4:16), *šmmwn* seems to have an emotional sense: appalment, numbed dismay; however, in view of the ambiguity of the cognate verb in the next clause one cannot be sure.

So (= in this way) *its land . . .* For this sense of *lm'n,* cf. comment on 4:17 end. The initial perception of this clause is: the anxious eating and drinking of the people will be a vivid particular embodiment of the condition of the crime-ridden land. But the clause is a good example of ambiguity arising from a choice (perhaps not conscious) of language rich in associations and possibilities of interpretation. Certain combinations yield a sense uncongenial to a result-clause relation with the preceding, and reduce *lm'n* to a vague, almost empty connective.

its land. The feminine suffix of *'rṣh* refers to Jerusalem (Kimhi); cf. *'rṣ y'zr* "the land (region) of Jaazer" (Num 22:5; also Josh 17:8; I Kings 4:10). It seems likely (but not certain) that the country of Judah rather than merely the region of Jerusalem is meant here; at any rate that is implied by the readings "the land" or "their land" (see text footnote), either of which is more natural.

shall be desolate (tšm) . . . *šmm* (*yšm*) *m-* can have various senses according to the ambiguity of both its elements; the following Ezekiel citations, very like our passage, illustrate them: "the land and all that filled it were *appalled at* [=because of] the sound of his roaring" (19:7); "the land will be *emptied of* what filled it" (32:15). If, guided by *šmmwn* "appalment" in the previous clause, we choose the first sense, then we may perceive "what fills it" (*ml'h*) as an ad hoc synonym of "lawlessness" (*ḥms*), on the strength of Ezekiel's frequent use of *ml'* with *ḥms* and murder (7:23; 8:17; 9:9 [one reading]; 11:6; 28:16—Flood story language [Gen 6:11, 13]). The sense will then be, the (population of the) land shall be struck numb with fear because of (=as punishment for) what fills it, namely, the lawlessness of its inhabitants. The relation to the foregoing expressed by *lm'n* is that spelled out above (comment to *So*).

If we are less venturesome, we will follow the second sense, which is better attested (Lev 26:43 *t'zb mhm* "be forsaken of them" || *bhšmh mhm* "be desolate [emptied] of them"; Zech 7:14), and render accordingly, "so the land will be desolate [emptied] of what [life and wealth] filled it, because of the lawlessness," etc. The ad hoc synonymy of *ml'h* and *ḥms* is replaced by the natural sense of each word—but at the cost of a switch from *šmmwn* "appalment" to *šmm m-* "be desolate [emptied] of," which attenuates the relationship between the two implied by *lm'n* "so." A third choice with *šmm* in the sense "be desolate" is to keep the synonymy, and play with the two senses of *m-*: either, "the land will be desolate *because of* what fills it, namely the lawlessness," etc., or "the land will be desolate [emptied] *of* what fills it, the lawlessness [or better: the wealth gained by crime (Amos 3:10)] of all its inhabitants."

20. The uncertainty about the scope of the calamity in the previous verse vanishes here in the face of "the inhabited cities . . . and the land." Similarly, the ambiguity of *šmm* is here canceled by the univocal *ḥrb* "be ruined," which here precedes it. The calamity will be country-wide devastation.

STRUCTURE AND THEMES

Since this and the foregoing passage both consist of symbolic acts, they are similar in form. After the revelation formula (vs. 17), comes (a) the command to perform the action (vs. 18). There follows (b) a command to relate its interpretation to the audience in the form of an oracle ("thus said Lord YHWH") (vs. 19aα). The interpretation (c) starts with the immediate reference of the act—how the people of Jerusalem will eat their meals anxiously (vs. 19aβ)—but moves through an indictment of all the population for lawlessness (vs. 19b) to a climactic prediction of a country-wide desolation (vs. 20). The passage ends with the recognition formula.

These parts are verbally interrelated. The items of the command (vs. 18), chiefly physical (quaking and trembling), include an indicator of emotion (anxiety) that links the command to the interpretation (vs. 19aβ). *'rṣ* and *šmm* recur in the second and third parts three times each, and their ambiguity and shifts in meaning provide the passage with unlooked-for fluidity; they are, as well, the key thematic terms. In vss. 19b and 20a the elements *šmm, 'rṣ* and *yšb* are arranged in a chiasm (abc cba) effecting closure of the threatening part of the oracle.

The structure serves the main theme: "He had threatened destruction to Jerusalem and its citizens [vs. 19]; he now adds the other cities of Judah which were still inhabited [vs. 20aβ] as if he said that no single corner should suppose itself free from slaughter" (Calvin).

Abarbanel and Fohrer regard our passage as depicting a situation following upon that of the preceding; the fright and desolation pertain to the survivors of the catastrophe who remain behind in the land of Israel. It appears more natural, however, to treat our passage as independent of what goes before it, and, like the similar meal symbol of 4:10f., 16f., a prediction of what would happen before the fall. Comparison of the phrase "inhabitants of Jerusalem on the soil of Israel" here with the post-fall "inhabitants of these ruins on the soil," etc. (33:24), also suggests that our passage deals with pre-fall Jerusalem.

While the meal symbolism of 4:10f. is of scarcity, here the prophet is to enact the symptoms of the terror that would seize the population in the face of the Babylonian onslaught. Constant, protracted emotions are said to be adjuncts of or substitutes for—i.e., present as regularly as—meals: "Go eat your bread in gladness, and drink of your wine in joy" (Qoh 9:7); cf. Ps 42:4; 80:6; Job 3:24. Zimmerli considers the prophet's trembling an ailment which he subsequently interpreted symbolically; nothing in the text suggests this. Why could Ezekiel not have felt himself ordered to act out the trembling as he was the even more arduous exercises of the siege-symbolism of chs. 4–5?

X. Discounting Prophecy
(12:21–28)

21 The word of YHWH came to me: 22 Man, what do you, on the soil
of Israel, mean by this proverb: "Time runs on and every vision
comes to nothing"? 23 So then, say to them: Thus said Lord YHWH:

I will put an end to this proverb;
they shall no longer use it in Israel!

Speak to them rather, "The time is at hand, and the event of every vision!"

24 For no longer shall [a]there be any idle vision
and empty divining[a] amidst the house of Israel.
25 For I, YHWH, will speak what word I will and it shall be fulfilled;
There shall be no more delay!
For in your time, you rebellious house, I will speak my word and fulfil it,
Declares Lord YHWH.

26 The word of YHWH came to me: 27 Man, the house of Israel say:

"The vision he has is of a far-off time,
about a distant future he prophesies."

28 So then, say to them: Thus said Lord YHWH:

There shall be no more delay!
Every word that I speak shall be fulfilled,
Declares Lord YHWH.

[a–a] Some mss. read *ḥāzon, miqsām* (absolute, not construct); render accordingly, "every vision be idle and divining [be] empty [or: and empty divining]."

COMMENT

12:22 *Man, what do you . . . mean.* We expect, after "Man" some such phrase as "say to the Israelites: [What do you mean . . .]." Instead, God's address to the culprits sets in directly (as in 18:2), as though the prophet were among them. Kimḥi aptly compares Exod 16:28, where God seems to include Moses in his rebuke to the people.

you, on ('al) *the soil of Israel.* As in 18:2: "What do you mean by using this proverb on the soil of Israel!" The proverb there reflects on God's justice; its citation by Jeremiah (31:28) proves that it was indeed current in the homeland. Others translate *'al* here "concerning (the land of Israel)," as in 36:6, but there the subject of the prophecy is indeed the land, while here the subject of the proverb is unfulfilled prophecy. We must assume that report of this proverb's currency in Judah had reached Ezekiel.

proverb. For *mašal* as a popular, often one-line, saying embodying a general truth, see W. McKane, *Proverbs,* OTL, pp. 22ff. The situation reflected on in the proverb must have been of long standing to have engendered a proverb; see the next comment.

Time runs on . . . Lit. "the days grow long." As the moment when the prophecy was uttered recedes further and further into the past without the prophecy's taking effect, its power peters out and it sinks into oblivion—a dead letter no one need worry about. (For the power of prophecy see I. L. Seeligmann, "Die Auffassung von der Prophetie in der Deuteronomistischen und Chronistischen Geschichtsschreibung," *Congress Volume, Göttingen 1977,* SVT 29 [Leiden: E. J. Brill, 1978], pp. 255ff.) From God's retort (vs. 25b) that fulfilment will surely come "in your time (lit. days)," it may be inferred that the "time" alluded to here is to be measured in lifetimes. Generations have lived under the shadow of unfulfilled prophecies; this circumstance has given rise to the disbelief epitomized in the proverb.

vision. I.e., prophecy. *ḥazon* is properly an optical phenomenon (*ḥaza* "see"; Dan 8:15ff.), but the term more often (as here) refers to verbal divine communication whether or not accompanying a vision (*THAT* I, p. 536; on this see Kaufmann, *Religion,* pp. 97ff.).

23. God's counter-proverb simply reverses the first verb of the proverb —*qar*^{e}*bu* "have drawn near" replacing *ya'ar*^{e}*ku* "grow long"—and substitutes the noun *dabar* lit. "word," but here content or event of prophecy, for the verb *'abad* "perish." The resulting sentence means, "The time of the event [realization] of every prophecy is near." The expression "the time is near" belongs to doom-proclamation, as in 7:7 *qarob hayyom*

(the plural *yamim* lit. "days" is used here to keep as close as possible to the language of the proverb; but see 22:4). When doomsday comes, the content of every prophecy will materialize; it will then be manifest that none lapsed.

The appearance in God's retort of a noun phrase where the proverb had a second verb clause is a free variation, of a piece with the variation of the first clause of vs. 25b in vs. 28 (described below). S invents a verb clause here ("and every vision will be [*nhw'*]"), and its spirit animates several critics who unnecessarily "emend" *dabar* into one or another verb (see *BHS*).

24. The epithets "idle vision, empty divining" are appropriated from the people's estimate of prophecy, and, in a way, admit its validity. The verse gives the ground of vs. 23a: why will the popular proverb go out of use? Because with the arrival of doomsday the woe-prophecies will cease being (regarded as) idle and empty! *miqsam* "divining" is a derogatory term; its use with reference to woe-prophecy reflects popular opinion. *ḥalaq* "smooth" (only here in a borrowed sense) is rendered according to a meaning attested in postbiblical Hebrew, "blank, empty" (Eliezer of Beaugency, Luzzatto).

According to this interpretation, the issue in this verse, as in the next, can only be the vindication of woe-prophecy; to that extent the ambiguity of the preceding verses, in which "every vision" may be taken to include weal-prophecy also, is resolved. It is striking, however, that the epithets are those normally attached to false weal-prophecy (this is most obvious in the standard vocalization, where "idle vision," "empty divining" are constructions identical with the epithets of false prophecy 13:6f.; it is slightly less obvious in the alternative reading [see text footnote], which, however, is easier and more in harmony with the idiom of the proverb). This has led many commentators (e.g., Cooke, Fohrer, Zimmerli, Wevers) to mistake our verse for an allusion to false weal-prophecy (they render *ḥalaq* as "seductive, flattering" in accord with other derivatives of *ḥlq*), and, in consequence, to excise it as out of context. (To be sure, the silencing of false prophecy when doom comes is an unavoidable—if incongruous—overtone of our verse.)

25. This verse elaborates on vs. 23b, at the same time giving the ground for the preceding verse. There will no longer be idle, empty (unfulfilled) prophecies because whatever word God speaks will without delay be fulfilled.

I . . . will speak . . . This sentence, which has been freely rendered, has a peculiar construction; comparison with its variant in vs. 28 is helpful:

(25)	*'dbr 't 'šr 'dbr* "I will speak what I will speak"	*dbr wy'sh* "a word that shall be done"
(28)	*kl dbry 'šr 'dbr* "All my words that I speak"	

The equivalence of these sentences is further suggested by their juxtaposition in both verses to "there shall be no more delay!" The first part of the passage from vs. 25 is an *idem per idem* construction (S. R. Driver, *Notes on the Hebrew Text and Topography of the Books of Samuel,* 2nd ed. [Oxford: Clarendon Press, 1913], pp. 185f., at I Sam 23:13) which here must be equivalent to a noun clause, "whatever I speak," to judge from the corresponding member of vs. 28. The *waw* of *wy'sh* functions as a relative, as in 14:7 "any man . . . who estranges himself [*wynzr*]"; cf. Gen 16:1 "a maid whose name [*wšmh* "that her name"] was Hagar"; Mal 1:10 "O that there were one among you that would close [*wysgr*]"; Job 14:5 "You have appointed him limits that he shall not pass [*wl' y'br*]." The context adds a certain urgency to the next clause: "it shall *soon* be done/fulfilled."

There . . . delay. The verb is feminine expressing a neuter (or abstract) subject (lit. "it shall [not] drag on"); cf. Num 14:41; Isa 7:7; 14:24; Jer 7:31 (GKC § 122 q; Joüon § 152 c).

27. "The house of Israel" are the exiles; "he" is Ezekiel.

28. *Every word.* The accents connect *kl dbry* with what comes before (as it were, "Every word that I speak shall not be delayed"), a dubious construction of *tmšk* "delay" whose subject is neuter (see above), not masculine plural (Luzzatto). The parallel of vs. 25 suggests our construction.

STRUCTURE AND THEMES

The two oracles in 12:21–25, 26–28 have the same basic structure: a popular saying is cited, followed by a divine response contradicting it (cf. 11:2ff., 14ff.). Both begin and end respectively with the formulas "The word of YHWH came to me: Man . . ." and "declares Lord YHWH"; in both God's response starts "So then, say to them: Thus said Lord YHWH."

The first, more complex oracle falls into two equal parts. Vss. 22–23 open with an angry question about the proverb in the land of Israel and close with God's counter-proverb. Vss. 24–25 consist of two *ki* "for" clauses, elaborating the grounds for God's retort. The two parts of the oracle are closely connected through a shared vocabulary: "every/any [*kol*] vision" (vss. 22, 23, 24), "time" (*yamim*) (vss. 22, 23, 25), "no longer/more [*lo 'od*]" (vss. 23, 24, 25), "word" (vss. 23, 25 [twice]). Second-person address opens the oracle (vs. 22) and closes it (vs. 25b); in between, Israel is spoken of in the third person. The piece is well-knit.

The second oracle is stripped down to the basic structure. However, its popular saying is more complex—a two-liner in chiastic synonymous parallelism, contrasting with the simple one-line proverb of the first oracle.

The second oracle shares much of the wording of the first: "vision," "time," and God's retort (an inverted variant of vs. 25a). It is something like an echo of the first; the relation of the two is best taken up after a discussion of their themes.

Common to both oracles are the dismissal of unfulfilled prophecy by the people and God's retort that his words will (soon) be fulfilled. The most important divergence occurs in the arguments for dismissing the prophecies; to these we now turn.

Other prophets record the skeptical public reception of their doom-oracles: Isaiah blames the wicked who say, "Let [YHWH] make haste, let him speed up his word for us to see it, let what YHWH planned soon come, so that we may know it" (5:19). Jeremiah complains, "See, they say to me, 'Where is the word of YHWH? Let it come!'" (17:15). The popular proverb of our first oracle differs in two ways from these sayings. Rather than a challenge, it is a "theological slogan" (McKane, *Proverbs,* p. 30)—a theory of desuetude based on generations-long delay in the fulfilment of prophecies. Moreover, it is framed in such general terms ("every/any vision") as to allow the inference that it applies to prophecies of weal and woe alike. "Prophetic words about the future . . . were self-contradictory. One moment they were promising salvation and freedom, and in the next breath they were announcing . . . gloom and disaster . . . The exaggerated pictures of blessing . . . had not as yet been fulfilled any more than had the descriptions of coming ruin . . . What was a sober realist to do but shrug his shoulders at all the unverifiable forecasts" (Eichrodt, *Ezekiel,* pp. 155f.); ". . . a frame of mind induced by the activities of false prophets, by the proven unreliability of prophecy and its inability to shed any light on the course of events" (McKane). While the proverb will allow such an interpretation, it is only with some strain that God's counter-proverb can be adjusted to it (e.g., by taking *dabar* to mean the "issue" of every prophecy, namely, the decision whether it was true or false). But two considerations plead against this interpretation: (1) Vss. 24–25, which give the ground for, and thus explain, what precedes, assert God's resolve to vindicate his word to "the rebellious house"; in the context of Ezekiel, that can only refer to hitherto unfulfilled prophecies of doom. (2) The next chapter deals at length with the false prophets of weal; far from supporting the view that they were discredited by the people, Ezekiel's fulminations against them show that they were widely believed and followed. Hence, despite the broad implication of the phrase "every vision" in vss. 22–24, its meaning in our context seems restricted to prophecies of doom; evidence of skepticism on the part of the people pertains to these only.

This first oracle, unlike the next one, does not concern Ezekiel's prophecies; it reacts to a proverb on the soil of Israel, and thus suggests the doom-prophecies of such as Jeremiah or Uriah as the immediate objects of skepticism (though, as observed above, the phenomenon of unfulfilled dooms was generations old). If so, we have here an acknowledgement almost unparalleled in Ezekiel, and rare in any of the classical prophets, that beside himself other true prophets were at work.

The second oracle answers a different mode of subverting prophecy, mentioned apparently for the first time in Amos 6:3: "[Woe to] those who put the evil day far off"; both Ibn Ezra and Kimḥi explain that verse by citing the popular saying in our vs. 27. Oracles of doom might be deferred—not canceled—for a generation or more because of the contrition of the condemned (I Kings 21:29 [Ahab]; II Kings 22:19f. [Josiah]) or God's long-suffering (see the summary in Maimonides, *Code, Yesode tora* 10.4, spelling out the implications of Jer 28:8f.). Hezekiah's punishment was expressly postponed, to his relief, until the time of his descendants (Isa 39:6f.). It was therefore possible to defuse Ezekiel's dooms without impugning their validity (as did the proverb of the first oracle) simply by "putting them far off." That is what the popular parallelistic epigram of the second oracle does.

Not only the thoughts, but also the locations of the epigrammatists in each of the two oracles diverge. The first addresses persons who are "on the soil of Israel"; the second addresses the exiles. Some critics regard these differences as enough to establish the separateness of the oracles: on two occasions the issue of delayed dooms arose and was dealt with similarly. Others think that we have here variant traditions of a single oracle. Since even the latter critics must suppose that the shapers of each of the traditions considered their version plausible, and since evidence outside of Ezekiel supports the viewpoints of both oracles, it makes little practical difference which hypothesis one adopts to account for their similarity.

XI. Substitutes for True Prophecy (13:1–23)

13 1 The word of YHWH came to me: 2 Man, prophesy against the prophets of Israel [a]who prophesy, and say to the prophets out of their own hearts[a], Hear the word of YHWH! Thus said Lord YHWH:

3 Woe to [b]the villainous prophets
who follow their whims[b]
without having seen a thing.
4 Your prophets, Israel, have become like jackals among ruins!
5 You have not gone up into the breaches
and made a fence about the house of Israel
so that they can stand firm in battle on the day of YHWH.
6 They utter idle visions and false divination
who say, "declares YHWH," when YHWH did not send them,
yet they expect to substantiate their word!
7 Surely it is idle visions you have uttered
and false divination you have spoken,
who say, "declares YHWH," when I never spoke.

8 So then, thus said Lord YHWH:
Because you have spoken idle things
and uttered false visions,
assuredly, I am coming at you,
declares Lord YHWH.
9 My hand will come upon the prophets
who utter idle visions and who divine falsehood;
they shall not be in the company of my people,
they shall not be listed in the register of the house of Israel,
and shall not reach the soil of Israel;
so you shall know that I am Lord YHWH—
10 For the very good reason that they misled my people,
saying, "All is well," when nothing was well.

a–a G "prophesy and say to them."
b–b G "those who prophesy out of their heart."

The people build a dry wall
and they daub it [c]with untempered plaster[c].
11 Say to those who daub on [d]untempered plaster[d]
that it will fall.
[e]Should there be[e] driving rain,
and you[f], hailstones, fall,
and a tempestuous wind burst forth
12 so that the wall falls,
you will surely be asked, "Where is the plaster you daubed on?"
13 Well then, thus said Lord YHWH:
I will make a tempestuous wind break forth in my fury,
and in my anger a driving rain will come,
and hailstones, in fury, for destruction.
14 I will demolish the wall that you daubed [c]with untempered plaster[c]
leveling it to the ground till its foundation is exposed.
When it falls and you perish within it
then you shall know that I am YHWH.
15 I will spend my fury on that wall and on those who daubed it with untempered plaster,
and [g]I will say[g] to you, Gone[h] is the wall and gone[h] are those who daubed it—
16 Israel's prophets who prophesy about Jerusalem,
those who utter visions of "All is well" for it,
when nothing is well, declares Lord YHWH.

17 And you, man, set your face toward the women of your people,
who play the prophet out of their own hearts, and prophesy against
them and 18 say: Thus said Lord YHWH:
Woe to those who sew cushions on the joints of every arm,
and make rags for the head of every stature
to entrap persons.
The persons of my people you entrap
and your own persons you maintain!
19 You profane me to my people
with handfuls of barley and breadcrumbs,

c–c G (S "so that) it will fall."
d–d Not in G S.
e–e G reflects Hebrew *whyh;* S *whnh.*
f G "I will give"; T *yat,* sign of accusative!
g–g S T "it will be said."
h S "where."

sentencing to death persons who should not die,
and to life persons who should not live,
as you lie to my people who listen to lies!
20 So then, thus said Lord YHWH:
I am coming at your cushions
where you entrap persons [d]like birds[d];
I will tear them off your arms
and set the persons whom you entrap free like birds.
21 I will tear your rags
and save my people from your clutches;
they shall no longer be prey in your clutches,
and you shall know that I am YHWH.
22 Because you fraudulently grieve the heart of the innocent man
whom I would not hurt,
and encourage the wicked man
so that he does not turn from his evil way and preserve
his life,
23 assuredly, you shall utter no more idle visions
nor divine any more divination;
I will save my people from your clutches
and you shall know that I am YHWH.

COMMENT

13:2. *prophesy against*. *'el* has this sense again in vs. 17, and in 21:2, 7, and thus interchanges with *'al* (e.g., 25:2). The loss of a distinction between these two prepositions is probably the effect of Aramaic, in which *'al* predominates and covers the meaning of both.

who prophesy. The tautology produces the effect, "who rant" (Davidson: "they prophesy, and that without limit: their mouths were always full of, 'the Lord saith'"). S suggests this deftly by adding an ethical dative *lhwn* after the verb (T. Nöldeke, *Compendious Syriac Grammar*, [London: Williams and Norgate, 1904], § 224), producing a sense "who love to prophesy, prophesy at will" (see the excellent summary of Hebrew usage of "ethical dative" in BDB, p. 515, def. i).

Alternatively, we may take a clue from *hmtnb'wt mlbhn* of vs. 17 and posit a corresponding base-phrase **hnb'ym mlbm* "who prophesy out of their own hearts" belonging to the following base sentence that has been broken up and the parts distributed among the a and b parts of this verse:

b * * *
hnb' w'mrt 'l nby'y ysr'l hnb'ym mlbm
a * * * * *
"prophesy and say to the prophets of Israel who prophesy
out of their own hearts"

G's reading recalls 34:2.

prophets out of their own hearts. mlbm "out of their hearts" is treated as a unit, the *m-* felt as fused with its noun (cf. *mrhwq* after a construct in Jer 23:23; GKC § 130 a; König, III, § 336 w). It replaces YHWH as the origin of prophetic authority (in the standing phrase *nby'y YHWH*) with the ordinary source of human figments. For our passage Num 16:28 is an antecedent: "YHWH has sent me [see our vs. 6, "YHWH did not send them"], and not out-of-my-heart." Cf. also Jeroboam's festival, invented "out of his own heart" (I Kings 12:33 *qre*), and Jer 23:16 "the vision of their own heart" spoken by false prophets.

3. *Woe to. hoy 'al* (*l-* [vs. 18]) serves in Ezekiel for the common extra-Ezekiel *'oy l-* (in Ezekiel only in 16:23). Further, *hoy* alone (34:2) = *'oy* alone (24:6, 9) = *'oy l-* "woe to."

villainous prophets. In Hebrew, a near anagram of "prophets out of their own hearts." *nabal* expresses religio-moral depravity; cf. Isa 32:6, with its additional similarities to our passage:

For the villain (*nabal*) speaks villainy (*n^e^bala*)
And his heart (*w^e^libbo*) plots evil
To act impiously
And to speak error (*to'a;* cf. *hiṭ'u* in our vs. 10) against YHWH.

whims. ru'aḥ is both the inspiriting that leads to prophecy (11:5) and the animating principle of "will" or "mind" (|| *leb* in 18:31; 36:26; with 20:32 cf. Jer 3:16; here too *ru'aḥ* parallels *leb* in vs. 2). "Follow after" (*halak 'aḥ^a^re*) is often pejorative, as in 20:16 (after idols), Jer 3:17 (willful heart). Our clause recalls the description of the false prophet in Micah 2:11:

If a man walking in delusion and falsehood (*holek ru'aḥ wašeqer*) should lie (*kizzeb:* cf. the frequent *kzb* in Ezek 13:6ff., 19) . . .

With these men, auto-inspiration and willfulness in pursuit of delusion replace obedience to a divine call.

without having seen a thing. So the ancient versions (G S T V) interpret our phrase. *lblty* is followed, unusually, by a perfect instead of an infinitive (but cf. Jer 23:14) and does not have its usual sense of "so as not." Moderns interpret the anomaly variously: "according to what they have not seen" GKC § 152 x, followed by Cooke and Zimmerli; "so that they (viz. the people [so Cornill]; the prophets [so S. R. Driver, *Tenses,* § 41. obs.]) can not see [the truth]"; G. R. Driver, *Biblica,* p. 150, supposes *ra'u* to be a noun like *śaḥu* (47:5), meaning "sight, seeing." I take *lblty* here as *lbly* "in a condition of not," noting the equivalence of the two in Deut 9:28 and Num 14:16; Job 14:12 and Ps 72:7.

4. Jackals scavenge in ruins (Lam 5:18); the sight of them making, or enlarging, breaches in tumbled walls was familiar (Neh 3:35). They thus benefit from and contribute to ruin. Israel, a religio-moral ruin, teems with jackal-prophets who batten on the decay, and by telling the people what they want to hear, hasten the end.

have become. The position and sense of *haya* is the same in 22:18.

5. A related image: cultivated vineyards and fields were protected from marauders by (stone) fences (Num 22:24; Isa 5:5; Prov 24:31; Ps 80:13). Israel lay defenseless before God's punitive stroke, for its integrity (fence) was destroyed (breached) by iniquity. The figure is spelled out in Isa 30:13: "This iniquity shall work on you like a spreading breach that occurs in a lofty wall." The prophet's task was on the one hand to warn the people of their iniquity (build a fence), and, on the other, to intercede with God on their behalf (stand in the breach). Ps 106:23 employs the latter figure in describing Moses' archetypal actions in the crisis of the Golden Calf (Exod 32):

> [God] would have destroyed them
> Had not Moses, his elect, stood in the breach before him
> To turn back his fury from destroying.

The figure recurs in 22:30, slightly different.

The images of vss. 4 and 5 are not the same, but their juxtaposition invites a unitary interpretation; so in the midrash (*Ruth Rabba, Petiḥta* 5): "As the jackal prowling the ruins keeps an eye on the passages [breaches] through which he can flee if a man appears, so you . . . did not go up into the breaches [to ward off God's blow] like Moses."

gone up into the breaches. The expression in 22:30 and Ps 106:23 is "stand in the breach" (so T here). "Go up" may be explained by the custom of running rams up ramps so as to break through middle and upper courses of walls (they would be thinner; see Y. Yadin, *The Art of Warfare in Biblical Lands*, 2 vols. [New York: McGraw-Hill, 1963], II, pp. 315, 422–25); defenders would have to "go up" into such breaches.

6. *yet they expect*. An indication that these prophets were sincere and believed in their mission. Some early commentators took *yiḥel* as transitive, "rouse expectation" (so in Ps 119:49).

to substantiate. Pi'el *qiyyem* is late (otherwise only in Esther and late Psalms; once in Ruth), replacing pre-exilic *heqim* in this sense; cf. Jer 28:6—whence the possibility is suggested that the subject of the infinitive is YHWH: "expect [him] to fulfil."

7. *who say*. Taking *waw* as a relative (see comment at 12:25, *wy'sh*).

9. *My hand will come upon* (hay^{e}ta 'el). Verbally identical with the phrase used for ecstatic possession (33:22; I Kings 18:46 = *hay^{e}ta 'al,*

Ezek 1:3), here the sense is hostile (*'el* as in *'ᵃlekem* of the preceding verse); those upon whom God's hand never came in prophetic seizure will experience his punishment—a trenchant pun.

in the company (sod) *of my people. sod* is used of a band of friends (Jer 15:17 "revellers"; 6:11 "youths"); Israel is depicted as an intimate circle to which these prophets will not gain access. The phrase recalls Gen 49:6, where Jacob abjures association with Simeon and Levi: "Let my person not enter their circle [*sodam*]."

register (kᵉtab). Another late word, used only in Esther and Ezra, Nehemiah ("genealogical lists," Ezra 2:62; Neh 7:64) and Chronicles. The reference here appears to be to a civil census list, rather than a heavenly "book [of life/the living]" alluded to in Exod 32:32f., Isa 4:3; Ps 69:29; Dan 12:1 (*THAT* II, pp. 172f.); compare the verdict passed on the false exiled prophet Shelemiah in Jer 29:32: "No descendant of his shall dwell among this people, nor will he see the good I am going to do to my people." Ezek 20:38 also threatens the wicked with excision from the community of those who return from exile.

10. *For the very good reason. ya'an ubᵉya'an* occurs only here, 36:3 and Lev 26:43.

misled (hiṭ'u). The root *ṭ'h* is the Aramaic and postbiblical Hebrew replacement of biblical *t'h* (*hit'a-* of false prophets, e.g., Jer 23:32); it is a hapax in the Bible.

dry wall (ḥayiṣ). Another hapax, the word occurs in *Mishnah, Shebi'it* 3.8: among agricultural activities forbidden in the fallow year was the terracing of ravines; however, it was allowed to build a *ḥayiṣ* in them, which was not mortared with earth. Accordingly, *ḥayiṣ* is an unimproved wall, *qir* (vs. 12) an improved (plastered) one (Ehrlich).

untempered plaster. tapel has been explained in several ways: (a) "anything that lacks an essential ingredient" (Rashi, at 22:28)—in Job 6:6, "insipid, tasteless"; in our context, "mud without chaff" (V), or "plain clay without straw" (T)—the organic material providing the essential binding ingredient for mortar and plaster (cf. C. F. Nims, "Bricks Without Straw," *BA* 13 [1950], 22ff.; S. Avitsur, *Man and His Work* [Hebrew] [Jerusalem: Karta, 1976], p. 134); (b) Whatever is daubed on —here the context requires something insubstantial, e.g., "whitewash"; taking *tpl* as equivalent to *ṭpl* "daub, smear on" (Mishnaic Hebrew *ṭᵉpela* "plaster"); so most moderns (e.g., BDB, GB, translations). I follow (a) because our passage evidently underlies Lam 2:14, "Your prophets uttered *šaw wᵉtapel* visions about you"; the pair of qualifiers is happily rendered by "empty [idle] and insipid [futile]." (One may compare the interchange in *Tosefta Berachot* 6.7 of *tᵉpillat tipla* "futile prayer" with *tᵉpillat šaw;* S. Lieberman, *Tosefta Ki-fshuṭah: Order Zera'im*, Part 1 [New York: Jewish Theological Seminary of America, 1955], p. 111, compares Lam 2:14.) A curiosity is the derivation from Arab "spittle" (Herrmann, Tur-Sinai, in B-Y) which hardly applies to Job 6:6.

As said expressly in 22:28, "they" who daubed the wall were the prophets: the people built the dry wall—a figure of their unfounded optimism, while the prophets daubed it with worthless stuff—their self-inspired predictions of well-being. Such a structure will offer no shelter from the storm (God's wrath).

Here and in the sequel, G S render *tapel* always as though it were *tippol* "it [fem., see ahead on vs. 14] will fall," syntactically very awkward, but calling attention to the assonantal play of the Hebrew.

11. *that it will fall.* The conjunctive use of *waw* is found, though infrequently (Gen 47:6 *wᵉyeš* = *ki yeš* "that there are"; see S. Loewenstamm and J. Blau, *Thesaurus of the Language of the Bible* [Hebrew] II [Jerusalem: Qonqordanṣia Tanakit, 1959], p. 439 [q, r]). G S render only one word here ("it will fall") raising the suspicion that their *Vorlage* had only *tpl; wypl* may then be an erroneous dittograph.

The first two conditional clauses are strange. One expects *wᵉhaya* (reflected in G) to start the condition (GKC § 159 g; T *yhy*). The apostrophe to the hailstones is very odd; G V and Abarbanel read *w'tnh* not as a pronoun but as a verb, "and I give (=produce)." The following two verbs may then be construed as in relative clauses—"hailstones, which fall . . . wind, which bursts forth." S recombines into a smooth sentence: "Lo! [as though *hnh* for *hyh*] I will give driving rain and falling hailstones and a tempestuous wind; and [the wall] shall be split . . ."

hailstones ('elgabiš). G "pelting-stones" (but in 38:22 "hailstones"), S and medievals, "hailstones"; only here and in 38:22, associated again with rain, fire and sulphur, from heaven. This is not the usual word for hail, and its relation to *gabiš* in Job 28:17f. (context of precious stones) is not clear. (Cf. the Akkadian pair *algames/šu—gamesu,* a kind of stone.) Ugaritic *algbṯ* ("24 talents of *a.*" in a list of commodities) is cognate.

burst forth. In midrashic Hebrew, *biqqa'* has this intransitive sense (B-Y, s.v.) and the vocalization may reflect later usage; one expects *yibbaqeaʿ* (nif'al: cf. Isa 58:8, of light).

13. *I will make . . . burst forth.* For a usually intransitive pi'el serving as a transitive, cf. *qinne* in Deut 32:21a; I Kings 14:22; *yiḥel* in Ps 119:49.

14. *leveling it to the ground.* In Lam 2:2 it is Judah's fortresses that have been "leveled to the ground," while in Micah 1:6 the foundations of Samaria are to be exposed. The language of this clause is thus more appropriate to massive demolition than to the fall of a mere wall; it facilitates the intrusion, in the next clause, of the reference to Jerusalem.

When it (fem.) *falls and you perish within it* (fem.). The reference is not to the wall (masc.) but to the city of Jerusalem (cf. 5:12). In its rendering of vs. 13, T had already supplied the political referents of the natural elements; here it perceives the shift from wall to city and extends it over the whole verse: "I will demolish the city [*qrt'*] in which you have prophesied falsely; I will cast it to the ground so that its foundations are exposed; it will fall and you will perish within it." Note that on this interpretation prophets in Jerusalem are referred to.

15. *I will say . . . Gone.* In contrast to the anonymous query of vs. 12, here it is God who speaks, making an authoritative assertion. S assimilates our passage more, T less, to vs. 12, but the complementary changes—"I will say" and "Gone"—bespeak a different message here, exemplifying Ezekiel's habit of varying when he repeats.

17. *play the prophet.* While both *nibba* (vss. 2, 16) and *hitnabbe* (here) are denominatives of *nabi* and mean "act as a prophet," *nibba* tends to be used for verbal prophesying, *hitnabbe* for the external behavior peculiar to prophecy (e.g., signs of possession). Derogation (I Kings 22:8, 18), aberration (Jer 29:26f.) and imposture (here) attach only to the latter. See *THAT* II, 16f.; M. Segal, *Mevo Ha-miqra* [Jerusalem: Kiryat Sepher, 1955], II, p. 240, esp. fns. 39, 40; R. Wilson, "Prophecy and Ecstasy," *JBL* 98 (1979), 321–37.

18–19. The practices and terms of these two verses are obscure; we have interpreted them as fortune-telling. *k^esatot* (sing. *keset*) are "cushions, pads" according to G S and tannaitic Hebrew (see below); BDB "fillet," i.e., magical bands (as cognate with Akkadian *kasū* "bind magically"), ignores this evidence. *'aṣṣile yaday* (*'aṣṣilot yad-* in Jer 38:12) is, according to a Syriac cognate and G S T "elbow" (in Jeremiah evidently "armpit"); properly "arm joint"; note that in vs. 20, the "cushions" are attached to the "arms" of the women. The anomalous plural *yaday* has analogues, collected by Kimḥi, *Mikhlol* 11a (ed. W. Chomsky, p. 221 and note on p. 373). *mispaḥot* looks like the plural of *mispaḥat* (Lev 13:6ff.) "scurf" (TpJ "peeling overlay"), from *spḥ* "add, attach to," whence may come G S "mantle, covering," followed by most moderns. But in tannaitic Hebrew (*Tosefta Baba Qama* 11.12, ed. Zuckermandel, p. 371, note) we find, "a pillow full of soft cloths and a cushion (*keset*) full of *mispaḥot* (variant in BT *Baba Qama* 119b: soft cloths)," whence S. Lieberman defines *m.* as "rags" (*Tosefet Rishonim* II, p. 104); so T *ptkmryn* (by which it also renders *ṭl'wt* in 16:17, "patches"). The use of this word for the head covering of the women will be insulting (that, like the "cushions" on their arms, the "rags" were on the heads of the women not of their clients, is the most natural sense of "your *m.*" in vs. 21. L. Ginzberg remarked the importance of the tannaitic usage as pointing to the late currency of these terms, since it cannot be supposed that biblical hapax legomena would otherwise be employed in tannaitic Hebrew for such everyday objects ("Beiträge zur Lexicographie des Jüdisch-Aramäischen," *MGWJ* 78 [1934], 28f.; he unconvincingly proposes "chopped straw" for *m.*). The attachment of these trappings to arms and head early evoked the Jewish phylacteries (by this single word the Origenic *ho hebraios* renders both Hebrew terms [Field]), which were vulgarly regarded as amulets (Aramaic *qmy'* as Ephraem Syrus renders *kstwt* [Smend]). Inasmuch as vs. 20 makes the "cushions" the instrument of "entrapment of persons" (see next paragraph), they are almost certainly magical appurtenances.

to entrap persons. ṣoded is an intensive of *ṣud* "hunt down" (not "kill"), probably with reference to many objects (*n^e^pašot* "persons"). A like phrase recurs in Prov 6:26, "a married woman can trap [*taṣud*] an honorable person [*nepeš*]" with her wiles; it is a figure for the enticement of gullibles. Theories based on the notion of the magical catching of disembodied souls (T. H. Gaster, *Myth, Legend, and Custom in the Old Testament,* pp. 615ff.) disregard the absence of evidence that *nepeš* ever has such a sense in Hebrew.

you entrap. Interrogative *h* followed by long consonant as in 18:29; 20:30 (GKC § 100 l; Joüon § 102 m), here expressing indignation; see comment at 20:4. The main contrast is "persons of my people" and "your own persons [selves]," emphasized by the balanced periphrasis (e.g., *n^e^pasot l^e^'ammi* instead of *napšot 'ammi*). The verbs connected with each object are not such direct contrasts: Do you think you can get away with entrapping my poor folk and making a living off their custom?

19. *profane me . . . with handfuls of barley . . .* The fortune-tellers degraded God by invoking him in their hocus-pocus (Mesopotamian diviners and exorcists regularly invoked deities; for a thoughtful discussion see H. Saggs, *The Encounter with the Divine in Mesopotamia and Israel* [London: Athlone Press, 1978], pp. 129ff.). Being so closely associated with "profanation," the barley and bread are to be taken, not as the paltry price of their services (so G, Eliezer of Beaugency), but rather as means of divination. Two possibilities may be considered: divination was performed with these materials—as, e.g., in Mesopotamia, by throwing flour on water (G. Contenau, *La Divination chez les Assyriens et les Babyloniens* [Paris: Payot 1940], p. 296; he compares Greek aleuromancy and alphitomancy—divination by wheat and barley meal). Alternatively, these grain items may have been offered to God in connection with divination (cf. the barley offering of Num 5:15); this view was developed by W. R. Smith, "On the Forms of Divination and Magic Enumerated in Deut. XVIII 10, 11, Part 1," *Journal of Philology* 13 (1885), 273–87; one might compare the modest offerings of honey, incense and cakes accompanying the Mesopotamian *namburbi* exorcisms (R. I. Caplice, *The Akkadian Namburbi Texts: An Introduction* [Los Angeles: Undena, 1974]). It is noteworthy that in Mesopotamia breadcrumbs are offered exclusively to ghosts (who figure there and in Israel in divination; A. L. Oppenheim, "Analysis of an Assyrian Ritual (KAR 139)," *History of Religion* 5 [1966], pp. 250–65).

20. *like birds.* A guess based on Aramaic *paraḥta* "bird" from *prḥ* "fly" (for the image, see Lam 3:52, "They hunted me down (*ṣaduni*) like a bird"); for *l-* "as" GB adduces Gen 23:17f.; Num 22:22; Deut 31:21; I Sam 22:13; Ps 48:4, none of which are entirely convincing. MT has the

word in both halves of the verse, construing it with "entrap." S G, on the other hand, reflect it only in the second clause, where it complements "I will release" (S "and make them fly away"); cf. the image of an escaping bird in Ps 124:7; Prov 6:5.

Before the second *lprḥt* the strange and redundant *'et nᵉpašim* occurs; it looks like a corruption. Cornill cleverly conjectured *lᵉḥopšim* "free" as the original reading, on the basis of the phrase *šillaḥ lᵉḥopšim* "set free" found in contemporary literature: Jer 34:9–16; Isa 58:6.

22. *grieve the heart. k'h* nif'al is construed with "heart" in Ps 109:16 ("the grieved in heart"); since the pairing of active hif'il with passive nif'al is common (*histir–nistar* "hide"; *hizhir–nizhar* "warn," *hiš'ir–niš'ar* "leave–remain"), this occurrence of hif'il *hak'ot* deserves more consideration than one would gather from recent critics who emend it to *hik'ib*. The ancient versions translate MT *hak'ot* and *hik'ib* "hurt" in this verse by the same term, but that is not ground for assuming they read the same verb in both places (the Authorized Version, working from MT, translates both "made sad").

STRUCTURE AND THEMES

The chapter is marked off as a single event by the revelation formula in vs. 1, which does not recur until 14:1; notwithstanding, on thematic grounds, there is a doubt as to its unity. The main section, A, on false prophets, begins with "Man" (vs. 2); it ends with the stereotypical "declares YHWH" (vs. 16). A subsection, B, about fortune-tellers follows, introduced by "And you, man" and concluding with the recognition formula "you shall know," etc. (vss. 17–23).

A, on false prophets, may again be divided in two: (1) the denunciation of counterfeit prophets ("Man" [vs. 2]—"you shall know," etc. [vs. 9]). Vs. 10, starting as the ground of punishment announced in vs. 9, shifts abruptly to a new theme in its middle—(2) the popular delusion of well-being fostered by false prophets, soon to be exploded by calamity (vss. 10–15, mostly taken up by the figure of the jerry-built wall). The conclusion (vs. 16) fuses expressions taken from the two parts of this section: "prophets of Israel who prophesy a vision" (1), "of 'All's well' when nothing is well" (2).

B, on fortune-tellers has a similar structure, though on a smaller scale: (1) a main oracle (vss. 17–21) and a restatement (vss. 22f.), whose conclusion resumes terms drawn from A ("idle," "divination") as well as from B. The halving structure with resumptive conclusion, so characteristic of Ezekiel, is well displayed—on a small scale within A, on a large in A and B. The following table sets forth the structural similarity of A and B.

		false prophets		**fortune-tellers**	
	(2)	Man, prophesy against the prophets . . . out of their own hearts . . .	(17)	And you man . . . against the women . . . who prophesy out of their own hearts and prophesy against them	
	(3)	Thus said Lord YHWH: Woe to	(18)	and say, Thus said Lord YHWH: Woe to	
1	(4–6)	[description of evil-doing; simile, metaphor]	(18–19)	[description of evil-doing; metaphor of hunting]	1
	(7)	Did not (*h^{a}lo*) . . .			
	(8)	So then, thus said Lord YHWH: Because . . . Assuredly, I am coming at you . . .	(20)	So then, thus said Lord YHWH: I am coming at . . .	
	(9)	[punishment] and you shall know that I am YHWH	(20–21)	[punishment] and you shall know that I am YHWH	
	(10)	For the very good reason that [offense, wall metaphor in	(22)	Because [offense, restatement of foregoing]	
	(11–12)	conditional statement; Will not (*h^{a}lo*)]			
	(13)	Well then (*laken*), thus said Lord YHWH	(23)	Assuredly (*laken*)	
2	(13–15)	[punishment]		[punishment; stated in terms drawn from main section and subsection]	2
		And you shall know that I am YHWH		and you shall know that I am YHWH	
	(14)				
	(16)	conclusion, resuming terms of both parts of section			

The verbal texture of the main components is similar, showing many repetitions of words as well as of phrases: vss. 1–9, prophets, prophesy, Israel, vision, divination, idle, false; vss. 10–15, plaster, fall (assonant with "untempered plaster"), end (*klh*); vss. 17–23, entrap/prey (*ṣwd*), persons, cushions, rags. There are also significant terms that cross the boundaries of the components and unite them (especially in the resumptive vss. 16 and 23), vision, my people (vss. 9f., 18f., 21).

The alternation between second and third persons in vss. 2–10 has given rise to a theory of fusion of two oracles. Rothstein (followed by

Cooke) gave priority to second-person sentences, since the third-person sentences seem to have a later vantage point—beyond the fall, looking to the restoration (3, 5[G], 6, 9; according to the *NAB:* 3, 4, 6, 9). But this theory cannot avoid manipulating the text even further in order to obtain consistency, and Herrmann and Zimmerli rightly give up the persons as a criterion. The theory is condemned by its necessitating the separation of "I am coming at you" (vs. 8, second person) from "my hand will come upon the prophets" (vs. 9, third person), in defiance of the rule that "I am coming at . . ." is followed by a sentence of punishment. The shift in persons in vss. 8–9 is paralleled in 26:2ff.; 28:21ff.; the amount of alternation here is remarkable (bespeaking rapid changes in the mental address of the prophet), but not the practice. Vs. 4, with its apostrophe to Israel, may well be an epigram incorporated by the prophet. From the viewpoint of its literary craft, the chapter shows a unified design.

Two substitutes for true prophets are denounced: counterfeit prophets in the exile (vss. 2–9) and in Jerusalem (vss. 10–15), and fortune-tellers (among the exiles?). Each in their own way vitiated the oracles of God and Ezekiel's mission. The counterfeits diverted the people's minds from the impending doom, and thus guaranteed it. The divine anger at them often breaks out in the prophecies of Jeremiah:

> They prophesy lies in my name; I have not sent them or given them orders or spoken to them. Lying visions, divination, nothingness, and the delusions of their heart they prophesy to you (14:14).

Jer 23 is particularly close in themes and language to our chapter.

> They speak the vision of their own hearts, not from the mouth of YHWH. I did not send the prophets, but they ran; I did not speak to them, yet they prophesied . . . I am coming at the prophets, declares YHWH, who make their tongues declare oracles; I am coming at those who prophesy lying dreams . . . and relate them, and mislead my people by their lies and their wantonness, whereas I never sent them . . . and they will do this people no good (23:16–32).

They are unaware of the "tempest of YHWH, the fury that has gone forth" against the wicked (23:19). They promise, "All will be well with you; no evil will befall you" (vs. 17); they "heal the fractures of my people superficially, saying, 'All is well' when nothing is well" (6:14; 8:11). Their effect is to "strengthen the hands of evildoers, so that they do not repent each one of his evil" (23:14). These counterfeits will die by sword and famine when Jerusalem falls (14:15).

Passages in Jeremiah's letter to the exiles denounce "prophets and diviners" among them who "beguile" them (Jer 29:15, 8f., 23, 28). The false hopes they inspired can be inferred from Jeremiah's insistence that the exile will be long, and that they must therefore settle down and build their lives in Babylonia. There was thus no difference between the exile and Jerusalem in this matter; both contained counterfeit prophets who thwarted the prophets of doom. And just as Jeremiah could fulminate against such men both at home and abroad, so might Ezekiel.

The two parts of Ezekiel's denunciation of the counterfeits have a common theme of illusory bulwarks against the coming calamity. First Israel is likened to a ruined vineyard (combining vss. 4ff.); the false prophets, instead of repairing its fence, like destructive jackals exploit the ruin for their own benefit, widening the breaches and exposing it helpless to the enemy. They keep Israel ignorant of their iniquity and defenseless before the divine anger, nor do they shield the people by interceding with God on their behalf. The second figure has the people building a dry wall to protect themselves, the prophets joining them in self-deception by plastering it over with plain mud, as if such a flimsy structure could withstand a rainstorm. Instead of telling the people how futile their hopes are, the prophets encourage them with more of the same, leaving them helpless on the day of wrath.

The poet who keened over fallen Jerusalem adopted the judgment and the idiom of Ezekiel:

> Your prophets uttered idle and insipid visions to you
> They did not expose your iniquity
> So as to restore your fortunes,
> But uttered to you idle and delusive oracles. (Lam 2:14)

Next, the prophet rebukes women who vitiated the effect on individuals of his warnings as a "lookout." By announcing God's sentences of death, he was to enable the condemned to repent and thus preserve their lives. These women did not warn but told fortunes; far from moving to action, they checked it, as useless in the face of predetermined destiny. Through divinatory rituals in which they invoked God, they usurped the prophet's privilege of declaring who would live and who would die (I Kings 14:1ff.; II Kings 1:6; 8:10; 20:1), and this on grounds that had no relation to the just deserts of their clients. So they wrongfully disheartened the innocent and encouraged the wicked, who credulously listened to their lies, turning away from the true messages of God in the mouth of Ezekiel.

Since the rites and appurtenances of these women gave them their hold on the people, particular attention is devoted to them in the prophecy. On their arms and heads the women attached what the prophet scoffingly calls cushions and rags; since it was by these that the folk were beguiled ("entrapped"), it may be surmised that they were divinatory paraphernalia, amulets, which when worn (like the priestly garments) lent special sanctity and power to the wearer (W. R. Smith). The grain items, used in a religious ritual in which God was invoked ("profaned" according to the censorious language of the prophet), may have been either a means through which the divine decision (of life and death) was disclosed (say, by being strewn on water), or, as seems more likely, offerings accompanying the prayers and invocations of the women; cf. Lev 2:14f. and the *todah*-breadcakes, Lev 7:12. If the latter, the belittling terms "handfuls" and "crumbs" would have more point—as insulting to their sacred offerings.

An incantation from the Babylonian Talmud (*Pesaḥim* 110a) has long been connected with our passage at least since the twelfth-century C.E. commentator R. Samuel b. Meir:

> Amemar [fifth century C.E.] said: The chief witch once said to me, if someone has run into witches he should recite this: "Hot dung in torn baskets into your mouths witches! May your heads be bald, may your crumbs fly away (*prḥ prḥyyky*), may your spices be scattered . . ."

L. Ginzberg (loc. cit.), followed by H. Yalon (*Quntresim le- 'inyene ha-lašon ha-'ivrit* II/1 [1938], 21), rendered "heads be bared," and understood it to mean, may your magic head-coverings (our *mispaḥot*) be removed—in accord with the rest of the line that wishes that these witches be denied their other magical appurtenances. Judging by the attention paid to them, it is the trappings, not the women, who are the objects of God's wrath, for they are a travesty of legitimate methods of inquiring into the future, and divert the people from belief in God. This silence with respect to the women contrasts with the law condemning witches and necromancers in Exod 22:17; Lev 20:27 (I Sam 28:9). Were these women "small fry," too trifling for God's attention?

The communal and the individual tasks fused in the "lookout" passage are here separated: the counterfeits correspond to the first, the fortune-tellers to the second. Taken together, they effectively nullify Ezekiel's work.

Among the denunciations of Israel in the first division of the Book of Ezekiel, this chapter stands out for its sympathy with "my people," (*'ammi,* seven times!), whom God is eager to protect from its self-serving misleaders. Such benevolence and such a portrayal of Israel as victims recur only in ch. 34—the censure, among prophecies of restoration, of Israel's past rulers ("Woe [to you], shepherds of Israel! . . ." cf. esp. 34:10: "I will save my flock from their mouths, so that they shall no longer be food for them," with our vs. 21). It is true that, as Jer 23 shows, denunciation of false prophets occurred in the pre-fall period; the terms of the "daubed wall" passage (vss. 10–15) are clearly also pre-fall. But what of the specific formulation of vss. 2–9? The future horizon is the return from exile, yet that need not indicate a post-fall standpoint: since prophets already exiled are referred to, their punishment can only take the form of excision from the restored community. Their offenses are described mostly in perfects (unlike Jer 23, in which participles and imperfects are common); to be sure, that can be paralleled in pre-fall oracles, especially with indictments (cf. ch. 22, esp. vs. 28), where Hebrew perfects = English present-perfects). Nonetheless, the preponderance of perfects evokes Lam 2:14, which is manifestly post-fall. When the verb tense is taken together with the differential sympathy toward the people and anger toward their misleaders, the possibility that in vss. 2–9 we have a post-fall version of a polemic against false prophecy gains weight (this on the assumption that before the fall only oracles of anger toward the people were given; but see ch. 18). The background of the oracle against the fortune-tellers is impossible to determine. The phraseological connection with the lookout task of the prophet suggests a pre-fall situation. We entertain, then, the possibility that the first part of the chapter is late; that the present design of the chapter is therefore editorial (maybe by the prophet); that linkage within the chapter was thematic—substitutes for true prophecy; while the placement of the chapter as a whole was determined by topical and verbal links between the end of ch. 12 and the first section of ch. 13 ("idle vision . . . divination").

There is a remarkable clustering of leprosy terms in the last two sections of the chapter: "plaster walls" (Lev 14:42, etc.; 39), *mispaḥat* (see commentary to vs. 18), "tear out (of clothing)" (Lev 13:56), *poraḥat* (Lev 13:42, etc.), "set free, release" (Lev 14:53, of a bird). Tur-Sinai (*Pešuṭo,* ad loc.) connected this with the magical paraphernalia of the women, which he conjectures were designed to inflict leprosy on their victims. Yet assonance need not mean semantic identity: *mispaḥat* and *poraḥat* do not mean here what they do in Leviticus, though the sound and the evocation are present. It is difficult to say what this assonance conveyed—perhaps that these persons and their doings were as unclean scurfs on the body of the people.

XII. God Will Not Respond
(14:1–11)

14 1 Some men of the elders of Israel came[a] to me[b] and sat down
before me. 2 The word of YHWH came to me: 3 Man, these men have
raised their idols in their thoughts and set their stumbling-blocks of
iniquity before their faces; am I supposed to respond to their inquiry?
4 Now speak to them and say to them: Thus said Lord YHWH:
Any man of the house of Israel who raises his idols in his thoughts
and sets his stumbling-block of iniquity before his face, and comes to
a prophet, I YHWH will oblige him with an answer—[c]coming with[c]
his many idols!—5 so as to catch the house of Israel at their thoughts,
they who have fallen away from me with all their idols!
6 So say to the house of Israel: Thus said Lord YHWH: Repent
and turn from your idols; from all your abominations turn your
faces!
7 For any man of the house of Israel or of the aliens who live
in Israel who falls away from me and raises his idols in his thoughts
and sets his stumbling-block of iniquity before his face, and comes
to a prophet to inquire of me by him, I YHWH will [d]by myself[d] oblige
him with an answer. 8 I will set my face against that man; I will [e]make
of him a sign and a byword[e] and cut him off from among my people
Israel; and you shall know that I am YHWH.
9 And if a prophet is so misled as to speak an oracle, I YHWH
have misled that prophet. I will stretch out my hand against him

[a] MT singular, all versions plural. *Minḥat Shay* at 23:44 notes eight cases of this verb in the singular where context requires plural; four of these are in Ezekiel: here and 20:38; 23:44; 36:20, all *plene* (with *waw*). It is supposed that the *waw* was wrongly copied before, instead of after, the *alef* (*wyb'w*, as in 9:2, etc.).

[b] S adds "to inquire of the Lord" as in 20:1.

[c–c] Q (*b'*) = T (*d'ty*); K (*bh*) "regarding it—regarding [*b*-] . . ." = S "[I the Lord will be a witness for him] regarding it [*bh*], regarding [the multitude of his idols]." G "in which [plural] his thought is entangled," an obscure rendering of a text close to ours (G at times renders *gillulim* by "thought(s)"; see Cooke's note here and at 6:4).

[d–d] Not reflected in S T (*bmymry* has nothing to do with MT *by*, but is a fixed adjunct of *mšt'l*—see T, vss. 3, 4; 20:3 end, 31 twice; 36:37); nor does G reflect *by*, but rather a text similar to the end of vs. 4 minus *gillulim*.

[e–e] Some editions read *wah^{a}šimmotihu* "I will desolate him"; G "I will make him a desert and a desolation."

and destroy him from among my people Israel. 10 Both shall suffer the same punishment, the inquirer and the prophet alike, 11 so that the house of Israel shall no longer stray from me, and no longer defile themselves by all their transgressions. But they shall be my people and I will be their God, declares Lord YHWH.

COMMENT

14:1. *sat down before me.* S's addition is based on 20:1. Some of the leaders of the community came on a particular inquiry; the prophet was directed to convey to them that their errand was fruitless.

3. *raised . . . thoughts. h'lw 'l lbm,* lit. "brought up onto their hearts"; the intransitive form appears in 38:11, "ideas *y'lw 'l lbk* will enter your mind" (lit. "will rise onto your heart"); cf. 20:32 ("onto your spirit"). The intransitive form is familiar from contemporary sources (II Kings 12:5; Jer 51:50; Isa 65:17); this passage expresses the deliberateness of their guilty thinking by using the hif'il, an otherwise unattested, but normal, transitive mode of expression. The phrase has been taken literally by some (e.g., J. Schoneveld, *Oudtestamentische Studiën* 15 [1969], 193ff.): "have applied (wore) idols to their breasts" (viz. amulets or tattoos); but when, in vs. 6, the men are urged to repent, the language is not that of 20:7, "cast away the loathsome objects before your eyes"—viz. the idols worshiped in Egypt—but "turn your faces away from your abominations"—a metaphor for disregarding what is only in the mind. "Face" serves again in vs. 8 for "regard, attention," this time for God's angry visitation upon these sinners. For "stumbling-block of iniquity" see comment at 7:19.

am I supposed to respond. 'iddareš is lit. "permit myself to be inquired of" (nif'al). The first *(h)'drš* stands for the infinitive *(h)hdrš;* Kimḥi accounts for the anomalous *'* by the desire to avoid two consecutive *h* sounds which would have resulted from the prefixed interrogative *ha-* (vocalized with long *a* according to rule, GKC § 100 m); cf. II Kings 6:21 *h'kh,* apparently for *hhkh* (infinitive) (Moshe ben Sheshet). The infinitive absolute strengthens the indignant tone of the question (GKC § 113 q).

4. *Any man . . .* For this formula (expanded in vs. 7) see Lev 17 where it repeatedly occurs, and Lev 22:14; the prophet's reply is couched as a general rule.

oblige him with an answer. Nif'al of *'nh* serves, as in Mishnaic Hebrew, to express (sarcastically here) a somewhat formal reply. The nif'al occurs probably under the influence of *nidraš* in vs. 3; its connotation is "answer for myself," that is, give a reply as I see fit, not in accord with the inquirer's query (Kimḥi).

coming with his many idols! Apparently an angry interjection. The text is uncertain (see text footnote [c–c]), inviting emendation of *bh/'* to *by* as at the end of vs. 7 (but others delete "with his many idols" because it is absent from vs. 7).

5. *catch . . . at their thoughts. tapaś* "apprehend in a [secret] crime" occurs in Num 5:13: of the suspected adulteress it is said that none witnessed her nor "has she been apprehended [*nitpaśa*]"—*in flagrante*. Our passage underlies Qumran *Hodayot* 4.19: "But you, God answer them, dooming them by your might . . . so that they may be caught in their thoughts [*ytpśw bmḥšbwtm*], for they have fallen away from your covenant." There is a triumphal note here, perceived by the medievals: "that the Israelites may know that I know their innermost thoughts" (Kara); "they hide their thoughts from me, but I will catch them at their thoughts. For I will lay bare before them their idolatrous thoughts and evil designs" (Kimḥi).

fallen away (nazoru) *from me*. The unusual verb (Isa 1:4) is commonly linked with *zar* "stranger" and translated "estranged themselves." In our passages it associates with *wynzr* in vs. 7 (see comment there) and *yt'w* in vs. 11; this evokes Ps 58:4 where *zoru* (a passive form, similar to our *nazoru*) is parallel with *ta'u* "go astray," favoring a derivation from *zwr* = *swr* "turn aside" (as in Aramaic; T frequently renders Hebrew *swr* by *zwr*). For the nif'al, cf. *nasog* (from *swg*) "fall away."

6. *and turn* (wahašibu). Usually transitive (Rashi and Ehrlich [Hebrew] supply "your thoughts"), it might be an incomplete anticipation of "turn your faces" at the end of the verse. Yet *šubu wahašibu* in 18:30, and *hašibu* alone in 18:32, suggest that the hif'il here is a longer, more emphatic variation of qal; cf. *zana/hizna* "fornicate" in Hos 4:10ff. "All" in the second part of God's exhortation is a characteristic means whereby the second of parallelistic lines reinforces, or carries further, what is said in the first (J. Kugel, *The Idea of Biblical Poetry* [New Haven: Yale University Press, 1981], pp. 47f.).

7. *or of the aliens who live in Israel*. The old formula (Lev 17:8, 10, 13; 20:2; 22:18) is kept despite its inappropriateness for the exilic community (contrast the renovated terminology of Isa 56:3 "the foreigner who has attached himself to YHWH") to lend the pronouncement the aura of ancient, general authority and applicability.

falls away from me. nzr is backformed from *nazoru,* as though its *n* were radical (cf. *nmltm* Gen 17:11 backformed from *nmwl* "be circumcised" from *mwl*), and is inflected (like it) in nif'al! Its conventional derivation from *nzr* "consecrate," as though it meant "separate himself from me," is artificial and pedantic. The equivalence of *me'alay* and *me'aḥaray* with these virtually identical verbs is paralleled by the use of both after *t'h;* cf. vs. 11 with 44:10.

of me by him (lo bi) . . . *by myself* . . . *him* (lo bi). The rhyming of these two clauses in Hebrew calls attention to their contrast; it entails stretching the sense of each of the rhyming elements alternately. For *lidroš lo* "to inquire by him (= the prophet)" the preposition *lo* must be equated with *'elaw* (*daraš 'el* = inquire by necromancy, Deut 18:11); *bi* is the object of *daraš*, as in the late texts I Chron 10:14; II Chron 34:26. G S V take the clause so; similarly some medievals. Alternatively, *lo* = "for him," viz., the inquirer—"that [the prophet] should inquire for him of me" (Kara, Cooke); this has the advantage of making *lo* in this and the next clause have the same reference, yet is somewhat unnatural.

bi of the second clause "by myself" gets this unusual meaning by association with *bi* of the first clause; the meaning is, I will oblige him with an answer directly, not through a medium.

8. *I will set my face against . . . and cut him off* . . . Adapted from a repeated formula of punishment in the priestly laws (e.g., Lev 17:10; 20:3, 6); the meaning is not expulsion from society or the cult community (Zimmerli, *ZAW* 66 [1954], 11–19), but early, untimely death (death—as indicated here [vs. 9] and elsewhere by the parallels; *IDB* s.v. "Crimes and Punishments," vol. I, pp. 734f.; so understood in talmudic times [*EJ* 10, s.v. "Karet"] and argued for the Bible by M. Tsevat, "Studies in the Book of Samuel. I," *HUCA* 32 [1961], 195ff.).

I will make of him. Rendering, with versions, as a pseudo-hif'il of *śim;* see J. Barth, *Die Nominalbildung in den semitischen Sprachen* (Leipzig: J. C. Hinrichs, 1894), pp. 119f.; GKC § 73 a; Joüon § 54 f, and B-Y 7558 for many postbiblical Hebrew examples (the versions do not support an emendation to qal). In some editions the sibilant is *š*, yielding "I shall make him desolate" (so Kara); cf. Deut 28:37: fallen Israel will be *l^{e}šamma ul^{e}mašal* "a[n object of] consternation and a byword." The connection with the sequel is not as easy, and the echo of *yašim* in previous verses is lost in this reading.

a sign. A warning, a lesson, as in Num 17:25 the sprouted staff of Aaron is to be preserved as "a sign to rebels" of the election of the priestly line. The doom of the inquirer will serve as a warning for all who would force themselves on God.

a byword. The plural, unexampled in this idiom (and hence emended into singular), is "of generalization or amplification" and occurs with other nouns denoting affective utterances; e.g., *k^{e}limmot* "insult" (Isa 50:6, paired as here with a singular *roq* "spittle"), *giddupim* "reproach" (Isa 43:28, paired with *ḥerem* "destruction"). See the extensive treatment in König, III, § 261 a–h, § 264 d; GKC § 124; Joüon § 136 g–j.

9. *is so misled as to*. For this sense of *putta*—to fall into error—see Jer 20:10, which Moffat excellently renders, "perhaps he will make a slip"; the implied agency—temptation, sin—is here startlingly identified in the next clause as God.

10. *suffer . . . punishment.* Lit. "bear [the consequence/penalty of] their iniquity"; see comment at 4:4.

11. The special charge of *ta'a me'aḥare* (YHWH) and *hiṭṭame* ("stray from [following] behind YHWH," "defile themselves") emerges from the pairing of each of these with *znh* "be unfaithful [of a wife]" in Hosea 4:12 (*zanah me'ahare* YHWH in Hos 1:2) and Ps 106:39. That we are in the field of the metaphor for covenant-breaking comes out even more clearly from the final clause, in which the classical expression of the covenant bond—"I their God, they my people"—appears (see Structure and Themes).

by all their transgressions. The pollution of transgressions in general (not only specific objects such as idols and the dead, or physical states, such as menstruation) recurs in 37:23; cf. Lev 16:16 on the scope of purgation of the Day of Atonement.

STRUCTURE AND THEMES

The oracle is introduced with a notice of the attendance of some elders on the prophet (cf. 8:1; 20:1) and the revelation formula (vss. 1–2). It runs from vss. 3–11 (to "declares YHWH") and consists of A (vs. 3), a justification for denying these men a response, followed by an abstract, general formulation in three paragraphs (B, C, D) of the offense and punishment of such Israelites.

In B (vss. 4–5), an initial statement of the case of the "idol-minded" inquirer and his punishment—vaguely worded—is followed by God's punitive purpose. Then comes an exhortation to repentance (vs. 6), in terms at once formulaic and specific to our passage (see below); this serves as a bridge to C (vss. 7–8), the second and chief statement of the offense. A new clause is added to the description of the offense, the object of the approach to the prophet is specified, and above all the punishment is detailed, ending with the recognition formula.

A complementary ruling on the case of a responding prophet is appended in D (vss. 9–10): his offense and punishment are set forth, with a résumé of the equal guilt of the inquirer and the prophet. The closing sentence affirms God's corrective and restorative purpose in all this.

Though D appears to be an appendix to A–C, it is integrated with what precedes, and thematically (see below) climaxes the oracle. Indeed, the entire oracle is highly integrated. The parallelistic description of the offense in A is repeated in B and C, each time with variation to avoid monotony: A—*'al libbam, nat^e^nu;* B—*'el libbo, yaśim;* C begins with an entirely new formulation. The subject gradually widens in scope: A—"these men"; B—"any man of the house of Israel"; C adds "and of the aliens who live in Israel." B's purpose clause uses only "thoughts [vs. 5]," the adjacent exhortation (vs. 6) speaks of "faces"; together the pair "thoughts—faces" (vss. 3, 4, 7) is constituted, and thus the heterogeneous exhortation is bonded to its neighbor. The terms *natan/śam panim* of the offense are echoed in *natan panim, *heśim* of the divine punishment (end of C). The divine punishment of the inquirer (C) and of the prophet (D) are couched in similar terms (for the pairing of *hikrit* and *hišmid* see, e.g., Isa 10:7), thus giving the ground for their equation in vs. 10 ("alike"). Moreover, the use of "my people" for the body out of which the culprits will be excised prepares for the climactic readoption of "the people" by YHWH (vs. 11b). Finally, there is the interesting progression of expressions of offense in B, C, and D:

NAZORU me‘alay (vs. 5)
YINNAZER ME'AḤARAY (vs. 7)
yit‘u ME'AḤARAY (vs. 11)

The (priestly) legal style of this oracle has been discussed above in the Structure and Themes section of the "lookout" passage. Here we note some striking affinities between it and Lev 17:

	Ezek 14	*Lev 17*
	"speak . . . and say . . ."	"speak . . . and say . . ." (vs. 2)
B.	the illegitimate inquirer (i): "any man of the house of I."	the illegitimate sacrificer (i): "any man of the house of I." (vs. 3)
	punishment	punishment (vs. 4b)
	purpose (*l^{e}ma‘an*)	purpose (*l^{e}ma‘an . . . w^{e}lo . . . ‘od*) (vss. 5ff.); cf. vs. 11 in our oracle
C.	the illegitimate inquirer (ii): "any man . . . and of the aliens . . ." "I will set my face against . . . and cut him off from the midst of my people"	the illegitimate sacrificer (ii): "any man . . . and of the aliens" (vs. 8); "that man shall be cut off from his people" (vs. 9); cf. the next case, "I will set my face against that person . . . and cut him off from among his people" (vs. 10)
D.	the unauthorized prophet: "they shall bear their guilt"	he who eats forbidden meat: "he shall bear his guilt" (vs. 16)

The structural analogy between these passages shows that the repetition in our oracle of B and C is normal for priestly legal style. The extent of the similarity suggests that the Leviticus passages may have been known to Ezekiel.

While God's refusal to answer the people accords with the traditional principle that sin silences the oracle (see comment to 7:26), the idea that the very resort of sinners to God is itself a mortal offense is singular. No less so is the fact that God's refusal to respond is conveyed in a response; to these sinners God does speak, if only to justify to them his silence.

Evidently more than a mere rebuff to ordinary sinners is being communicated.

The prophet refrains from charging his audience with open idolatry; he reads it in their minds. Modern commentators have interpreted this as an attribution of "syncretism," the worship of YHWH alongside alleged deities of the popular religion, a kind of "halting between two opinions"—but the prophet does not say that. Overtly, it would appear, the people's conduct had been blameless; indeed had they been idolaters no reason can be found for ignoring it until this moment of recourse to YHWH. Since when did YHWH tolerate idolatry in Israel so long as the culprits refrained from seeking his oracles? That the elders came to Ezekiel for an oracle shows that in their own estimate they were true devotees of YHWH, worthy of his attention. God's indignant response shows how gravely he and his people differ in their conceptions of the religious reality. The situation resembles that of ch. 20: there too some elders come on an inquiry; they are rebuffed, and the thought of assimilation to the idolatrous nations is imputed to the people (vs. 32: "what has risen onto your spirits"). There too interpreters have translated into empirical reality what the prophet charges to the people's thoughts; but can it be that simple? Is it plausible that subverters of YHWH's authority would have sought an oracle from him from the zealot Ezekiel?

The "idols" in the people's thoughts and "before their faces" must be a rubric for an unregenerate state of mind. The assurance, fed by the false prophets, that all was well between Israel and YHWH, confirmed the people in their course, a course which, as the exile had proved, stood under God's condemnation. To presume that normal relations existed between Israel and its God in these circumstances was infuriating obtuseness. God was present among the exiles only "as a small sanctuary"; here Ezekiel defines that conception in an original manner. Communication between heaven and earth moves in one direction only. For his own purposes, God sends warnings, exhortations, announcements of doom to the people; he will not be accessible for human purposes. There will be no heavenly response to man's requests for allaying anxiety, no benevolent condescension to movement initiated from below—not before "their uncircumcised heart shall humble itself" (Lev 26:41).

The drastic consequences with which both parties to the offense are threatened underlines the fury aroused by the people's incomprehension of their iniquity and their rejected status in the eyes of YHWH; such incomprehension is revealed by their confident assertion, cited by Jeremiah, "YHWH has raised up prophets for us in Babylon" (29:15). But the presence among the exiles of respondents in YHWH's name required special explanation. Jeremiah points to the false prophets in order to extenuate the people's guilt (14:13); in 4:10 he accuses God of misleading the people through them (the common misunderstanding of this passage is rectified in Y. Muffs, "Tefillatam šel nevi'im," *Molad* [Hebrew] 35–36

[1975], 206ff.). For Ezekiel, the illegitimate prophet is himself a victim and sign of God's fury. This goes further than Deut 13:2ff., which interprets the confirmatory signs of a subversive prophet as a test of the people's loyalty to YHWH; further also than I Kings 22:20ff., in which a "lying spirit" is commissioned to enter Ahab's prophets in order to assure his death in battle (we are not told that those prophets suffered any penalty, human or divine). Our passage ascribes the error of a prophet in responding to inquiry to divine misguidance. The obtuseness of the Israelites, including prophets, is culpable, and God punishes it by corrupting the spring of inspiration, leading inquirer and respondent alike to destruction. Again, ch. 20 provides a parallel: in order to punish the guilty Israelites God gave them (misled them with) bad and fatal laws "so that I might desolate them" (vss. 25f.). This conception of divine interference with human freedom in order to punish is not peculiar to Ezekiel, only its drastic expression is (for the issue, see Y. Kaufmann, *Religion,* pp. 75f.; W. Eichrodt, *Theology of the Old Testament* [trans. J. A. Baker] [Philadelphia, 1967], II, pp. 178ff.). Its counterpart is a similar, eschatological interference in order to redeem Israel once for all from sin—the doctrine of the new heart (11:19f.; 36:26f.).

How far the bond between God and Israel had been dissolved in the present is indicated by the prediction (at the end of vs. 11) that only after the purge "they shall be my people and I will be their God." This formula has its matrix in Exod 6:7, where God commands Moses to tell the people of his intention to rescue them and adopt them: "and I will take you for my people and I will be your God." It recurs in the description of the ultimate bliss in the covenant blessings of Lev 26:12: "I will walk among you, and I will be your God and you shall be my people." Derived from the terminology of marriage and adoption (Y. Muffs, "Studies in Biblical Law, IV: The Antiquity of P," mimeographed [Lectures held at the Jewish Theological Seminary of America, New York, 1965]), the formula is a deuteronomic commonplace (M. Weinfeld, *Deuteronomy,* p. 327). As the essential expression of the bond between Israel and its God, Jeremiah repeats it in his recall of God's expectation at the Exodus (7:23; 11:4) and in his predictions of ultimate reconciliation (30:21; 32:27ff.). Ezekiel uses the formula only in visions of the future. Its first use was in 11:20, introducing the "new heart" theme; when the theme is elaborated in ch. 36 it recurs (in vs. 28) in the proclamation of the ideal relationship between God and Israel. Our passage may be paired, in turn, with 37:23, where purification from idols, loathsome things, and transgressions fulfils the condition for restoring the ideal bond, expressed again by the same traditional formula.

This oracle carries a heavy ideological cargo, more subtle than most. In language redolent of old priestly law, Ezekiel promulgates a new theological ordinance (*tora*) defining for his time and place strictures on contact with God, strictures arising from the people's "idolmindedness." We understand that to be a rubric for the people's unregenerateness, nourished by misguided assurances of God's favor given them by the prophets denounced here and in the prior oracles. But prophets and laity who force themselves upon God, oblivious of their condemned status, will be destroyed. Yet God's immediate punitive purpose has an educative final aim —to bring the errants back to him. What cannot be now will then be, when YHWH and the people are once again joined, as at the beginning, by a bond of mutual allegiance.

XIII. An Exception to the Rule (14:12–23)

14 12 The word of YHWH came to me: 13 Man, if a land sinned
against me by committing trespass, and I stretched out my hand
against it, and I broke its staff of bread and let famine loose against
it, cutting off man and beast from it, 14 and these three men were
in it—Noah, Daniel and Job, by their righteousness they should [a]save
themselves[a], declares Lord YHWH.

15 If I caused wild animals to pass through the land and bereave
it so that it became a desolation with none passing through it because
of the animals, 16 [b]these three men being in it, by my life, declares
Lord YHWH, they should not save sons or daughters; they alone
should be saved while the land became a desolation.

17 Or I brought a sword upon that land, and decreed, A sword
shall pass through the land! and I cut off man and beast from it,
18 and these three men were in it, by my life, declares Lord YHWH,
they should not save sons or daughters, but they alone should be
saved.

19 Or I let a plague loose upon that land and I poured out my fury
upon it with bloody death, cutting off man and beast from it, 20 and
Noah, Daniel and Job were in it, by my life, declares Lord YHWH,
they should not save a son or a daughter; by their righteousness they
should save themselves.

21 Now then, thus said Lord YHWH: The more so when I have let
loose against Jerusalem my four evil scourges—sword, famine, wild
animals, and plague—to cut off man and beast from it! 22 And yet
survivors will be left in it who will [c]be brought[c] out—sons and
daughters; yes they will come out to you, and when you see their
ways and their deeds you will be consoled for the evil I brought upon
Jerusalem, all[d] that I brought upon it. 23 They shall console you when
you see their ways and their deeds, and you shall know that not for
nothing did I do all that I did to it, declares Lord YHWH.

[a–a] G "be saved" (as in vss. 16, 18).
[b] Heb. mss., G S "and . . . were."
[c–c] G S "bring."
[d] G adds "the evil."

COMMENT

14:13. *sinned . . . trespass.* For the sequence, cf. the priestly law of Lev 5:21. Inasmuch as the hypothetical land of vss. 13–20 is not specifically that of Israel, this will be the only passage in Hebrew Scripture in which "trespass (against YHWH)" is predicated of a non-Israelite subject. Since the term refers to misappropriation or violation of the holy things or oath of YHWH (J. Milgrom, *JAOS* 96 [1976], 236ff.), properly speaking, only those who know YHWH can be guilty of trespass against him. However, note that in Jer 50:14 and Ezek 16:50 the wrongdoing of gentiles toward YHWH is also described in terms used otherwise only of Israel. This is either a glimmer of a religiously more unified view of mankind than is usual for Ezekiel, or a coloration of the hypothetical by the underlying reference (and later explicit application) to Jerusalem.

staff of bread . . . famine. See at 5:16; for the latter expression see Amos 8:11.

14. *Noah, Daniel and Job.* The biblical Noah and Job are expressly paragons of virtue (Gen 6:9; Job 1:1) of extra-Israelite antiquity (for the antique setting of Job, see N. Sarna, "Epic Substratum in the Prose of Job," *JBL* 76 [1957], 14f.); the biblical Daniel, a hero of Jewish loyalty and a wiseman contemporary with Ezekiel (according to Dan 1:1–6) appears strangely between them (Bar Hebraeus justly wondered at the chronological disorder of the listing). The plausible inference that this *dn'l* (the Jew is spelled *dny'l*) was also an ancient gentile worthy (see, e.g., Smend; hence the aptness of comparing the king of Tyre to him, in 28:3), barely enforced by the occurrence of a Danel as the uncle and father-in-law of the antediluvian Enoch in Jub 4:20, received support from the discovery of the Epic of Aqhat among the literature of Ugarit. The father of the tragic hero Aqhat is a king, Dan'el (*dn'il*), who is described as the ideally righteous ruler "who judges the cause of the widow and adjudicates the case of the fatherless" (*ANET*³, pp. 151a, 153a; for the story see the delightful retelling by Gaster, *The Oldest Stories in the World* [Boston: Beacon Press, 1958], pp. 175ff.). It is supposed that this ancient character survived in various embodiments among the Canaanites and Israelites; in Ezekiel's time he combined the righteousness of his Ugaritic form with the wisdom of his later Jewish form.

The non-Israelite character of the three worthies accords with the generality of the doctrine of retribution taught here, and with the foreign backgrounds against which such sapiential issues are commonly presented: the Garden of Eden story about the origin of sin and trouble; the judgment of Sodom and Gomorrah, which might have been averted by the presence of ten righteous men in the cities (is our passage a rejection of that doctrine?); the story of Jonah showing the power of repentance; cf. Kaufmann, *Religion,* pp. 283, 297). Here they serve to underline the ruthless, rigorous discrimination God exercises when he punishes a wicked community: not even the—in themselves undeserving—sons and daughters of such paragons would be spared for the sake of their fathers, who could do no more than save themselves.

(Modern theories have unnecessarily complicated the subject of the three worthies. The likelihood that Noah's name occurs as a divine element in Amorite names of the nineteenth and eighteenth centuries B.C.E. adds nothing to understanding the present reference to Noah; see M. Noth's critical assessment of J. Lewy's theory in *VT* 1 [1951], 254ff. Ezekiel's Noah is solely and adequately explained by the role of the so-named worthy in the biblical Flood story; in Isa 54:9, composed probably a few decades after Ezekiel, Noah is expressly connected with the Flood, and there is no ground for imagining a divergent Israelite tradition about another Noah in Ezekiel. S. Spiegel accounted for the connection between the three by their relation to "sons and daughters": as Noah saved his sons, so Job got back his children [according to Spiegel, prayed them back from death], and Dan'el got back Aqhat [according to Spiegel's reconstruction; see *Louis Ginzberg Jubilee Volume,* pp. 305–55]. Though scholars have not been convinced by Spiegel's tour de force, some continue to regard the relation to their children as the common aspect of the three. Job, writes Eichrodt, is connected with the other two "by having undergone the same fate of helplessly seeing disasters come upon his own children." Such diametric opposition to Spiegel's view suggests that the attempt to ground the motif of children in the legends of the three is misguided. For a different explanation of the motif see Structure and Themes.)

save themselves. niṣṣel "save" is an anomaly; elsewhere the pi'el of this verb means only "strip, pluck clean," but it occurs too rarely for us to reject the meaning "save" here. Note how the hif'il–pi'el sequence of *hišliᵃḥ–niṣṣel* in vss. 13f. is answered by the pi'el–hif'il sequence in vss. 19ff., *šillaḥ–hiṣṣil;* see Structure and Themes. G assimilates the anomaly to the passive forms of vss. 16, 18.

15. *If.* Though *lu* serves mostly to introduce hypotheticals not likely to be realized, it sometimes (as here) serves for ordinary cases; Gen 50:15; Micah 2:11.

16. It is hard to decide whether the absence of *waw* at the start of this verse is a copyist's error or a deliberate variation, of which our passage shows so many examples.

19. *bloody death* (lit. "blood"). Ezekiel regularly combines plague and blood(y death): 5:17; 28:23; 38:22.

21. *The more so.* "If by one of these four scourges I lay waste a land of

the gentiles, how much more so when I bring all four on one of those lands! And against Jerusalem I have indeed let four loose, yet I will not annihilate it" (Kimḥi).

22. *brought out.* In Jer 38:22 the identical form (*muṣa'im*) qualifies the members of the royal family who were led off into captivity.

sons and daughters. In apposition to the preceding. The meaning of these words here is conditioned by their use in the last three hypothetical cases where they refer to the undeserving children of Noah, Daniel and Job who would not survive the doom of their land. Here, on the contrary, it is said that only undeserving persons would survive the fall of Jerusalem and be led out to the exiles—those in the class of the "sons and daughters" of the hypothetical cases. The reasons for this astounding breach of rule are immediately stated.

The reading of G S "who will bring out" (as from *hammoṣi'im*) makes the survivors proper one group and their children adjunct to them—paralleling the situation in the hypotheticals (the three worthies on the one hand, their children on the other). Initially pleasing, this reading, on reflection, is bewildering: are the "survivors proper" wicked or righteous? Aside from the structural reward of reading them into the application to Jerusalem, what purpose do they serve alongside the "sons and daughters" whose wickedness is assured? MT proves to be the more economical and clearer reading.

Zimmerli makes the fine point that in contrast to the hypotheticals, the application to Jerusalem uses verbs of the root *yṣ'* "go out" rather than *nṣl* "save"; the positive connotations of the latter verb are unsuitable in connection with the survival of these wicked.

deeds. *'ᵃlilot,* usually paired with *derek* "way," is always pejorative in Ezekiel (e.g., 20:43f.; 21:29)—as is its cognate *ma'ᵃlal* in Jer (7:3, etc.).

all that I brought . . . This clause is felt to be in apposition to "the evil," which is the logical object of the preceding "I brought"; as appositional to an object it is preceded by *'et* (for a different and more cumbersome interpretation of *'et* see J. Blau, *VT* 4 [1954], 11). G assimilates our clause to the preceding; MT assimilates it to the end of the next verse ("all that I did").

23. *not for nothing.* As 6:10.

STRUCTURE AND THEMES

The oracle sets in with the revelation formula, but oddly lacks the message formula ("say, Thus said YHWH . . ."), although vs. 21, which introduces the second part of the oracle (presupposing the first part), does have it. (The versions all agree with MT; there is irreducible inconsistency and variety amidst the repetitions and formulas of Ezekiel; he was not a machine.) The message divides into two: vss. 13–20, four hypothetical cases formulated in a patterned, legal style containing a doctrine of retribution, and vss. 21–23, the exception to the doctrine in the case of Jerusalem. The hypotheticals lead up to the application, and the application get its punch from contradicting the doctrine they set forth; clearly, the combination of the parts of this oracle is primary.

Ezekiel's style of repetition was never better displayed. Each of the four cases consists of a seven-member statement; three members describe the scourge and its devastation, three the inability of the three worthies to save even their own children's lives, but only their own; one member, variously located, contains the formula "declares YHWH," in three out of four cases preceded by an oath. Despite this pattern, no two statements of the case are the same; while the common purpose of all the changes is to sustain attention, several of the variations seem to have special significance. Thus while in the last three cases two of the three members dealing with the worthies are devoted to their (in)ability to save, in the first case only one member is about saving, the others (preceding it) are taken up with introducing and naming the worthies. The divergence of the second case from the pattern of the first is greater than that of the others: its first two lines are longer, while the third line describing devastation is not only shorter, but located at the very end. A new oath clause appears, negating the ability of the worthies to save even their own children; the oath and subsequent repetition of the entire clause in the rest of the cases indicates the weight attached to this negation. The pattern-changes in the second case not only prevent monotony, but alert the hearer (or reader) to this fresh item. Subsequent variations of the sworn negation keep its freshness: it is first formulated as an "if" clause, normal for negative oaths (GKC § 149; Joüon § 165), it next appears as a straight negation (*lo*), and finally as an "if" clause with the objects in the singular for emphasis ("[not even] a single son or daughter"). Several features of the fourth case connect it with the first: the naming of the worthies, the verbs "let loose" and "save themselves" (with the pi'el–hif'il inversion commented on at vs. 14), the phrase "by their righteousness"; the whole section is thus contained in an envelope.

Emphatic *ki* ("now then") turns the oracle to the application (vss. 21–23) in ordinary prophetic style. If the patterned regularity and legal style of the four cases suggested the inevitability and consistency of God's dealing with wicked lands, the break in the formulation of his dealing with Jerusalem conforms with the surprising contradiction between the doctrine of the cases and the fate of Jerusalem's inhabitants. The organic relation of the contradiction to the doctrine comes out not only in its troublesome use of "sons and daughters," but in its deliberate avoidance of any form of *nṣl* "save"—for which *ytr* "be left," *plṭ* "survive" and *yṣ'* "come out" are substituted. God has no saving purpose in contradicting his principle of retribution in Jerusalem's case, but a grim didactic one, whose utter novelty justifies its emphatic, repeated formulation in vss. 22–23. We note that in the (partly chiastic) repetition in vs. 23 a novel element appears, having no correspondent in vs. 22: the result clause, "and you shall know that not for nothing . . ." (note how *niḥḥam* "console" is a phonetic quasi-inversion of *ḥinnam* "for nothing" [or a semantic quasi-equivalent of *lo ḥinnam*]).

The thematic and linguistic relation of the two parts of the oracle speak for its integrity; interpretation must start from the surprise ending toward which the whole is oriented. "Sons and daughters" will, against the settled principle of divine retribution, survive Jerusalem's fall, but only to vindicate God's judgment. To what is this a response? Spiegel observed that "in 24:21 the prophet plainly told the parents in Babylonia, separated from their children in Palestine: 'Your sons and daughters *whom ye have left behind* shall fall by the sword.' Ezek 14:12ff. would seem to . . . bespeak the anxiety felt among the captives for their children in Judaea" (*Louis Ginzberg Jubilee Volume,* pp. 320f.). This assumption explains the unique prominence in the oracle of "sons and daughters"; those of vs. 22 are not a troublesome reflection of the previously mentioned sons and daughters in the hypotheticals, but, on the contrary, are (thinly veiled) the real sons and daughters of the exilic audience. The hypotheticals have been framed to include children because of the exiles' actual concern over their children. Now it was inferable from Abraham's famous plea on behalf of Sodom that even a few righteous might save a city, or that, at the least, one righteous man (Abraham) might save even his undeserving kin (Lot and his daughters; cf. Gen 19:29). The exiles might plausibly have banked on such a doctrine, for surely there were among Jerusalem's prophets and priests some righteous who could protect the city, or among the exiles some whose sufferings had purged them in the sight of God. Might there not thus be hope for the kin left behind in the homeland? Against such a hope the prophet counterposes his argument. The true doctrine of retribution (to be spelled out in ch. 18) is that even paragons of virtue (the likes of whom do not exist in the depraved city or among the exiles) could not save any but themselves in a general doom; the exiles hold to wrong doctrine and therefore to a vain hope. Nonetheless it was true that there would be survivors, as Ezekiel several times proclaimed (6:8; 7:16; 12:16), and as the curses of the covenant had predicted (Lev 26:39ff.). The prophet now brings that article of faith into the context of parental anxiety through a wry linguistic innovation: the survival of depraved sons and daughters and their arrival among the exiles would "console" the parents, not through relief at their escape, but by allaying the exiles' doubts about the justice of Jerusalem's fate! In the prophet's overriding concern for theodicy, he transforms every situation into a witness to God's justice; only the vocabulary betrays the underlying human anguish that is overlaid by and submerged under the prophet's theocentrism.

(That Ezekiel predicts a remnant alongside his announcement of total annihilation is not so startling an inconsistency as those make it out to be who regard vss. 22–23 as post-fall amendments to the oracle in the light of the actuality of survivors [e.g., Spiegel, Wevers; cf. Herrmann and Cooke]. Jeremiah expounds such an inconsistency in a single breath in an oracle to the Egyptian diaspora which, since it seems never to have come true, can hardly be emended by chopping off the inconsistency as a post-event addition: [27] "I will be watchful over them to their hurt . . . all the men of Judah in the land of Egypt shall be consumed by sword and by famine until they perish. [28] Only the few who survive the sword shall return . . . to the land of Judah; then all the remnant of Judah . . . shall know whose word will come true, mine or theirs!" (Jer 44:27f.; cf. vs. 14). Note that the "inconsistent" survivors serve, as in Ezekiel, to vindicate God. Now it is true that critics have not hesitated to declare Jer 44:28 "prophecy after the event" (Rothstein [*HSAT*], Rudolph [HAT], Hyatt [IB])—meaning by "event" the actual repatriation of some exiles. But that is not what vs. 28 signifies; it speaks of "survivors" (*p^eleṭa*) of a massacre (vs. 27) about which Coutourier correctly says we know nothing (*The Jerome Bible Commentary,* ed. R. E. Brown et al. [London, 1970]). Vs. 27's massacre is plainly a romantic notion of precisely the same order as the "inconsistent" survivors of vs. 28—both belong to the ideal world of just deserts and vindication of God. To sift out of vs. 28 evidence for a (peaceful) repatriation, while ignoring the plain drastic sense, then to turn and declare the verse a "prophecy after" the manufactured "event"—all because of its inconsistency with vs. 27—is a solution at least as problematic as the problem it is supposed to solve. The prophetic message of the age of the fall is ridden by a momentous arch-inconsistency: the assurance of the final dissolution of Judah owing to its breach of covenant, opposed to God's promise of an eternal bond with his people. This is the father of all the others, including the rather minor ones presently under discussion.)

In the outpouring of invective against Jerusalem at the end of ch. 5, the four scourges (lit. judgments) are listed in the order: famine, wild animals, plague/blood, and sword. The core consists of the trio, sword, famine, and plague (see comment to 6:11), to which wild animals have been added on the basis of Lev 26:22f. (How far Ezekiel assimilated animals to the original trio comes out in 33:27, where he forms a unique series of sword, animals, and plague; he may have known Hosea 2:20, animal and sword.) With that, the scourges reached four, a number favored in Ezekiel (see the divine vehicle of chs. 1 and 10 and M. Pope, s.v. "Number," *IDB* [3], p. 565a) and used of destroyers in Jer 15:3 ("four 'families': sword for killing, dogs for dragging off, fowl of heaven and beasts of earth for consuming and destroying") and Zech 2:2–4 ("four horns to scatter Judah"). It is characteristic of tradition-bound Ezekiel (contrast the combinations of the other prophets) that he expresses his individuality by preserving the marginal liberty of disposing the members of these series with a greater variety than is found elsewhere (e.g., Jer keeps to the traditional order of the trio almost always, Ezekiel has it in 6:11 and 12:16, but changes it in 6:12 and 7:15, while every listing of the four scourges is different (5:17; 14:13–19; 14:21).

XIV. The Vinestock and Jerusalem
(15:1–8)

15 1 The word of YHWH came to me:
2 [a]Man, what, of all trees, becomes of the vinestock,
the vine branch, that belongs among the trees of the forest?
3 Can wood be taken[b] from it to make something useful?
can one take a peg from it on which to hang any vessel?
4 See, it has been consigned to the fire as fuel;
When the fire devours its two ends, and its inside is charred,
is it fit for anything useful?
5 If when it was whole it could not be made into something useful,
how much less when fire devours it and it is charred
can it yet be made into some useful thing!
6 Well, then, thus said Lord YHWH: as the vinestock among the
trees of the forest which I have consigned to the fire as fuel—so have
I consigned the inhabitants of Jerusalem. 7 I will set my face against
them; they have escaped from the fire but fire will devour them; and
you shall know that I am YHWH, when I set my face against
them. 8 I will make the land a desolation because they committed
trespass, declares Lord YHWH.

[a] G adds "And you."
[b] G T "they take," as in the next clause, where Hebrew is lit. "they take."

COMMENT

15:2. *what, of all trees, becomes of the vinestock*. Cf. *ma yihyu ḥ*[a]*lomotaw* (Gen 37:20) "What will become of his dreams." So G *ti an genoito to xylon tēs ampelou* "what is to become [of] the tree of the vine"; S *mn' nhw' lqys' dgpt'* "what shall become of . . ."; Rashi: "What is its end [= how does it end up] of all the other trees." All these take *mi-* (of *mikkol*) in a partitive sense, "out of, differently from [all other trees]"; cf. T "How differs [*mh šn'*] the vine tree from all trees." The question asks about the fate of the vinestock, how its career and final disposition set it apart from other trees. Hebrew *'eṣ* serves for "tree" and "wood"; while in vs. 3 it must mean "wood" and at the end of vs. 2 it must mean "trees [of the forest]," moderns vacillate in the other occurrences, with most favoring "wood of the vine" for *'eṣ haggepen* (we render it "vinestock"—the woody stem and branches).

Most moderns take *mi-* in a comparative sense and render "How is the wood of the vine better than . . ." or the like (*RSV, AV, NEB,* NJPS). But this ignores the verb *yihye* and is not picked up in the sequel (vss. 3ff.), which dwells on the use of the vine's wood rather than its comparison with other trees. This interpretation imports into the opening of the oracle a polemic against the pride of the Judahites (supposedly expressed by the figure of Israel as a vine) that is not found anywhere else in it.

the vine branch. z^e^mora is specifically a cut off branch of the vine (I. Löw, *Die Flora der Juden,* I, pp. 71f.; *zamar* "prune a vine"), hence it cannot be connected to the preceding *'eṣ* (as already in G) in the general sense "wood of any branch" (e.g., Zimmerli, NJPS), but must be in apposition to "vinestock" of the first clause. The combination with *'es* commends itself as a solution to the otherwise anomalous masculine verb *haya;* but the anomaly of feminine *z^e^mora* with masculine *haya* has its parallels (Joüon § 150 b, k; on all the foregoing, see G. R. Driver, *Biblica* 35 [1954], 151, but beware of fn. 3!).

belongs among. I.e., is counted as one of, following Ehrlich; for this sense of *haya b-* see, e.g., Prov 22:26; 23:20. Though reckoned among "the trees of the forest," how different is its destiny! Many moderns follow Rashi, Kimḥi, in taking the vine (or at least the vine branch) to be wild ("of the forest"), but the phrase "trees of the forest" seems to mean no more than "the class of trees" (as "fowl of heaven," "fish of the sea"). There is no distinction to be made between wild and cultivated vines with regard to their wood, which alone counts here.

3. *be taken . . . one take.* The active-passive variation occurs with *'aśa* in this verse and vs. 5, and with *natan* in vss. 4 and 6; cf. *nṣl* in 14:14, 16, etc. (The versions are inconsistent in rendering such fine points; here, e.g., G and T ignore, but S reflects the distinction.)

4. *See, it has been consigned.* It is destined to serve as fuel "by a law of nature, as it were"; so Cooke, on vs. 6, where indeed God speaks as the author of that "law." In spite of vs. 6, some moderns take this clause as a hypothetical, referring to a specific case ("Now suppose it was thrown into the fire as fuel" [NJPS; cf. *AV, NEB*]), tailored to Jerusalem's situation (along with the rest of the verse). But not only is consignment to the fire as fuel a general rule with vine prunings (see Structure and Themes), even the particular circumstances related in the following clause describe what must have been a common occurrence.

When the fire devours its two ends. Ashes of vinewood fires must commonly have contained such partly consumed branches, which would have been collected for reuse. (Apparently such charred but still combustible wood is the *peḥam* "charcoal" that burns into *geḥalim* "cinders" in Prov 26:21; see S. Krauss, *Qadmoniyot Ha-talmud* II/1 [Tel Aviv: Dvir, 1929], pp. 131ff.) Recommittal to the flames fits the comparison in vs. 6 to the successive calamities suffered by Jerusalem. However, the figure was understood otherwise in *Shabbat* 20a, where this verse serves to prove that once fire has so extensively taken hold of a piece of wood, the presumption is it will burn on without further tending: "If its two ends have been devoured by fire, then surely its inside is scorched—has lost its moisture and is parched" (Rashi, ibid.). At that stage, any destination other than as fuel is even more definitely excluded; the comparison with Jerusalem will then be to its ineluctable destruction.

Our inclination to seek a basis for the figure in everyday life rather than in events is only strengthened by the inconclusive attempts of medievals and moderns to find historical referents for "the two ends" and the "inside"; e.g., Jehoiakim's exile (based on the dubious Dan 1:2), Jehoiachin's exile, Zedekiah's doomed state (Rashi, Kara); the exiles of transjordanian Israel, Ephraimitic Israel, and Jehoiachin (Abarbanel); Israel's exile, Jehoiachin's exile, Jerusalem's "scorched" state (Fohrer). As soon look for specific allusions in Isa 42:25 "It blazed on him all about . . . It burned in him . . ."

6. *as the vinestock*. The strained English syntax mirrors the Hebrew. The sentence begins with *ka'ašer* "as," which normally introduces a verb, but instead of the verb following immediately it appears farther on only in a relative clause ("which I have consigned to the fire . . .") qualifying a noun ("the vinestock . . .") that has forced its way into the foreground. Two purposes appear to be in conflict: (1) comparison of the fate to which God has consigned the Jerusalemites to that to which he has consigned the vinestock ("As I have consigned the vinestock . . . to the fire . . . so have I consigned . . ."); (2) opening the consequential part of the oracle (after *laken*) with a symmetrical echo of its beginning (vs. 2) in order to highlight the link between them ("Like the vinestock [**ke'eṣ haggepen*] among the trees ['*eṣ* used collectively, as in 47:7—a varying repetition of *'aṣe* of vs. 2] of the forest . . . so have I made [a different nuance of *natatti*, as in vs. 8] the inhabitants of Jerusalem"). The syntax has suffered under the strain.

7. *and you shall know*. Addressing the exiles.

STRUCTURE AND THEMES

The oracle is divided in two: A (vss. 2–5), a reflection on the ill-fated vinestock, and B (vss. 6–8), a comparison to it of the inhabitants of Jerusalem. The style of A approaches the poetic; vss. 2 and 3 are parallelistic, in each the second clause is longer than the first. Vss. 4–5 are repetitive—devouring by fire and the reference to usefulness recurring each three times (never in precisely the same form!). Vs. 6 opens with *laken* heralding the consequential part of the oracle, the comparison with Jerusalem (*ka'ašer . . . ken*). The comparison (vs. 6) is followed by a metaphoric announcement of Jerusalem's destruction (burning) (vs. 7) concluded by the recognition formula addressed to the exiles. This, in turn, is followed by an afterwave (vs. 8) (see the discussion of this phenomenon in ch. 6, Structure and Themes; moderns regard it characteristically as a sign of later addition); *b^{e}śumi panay* resumes *w^{e}natatti panay* and leads into the final nonmetaphoric proclamation of Jerusalem's destruction, terminated by the formula "declares Lord YHWH." Echoes of the oracles of ch. 14 occur in these verses: *natan panim* recalls 14:8; vs. 8 echoes 14:16 ("desolation") and 14:13 ("commit trespass").

A and B are each compacted together: A by the parallelism and repetition already mentioned; B by the fourfold repetition of *natatti* (consigned [twice, vs. 6], set [vs. 7], make [vs. 8]). A is bound to B by shared motifs and terms: vs. 6, which specifically compares the vinestock's fate to Jerusalem's, and introduces fire into B (vss. 6, 7); and the passive-active sequence of *natan* in vss. 4 (A) and 6 (B), by which *natatti* is introduced in B. Such a density of common features and continuities speaks for the literary integrity of the oracle.

The didactic meditation on the ill-fated vinestock is framed as a series of rhetorical questions flowing from the central assertion, "See, it has been consigned to the fire as fuel" (vs. 4a). This is a statement of general validity, opposing the vinestock to all other woods, as indicated by its theological grounding in vs. 6, and was so understood by G and S, which introduce it by limiting particles (*parex* "except, save"; *'l'* "only"). To no useful work has the vinestock been appointed (vs. 3), but only as fuel for fire. A fresh detail appears in G's whimsical rendering of *šny qṣwtyw* in the next clause: "what is annually (*š^{e}ne* as from *šana* "year") pruned off it (*q^{e}ṣotaw* as though from *qṣṣ* "cut off") the fire devours." Here is a glimpse of ancient reality that is further illuminated by John 15:2:

> He cuts off any of my branches
>   that does not bear fruit,
> But any that bears fruit he trims clean
>   to make it bear more fruit.

Two annual prunings are alluded to, the first in late winter, the second in summer (R. Brown, AB, ad loc.). These yielded heaps of vine twigs, which were collected into *ḥ^{a}bile z^{e}morot* "bundles of vine branches" (*Mishnah Sanhedrin* 7.2; BT *Abodah zarah* 18a) used to fuel fires. For proper appreciation of the argument of vss. 4b–5, it need only be observed that a frugal peasantry could be counted on to exploit fully the materials of the environment; hence it was enough that a wood could not be made into work articles to ensure that it would serve as fuel. The insistence on the inutility of vinewood in vss. 4–5 is equivalent to condemning it to the fire, since that was the sure consequence of its unsuitability for industrial purposes.

Part A of the oracle is, then, based on observed, everyday practice, contains no artificial facts tailored to fit history, and therefore does not betray its application prematurely. The construction of vss. 2–5 is deliberate. Vss. 2–3 oppose the vinestock to other trees (*'eṣ* four times) by rhetorical questions indicating its uselessness for any work. This leads to the conclusion (vs. 4a) that its assigned destiny is to serve as fuel for fire. The career of the vine branch as fuel is then considered. Once the fire has laid hold of it so that even its inside is charred, its uselessness is even more firmly assured (for anything save fuel, to which it has been devoted). Here the meditation stops without portraying the final stage of the vinestock's reduction to ashes. That is postponed, and the hearer's attention kept, for the next part of the oracle—the comparison.

Comparison of the vinestock to Jerusalem (a surrogate for Judah/Israel) is a grotesque distortion of the traditional use of the vine as a figure for Israel. The figure of the vine aptly expressed several aspects of Israel's relation to its God. As the vinedresser lovingly cultivated his vineyard, expecting a good reward, so God cultivated and tended Israel, expecting its faithful obedience (Isa 5:1–7); as the vinedresser transplanted shoots into good soil, so God transplanted Israel from Egypt to Canaan (Ps 80:9). Israel was God's "beloved planting" (Isa 5:7). While this figure was used in eulogistic self-description in Israel's prayers ("Turn . . . and attend to this vine!" Ps 80:15), prophets turned it to polemical purpose: both Isaiah (5:1ff.) and Jeremiah (2:21) spoke of the disappointment of the divine vinedresser, whose labors yielded only bad grapes. But Ezekiel's imagination seized upon an as yet unexploited aspect of the figure. Why speak of fruit at all, when the only appropriate element of comparison was the base wood of the vine whose destiny was destruction?

The application introduces the comparison with a resumption of the statement concerning fire as the destination of the vinestock (vs. 6). The hearer had been left contemplating the partly burned vine branch and its manifest inutility. The prophet now proceeds to the final step: Jerusalem had been partly burned (Jehoiachin's exile), and though it had escaped, it was doomed to be recommitted to the flames. What was left suspended in the meditation on the vinestock is resolved brutally in the comparison: partly burned Jerusalem will be devoured completely by the fire next time.

As soon as the comparison with Jerusalem is broached, the reflection on the vinestock is transformed into something like an allegory. The prophet pursues one topic only—the one he introduced in the opening verse, namely, the ultimate fate of the vinestock—annihilation. But as an allegory, the vinestock has several other implications. Unlike the disappointing bad grapes of the vineyard allegory, the vinestock is by nature and origin worthless as wood and destined for the fire; the analogous implication of Israel's "congenital" baseness, a major theme of Ezekiel, begs to be drawn out. The vinestock is set apart from other trees by its worthlessness; an analogy to Israel's moral inferiority to the nations, another theme of the book, lurks here. However, none of these receives attention; the focus is from the start on career and destination, as the single explicit point of comparison with Jerusalem. Various scholars have, nonetheless, seized upon one or another of the implications (influenced, to be sure, by the comparative interpretation of the leading question of vs. 2; see Zimmerli's strictures against Baumann). Of these, W. A. Irwin stands out for his insistence that the present course of the argument is wrong. Vss. 2–5 say that "vine-wood is worthless in any case . . . when a piece has been burned it is out of the question to set any value on it." But vss. 6ff. focus "not on the nature of the vine-wood, but on the fire which has burned this particular piece . . . This writer missed the main idea of the oracle that vine-wood is worthless; instead he snatched at the figure of burning fire and so gave a totally diverse pronouncement. There is nothing in common between oracle and interpretation save their use of the symbols of vine-wood and fire. The interpretation is false [and therefore not the prophet's]" (*The Problem of Ezekiel,* p. 43). This example of imposition of an external standard on a text would hardly be worth citing had it not impressed even the latest commentators. Zimmerli courteously demurs, but Wevers must admit Irwin's main contention that "the prophet does not elaborate the central comparison logically." We have not found Ezekiel's logic unequal to his purpose.

XV. Jerusalem the Wanton
(16:1–63)

16 1 The word of YHWH came to me: 2 Man, inform Jerusalem of
her abominations, 3 and say: Thus said Lord YHWH to Jerusalem:
Your origin and your birth were in the land of the Canaanite;
your father was an Amorite, your mother Hittite. 4 As to your birth:
on the day you were born, your navel-string was not cut, you were
not washed smooth[a] with water, you were not rubbed with salt or
swaddled. 5 No one cared enough about you to do any of these things
for you out of pity for you, but you were left to die in the field,
spurned, on the day you were born. 6 I passed by and saw you
wallowing in your blood, and I said to you, "In your blood, live!"
[a]I said to you, "In your blood, live!"[a] 7 [b]I made you flourish[b] like the
plants of the field; you grew and matured, and developed the loveliest
of adornments—your breasts were well formed and your hair had
sprouted; but you were stark naked. 8 I passed by and saw that you
had reached the age of lovemaking, so I spread the edge of my garment over you and covered your nakedness. I pledged myself to you
and entered into a covenant with you—declares Lord YHWH—and
you became mine.

9 Then I washed you with water and rinsed your blood off you and
anointed you with oil. 10 I clothed you in embroidery and shod you
in leather and turbaned you in linen and covered you with silk.

11 I decked you with ornaments, putting bracelets on your arms and
a necklace on your throat. 12 I put a ring in your nose, earrings in
your ears and a glorious crown on your head. 13 So you were decked
in gold and silver, your clothes were linen, silk and embroidery; you
ate the finest flour, honey and oil. You were very, very beautiful, fit
to be a queen. 14 You became famous among the nations for your
beauty, made perfect by my splendor which I bestowed upon you—
declares Lord YHWH.

15 Then, confident of your beauty, you harloted on your fame, and
poured your harlotry on anyone who passed by—it was his!

a (a–a) Not in G S.
b–b G (S) "(and) grow."

16 You took some of your clothes and made gaily-colored shrines
and harloted on them—such things will never be! 17 You took your
glorious articles, of my gold and my silver that I gave you, and made
yourself male images and harloted with them. 18 You took your
embroidered clothes and covered them. My oil and my incense you
set before them. 19 My food that I gave you—the fine flour, oil and
honey that I fed you—you set before them for a soothing savor;
it was so!—declares Lord YHWH.

20 You took your sons and your daughters that you bore me and
sacrificed them to them for food. As if your harlotry was not enough,
21 you slaughtered my sons as an offering and delivered them over to
them! 22 And with all your abominations and your harlotry you did
not remember the time of your youth when you were stark naked,
wallowing in your blood.

23 After all your evil—woe, woe to you! declares Lord YHWH—
24 you built yourself a platform and made yourself a height in every
square. 25 At every crossroad you built your height and you made
your beauty abominable by opening your legs to anyone who passed
by. Increasing your harlotry, 26 you harloted with the Egyptians,
your big-membered neighbors; you increased your harlotry to vex
me.

27 So I stretched out my hand against you and cut your rations,
and subjected you to the will of your enemies, the Philistine women
who were ashamed of your depraved way. 28 Unsatisfied, you harloted
with the Assyrians; you harloted with them but were still not satisfied.
29 So you extended your harlotry to Merchant-land, Chaldea, but you
were not satisfied with that either.

30 How hot your ardor is—declares Lord YHWH—to have done
all these things, the deeds of a headstrong harlot: 31 to have set up
your platform at every crossroad and made your height in every
square. Nor were you like other harlots, in that you scorned hire.
32 [c]O adulterous wife, who while married to her husband takes
strangers! 33 Every harlot receives gifts, but you gave your gifts
to all your lovers, paying them to come to you from all around, in
your harlotry. 34 You acted contrary to other women, in that you
harloted though not sought for harloting, and you paid hire, no
hire being paid to you; yes, you were the contrary!

35 Now then, harlot, hear the word of YHWH! 36 Thus said Lord
YHWH: Because your juice was poured out and your nakedness

[c] G "the adulterous woman like you from her husband taking hires [as from Hebrew *'tnnm*]."

exposed in your harlotry with all your lovers, and on account of all
your abominable idols, and in accordance with the blood of your
children which you gave them— 37 Now then, see, I am gathering all
your lovers to whom you were so sweet—and with all you loved all
you hated also—I am gathering them against you from all around.
I will expose your nakedness to them and they shall gaze upon your
nakedness. 38 I will condemn you to be punished as an adulterer
and a murderer, and turn you into a bloody object of fury and
passion. 39 I will hand you over to them and they shall demolish
your platform and tear down your heights. They shall strip you
of your clothes and take all your glorious articles, leaving you
stark naked. 40 They shall summon a crowd, who shall stone you
and hack you with their swords. 41 They shall burn [d]your houses in[d]
fire and inflict punishment on you in the sight of many women.
Thus I will put an end to your career as a harlot, nor will you pay
hire any more. 42 I will spend my fury against you and my rage at
you shall subside; I will grow calm and not be vexed any more. 43 Because you did not remember the time of your youth and were not in
dread of me in all these matters, see, I am holding you to account
for your ways—declares Lord YHWH; have you not acted depravedly
on top of all your abominations?

44 See, quipsters will apply to you the quip, "Like mother like
daughter." 45 You are the daughter of your mother, who spurned her
husband and her children, and the sister of your sisters[e], who spurned
their husbands and children—you daughters of a Hittite mother and
an Amorite father! 46 Your big sister Samaria and her daughters
who live on your left, and your little sister who lives on your right,
Sodom and her daughters— 47 did you not follow their ways and
commit their abominations? Very soon you became more corrupt
than they in all your ways.

48 By my life! declares Lord YHWH, your sister Sodom and her
daughters did not do as you and your daughters did. 49 This was the
sin of your sister Sodom: she and her daughters had pride of satiety
of bread and careless ease, and did not sustain the poor and needy.
50 They grew haughty and committed abomination before me, so I
removed them when I saw it. 51 As for Samaria, she did not commit
half the sins you did. You committed more abominations than they,
making your sisters look righteous by all the abominations you
committed.

[d–d] S "you in the midst of" (as from *btwk*).
[e] See comment.

52 Then bear the disgrace of having justified your sisters; because the sins you committed were more abominable than theirs, they look righteous in comparison! Then be ashamed and bear your disgrace, having made your sisters look righteous! 53 I will restore their fortunes—the fortunes of Sodom and her daughters, and the fortunes of Samaria and her daughters—and [f]the fortunes of your captives[f] among them, 54 so that you may bear your disgrace and be disgraced at all you did, in giving comfort to them. 55 When your sister Sodom and her daughters are restored to their former state, and Samaria and her daughters are restored to their former state, you and your daughters will be restored to your former state. 56 Did not your sister Sodom serve you as a byword during your proud days, 57 before your own evil was exposed—now the reproach of the Aramean women and all who are around them, the Philistine women who despise you on every side. 58 You must bear your depravity and your abominations, declares YHWH.

59 Truly thus said Lord YHWH: I will do to you in accord with what you did when you flouted the curse-oath and violated the covenant. 60 But I will remember the covenant I made with you in the time of your youth, and I will establish an eternal covenant with you. 61 And you will remember your ways and will feel disgraced, when you receive your big sisters with your little ones—for I will give them to you as daughters, though not because of your covenant. 62 I will establish my covenant with you and you shall know that I am YHWH. 63 So you will remember and be ashamed and not be able to open your mouth again because of your disgrace, when I absolve you from all you have done, declares Lord YHWH.

f–f G "I will restore your fortunes" (reflecting *wšbty šbwtk*).

COMMENT

16:2. *Inform.* T *'wkḥ . . . wḥwy* "Arraign . . . and declare" (identical with its rendering of the sequence *šapaṭ . . . hodiaʿ* in 20:4; 22:2) captures the forensic allusion: the prophet is to proclaim to Jerusalem God's charge against it, followed by his sentence (for a recent survey and critique of literature on this motif—which generally ignores Ezekiel—see K. Nielsen, *Yahweh As Prosecutor and Judge* [Sheffield, England: Department of Biblical Studies, University of Sheffield, 1978]). Forensic *hodiaʿ* reappears in Job 10:2; 13:23 ("Let me know what you sue me for!").

3. Since the city Jerusalem is addressed—symbolizing Israel—its pagan antecedents are exploited for reprobating the people. "Land of the Canaanite" (instead of the usual "land of Canaan") emphasizes the pagan pedigree; biblical ethnography connects Canaanites, Amorites and Hittites very closely, and these three to the Jebusites, the pre-Israelite inhabitants of the city (Gen 10:15f.; Judg 19:11f.; II Sam 5:6). B. Mazar combines the meager data on pre-Davidic Israelite contact with Jerusalem (including traditional data that Ezekiel may have known) thus:

> In Joshua's time, Adonisedeq, king of Jerusalem, headed an alliance of Amorite kingdoms in the south of the country [Josh 10:1, 3]. After Joshua's death (second half of thirteenth century B.C.E.), the city was razed and the Amorite element wiped out [Judg 1:8ff.]. The Jebusites, apparently belonging to the Hittites and their satellites, migrated from the north during the first half of the twelfth century B.C.E., after the destruction of the Hittite empire. This is the background of Ezek 16:3 (*Jerusalem Through the Ages* [Hebrew] [Jerusalem: Israel Exploration Society, 1968], p. 4).

Your origin (mkrtyk). G S "your root"; the Hebrew word recurs only in 21:35; 29:14, and is of unknown derivation. The plural of this and the following noun (*mldtyk* "your birth") expresses the multiple elements comprising the concept (GKC § 124 f; Joüon § 136 i, fn.). The double rubric introduces all that follows in vss. 3–5, while "your birth" is repeated before the particular account of the girl's birth. A similar procedure occurs in 1:8b: "faces and wings," with "faces" repeated in vs. 10.

an Amorite. Disregarding the article of *h'mry,* insinuated under the influence of the preceding *hkn'ny,* where it is regular with a gentilic used as a collective (GKC § 126 m); cf. *'mry* in vs. 45.

4–5. Talmudic rabbis deemed these operations on the newborn so vital that they expressly permitted them even in violation of the sabbath (BT *Shabbat* 129b; see commentary of R. Nissim of Gerona). In modern times Arab midwives in Palestine were observed, after the cutting of the navel cord, dressing the infant's body in a mixture of salt and oil. Salt was rubbed on for seven days after birth in the belief that it toughened the child's skin and worked beneficently on his character. The infant was swaddled immediately and kept so for forty days to six months to "straighten out" or "set in place" its limbs (E. Grant, *The People of Palestine* [Philadelphia–London: J. B. Lippincott, 1921], p. 66; H. Granqvist, *Birth and Childhood Among the Arabs* [Helsingfors: Söderströms and Co., 1947], pp. 74, 93–101, 243; J. Morgenstern, *Rites of Birth, Marriage, Death . . . Among the Semites* [Cincinnati–Chicago: Hebrew Union College, 1966], pp. 8f.).

Lengthened *r* (*kŏrrat šŏrrek*) is occasionally attested (GKC § 22 s;

Joüon § 23 a). *kŏrrat* "was cut" is qal passive (GKC § 52 e; Bergsträsser II § 15 c) with lengthened *r,* as in the following noun, instead of the expected *korat* as in Judg 6:28. *ruḥaṣt* "you were washed" and *ḥuttalt* "you were swaddled" are the same (the derived *ḥᵃtulla* "swaddling clothes" is in a noun pattern based usually on qal); the association of a hofʿal infinitive absolute with the latter (*hoḥtel*) is due to the preceding *humleᵃḥ* (on the mixing of conjugations with infinitive absolutes see GKC § 113 w; Joüon § 123 p).

The hapax *lᵉmišʿi* (T "to be cleansed") has been variously explained. G. R. Driver, in *Studies in Old Testament Prophecy,* pp. 63ff., takes it as an Aramaizing verbal noun of Aramaic *šʿy* "daub, smear" (according to Rashi and others a by-form of *šʿʿ* "smooth over"). Ibn Janaḥ (*Haschoraschim*) s.v. "*mšʿ*") compares Arabic *mašaʿa* "cleanse" (on the occasional equivalence of Arabic *š* and Hebrew *š,* see C. Brockelmann, *Grundriss der vergleichenden Grammatik der semitischen Sprachen,* I [Berlin: Reuther and Reichard, 1908], § 167 δ, who attributes it to contact of the sibilant with a velar). The form remains anomalous. Omission in G S may be due to perplexity.

The practice of exposing infants is attested in the Sargon legend (*ANET*³, p. 119), in the Bible—the cases of Ishmael and Moses, both forced on mothers in dire distress (the midrash incorporates our passage in a legend of the miraculous survival of all the male Israelite babies born in Egypt and abandoned by their mothers in the fields [BT *Sotah* 11b; L. Ginzberg, *Legends of the Jews* (Philadelphia: Jewish Publication Society of America, 1910), II, pp. 257f.]), and, for baby girls, in pre-Islamic Arabia—because of poverty or fear of disgrace (denounced by Muhammad in the Koran, 81.8; 16.60f.; 17.33; 6.138, 141, 152; see the vivid account in C. M. Doughty, *Travels in Arabia Deserta* [New York: Boni and Liveright, (1926?)], pp. 239f.). Classical lawgivers and philosophers recommended the exposure of unwanted, ill-formed or weak children (Plutarch, Lycurgus, 16; Plato, Republic 5.459–61; see W. Lecky, *History of European Morals* [London: Longmans, Green & Co., 1877], II, pp. 24ff.). Here no motive is given for the exposure; from vss. 44f. one may infer only the viciousness of the parents.

That *hišlik* means "expose" was argued by M. Cogan, "A Technical Term for Exposure," *JNES* 27 (1968), 133ff.; he cites, among others, Gen 21:15 (see Ehrlich).

spurned. Lit. "in a spurning of your person"; this interpretation of *goʿal* is supported by the use of the verb *gaʿal* in vs. 45 (Ehrlich). Medievals interpreted "in the filthiness of your person" (cf. *nigʿal* "polluted," I Sam 1:21) according to Mishnaic Hebrew and Aramaic.

6. *"In your blood, live!"* Although befouled and uncared for you shall not die (Eliezer of Beaugency, Rashi). The repetition does not appear in G, hence moderns regard it as a dittograph ("that no exegetical art can make tolerable," Cornill; a genuine repetition would have in-

volved only "in your blood live," Ehrlich). The situation parallels the case of Ps 130:6c: *šomrim laboqer* is not repeated in G; Ehrlich (*Die Psalmen* [Berlin: M. Poppelauer, 1905]) avers that a genuine repetition would have been *miššomrim;* Gunkel (*Die Psalmen,* 5te Auflage [Göttingen: Vandenhoeck & Ruprecht, 1968]) declares it clearly an error. But just as Kraus (*Psalmen,* BKAT, 2te Auflage, 1961) considered the Psalm repetition an "emphatic underlining of fervent yearning," so medievals and Davidson saw here an emphatic manner of speaking, to stress the great act of God's pity. G's shorter text, even if it is based on a Hebrew *Vorlage,* is not necessarily more original.

The plural *damayik* "your blood" follows the usage in priestly laws dealing with bloody body issues: Lev 12:4f.; 15:19; 20:18; but note that in vs. 22 a singular appears (*damek*). For a similar vacillation with *taznut,* see vs. 15.

7. *I made you flourish.* If one takes the Hebrew in its usual sense, the rendering is "I made you myriad"—apparently an intrusion of the reality behind the metaphor (the great increase of Israel in Egypt?). Eliezer of Beaugency and Ehrlich (Hebrew) avoid this by positing the sense "growth" for *r^e^baba* (a verbal noun from *rbb* "grow"); as *natan* + object + *dam* means "make [an object] bloody" (vs. 38), so *natan* + object + *r^e^baba* means "make [an object] grown" (cf. S. R. Driver, *Tenses,* § 189 obs. [p. 252]). According to this suggestion, the comparison with "verdure [*ṣemaḥ* lit. "sprouts"] of the field" expresses not quantity (like "grass of the field," Job 5:25), but healthy growth: "As the sprouts of the field need nothing of the aforementioned care, so you, without any of those attentions, grew to maturity" (Eliezer of Beaugency). Note how *ṣemaḥ* is echoed in *ṣimme^a^h* "sprouted" (cf. body hair)—referring to development rather than multiplication.

developed the loveliest of adornments. ba b- "come with" = bring, produce (like its Arabic equivalents, W. Wright, *A Grammar of the Arabic Language,* 3d. ed. [Cambridge: Cambridge University Press, 1955], p. 159 c); see I Kings 13:1; Ps 66:13; Prov 18:6 (cited by KB^3). The "loveliest [lit. adornment] of adornments" are the signs of sexual ripeness—breasts and bodily hair. In an ancient Sumerian sacred marriage poem (S. N. Kramer, *The Sacred Marriage Rite* [Bloomington: Indiana University Press, 1969], p. 98), companions of the goddess boast:

> "Lo, high [?] is our bosom,
> Lo, hair has grown on our vulva,
> At the lap of the bridegroom let us rejoice."

The verse evokes Mishnaic Hebrew *hebi'a simanim* "she developed signs (of puberty)," namely, breasts and body hair (*Mishnah Niddah* 5.7ff.; *Tosefta Niddah* 6.4ff.). The erotic attraction of maiden breasts is alluded to in Ezek 23:3, and of women's breasts in *Mishnah Sotah* 1.5 and BT *Berakot* 10b (the "glory of woman's beauty" is her bosom).

Although this reading is attested in G S (misreading *'ry 'rym* "city of cities"), the peculiarity of its application of "adornment" to physical features and the subsequent adorning of the woman by God (vs. 11) have led most moderns to emend *b'dy 'dyym* to *'ad / be'et / be'iddim* "[you arrived] at / the time of / menses" (Isa 64:5). It is remarkable that among the Jews menses are not listed among the signs of puberty; nor would their mention here suit the erotic context.

your breasts. MT has no pronoun, nor does *roš* "[your] head" (vs. 43) or *berit* "[my] covenant" (vs. 59). Such omission is idiomatic (e.g., see 25:6); that G supplies a pronoun in all these cases may be only a translation technique, not a reflection of a different *Vorlage.* (A dual suffixed body member is juxtaposed to a single unsuffixed one in Lam 2:15; 3:41.)

you were stark naked. Lit. "you [were] nakedness and bareness"; on such apposition, where substantives are employed as predicate adjectives, see Driver, *Tenses,* § 189 (2) (where *'al tehi meri* of 2:7 is also discussed).

8. *age of lovemaking. dodim* is specifically sexual lovemaking (Ezek 23:17; cf. Prov 7:16; Song of Songs 4:10; 7:13).

Covering a woman with a garment expresses acquiring her, Ruth 3:9. Cf. *Mishnah Peah* 4.3: "If a poor man threw himself upon [the crop] and spread his cloak over it [in order to claim it], he is removed therefrom." In early Arabia too throwing a garment over a woman symbolized acquiring her (A. Guillaume, *The Life of Muhammad: A Translation of Ibn Isḥāq's* sīrat rasūl allāh [London: Oxford University Press, 1955], p. 515; cf. J. Wellhausen, "Zwei Rechtsriten bei den Hebräern," *Archiv für Religionswissenschaft* 7 [1904], 40f.; a modern counterpart appears in H. Granqvist, *Marriage Conditions in a Palestinian Village,* II [Helsingfors: Akademische Buchhandlung, 1935], p. 81, fn. 3). Since it is understood that henceforth the woman shall be covered to all except her husband, Deut 23:1 can express the illicitness of relations with the wife of one's father as "uncovering the edge of the father's garment" (see Ehrlich; see also R. Patai, *Sex and Family in the Bible and the Middle East* [Garden City, N.Y.: Doubleday, 1959], pp. 197f.).

I pledged myself to you. This refers to YHWH's promise to be Israel's God, mentioned in 20:5 ("I solemnly swore to them saying, I, YHWH, am your God"—in turn an echo of Exod 6:1–8, especially vs. 7). This is another way of phrasing the divine side of the double obligation clause "You shall be my people and I will be your God" (see ch. 14, Structure and Themes). The human side of that clause is expressed here at the end of the verse through "and you became mine." In using the marriage metaphor, our passage returns the covenant-establishing clause to its matrix, the solemn words that constituted marriage or adoption; see e.g., the Elephantine marriage declaration of the husband, "She is my wife and I am her husband," discussed by R. Yaron, *Introduction to the Law of the*

Aramaic Papyri (Oxford: Clarendon Press, 1961), pp. 46f. (and cf. the reconstruction of the Israelite formulas in M. A. Friedman, "Israel's Response in Hosea 2:17b: 'You Are My Husband'" [Hebrew], *Bar-Ilan Annual* 16–17 [Ramat Gan: Bar-Ilan University, 1979], pp. 32–36; English summary, pp. 129f.). Nowhere but in Ezekiel is this declaration called an oath. This has been explained by assuming that marriage in ancient Israel was actually conceived of as a mutual "covenant" with each side swearing fidelity to the other, hence Israel's covenant with God could be described in terms of such a mutual marriage oath. The two passages on which the theory is based (Mal 2:14; Prov 2:17) may be otherwise interpreted, however (J. Milgrom, *Cult and Conscience,* pp. 133f.). In fact, nowhere is marriage expressly called a covenant or the husband charged with an oath. The origin of the oath image here—and in the parallel in 20:5—seems rather to be a fusion of the divine oath to the patriarchs to give their descendants the land of Canaan (e.g. Gen 26:3; Deut 1:8, etc.) and the solemn declaration of mutual obligation connected with the Exodus and covenant with the people (in the priestly writings and Deuteronomy). This fusion is clear in 20:6, where the "raising of the hand" (in oath) is connected with a promise of land-giving to the people in Egypt (see comments there). Ezekiel disregards the patriarchal tradition in his historical surveys (see Structure and Themes), but the conception of a divine oath to Israel as an element in the covenant with the people betrays his awareness of the tradition.

Through the terminology of oath and covenant, which does not belong to the realm of marriage, glimmers the reality underlying the metaphor.

9. *I washed you.* The woman is now given all the care she lacked when she was born, and much more. The first three items—washing, anointing, and covering—parallel the deprivations of vs. 4, end ("rubbing with salt" involves oil). The blood rinsed away is, in the telescoped vision of the allegory, her birth blood that still clung to her. Some medievals (Ibn Caspi, Abarbanel), and all moderns who emend *'dyym* in vs. 7, take it to be menstrual blood.

10–12. Embroidery belongs to the dress of princesses (Ps 45:15) and booty taken for noblewomen (Judg 5:30); much of the cloth of the tabernacle consisted of such work (Exod 26:36; 27:16; 28:39, etc.). *taḥaš,* out of which the foundling's shoes (and the tabernacle cover Exod 26:14; Num 4:6) were made, seems to be cognate with Akkadian *dušu* (**tuḥšia*) "goat/sheep leather [dyed and tanned the color of *dušu*-stone]" out of which luxury boots and sandals were made (*CAD;* the suggestion to combine with *taḥaš* courtesy of H. Tadmor). This seems preferable to Bodenheimer's connection with Arabic *daḫs* "dolphin" (or dugong, *IDB* s.v. "Fauna," p. 252a). The verb *ḥabaš* is normally used of winding on headgear (Ezek 24:17)—in Exod 29:9, of the priests' headgear, likewise of linen (Exod 39:28). The traditional rendering of *meši* has been "silk" since at least the time of the tenth-century C.E. Karaite, David b.

Abraham Alfasi (so, too, Ibn Janaḥ), but (a) it is doubtful whether silk was known in western Asia in the sixth century B.C.E.; the earliest Western allusion to silk being in Aristotle (fourth century B.C.E.)—of a sort produced on the Aegean island of Cos (G. Sarton, *A History of Science* I [Cambridge: Harvard University Press, 1952], p. 336); (b) G S render by "[fine] veil [of hair]" ("with which women cover their faces so that they can see without being seen" [Bar Hebraeus]). To the usual derivation from Egyptian *msy,* a kind of clothing, C. Rabin added the alternative of Hittite *maššiya* "veil, shawl" (in *Studies in the Bible Presented to . . . M. H. Segal* [Hebrew], ed. J. M. Grintz and J. Liver [Jerusalem: Israel Society of Biblical Research/Kiryat Sepher, 1964], p. 172). Bracelets and a ring are bridal gifts in Gen 24:22; a gold necklace adorns Joseph as vice-regent (Gen 41:42). The "glorious crown" (in Isa 62:3 || "royal turban") indicates that the woman is a queen—as vs. 13 shows, a real not a ceremonial one (as though brides were queens [Patai, *Sex and Family,* p. 66]; against the theory that in ancient Israel bride and groom were "king and queen" for the wedding week, see M. Pope, *Song of Songs,* AB, pp. 141–44).

Most moderns take this finery to be the bridal outfit (cf. Granqvist, *Marriage* II, p. 44, for close comparison), but since the wedding has already occurred (vs. 8b), it is more likely to be the clothing with which the royal husband dowers his wife for life (see Structure and Themes).

13. Flour, honey and oil are the components of "my bread" in vs. 19; cf. Exod 16:31, where the taste of the manna was like "wafers made in honey" (Num 11:8, "cream of oil"), and also the unleavened cakes of the meal offering—made of "fine flour . . . soaked in oil" (honey, being leavened, was forbidden in offerings, Lev 2:4 [11]).

fit to be a queen. Lit. "fit for royalty" (*m*ᵉ*luka*). The fitness of beauty for royalty is a commonplace: Ps 45:3 (addressed to a king): "you are the most beautiful of men" (cf. Isa 33:17) and the archetypal David (I Sam 16:12, 18; 17:42), and his son, Absalom, whom the people followed (II Sam 14:25). For later Jewish literature, see S. Leiter, "Worthiness, Acclamation and Appointment: Some Rabbinic Terms," *Proceedings of the American Academy for Jewish Research* 41–42 (1973–74), 137ff. This climactic clause (Cooke) is strikingly assonant with 15:4 end, lit. "is it fit for work" (*m*ᵉ*laka*), the more reason for not striking it just because it is absent in G.

14. "Beauty" (*yopi*), "perfect" (*kalil*), "splendor" (*hadar*) recur together in 27:3, 4, 10, in the dirge over Tyre.

15. The sequence "you were confident of [*b*ᵉ-] your beauty and you harloted on account of [*'al*] your fame" recurs very similarly in 28:17: "your heart was haughty because of [*b*ᵉ-] your beauty; you corrupted your wisdom on account of [*'al*] your splendor." In each case the first clause describes the mental attitude that prepared the way for the evil of the second, committed as a consequence of fame and splendor.

your harlotry. The suffixes of this noun fluctuate freely between those of the singular (*-tek,* vss. 26, 29) and the plural (*-tayik* 15, 20, 22, 25, 34, 36)—as though the *ut* abstract formative were the feminine plural *ot* (GKC § 91 l; Joüon § 94 j).

it was his! Namely, your harlotry; an exclamation of disgust, formulated as a contrast to "you were mine" at the end of vs. 8, the first of three such exclamations; see vss. 16 and 19. Jussive stands for imperfect (GKC § 109 k; Joüon § 114 l), and masculine verb with a feminine subject is not infrequent with *haya l*ᵉ- (Joüon § 150 k, l). The versions vary widely, reflecting either textual or exegetical uncertainty: G S omit; T assimilates to the end of vs. 16 rendering *lo* as negative; an Origenic reading, "his you were" (as from *thy*), sharpens the contrast with the end of vs. 8.

16. With this and the following verses, compare the cajolery of the adulteress in Prov 7:16: "I have decked my couch with coverlets, / with striped cloths of the yarn of Egypt. / [17] I have perfumed my bed with myrrh, aloes and cinnamon." In our verse, shrines (*bamot*) (at which foreign gods were worshiped, II Kings 21:3) replace the bed—the referent intruding again, recalling Isa 57:7. To be sure, both this and the Isaiah passage are generally thought to allude to sacred prostitution; O. Eissfeldt, who explains all the terms for "elevations" in our passage as the raised bed or pedestal on which this rite was performed, considers "harlotry" to have a double meaning (prostitution in the cult of foreign gods; *JPOS* 16 [1939], 286–92 = *Kleine Schriften* II, pp. 101–6).

such things will never be! Lit. "not coming things [Isa 41:22] and it will not be"—hardly coherent, perhaps an idiom. The versions reflect these graphs, interpreted variously.

17. On conversion of precious metal into idols, see 7:20. It is hard to ascertain the specific sense of this accusation: is it worship of any and all images, including that of a female Asherah—"male" through the exigency of the metaphor (just as below allies are "male" and enemies "female") —or worship of male gods only (e.g., Baal), or of "phalluses belonging to the Canaanite fertility cult" (Ehrlich and followers) supposedly alluded to in Isa 57:8 as well?

18. Mesopotamia and Egypt offer examples of the ritual clothing of the cult image and the daily offerings, including honey, incense and oil (B. Meissner, *Babylonien und Assyrien* II [Heidelberg: C. Winter, 1925], pp. 85ff.; J. Černý, *Ancient Egyptian Religion* [London: Hutchinson's University Library, 1952], pp. 101f.). Such allusions to Israelite idolatrous practices are unique in the Bible.

19. "My bread that I gave you" is explained (since no prior mention was made of "bread") by the appositional relative clause (without *'ᵃšer*) "[the] flour . . . [that] I fed you" (so, too, V); all this is a *casus pendens,* and the following clause, its predicate, is introduced by *w/u-* "you put it," etc. (Driver, *Tenses,* § 123).

20–21. Cf. Jer 3.24: "The Shame (= Baal) has eaten up the property of our fathers since our youth—their flocks and herds, their sons and daughters." Child sacrifice in the Valley of Ben-Hinnom is referred to in Jer 7:31; 19:5 ("burning their sons and daughters in fire"); 32:35 ("delivering [lit. making pass over] their sons and daughters to Molech); it was one of the practices Josiah abolished in his reform (II Kings 23:10: "he polluted the tophet which was in Valley of Ben-Hinnom so that none should deliver his son and daughter by fire to Molech"). Ezekiel uses the full "deliver by fire" (*heʿebir baʾeš*) in 20:31; here the abbreviated "delivered" is amply defined by "slaughtering [for them to eat]" in vss. 20f. (see 23:37 "deliver their sons . . . to them to eat"). Kings Ahaz (II Kings 16:7) and Manasseh (II Chron 33:6) are taxed with this practice, and II Kings 17:17 ascribes it to the northern kingdom in the preceding century as well. Whether or not elsewhere "to make pass over by [or through] fire" means dedication (so M. Cogan, *Imperialism and Religion*, pp. 77–83; M. Weinfeld, "The Worship of Molech and of the Queen of Heaven and Its Background," *Ugarit-Forschungen*, 4 [1972], 133–54; 10 [1978], 411–13—against the strictures of M. Smith, "A Note on Burning Babies," *JAOS* 95 [1975], 477ff.), in Ezekiel and Jeremiah child sacrifice is meant (on the evidence for this practice, see A. Green, *The Role of Human Sacrifice in the Ancient Near East* [Missoula, Mont.: Scholars Press, 1975]). From the heated denials of Jeremiah (passages cited above) that YHWH ever commanded it, it can be inferred that in the seventh century B.C.E., it was part of the worship of YHWH (G. B. Gray, *Sacrifice in the Old Testament* [Oxford: Clarendon Press, 1925], pp. 87f.; cf. Green's tortured discussion, pp. 173–79). By branding the recipient of this sacrifice "Baal" or "Molech," Jeremiah denies its legitimacy in the worship of YHWH.

The connection of the last two words of vs. 20 with what follows was suggested by Eliezer of Beaugency and Ehrlich.

22. The final *hayit* is similar to the verse-ending *hayu* in 22:18. G "you lived" (*ḥayit*)—doubtless an echo of *bdmyk ḥyy* in vs. 6b—crowds the sentence with a reference to God's rescue, whereas the point of MT is to evoke the perilous, bloody condition of the woman before God's intervention (vs. 6a).

23. *After all your evil—woe, woe to you!* . . . For, instead of desisting and repenting, you built . . . (vs. 24). Cf. Jer 3:7: "I thought, After she has done all these things she will return to me; but she did not return."

24. *platform* (geb) . . . *height* (rama). These terms are commonly taken as synonyms for "high place" ("shrines," vs. 16), with the evocation of the lascivious rites alluded to in the comment to vs. 16 (P. H. Vaughan, *The Meaning of 'BĀMĀ' in the Old Testament* [London and New York: Cambridge University Press, 1974], pp. 29ff.); in that case, the referent intrudes into the metaphor again. But G consistently renders the first term as "brothel"—recalling the *qubba* of Num 25:8 and post-

biblical Hebrew (on the affinity of the roots *gb*(*b*), *qb*(*b*), etc. see H. L. Fleischer in J. Lewy, *Chaldäisches Wörterbuch über die Targum . . .* [Leipzig: Baumgartner, 1881], I, p. 421a), while vacillating in the case of the second term among "public notice" (vs. 24), "brothel" (vs. 25) and "pedestal" (vs. 31); Herrmann made the attractive conjecture that *rama* means "[harlot's] stand or booth."

The proliferation of these establishments (vss. 24b–25a) recalls the accusation against Ahaz that he built altars to foreign gods "in every corner in Jerusalem" (II Chron 28:24).

25. *opening*. The rare root *pśq* appears once in qal (Prov 13:3 "he opens his lips"—of a voluble person) and once again here in pi'el (frequentative); the sense is of opening or parting what is usually closed. It is common in postbiblical Hebrew and Aramaic (*psq*), in the sense "split, cut."

26–29. Harlotry as a metaphor for alliances with foreign nations is discussed in Structure and Themes. The nations are listed in order of Israel's contact with them, and comprise allies (males) and an enemy (female) of Judah–Jerusalem. The liaison with Egypt (see next chapter) is traced back in 20:7f.; 23:3 to Israel's beginnings (there cultic disloyalty is derived from contact with Egypt); ever since the Assyrian period, Israel and Judah constantly applied to Egypt to aid against the Mesopotamian power: King Hoshea of Israel (II Kings 17:4; "So" = Sais [H. Geodicke, "The End of So [*Sô'*], King of Egypt," *BASOR* 171 (1963), 66]), and the Judean kings, Hezekiah (Isa 20; 30:1–5; 31:1ff.; *ANET*³, p. 287d), probably Jehoiakim (II Kings 24:7; cf. A. Šanda's commentary in Exegetisches Handbuch zum AT [Münster: Aschendorff, 1912]), and Zedekiah (Ezek 17). The Philistines, Israel's ancient rivals for control of the country (Samson, Saul, David stories), continued to worry the Judahites during the Assyrian period (J. Greenfield, *IDB* s.v. "Philistines," pp. 793f.); Ahaz suffered from them (II Chron 28:18) and Hezekiah's realm was diminished in their favor by victorious Sennacherib after he crushed the rebellion in Palestine at the end of the eighth century B.C.E.: Sennacherib awarded to the faithful Philistine cities Ashdod, Ekron, and Gaza (= "Philistine women") the Judean territories adjacent to them; *ANET*³, p. 288a. This territorial trenching on Judah appears to be the specific allusion in vs. 27 (proposed by O. Eissfeldt, *Palästina-Jahrbuch* 27 [1931], 58–66 [= *Kleine Schriften* I, pp. 239–46]).

Judah's "affair" with Assyria began when Ahaz sent a "present" (*šoḥad*, cf. *šaḥad* in vs. 33) and an offer of vassaldom to Tiglath-pileser III, seeking his help against an Israelite-Aramean attack (II Kings 16:7ff.; Isa 7 – 8); for the next century, Judah remained an Assyrian vassal, with interludes of rebellion under Hezekiah. Judah's last "lover" was "Merchant-land" Babylonia ("Canaan" = merchant, a usage based on the commercial eminence of the Phoenicians [= Canaanites; Gen 10:15]; see Hos 12:8; Zeph 1:11; Zech 14:21; Prov 31:24 and M. Astour,

"The Origin of the Terms 'Canaan,' 'Phoenician,' and 'Purple,'" *JNES* 24 [1965], 346ff.; in Ezek 17:4 Babylon bears the epithet "city of traders"). Hezekiah inaugurated the connection when he received the emissaries of the Babylonian rebel against Assyria, Merodachbaladan (II Kings 20:12ff.), evidently as part of his own defection from his overlord. Josiah may be presumed to have coordinated his policy against Egypt, which led to his death at Megiddo, with Babylonia and the Medes who had brought Assyria to its knees (II Kings 23:29; Josephus, Antiq. 10.5.1). Subsequently Nebuchadnezzar subjugated all of western Asia, including Judah.

It was a fact, then, that the relations of Israel and Judah with the three great kingdoms of the region all began with alliances pursued in the hope of political and military security. Isaiah preceded Ezekiel in opposing alliances with these same three nations.

26. *big-membered. baśar* "flesh" is a euphemism for penis in Gen 17:13; Lev 15:2ff. (priestly writings).

27. *will.* Or "appetite, greed" (cf. Exod 15:9)—abstracted from the concrete sense "throat" that *nepeš* has, e.g., in Isa 5:14 ("Sheol has widened its *nepeš* / opened wide its mouth"). Our phrase is a more vivid expression than *natan* X *bᵉyad-* "deliver X into the hand [power] of"—by which S T render it; it connotes the eagerness of the Philistines to "devour" their victims (cf. Ps 27:12; 41:3).

your depraved way. The unusual location of the suffix on the first word of a construct sequence recurs in Ezek 18:7 and 24:13; the same in Num 25:12 "my covenant of well-being," which contrasts with the normal construction of this phrase in Isa 54:10 (see König, III, § 277).

zimma "depravity" (lit. "evil device") includes murder (Hos 6:9) but especially unchastity (Lev 18:17; Judg 20:6; Jer 13:27). In 16:43, 58 and in 23:27, 29, 35 it serves as an aggravating synonym of *to'eba* and *taznut.*

28. *harloted with them. zana* is construed with direct object in Jer 3:1; Isa 23:17f.

30. *How hot your ardor is.* Following the medieval Karaite poet cited by F. Stummer (*VT* 4 [1954], 34–40), who used our expression in the line "*'amula libbati* like flaming fire"; Stummer translated it "fever-hot is my heart," citing Zorell's comparison of Hebrew *'ml* with Arabic *mll* "be hot." But *libba* seems to fuse *labba* "flame" (Exod 3:2) and *leb* "heart," and hence is better rendered "ardor." Since the appearance of Aramaic *mly/' lbt-* "be filled with wrath against" in the Elephantine papyri (A. Cowley, *Aramaic Papyri of the Fifth Century B.C.* [Oxford: Clarendon Press, 1923], ⋇37.11; ⋇41.4) and the Asshur ostracon (*KAI* 233.19) —evidently borrowed from Akkadian (S. H. Kaufman, *The Akkadian Influences on Aramaic* [Chicago and London: University of Chicago Press, 1974], p. 66)—our *'mlh lbtk* has been so interpreted: "how filled am I with wrath against you" (B. Porten, *Archives from Elephantine* [Berkeley and Los Angeles: University of California Press, 1968], p. 269,

fn. 12). MT may be retained with doubling of *l 'ᵃmulla* (pu'al) or revocalized *'emla;* for final *'* vocalization of final weak forms (derived from final *'*), see GKC § 75 pp; Joüon § 78 g.

headstrong (šlṭt). Lit. "ruling"; i.e., who does what she pleases, being subject to no one (Kara). J. C. Greenfield (*Eretz-Israel* 16 [1982], 56–61; English summary, 253*) proposes the meaning "a woman authorized to dispose at will" of the property endowed her by her husband; this is based on the meaning of *šl(y)ṭ b-* in Elephantine, Aramaic (Y. Muffs, *Studies in the Aramaic Legal Papyri from Elephantine* [Leiden: E. J. Brill, 1969]; consult index s.v. *"šlṭ,"* p. 231). The proposal would gain if it could be shown that *šlṭt* described the wanton with regard to the following, rather than to the preceding activities. Like other derivatives of *šlṭ* that cluster in late biblical Hebrew, *šlṭt* is probably an Aramaism, a revival of an early usage (Gen 42:6) under Aramaic influence (Aramaic *šlṭ* = monarchic Hebrew *mšl;* cf. Wagner, *Aramaismen* ⋕ 306–9).

31. For the plural suffix on *bbnwtyk* see comment to 6:8 "when you are scattered."

in that you scorned hire. Despite the reservations of B-Y, p. 5961b, fn. 5, this interpretation is justified. Infinitive with *l* frequently explicates a preceding verb, having the force of a gerund ("—ing," "by/in —ing"); GKC § 114 o; Joüon § 124 o. For example: "they caused the whole congregation to complain against him *lᵉhoṣi* by [their] spreading calumnies about the land" (Num 14:36); "he revealed his powerful works to his people *latet* by [his] giving them the heritage of nations" (Ps 111:6). Here, "you were not like a[ny other] harlot" is explicated by *lᵉqalles* "in [your] scorning"; what has confused interpreters is the unusual positive explication by the infinitive of a negative verb (*lo hayit*). The versions wrongly take the infinitive as having "a[ny other] harlot" for its subject, and variously misunderstand *lqls* (though they correctly translate *ytqlsw* at 22:5): G S "like a harlot who collects [*llqṭ?*] hire"; V "like a harlot by disdain increasing price"; T "who profits from wages."

32. *O adulterous wife* (for *wife* cf. Prov 30:20). Pi'el of *n'p* recurs in 23:37 and clusters in Jeremiah and Hosea, the literary antecedents of so much in Ezekiel.

while married to. taḥat means "under the control, authority of [a husband]" in 23:5 and Num 5:19f., 29 (priestly source).

takes strangers. Addressed to this woman, "takes" may mean not merely "receives" but "procures" (see next verse). *zarim* "strangers" has, as its first sense, men outside the marriage bond (cf. its use in the identical metaphor in Jer 2:25; 3:13; see feminine *zara* in Prov 2:16; 5:3, etc. and *zarim* of bastards in Hosea 5:7). It also has overtones of foreign nations (Ezek 7:21; 11:9; Lam 5:2) and foreign gods (Deut 32:16, where it || "abominations")—thus in a word it embraces the whole range of infidelities referred to in our passage. For the uncommon *'et* with indeterminate noun, see 43:10 and GKC § 117 c, d; König, III, § 288 g–h.

This interpretation of MT (Rashi's) satisfies the second-person address context and takes *taḥat* in the sense of its parallel in 23:5. The resulting disagreement between the implied second person of the vocative and the third-person verb (*tiqqaḥ* "she takes") is uncommon but not without parallel (Isa 22:16; 47:8a; 54:1 [yet none of these have a vocative consisting of a determined noun phrase as here]; see König, III, § 344 l). The anomalies of MT raise doubts about its soundness.

G maintains the address by an explicatory insertion of "like you"; it stumbles over *taḥat* ("from"), but at the verse end reads *'tnnym*. G's *Vorlage* seems to have read, "The woman who commits adultery while married to her husband takes hires," and may be regarded as an alternative to vs. 33a. Was there also a reading in vs. 33b of *'tnnyk* for present *'t ndnyk?* As vs. 33a is (quite properly) in the third person, so is this hypothetical *Vorlage* which eventually was conflated with it. The corruption of *'tnnm* to *'t zrym* may have been facilitated by misunderstanding *taḥat* as "instead of" (e.g., Num 3:12, 45, where *laqah* X *tahat* Y = "take X instead of Y"); that is indeed how Kara interprets our passage: "You are like [cf. G!] an adulterous woman who forsakes the mate of her youth and instead of her husband takes strangers." The multiple apt connotations of *zarim,* noted above, assured its survival as an enrichment of the text.

33. The hapaxes *nede* and *nadan* "gift" (G S T V render as *'etna(n)* in vss. 31, 34) appear to be morphological variants like *'etnu* and *'etnan* (Hosea 2:14; 9:1), "harlot's hire" (Moshe ben Sheshet compares also *'ᵃdi* and *'ᵃdanim* "ornament[s]," II Sam 1:24). J. C. Greenfield supposes wholly different words: *nadan,* from Akkadian *nidnu* "gift," particularly that given by the groom to the bride; *nede,* from Palestinian Aramaic *ndy* "bring, give." The sense seems clear enough: all harlots receive gifts, but you gave your dowry (my gifts to you) to all your paramours. "You paid" renders *šaḥad* cognate with *šoḥad* "bribe," or better "gift" given to move one to do something he may not have otherwise done. The verb is used of international relations in II Kings 16:8.

34. *You acted contrary*. Lit. "There was in you the contrary," but at the verse end this is stepped up to lit. "You became the contrary," that is, the embodiment of contrariety.

in that you harloted . . . We construe this clause according to its evident parallel in the next part of the verse: *taznut* is used here as a verbal noun || *tet* in the next clause; *zunna aḥarayik* "you were sought for harloting" || *nittan lak* "was given to you."

36. *your juice was poured out*. A reference to female genital "distillation" produced by sexual arousal. *nᵉḥuštek*—the versional renderings "your copper" guarantee the graph—is evidently the cognate of Akkadian *naḫšāti* "morbid genital outflow [of a woman]," from *nḫš* "be abundant,

overflowing" (M. Greenberg, in *Essays . . . in Memory of Jacob Joel Finkelstein,* pp. 85f.). Medieval guesses connected it with an obscure Mishnaic term *nᵉḥusto šellᵉtannur* "the bottom of an oven," which A. Geiger adopted (*Urschrift und Übersetzungen der Bibel,* 2te Auflage [Frankfurt: Madda, 1928], pp. 391ff. [Hebrew translation, *Ha-miqra ve-targumav* (Jerusalem: Bialik Institute, 1949), pp. 251f.]). Citing T S, Geiger emended the preceding word to *ḥošpek* and the following to *wattᵉgalli,* arriving at "you exposed your nether parts and uncovered your nakedness." Moderns generally follow suit, but the Akkadian cognate above-mentioned opens the possibility of interpreting the text as it stands. (T "your pudendum was exposed and your shame revealed" repeats itself at vs. 37 and 23:18 as the stock rendering of several like expressions, regardless of their precise wording; it cannot therefore be relied upon for emending our passage.) This may be the earliest instance of what became a motif of hypersexuality in erotic literature.

in accordance with the blood. "You will be sentenced to a punishment in accord with that (*kᵉ'oto*) sin, measure for measure: you did not spare your children . . . nor shall I on my part spare you . . ." (Kimḥi). G, and some T mss., "in the blood" and so patently Rashi ("in [for] the iniquity of the blood . . ."); but this is an easier reading, and Ezekiel prefers *kᵉ* in defining dooms: *kidᵉrakayik* "in accordance with your ways" (7:3, 8f.; 24:14). *Minḥat Shay* observes vacillation in copies between *k* and *b,* with the better copies showing *k;* he cites Profiat Duran's *Maʿᵃśe epod,* ch. 14 [Vienna edition, 1865, p. 82], for the occasional interchangeability in meaning of the two prepositions (e.g., Zech 2:10; Jer 18:17; Hosea 7:12; in each of these, ms. or versional variation occurs).

37. *you were so sweet.* MT is backed by G, who mistranslates "intermixed" (from a homonymous root); moderns prefer to emend to *'agabt* "you lusted after" according to 23:9, etc. The following reference to "all you hated" apparently alludes to the Philistines (vs. 27), who indeed were later condemned for taking revenge on Judah (25:15). Cf. 23:22, 28, where the "hated" are former paramours.

expose nakedness . . . they shall gaze. The public degradation of a harlot by exhibiting her naked is mentioned in Hos 2:12; Nahum 3:5; Jer 13:22, 26. A modified form appears in *Mishnah Sotah* 1.5, inflicted on a suspected adulteress before her trial (as here); the rationale expressed there—"She exposed herself for sin, God therefore exposes her"—fits our case, for this humiliation corresponds to the indictment of vs. 36a. Such uncovering of nakedness or turning back clothing is distinct from the stripping of the adulteress, which occurs after her conviction (vs. 39).

38. *bloody object.* Similarly 35:6 "I will make you [= turn you into] blood"; her end is like her beginning, "weltering in her blood." Fury and passion (cf. 5:13) pertain to a betrayed husband; cf. Prov 6:34 "the fury (*ḥema*) of the husband will be passion[ate] (*qin'a*)."

39. That God delivers the woman to her peers (including her paramours) for punishment seems to color the figure again in accord with the reality (foreign nations would ravage Judah). The angry threat of Hosea 2:5—"lest I strip her naked and leave her as on the day of her birth" (note how the end of Ezek 16:39 echoes the childhood nakedness of the woman in vs. 7)—presumably reflects more closely what happened to such a woman: her husband (or the males of the family) inflicted the punishment, symbolizing the withdrawal of all her husband's goods and gifts from her. Contracts from Nuzi (fifteenth century B.C.E., north Iraq) specify that if a wife divorces her husband, she will "go out naked"; if she leaves him for another man, "my sons shall strip the garments off my wife and expel her out of my house" (C. Gordon, "Hos 2:4–5 in the Light of New Semitic Inscriptions," *ZAW* 13 [1936], 277ff.). A Jewish Aramaic incantation "divorcing" the demoness Lilith declares, "naked you are sent forth, unclothed" (J. Montgomery, *Aramaic Incantation Texts from Nippur* [Philadelphia: University Museum, 1913], #17, p. 190). Tacitus tells that the ancient Germans left the punishment of an adulteress to her husband; "he shaves off his wife's hair, strips her in the presence of kinsmen, thrusts her from his house and flogs her through the whole village" (Germania 19).

40. After all her possessions have been taken from her, she will be executed (Lev 20:10) by stoning (Deut 22:23f.)—a public mode of punishment expressing the outrage of the community—(H. Cohen, *'al 'oneš haseqila* [Bar-Ilan University, 1962])—then her corpse will be hacked (the hapax *bataq* is cognate with Akkadian *bataqu* "cut, sever [limbs]" [*CAD*]). This unexampled action recalls the early English multiple punishment for high treason, ending with cutting up the culprit's body into quarters (W. Blackstone, *Commentaries on the Laws of England,* IV [rpt. Boston: Dover, 1962], p. 88).

The executioners are a *qahal*—a term used for an assemblage of armed forces (17:17; 26:7; 32:3, 22f.; 38:4, 7, 13, 15) as well as for crowds (27:27, 34). In the restatement of the allegory in 23:24, it serves for the assemblage of peoples attacking Jerusalem. Hence *qahal* here (and in the || 23:46f.) probably intrudes reality into the metaphor once again: armies would overwhelm Jerusalem (contrast J. Milgrom, "Priestly Terminology and the Political and Social Structure of Pre-Monarchic Israel," *JQR* 69 [1978], 73, who regards our passage as evidence for the postexilic substitution of *qahal* for pre-exilic *'eda* as the title of public body exercising judicial functions [in Lev 24:16 it is the *'eda* that stones]).

41. *They shall burn your houses in fire.* So, too, 23:47. Another intrusion of reality into the figure; Jeremiah was constantly threatening Jerusalem with capture followed by burning (e.g., 32:29; 34:22; 37:8; 38:18). A fixed formula of Assyrian royal inscriptions reporting a successful campaign against a resistant or rebellious city is "I destroyed, tore down, burned down city X." This expected fate did overtake the city; II

Kings 25:8ff. tells how after its fall it was systematically burned down and demolished. S's attempt to retain the figure (text note [d–d]) fails, since its implied reading of *btwk* "in the midst of" instead of *btyk* "your houses" yields unidiomatic Hebrew; one does not burn "inside" but "in/with" (*b*ᵉ[*mo*]-) fire.

in the sight of many women. "Women" = nations (5:8); the world is divided into Jerusalem's "paramours" (allies)—males, and all others who are (at least potential) rivals or enemies—hence, females; cf. "the Philistine women" of vs. 27.

42. Cf. 5:13; not a consolation (and hence out of place) but a notice that God will not rest until he has inflicted the extreme penalty.

43. *were not in dread of me.* The negative particle at the beginning of the verse governs this second verb as well (Eliezer of Beaugency, Ehrlich [Hebrew]; see further at 11:11). Since *ragaz* || *paḥad* (Jer 33:9), our expression is comparable to *w*ᵉ*lo paḥdati 'elayik* "awe of me is not upon you" (Jer 2:19). For the construction *ragaz l*ᵉ "tremble on account of" Ehrlich compares Isa 14:9. G S T render as a transitive "you enraged me," the normal sense of hif'il, to which most moderns emend. *darkek b*ᵉ*roš* lit. "your way on [your] head" calls up *b*ᵉ*roš kol derek* lit. "at the head of every way" in vs. 31: punishment mirrors crime.

44. *Like mother.* Lit. "like her mother"; the lack of mappiq in the suffix *h* is not uncommon before *bgdkpt* (GKC § 91 e; Joüon § 94 h); cf. 24:6; 47:10.

45. The depravity of the Amorite and Hittite is assumed: "they spurn their husbands and commit adultery with other men; they spurn their children and slaughter them for Molech" (Eliezer of Beaugency); cf. Lev 18:27; 20:23 (with specific reference to sexual offenses linked with Molech worship). Since the daughter's depravity derives from bad heredity, her mother's behavior is wholly assimilated to hers (though it is nowhere described to have been so).

the sister of your sisters. *'*ᵃ*ḥot*- (the normal singular) serves as plural here and in vss. 51, 52, 55, 61 with only one instance of the form *'aḥyot*- that serves as the regular postbiblical Hebrew plural (vs. 52); the suffixes of *'*ᵃ*ḥot* (plural) vacillate between those normally attached to singular nouns (*-k;* vss. 45, 51 [*ktib*], 52 [note same attached to ᵃ*ḥyot*-!]) and those attached to plurals (*-yk;* 51 [*qre*], 55, 61); see B-L § 28 s, q′; § 78 c for historical explanation.

The verse introduces a new theme—sibling depravity. The sisterhood of Samaria, whose similarity to Jerusalem is a matter of record (cf. Hos 5; II Kings 17:19), is justified; that of Sodom, however, is based not on any resemblance in sin, but on the fabled iniquity of that city, which is exploited for the invective.

46. Samaria is "big" in size, not age; younger than Jerusalem, it stands for the northern kingdom, much larger than Judah (for which Jerusalem stands). Sodom is "little" in size, not in age, since it was destroyed before

Judah ever existed. "Daughters" is the regular epithet of towns (hamlets) included in the territory of a main city (Ezek 26:6—of Tyre; 30:18—of Tahpanes; often in the city lists, e.g., Josh 15:45; Neh 11:25ff.). "Left" = north and "right" = south of one facing the rising sun (one who is oriented).

47. *did you not.* Taking *w^elo* as a rhetorical question—as in vss. 43 and 56. G S take it as an indicative negative extending to the next verb as well: "You did not follow . . . or commit" (R. Weiss, *Shnaton* 2 [1977], 89).

Very soon. Lit. "in but a short while"; temporal *kim'aṭ* occurs in Isa 1:9, "We should soon have become like Sodom"; Ps 81:15, "I would soon bring their enemies low" (both adduced by Ibn Janaḥ). The hapax *qat* has an Arab equivalent meaning "only, solely," and serves to intensify the adverb ("soon"). For the thought of this verse cf. 5:5ff., where it is asserted that Jerusalem was worse than her neighbors.

49–50. The proverbial prosperity of the cities of the plain (Gen 13:10, "like the garden of YHWH") nurtured in them pride and callousness, ending in their committing abomination (sodomy [cf. Gen 19:5f.] is *to'eba* in Lev 18:22; 20:13). Prosperity as a cause of iniquity is a Deuteronomic theme, e.g., Deut 8:12; 32:15. The expressions "satiety of bread and careless ease" (the latter a construct pair of synonyms, Avishur, *Construct,* p. 163) stand in apposition to "pride" (*ga'on*)—the subject of *haya*—and explicate it; cf. Gen 15:12 *'ema ḥ^ašeka nopelet* "a terrifying darkness fell [singular]," where "darkness" is both an accompaniment and component of the preceding "terror." Ehrlich simply revocalizes *g^e'on* (construct) "pride of." Note how *tigb^ohena* is assimilated in form to *ta'^ašena* (normally *tigbahna*).

when I saw it. Evidently a reminiscence of "Let me go down now and see . . ." (Gen 18:21; so Rashi). S renders so; G "according as I saw"—apparently, "as I saw fit" (so Kimḥi's first explanation). Some copies and G mss. read "as you saw," anticipating the allusion below (vs. 56) to Jerusalem's using Sodom as a byword. In its way, Jer 3:7f. also utilizes the motif of Jerusalem's witnessing her sister's punishment—in vain.

51–52. For the thought cf. Jer 3:11: "Wayward Israel has proven herself more righteous than faithless Judah." Characteristically, Ezekiel carries the thought to an extreme: Jerusalem is here the active subject; let her be mortified for having "made her sisters [look] more righteous than she," for having indeed (inadvertently) interceded (*pillalt*) on their behalf, for having, finally, provided them comfort (see vs. 54)! *ṣaddeqtek* is feminine infinitive construct of *ṣiddeq* (patterned like *yass^era,* Lev 26:18).

53–55. Inasmuch as Jerusalem has debased herself more than her sisters, a decision of God to forgive and restore her must in all fairness entail the same for her sisters. But since she boasted of her superiority (see vss. 56f.), elevating them to her level must be humiliating to her. Furthermore, the cases of her sisters being better than hers, their restoration will take precedence over hers (note the order in vss. 53, 55), so that hers can be said to be incidental to theirs ("among them"). Jerusalem's pride is thoroughly deflated. A. Soggin discusses the expression *šub* *š^ebu/it* judiciously in *THAT* II, pp. 886ff. "Restore fortunes" (both words deriving from *šwb*) rather than "return captivity" (the second word as from *šby*) is indicated by Job 42:10 and the Aramaic parallel, "the gods restored the fortunes (*hšbw šybt*) of my dynasty" (Sefire inscription III 24f.; J. C. Greenfield, "Stylistic Aspects of the Sefire Treaty Inscription," *Acta Orientalia* 29 [1965], 4), but the exact sense of the verb (why qal? contrast Aramaic haf'el) remains unclear. The expression recurs in 29:14 (of Egypt) and 39:25 (of "Jacob"); it is far more frequent in the restoration oracles of Jeremiah (chs. 30–33).

the fortunes of your captives. Taking the second word *šbyt* as a derivative of *šby* "capture" (so in Num 21:29); but G's rendering of the first word as from *wšbty* (text note [f–f]) is appealing, for thereby the second part of the sentence fully corresponds to the first (MT will have arisen by a mistaken metathesis under the influence of the preceding repeated *šbyt*). Yet see vs. 55.

54. *giving comfort.* Your misfortune gave them the solace of company in their own; so 32:31 speaks of Pharaoh's consolation at seeing all the other kings lying in Sheol when he arrives. Alternatively, your extreme wickedness gives them room to extenuate their behavior.

55. Note how an artificial distinction is made in *b*'s verb *t^ešubena,* so that the shift to second person be clearly marked all through the last clause.

56. *a byword.* Lit. "a report in your mouth"; did you not smugly hold up the cities of the plain as an object lesson in your prosperous days? The viciousness of Sodom and its condign punishment were such popular commonplaces that prophets habitually referred to them (Amos 4:11; Isa 1:9f.; 3:9; 13:19; Jer 49:18; 50:40).

57. *now the reproach.* Surmising that *k^emo 'et* = *ka'et* "now," Judg 13:23; Num 23:23. G "as now you are a reproach" probably reflects MT, but has stimulated various emendations (*kmwh 'at ḥrpt* "like her you are the reproach"). For the thought, compare vs. 27 above.

Aramean = G "of Syria," but S reads "Edomite," attractive in the light of 25:12 (note the preceding reference to Philistines in vs. 15) and 36:5 ("hearty contempt" of the Edomites); the Arameans are not elsewhere found among Jerusalem's enemies.

59. *what you did.* As you turned your back on me, so will I forsake you; as you flouted your obligations to me, so will I ignore mine to you. As the sequel shows, this phrase does not mean that God will violate his covenant (much less flout the curse-oath—which he never took!), but that he will show the same harshness toward Jerusalem as she did toward him when she violated the covenant and flouted the curse-oath. The conception is the same as in Lev 26, where the people's "contrariness" is an-

swered by the like on the part of God (Lev 26:23, 27, 40f.). But particularly illuminating is the opening passage of that section (Lev 26:14–16aα): if you spurn my laws and "violate my covenant, I on my part will do this to you . . ." Interpreters are divided as to the reference of "this," is it to the preceding misdeeds of the people, or to the following punishments? Since vs. 44 declares that even in exile God will maintain his covenant, clearly "I will do this to you" cannot mean violate my covenant with you. Hence most moderns take the easy solution and make "this" refer forward to the following punishments, but the Hebrew by no means indicates this. In fact all the Jewish commentators who interpret it (many do not) take it as a backward reference (see Abarbanel, Sforno, Malbim, Hoffman); Ehrlich is typical: "If Israel behaves in such a way as to break the covenant with YHWH, YHWH will do similarly and behave toward them contrary to his covenant obligations." Ezekiel's language here may be taken to mean the same.

curse-oath . . . These terms are drawn from the Deuteronomic conception of the covenant (made in the Plains of Moab) as having been confirmed by Israel through self-imprecations conditional upon violating the covenant (Deut 29:11, 13, 18ff.; on the first millennium Near Eastern background, see Weinfeld, *Deuteronomy,* pp. 62f., 102ff.). Once again the real reference of the metaphor intrudes (cf. above, vs. 8, where God's oath to the patriarchs is alluded to).

The verse recapitulates the punishment of the adulteress and her offense by way of a setting for the antithesis which follows (see Structure and Themes).

60. *But I.* The pronoun appears in Hebrew after the verb, thus doubly emphatic; unlike you, I will remember my former covenant with you. So again vs. 62: unlike you, I will maintain my covenant with you.

I will establish (whqmwty). Unlike the phrase *karat b^e^rit,* which refers always to the making of a new covenant (so 34:25; 37:26—with reference to "the covenant of peace," a divine boon of the new future order), *heqim b^e^rit* usually means "maintain a covenant" already concluded (Gen 17:19, 21: I will bless Ishmael, but my covenant *'aqim* with Isaac; Lev 26:9: I will make you fertile and numerous, and *h^a^qimoti* my covenant with you; Deut 8:18: *l^e^haqim* his covenant that he swore to you), although many believe that it also has the sense of establishing a new covenant (e.g., in Gen 6:18; Exod 6:4). In our passage, the continuity of the "eternal covenant" with "the covenant of your youth" is suggested by remembrance of the latter serving as the motive of the former. *heper* of vs. 59 and *heqim* of vs. 60 will thus be antonymous verbs with the same *b^e^rit* as object; cf. the identical antonymy in Num 30:14–16. Yet the language is equivocal enough to leave open the possibility of a disjuncture between the two. Clearly declared is the origin and basis of the "eternal covenant" in God's memory of "the covenant of your youth"; in the future as in the past, God's tie with Israel will be self-motivated, an expression of his concern and his nature, rather than of any quality or merit of Israel; see Structure and Themes.

61. *when you receive.* As an inheritance or a gift; for this use of *laqaḥ,* see Num 34:14f.; especially Josh 13:8 and 18:7 in which the sequence *laqaḥ . . . natan* occurs. G "in my taking"(= when I take) follows the usage in vss. 16ff. where *laqaḥ* is a preliminary to further action. "Sisters" in the plural refers to Sodom and her "daughters," and Samaria and hers, all of whom will become "daughters" (dependencies) of restored Jerusalem.

The last clause is unclear. I follow T "though you did not observe the Torah," which Rashi adapts to the language of the text: "not because you have kept the covenant, but through my constancy." Ehrlich (Hebrew): "Judah will surely be ashamed when it sees that its God has maintained the covenant and even dealt with it beyond the letter of the law when he gave it more than he promised [namely, Sodom]—while it did not even uphold the terms of the covenant."

63. *be able to open your mouth.* Lit. "have an opening of the mouth" (see at 3:27, "I will open your mouth"); the sense here is: be able to assert yourself, with evocation of vs. 56—Jerusalem's haughty citation of Sodom (and, by inference, of Samaria also).

when I absolve you. For *kipper l-* in this sense see Deut 21:8 "absolve your people!"; Isa 22:14 "you shall never be absolved of this iniquity" (lit. this iniquity shall never be absolved for you). It is remarkable that the usual sequence of shame leading to repentance and expunging of sin by God is reversed here (J. Milgrom, *Cult and Conscience* [Leiden: E. J. Brill, 1976], p. 120, fn. 43a, errs in including our passage among the "uniform teaching of the prophets" that repentance expunges sin.)

STRUCTURE AND THEMES

This longest prophecy of the book—sixty-three verses between one revelation formula (16:1) and another (17:1)—has three divisions. After the command to arraign Jerusalem for her abominations (vs. 2), comes A (vss. 3–43), an extended metaphor of the nymphomaniacal adulteress; B (vss. 44–58), the invidious comparison of Jerusalem to her sisters Sodom and Samaria; and C (vss. 59–63), a coda foretelling the mortification of restored Jerusalem before covenant-true YHWH. Each division ends with an epitomizing sentence concluding with the formula "declares (Lord) YHWH." That formula, affirming the divine authorship of a passage and thus appropriately occurring at a terminus, seems to mark the subunits within each division as well (beginnings and endings).

A consists of a detailed bill of indictment, introduced by "and say: Thus said Lord YHWH" (vs. 3) and running on to vs. 34, and a sentencing ("So harlot, hear the word of YHWH; thus said Lord YHWH: Because . . ." (vss. 35–43). (For a similar structure, see ch. 34: indictment, vss. 2–6; consequence, vss. 7ff.) The formula "declares Lord YHWH" further subdivides A as follows:

A1 An abandoned baby girl is saved and possessed by YHWH (vss. 3–8). The narrative moves in vivid episodes from the birth and exposure of the baby (vss. 3–5, abounding in negatives; note the *inclusio* formed by the expression "on the day of your birth"), to God's first notice of the infant, in which he preserves her and lets her grow to nubile ripeness (vss. 6–7), to his second notice when he takes her and pledges his troth (vs. 8). Forsaken by her natural parents, she is saved alive by a gracious divine savior, who covenants with her.

A2 She is provided for splendidly and becomes a famous beauty (vss. 9–14). God lavishes on her the care her parents denied her (vs. 9 contrasts with vs. 4); he clothes and adorns her (vss. 10–12) to indulgence (in vs. 13 she, not God, is the subject), and declares that her renowned beauty is his doing (vs. 14).

A3 She spends her endowment on fornication (vss. 15–19). After a general indictment (anticipating A5; vs. 15b = vs. 25), vss. 16–19 describe how she used her gifts for the making and tending of "male images." *watihyi li* "you became mine" at the end of vs. 8 reverberates in the exclamations of outrage at the end of vss. 15, 16, 19.

A4 She sacrifices her children to the images (vss. 20–22). Not content with infidelity, she murdered her children to feed her images, forgetful of her bloody plight as a baby, from which she had been saved. Her filicide evokes her own verging on death, when, naked and bloody, she was a victim of her own parents' cruelty.

A5 She fornicates with every passerby (vss. 23–29; here and in the following section, A6, "declares Lord YHWH" is in the opening line of the section). Vss. 24f. heighten the language of vss. 15f.: instead of a single term (*bama*) come two (*gab, rama*); multiple locations are mentioned, an obscene gesture, and the "extension" of harlotry. A new level of outrage has been reached, with human males instead of idols as paramours. Along with "male" partners, "female" enemies appear—filling out the register of Jerusalem's international contacts. Repeated "you were not satisfied" at the end of the section underlines the woman's abandoned frenzy and prepares the sequel.

A6 The contrariety of the nymphomaniacal harlot (vss. 30–34; she is now called a *zona* "harlot"—a grade lower than "one who fornicates" [*tizni*]). The resumption of vss. 24–25a in vss. 30–31a ends by announcing the theme of contrariety: "You were not like other harlots . . ." Reflecting this, vss. 33f. are constructed antithetically; vs. 34 is strongly patterned: two phrases with *hepek* "contrary" form an *inclusio,* and the two central verb clauses are each chiastic ([verb(-object)-object-verb]). Thematic "harlot's hire," announced in vs. 31b, resounds in the highly alliterative penultimate verb clause of the final sentence (vs. 34).

A7 God sentences her to violent death (vss. 35–43). After a summons to the harlot (vs. 35), a message formula opens the verdict: a summary of offenses (vs. 36) is followed by a list of consequences—public exposure (vs. 37), condemnation to punishment for adultery and murder (vs. 38), and delivery to the mob for pillage and lynching (vss. 39–41). Only then will God's wrath subside (vs. 42). An afterwave, evoking the beginning of the prophecy (the woman's forgetfulness of her youth[ful covenant and its benefits]), rounds off the sentence. In the rhetorical question that follows "declares Lord YHWH" (vs. 43), *zimma* combines with *darkek* preceding the formula to evoke vs. 27, in which the shame of the Philistine women at Jerusalem's depraved conduct (*darkek zimma*) is mentioned. The question seeks to bring home to Jerusalem that she has heaped up wickedness in brazen insouciance. The overtones of vs. 27, with its contrast of more virtuous gentiles and its motif of shame, foreshadow the next division of the prophecy.

B is dominated by comparisons unfavorable (that is, causing shame) to Jerusalem. The thought moves quickly from the opening epigram ("like mother like daughter") through an implicit "like mother like daughters" to the explicit equation of the three sisters, which is the point of departure for the division.

B1 Jerusalem is the worst of three depraved sisters (vss. 44–47). The perfidious family is introduced: "mother" and "mother-father" not only form an *inclusio* (vss. 44b–45) but connect B1 with A1 (note the inversion of the parents); the sisters are identified (vs. 46) and Jerusalem is said to have soon outdone them in wickedness (vs. 47)—a bridge to what follows.

B2 Jerusalem must be ashamed over having made her sisters look righteous, and over being restored only as an adjunct to their restoration (vss. 48–58). Sodom stands at the beginning and at the end of this section (vss. 48–50, 56f.), for as a byword of corruption its "vindication" by Jerusalem is the latter's most stinging humiliation (note the association of "pride" with each). The sequence of vss. 53–55 is: restoration of the three, with Jerusalem "among them" (vs. 53), which equalization comforts them and disgraces her (vs. 54); the three will attain to their former states—an implicit curb on Jerusalem's dream of hegemony over the land of Israel—and a preparation for the sequel. (Vs. 58 echoes vs. 43 [*zimma, to'eba*].)

C Recovenanted and re-endowed beyond her former state, Jerusalem will feel shame at remembrance of her past (vss. 59–63). Starting with *ki* plus message formula, which serves often to introduce a new turn (see at 14:21), this coda is at once a climax and a resolution: a climax in terms of God's victory over human obduracy, and a resolution in terms of Jerusalem's reformation and acknowledgment of her abominable conduct as shown by her deep shame. Themes of A (covenant of youth) and B (sisters, shame) are tied together in a sublime catharsis.

Though B is evidently a new turn, it is dependent upon A: it assumes the reader knows the identity of the wanton (she is never identified in B), the baseness of her parents, and her abominations (which though alluded to are not described). (As to the question of the "resurrection" of the executed wanton in this section, compare pp. 262–63 above on the inconsistency pervading all the doom-restoration prophecies.) The temporal setting of B is determined by the equal footing of all three sisters; Jerusalem has joined the others in the limbo of has-beens awaiting restoration. What was threatened in A has occurred. C marks a further advance of the historical horizon, beyond the restoration to a new dispensation in which the two "sisters" will be subject to Jerusalem. C's dependence on B (sister motif) and A (covenant of youth) is manifest. The prophecy thus moves in a cumulative chronological sequence.

The prophecy is united through several continuities, some of which undergo transformation. The family theme runs through all three divisions; an ever-changing aspect is "daughters"—in vs. 20 children; in vs. 27, women (= enemies); in vs. 46 and throughout B, dependencies; lastly, the surprise transformation of "sisters" (vs. 61). Shame occurs in A only in the Philistine women (vs. 27), but in B and C in Jerusalem. Common to A and B (where it is more frequent) is the term "abomination"—answering to the charge laid on the prophet in vs. 2. The wanton does not "remember" her youth in A (vss. 22, 43), but God does in C (vs. 60), while after her reformation she "remembers" her evil ways (vs. 61).

The most pervasive feature of the prophecy is contrast or antithesis. The life course of the wanton starts with rescue from early death, soars to the peak of beauty and fame, then plunges to the depths of degradation and bloody death (A). B continuously compares and contrasts the wanton's acts and fate with those of her sisters. C foretells Jerusalem's shame at the contrast between her past behavior and God's future graciousness. The brazen adulteress who does not blush at any perversion (A) learns shame (B) and when chastened is mortified by her past (C). God, whose fury unleashes savage retribution (A), appears in B as tempering redemption with humiliation, and finally (in C) as graciously absolving from all sin.

The parts of each division are closely interconnected. To begin with A: what the child's parents withheld from her, God gave her without stint. The "field" was to be her death-site; after God's reviving command it is part of a simile for her flourishing growth, like "the plants of the field." "Stark naked" describes the woman arrived at nubility, ready to receive God's lavish endowment; "stark naked" describes her stripped of her last bit of clothing on the verge of her execution. In between, the prophet pauses in his account of how she squandered all she had on "male images" to denounce her forgetfulness of her childhood when she was "stark naked," wallowing in her blood.

Contrasts are highlighted by the use of repetition. God "passed by" and preserved her alive; he "passed by" again when she came of age and took her; she on her part pressed her favors on "anyone who passed by." A series of six (or seven) verb clauses particularizes the gifts God made to the woman ("I clothed . . . I shod . . . I bound . . ." etc.); six corresponding sentences relate how she squandered them—and her children—on her "male images" ("you took . . . and made/put . . ."). Her blood, in which she lived through God's word, reverberates in the blood of her children which she slaughtered for her idols. God covered her nakedness, but her nakedness was exposed in her harlotry, so God will hand her over to executioners who will expose and see all her nakedness.

The key term in the tale of the harlot's progress is *znh* "to harlot, fornicate" (occurs, with its derivative *taznut* twenty times), which describes offenses increasingly heinous. Fornication with idols was "too little," so she killed her children for them. Idols too were not enough, so she "extended (=increased) her harlotry" (three times in vss. 25–29) to male neighbors—without ever finding satisfaction (three times in vss. 28–29). Her nadir of degradation, paying out hire instead of receiving it, is dwelt upon in several antithetical sentences (vss. 31b–34). The verdict on her conduct is an outpouring of accumulated rage, heaping up items of indictment and measures of punishment.

Alongside the climactic structure, lurid images and shocking language serve to sustain this long, verbose diatribe: fornicating with male images, slaughtering children for them to eat, spreading legs for every passerby, "your 'juice' was poured out," a bloody object of fury and passion, "hack you with their swords." The prophecy also contains a good number of rare or unique words and grammatical anomalies.

Unique words (including words found again only in Ezekiel; followed by verse number):

mkrt (3), *lmš'y* (4), *hmlḥ, hḥtl/ḥtl* (4), *g'l* (5), *mtbwsst* (6), *mšy* (10), *tznwt* (passim and in ch. 23 only), *pśk* (25), *mh 'mlh lbtk* (30), *ndh, ndn* (33), *šḥd* (verb, 33), *nḥšt* (obscene, 36), *btq* (40).

Rare words or usages:

mldt (plural) (3), *rbbh* ("growth," 7), *rbh* ("grow up") *'dy 'dyym, 'rm w'ryh* (7), *'gyl* (12), *ṭl'wt, l' b'wt wl' yhyh* (16), *gb, rmh* (obscene, 24), *gdly bśr* (26), *znh* with accusative (28), *qls* (31), *hpk* (noun, 34), *znh* (passive, 34), *rgz l-, h'* (43).

Grammatical anomalies:

Second-person feminine singular verb afformative *ty* (*k^{e}tib*)—13, 18, 22, 31 (twice), 43 (twice); plural suffix *-yk* on substantives ending in *ut* (*ot*)—15, etc., 31; doubled *r*—4 (twice); assimilation in noun pair *ššy wmšy*—13.

Some of these rarities are due to topics not otherwise taken up (care of the newborn, the argot of whoring), others may be a colloquial level of language. To the latter we may account exclamations, Akkadianisms (*ndn, btq, nḥšt*—also perhaps argot), and Aramaisms (afformative *ty* [cf. E. Y. Kutscher, *The Language and Linguistic Background of the Isaiah Scroll* (Hebrew) (Jerusalem: Magnes Press, 1959), pp. 20f., 142f.], *pśk, ml' lbt-*, perhaps *qls*). The penchant for plural forms (*mldwt, mkrt, dmy-, rmwt* [39], second-person feminine plural suffixes on *-u/ot* nouns) suits the turgid style of the passage.

Choice of language thus combines with climactic structure and antithesis to produce a sensational effect that does not flag despite the length of the passage.

The transition from A to B is made by the quip, "Like mother like daughter," which facilitates the shift in focus to the three "(daughters/) sisters," and to the antithesis Jerusalem—Sodom (and Samaria) that dominates B. The point of this antithesis is its inversion of the traditional evaluation of Sodom relative to Jerusalem, the latter's pride replaced by the reproach of making her notorious "sister[s]" look righteous by comparison. The linguistic features of A continue in B: unique and rare words (*qt, pll, šmw'h* "byword," *kmw 't* "now"), an Aramaism (or Akkadianism, *šwṭ* "despise"), second-person feminine singular *ty* verb afformative (vs. 51, perhaps vs. 50), morphological assimilation (vs. 50) and other irregularity (in the inflection of *'ḥwt*). Style and linguistic texture confirm the connection of B to A.

The bridge from B to C is *ka'ašer 'aśit* (vs. 59) "as you have done," which echoes *kol/ka'ašer 'aśit* in vss. 48, 51, 54; here the clause is defined as violation of the covenant, introducing the main theme of the coda (*berit*, vss. 60 [twice], 61, 62). Around the covenant the prophet constructs his final contrast—the faithfulness of God despite the faithlessness of Jerusalem, expressed in his ultimate eschatological bounty, which will shame her into silence. Even this brief division has its unusual term, *pitḥon pe* (vs. 63).

The coherent structure, the progressive temporal sequence, the homogeneous style and linguistic texture, and the intricate connection of the parts of this prophecy give it an architectural aspect; such flaws as exist are overborne by the great design. Once again we observe the "halving" pattern: a theme (A), a variation on it (B), and a conclusion in which elements of both are fused (C).

"Make known to Jerusalem her abominations" embodies the main issue of this complex oracle: Jerusalem is oblivious to her shame (in Jer 2:23 she denies it), hence the prophet must confront her with her appalling record. The passage through time distinguishes this indictment from the preceding ones. It is the first of three surveys of Israel's history (chs. 16, 20, 23) and the most impressive: its metaphor is worked out more elaborately and in more directions than that of ch. 23 (ch. 20 has no metaphor); it takes in more history than ch. 20; neither of the other two can match its structure and rhetoric. We turn now to its themes.

The figure of Israel as YHWH's wife derives from the cardinal commandment that Israel worship YHWH alone. To that demand of exclusive fidelity, the obligation of a wife to her husband offered a parallel. Certain usages in the Torah already reflect the figure. In the Decalogue and the smaller "Covenant Code" YHWH is called *qanna* "passionate, jealous" toward those who break faith with him (Exod 20:5; 34:14). In Num 5:14, 30 the related noun *qin'a* and verb *qinne* describe the agitation of a husband suspicious of his wife's fidelity (cf. Prov 6:34). Apostasy is expressed by *zana* "go whoring" in Exod 34:14f. and Num 15:39 (whence Ezek 6:9; on the foregoing see the luminous remarks of G. Cohen, "The Song of Songs," in *Samuel Friedland Lectures, 1960–1966* [New York: Jewish Theological Seminary of America, 1966], pp. 1–22; esp. pp. 4ff.). The prophetic development of this figure is built upon this early foundation. The first recorded use of it is in Hosea's denunciation of the northern kingdom. "Arraign your mother [= the kingdom of Israel]," he cried to her "children" (= citizens), ". . . for she is not my wife, and I am not her husband" (= a formula of divorce; cf. Muffs, "Studies in Biblical Law, IV," pp. 4ff.):

> Let her remove her harlotry from her face and her adultery from between her breasts, lest I strip her as on the day of her birth . . . Their mother has fornicated . . . for she said, Let me go after my lovers who give me my bread, my water and my wool, my flax, my oil and my drink . . . She did not realize that it was I who gave her grain, new wine and oil; the silver I gave her so much of, and the gold, they made over to Baal! So I shall take back my grain in its season and my new wine in its time, and pluck off my wool and flax so that it does not cover her nakedness. Now will I uncover her shame in the sight of her lovers, and no one will save her from my hand . . . I will desolate her vines and fig-trees, of which she said, They are my wages which my lovers paid me (Hosea 2:4–14).

This is a manifest forerunner of the imagery of our prophecy. Israel is an unfaithful wife; having received bounty from her God, she attributed it to others, on whom she spent it (this motif derives ultimately from the story of the Golden Calf, made out of the gold objects God disposed the Egyptians to give the departing Israelites; cf. also Deut 32:15). God will punish her by stripping her and exposing her naked to her lovers. There is no time perspective in Hosea (how Ezekiel expanded the simile "as on the day of your birth"!), no political "harlotry," and no maniacal perversity and insatiability.

Jeremiah took up the image. In 2:20–25 he brands Israel's illicit cults as harlotry and pursuit of "strangers" (see our vs. 32). But it is in ch. 3 that he speaks in terms familiar from Ezekiel:

> You have fornicated with many "friends." Look around at the hills and see, where have you not been laid? You waited on the roads for them . . . and polluted the land with your fornication and your evil . . . You have the forehead of a harlot; you refuse to be ashamed . . . She fornicated

> with wood and stone . . . Know your iniquity, for you have rebelled against YHWH your God, and scattered your favors [lit. ways] among strangers under every green tree (3:1–13).

Promiscuity in many places (the shrines to foreign gods), brazen shamelessness, wood and stone, scattering of favors upon strangers—these features in Jeremiah's figure bring her to within a step of Ezekiel's wanton.

The extension of the figure to alliances with foreign nations came to Ezekiel by the same route. Other prophets denounced reliance on foreign powers as an insult to God (Isa 7–8 [Assyria]; 30–31 [Egypt]), but it was Hosea who, after railing at Israel for "straying" from God after Egypt and Assyria ("like a silly dove"; 7:11–13), brands its pursuit of alliances as "offers of love" (8:9). Just over a century later, Jeremiah foretold Judah's disappointment by Egypt as it had been earlier disappointed by Assyria "for YHWH has spurned those you trust" (Jer 2:36f.); then, following Hosea, he calls Judah's allies her "lovers" (22:20, 22 [*ro'ayik* "companions" as in Prov 29:3]; 30:14; cf. Lam 1:19). Ezekiel not only adopted this imagery from his predecessors, but spelled out the "sexual attractiveness" of the lovers in characteristic vividness (vs. 26; cf. 23:6ff.). By seeking its security in alliances with earthly powers, Israel has broken faith with YHWH, "fornicating" with the gentiles (cf. the nonfigurative language of 29:16).

By extending the metaphor in time, Ezekiel provided the adulterous wife of Hosea and Jeremiah with a biography. The impulse to do so came from theodicy. The imminent destruction of the "last remnant of Israel" was a catastrophe that demanded a correspondingly enormous sin to justify it. The doom prophets of the age supplied it by summoning up the accumulated sin of Israel's entire history: Jerusalem and Judah would be eradicated "because they have done what is evil in my sight and have been vexing me from the day that their fathers came out of Egypt to this day" (II Kings 21:15—a comment on Manasseh's reign). During Jehoiakim's reign Jeremiah denounced the people for having "gone backward, not forward, from the day your fathers left the land of Egypt until today" (7:24f.). In Ezek 20:8ff. and 23:3, 19, our prophet carries back Israel's rebellion against YHWH to its Egyptian sojourn. Here he follows a different tack; by starting from the very origins of the people (Hos 2:5 may have suggested this) the effect of the denunciation is heightened.

The infant castaway foundling, known from life and story, serves to represent the weakness verging on death of Israel's natural state at its beginnings (cf. the opening line of the farmer's liturgy, "My father was a fugitive Aramean," Deut 26:5). Her desperate plight throws into relief God's gratuitous kindness. His finding her in the "field" resembles the depiction in the poem of Deut 32:10 in which God finds Israel "in the wilderness, in the empty, howling desert," and the purport is the same: to start the account of God's relation to his people with a situation best designed to enhance his beneficence toward them and illustrate his providential and tender care of them (S. R. Driver, *Deuteronomy,* ICC, p. 356) —the blacker to paint their subsequent apostasy. (R. Bach [*Theologische Literaturzeitung,* 1953, p. 687] sought in Hos 9:10; 10:11; Deut 32:10 and in our passage an aberrant tradition of Israel's foundation, which portrayed the desert age as a time of harmony between God and Israel, and knew nothing of the patriarchal or Sinai tradition; but this makes too much of a poetic picture, drawn for the sake of antithesis, and is justly criticized by W. Rudolph, *Hosea,* KAT, p. 185, fn. 5.) The prophet ignores the traditional ancestors of Israel, the patriarchs, precisely because they gave honor and encouragement to the people (cf. the post-fall reliance on Abraham's covenant in 33:23ff.); he chooses instead the pagan antecedents of Jerusalem, thus providing a motive for the cruel abandonment of the infant (necessary to highlight God's kindness) and a hereditary ground for her future dissolute conduct.

Moderns have regarded the story of the exposure, preservation, and eventual marriage to royalty of the foundling as too detailed and too remote from Jerusalem's history to have been a creation of the prophet.

> The detailed story of the exposure of the girl and her growth amidst the plants of the field [?] defies interpretation in connection with the destiny of Jerusalem. Here one can palpably feel how Ezekiel has adopted material derived from elsewhere. There existed a story about a girl exposed in the wilderness right after her birth; uncared for, she was given over to die. While she weltered in the blood that still covered her from birth, a man came by who granted her life. Ezekiel says in his adaptation that it was YHWH; but since the man granted life to the girl by his word, it must originally have been a magician. The girl grew up, thanks to the magic word, and became a robust maiden; but no clothes covered her. Again blood appeared on her—the first blood of her puberty. Someone else came by again, according to Ezekiel it was YHWH again; but the sequel in which the girl is elevated to royalty indicates that the story meant the man to be a king. But if the two passersby were really from the first identical—and that is not self-evident—we must suppose a magician-king, who now beholds in all her glory the product of his lifegiving word—perhaps to his own surprise. He falls in love with the girl, covers her with his own garment, and takes her in marriage. He brings her home, adorns her with costly garments and sets a crown on her head. Thus the poor rejected girl becomes a queen and her beauty becomes renowned among the nations. All this is evidently fairy-tale material with strong oriental coloration. We may assume the fairy-tale nature of this narrative with complete certainty . . . (H. Gunkel, *Das Märchen in Alten Testament* [Tübingen: J. C. B. Mohr, 1917], pp. 115f.).

Comparison of the ground-scheme of exposure stories casts doubt on this assessment. The typical foundling is a *Wunderkind* destined for greatness; indeed the reason for the story is the eventual greatness of its hero (ine), which it enhances. The child's abandonment is forced on the parent(s) by shame or necessity. It grows up under foster tutelage, betraying unsuspected qualities even before its true identity is revealed (G. Binder, in *Enzyklopädie des Märchens* [Berlin: de Gruyter, 1977], s.v. "Aussetzung" [Band 1, ss. 1048–65]). Ezekiel's story, on the contrary, is designed to account for and illustrate baseness—an unexampled motive of exposure stories. The parents' abandonment of their child is wanton cruelty (inherited by the child); her remarkable qualities are not hers but reflect YHWH's glory that he has bestowed upon her. It is not she that is wonderful, but the care and gifts lavished on her by YHWH. There may be a relation between Ezekiel's story and the scheme of exposure tales, but it is one of inversion; on that supposition, the relation makes some sense. But it remains a question whether, given all the pre-existent ingredients—the metaphor of the adulterous wife, the view of the radical evil of Israel, the practice of exposure—the origin of this story is better explained by inversion of a folk-motif than by the free inspiration of the prophet.

A peculiar detail of the story inclines one to the second alternative.

The assertion that the tale is remote from Jerusalem's history loses most of its weight when it is realized that Jerusalem stands for Israel; God entered into a covenant only with the people, never with the city (vs. 8). On the contrary, it would seem that only on the basis of Israelite history can the details of God's passing by the girl twice and the untended interval between be explained. In the scheme of exposure stories, between the foundling's rescue and revelation, it lives under the care of a guardian. Here the girl grows up so untended that her body remains filthy till the time of her marriage. God's abandonment of the girl after he commanded her preservation until her nubility is an artificial adjustment of the narrative to the Exodus tradition. During the long interval of the Egyptian bondage, Israel flourished and grew, apparently forsaken by its God, until the time of redemption arrived, when it was taken by God to be his people (the child's abandonment in the "field" and its development "like the plants of the field" recall the Israelites' labor "in the field" and God's wonders worked against Egypt, "the field of Zoan" [Exod 1:14; Ps 78:43]). The further inference may be ventured that the rejection of the child by its Canaanite parents somehow refers to the forced emigration of Jacob's family into Egypt because of famine in Canaan, where they were providentially sustained (Gen 45:7; 50:20). Gunkel's puzzlement over the identity of the two passersby indicates a problem in the reconstruction of his hypothetical fairy tale that is obviated by taking the plot to reflect, roughly as is Ezekiel's habit in his historical surveys, the outlines of the traditional account of Israel's beginnings as a people.

Having proceeded this far contrary to the fairy-tale interpretation, one is tempted to match the other details in the story with items in the early historical tradition. Is the concurrence of items used in building the tabernacle and outfitting the priests with the ornaments of the woman accidental? The fantastic lengths to which one may be led in this direction—and an appreciation of the motive of Gunkel's approach if not of its results—emerge from a glance at T to vss. 3–14:

> [3] Your sojourning and birthplace was of the land of the Canaanite; there I revealed myself to your father Abraham [in the covenant made] between the pieces [Gen 15] and informed him that you would go down to Egypt, with an upraised arm I would redeem you, and through the merit of your fathers I would expel the Amorites before you and destroy the Hittites. [4] Moreover when your fathers went down to Egypt, sojourners in a land not theirs, enslaved and afflicted, the congregation of Israel was like an infant abandoned in the field, whose navel-cord was not cut [. . .] [5] Pharaoh's eye did not pity you to do even one kindness to you, to give you rest from your slavery, to have mercy on you; but he issued against you a decree of annihilation, to throw your males into the river, to make you perish, at the time you were in Egypt. [6] And the memory of the covenant of your fathers came before me, and I revealed myself in order to redeem you, for I saw that you were afflicted in your slavery, and I said to you, Because of the blood of circumcision I will pity you, and I said to you, Because of the blood of the paschal sacrifices I will redeem you. [7] Myriads like the plants of the field I made you, and you grew numerous and powerful, and became generations and tribes; and because of the righteous deeds of your fathers, the time for redeeming your congregation arrived, for you were enslaved and afflicted. [8] Then I revealed myself to Moses in the bush, for I saw that the time for redeeming you had arrived, and I sheltered you with my word and I removed your sins, and I swore by my word to redeem you as I swore to your fathers, said the Lord God, that you might become a people serving me. [9] And I redeemed you from the slavery of Egypt and removed harsh tyranny from you, and led you to freedom. [10] And I clothed you in embroidered garments of your enemies' valuables, and I put gorgeous shoes on your feet, and consecrated some of you as priests to serve me in turbans of linen, [and] the high priest in many-colored clothes. [11] And I adorned you with the ornament of the words of the Torah written on two tables of stone and given by Moses, and consecrated you with the holiness of my great name. [12] I placed my ark of the covenant among you, with my cloud of glory shading you, and an angel commissioned by me leading you at your head. [13] And I set my tabernacle in your midst, adorned with gold and silver and curtains of linen and many-colored and embroidered stuff, and I fed you manna as good as fine flour and honey and oil; so you grew very very rich and powerful, and you prospered and ruled every kingdom.

The wicked sisters, the theme of B, reappear (i.e., two of them do) in ch. 23; they occur first in Jer 3:6ff., a passage dated to Josiah's reign. Jeremiah extends the Hoseanic figure of the faithless wife (used in the immediately preceding vss. 1–5) to Israel and Judah, representing the related kingdoms as sisters.

> You saw, did you not, what that apostate Israel did—how she went up onto every high hill and under every leafy tree, and fornicated there . . .

> And that faithless one, her sister Judah, saw this. She saw [reading *wtr'*] that it was precisely because Israel . . . had committed adultery that I turned her out and gave her a bill of divorce. Nevertheless her faithless sister Judah was not afraid, but went herself and fornicated too . . . Apostate Israel has shown herself more in the right than faithless Judah (Jer 3:6–11).

In Ezekiel's adaptation, the sisters represent cities (determined perhaps by his focus on Jerusalem), but their portrayal in our oracle differs markedly from that of ch. 23—yet in each showing features derived directly from Jeremiah. Thus, in ch. 23, only two sisters figure, as in Jeremiah, and they have a history of infidelity that goes back to the sojourn in Egypt (unlike our passage, but cf. 20:7–8). In our passage, there are three sisters—Sodom is added—and while all have "spurned their husbands" none is explicitly YHWH's spouse; this point is muffled in order to accommodate Sodom, which was never "married" to YHWH (whose sin is accordingly not infidelity). Over against this major difference from Jeremiah and Ezek 23, the central point of our passage—namely, Jerusalem's "justification" of her sisters by her wickedness—is an almost literal adoption of a motif in Jeremiah elaborated here but ignored in ch. 23. Indeed it was only to heighten the disparaging comparison of Jerusalem that Sodom was adopted as a sister and given precedence over Samaria in the argument. We conclude that our passage and ch. 23 are independent adaptations of Jeremiah's theme, each selecting different aspects for elaboration. We shall soon see why the "justification" motif was chosen here.

The covenant theme of the coda (C) is ambiguous and liable to be confused with other eschatological covenants mentioned later in the book. The covenant enforced by curse sanctions (vs. 59) imposed obligations on Israel which she violated. The "covenant of your youth" (vs. 60) to be remembered by YHWH is his unilateral pledge made to Israel (in Egypt, according to 20:5, but incorporating promises made to the patriarchs; see comment). YHWH averts that despite Israel's violation of its obligation, he will be mindful of his and will (re)establish *whqmwty* (it as) an eternal covenant with Israel in the future.

Now in 34:25, Ezekiel mentions a new future "covenant of peace" which God will make (*krt*) with Israel; when this is iterated in 37:26 it is further qualified as an eternal covenant. Critics have noted that elsewhere in Ezekiel *krt* alone is employed for making a covenant (17:13); combining this with the preceding data, they have concluded that Ezekiel's concept of the eschatological covenant between YHWH and Israel regarded it as a new beginning, not a continuation of the old covenant, and that his term for making it was *krt,* not *hqym.* It follows that our passage is not from Ezekiel. The supposed discord vanishes however, when the covenant of 34:25 is correctly understood not as the grand bond between God and people, but as a specific assurance of everlasting physical security in the land. In future, the contingent blessing of Lev 26:6 that obedience would be rewarded by God's "granting peace in the land, and you shall lie down untroubled by anyone; I will rid the land of vicious beasts and no sword shall pass through your land"—that blessing would be realized forever: "I will make with them a covenant of peace, and I will rid the land of vicious beasts, so that they can dwell secure [even] in the wilderness, and sleep [even] in forests" (Ezek 34:25). That is indeed a new covenant, never before made (*krt*); its subsequent qualification as eternal, if not a borrowing from our passage, is no more significant than the identical qualification of several such specific covenants in the priestly writings: the sabbath (Exod 31:16); the priestly emoluments (Num 18:19); the hereditary privilege of a priestly family (Num 25:13). It does not signify that the "covenant of peace" is the great link between God and Israel thus repeating in different terms the purport of 16:60, 62. Rather, our passage will, with 20:37, be the only reference to the great eschatological covenant using the term *b^e^rit* (the other references use the double adoption/marriage formula, 11:20; 14:11 [see Structure and Themes], etc.). The use of *hqym* (vs. 60), taken with the explicit reference to the ancient covenant, suggests that—whether or not it is conceived as a continuation of it—the eschatological covenant will reaffirm the ancient one. Nothing in this passage indicates a hand other than Ezekiel's.

Critics generally regard B and C as subsequent accretions to the core prophecy in A. The setting of A is clearly pre-fall; the punishment of the city is still to come (= ch. 23). In B, however, the punishment has occurred; the three sisters are compared as being on an equal footing of political dissolution remediable only by a future act of God. Since the implied setting is post-fall, critics suppose that to be the time of composition as well. In C, the mere restoration of Jerusalem predicted in B is superseded by its hegemony over its sisters; this, critics argue, is an even later addition, comparable to the latest prophecies of consolation (e.g., 37:24ff.).

Rhetorical and psychological considerations are advanced in support of the accretional view of the chapter. Would a single creative moment contain so extreme a shift in mood from the furious denunciation of A to the serene and sublime reconciliation of C? Furthermore, would not the consolatory aspects of B and C defeat the purpose of the arraignment? From the doom-prophet's viewpoint, the unregenerate audience does not deserve to be comforted; comfort pertains to a brokenhearted, despairing post-fall audience. The analogous sequence of ruthless threats of doom and assurance of God's reconciliation with contrite survivors in Deut 28–30 and (even more closely related to Ezekiel) in Lev 26 is not an effective check to this reasoning, which simply nullifies this counterevidence by subjecting it to the same disintegrating analysis (e.g., O. Eissfeldt, *The Old Testament: An Introduction* [New York and Evanston: Harper & Row, 1965], pp. 237f., on Lev 26:40–45; G. von Rad, *Deuteronomy*, OTL, p. 183, on Deut 30). That prophetic (and Torah) covenant theology could not regard the destruction of Israel as YHWH's final word; or that the reversal in mood reflected a catharsis induced by giving voice and vent to rage, allowing the underlying permanent bond of YHWH with Israel to reassert itself; that accordingly there may be a parallel here to the familiar prayer phenomenon of the metamorphosis of anguished lament into serene confidence (F. Heiler, *Prayer,* trans. and ed. by S. McComb and J. E. Parks [London, New York, Toronto: Oxford University Press, 1932], pp. 260ff.)—these possibilities await exploration as alternatives to the literary-historical explanation of the sequence of thoughts in our chapter and analogues.

We need not await a decision in this matter in order to appreciate, finally, the unifying function of two alternating themes that converge climactically in the coda: original or secondary, the sense of a single grand movement from start to finish of this long oracle owes much to its permeation by these two themes.

From the latter phases of the oracle it emerges that the terrible arraignment of the wanton aims beyond her sentencing to her reformation; she must come to realize her guilt. "In every criminal trial, the primary object is to elicit a confession of guilt from the culprit. Confession is the best guarantee that the sentence fits the offender, and that the court has not committed a miscarriage of justice" (H. J. Boecker, *Redeformen des Rechtslebens im Alten Testament* [Neukirchen-Vluyn: Neukirchener Verlag, 1964], p. 111). To that end, two faculties this wanton abnormally lacks must be generated in her: memory and shame. By following the themes of *zākar* "remember" and *bwš/klm* "shame" we may trace the wanton's progress.

Israel's duty always to remember YHWH's redemptive and sustaining deeds (particularly in her prosperity) as the chief motive of obedience to his commandments is a Deuteronomic commonplace (5:15; 8:2–18; 11:15; 16:12; 24:18, 22; 32:5). The priestly writings, on the other hand, extol YHWH's remembrance of his covenant as a feature of his trustworthiness (Gen 9:15f.; Exod 2:24; 6:5). Especially germane is the epilogue to the covenant curses in Lev 26:42ff. At the sight of the remnant of penitent exiles—

> Then I will remember my covenant with Jacob; I will remember also my covenant with Isaac, and also my covenant with Abraham . . . Yes even then when they are in the land of their enemies I will not spurn or reject them so as to destroy them violating my covenant with them; for I YHWH am their God. I will remember in their favor the covenant with the ancients, whom I freed from the land of Egypt in the sight of the nations to be their God, I YHWH.

Our oracle contrasts human dereliction toward this duty with divine fulfilment of it. Wanton Jerusalem did not, in her willfulness, remember her lowly beginnings and all that she owed to God (vss. 22, 43), for which she paid the ultimate penalty. But YHWH will remember the "covenant of her youth" (vs. 60) and restore the prodigal to a glory greater than her former state. The effect will be to awaken in her a memory of her former abominable behavior, and she will be ashamed.

Jeremiah preceded Ezekiel in deploring the shamelessness of the Judahites; they have "the face [lit. forehead] of a harlot; they will not feel disgrace" (3:3; cf. 6:15; 8:12). The characteristic phrase of confession Jeremiah puts into the mouth of the contrite people is "We feel shame and disgrace" (3:25; 31:19). In the arraignment division of our oracle (A), the shamelessness of the wanton is too amply displayed to need explicit mention; the Philistines' "shame" at her conduct underscores her lack of it (vs. 27). In B, however, the wanton is repeatedly summoned to feel shame in a situation designed to elicit it even in her: she is unfavorably compared with her siblings, especially to "sister" Sodom, toward whom she had always felt superior. Sibling rivalry gives occasion for her first experience of shame—really humiliation over having made her disdained sisters look righteous by comparison with her. This prepares a faculty within her which, in her final stage of restoration, can respond to God's undeserved favor with penitential shame over all her past offenses.

This theme is related to the self-loathing predicted in 6:9; see discussion of both there. In 36:31f., shame and self-loathing are combined; thereafter only shame and disgrace occur (39:21; 43:10; 44:13). Their appearance in Jeremiah's formulas of confession accounts for their presence in Ezekiel's restoration prophecies: shame and disgrace over the past bespeak the new, impressionable, contrite heart that will animate the future Israel.

With the awakening of wanton Jerusalem's memory of her wicked past and her brokenhearted shame over it foretold in the coda, the purpose and goal of the condemnation, which at the start of the oracle the prophet was charged to proclaim, have been achieved.

XVI. The Fable of the Two Eagles (17:1–24)

17 1 The word of YHWH came to me: 2 O man! Pose a riddle and
tell a fable to the house of Israel, 3 and say to them: Thus said Lord
YHWH:

A great eagle—
great winged,
long-pinioned,
Full of feathers,
decked in embroidery—
came to Lebanon.
He took the crown of a cedar,
4 its topmost shoot he plucked;
He brought it to the land of Canaan
in a city of traders he set it.
5 He took a seed of the land
and put it in a seed-field—
A slip[a] beside abundant water,
like a willow, he set it.
6 It sprouted and became a spreading vine of lowly stature,
Its branches to be turned toward him,
its roots to be beneath him.
So it became a vine
producing rods
and growing boughs.
7 There was another great eagle,
great-winged and many-feathered,
And see! This vine
twined[b] its roots about him,
And grew its branches toward him
to be watered, from the bed where it was planted.

[a] Not in G S.
[b] Some oriental mss. have Q: *knfh*.

8 In a good field,
by abundant waters
it was planted,
To produce branches,
and to bear fruit,
to become a majestic vine.
9 Say: Thus said Lord YHWH: Will it prosper?
Surely its roots he will tear out,
and cause its fruit to rot and wither—
every leaf it sprouted shall wither—
And with no great strength or large army
to hoist it from its roots.
10 Although it is planted will it prosper?
Surely but touch it
the east wind,
it will wither up,
On the bed where it sprouted it will wither.

11 The word of YHWH came to me: 12 Say now to the rebellious
house: Surely you know what these things mean! Say:

The king of Babylon came to Jerusalem, and took its king and
officers and brought them to Babylon. 13 He took one of the seed
royal and made a covenant with him, and imposed a curse-oath on
him (and he took the leading men of the land)[c] 14 to be a lowly
kingdom, not to exalt himself, to keep his covenant that it might
endure. 15 But he rebelled against him, sending his emissaries to
Egypt to obtain horses and a large army; will he prosper? Will he
escape who does these things? Will he violate a covenant and escape?

16 By my life, declares Lord YHWH! Surely in the place of the
king who crowned him, whose curse-oath he flouted and whose
covenant with him he violated—in Babylon he shall die. 17 And with
no great force or large assemblage will Pharaoh deal with him in
battle, when ramps are thrown up and a siege-wall built for cutting
down many lives. 18 He flouted the curse-oath to violate the covenant
—although he gave his hand to it yet he did all these things!—he
shall not escape!

19 Now then, thus said Lord YHWH: By my life, surely my curse-
oath that he flouted and my covenant that he violated—I will
requite it on his head! 20 I will spread my net for him and he will be
caught in my trap; I will bring him to Babylon and enter into judg-

[c] See comment.

ment with him there for the trespass he committed against me.
21 All his fugitives[d] among all his divisions will fall by the sword, and the survivors will be scattered to the winds. And you shall know that I, YHWH, have spoken it.

22 Thus said the Lord YHWH:
But I will take
of the lofty crown of a cedar [e]and put it[e];
of its topmost shoots I will pluck a tender one;
And I will plant—
on a high and towering mountain
23 in the mountainous heights of Israel I will plant it.
It will bear branches
and produce fruit
and become a noble cedar.
Every bird of every wing
shall dwell beneath it;
in the shadow of its branches they shall dwell.
24 And all the trees of the field shall know that I, YHWH,
Have lowered the high tree
have heightened the lowly tree
Have withered the green tree
and have made the withered tree bloom;
I, YHWH, have spoken and have done it.

[d] Following Q: *mbrḥyw;* versions seem to render *mbhr(y)w;* see comment.
[e–e] Not in G S.

COMMENT

17:2. "A *ḥida* [riddle] is an obscure saying from which something else is to be understood, while a *mašal* [here, fable] is a likening of one matter to another—so this *mašal,* in which the king is likened to an eagle, is at the same time a *ḥida,* since none but the discerning can understand it" (Kimḥi). The essence of the *ḥida* was opaqueness and mystification, while that of the *mašal* was illumination (W. McKane, *Proverbs,* OTL, p. 267). While the two terms appear in parallelism (Ps 49:5; 78:2; Prov 1:6) they are not interchangeable (as Judg 14:12ff. and I Kings 10:1 show); here they may point to the two levels on which the fable moves; see Structure and Themes.

3. *A great eagle.* The article of *hannešer* (as of *ha'erez* at the end of the

verse indicates "incomplete determination"; viz. "a certain eagle." It is used in parables (II Kings 14:9) and comparisons (Num 11:12); GKC § 126 q–t; Joüon § 137 m–o; König, III, § 299 h–i.

"Full of feathers" and "decked in [lit., "who has"] embroidery" suggest the golden eagle, whose neck and legs are fully feathered, and whose neck feathers (hackles) are golden and shaped like lanceheads. These characteristics exclude the griffon vulture, which resembles the eagle in build and flight characteristics and is also called *nešer*. For the symbolism of the eagle, see p. 56. To what was said there of its royal features must be added its use as a figure for divine protection on the one hand (Exod 19:4; Deut 32:11), and on the other, for a powerful, speedy, alien conqueror (Deut 28:49; Hab 1:8; Jer 4:13).

Lebanon. The Lebanon mountain range was, in ancient times, wooded with cedars, coveted and exploited equally by Egypt (e.g., *ANET*³, p. 243), Mesopotamia (e.g., *ANET*³, p. 307; Isa 37:24) and Israel (I Kings 5:28). In biblical literature, Lebanon's cedars symbolized (royal) majesty (Judg 9:15; I Kings 5:13; II Kings 14:9; Isa 10:33f.; Song of Songs 5:15). Since Jerusalem was on a mountain, and one of the royal buildings was "The house of the forest of Lebanon" (I Kings 7:2; named after the cedar used in its construction), it was possible to refer to the dynastic seat of the Davidides as "Lebanon" (Jer 22:6, 23), as is done here.

4. *shoot. yᵉniqa* lit. "suckling"—concrete, of an abstract noun pattern, as *nᵉṭiša* "tendril" (Jer 5:10); in vs. 22 the participle pattern *yoneqet* occurs, with which cf. *nobelet* "unripe cast-off fruit" (Isa 34:4). The royal scion (newly crowned) is compared to a twig growing from the main stock in Isa 11:1.

land of Canaan. Ambiguous; see comment to 16:29. Transplanted cedars were a feature of Assyrian royal gardens (Tiglath-pileser I, Luckenbill, *ARAB* § 254; Assurnasirpal, *ANET*³, p. 559a; cf. A. L. Oppenheim, "On Royal Gardens in Mesopotamia," *JNES* 24 [1965], 328–33).

5. *seed.* While it is possible to start a vine from seeds (Deut 22:9), one commonly planted (*naṭaʿ* or *šatal*) a shoot (*kanna,* Ps 80:16); hence *zeraʿ* "seed" may here refer to a seedling (Lang, *Kein Aufstand,* p. 31); cf. Isa 17:10 *zaraʿ zᵉmora* "sow[!] a shoot." The eagle took pains to locate the plant in the most promising site: a fertile ("seed-")field, abundantly watered. Although modern viticulture does not regularly employ irrigation (U. Feldman, *Ṣimḥe ha-tanak* [Tel Aviv: Dvir, 1956], p. 23), our passage, like Isa 27:3 ("I water it every moment"—of God caring for his vineyard Israel), expresses the solicitude of the vinedresser by exaggerating his attention to the water supply of the vine.

slip. qaḥ is a hapax, ignored by G S and generally thought to be an error (for some verb?). The best interpretation of the graph is through Akkadian *qū* "plant" (cf. Syriac *qwḥʾ* "stem, stalk"); in the language of the Ethiopian Falashas, a waterside plant used instead of ritual willows is called *qaha* (I. Löw, *Die Flora der Juden,* III [Wien und Leipzig: R. Löwit Verlag, 1924], p. 326).

like a willow . . . Mishnaic Hebrew *ṣpṣp(h/t)*, like Arab *ṣafṣāf,* denotes various members of the Salicaceae family—willows and poplars—whose habitat is by streams and rivers or in flood plains; for details of dialectic and geographic divergences see Löw, *Flora* III, pp. 322ff.; J. Felix, *Plant World of the Bible* [Hebrew] (Tel Aviv: Masada, 1957), pp. 113–16; S. Lieberman, *Tosefta Ki-fshutah,* part IV, Moed, pp. 858f. It may also be relevant for our comparison that the growth and maturation of seedlings of this family is very rapid (Encyclopedia Britannica, 15th ed., Macropaedia, vol. 16, s.v. "Salicales," p. 181). The expression of the comparison is through a second accusative of *śim* "which denotes the ideal or real effect that the given action works on the first accusative": viz. he set it (the shoot) so as to be effectively—in an ideal sense—a willow (in that it drank abundant water; cf. in 19:5, "she set up her cub effectively as a lion"; Zech 7:12, "set their hearts up effectively as diamond"; 12:2, "set Jerusalem up effectively as a cup of poison"; König, III, § 327 t–v).

Another interpretation of *ṣpṣph* connects it with *ṣwp* "swim, float" and takes it as a synonym of and in apposition to "abundant water," namely "irrigation ditches" (Kara, Eliezer of Beaugency, Lang).

6. *It sprouted and became.* A smoother reading is obtained by vocalizing the two verbs as jussives *wᵉyiṣmaḥ wiyhi* "that it might sprout and become"; for the construction see Lam 1:19 (*wyšybw*) and Joüon § 116 e.

spreading vine. srḥ is "sprawl" (of men, Amos 6:4), "overrun limits" (of cloth, Exod 26:12f.); in 23:15 men "flow over with respect to [*sᵉruḥe*] turbans," i.e., wear flowing (pendant) turbans. The sense here is that the vine flourished.

growing. As in 44:20 "grow (*šillaḥ*) long hair."

7. *another.* So G; MT *'ḥd* = "another" as in 19:5, or is an error for *'aḥer*.

twined. So rendered by G S; cf. Arabic *kafana* "wrap [in shrouds]"; others compare Aramaic *kfn'* "famine" and render "stretched hungrily" (BDB). The mss. variant *knph* is explained by Kimḥi through Aramaic *knp* "gather."

from the bed. Despite its being in a well-watered bed, from that bed the vine twined its roots around the other eagle. The connection of the phrase with the distant verbs "twined" and "grew" accords with Hebrew syntax, e.g., Gen 41:57 ("to Joseph" is connected with "came"); this and other examples (which must be discriminated from the mass there collected) are found in Ibn Janaḥ, *Ha-riqma,* chs. 33–34; cf. also A. Sperber, "Biblical Exegesis: Prolegomenon to a Commentary and Dictionary to the Bible," *JBL* 64 (1945), 117ff. (particularly apposite are Exod 14:30,

"Israel . . . [safe] on the seashore," and II Sam 11:2, "He being on the roof saw . . ."). *RSV* joins the phrase to the next verse, accepting Ehrlich's emendation of *šᵉtula;* see next comment. More recent renderings (*NAB,* NJPS, Lang) take *me-* comparatively: "That he might water it more than the bed where it was planted"; but the comparative usually goes with expressions (verbs or adjectives) containing or implying quality—unlike "to water it" (König, III, § 308 b; in c some exceptions are listed, to which our passage might be added if there were no alternative—but there is!).

8. "The vine really made a very big mistake, for when it was beneath the first great eagle 'it was planted in a good field . . . to become a majestic vine'" (Abarbanel and medieval commentators). By this interpretation, all of vs. 8 expostulates against the vine's folly and ingratitude in the face of the optimal prospects offered it by the first eagle. Others, however, take the infinitive series in vs. 8b to express the purpose of the vine's change of allegiance, with vs. 8a parenthetic; so NJPS: [7]". . . and this vine now bent its roots in his direction . . . that he might water it more than the bed where it was planted—[8] though it was planted in rich soil beside abundant water—so that it might grow branches . . . and be a noble vine." (Herrmann makes vs. 8a a gloss.)

Another issue is the meaning of *šᵉtula* in vss. 8a and 10. A supposed distinction between *naṭa'* "plant" and *šatal* "transplant" (BDB) underlies the modern notion that the second eagle transplanted the vine (Ehrlich emends in vs. 8 to *wᵉhu šᵉtalah* "he transplanted it," followed by *RSV;* NJPS renders "transplanted" in vs. 10 only). But aside from the (artificial?) distinction of the midrash on Ps 1:3 cited by Ehrlich from BT *Abodah Zarah* 19a, no biblical data can be adduced for this distinction; just as *naṭa'* serves in Ps 107:37 for planting a vineyard, so in Ps 80:9 it serves for transplanting a vine, while *šatal* serves in Ezek 19:10 and 13 indifferently for the first and second planting of a vine. None of the biblical uses of *šatal* require "transplant" (except, perhaps, Ezek 19:13); some—Ezek 17:22 for example—require "plant"; most are best rendered simply by "plant" (GB, B-Y). As for the notion itself, neither the referent (fickle Judah) nor the figure (vine) signaled defection by change of location; they reached out from where they were in a new direction—an idea perfectly figured in vss. 6 and 7b.

The trend of these moderns has been to supply a motive of self-improvement to the vine's defection. But nothing in vss. 5–7 suggests that the first eagle begrudged the vine anything that would enhance its glory—as a vine. On the contrary, he took care to plant it in a fertile field and beside an abundant supply of water; his only requirement was subservience. It is going beyond the text to say that the vine was motivated by discontent at some unexpressed check on its growth. Vs. 6 ends with the new vine thriving; no motive is given for its sudden shift in allegiance in vs. 7, indicating that it was gratuitous. The rationale found by some moderns in vs. 8 confuses the issue by (at least partially) justifying the vine and retrospectively denigrating the first eagle; it also weakens the climax obtained when vs. 8b is taken as the destiny intended by the first eagle for the vine—now forfeited. The idea that the first eagle wished the vine well is supported by the parallel of God's intention regarding the cedar's twig in vs. 23, except that the eagle's plan was thwarted while God's will succeed. Accordingly, we are to understand that although at the time of its defection the vine had developed only "rods and boughs" (vs. 6c), had it remained loyal it would have attained to branches, fruit, and majesty (vs. 8b). *RSV*'s substitution of "branches" (*p'rwt*) for "fruit" (*pry*) in vs. 8b misses the climactic expression of a lost opportunity. By turning its back on its benign master and his benefits, the ungrateful vine lost forever the chance of developing the viny majesty he had intended for it.

9. Moderns supply interrogative *h-* before the verb *tṣlḥ* (as in vss. 10, 15), supposing it was haplographed (due to preceding YHWH); for the omission of interrogative *h-*, see, however, GKC § 150, esp. fn. 1).

cause . . . to rot (yᵉqoses). Mishnaic Hebrew *qasas* "turn sourish (of wine)"—e.g., *Maaser Sheni* 4.2, in parallel with fruit rotting and coins rusting; evidently this verb pertains to viticulture (Löw, *Flora* I, pp. 100f., connects it with *qśqśt* "scales" and renders our verb "make [its fruit] scaly"). The following *wybš* "and it will wither," intransitive, lends weight to G S rendering *yqwss* "will putrefy," in which case the accusative sign *'t* stands before "its fruit" under the influence of the preceding active verb *ynq*. See below at vs. 21. For intransitive *polel*, cf. *yᵉmolel wᵉyabeš* "it languishes and withers (of grass)," Ps 90:6. T, medievals and moderns take it as "cut off," related to *qss*.

every leaf. Lit. "[With respect to] all the leaves of its sprouting it [the vine] will wither"; the noun phrase is a specification (*tamyiz* in Arabic) of the verb (Joüon § 126 g). The hapax *ṭarpe* is an Aramaism (Aramaic *ṭrp'* "leaf" appears here in S T), apparently unrelated to *ṭarap* "plucked" in Gen 8:11: *'ly zyt ṭrp* "a plucked olive leaf" (most telling are T Onkelos, S translations of *ṭrp* as *tbyr* ["broken-off"] and *'ḥyd'* ["held"] respectively).

And with no great strength or large army. An insinuation of the reality into the figure; it will take no great force for the eagle to sever the vine from its roots. *lᵉmaśśot* "to hoist" is an Aramaic-like qal infinitive of *nś'*, with prefixed *m* (cf. *maśśo*, II Chron 19:7) and *-ot* ending of late Hebrew final *'* verbs (GKC § 74 h).

10. *east wind*. A new figure: though the vine is planted in a fertile and well-watered bed, the touch of the east wind will wither it. The thought resembles that of Hos 13:15: "For though he flourish among reeds (= swampland), the east wind—a wind of YHWH—shall blow up from the wilderness, and his source shall fail and his fountain dry up." Lang,

Kein Aufstand, pp. 45f., defends the originality of this new image (against, e.g., Zimmerli), comparing the "eagle-like" Pazuzu demon of Mesopotamia, which represented the baleful malaria-bearing southeast wind (*ANEP*² ※659). The biblical associations of the east wind are however not so much demonic as instrumental of YHWH's will: such is the east wind of the Exodus narratives (Exod 10:13; 14:21; cf. Ps 78:26), Jonah (4:8), and the above-mentioned Hosea passage. For the present, we note that vs. 10 describes the destruction of the vine through a more "spiritual" instrumentality than vs. 9. The infinitive absolute *yaboš* after the finite verb is rare (Gen 19:9; Josh 24:10; König, III, § 220 a).

12–15. The fable interpreted. After calling on his audience to consider the meaning of the fable (for the force of "surely you [lit. do you not] know" see Zech 4:5, 13 and Judg 15:11; Isa 40:21, 28; II Chron 32:13), and allowing an interval to do so, the prophet is to resume his speech ("Say") by explicating it. The first eagle—grander than the second—is Nebuchadnezzar, king of Babylon; Lebanon is Jerusalem; the crown of the cedar and its topmost shoot are the royal court and the king (Jehoiachin), who were exiled and held captive in Babylon (land of merchants, city of traders). All this is summarized in the laconic account of II Kings 24:11–15. The eagle's favors toward the native seedling elaborate the annalist's bare, but significant datum, that following Jehoiachin's voluntary surrender, Nebuchadnezzar allowed the Judahite monarchy to continue reigning, appointing the Davidide Zedekiah (Jehoiachin's uncle) to the throne (24:17). From this prophecy only we learn that the vassaldom of Zedekiah was defined by a sworn treaty, enforced by curse-sanctions (Akkadian *adê u māmīt; CAD* s.v. *"adû"*; see, also, Structure and Themes). The last clause of vs. 13, "and he took the leading men of the land," seems to belong before the last clause of vs. 12 (cf. II Kings 24:15); placed there it would chiastically close the sentence concerning the deportation: *wyqḥ—lqḥ*). Ehrlich, following Kimḥi (without citing him), keeps the clause in vs. 13 by interpreting it as the seizure of hostages of the noble Judahite families to guarantee the vassal oath. *'ele* "leading men" lit. "rams"; for this metaphor (also in Exod 15:15) cf. *'lm* in a third-century B.C.E. Phoenician inscription from Ma'ṣub (*KAI* ※19, l. 2) and the Ugaritic "bulls, gazelles" = nobles, in KRT iv 6–7 (J. Gibson, *Canaanite Myths and Legends* [Edinburgh: Clark, 1978], p. 92, fn. 6). The second (less splendid) eagle is the king of Egypt (Psammetichus II); roots and branches reaching toward it for water are Zedekiah's emissaries seeking Egyptian auxiliaries and cavalry.

15b–18. *Will he prosper.* This echoes vs. 9, the sequel spelling out the real meaning ("will he escape," etc.). Tearing out roots and hoisting from roots so that the vine withers refer to the transportation of Zedekiah to Babylon, where he will die (and so it was; cf. Jer 39:7; 52:11). The small force sufficient in vs. 9 to uproot the vine is skewed in vs. 17 to mean the small force to be supplied by Pharoah to oppose Nebuchadnezzar at the siege of Jerusalem (cf. Jer 37:5; *'aśa'ot-* "deal hostilely with" 7:27; 16:59; 22:14; 23:25, 29; 39:24, hence the antecedent of *'oto* "him" cannot be the expected one—Zedekiah). Smend is not troubled by the skewing, and the "(horses and) large army" of Egypt mentioned in vs. 15 have already obscured the earlier connection of this phrase with the first eagle (Babylon) in vs. 9. (To be sure, medievals [Rashi, Kara, Kimḥi] interpreted the "enigmatic" vs. 9 by the clear vs. 17: "'Not with great strength or a large army' will the *second* eagle come *to their aid* . . . to *confront those who* uproot and transport it from its roots" [Rashi, emphasis added]; thus the tension between vs. 9 and vs. 17 is obviated—but the crucial, italicized words must be supplied!) Yet the prescient anticipation of Pharaoh Hophra's futile sally casts doubts on the originality of the text of vs. 17, as the mistaken anticipation of the first eagle's easy conquest of the vine in vs. 9 tends to confirm its originality. All is resolved by regarding "Pharaoh" in vs. 17 as secondary. Originally, then, vs. 17 will have agreed with vs. 9: the Babylonian "eagle" would need no large force to deal (hostilely) with Zedekiah (the expected antecedent of *'oto*) during the siege. When events contradicted this prediction, the flexibility of the Hebrew allowed a new appreciation of the sentence as a hitherto unperceived reference to Pharaoh's vain gesture (e.g., *y'śh* = impersonal "one will deal"; *'tw* refers to Nebuchadnezzar). The clarifying gloss "Pharoah" was inserted into the interpreting vs. 17, while the enigmatic vs. 9 could be left alone. The glossator (perhaps the prophet) might have expected his readers to read back into vs. 9 his new insight into vs. 17; medieval exegesis justified this expectation (see Greenberg, *JBL* 76 [1957], 308f.).

covenant with him. The accents link "with him" to the following "in Babylon and so forth" which can only mean that Zedekiah and Nebuchadnezzar would die together (= at the same time; cf. *mut 'im* I Sam 31:5; Job 12:2)—and that is indeed how Abarbanel takes it. Since this precision seems pointless, Ehrlich's suggestion to take "with him" with what precedes has generally been adopted (cf. the idiom of Lev 26:44; Judg 2:1, etc.).

he gave his hand. A gesture of promise and compact: II Kings 10:15 (see J. Montgomery, *Kings,* ICC); Ezra 10:19; I Chron 29:24; II Chron 30:8. In Lam 5:6 the phrase may also mean this (so Hillers, *Lamentations,* AB), though it is usually understood there as a gesture of begging (so T here!).

19. *my curse-oath . . . my covenant.* When II Chron 36:13 reports that Nebuchadnezzar imposed the vassal oath on Zedekiah with invocation of YHWH, he probably is interpreting this passage, making "my curse-oath" of this verse and "his curse-oath" of vs. 16 (translated "whose oath") one and the same (G S actually have "my oath . . . my covenant" in vs. 16 as well). Medievals and moderns follow suit; but see Structure and Themes.

I will requite it (masc.). For the disaccord of the suffix with the feminine *'lh* and *bryt,* cf., e.g., Exod 11:6 ("like it"); Jer 51:46 ("after it"); facilitated here by the general reference of "it" to the offense, rather than specifically to the curse-oath or covenant.

20. An echo of 12:13, adding "his trespass . . ." by way of allusion to the oath violation (J. Milgrom, *JAOS* 96 [1976], 238). The last clause ("for the trespass . . .") is construed (without a preposition) as an accusative of specification ("of determination of the sphere," Brockelmann, *Syntax* § 102; König, III, § 328); cf. I Sam 12:7b, where *'et* appears.

21. *fugitives.* Taken so, as a hapax from *brḥ* "flee" by various later Greek versions and Syro-Hexapla; other Greek versions and S T reflect the commoner *mbḥr* "choice [troops]" (23:7; Dan 11:15). G lacks the entire phrase. J. Blau explains the unusual preposed *'et* as due to perceiving *mbrḥw,* the subject of "fall [by the sword]", as an object (*VT* 4 [1954], 9).

will be dispersed (yippareśu). An unusual verb (pi'el in Zech 2:10) evidently chosen to form an *inclusio* with *wpršty* (vs. 20) around the description of the rout.

22. *lofty crown.* The stress on height—also in the following expressions, "towering mountain," "mountain heights" (vs. 23)—forms a contrast with the lowly vine of vs. 6. The splendor of the future restored scion of David in Jerusalem is signified.

and put (*it*). The sequence of "take—put" recalls vs. 5, but "put [it]" is awkward here, is (therefore?) absent in G S, and unwantedly anticipates "and I will plant" in the sequel. Perhaps it is a variant doublet of the latter misplaced here.

23. *fruit.* This fabulous cedar, unlike present-day real ones, will bear fruit (Lang). Needless expedients have been proposed in order to avoid this marvel: e.g., change *pry* "fruit" to *p'rwt* "boughs" or interpret it as "foliage." With this future fructification of the cedar, cf. the midrashic view that at the creation even the trees presently barren bore fruit; only after Adam's sin were they cursed with fruitlessness (*Bereshit Rabba* 5.9; *Aboth deRabbi Nathan* B 42 [ed. Schechter, p. 117]). The terms used of the cedar's flourishing are those of the vine's unrealized prospect (vs. 8b).

Every bird of every wing. Taken from the Flood story (Gen 7:14), the phrase stresses the great number and variety of fowl that will shelter in the great cedar. In the fable, great birds lord it over victimized plants, here a great tree provides for myriad birds. There, branches were lowly and needy; here they are lofty and sheltering. Since birds are the accouterments of cedars ("cedars of Lebanon . . . there birds nest," Ps 104:16f.), they are meant here literally, and serve to illustrate the ampleness of the cedar. They are not a figure for the nations; those are represented by "the trees of the field" in the next verse. Likewise in 31:6, birds and beasts are real, and separate from "the nations," and in 31:13ff.

"trees of water/the field" represent the nations as distinct from birds and beasts which are real.

24. This closing verse is a greatly expanded recognition formula, framed by the parts of a modestly expanded formula: "All . . . shall know that I, YHWH, have spoken and have done it" (= have decreed that it be and have brought it about) as in 37:14. This modestly expanded formula has been split, so that "All . . . shall know that I, YHWH" precedes the recitation of his mighty deeds, while "I, YHWH, have spoken and have done it" concludes it triumphantly.

" 'Have lowered the high tree'—the nations who dominated Israel; 'have withered the green tree'—Zedekiah and his offspring; 'and have made the withered tree bloom'—Jehoiachin, who went into exile childless, will father Zerubabel in Babylon, who will eventually rule Judaea as governor" (Rashi). This typical medieval particularization goes beyond the text, which uses the reversal language of doxology celebrating God as sovereign over men's fortunes (I Sam 2:4ff.; Ps 113:7ff.; Dan 2:22). Indeed, since these reversals are here stated in terms drawn from the vine imagery of the fable, they most likely all refer to the Davidide line—lowered, it shall be raised high; withered, it shall be made to bloom again. Cf. the (evidently) identical objects of the reversing verbs of Deut 32:39 (God's self-praise).

STRUCTURE AND THEMES

The two revelation formulas of this prophecy—one at its start, before the fable (vs. 1), and one in its middle, before the interpretation (vs. 11)—underline the symmetry of fable and interpretation (A. Rivlin, *Beth Mikra* 54 [1973], 344; somewhat comparable are 12:8; 21:6); the two concluding formulas (vss. 21, 24) round off the main body—a doom prophecy, and the coda—a consolation. Divisions of the oracle are further articulated by the messenger formula (vss. 1, 19, 22) and oaths (vss. 16, 19) as will emerge in the sequel.

Duality pervades the prophecy: fable and interpretation, two eagles, two plants, two modes of punishment, two planes of agency (earthly and divine), doom and consolation. With this duality agrees the double command with which the oracle opens: "Pose a riddle and tell a fable"—an indication that more is here than meets the eye. As a whole, the bipartition of the oracle—in this case, poetic fable and prose interpretation—with an added coda evoking its beginning (poetic and in terms of the fable) is a familiar pattern (chs. 13, 16).

The detail of the structure is as follows:

A. The fable/riddle (vss. 1–10). The revelation formula is followed by a command to tell a fable, introduced by the messenger formula (vss. 1–3a).

A1. The offense. What follows is marked as poetry by its measures (changeable though they are), its parallelisms and repetitions, and its devices (chiasm, assonance; for a suggestive treatment see Rivlin's study, *Beth Mikra* 54 [1973], 342–59). A great eagle arrives at a mountain (vs. 3aβ–bα, two lines, whose stress-count is a staccato 2:2:2, 2:2:2; *gadol–gedol;* wings || pinions || feathers; first line has chiastic vowel pattern; each phrase has article); he crops a cedar-top and removes it to a merchant-city (vss. 3bβ–4b, two lines, 3:3, 3:3, parallelism, chiasm). He then plants a native seed in optimum conditions (vs. 5, two lines, 3:3, 3:2; *zera'–zara'*) intending it to be a subservient but thriving vine; and it thrives (vs. 6, three lines, 6 [1 + 5], 3:3, 2:2:2—variations of diminishing length on six stresses, ending of episode staccato as beginning, parallelism). Another, less imposing eagle appears, to which the vine, surprisingly, appeals (vs. 7, three lines, 3:3, 3:3, 3:4, but lines 2–3 are not segmented; parallelism between them; variation on terms of first eagle's tale—*rab/male; pana/kapan*), though it lacked nothing in order to prosper (vs. 8, two lines, 2:2:2, 2:2:3, staccato, climactic repetition of vss. 5, 6c with heightened variants *ṭob, šetula, peri, 'addaret* [contrast *sorahat* of vs. 6a]). We note that the first eagle alone is active, and in his tale the plants are passive or supine; the second eagle is merely there, while in his tale, it is the vine that is active—the eagle serving as a temptation the vine cannot resist.

A2. The punishment (vss. 9–10). After an introduction resembling vs. 3aα, a series of rhetorical questions (*halo* amounts to an asseveration) urges the hearers to realize the consequences of the offense. (a) The first eagle will uproot the vine so that it withers, and he will need no great force to do so (vs. 9a contains the introductory formula and the rhetorical "Will it prosper?" outside the lines of poetry; the rest of vs. 9 has two lines, 3:3:3 [each segment ending with a verb]; 3:3—*šorašeha* frames this section). (b) The east wind's touch will wither it (vs. 10, three lines, 3, 2:2:2, 3; repetition of "Will it prosper," *ybš* [cf. vs. 9b]). The poetic measure of the latter part of vss. 9–10 is hard to determine, and it is mainly through the repeated forms of *ybš* that the segments are identified.

B. The interpretation (vss. 11–21). In a new revelation, the prophet is instructed first to ask his audience to consider the meaning of the fable (vss. 11–12a), then to tell it. It unfolds on two planes.

B1. On the earthly plane (vss. 12b–18), the decipherment of the fable (vss. 12–15) shows its correspondence to the relations of the kings of Judah to the kings of Babylon and Egypt; the offense of the Judahite is exposed (vss. 12b–15a = A1), and the question put rhetorically, "Will he prosper/escape?" (vs. 15b = 9a). Thus far the plot involves human actors only (as A1 involved only eagles and plants).

The punishment that the Babylonian king will inflict on the Judahite for his treachery is then described (vss. 16–18); it goes beyond the uprooting (exile) foreshadowed in the fable, to Zedekiah's death in captivity. This is in line with the practice noted in chs. 5, 12 and 15, where the interpretation of a figure advanced beyond the scope of the figure; this need not imply accretion. Although the actors in the punishment passage are still human (Nebuchadnezzar, Zedekiah, and [later] Pharaoh), the whole is framed as an oath of God ("By my life, declares Lord YHWH"), who is therefore involved as guaranteeing the execution of punishment. The passage ends with an affirmation that the violator of the covenant shall not escape (vs. 18), answering the rhetorical questions of vs. 15b (relation to the question is indicated by the inversion of its parts).

B2. The interpretation then rises to the divine plane: God will vindicate his curse-oath and covenant (vss. 19–21). Just when the meaning of the fable seems to have been exhausted, *laken* (vs. 19) advises us that only now have we arrived at the consequential part of the oracle. A messenger formula announces the new message, which begins with a second oath by God, that he shall requite Zedekiah for violation of his (God's) curse-oath and covenant. Capture, exile and judgment in Babylonia (and here the dispersal of the Judahite army is added as well) are attributed to God. This passage appears to depict the celestial plane of the earthly events predicted in B1. As the mere agent of God, the Babylonian king has disappeared; God alone is the author of punishment, and when it occurs it will be recognized as his decree (vs. 21b). The two planes of punishment in the interpretation recall the double agency of punishment in the fable: eagle and wind (A2 [a][b]).

C. The coda: a prophecy of restoration (vss. 22–24). To the prediction of God's punishment is attached a forecast of his renovation of the kingdom of Judah, without a new revelation formula—and hence as a continuation, yet with a messenger formula—and hence as a discrete message. This passage is again poetic, with all the above-mentioned features of poetry; characteristic of the first two verses (22–23) are tristichs whose last stich is resumptive-climactic and one stress longer than the preceding—symbolic of increase. Line structure and imagery draw on the fable for precedent. The coda falls into two parts: C1. God's new planting of a cedar-shoot (vss. 22aβ–23aα, 2:3[omitting *w*ᵉ*natatti*]:4, 2:3:4, each augmenting tristich framed by *wqtlty 'ny—'qtl* emphasizing the activity of God the speaker, parallelism) and its thriving (vs. 23aβ–b, 2:2:3, 2:2:3 tristichs of a different augmenting pattern, note the frame *wšknw—tišknh*); C2. Universal recognition of God as the reverser of national fortunes (vs. 24, an expanded recognition formula is broken up to frame two sets of antitheses [lower—heighten, wither—bloom], each 3:3). Drawing its imagery from the fable and its theocentrism from the upper plane of the interpretation, the coda serves to bind together all the chief elements of the oracle.

The structure of this prophecy may be diagramed as a spiraling progress of characters and planes as follows (clockwise, starting from the fable):

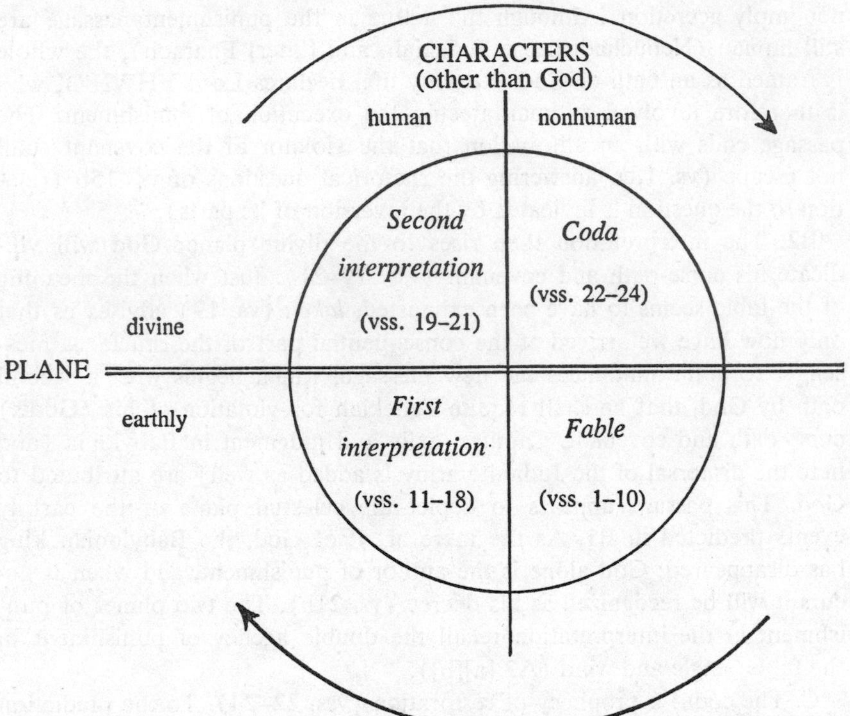

Medieval and modern exegetes regard the lesson of this oracle (minus the coda) as unitary: the fatal culpability of Zedekiah in breaking his vassal oath to Nebuchadnezzar. Assessment of the art of the fable is generally confined to the observation that it is overly tailored (not, however, because human actions and motives are ascribed to nonhumans; that is the way of fabulists): e.g., eagles are not stationary so that vines can grow under, or twine about, them. This appreciation of the oracle depends on the reflection of vs. 19 in II Chron 36:13: among Zedekiah's offenses the Chronicler counts his rebellion against Nebuchadnezzar, "who made him swear an oath by God." It is likely that the source of that allegation was this oracle since no other allusion to such an oath exists; but the Chronicler's interpretation trivializes the leap from plane to plane in vs. 19 that the unprejudiced reader senses as momentous. Worse, it impedes appreciation of the ambiguity present in the fable, which is exploited in the planar leap.

How would the first hearer of the fable, who did not know its interpretation, decode it on the basis of familiar biblical imagery? He might, of course, anticipate the correct decoding; on the other hand he might light upon alternatives which would almost yield a coherent solution. The grand eagle might be YHWH—as in the figures of Exod 19:4; Deut 32:11; the cedar—Israel (Num 24:6); Canaan—the real land so named; the planting and care of the vine—God's installation of Israel in its land (Ps 80:9–12); the lesser eagle that does not act but only tempts to infidelity—a foreign deity; the vine's appeal to it for sustenance—apostasy; the first eagle's (and the east wind's) destruction of the vine—God's punishment (Isa 5:5f.; Ps 80:13f.; Hos 13:15). Such a partial decoding—Lebanon and the double planting of the first eagle remain unaccounted for—would indeed be the one most ready to hand, considering Ezekiel's regular themes. The ambiguity of most of the terms in the fable allows such a misconstruing and justifies its being entitled a riddle as well as a fable; the prophet's challenging "Surely you know what these things mean!" points to the possibility of misunderstanding.

To one who had worked out an interpretation along these lines the true decoding (B1) would appear as an illumination and a surprise—the former because it would take account of all the terms of the fable, the latter because for once the prophet had gotten off his theocentric hobbyhorse and had dealt with human events! The effect would be to drive home a dreadful premonition: Zedekiah's defection from his Babylonian overlord must earn a terrible revenge; Nebuchadnezzar could not possibly allow such a breach of a sworn vassal-treaty to escape unpunished.

And now, just when the hearer was satisfied that he had gotten the point, *laken* puts him on notice that the chief consequence of the oracle is still to come. According to the accepted view (based on II Chron 36), the climax of the oracle consists of God's identifying the Babylonian king's treaty enforced by oath as his own. M. Tsevat (*JBL* 78 [1959], 201–4) has argued that Nebuchadnezzar made Zedekiah swear allegiance to him by YHWH when he appointed him king; that, furthermore, Ezekiel—uniquely among the prophets—regarded that extorted oath as binding. Tsevat ascribes to Ezekiel the singular doctrine that even such an oath is protected by the absolute injunction to honor one's word found in Lev 5:4 with respect to individuals. "The law . . . has its place in the life of the individual; . . . Ezekiel . . . applies it . . . in the relation between the imperialist state and its captive vassals . . . No longer do two standards prevail" (p. 204). Now, that Nebuchadnezzar (or any neo-Babylonian king) imposed on his vassals an oath of allegiance by their own gods is otherwise unknown. The neo-Assyrian evidence cited by Tsevat (added to by R. Frankena, "The Vassal Treaties of Esarhaddon and the Dating of Deuteronomy," *Oudtestamentische Studiën* 14 [1965], 131; M. Cogan, *Imperialism,* pp. 46f.) is mostly supplied by conjectural fillings-in of lacunae. There is one clear case of the Assyrian king Esarhaddon including Phoenician gods in the curses sanctioning his treaty with Baal of Tyre

(*ANET*³, p. 534); but that appears as a special concession (see Cogan). The only evidence for neo-Babylonian practice is II Chron 36—probably based on the Chronicler's understanding of our Ezekiel passage and therefore no independent witness (Mendenhall, cited by Zimmerli, bases himself on nothing else).

But even granting the possibility that Nebuchadnezzar did adjure Zedekiah by YHWH, is the natural sense of vs. 19 that YHWH solemnly makes that oath his own? We understand that the Chronicler, intent on gathering all possible support for his theodicy, should have read this meaning into our verse; we recall how in II Chron 35:22 he explained Josiah's untimely death by the invention of "an oracle of God," defended by Necho, which the Judahite king spurned. But what other compelling reason is there for turning Ezekiel into a zealous partisan of Nebuchadnezzar's interested doctrine of the validity of an extorted oath by YHWH? The natural—indeed the obvious—construction of vs. 19 is to make "my curse-oath . . . and my covenant" in YHWH's speech refer to his covenant with Israel (as in 16:59), which the king was held responsible to maintain.

Indeed, the historian of the Book of Kings holds it as established doctrine that the kings are responsible for covenant violations of their kingdoms (I Kings 12:28ff.; 14:15f.); public violations of the Torah of Moses are laid at the door of Manasseh (II Kings 21:8–11). Ezekiel so far shares this view as to blame the religious "straying" of Israel on the dereliction of its kings (34:6). As for Zedekiah, II Kings 24:18 judges him "evil in the sight of YHWH," and in Ezek 21:30 the prophet brands him a "desecrated, wicked man."

There is, then, warrant for taking vs. 19 according to its natural sense, and seeing in all of B2 a shift from earthly to divine matters. Both fable and its earthly interpretation are suddenly transposed into an allegory of the relation between God and (the king of) Judah. The earthly suzerain, Nebuchadnezzar, will not let rebellious Zedekiah get away with his treachery, how much less will the divine sovereign countenance the Judahite's breach of faith with *him*.

By this understanding of the course of the oracle, two turnabouts are assumed in the audience perception of it. What may vaguely have been thought to be an allegory of apostasy is interpreted as wholly political; but then the political transaction is used as a model from which a theological analogy is drawn. Justice is thus done (1) to the ambiguities of the fable—whose glimmerings of a divine reference are thus affirmed, and whose riddle quality is now realized; (2) to the structure of the oracle, whose consequential *laken* passage now receives its full weight; and (3) to the thought of Ezekiel, which is now freed of the idiosyncratic burden of questionable validity imposed on it by the Chronicler-Tsevat interpretation.

All parts of the prophecy are now mutually illuminated: the fable is truly a riddle (*ḥida*)—solved by identifying its human referents, all on an earthly plane. Then an allegorical cast is thrown on both by the rise to the divine plane of interpretation; that is, all the preceding political transactions are but a "likening" (*mašal*) to the relations between God and the Judahite king. (Note the correspondence between the sequence of *ḥida* and *mašal* in vs. 2 and their literary realization [suggested by Lou Levine of Toronto].)

Finer points emerge: the dual agents of punishment in the fable (eagle and wind) presage the earthly and divine planes of the real punishment of Zedekiah. Moreover, the divine oath introducing the earthly interpretation of the fable, and expressing God's guarantee that the human suzerain will vindicate his violated compact, is given a new dimension by the parallel oath introducing the divine plane of events. Events on the two planes are indeed parallel and simultaneous: for his own reasons Nebuchadnezzar will punish the Judahite rebel, but in so doing he will (all unknown to him) be executing the design of the divine architect of history upon the king responsible for violation of his covenant with Judah. This brings us to the coda.

The coda is not only the planar correspondent of the fable (poetic, and with nonhuman characters), it is the diametric divine counterpart of the earthly arrangements made by the king of Babylon (see diagram). Without the coda, God appears only in the character of destroyer, the divine correspondent to the Babylonian king in the role of outraged overlord. To the constructive arrangements of the earthling no analogue on the higher plane appears. The coda supplies that lack; not only is it a planar analogue of the fable, but it portrays God as undoing and superseding the order of the earthling, reversing its every effect. The revolutionary character of God's deeds is highlighted by the emphatic pronouns "*I* will take," "*I* will plant," and the antitheses of vs. 24.

This prophecy has thematic and verbal links with the preceding one. The theme of faithlessness to the covenant dominates both; indeed, the proximity of the expression "violate covenant and flout curse-oath" in 16:59 to our oracle provides a clue for our understanding of that expression in vs. 19. Only in these two oracles does this terminology appear. Incidental contacts, common to these two oracles alone (and suggesting they were composed at about the same time), are the terms *riqma* "embroidery" and "Canaan" for Chaldea.

If our surmise is correct concerning the secondary character of "Pharaoh" in vs. 17 and the occasion of its entrance into the text, the body of this oracle will have predated the siege of Jerusalem. The embassy to Egypt (vs. 15) belongs to the very beginning of the rebellion, during the last days of Psammetichus II (see Introduction, pp. 12–13). The prediction of the rout of Zedekiah's forces, his capture, captivity and death in Babylon echo 12:13–14 and do not necessitate a post-fall date; see the detailed discussion in the comments to those verses. That the particular horrors of Zedekiah's fate—the slaughter of his children and his blinding—are not mentioned points to a date of composition before the fall of the city.

Critics are almost unanimous in regarding the coda as a post-fall consolation, of a piece with the visions of chs. 34–48. As in the case of the coda of ch. 16, they question the suitability of a restoration oracle in a doom context. There are two issues: did Ezekiel prophesy consolations before the fall? Is this consolation pre-fall? Lang, *Kein Aufstand,* pp. 84ff., has pointed to the incidental restoration prophecies in 11:17f.; 13:9 as evidence that Ezekiel (like Jeremiah, ch. 24) anticipated a restoration well before the fall. We have argued that the restoration coda of ch. 16 is integrally related to the dooms preceding it. Here it is less obvious that the coda is necessary to the message of the body of the oracle, unless it is maintained that the rise to the divine plane of events entailed the assertion of YHWH's superiority over all earthly kings in the constructive as well as the destructive dealing with kingdoms. But before deciding that the coda is late, we must give due consideration to the fact that in post-fall restoration prophecies anxiety over the damaged reputation of YHWH appears as a motive of God's healing acts (36:20ff.; 39:25ff.); that theme is hardly present here. In language and conception the coda suits the body of the oracle, and completes it; there is no ground for doubting its Ezekielian provenience. But whether it was from the first the denouement of the doom oracle, cannot be answered decisively, though its literary fit is perfect.

XVII. Divine Justice and Repentance (18:1–31)

18 [1]The word of YHWH came to me: [2]What are you doing bandying this proverb on the soil of Israel, "Fathers eat unripe grapes and
their sons' teeth are set on edge"? [3]By my life! declares Lord YHWH,
you shall have no more occasion for bandying this proverb in Israel!
[4]See, all persons are mine; the person of the father and that of the
son are alike mine; it is the person who sins that shall die.

[5]If a man is righteous and does what is just and right— [6]he does
not eat on the mountains, or look for help to the idols of the house of
Israel; he does not defile his fellowman's wife, or approach a menstruous woman; [7]he wrongs no one; he gives back his debt-pledge; he
takes nothing by force; he offers his bread to the hungry and covers
the naked with clothes; [8]he does not lend at interest or collect with
increase; he keeps clear of injustice, and arbitrates faithfully between
men; [9]he follows my laws and observes my rulings, acting faithfully[a]
—he is a righteous man; surely he shall live, declares Lord YHWH.

[10]If he begot a violent son, a blood-shedder / who did any one
of these things / [b] [11]who did none of these things, but ate on the
mountains, and defiled his fellowman's wife, [12]wronged the poor and
needy, took things by force, did not return pledges, looked for
help to idols, committed abominations, [13]loaned at interest and
collected with increase—shall he live? He shall not; having committed
all these abominations, surely he shall [c]be put to death[c], his blood
being on him.

[14]Now, if he begot a son who saw all the sins his father committed
and, taking thought[d], did not do such things— [15]he did not eat on
the mountains, or look for help to the idols of the house of Israel;
he did not defile his fellowman's wife; [16]he wronged no one; he

[a] MT *'ᵉmet;* G "them" (as from *'otam*); cf. MT of vs. 19.
[b] So S, ignoring *'ḥ* (perhaps a scribe's false start of following *m'ḥd*); G "who commits sin."
[c–c] Some Hebrew mss., S T V "die."
[d] G "he was afraid" (as from *wyr'*).

took no pledge, and seized nothing by force; he offered his bread
to the hungry and covered the naked with clothes; 17 he [e]avoided
harming the poor[e]; he did not take interest or increase; he observed
my rulings and followed my laws—he shall not die for the iniquity
of his father; surely he shall live. 18 His father, having withheld what
was due, taken [f]his brother's goods[f] by force, and done what was
not good among his people, died for his iniquity. 19 You say, How is it
that the son did not suffer for the iniquity of his father? Why, the son
did what was just and right; he carefully observed all my laws; surely he
shall live! 20 It is the person who sins that shall die; a son shall not
suffer for the iniquity of his father, and a father shall not suffer for the
iniquity of his son. The righteousness of the righteous man shall
redound to him and the wickedness of the wicked one shall redound to
him.

21 And if the wicked man turns back from all the sins he has
committed, and observes all my laws, and does what is just and right,
surely he shall live, not die. 22 All the transgressions he committed
shall not be held against him; through his righteous acts he shall
live. 23 Do I at all desire the death of the wicked man, declares
Lord YHWH, and not rather that he turn back from his ways and
live?

24 And when the righteous man turns back from his righteousness
and does wrong, committing all the abominations that the wicked man
did, shall he live? No regard will be paid to all his righteous acts;
for the trespass he committed and the sins that he sinned—for them
he shall die. 25 You say, The way of the Lord does not conform to
rule! Listen here, house of Israel, is it my way that does not conform
to rule? Surely your ways do not conform to rule! 26 When a righteous
man turns back from his righteousness and acts unjustly and dies for
it, for his unjust acts he shall die. 27 And when a wicked man turns
back from his wicked acts and does what is right and just, he has
preserved his life; 28 he took thought and turned back from all the
transgressions he committed; surely he shall live, not die. 29 The house
of Israel say, The way of the Lord does not conform to rule; is it my
ways that do not conform to rule, O house of Israel? Surely your ways
do not conform to rule!

30 So then I shall judge you each according to his ways, O house

[e–e] G reflects *'wl* "iniquity" for MT *'ny* "poor man," hence "he keeps clear of iniquity" as in vs. 8.

[f–f] G reflects text identical with that of vs. 12, viz. *gzlwt* "things taken by force" for MT *gzl 'ḥ*.

of Israel, declares Lord YHWH. Turn back and face about from all your transgressions, and let it not be your stumbling-block of iniquity! 31 Cast off all your transgressions that you have committed, and make yourselves a new heart and a new spirit; why should you die, O house of Israel? For I do not desire the death of anyone, declares Lord YHWH, so face about and live!

COMMENT

18:2. *What are you doing bandying* (mh lkm 'tm mšlym). The construction is as in Jonah 1:6, *mk lk nrdm* "What are you doing asleep?" (Joüon § 127 a, 161 i; König, III, § 412 i)—only here the pronoun *'attem* is added to emphasize the inappropriateness of the proverb to them ("you of all people!"). G without *'tm* and S without *lkm* reflect more ordinary constructions than MT (cf., e.g., 12:22a).

on the soil of Israel. Word had reached Ezekiel of the currency of this proverb in the homeland (cf. 11:3, 15; 12:22; 33:24)—independently attested by Jer 31:28, it may have been current among the exiles too.

eat . . . are set. Imperfect verb forms, normal in maxims (e.g., Exod 23:8, "bribes blind . . . pervert . . ."). In Jer 31:28 the first verb is perfect either as denoting anteriority (the fathers, having eaten unripe grapes) or simply because the two verb forms may interchange in maxims (Job 3:17; Prov 14:1; 19:24; Driver, *Tenses,* § 35; Joüon § 112 d, 113 c). The article of *hbnym* (not in Jeremiah) denotes the possessive "their sons" (Joüon § 137 f [p. 422, I.2]), so, too, in vs. 20. The variations between the formulations here and in Jeremiah are such as are to be expected in oral transmission.

The general meaning of the proverb is given in T's paraphrase: "Fathers sin and sons are smitten"; the particular meaning depends on the sense of the rare verb *qhy* (*tqhynh*), rendered by G *egomphiasan* "ached (of teeth)" (in Jeremiah G has *hemodiasan* "be set on edge [teeth, from acid food]"), by V *obstupescunt* "became senseless, numb." Hebrew *qhy* (= Aramaic *qh'*) means "become blunt, dull" (Qoh 10:10, of an iron tool; in later Hebrew also of senses). Two citations from the Oxford English Dictionary illustrate the difficulty of defining precisely the unpleasant sensation conveyed by "on edge," which has translated *tqhynh* since Wyclif (fourteenth century) "A grene grape greueth [= grieveth] the rotes and synewes of the teeth wyth colde soo that they make the teeth an egge [= on edge]" (1398); "*Dentium stupor* [numbness], a bluntness of the teeth, when with eating of . . . sowre things they be out of edge"

(1585). Prov 10:26 compares the effect of vinegar on the teeth with that of smoke on the eyes. Tur-Sinai ingeniously explained our *qhy* as "have nothing to eat"—the proverb meaning, since the fathers ate up the unripe grapes, their children had nothing left to eat (see B-Y, pp. 5800ff., esp. the notes). But why should the maxim single out adults as blameworthy for eating unripe grapes and their children as suffering therefrom when, in fact, the custom of eating unripe grapes in Palestine-Syria is attested in early and late sources as widely popular in spite of the unpleasant effect on the teeth (*Mishnah Shebi'it* 4.8; Löw, *Flora,* I, pp. 76f.; Dalman, *AuS,* IV, p. 345; G. Crowfoot and L. Baldensperger, *From Cedar to Hyssop* [London: The Sheldon Press, 1932], pp. 10, 26; E. Grant, *The People of Palestine* [Philadelphia: J. B. Lippincott, 1921], p. 81). On the contrary, the first part of the proverb states a commonplace, innocent event, and it is only the second clause that expresses a monstrosity (sarcastic folk humor, Herrmann called it)—conveying through this thin veil resentment at a divine order (or disorder) in which the evil consequences of fathers' actions are borne by their sons. Freedman points out privately that the proverb-sayers accept the basic idea that sin deserves punishment, and that in fact it is punished. Their complaint is that the wrong people get punished; it does not matter to God who suffers so long as the balance of sin and punishment is kept.

3. *you shall have no more occasion.* ". . . because I will teach you the rule by which I judge you and you shall no longer err respecting it" (Kimḥi, Abarbanel).

4. This sentence appears to take the form of a syllogism, but the meaning of the premises and their relation to the conclusion are not perfectly clear. The argument seems to say: Since I, as the dispenser of life, own everybody; since, therefore, I have an equal stake in fathers and sons (or: therefore fathers and sons are alike to me); hence sinners appear to me not as fathers or sons but simply as sinful individuals, and as such each takes the consequences only for his own conduct. This denies that any person is morally an extension of another; God does not "get at" a sinner through his son, nor does he impose punishment on the son as a "limb" of his father. The sinner, like everybody, is a discrete moral entity in God's sight; he is not a father or a son (following Abarbanel).

shall die. On "life" and "death" in this oracle, see Structure and Themes.

5. *what is just and right.* This generality is particularized in vss. 6–8 and restated in legislative terms ("laws, rulings") in vs. 9; see Structure and Themes.

6. *eat on the mountains.* Mountains are mentioned in 6:13 (cf. 20:28; 34:6) as the site of idolatrous sacrifices from which meals were eaten; for the unity of two clauses in vs. 6a Freedman, privately, aptly compares the sequence of worship and feasting in the Golden Calf story (Exod 32:6).

Since the expression is peculiar to Ezekiel (again only in vss. 11, 15; 22:9), it has been proposed to emend it, in accord with 33:25, to the more familiar cult offense of "eating on the blood" (*hdm* for *hr*[*y*]*m*). But it is perverse to adjust a repeated, unusual, textually firm expression to a single, commonplace, and hence textually dubious one.

look for help. Lit. "lift his eyes," so in 23:27 (to Egypt), and in Ps 123:1 (to God; cf. 121:1); cf. Lev 19:4, "Do not look [*tpnw* lit. face] to the idols [*'lylm*]." Is the proximity of "mountains" and "lifting one's eyes" in this verse a deliberate evocation of the pious gesture of Ps 121:1, here put into a context of apostasy?

defile. ṭm' is used for violation of chastity in 22:11; 23:13, 17; 33:26; so, too, in Gen 34:5 and in the ordeal of the suspected adulteress in Num 5:14, 27ff.

menstruous woman. The abstract *nidda* "(menstrual) impurity" serves here as concrete substantive, in apposition to *'šh* (cf. *'šh zwnh* "a harlot woman," 16:30), as regularly in Mishnaic Hebrew (*Mishnah Niddah* 4.1, in plural!). "Approach" is a euphemism for sexual intercourse (Deut 22:14; Isa 8:3; cf. Lev 18:14); the full expression is in Lev 18:19: "Do not approach a woman in her menstrual impurity so as to 'uncover her nakedness' (= cohabit with her)."

7. *wrongs.* Again in 45:8; 46:18, *hona* denotes specifically doing a (usually helpless) person out of his property (Jer 22:3), e.g., by overreaching (Lev 25:14, 17).

his debt-pledge (ḥᵃbolato ḥob). Construing the unique phrase as *ḥᵃbolat ḥobo;* see comment on *drkk zmh,* 16:27. *ḥblh* is a feminine of *ḥᵃbol,* vss. 12, 16 (cf. the alternates *gzlh/gzl,* vss. 7, 18); *ḥob* is Aramaic and Mishnaic Hebrew "debt" (in earlier Hebrew *nšy,* II Kings 4:7); both are hapaxes. Since the verb *ḥbl* occurs in the admonition of Exod 22:25 to restore at nightfall a garment taken in pledge, many understand "give back" here in that sense. But the connection with the next clause suggests that dutiful restoration of the pledge after repayment of the debt is meant (Ibn Caspi). Milgrom, *Cult and Conscience,* pp. 95ff., argues for the talmudic view that *ḥbl* refers to distraining property of a defaulting debtor to ensure his repayment (see Rashi at Exod 22:25; Milgrom's treatment of our passage on pp. 90f. could be clearer; see also I. L. Seeligmann, "Lending, Pledge, and Interest in Biblical Law and Biblical Thought," *SBANE,* Hebrew part, pp. 183–205, esp. pp. 191–95).

takes . . . by force. Lev 5:21, 23; 19:13; Isa 3:14; for the meaning of this expression, often rendered "rob," see Milgrom, *Cult and Conscience,* pp. 89–94.

bread . . . clothes. These positive actions, having no specific legal background, pertain to brotherly solidarity with the unfortunate; see Isa 58:7 and Job 22:7; 24:10; 31:16–22 (in the first two Job passages reference is also made to the poor man's pledge). As common human virtues they were recognized outside Israel as well; in his autobiography the Egyptian official Harkhuf (end of third millennium B.C.E.) boasts: "I gave bread to the hungry, clothing to the naked" (M. Lichtheim, *Ancient Egyptian Literature,* I [Berkeley: University of California Press, 1973], p. 24).

8. *interest* (nšk) . . . *increase* (trbyt). Manifestly related to Lev 25:36f., where alone *lqḥ, ntn* plus both terms appear (cf. Prov 28:8). The distinction between *nšk* and *trbyt* (*mrbyt, rbyt*) is not clear. According to Tur-Sinai (B-Y, s.v. *"rbyt,"* note), "the two terms refer to the two aspects of usury—it bites (*nošek*) out of the property of one party and increases (*marbe*) that of the other"; he cites D. H. Müller's complementary view that at bottom these constitute a fixed pair denoting a unitary concept, like later Hebrew *maśśa umattan* "carrying and delivery," *miqqaḥ umimkar* "buying and selling," both of which mean "commerce, business." Eliezer of Beaugency comments here: "Since throughout this passage *nšk* is associated with the act of lending while *trbyt* is connected with the act of collecting, it is to be inferred that the first is a reduced weight, sum of money, or measure; i.e., the lender takes a bite (*nšk*) out of the amount stipulated when he makes the loan, whereas he demands the full measure or weight in repayment." This underlies NJPS, "advance and accrued interest," but S. Loewenstamm argues that *nšk* is interest on a loan of money, while *trbyt* attaches to a loan of victuals (*"nšk* and *m/trbyt," JBL* 88 [1969], 78–80); note also that Lev 25:36f. fails to distinguish the verbs as here.

keeps clear of. Lit. "keeps back his hand from" (20:22; Lam 2:8; Ps 74:11). For the association of *'wl, 'śh* and *mšpṭ* in the two parts of this verse Kimḥi rightly cites Lev 19:35, "Commit no injustice in judgment" (*l' t'św 'wl bmšpt*). The terms have been recombined here and, in the context of a layman's everyday affairs, *mšpṭ* bears the different sense of "arbitration, decision, settlement." Ezekiel's unusual *mšpṭ 'mt* "faithful (honest?) arbitration" was taken up in Zech 7:9 (8:16).

9. *follows* (yᵉhallek). Here pi'el (Ps 142:4), more poetic than vs. 17's qal (*halak*); for the interchange cf. Ps 81:13–14. Such formal variations mitigate the repetitiousness of this oracle (*ḥblh/ḥbl*, tense changes, etc.). The formulaic expression of obedience (cf. 5:6; 11:20; Lev 26:3) sums up the preceding actions in terms of a canon of divine laws that enjoin them.

acting faithfully. *'śh 'mt* is a rare, late usage (Neh 9:33 [of God]; II Chron 31:20); in the light of vs. 19b, G "to do them" (*'otam*) appears preferable, MT having arisen therefrom under the influence of *'mt* in the preceding verse.

10. *If he begot.* A hypothetical sentence with perfect form of the verb in the protasis (so, too, in most of the sequel down to vs. 17); see note to 3:18 and contrast the treatment by Driver, *Tenses,* § 149 (the analogy

with vs. 14 indicates that, contrary to his view, our *w^eholid* is not perfect consecutive but ordinary perfect).

a violent son, a blood-shedder. These extreme antonyms of *ṣaddiq* replace the usual *raša'*—employed in vss. 20ff.—and signal a polarizing trend throughout this passage. For *pariṣ,* see 7:22; Jer 7:11 ("a den of robbers"); "shedder of blood" is a favored phrase of Ezekiel: 16:38; 22:3, 27; 23:45; 33:25.

/who did . . . things/. *'ḥ* is awkward; S ignores it, while T's "to his brother" would have been expressed by *l'ḥyw*. The graph seems to be a mistaken start of *m'ḥd* and must be disregarded; the rest of the clause is patterned after Lev 4:2; 5:13 and appears to be a(n inferior) variant of the next clause. These variants arose as alternative solutions to the puzzle of how to negate a list containing both positive and negative statements. Ibn Caspi attempts to keep them both: the wicked son "did any one" of the offenses avoided by the righteous one, and "did none" of his virtuous acts. The sequel *ki gam* "but also" attaches to the second alternative and makes the wicked son a polar opposite of his father.

12. *the poor and needy*. Chiefly a Psalms idiom (Ps 12:6; 35:10; 37:14, etc.; also Deut 24:14; Jer 22:16; and Ezek 16:49); not previously used in vs. 7, its use here underlines the malevolence of the man, who picks on unfortunates to persecute.

13. *his blood being on him*. That is, he has only himself to blame, since he chose to do evil (cf. 33:4f.). The original force of this expression, found in such sentences of judicial execution as Lev 20:9–27, was to exculpate legal executioners from bloodguilt (see K. Koch, "Der Spruch 'Sein Blut bleibe auf seinem Haupt' . . . ," *VT* 12 [1962], 413); and although no human executioner appears in our passage, the verb *yumat* "he shall be put to death" associated with this phrase in its primary context is retained. We expect the non-agential *yamut* "he shall die" (as in vss. 21, 24, 27), used normally for divine as well as for royal dooms (I Sam 14:39, 44; 22:16)—even when the latter are accompanied by the exculpatory formula (I Kings 2:37); there is mss. and versional evidence of *yamut* here.

14. *taking thought*. As in Qoh 7:14; so again in vs. 28. *wyr'h* is distinguished in form and meaning from the verse-initial *wyr'* "he saw"; this artifice is absent in G, whose rendering "and was afraid" (as though from *wy[y]r'*) yields a commonplace sequence "see—be afraid" (e.g., Isa 41:5; Zech 9:5) which gets the critics' votes. MT implies a higher motive —reflection—for the son's choice of a righteous course and the repentance of the wicked man in vs. 28.

16. *he took no pledge*. Such scrupulousness, going beyond the standard of vs. 7, is the polar counterpart of the special malevolence exhibited by the father in vs. 12a (see comment).

17. *avoided harming the poor*. Lit. "from the poor [*m'ny*] he turned

back his hand" (= desisted [from harming; cf. 20:22]—so medievals); MT's left-handed praise was improved on in S T by supplying a negative: "he did *not* withhold his hand [from helping]." Eliezer of Beaugency simply glossed *m'ny* "from injustice," in accord with vs. 8, and thus arrived at the text reflected in G's rendering. MT's error (for so it is) seems to have arisen from the attraction of "poor" to the preceding "hungry" and "naked"; the three are combined in the strikingly similar Isa 58:7.

18. *withheld what was due. 'šq* differs from *gzl* (Lev 19:13; Micah 2:2; Jer 21:12; 22:3) in that the illegally held property came into (or was initially in) the culprit's possession legally (e.g., wages due a laborer); see Milgrom, *Cult and Conscience,* pp. 98f.

his brother's. gezel 'aḥ is a unique expression, embodying the idea that "all Israel are brothers, as it is said, 'till your brother comes seeking it'" (Deut 22:2, where "your brother" is an Israelite "whom you do not know"; so Kimḥi). G does not represent *'ḥ;* S T do.

what was not good. A litotes for "evil" characteristic of sapiential idiom (Prov 16:29; 17:26; 18:5; 19:2, etc.).

his people. 'amaw is an early term fixed in formulas (*n'sp 'l*—"gathered [in death] to—"; *nkrt m[qrb]*—"excised [for sin] from [the midst of]—") with the meaning "his kinsfolk"; otherwise it is rare and not distinct from *'ammo* "his people" (A. R. Hulst, *THAT* II, pp. 297ff.).

19. *You say.* Since "you" are those who bandy the proverb, and hence resent the attribution of guilt, it is hard to imagine them raising such an objection. (*naśa b-* does not have its usual meaning "share in, alleviate the burden of" [Num 11:17; Job 7:13], since that is not at issue; *b-* replaces the normal *'t* [see Num 14:33f.] under the influence of the adjacent *b'wn* in vss. 17f.) The question seems rather a provocative one: how is it that your model does not conform with the reality that innocent children do bear their parents' punishment, as we attest from our own experience! "[Ezekiel] does not mean that they contended about the right, but about the fact" (Calvin). The answer is: the son in the model—unlike you—was really innocent! This colloquy may not reflect any actual reaction to the speech of the prophet but a rhetorical device for stressing the gap between the people's notion of God's conduct (he punishes the innocent, as the proverb says) and the revealed divine rule of retribution, which is repeated in the following verse.

20. *a father . . . not . . . for . . . his son.* This supererogatory balancing clause, which goes beyond the issue raised here (nor is reverse attribution of guilt ever an issue in Scripture), recalls the structure of the legal rule in Deut 24:16, "Fathers shall not be put to death on account of sons, nor sons be put to death on account of fathers; each shall be put to death for his own offense." The initial Deuteronomic clause also seems to go beyond the actual obnoxious practice; cf. II Kings 9:26 and 14:6, where it is only a question of the sons of criminals (and so, too, the Hit-

tite practice; *ANET*³, pp. 207f.). We understand the balancing clauses to be a rhetorical device for emphasizing the dissociation of generations from each other's guilt. Ibn Caspi offers another interpretation of the inclusion of the "irrelevant" clause in Ezekiel (which applies to Deuteronomy as well): "Just as it is agreed and taken for granted that fathers do not suffer for their sons' offenses, so it is that God does not punish sons for their fathers'.

The literary connection of Ezekiel's theological principle to Deuteronomy's legal one is suggested by the strict inversion of parts:

Deut 24:16		Ezek 18:20	
not fathers for sons	1	who sins dies	3
not sons for fathers	2	not son for father	2
each dies for his own sin	3	not father for son	1

—a parade example of Seidel's rule that literary reference is indicated by inversion. The "normal" sequence "fathers—sons" appears in initial position in Deuteronomy; this suggests that Ezekiel was the borrower (cf. Ezek 5:10, a different adaptation of Deuteronomy's balanced clauses, without inversion).

shall redound to. Lit. "shall be upon."

21. The relation of the new stage of the argument to the preceding is stated thus by Eliezer of Beaugency: Even if one is wicked, should he reform himself he will not suffer for his former iniquity; how much less, then, shall a son, who is a separate person from his father, and who never sinned, suffer on account of an evil father!

24. *shall he live?* "He shall not! How much less, then, shall the righteousness of the father of a wicked son—a son who from his beginnings was wicked—be counted in favor of that son"; thus again does Eliezer attempt to relate the new argument to the old. Relative to the desire of God that the wicked repent and live, this argument is supererogatory and must be understood as serving rhetorically to underscore the cancellation of one's past record by a reversal in conduct; it is analogous, then, to "a father shall not suffer for the iniquity of his son" in vs. 20.

25. *does not conform to rule* (lo yittaken). *tkn* in qal (Prov 16:2) and pi'el (Isa 40:13) means "determine" the measure, content, or character of something. Ezekiel cites this expression (again in vs. 29; 33:17) always as a popular protest following his explication of the rule that God judges solely according to one's present state. The phrase is usually interpreted "not right, fair," i.e., adjusted to standard (among the versions—G T S; also BDB, NJPS), and so a nonfigurative equivalent to the proverb —a protest against the unfair transfer of punishment from sinners to their children. More in accord with the attested sense of *tkn* is the sense "determined" or, better (as tolerative nif'al), "determinable," i.e., God's way is erratic, arbitrary; so long as someone suffers punishment he does not care whether or not it is the sinner.

The prophet angrily retorts in God's name: My way is erratic? It is your way that is erratic, that conforms to no rule, but is "twisting" (Prov 19:3), crooked (Ps 146:9), perverted (Prov 21:8)—the description of the ways of the wicked. Medievals and some moderns interpret the people's protest as directed against the prophet's statement of the rule of divine retribution (Davidson: "The prophet's principle of the freedom of the individual and his independence was a novelty running counter to cherished notions of that age . . ."); if so, this was not the same audience who bruited the proverb!

26. *for it.* The pronoun is plural in Hebrew; cf. *bahem* "for them" in 33:18—in both cases implicit iniquitous acts are referred to.

29. There is disaccord between the plural subject (*drkykm*) and the singular verb (*ytkn*) in the last clause; mss. and versions variously adjust the one to the other. The orderly sequence in vs. 25 of divine way in the singular and people's ways in the plural breaks down in this verse.

30. *Turn back and face about.* See comment at 14:6 to "and turn" (the translation of *hšybw* by "face about" results from local exigency and does not imply adoption of the first alternative offered there).

and let it—namely, your impenitence (Kimḥi)—*not be your stumbling-block of iniquity!* For the preference of this construction of *mkšwl ʿwn* to "and let not iniquity be your stumbling-block" (see, e.g., *RSV, NEB*), see comment at 7:19, where the phrase is explained as "the iniquitous cause of downfall."

STRUCTURE AND THEMES

Plain as it seems when taken part by part, this prophecy challenges the interpreter who seeks to grasp it as a whole. Its two themes—the principle of individual retribution and God's constant readiness to accept and save penitents—are juxtaposed rather than expressly connected; the connection must be supplied. The meaning and function of the interpolated citations must be worked out. The contrast of the ideas of this prophecy with others in this book and elsewhere in Scripture must be confronted. Finally, the relation of this prophecy to its parallel in 33:10–20 calls for comment. We begin with an account of its structure.

After the revelation formula (vs. 1), God's admonition sets in without an address or a message formula, as though the prophet were among the admonished. The proverb about sons suffering for their fathers' misdeeds (vs. 2) opens the first, longest section of the oracle, which consists of its (theoretical) refutation (vss. 3–20). In the second section the principle of God's justice, namely, that the past does not determine the evaluation of the present, is extended into the life of the individual; it is the basis of the doctrine of the constant availability of repentance (vss. 21–32). The conclusion of the second section (beginning with *laken*) binds both sections: since each person is judged on his own record, the audience is summoned to repent and live (vss. 30–32). A feature of this oracle is the interweaving of its parts with an absence of clear formal boundaries.

A. The principle of individual retribution (vss. 3–20). The boundaries of this section are marked by the two statements of the principle in vs. 4 and—inverted (Seidel's rule) and elaborated—in vs. 20. However, the terms of both vss. 4 and 3 hark back to the proverb in vs. 2; hence our paragraphing. If in this analysis we nonetheless chose to begin the section with vs. 3, it is by preferring form over content, since, strictly speaking, God's refutation begins with his oath in vs. 3. Similarly, the closing statement of the principle ends in vs. 20bα; the rest of vs. 20b is a bridge to the second section, which we retain in the first for convenience.

From God's ownership of every person the grand principle is derived that only the sinner shall die (vs. 4). This is illustrated by the fates of three generations. The description of the traits of the first generation serves as the standard definition of the righteous man, who earns life (vss. 5–9); that of the second generation, its antithesis, defines the wicked man, who is condemned to death (vss. 10–13); the third generation—the righteous son of a wicked father—is, in the estimate of the users of the proverb, equivalent to themselves. For the sake of illustrating the supererogatory "a father shall not die for . . . his son" (see comment to vs. 20) the first two generations are required; for refuting the proverb only the last two are pertinent. Hence the ensuing argument focuses on them, utilizing a possibly fictitious audience stricture (vs. 19a) to emphasize and restate the principle of the moral autonomy of the generations. The detailed justification for the disparate fates of the last two generations (vss. 18, 19b), the interpolated stricture, followed by the climactic restatement of the opening principle (vs. 20)—all show that in vss. 18–20 the pith of the argument resides; the proverb has been refuted in principle.

Throughout the first section the father-son contrast prevails in accord with the terms of the proverb. But in the final clause of vs. 20 the principle of retribution is rephrased with a new contrasting pair: "righteous(ness)" and "wicked(ness)," as if to say that in judgment God recognizes no fathers and sons, only righteous and wicked. These new terms serve as a bridge to the next section, in which they predominate.

B. God's constant readiness to accept and save penitents (vss. 21–32). Following the clue of A's structure, we identify the boundary markers of B as vss. 23 and 32—a statement and a restatement of its essential doctrine. The former appears as a conclusion from a premise (repentance expunges past sins) and is phrased as a rhetorical question: "Do I at all desire the death of the wicked man . . . ?" The latter closes the consequential part of the oracle in the form of a declaration and an exhortation: "For I do not desire the death of anyone . . ."

To the premise and conclusion comprising the primary statement of doctrine (vss. 21–23) a further proposition is attached: reversion from righteousness expunges past merits (vs. 24)—a logical outcome of the doctrine and a triumph of consistency, even if it is properly irrelevant to the chief interest of the oracle in encouraging repentance. A popular cavil at God's arbitrary conduct is then cited and turned back on the cavilers, with the reassertion of the rule that retribution conforms strictly with a person's present state (vss. 25–29). The structure of B so far is:

B1	Doctrine	a. repentance expunges past sins
		b. God desires repentance
		c. reversion expunges past merits
B2	Cavil and	d. not God's ways but yours are perverse
	retort	c′. reversion expunges merits
		a′. repentance expunges past sins
		d′. not God's ways but yours are perverse

Note how a and c of B1 are woven—inverted!—into B2, with a′ (vss. 27f.) twice as long as c′ (vs. 26; contrast the equality of a and c), betraying an emphasis on the doctrine of repentance. Note also the envelope of d–d′, marking off this repartee as a discrete unit while stressing the rigorous consistency of God as opposed to the people's perversity.

The theoretical refutation of the proverb is now complete; from this viewpoint, the turned-about cavil of B2 corresponds to the rejected proverb in vss. 2–3. But the prophet drives on to draw the practical conclusion from his exposition. For what ultimately stirred God's indignation was not a mere error in cognition but the corrosive moral consequence implicit in it; its remedy is now announced.

B3. A call to repentance (vss. 30–32). The conclusion of the oracle opens with the customary *laken* (vs. 30) and a résumé of the doctrine of A: each person is judged for his own—not his father's—conduct (note how "his ways" of vs. 30a connects with "my, your ways" of vs. 29). Then the essential affirmation of B (*bšwbw . . . wḥyh* "that he turn . . . and live," vs. 23) is transformed into imperatives, divided and augmented to form a staircase envelope for the climax of the oracle:

šwbw whšybw "turn back and face about" (vs. 30b)
whsybw wḥyw "face about and live" (vs. 32b)

Within the envelope are urgent appeals to repent; they are capped by God's definitive negation of his ill will toward man ("For I do not desire the death of anyone")—a heightened rephrasing of the rhetorical question of vs. 23—followed by the command to repent and live (vs. 32).

Once again the "halving" structure of Ezekiel's oracles appears, with a conclusion characteristically resuming both parts. The general correspondence of the elements of A and B (though differently proportioned) is noteworthy:

A	B
proverb, first statement of doctrine of retribution (vss. 2–4) and its illustration (vss. 5–18)	first statement of God's good will toward penitents, within presentation of doctrine of judgment according to present state (vss. 21–24)
people's stricture (vs. 19)	people's cavil and God's retort (vss. 25–29)
restatement of doctrine (vs. 20)	practical consequences of doctrines of A and B with restatement of God's good will toward penitents (vss. 30–32)

As befits a disputation, this prophecy is full of rhetorical effects. Section A is didactic; its style is predominantly impersonal case-law; the only personal note is the suffix "my" attached to "laws" and "rules" in vss. 9, 17, 19. In B1 and B2 the impersonal style is joined by God's revelation of his good will, couched in rousing rhetorical questions (vs. 23), and impatient expostulation with the audience, again in rhetorical questions (vss. 25, 29). In B3 the impersonal style is entirely replaced by God speaking for himself in strong asseverations (note the repeated "declares Lord YHWH" in vss. 30, 32) and imperatives. A clear gradation of passion pervades the oracle, reaching a climax at the end.

Emphatic devices known from previous oracles abound: repetition, with often significant variation (e.g., the heightening of "one" in vs. 7a to "poor and needy" in vs. 12a in order to blacken the wicked man; "gives back" in vs. 7a to "does not take" in vs. 16 in order to ennoble his righteous son); juxtaposed contrasts (throughout); chiastic inversion or otherwise bonding of sections through verbal links. A sense of engagement with the audience is maintained by repeated interpolation of their alleged strictures and objections (vss. 19, 25, 29).

In order, as it were, to clinch the argument, it is extended time and again beyond the immediate need. In the proverb the father's guilt is laid upon the son, the direction imputed guilt regularly takes in the Bible and elsewhere in the ancient Near East (on Deut 24:16, see discussion below); but in the climactic summation of vs. 20 the moral autonomy of the generations is declared to run backward as well as forward: sons shall not suffer for fathers, *nor fathers for sons*. This principle is a full and sufficient theoretical rebuttal of the accusation implied in the proverb, but in the next section (B1) it is extended by logical consistency into a new principle: one's own past does not determine one's present status with God. In this form it anticipates a concern that can arise only in the minds of those who have been persuaded by the argument of A: if, indeed, there is no imputed guilt, then we must be suffering for terrible sins of our own; what hope, then, is there for us (=33:10)? The anticipated concern would, in turn, be met adequately by the assurance that a wicked man's repentance causes his evil record to be expunged so that he may live. But, again, the argument is carried on to the complementary and, properly speaking, irrelevant case of the backsliding righteous man. This extension can be justified only as a rhetorical device designed to depict God's way with men as bound by the strictest conformity to rules, the diametric opposite of what the people imagined it to be.

Evaluation of the relation of B (vss. 21–32) to the parallel in 33:10–20 must weigh the more evident aptness of the argument there against signs of the derivative character of that passage; in addition, the rhetoric of the present oracle must be taken into account. There is no doubt that the affirmation of the expungeability of a wicked past and the assurance of life to the penitent better answers to the despair expressed in 33:10 ("Our transgressions and our sins are upon us; how then shall we live?") than to the proverb that gave occasion to our oracle. Did that affirmation first arise in connection with the saying of ch. 33, only later to be attached to our A? A case can be made for that view of the relation of the ideas of the two oracles. But it will hardly account for the literary facts. Too many elements in B are connected with A for B to have been transplanted from elsewhere; to regard ch. 33 as the origin of B is even less likely in view of the poor connection of certain of B's elements found in ch. 33 with the saying of 33:10. Thus, the complaint about God's way being arbitrary (18:25, 29; 33:17, 20) belongs to recrimination (A's proverb) rather than to the despair of those who admit being guilty (ch. 33's saying); similarly, the affirmation that God will judge each according to his ways (18:30; 33:20) is a rebuttal of the charge that he judges men by the ways of others rather than a remedy for despair at being trapped by one's own record of evil. We conclude, then, that B is a continuation of A, and its repentance theme was spun out of the principle of A by way of drawing out its consequences. In order to serve later as a retort to the saying of despair (33:10), B was recast and supplied with other ingredients of our prophecy (cf. 33:14b–15 with 18:5, 7) and of others (see comments there). The reuse and combination of elements of ch. 18 in the mosaic of ch. 33 is a good example of Ezekiel's practice of both mixing wines and putting old wine into new bottles.

The proverb that occasioned this oracle was not peculiar to the exiles but was current in Jerusalem as well (Jer 31:29–30). It expressed resentment against the notion that a man's family might be punished for his misdeeds, as though they were extensions of him, and mortgaged for his good behavior. This notion governed the treatment of rebels against human and divine authority in Israel and outside it. The practice is vividly described in the Hittite "Instructions for Temple Officials":

> . . . if a slave causes his master's anger, they either kill him or they will injure him . . . or they will seize him, his wife, his children, his brother,

> his sister, his in-laws, his kin . . . If ever he is to die, he will not die alone; his kin will accompany him. If then . . . anyone arouses the anger of a god, does the god take revenge on him alone? Does he not take revenge on his wife, his children, his descendants, his kin, his slaves, and slave-girls, his cattle (and) sheep together with his crop, and will utterly destroy him? (*ANET*[3], pp. 207–8; cf. also the plague prayer of Mursilis, ibid., p. 395, § 9)

In Israel, kings took such measures against rebels (I Sam 22:19; II Kings 10:1–11), as did Nebuchadnezzar against Zedekiah (II Kings 25:7). A progressive ruling of Deut 24:16 outlawed the practice (for the history and legal significance of this ruling, see M. Greenberg, in *Y. Kaufmann Jubilee Volume,* ed. M. Haran [Jerusalem: Magnes Press, 1960], pp. 20–27), and King Amaziah of Judah is cited as having spared the children of his father's assassins in obedience to it (II Kings 14:6). But that God might punish the children of those who rebelled against him remained an article of faith throughout the biblical period (Exod 20:5; Deut 5:9; cf. Jer 18:21; Job 27:14). The justice of "horizontal" collective punishment of a society that contains offenders was challenged several times, and examples of divine scrupulousness in this matter occur; see 9:4; in 14:16 not only are the righteous singled out for deliverance but their (grown) children are treated independently of them—an anticipation of the principle of the present oracle. Moses and Aaron cry out, "Will one man sin and you be incensed at the whole congregation?" (Num 16:22). The sons of Korah did not perish with their rebel father (Num 26:11; see TpJ). But the solidarity of the family was so strongly felt that "vertical" generational collective punishment was nonetheless accepted.

Ezekiel's generation, however, were conscious of their religious superiority over their ancestors of the time of Manasseh and Amon. That the decline in national fortunes started in the reign of the just and pious Josiah and continued unabated to the time of Zedekiah challenged God's justice. Not even the author of Kings, who scraped up sins to explain the exile, could find in the "evil" of the kings after Amon reason enough to explain it; he must invoke "the sins of Manasseh" in order to explain the decision to destroy Judah (II Kings 21:11ff.; 23:26; 24:3f.; cf. Jer 15:4). Precisely in the wake of good King Josiah's reformation did Judah's political fortune sink so low as to have its royal succession determined by the Egyptian Pharaoh (II Kings 23:33f.). A train of setbacks followed: vassalage to Nebuchadnezzar (24:1), the conquest of Jerusalem and exile of King Jehoiachin and the aristocracy, and the Babylonian appointment of Zedekiah over Judah (vss. 8–17). If, after the final collapse in 586, a man of faith could lament, "Our fathers have sinned and are gone; we have suffered for their iniquity" (Lam 5:7), it is little wonder that earlier, more assertive souls witnessing the agony of their country coined the bitter proverb cited both by Jeremiah and Ezekiel.

Contrary to Ezekiel, Jeremiah tacitly admitted the validity of the proverb. In the present dispensation, made harsh by Israel's obduracy, God uses his prerogative against the children of apostates (who, though not so bad as their fathers, still do not have clean hands); only in time to come ("in those days") as part of the "new covenant" God will abandon this harsh measure. Then, but not now, "he who eats unripe grapes, his teeth shall be set on edge," and the proverb will no longer be used.

Ezekiel, on the other hand, demands that the proverb be given up at once; it gives a false picture of God's conduct now. To him the proverb means that its users regard themselves as innocent. Accordingly, he defines innocence and affirms that its reward of "life" cannot be canceled by parental guilt. He announces that the restriction put by Deut 24:16 on the scope of human punishment applies to divine justice as well. "Moses said, 'Visiting the iniquity of fathers upon the sons,' but Ezekiel came and annulled it: 'It is the person who sins that shall die'" (R. Jose bar Ḥanina, Palestine, third century C.E. [BT *Makkot* 24a]). Note, however, that God's scrupulous discrimination between the fates of generations operates in a context of men diametrically opposite in their conduct. Understanding the proverb in black and white terms, Ezekiel couches his response similarly: all-righteous son, all-wicked father ("he does none of these things"; another manner of rigorousness is reflected in the preceding variant, "he does even one of these [offenses]"—i.e., to commit even one offense is to lose the status of righteousness). Such a simplification of the issue through ideal norms serves to bring out God's principle of individual retribution with utmost clarity. Its practical importance emerges in B.

If, indeed, the proverb was true, and God exempted himself from the ordinary standard of justice by punishing innocent sons for their fathers' offenses, demoralization could hardly be averted. Now, while Ezekiel held no hope out to the homelanders, he did anticipate the reformation and restoration of the exiles (e.g., 11:16, 18). According to the established view set out in Lev 26:41; Deut 4:29; I Kings 8:47f.; Jer 29:12f., the chastisement of exile was supposed to soften Israel's obduracy till they turned back contritely to their God. That could come about only on the basis of trust in God's justice; so long as the view of God's way reflected in the proverb prevailed, there was little prospect of repentance. The basic issue raised by the proverb was practical rather than theoretical; there were vital behavioral consequences at stake; hence the static-didactic A section must be complemented by the dynamic-volitional B section.

B opens with a leap: anticipating a second cause of despair that might arise even after—indeed, precisely from—acceptance of the grand principle of A, the prophet moves from intergenerational moral autonomy to the liberation of the individual from the burden of his own past. If the current generation's troubles were for their own sins, and these were as heinous as Ezekiel had made them out to be all along, what hope had they of being reconciled with God and accepted back into his favor, i.e., of winning "life"? In response to this anticipated need (made explicit in 33:10), Ezekiel adds a correlate to A's principle, based on God's "proprietary interest" in each person: God's benevolent desire that even the wicked should live and not die, for which reason he allows men to expunge their records by turning over a new leaf. This furnishes the ground for the urgent appeal to repentance with which the oracle ends.

Ezekiel joins Hosea (e.g., 14:2) and Jeremiah (3:12, 14, 22; 18:11, etc.) in proclaiming God's call to the nation to repent (in Jer 25:5; 35:15 this call is represented as the main burden of all prophecy). But none of his predecessors buttressed his call with the theological postulates enunciated here. Nowhere else is the constant availability of repentance guaranteed by God's avowal of his desire that men live and not die (contrast I Sam 2:25, "for YHWH desired to put them to death," and the endless dooms of the prophets). Peculiarly far-reaching is the human capacity presumed in vs. 31 to "make yourselves a new heart and a new spirit." Not only is Ezekiel alone in ascribing to man such a capacity, but within Ezekiel's prophecies it is proclaimed only here. Elsewhere the prophet enlarges on the people's incorrigibility (e.g., chs. 16; 20), while in 11:19 and 36:36 it is expressly God who will create a "new heart and new spirit" in the redeemed of the future. This singular empowering of the people, so contrary to the general mood of the book, is of a piece with the liberating, encouraging tidings of this oracle, designed as an antidote to despair.

It is true that the principles of retribution and repentance that Ezekiel enunciated are highly theoretical and hardly take realities into account. "He simply denies, on theological grounds, that there may be any discrepancy between what is supposed to be and what actually is, or has been. In this respect there seems to be more than a mere family resemblance between him and the friends of Job" (Freedman, privately). Nonetheless, his adamant imposition of the yoke of intelligibility upon events answered the needs of the hour. Under the stress of the fall of Jerusalem, the exiles evidently accepted his view of their spiritual state. The proverb about the unripe grapes was replaced by "Our transgressions and our sins lie upon us . . ." (33:10). "Our sins" and not "our fathers' sins"; Ezekiel had carried his point.

Ezekiel's message was for the nation—that is, the exilic continuation of the nation that he regularly calls *bet yisra'el* (vss. 25, 29–31; cf. 3:4 with 3:11). Neither the singular used in the legally styled descriptions of the righteous and wicked in vss. 5–17 nor the selection of behaviors implies a shift in focus from national community to individual souls, or even from a homeland perspective to an exilic one (on the former issue, see Structure and Themes; the latter notion is held, e.g., by Eichrodt). Nor is there anything in the proverb that requires a post-fall date, since the pre-fall misfortunes of Judah alluded to above are quite enough to account for its bitterness. An argument for the pre-fall date of the oracle and its address to the nation (of exiles) may be gathered from a study of the list of behaviors, to which we now turn.

The list appears in three variations: the basic list in vss. 5–9, its much-abbreviated negative in vss. 10–13, and its nearly full restatement in vss. 14–17. All start and end with generalities, between which the particulars are listed; the relation of the three lists is as follows:

righteous (*vss. 5–9*)	*wicked* (*vss. 10–13*)	*righteous* (*vss. 14–17*)
does what is right and just	did none of these	did not act so
1 not eating on mountains	1	1
2 looking to idols	6	2
3 adultery	2	3
4 menstruant	—	—
5 maltreatment	3	4
6 pledge	5	5
7 robbery	4	6
8 hungry	—	7
9 naked	—	8
10 interest	7	10
11 wrongdoing	—	9 [emended]
12 arbitration	—	—
observes laws	committed abominations	observed laws

Such variation, Wevers has noted, argues against taking this list as some kind of well-known standard, like the Decalogue. On the contrary, both in scope and language it bears the personal mark of Ezekiel. It combines a priestly interest in ritual (cultic and sexual pollutions) and a prophetic emphasis on the sociomoral virtues; although ritual stipulations have precedence (as in the Decalogue), the sociomoral ones are twice their number. Compared with the Decalogue, Ezekiel's list is more specific in its moral items but less comprehensive and suggestive; it is formally composed of indicative verb sentences, not commands. Other comparable lists describe the ideal man "who may sojourn on God's holy mountain" (Ps 15 at length; briefly Ps 24:3f.; cf. Isa 33:14b–16)—but they are remarkably divergent from Ezekiel's list and lack ritual qualifications. Formally, Isa 33 uses only participial clauses, while the two Psalms passages mix participial and verbal sentences. One might also compare the brief prophetic epitomes of righteousness (Amos 5:13, 15; Isa 1:16f.; Micah 6:8), also lacking ritual items; formally, Amos and Isaiah are couched in imperatives, Micah in infinitive clauses. Thus, there is a wide variety of comparable lists, and little reason to suppose a single archetype, or even life situation, from which all evolved. Ezekiel's list is the longest and its analysis yields results consonant with the character of the man and his prophecy.

A fruitful comparison can be made between our list and that of Jerusalem's crimes in ch. 22:

vs. in ch. 22		*ordinal no. here (or vs.)*
6	bloodshed	vs. 10
7	parents	—
	'šq	vs. 18
	maltreatment	5
8	desecration of sancta	—
	and sabbath	—
9	slanderers (?)	—
	eating on mountains	1
10	father's wife	—
	menstruant	4
11	adultery	3
	daughter-in-law	—
	sister	—
12	bribery	—
	interest	10
	gain by violence	cf. 7

The family resemblance of these lists cannot be missed, and it supports the impression made by our list of being Ezekiel's creation. The differences are accountable to the fact that our list is of virtues (and hence contains nos. 8, 9, 12), while ch. 22 is a bill of indictment (hence the addition of desecration and sexual offenses; see comments to ch. 22). But the overlap with our list occurs first in categorization and second in specifically identical items: cult—1; sex—3, 4; society—5, 10, 22:10, 18. The divergences are not such as can be accounted for by geographical or social conditions. It cannot be claimed that the list of ch. 18 was tailored for individuals or for exiles, in contrast to a communal orientation of ch. 22. Moreover, the inclusion of "eating on the mountains" in both lists, an offense peculiar to those living in the homeland, shows that they both have a pre-fall orientation.

A study of the details of our list reveals a distinctive perspective. The general statements that provide its frame are strikingly different: the key clause of the opening generality is *'śh mšpṭ wṣdqh* "do what is just and right" (vs. 5); the key terms of the closing one are *hlk bḥqwty, šmr/'śh mšpṭy* "follow my laws, observe/perform my judgments (rulings)" (vss. 9, 17). While the two are combined and identified in vs. 19—"the son did what was just and right; he carefully observed [*šmr wy'śh*] my laws"—in origin they each have quite different referents.

"Doing what is just and right" defines the divine and royal standard of conduct. It is "the way of YHWH" (Gen 18:19); it is how he acts and what he desires (Jer 9:23; Ps 99:4). As God's elect, the king must embody this ideal; the paragons David (II Sam 8:15) and Solomon (I Kings 10:9) did, and Jeremiah insists on the obligations of present and future

Davidides to do so too (Jer 22:3, 15–17; 23:5; 33:15). In 22:3 Jeremiah spells out to the king the meaning of the phrase in these injunctions: "Save the robbed one from him who oppresses him; poor man and widow do not maltreat; do not act lawlessly, and do not shed innocent blood in this place."

Such itemization enables us to see how continuous with common ancient Near Eastern conceptions was Israel's conception of the divine and the monarchic ideal. To take only a few Mesopotamian examples: King Ur-Nammu of Ur (end of third millennium B.C.E.) ruled in accord with his god's "equity and truth" (*ANET*³, p. 523c; for this Sumero-Akkadian equivalent of *mšpṭ wṣdqh,* see *CAD* s.v. *"kittu,"* the citations about gods and kings); Lipit Ishtar, king of Isin (beginning, second millennium), and Hammurabi of Babylon (early second millennium) regarded themselves as elected by the gods to establish justice in their lands (*ANET*³, pp. 159c, 164b), the latter specifying, "in order that the strong might not oppress the weak, that justice be dealt the orphan and widow" (ibid., p. 178a). Peculiar to Israel is the democratization of the ideal; both Gen 18:19 and Amos 5:24 require the entire community—not merely the king—to "do what is just and right"; each individual was expected to conform to the royal standard (cf. also Jer 9:23).

To "follow my laws and observe my rulings (judgments)" (so, too, 5:7) is priestly language found in the "Holiness Code" (e.g., Lev 18:4), there summarizing what is required of the Israelite (Lev 26:3, 14f.). It was appropriate that Ezekiel should fuse the democratized ancient royal ideal of doing what is just and right—"the way of YHWH"—with the divinely ordained "laws and rulings"; by so doing he expressed his conception that the "laws and judgments" were essentially the details of "God's way." The fusion was facilitated by the substantial overlap of the two (cf. Jer 22). The linguistic affinity of the items in our lists to ordinances of the law corpora of Exodus, Leviticus, and Deuteronomy (see comments) points to such corpora of God's revealed rules (*torot*) as the referent of Ezekiel's generalization: "he follows my laws and observes my rulings" (vss. 9, 17). The priest-prophet's orientation toward *torah* meant that for him the ancient ideal would be embodied in *torah*-like individual stipulations.

As we have already noted, lists of righteous behaviors of various form and content exist elsewhere in Scripture. What may be said of their origin? Simlai, a third-century C.E. Palestinian sage, arranged several lists in an ascending order of terseness:

> 613 commandments [a traditional number of unknown provenience] were conveyed to Moses . . . David came and summed them up as eleven [Ps 15] . . . Isaiah came and summed them up as six [Isa 33:15] . . . Micah came and summed them up as three [Micah 6:8] . . . Isaiah came and summed them up again as two: "Thus said YHWH: Observe what is

right [*mšpṭ*] and do what is just" [*ṣdqh*] [Isa 56:1]; Amos came and summed them up as one: "Seek me and live" [Amos 5:4] . . . [another opinion:] Habakkuk came and summed them up as one: "The righteous shall live by his fidelity" [Hab 2:4] (*Makkot* 24a).

Simlai seems to have a philosophical motive in seeking to discern increasingly higher generalities in these passages. Earlier, such a motive seems to underlie the colloquy between Rabbi Akiba and Ben Azzai on the most general principle of the Torah (Akiba: "You shall love your neighbor as yourself"; Ben Azzai: "This is the book of the generations of Adam . . . in the image of God he made him," *Sifra* at Lev 19:18). Earlier still, Jesus and the bookmen had a similar colloquy where Jesus proposed two great principles, "Hear O Israel . . . the Lord is one," and "You shall love your neighbor . . ." (Mark 12:28–34 and parallels). That such exercises had a pedagogical-practical purpose can hardly be doubted. Once, in fact, Jesus produces a list based mainly on the "second tablet" of the Decalogue in answer to the question, What good deeds must be done to gain eternal life? (Matt 19:16–22 and parallels). This motive brings us back to some of the above-cited passages in Hebrew Scripture: "gaining life" is the common concern of our Ezekiel passage, Amos 5:4, and Hab 2:4. This is not the "eternal life" of the New Testament passage, but, as everywhere in ancient Israelite thought, this-worldly enjoyment of good things. Lev 18:5's commendation of God's laws for bestowing life on those who observe them (cited in Ezek 20:11) is equivalent to Deuteronomy's motive clause, rewarding observance with "that you shall live and possess the land" (16:20; cf. 30:19f.), or "that you shall live, and it go well with you, and you will have a long life in the land that you are possessing" (5:30; 8:1).

Epitomes of virtuous behavior were formulated, then, for public education in the essential requirements for a blessed life. One such epitome appears to have been the Decalogue, which tradition made a central constituent of the covenant at Sinai. The Decalogue was depicted as a divine revelation to the people, and in that character resembled most other examples cited above, which are prophetic proclamations to the people. The contexts of the Amos, Micah, and Isaiah passages are, in one way or another, the worship at the temple; this is natural, since the main motive of worship was vital renewal at the source of blessing. The prophets exploited the popular attachment to worship in order to proclaim their epitomes of what assured life. Ps 15, 24, and Isa 33 are temple-centered as well, prescribing the conduct required for "sojourning" in the sacred precinct. The existence in Greece and Ptolemaic Egypt of temple inscriptions stating ritual and moral qualifications for worshipers offers a certain analogy (M. Weinfeld, "Instructions for Temple Visitors in the Bible and in Ancient Egypt," *Egyptological Studies* [*Scripta Hierosolymitana* 28], ed. S. Israelit-Groll [Jerusalem: Magnes Press, 1982], pp. 224–50).

Moderns, beginning with S. Mowinckel, have posited a dramatic "temple-entry liturgy" as the Israelite life setting for the rise of this type of list. It is supposed that priests were its authors and executors: to the pilgrim intent upon entering the sacred courts a checklist of qualifications was presented; upon his affirmation that he had these, he was declared "righteous" and allowed to enter (see simply Zimmerli). This hypothetical construct has no parallel outside of Israel; no trace of it appears outside the alleged evidence for it in these biblical lists. (The Egyptian "protestation of guiltlessness" [*ANET*³, pp. 34ff.] by the dead before a court of forty-two gods in order to be found worthy of eternal life, though it has been adduced as an analogue, is closer to the New Testament passages cited above; it has nothing to do with worshiping at a temple.) The question form of such passages as Ps 15, "Who may sojourn/ascend," etc., points to sapiential literature as its model; one may compare both the form and substance of the wisdom passage of Ps 34:13f. (on which see H. Gunkel, *Die Psalmen* [Göttingen: Vandenhoeck & Ruprecht, 1929], p. 143; N. H. Ridderbos, *Die Psalmen*, BZAW 117 [Berlin: de Gruyter, 1972], p. 249):

> Come, sons, listen to me;
> I will teach you the fear of YHWH
> Who is the man who desires life [*ḥpṣ ḥyym;* cf. our vss. 23, 32]
> Who loves years in which to experience good?
> Keep your tongue from evil,
> And your lips from speaking guile;
> Shun evil and do good;
> Seek amity and pursue it.

Note the key notion of "desiring life." It is to be concluded that the practice of epitomizing the virtues of a godly life—basically, the definition of membership in the community of YHWH's devotees (so Weinfeld)—had various life settings, all pedagogic. Ezekiel's priestly learning and his prophetic antecedents provided him with a variety of models to follow. For the definition of the righteous man he chose the casuistic form widely used in priestly definitions; for an example, see Num 35:15b–21 (cities of refuge are for the accidental homicide; but if one killed in this or that fashion or circumstance, *roṣeᵃḥ hu mot yumat haroṣeᵃḥ* "he is a murderer; that murderer shall be put to death"). Zimmerli calls the phrase *ṣaddiq hu* "he is righteous" in our vs. 9 a declarative formula, in accord with his theory of an entry liturgy; the priest declares the worshiper qualified to enter the sanctuary and worthy of life. But it is not clear why a declaration should be in the third person and not in the second (as, e.g., Gen 29:14; 49:3; I Sam 15:13; 24:18; 29:9, etc.). That our *ṣaddiq hu* is rather definitional seems to be necessitated by the context, which starts out with the postulation "If a man is righteous" (vs. 5), continues with the enumeration or definition of the qualities that make him so, and ends with the summation "he is righteous, he shall live." In sum, the inspiration to compile such a list as we have in ch. 18 is pedagogic. The specific items listed in ch. 18 derive mostly from collections of God's "laws and rulings" in the custody of priests. But the predominance of sociomoral injunctions stems from the distinctively prophetic appreciation of them as the essence of God's requirement of Israel.

XVIII. A Dirge over the Kings of Israel (19:1–14)

19 1 And you, recite a dirge over the chiefs[a] of Israel 2 and say:
What a lioness was your mother,
couching among the lions,
Rearing her cubs
among the young lions.
3 She raised up one of her cubs—
he became a young lion;
He learned to tear prey,
he ate men.
4 Nations heard about him—
he was caught in their snare;
They led him in shackles
to the land of Egypt.
5 When she saw that she waited in vain,
that hope was lost,
She took another of her cubs,
appointed him a young lion.
6 He walked among lions,
he became a young lion.
He learned to tear prey,
he ate men.
7 He knew[b] his widows
and desolated their cities;
The land and all that was in it were appalled
at the sound of his roaring.
8 Nations set upon him
from provinces roundabout;
They spread their net for him,
he was caught in their snare.

[a] G singular.
[b] G "he grazed" reflects *wyrʿ* (for MT *wydʿ*).

9 They put him, shackled, in neckstocks
and led him to the king of Babylon—
led him in toils,
So that his voice would no longer be heard
on the mountains of Israel.

10 Your mother was like a vine, in your blood,
planted by water;
She was fruitful and ramified
because of abundant water.
11 She had mighty boughs[a]
for scepters[a] of rulers;
Its stature towered
among the clouds;
It was conspicuous for its height
with its many branches.
12 But she was uprooted in fury,
hurled to the ground;
The east wind
dried up her fruit,
They broke off and withered,
Her mighty bough—
fire consumed it.
13 Now she is planted in the wilderness,
in a parched and thirsty land.
14 Fire came out of the bough of her shoots,
it consumed her fruit;
No mighty bough remained on her,
no scepter for ruling.
This is a dirge, and it became[c] a dirge.

[c] G S "will become."

COMMENT

19:1. *chiefs.* Several kings (*nśy'*, cf. at 7:27) of Judah are alluded to in the dirge. But since the suffix pronoun in *'mk* "your mother" in vs. 2 is singular, G's reading "chief" is attractive; MT plural may have risen through adjustment to the sequel. Since "chiefs of" ends in *y* and "Israel" begins with *y,* it is also possible that these variations arose mechanically: if MT is secondary, it is explicable as a dittography of the *y* of "Israel"; if G is secondary, it is explicable as a haplography of one of the two *y*'s (Freedman, privately).

2. *What a lioness.* This is a conjecture, since elsewhere exclamatory *mh* appears only with a qualitative substantive or verbal, e.g., *mh ṭwbw* "how good are!" Yet it is preferable to the vapid "What was your mother? a lioness," etc.

your mother. One of the last kings of Judah is addressed, either Jehoiachin—exiled but hopeful of restoration—or Zedekiah, the reigning incumbent. In Ezekiel's dirges the bewailed persons are normally the ones addressed (26:17f.; 27:3ff.; 28:12ff.; 32:2, 18, 28). On the identification of the mother, here and in vs. 10, see Structure and Themes.

lby' is vocalized (*l*ᵉ*biyya*) as feminine of **lby,* with ' indicating the feminine, in the Aramaic manner, instead of *h* (cf. *ṣ*ᵉ*biyya* [*ṣbyh*] "roe" from *ṣby*).

Moderns (e.g., *BHS*) divide the verse into two 3:2 lines, thus:

mh 'mk lby' / byn 'rywt	What a lioness your mother, among lions!
rbṣh btwk kprym / rbth gwryh	She couched amidst young lions, she reared her cubs.

While this adjusts the meter of both lines to the prevailing 3:2 characteristic of dirges (though not rigidly adhered to!), it runs counter to the distinction made in this piece between *'ryh* and *kpyr.* Generally, the latter is indistinguishable from other terms for lion, e.g., Isa 5:29 (|| *lby'*); Jer 51:38, Amos 3:4 (|| *'ryh*); but here (vss. 3, 6) *kpyr* marks the stage of young adulthood into which the cub grows. In vs. 2, then, MT's line division, which our translation follows, fittingly places the lioness among lions (*'rywt*) while having her rear her cubs in the company of *kpyrym* "young lions," which they might emulate. The lions are evidently the Judahite royalty and nobility.

3. *raised up. h'lh* "lift up, raise," is not attested elsewhere either as "rear (a child)" or "elevate" in rank—the two senses most suitable for this context. Since vs. 5 shows the determining role of the mother in kingmaking, MT's unusual reading is to be preferred to S's simplification "one of her cubs grew" (as from *wy'l*). It also agrees with nature, since the cubs learn to tear prey by imitating their elders, and since it is the lioness that does much of the hunting, often with her cubs (Freedman, privately). Gen 49:9 *mṭrp bny 'lyt* "you have grown, my son, on prey" seems to underlie this and the next line.

4. *heard about him.* Wevers justly compares II Kings 19:9 for this sense of *šm' 'l.* Kara and Menahem bar Shim'on gloss as "gathered against him," like moderns who read the verb as hif'il or pi'el (Jer 50:29; I Sam 15:4); it must then follow that either "nations" is the object and a sub-

ject must be supplied (Zimmerli: God) or "nations" is the subject and an object (say, hunters) must be supplied.

snare. T "net"; so Menahem bar Shim'on—cf. vs. 8. M. Held argues for this sense here and in similar contexts (*JANES* 5 [1973], 181ff.) as opposed to the usual rendering "pit," which is defended by Lang, *Kein Aufstand,* 97f. Lions were, in fact, hunted both ways.

shackles (ḥḥym). G S "halter, muzzle"; T "chains" (so Menahem bar Shim'on). The parallel in vs. 9 suggests a kind of restraint, as does II Chron 33:11 (*ḥwḥ;* G "bonds"; T "manacles"; see Held, op. cit., pp. 183ff.), and the association of *ḥḥ* with rings (*nzm, ṭb't*) in Exod 35:22. On the other hand, fusion with *ḥwḥ* "nettle" as a piercing object appears not only in II Chron 33:11 but in the expression "put a *ḥḥ* in the jaw" (Ezek 29:4; 38:4; cf. Job 40:26) and the "nose" (Isa 37:29/II Kings 19:28—G, Kimḥi "hooks"). Ancient practice backs both interpretations, as appears in an inscription of Assurbanipal in which he claims to have "pierced the cheek" of a captive king, "put the ring to his jaw, placed a dog collar around his neck and made him guard (at a gate of Nineveh)," *ANET*[3], p. 300a. The relief of Esarhaddon showing him holding two royal captives with ropes fastened by rings to their lips has been compared (*ANEP*[2] ⋡447).

5. *she waited in vain.* Medievals and moderns assume this unprecedented sense for nif'al of *yḥl* "hope, wait for"; Smend helpfully compares the Syriac cognate *'wḥl* "be exhausted," *'wḥl 'l* "despair of." The meaning is: when the lioness saw that her son would never return from Egyptian exile.

7. *He knew his widows.* A strange expression; since *yd'* can mean "have (the experience of)"—as in Isa 47:8, "I shall not know bereavement; Qoh 8:5, "shall not know misfortune"—this might mean "he counted his widows" (like an Indian brave counting his scalps); Moses Kimḥi (cited by Menahem bar Shim'on) gave such an explanation. Most medievals understood *yd'* sexually: "he raped their widows," thus transgressing the bounds of the imagery. T "he laid waste their castles" was explained by Kimḥi on the basis of *yd'* "break, chastise" as in Judg 8:16 (cf. J. Barr, *Comparative Philology and the Text of the Old Testament* [Oxford: Clarendon Press, 1968], pp. 19ff., citing D. Winton Thomas), and *'lmnwt-* = *'rmnwt-* "castles," as in Isa 13:22; this strained interpretation also violates the imagery (it is therefore not substantially promoted by reading *wyr'* "he shattered" [from *r' '*], reconstructed from G "he grazed" [from *r'h*]). Luzzatto hesitantly proposed the emendation *wyrb* "he multiplied, made many," which is conform to 22:25, a context related to our passage (cf. also Jer 15:8, "their widows shall be more numerous . . ."); the suffixed "his widows" means that he was the cause of their widowhood, as "your corpses" in 11:6 means that "you" caused their death.

Actually, G's reflex of *wyr'(h)* "he grazed, fed on" fits curiously the immediately preceding sequence *ṭarap* "he tore prey" and *'akal* "he ate."

Ch. 34:2, 10 denounces the "shepherds" (kings) of Israel *haro'im 'otam*—a phrase whose perfect ambiguity emerges in vs. 10b: "the shepherds shall no more [*yr'w 'tm*] tend themselves / graze on them; but I will rescue my sheep from their mouths and they shall no longer be food for them." The resultant parallel here between *r'h* "feed on, devour" and *hḥryb* "depopulate" (see next comment) evokes *wr'w . . . bḥrb* of Micah 5:5, "they shall lay waste (lit. devour; cf. Jer 6:3) . . . with the sword" (M. Margolis, *Micah* [Philadelphia: Jewish Publication Society of America, 1908], ad loc.). A lion as the subject of *r'h* is, to be sure, unexampled; does the play on "shepherds" (kings)/"devourers" lurk behind it? Yet note Jer 2:14–16, with its sequence "spoil . . . lions sounding their voice" . . . *yr'wk qdqd*—OJPS: "shall feed on thy crown."

desolated. That is, depopulated—for this sense of *hḥryb* see Zeph 3:6, "I made their streets desolate, without any passerby" (so, too, Jer 2:15). The possessive of "their cities" is awkward; it can only refer to the collective *'dm* "humans" in the previous line.

Wevers regards this line as secondary for having abandoned the figure of the lion. But the figure of lions desolating cities occurs in Jer 2:15; does something like the plague of lions mentioned in II Kings 17:25 underlie this figure? A striking parallel to the Kings passage is Assurbanipal's account of his deliverance of his people from such a plague; in the following excerpt, evocations of our vss. 6–9 are italicized:

> The young of the lions grew up (*lit.* throve) therein (in forests and marshes) . . . They became fierce and terrible through their devouring of herds, flocks, *and people. With their roaring the hills resound* . . . They keep bringing down the cattle of the plain, they (keep) shedding the blood of men . . . *The villages are in mourning* day and night . . . (Luckenbill, *ARAB* II, § 935).

8. *set upon him. ntn* here has the military sense of its synonyms *śym* (in 23:24; I Kings 20:12) and *šyt* (Ps 3:7).

provinces. mdynh is a pre-exilic Aramaism (M. Wagner, *Aramaismen*, ※152, p. 72), attested in I Kings 20:14ff., Lam 1:1, and frequently later.

9. *neckstocks.* Akkadian *šigaru,* see I. Gelb, "Prisoners of War in Early Mesopotamia," *JNES* 32 (1973), 86; M. Held, op. cit., p. 184; *ANET*³, p. 298a, "pillory." T translates correctly by *qwlryn,* from Latin *collare* "neck-iron."

in toils. That is, nets, as in Qoh 9:12. An alternative reading *mᵉṣadot* "fortresses" (see *Minḥat Shay*) underlies Rashi and Menahem bar Shim'on, who gloss "to imprison him there" (cf. G S "prison").

The verb *yb'hw* occurs twice in this verse, the first time with *w*-consecutive (as expected), the second time without; yet, as echoing the first verb, the second is clearly equivalent to it temporally. Is the first verb's *w*-doing double-duty (as the copula in Gen 37:7 *whnh tsbynh*) or is the old preterit sense of the "imperfect" being realized as often in high prose and poetry? (G. Beer and R. Meyer, *Hebräische Grammatik* II [Berlin: de Gruyter, 1955], pp. 120f.; cf. König, III, § 368 h–k).

10. *in your blood* (bdmk). Cf. 22:4, "of the blood (*bdmk*) that you shed you are guilty," on the basis of which Eliezer of Beaugency writes: "Your mother . . . that is, the kingdom of Judah, became lowly as a vine on account of the blood you shed . . . yet in spite of the evil I brought on her I allowed her to survive [planted by abundant water, as above, 17:5f.]." This effort, the best of the medievals, does not solve the puzzle of *bdmk;* its appeal to the opprobrium connected with the vine in ch. 17 is out of place here. G surprises us with "like a sprig on a pomegranate." J. Bewer's emendation is notable: *bdm k[y]* "(like a vine [full]) of shoots because (planted)," etc., *JBL* 72 (1953), 159; cf. M. Dahood in *Biblica* 56 (1975), 96f., who ascribes the sense "which" to *ky:* "(a ramified vine) which (was planted)." The word remains a crux.

11. *boughs for scepters.* An allusion to the many royal scions of Josiah? The use of *'l* as "fit for" is unusual; Ehrlich cites Jer 33:4, but that passage is uncertain. In the light of the next line (vs. 11aβ: "its"), the plural forms *mṭwt, šbṭy* have been interpreted as a singular—the "plural of amplification" (so Ehrlich [Hebrew]) or of "majesty" (Brownlee, cited by Lang; for these terms, see GKC § 124). G renders both terms by a singular, and moderns propose to emend the verb and the nouns accordingly (*wyhy, mṭh, šbṭ*). But MT seems simply to move from an allusion to many kings in this line to the one final king of the dynasty in the next line, whose self-aggrandizement led to the collapse of the state.

Its stature towered . . . clouds. That *'btym* is clouds seems assured by the echoing passages 31:3, 10, 14 (*'el ben* = our *'al ben*) said of the crown of a cedar (*'bwt* "cloud" in II Sam 23:4 too), as against medievals who take it to mean "many-branched tree" (Rashi, Eliezer of Beaugency; cf. 20:28). The masculine "its (his)" has been taken to refer to the vine —masculine in II Kings 4:39; Hosea 10:1 (*gpn bwqq* "fertile vine"; otherwise Freedman-Andersen, *Hosea,* AB)—but the return to feminine in the next line makes that doubtful. The natural antecedent is (one of) the bough(s) of the preceding line. Some moderns seek to get rid of the difficulty by regarding this line as an addition inspired by 31:3, etc., but the sequel indicates its originality: if vs. 12a speaks of the vine's being hurled to the ground, it must previously have risen above it—and only our line describes that rise. That *gbh* (vs. 11aβ–b) and *hšlk 'rṣ* (vs. 12a) reappear in 28:17 as a contrasting pair also argues for the originality of their combination here. Moreover, without vs. 11aβ–b, we should lack the reason for the vine's downfall—its hubris (for substance and language, 31:10–14 must be compared).

12. *hšlk (l)'rṣ* "hurl (from the sky) to the ground" also occurs in Lam 2:1, with God as subject and "Israel's glory" the object. Cf., also, the remarkable verbal similarity between vs. 12aα and Deut 29:27.

The east wind dried up her fruit. As in 17:9–10. The plural verbs "they broke off and withered" have no subject in the immediate vicinity; medievals refer to "its boughs" and "its branches" of vs. 11—too remote for comfort. Perhaps the collective "fruit" is the subject (Ehrlich revocalizes it to read *poreha* [otherwise unattested], plural of *pora* "its branches"; others emend to *badeha* "its rods," as in vs. 14. Freedman privately suggests that since vs. 12aβ ("the east wind . . .") and b ("her mighty bough . . .") form a chiastic envelope around the two third-person plural verbs, the latter are linked to both environing nouns—fruit and bough. For the consuming fire, cf. the vine of 15:4f.

13. *Now . . . wilderness.* This is generally understood as a reference to the exile of Jerusalem (or the royal house), the wilderness being an emblem of the inhospitable foreign soil. A. Caquot (*Semitica* 14 [1964], 13) took it as a reference to the ruined and parched native plot of the vine (cf. 17:10); but, having been uprooted (vs. 12a), is it likely that the vine was described as still planted in its original plot?

14. Fire breaking out in the mighty bough and destroying the fruit of the vine recalls the image of Jotham's fable, in which the worthless bramble causes a fire that consumes the cedars of Lebanon (Judg 9:20). Here the vine's fruits are destroyed by the fault of the bough (= the people through the sin of the king).

This is a dirge. As communicated to Ezekiel (vs. 1), and *it became a dirge* actually employed as such after the events alluded to in it happened; the last clause anticipates the reality, using the prophetic perfect (as do all verbs from vs. 12 on). G S, with their simple future, agree with the similar expression in 32:16.

STRUCTURE AND THEMES

This passage, with its new theme of Israel's (mis)rulers and its short lines—preponderantly 3:2, a common dirge meter—is clearly marked off from what precedes, despite the absence of regular opening formulas (contrast the dirges in 27:1ff.; 28:11ff.; 32:1ff., 17ff.). The opening "And you" (G adds: "son of man") normally belongs to a subdivision and gives the passage an appearance of continuing the preceding oracle (on the connection with chs. 17 and 18, see end of this section). The dirge closes with vs. 14a; it is followed by a brief colophon that, together with vs. 1, forms a frame: "Recite a dirge . . . This is a dirge . . ."

The passage falls into two sections, each beginning with the address "Your mother" (vss. 2, 10), the figure changing from lions in the first section to a vine in the second. The lines of the first section are more regular (mostly 3:2) than those of the second (mostly not 3:2) and its style more "poetic": in the vine allegory more nonsegmented lines occur (seven of twelve)—lines whose second part completes the first syntactically (vss. 10, 11, 12aβ, 12bβ) instead of being an echo or a syntactically independent complement of it (as are ten of the sixteen lines of the lions allegory).

The first section (vss. 5–9) again falls into two parts: vss. 2–4, the lioness and her first cub; vss. 5–9, the lioness and her second cub. Freshness is imparted to the essentially repetitive second story through parallelistic expansions, making it twice the length of the first (vs. 3a || 5b, 6a; vs. 3b || 6b, 7; vs. 4a || 8; vs. 4b || 9a–b). The closing line (vs. 9bβ "so that . . .") binds the two parts by echoing words of the first part—*šmʿ* (vs. 4) and *yiśraʾel* (vs. 1).

The second section (vss. 10–14) differs in structure and focus: a mother and her issue are again present, but since these are a vine and her mighty bough(s) (see comment to vs. 11), their fates are more closely linked than in the case of the lioness and her cubs. The subject of the narrative is the vine (except for vs. 11aβ–b): vss. 10–11 tell the past glory of the well-watered vine and her soaring bough(s); vs. 12 relates her fall and desiccation; vs. 13 describes her present, final state of desolation. The vine is "overkilled": she is uprooted and hurled to the ground (vs. 12aα); the east wind withers her fruit (vs. 12aβ) and fire consumes her mighty bough (vs. 12bβ). Planted in parched wilderness (vs. 13)—which alone would have sufficed to kill her—fire then spreads from her branches to her fruit (vs. 14). Such an accumulation recalls the fate of the vine of ch. 17, first uprooted by the eagle, with all dire consequences, then withered by the east wind; one also thinks of the multiple punishments inflicted on the harlot of 16:40. Logic is set aside in order to express boundless fury about to be unleashed upon the wicked rebels.

Since the dirge is over "the chiefs of Israel," the pronominal reference in "your mother" must be to one of the kings. The usual procedure is to address the lamented person and describe his fate (see the above-listed laments); here the fate of the kings is narrated from the viewpoint of their mother. If in the first section this anomaly is mitigated by the extensive accounts of her cubs' careers, in the second the mother's fate—in suspense at the end of the preceding passage—becomes almost the sole subject of the narrative. What is titled a dirge over Israel's chiefs turns into a depiction of a pathetic mother ruined by the self-aggrandizement of her issue. This dominance of the mother in the figures must be accorded its due in determining her identity.

Neither medieval nor modern commentators have arrived at a consensus regarding the referents of the figures in the allegories. Only the first cub-king can be firmly identified: he stands for Jehoahaz, son of Josiah and Hamutal; crowned by the people after his father's death, he was almost immediately deposed by Pharaoh Necho and brought in fetters to Egypt (II Kings 23:30–34). The capture and deportation to Babylon of the second cub-king fits the cases of Jehoiachin, son of Jehoiakim and Nehushta (24:8ff.), and (still in the future from Ezekiel's perspective) Zedekiah, son of Josiah and Hamutal (I Chron 3:15; II Kings 24:18ff.).

A decision in favor of Jehoiachin can invoke the analogue of Jeremiah's two laments in ch. 22: in vss. 10–12 Jeremiah sympathizes with the cruel fate of Jehoahaz, condemned to die in exile, while in vss. 24–30 he foretells, with emotion, the fate of Jehoiachin to die in a foreign land, never to see a descendant of his on the throne of David. The combination of piteousness and humiliation in these two figures, and the balance of their ignominious fates—the one deported to the west, the other to the east—makes them fit themes for a poetic dirge. According to this interpretation of the cub-kings, their mother-lioness will be an emblem of the nation (T "the congregation of Israel") or the dynasty (cf. Hos 2:4; Ezek 16; 23:2; Isa 50:1).

No identification of the royal figure(s) represented by the "mighty bough(s)" of the second allegory imposes itself immediately; the textual uncertainty about the number of boughs referred to precludes sure identification. The final scene of the burnt vine planted in the desert, stripped of the capability of growing any more scepters for ruling is most naturally taken as a picture of the impending end drawn as though already accomplished. The mighty bough whose hubris is punished on the whole vine will be Zedekiah, who failed at the big power game. Unlike the past failures of the mother's issue, the future one will bring ruin on her as well—she representing again the nation or the dynasty. According to this interpretation, then, the two allegories are in chronological sequence.

A more literal approach identifies the mother as Hamutal, wife of Josiah and mother of both Jehoahaz and Zedekiah. From the role assigned to the lioness in the elevation of her two cubs it is inferred that Hamutal must have been a power in court politics (no other evidence for this exists). Since, according to this view, anticipation of the future fate of Zedekiah already appears in the story of the second cub, the vine allegory must go over the same ground.

Another view finds in brutal Jehoiakim a more fitting referent for the vicious lion of vss. 6–7 (cf. Jer 22:13–17; 26:21–23) than the ephemeral Jehoiachin, whose three-month reign could hardly have given him scope to achieve such a reputation. The earliest proponent of this view may have been the Chronicler who, accordingly, reports that Nebuchadnezzar "bound him [Jehoiakim] in fetters to lead (G, I Esdras 1:38 "and led") him to Babylon" (II Chron 36:6, whence, it would seem, Dan 1:2 derived an exile of Jehoiakim; W. Rudolph argues unconvincingly that "to lead" implies that Jehoiakim did not actually undergo deportation but was only threatened therewith [*Chronikbücher,* HAT (1955), p. 335). For another instance of the Chronicler's invention based on a verse in Ezekiel, see at 17:19. But it seems misguided to look for a strict historical correspondent for the second vicious lion when the first vicious lion is manifestly stereotypical; for could Jehoahaz really have won a reputation of being a maneater in three months?

The allegory appears to be schematic, with fidelity to history subordinated to the elegiac theme of onetime glory turned into disgrace and ruin. The lioness and the vine stand for the glorious source out of which calamitous issue sprang. To take them as a particular queen mother—Hamutal—at once reduces their pathetic grandeur while gratuitously enhancing a wholly obscure person. It needlessly commits one to a specificity in interpretation of the second cub-king and the mighty bough(s) beyond that which the data allow, thus shifting attention from their typical features to historical details that the allegory is not meant to illumine. It is best, then, to take the "mothers" as a collective emblem (e.g., Israel, Judah, Jerusalem, or the royal house), and turn our efforts to determining what the ensemble of these figures in this particular form of a dirge signifies.

The standard dirge eulogized the person lamented, contrasted his splendid former state with his miserable latter one, and offered him various consolations (E. Jacob in *IDB,* s.v. "Mourning"). In the prophetic adaptation the glorious past of the lamented is depicted censoriously so as to give the ground for his fall (e.g., Isa 14:4–21, and the rest of Ezekiel's dirges). In our case the predatory nature of the cub-kings and the soaring of the bough(s) seem such natural attributes that some moderns have thought that the prophet sympathized with the lamented, that we may hear in this dirge the sigh of a patriotic heart (Smend, Cooke). This would be a striking departure from all Ezekiel preached about king and kingdom; study of the figures and the language of the oracle does not recommend this interpretation.

The poetic figure of a ravaging lion underwent a metamorphosis in prophecy. It is a heroic emblem in Jacob's blessing of Judah (Gen 49:9), Moses' blessing of Gad (Deut 33:20), and Balaam's characterization of Israel (Num 23:24; 24:9). The terms of the blessing of Judah, in particular, are so similar to those of our dirge as to suggest a genetic relation: in common are *gur* "cub," *'ryh* "lion," *ṭrp* "prey," *'lh* "rise," *rbṣ* "couch," *lby'* "lion(ess)," *šbṭ* "scepter," *gwym* "nations," *gpn* "vine," and *dm* "blood." In Psalms, on the other hand, lions appear as an emblem of the wicked enemy (e.g., 7:3; 17:12), while in Prov 28:15 "A roaring lion, a ravenous bear is the wicked ruler of a poor people." Prophecy likewise employs the lion as a figure of fierce cruelty. J. M. P. Smith described the use in Nahum 2:12–14 thus: "Under this figure, the prophet has presented . . . a picture of the ferocity and rapacity which characterized the Assyrian conqueror in his treatment of defeated peoples" (*Micah, Zephaniah,* etc., ICC). Again we remark the number of terms held in common by Nahum 2 and our oracle: *'rywt, kpyrym, lby', gwr, ṭrp,* and the phrase *l' yšm' 'wd qwl* "the voice of—shall no longer be heard." In Zephaniah we find the first application of the figure to Israel's rulers (3:3):

> Her officers in her midst are roaring lions;
> Her rulers, wolves of the steppe;
> They leave no bone until the morning [?]

Jacob's endowment of Judah with royalty evidently hovered in Ezekiel's consciousness as he composed this dirge over Judah's rulers; however, he subverted the terms of the blessing (as he did the figure of the vine in ch. 15), inspired, perhaps, by the language of Nahum and Zephaniah. That he intended the lion to be a pejorative figure is indicated by its outrageous conduct: "he ate humans . . . he desolated their cities." Moreover, Ezekiel employs similar language when, in 22:25, he describes the kings of "the bloody city" Jerusalem (the epithet belongs to Nineveh in Nahum 3:1):

> Her chiefs [so read!] are in its midst like a roaring lion, tearing prey; they eat people, they take wealth and precious objects; they multiply widows within it.

Far from expressing "the lion's sovereign freedom" (Luzzatto), such language accords with Ezekiel's previous denunciations of Jerusalem's lawlessness and her murderous aristocracy (9:9; 11:6f.). By depicting the victims as human, the poet may be alluding to the idea expressed in 11:6 that the victims were better than their slayers; the humanness of the lion-hunters also accords with Ezekiel's theme of the moral superiority of the gentiles to Israel.

In the image of the vine, occurring for the third time (after chs. 15 and 17), the prophet repeats earlier expressions: the vine is planted by abundant water; it produces much fruit and many branches; it is uprooted and it is withered by the east wind (ch. 17), and then consumed by fire (ch. 15). But instead of representing worthless and wicked people, this vine "mothers" the bough whose presumptuousness brings ruin to all. Though on the surface it might appear that the terms of the story are morally neutral, what is evoked by the language of vs. 11aβ–b is unmistakably pejorative. "Highness of heart"—haughtiness—is an offense whose gist is forgetting God and usurping his place (cf. Deut 8:14). In prophecy *gbh* "be high" can, by itself, express this idea: e.g., "the women of Zion are haughty" (*gbhw,* Isa 3:16); Sodom and her daughters were haughty (*wtgbhynh,* Ezek 16:50); in metaphor, physical height is the equivalent: "I have brought the high tree low" (17:24). To God alone belongs height; hence his temple mount is "a high, towering mountain" (17:22; cf. 40:2). An ear attuned to prophetic idiom (or sapiential idiom, for that matter: Prov 16:18; 18:12) will detect an ominous note in the depiction of the vine's mighty bough towering among the clouds—a note of pride that goes before a fall. The premonition is confirmed in vs. 12, where it is said that the vine was uprooted and flung to the ground and a fire consumed its mighty bough. The consequential punishment of vs. 12 confirms our interpretation of vs. 11aβ–b as an account of guilt and speaks for its originality against those who would delete it for metric reasons. In none of the previous uses of the figure was the vine hurled to the ground (even when, as in 17:9, it was uprooted), because only here—in vs. 11aβ–b—

did it soar to the sky; and in no other passage did fire consume its bough, because only here is the bough, which reared itself skyward, the guilty member.

Some have taken this oracle to be a continuation of the eagle-cedar-vine allegory of ch. 17; the two are indeed similar. But our dirge differs from the political allegory of ch. 17 in its distinguishing between generations (parent-offspring) and its moral grounds for punishment (cruelty, pride), instead of the political ground of ch. 17. Both features reflect something of the themes of the intervening ch. 18. In the light of 18:10, "a violent [*pryṣ*] son," it is also interesting that Isa 35:9 parallels "lion" with "a violent [*pryṣ*] beast"; could the unusual adjective in ch. 18 have triggered the lion figure of ch. 19?

With regard to the dating of this dirge, it must be noted that the depiction of the final ruin of the kingdom as already accomplished is no ground for assigning its composition to post-fall times. The prophetic past is particularly common in dirges (e.g., Amos 5:2), a signal instance being Ezekiel's dirge over the king of Tyre, 28:12–19; Tyre and its king never were destroyed by the Babylonians.

XIX. Threat of a Second Exodus
(20:1–44)

20 1 In the seventh year, in the fifth month, on the tenth of the month,
some of the elders of Israel came to inquire of YHWH, and they sat
down before me. 2 The word of YHWH came to me: 3 Man, speak
to the elders of Israel and say to them: Thus said Lord YHWH: Is
it to inquire of me that you have come? By my life, I will not respond
to your inquiry, declares Lord YHWH.

4 Will you arraign, will you arraign them, man? Make known to
them the abominations of their fathers! 5 Say to them: Thus said
Lord YHWH:

On the day I chose Israel,
  solemnly swearing to the progeny of the house of Jacob,
    and making myself known to them in the land of Egypt;
  solemnly swearing to them, saying,
    I, YHWH, am your God—

6 on that day I solemnly swore to them to bring them out of the
land of Egypt to a land I had searched out for them—flowing with
milk and honey, the most desirable of all lands; and I said to them:
Throw away, each of you, the loathsome things before your eyes,
and do not defile yourselves with the idols of Egypt; I, YHWH,
am your God! 8 But they defied me and were unwilling to listen to
me; none threw away the loathsome things before their eyes, nor
did they abandon the idols of Egypt. I thought to pour out my
wrath on them, to spend my anger on them in the midst of the land
of Egypt; 9 but I acted for the sake of my name, that it should not
be desecrated in the sight of the nations among whom they were,
before whose eyes I made myself known to them, to bring them out of
the land of Egypt. 10 So I took them out of the land of Egypt and
led them into the wilderness.

11 I gave them my laws and my rules I made known to them, by
observing which man shall live. 12 I also gave them my sabbaths,
to serve as a sign between me and them, that it might be known that it
is I, YHWH, who sanctify them. 13 But the house of Israel defied

me in the wilderness: they did not follow my laws, they rejected
my rules, by observing which man shall live, and they desecrated
my sabbaths greatly. I thought to pour out my wrath on them in
the wilderness, to annihilate them; 14 but I acted for the sake of
my name, that it should not be desecrated in the sight of the nations
before whose eyes I had brought them out. 15 Yet I did solemnly
swear to them in the wilderness not to bring them to the land that
I gave them[a]—flowing with milk and honey, the most desirable
of all lands— 16 because they rejected my rules, and my laws—they
did not follow them, and they desecrated my sabbaths, for their
hearts went after their idols. 17 Yet my eye spared them so I would
not destroy them; I did not make an end of them in the wilderness.
18 I said to their children in the wilderness: Do not follow the
laws of your fathers, do not observe their rules, and do not defile
yourselves with their idols. 19 I, YHWH, am your God: follow my
laws, be careful to observe my rules, 20 and sanctify my sabbaths,
that they may serve as a sign between me and you that it may be
known that I, YHWH, am your God. 21 But the sons defied me: they
did not follow my laws, they were not careful to observe my rules, by
observing which man shall live; they desecrated my sabbaths greatly.
I thought to pour out my wrath on them, to spend my anger on them
in the wilderness; 22 [b]but I drew my hand back[b], acting for the
sake of my name, that it should not be desecrated in the sight of
the nations before whose eyes I brought them out. 23 Yet I did
solemnly swear to them in the wilderness to scatter them among the
nations and disperse them through the lands, 24 because they did
not observe my rules, they rejected my laws, they desecrated my
sabbaths, and their eyes were after the idols of their fathers. 25 And
I also gave them laws not good and rules by which they could
not live, 26 defiling them by their gifts, in that they delivered
up every first issue of the womb, so that I might desolate them,
so that they might know that I am YHWH.

27 Speak, then, to the house of Israel, man, and say to them:
Thus said Lord YHWH: In this, too, your fathers showed contempt
for me, committing trespass against me: 28 When I brought them to
the land that I solemnly swore to give them, they saw every high hill
and every leafy tree, and there they made their sacrifices, there they
placed their vexatious offerings, there they set their soothing savors,

[a] "them" in G S, but not in MT.
[b–b] Not in G S.

there poured their libations. 29 I said to them: What is the high-place
you hie to?—and it is called high-place to this day.

30 Say, then, to the house of Israel: Thus said Lord YHWH:
You defile yourselves in the manner of your fathers, you go whoring
after their loathsome things; 31 you defile yourselves by the offer
of your gifts and by delivering up your sons to the fire—your
idolatries of all sorts—to this day; shall I then respond to your
inquiry, house of Israel? By my life, declares Lord YHWH, I will
not respond to your inquiry!

32 And what has entered your minds shall never, never be, your
thinking, "We will become like the nations, like the families of the
earth, serving wood and stone." 33 By my life—declares Lord
YHWH—with a strong hand, with an outstretched arm and with
outpoured fury I will be king over you! 34 I will take you from among
the peoples and gather you from the lands through which you have
been scattered, with a strong hand and an outstretched arm and outpoured fury. 35 I will lead you into the wilderness of the peoples, and
enter into judgment with you there, face to face. 36 As I entered into
judgment with your fathers in the wilderness of Egypt, so will I enter
into judgment with you, declares Lord YHWH. 37 I will make you
pass under the staff and lead you [c]into the obligation of the covenant.
38 I will purge[c] you of those who rebel and transgress against me; I
will take them out of the land of their sojourn, but they shall not
come onto the soil of Israel; and you shall know that I am YHWH.

39 As for you, O house of Israel, thus said Lord YHWH: Each of
you go worship his idols, and afterward, if you do not listen to
me . . . And you shall not desecrate my holy name any more with
your gifts and your idols. 40 For in my holy mountain, in the high
mountain of Israel, declares Lord YHWH, there shall all the house
of Israel worship me, all of them, in the land; there I will accept
them, and there I will require your contributions and your choice
offerings, with all your holy things. 41 With a soothing savor I will
accept you, when I take you from among the peoples and gather you
from the lands through which you have been scattered; and I will
assert my sanctity through you in the sight of the nations. 42 And you
shall know that I am YHWH, when I lead you onto the soil of Israel,
the land I solemnly swore to give to your fathers.

43 Then you will remember your ways, and all your misdeeds by
which you defiled yourselves, and you will loathe yourselves for all

c–c G "in by number. And I will pick out of"; no reflection of MT *hbryt*.

the evil things that you did. 44 And you shall know that I am YHWH, when I act on your behalf for the sake of my name, and not according to your evil ways and your corrupt deeds, O house of Israel—declares Lord YHWH.

COMMENT

20:1. The year is 591; the date, 10 Ab (14 August [Parker-Dubberstein]), coincides with that of Jer 52:12 for the burning of the temple five years later; the portent is noted by Kimḥi. The errand on which the elders came to the prophet is as unknown as in the analogous cases of 8:1 and 14:1. A. Malamat (SVT 28 [1975], 130) connected it with the "false prophet" Hananiah's restoration prophecy (Jer 28:3f.), whose fulfilment would have been due just then (according to Malamat's plausible chronology; see table at end of his article). For discussion, see Structure and Themes.

3. On God's refusal to respond to sinners, see at 7:26 and ch. 14, Structure and Themes.

4. *Will you arraign.* Repeated in 22:2; 23:36; in all cases T renders unusually by *htwkḥ* "will you rebuke" instead of by a form of *'tpr' mn* "punish"—its normal equivalent of *špṭ*. "Arraign" comes closest to the intention, which is that the prophet bring a bill of indictment. Interrogative *h-* here conveys impassioned or indignant affirmation, as in I Sam 2:27; Jer 31:20 (BDB, p. 210a, def. c).

of their fathers. But according to vss. 30f., the present generation continues the way of their ancestors; this oracle, then, presents in realistic terms of generations the messages of chs. 16 and 23, in which Israel's continuous sin is allegorized as the career of a single wanton woman.

5. *On the day I chose Israel.* This is the only occurrence in Ezekiel of *baḥar,* the key Deuteronomic term for God's relation to Israel (Weinfeld, *Deuteronomy,* p. 127). For the Deuteronomist, election was "a dialectical process: it bespeaks the love of YHWH and requires loyal obedience on the part of his people. The word that establishes the relationship issues from YHWH, but it unmistakably demands a response from Israel who are addressed" (H. Wildberger, *THAT* I, p. 286). The verses that follow exemplify this two-way process perfectly. Wildberger suggests that Ezekiel's general avoidance of the term *baḥar* may stem from the complacency the doctrine of election was liable to foster—of which Deuteronomy, too, is apprehensive; cf. Deut 7:7f.; 9:4ff.

solemnly swearing. Lit. "I lifted my hand"; so again 36:7, with oath particle *'m* (cf. Jer 44:26), and 47:14; cf. also Num 14:30; Deut 32:40. The closest parallel in substance and language is Exod 6:8.

"On the day . . ." (vs. 5) and "on that day" (vs. 6) are paired again in 24:25f., from which passage it emerges clearly that the first clause is incomplete and is resumed and completed by the second. Accordingly, vs. 5 is preparatory for vss. 6f.; the highly charged "chose" is developed in two stages: vs. 5aβ–b, the general terms of God's commitment to Israel (God's initiative is primary); and vss. 6f., the details, including the demand for a reciprocating commitment. Vs. 5aβ–b consists of two parallel lines explicating the election as consisting of an oath and a self-revelation of YHWH as Israel's God. While in the first line each of these acts is expressed separately (*w'ś' ydy, w'wd'*), in the second the two are merged as though the substance of the oath was the assertion of YHWH's Godhood in Israel (this recalls 16:8b, where God takes an oath and covenants with the foundling, whereupon she becomes his). Only in the next stage of development (vss. 6f.) is each act clearly distinguished. The effect of this gradual unfolding of *baḥar* is to underscore its weight and the complexity and close relation of its elements.

6. The solemn oath of vs. 5 is now revealed as pertaining to the gift of a choice land for Israel; see, again, Exod 6:8—and note how Ezekiel, in contrast, makes the Israelites in Egypt, not the patriarchs, the recipients of the oath.

Ezekiel's disregard of the patriarchs is perhaps deliberate (for his acquaintance with them is proven by the term "house of Jacob" in vs. 5 and the reference to Abraham in 33:24), chosen for the effect gained by juxtaposing God's total gracious commitment to Israel with Israel's total rejection of him from their first encounter with him as a nation, which was in Egypt. Ezekiel could not well have started Israel's career of apostasy with the patriarchs, the archetypal pious recipients of God's blessings. On this, see the discussion in Brin, *Studies,* pp. 160ff.

I had searched out (tarti). In Pentateuchal traditions *twr* is used of God's advance scouting for campsites during Israel's trek through the wilderness (Deut 1:33; in Num 10:33 it is the ark that scouts), and of the twelve spies who spied out the land for the Israelites (Num 13:1, 16, etc.). The two motifs are here poetically combined in the depiction of God reconnoitering the earth to find the choicest land for Israel. Notably, *twr* also occurs in Num 15:39, a passage that reverberates through the first part of this oracle. *ṣby,* properly "desire" (cognate with Aramaic *ṣb'* "desire"; in Ezek 7:20 "glory"), as applied to the land (cf. Dan 11:16, 41 *'rṣ hṣby*), is synonymous with *'rṣ ḥmdh* (*ḥmd* "covet") of Jer 3:19 (followed by *nḥlt ṣby ṣb'wt gwym* "the heritage [consisting] of what is most desired by the nations") and *'rṣ ḥpṣ* (*ḥpṣ* "desire") of Mal 3:12. Such epithets, attested no earlier than the late monarchy, apparently belong to the patriotic sentiment of the time (cf. Deut 8:7–10) and surpass the traditional "land flowing with milk and honey" (also in Jer 11:5; 32:22), found in the Pentateuchal sources, especially in connection with the promise of land: Exod 3:8, 17; 13:5; 33:3; Lev 20:24; Num 13:27; 14:8; Deut 6:3; 11:9; 26:9, 15; 31:20.

7. YHWH's self-presentation as Israel's God is followed by its negative implication: the injunction to abandon Egypt's idols (for the pattern of twofold admonition ending with the sanction, "I, YHWH, am your God," cf. Lev 19:3). No such injunction given in Egypt is recorded in the Pentateuch or elsewhere. Josh 24:14 alludes to ancestral foreign gods worshiped in Mesopotamia and Egypt, and still with the Israelites in Joshua's time; this comes closest to Ezekiel, and it does not refer to an admonition to stop worshiping Egypt's idols. A midrash combines our passage with the allusion in I Sam 2:27 to a divine revelation to Eli's forefathers in Egypt, inferring that Aaron preceded Moses as a prophet in Egypt and proclaimed this admonition (*Tanḥuma Shemot* 27; cf. Rashi at I Sam 2:27). Antedating Israel's rebelliousness to the Egyptian sojourn is consistent with Ezekiel's portrait of original corruption in chs. 16 and 23. Remarking the silence of the sources regarding this primordial sin, Rashi comments: "God evidently suppressed his resentment over it for close to 900 years—from the time they were in Egypt to Ezekiel's day—overmastered by his love toward the people. But it reawakened because of their excessive sinfulness, illustrating the proverb 'Hatred wakens quarrels, but love covers all offenses' (Prov 10:12)" (based on *Leviticus Rabba* 7.1).

I, YHWH, am your God! To me you must cleave and me only worship (Eliezer of Beaugency, following Deut 13:5).

The loathsome things before (lit. *of*) *your eyes.* Cf. vs. 24, "their eyes were after the idols of their fathers." With "eyes" goes "heart" of vs. 16, and the phrase "you go whoring after their loathsome things" of vs. 30: all derive from and expand on Num 15:39, "so that you not go roving (*ttwrw* "reconnoitering") after your hearts and after your eyes, after which you go whoring."

8–9. Since YHWH made known to Pharaoh his intention to free Israel from Egypt (according to the priestly strand of the Exodus tradition, e.g., Exod 6:11; contrast 3:18 and 5:1), he could not now destroy them without injuring his reputation. This consideration, urged by Moses on God, obtains Israel's release from punishment after the Golden Calf episode and the fiasco of the spies (Exod 32:12; Num 14:15f.; Deut 9:28). Having derived it from the wandering traditions, Ezekiel antedates its operation to the Egyptian sojourn, where he places Israel's first rebellion.

In the sequel, when God's regard for his reputation restrains his deadly fury, he nonetheless inflicts punishment of a sort on the rebels (vss. 14f., 22f.); by analogy, the midrash inferred that the wicked in Egypt (most of the Israelites) were, in fact, destroyed during the plague of darkness—which was produced so that the Egyptians could not witness the disaster and gloat (*Mechilta, Pisḥa* 5; cited here by Kimḥi). The midrash is so far true to the spirit of this passage in that Ezekiel represents the Israelites at large as unwilling to separate themselves from Egypt's gods—unwilling to be redeemed on YHWH's terms. The Exodus was not something they sought but was imposed on them for YHWH's own purpose. This conception will be echoed in Ezekiel's depiction of his contemporaries in vs. 32 and the motive of the future redemption in vss. 33–34.

11. *I gave them.* At Sinai, as Neh 9:13f.—in evident dependence on our passage—interprets it (in accord with the priestly idea that the bulk of the laws was given through Moses at Sinai, Lev 26:46; for the sabbath, see Exod 31:12ff.).

by observing which man shall live. Lit. "which man will observe and live through them." The phrase and its context are genetically related to Lev 18:5 (the only occurrence of the phrase outside this prophecy); the combination of observance and life occurs in Ezek 18:9 and the phrase "laws of life" in 33:15. The laws are intended to bring life; obedience to them makes man the beneficiary of their virtue (cf. Deut 6:24f.). Deut 30:15–19 states forcefully that to follow the commandments is to choose life and blessing; not to follow them is to choose death and the curse. This iterated phrase (here, vss. 13, 21) stresses God's initial good will toward Israel, to be replaced by retribution in the face of their obduracy (vs. 25).

12. *that it might be known.* By Israel and others; the subject of the infinitive being indefinite ("for one to know"), it has the effect of a passive. Cf. Exod 9:16, "that my fame be recounted"; Num 9:15, ". . . was erected"; Isa 18:3, ". . . is raised . . . is blown"; Jer 25:34, "to be slaughtered"; Ps 67:3, "that . . . be known" (=to make known; as here).

The purpose clause is a virtual citation of Exod 31:13: observance of God's sabbaths (his, because he rested on that day [Exod 31:17, based on Gen 2:2f.]) is a token that he consecrated Israel to him. "It is an important sign for them that I gave them my rest day for their own rest—a manifest testimony to my consecrating them to me" (Rashi). Note that when this purpose clause is repeated in vs. 20 the last phrase is replaced by "that I, YHWH, am their God"; consecration to YHWH and having him as God are equivalent.

Singling out the sabbath from all the laws attests to its significance as a distinguishing feature of YHWH's people. While the sabbath is mentioned in later oracles (22:8, 26; 23:38) and its sanctification is a duty of the priesthood in the future state (44:24), its importance here seems greater, comparable only to that assigned to it in Jer 17:19–27; Isa 56:2, 4, 6; Neh 13:18. Cooke regards the emphasis as disproportionate and therefore secondary (by a "scribe zealous for the Law"), and Eichrodt ascribes it to a priestly glossator arguing its theological foreignness to Ezekiel (in *Lex tua veritas,* pp. 65–74—but the disappearance of the sabbath in the latter part of the oracle is not, as Eichrodt asserted, suspicious; Eichrodt overlooked the disappearance of "laws and rules," from which their secondary character is surely not to be inferred). Yet the emphasis laid on the sabbath in this oracle is not inordinate when account is taken of the prominence given here to Israel's propensity to assimilate to the nations (esp. vss. 32f.). As a distinctively Israelite custom, the sabbath may well have become a touchstone of loyalty to YHWH from the time of the assimilatory reforms of Manasseh onward. On this ground the fitness of Jer 17's estimate of the fateful importance of the sabbath for the late preexilic situation in Judah may be also defended (M. Greenberg, *'Iyyunim be-sefer yirmeyahu* [n.p. 1971], II, pp. 27–37). Ezekiel portrayed Israel's origins, in his typical fashion, as reflecting the crises and issues of his time.

13–17. The schematic presentation ignores all the particulars of the Pentateuchal traditions; conflicts with the traditions may be due to the schematization, or to Ezekiel's not knowing them as we have them. Violation of God's laws by the generation of the Exodus occurred in the worship of the Golden Calf (Exod 32) and the disregard of the sabbath in the manna episode (Exod 16). God intended to annihilate the people because they worshiped the calf, and again because they mistrusted his ability to deliver the Canaanites into their hands (Num 14). In both cases Moses dissuaded him by appeals to his self-interest, prominent among them being regard for the injury to his reputation that would result from Israel's destruction. But after the second episode God swore that the Exodus generation would not live to enter the promised land.

That God spared the people (vs. 17) has been interpreted as an expression of pity on the basis of Ps 78:38, "But he, being merciful, forgave iniquity and would not destroy" (Davidson). However, there is no room in this oracle for any motive of divine action other than concern for the authority (sanctification) of the divine name; *ḥus 'al* here means no more than to spare, i.e., not to inflict destruction upon. (Ezekiel explicitly ascribes a tender sentiment to God only in 39:25, *riḥem* "have compassion for.")

18–20. No such divine call (through a prophet, presumably) is found in the Pentateuchal traditions, but the idea that God continually summoned his wayward people to return to him through a succession of prophets is a commonplace of Deuteronomic historiography and Jeremiah; see Structure and Themes.

21–22. The repetition of the scheme of vss. 13–14 with respect to the wilderness generation has no antecedent in our Pentateuch traditions; these do not identify the offenders in the episodes of rebellion after the condemnation of the Exodus generation as belonging to the next generation (e.g., the sabbath-breaker, Num 15:32ff.; Korah's rebellion and its aftermath, Num 16–17; idolatry at Shittim, Num 25). Nor is there a known source for the idea that God thought to destroy them but relented for his name's sake; has Ezekiel adapted to his scheme the account of Num 14, in which Moses dissuades God a second time from destroying fickle Israel (according to our narrative, still the Exodus generation)?

22. *drew my hand back.* That is, refrained from acting on my intention; for the idiom see Lam 2:8; Ps 74:11, and cf. "curbed (lit. drew back) his wrath" in Ps 78:38, also of God's sparing the rebels in the wilderness. Since the clause does not appear in G S, moderns have declared it an addition, noting that it differs from the parallels in vss. 9 and 14. It may be that the *Vorlage* of G S lacked these words, but that is still not a decisive argument against their authenticity, since it is precisely in character for repetitions in Ezekiel to show such variation (cf. *trty* [vs. 6]—*ntty* [vs. 15]; the final clause of vss. 12 and 20; *lklwt 'py bhm* [vs. 8]—*lklwtm* [vs. 13]—*'śyty 'wtm klh* [vs. 17]—*lklwt 'py bm* [vs. 21]; vs. 16—vs. 24). "I drew back my hand" is here an out-of-pattern parallel to "My eye spared them so I would not destroy them"—also unique—in vs. 17. The grammatical objection that *whšbty* as a perfect consecutive violates syntax (Zimmerli, Eichrodt) is mistaken; the penultimate stress shows it to be ordinary perfect (in contrast to, say, *whqmwty* of 16:60), which, in accord with Ezekiel's loose style, occasionally appears where the rule calls for imperfect consecutive (e.g., 13:6, 8; 19:12b; 25:12; 37:2, 7, 10; 40:24, 35; 41:3, 13; 42:15); this may show the influence of Aramaic, which does not have consecutive tenses.

23. The Pentateuchal traditions are silent about this remarkable oath to exile the people, taken by God even before they entered the land. But Ps 106:27 refers to it (read the first word *wlhpyṣ* [|| *wlzrtm*] as here) in connection with the episode of the spies, where, fittingly, it is Israel's punishment for rejecting the "desirable land" (vs. 24; this is reflected in TpJ to Num 14:1: *"The people wept that night* and that night was appointed for them for weeping for generations to come"; cf. *Taanit* 29a, which makes the ninth of Ab the fateful date of God's oath in the wilderness and of the destruction of the first and second temples; cited by Kimḥi here). By placing this oath after the apostasy of the wilderness generation, Ezekiel depicts it as punishment for the threefold rebellion he has described in vss. 8, 13, and 21. Since the people proved to be confirmed rebels, God sealed their fate even before they entered the promised land; it was only a question of time till that fate was realized. Comparable is the condemnation of the Amorites in Gen 15:13–16: in Abraham's time the iniquity of the Amorites already justified predetermining them to expulsion after four hundred years—during which centuries their measure of iniquity would be filled, thus justifying the decree. How God saw to it that his decree of exile against Israel would be warranted by a full measure of guilt is described in the following verses.

25–26. Because Israel consistently rejected God's good, life-giving laws, God's condign punishment was to replace them with not-good laws, by observing which one would gain not life but death (the circumlocution *lo tobim* conforms with *lo yiḥyu bahem;* cf. 18:18; 36:31). These are then exemplified by child sacrifice, at once a murderous pagan practice and an abomination worthy of severest condemnation. By this anti-gift God only confirmed the people in their choice of laws countering God's (cf. vss. 18f.); this choice led them inevitably to adopt the deadly laws of the pagans (cf. Deut 12:31, which illustrates the pagan mode of worship by the custom of burning children).

The shocking idea that God misleads those who anger him into sin, for which he then destroys them, already appeared in 14:9 (the misled prophet); thence is proven the error of the modern evasive rendering of *lm'n 'šmm* here as "so that I might horrify them" (*RSV, NEB,* Cooke, Zimmerli et al.). It is essentially the same as God's hardening of Pharaoh's heart so that his ruin might be a lasting object lesson (Exod 9:16; 10:2); or the charge to Isaiah to "dull the people's mind, stop its ears, and seal its eyes, lest, seeing with its eyes and hearing with its ears, it also grasp with its mind and repent and heal itself" (Isa 6:9ff.); or the complaint of Isa 63:17, "Why, YHWH, do you make us stray from your ways, and harden our hearts not to fear you?" (cf. also I Kings 18:36b; M. Greenberg, "'You have turned their hearts backward,' I Kings 18:36," in *Studies in Memory of J. Heinemann* [Hebrew] [Jerusalem: Magnes Press, 1981], pp. 52–67, reviews the exegetical history of such passages). T mitigates the language: "I removed them [from me] and delivered them into the power of their stupid impulse; they went and made decrees that were not right" (cf. Ps 81:12f., "But my people would not listen to me . . . so I let them go after their willful heart, that they might follow their own devices"). Davidson follows suit: ". . . for what we now speak of as permitted by God is in the OT often attributed to His direct agency. As a judicial punishment . . . He left them to follow their own ideas, which they came to attribute to His authority."

Moderns, seeking a historical basis for the allegation of vs. 25, have found it in such a categorical demand as Exod 22:28b (34:19): "You must give me the firstborn of your sons" (in 13:1, "the first issue of the womb"); on this supposition, the practice of redemption ordained in 34:20 and 13:11–13 is assumed to be a later modification of this originally harsh rule making over all firstborn males as sacrifices to the deity. Outside of our passage no evidence for such an interpretation of these laws, or for such a practice, exists; indeed, it is intrinsically improbable. On the other hand, our vs. 25 was not spun out of thin air. The polemic against child sacrifice (to YHWH) in Deut 12:29ff.; Jer 7:31; 19:5; 32:35 indicates that at least from the time of the last kings of Judah it was popularly believed that YHWH accepted, perhaps even commanded, it. The abovementioned laws declaring all firstborn males the property of YHWH (to be "transferred" [*h'byr*] to him) signified their naturally dedicated status; normally they were to be redeemed, but their peculiar fitness for sacrifice as a token of extraordinary devotion in emergencies appears to have been widely held (II Kings 3:27; Micah 6:7; see further comment at 16:20). Unique to our passage is the fusion of terms drawn from the firstborn law (*h'byr kl pṭr rḥm* "transfer every first issue of the womb") with that of burning children (*h'byr b'š,* vs. 31), resulting in the unprecedented and incredible charge that Israelites regularly offered up every firstborn as a sacrifice—a manifest exaggeration.

27. *Speak, then* . . . Vss. 27–29 in some way cap the list of Israel's provocations; *laken,* indicating consequence, here may express climax. For other rhetorical uses of *laken* (e.g., emphasis, urgency) see 11:7; 36:5–7.

showed contempt . . . *trespass.* Only here and in Num 15:30 does *giddep* refer to acts; otherwise it refers to words ("revile"—II Kings 19:6, 22; Ps 44:17; cf. *gdwph* in Ezek 5:15). The "trespass" (*m'l*—violation of sancta; J. Milgrom, *JAOS* 96 [1976], 236–47) consisted in violating the provision of a single sanctuary. Milgrom assumes that the priestly sources (to which the term belongs) premised "that the tabernacle would continue as a roving sanctuary in the land" (ibid., p. 237, fn. 9); that may be, but it cannot be inferred from our passage, since Ezekiel might have combined the priestly term *m'l* with the Deuteronomic law—from which our *gb'h, rm-* and *'ṣ* in vs. 28 plainly derive (Deut 12:2). From Ezek 6:13 it appears that "idols" (*gillulim*) were the object of worship at the local shrines (*bamot*); however, Ezekiel included in "idolatry" illegitimate modes of worshiping YHWH; see Structure and Themes.

28. *vexatious offerings. k's qrbn-* "vexation of offering" is the equivalent of *qrbn k's-* "offering of vexation, vexatious offering." Other inverted construct pairs are *šny twl't / twl't šny* (Lev 14:6; Exod 25:4), and *mbṭḥ 'z / 'z mbṭḥ-* (Prov 14:26; 21:22).

29. *What is the high-place* (habbama) *you hie* (habba'im) *to?* So Moffatt cleverly renders the pun, to call attention to which the Hebrew attaches an unnecessary article to the second word, assimilating it to the first. A similar pun occurs in the Talmud on zimma (Lev 19:29)—*zo ma hi* "this woman, what is she?" (*Nedarim* 51a). Moderns regard this pun as unbefittingly frivolous and hence secondary (Eichrodt: "an etymological joke . . . One need not expect any . . . profundity . . . in such glossatorial puns"); however, the ancients had no qualms about the use of paronomasia even in the most serious context. (Aristotle, *Rhetoric,* Book II, ch. 23.28 [trans. W. R. Roberts, in *The Basic Works of Aristotle,* ed. R. McKeon (New York: Random House, 1941)], calls it "to draw meanings from names.") "But it may have its place in grave and excited speech, giving it a tinge of sharpness and sarcasm. Thus Demosthenes . . . wields the play upon words as a mighty weapon of his *deinotēs* [cleverness], and in a similar manner was it employed by the greatest prophets in their most earnest sermons" (Casanowicz, *Paronomasia,* p. 13).

The question insinuates reproach or contempt; cf. II Kings 9:22, *mh hšlwm* "what peace!" (the other examples in BDB, p. 552 b, def. c, have a demonstrative, e.g., I Sam 29:3, *mh h'brym h'lh* "what are these Hebrews [doing here]!"). The punning question reflects the disrepute into which the word *bama* had fallen among circles influenced by Deuteronomy. Like *maṣṣeba* "pillar," formerly licit (e.g., Gen 28:18, 22; 31:13; Exod 24:4) but banned in Deuteronomy (16:22; cf. II Kings 17:10), *bama,* formerly licit (I Sam 9:12ff., but also denoting gentile shrines, Num 21:28; 33:52), is in Deuteronomistic literature reserved for gentile or illegal Israelite shrines—i.e., Israelite places of worship outside of the Jerusalem temple. This usage is reflected in Ibn Caspi's comment here (which explains the contemptuous pun): "[*bama*] is not employed anywhere in the Torah or the rest of Scripture of a site dedicated to God [! cf. I Sam 9:12ff.], only *mizbeaḥ* [altar] or *miqdaš* [sanctuary]. The prophet censures their having a place of congregating called *bama* . . . as though saying, Why do you come to a site called *bama* after the manner of the gentiles?" The imitation etiological notice (for the genuine article see, e.g., Gen 26:33) grounding the current term *bama* in God's reproachful query hints, through its formulaic ending "to this say," at the currency of the issue of legitimacy of *bama*-worship at the time of this oracle.

31. *your idolatries . . . sorts. lkl* has the summarizing, generalizing force also found in 6:9 (BDB, p. 514 b, def. [d]). Others follow Ehrlich, who connects *l-* with *nṭm'* ("defile yourselves with all your idols"), but Ezekiel regularly uses *b-* with that verb—as in vss. 7, 18, 30, 43 of this oracle, and in 23:7, 30; 37:23 (in 44:25 *l-* means "for").

32. *We will become.* An echo of I Sam 8:20 (see Structure and Themes), expressing the wish of the people, not their despair (as Herrmann, Zimmerli, and others take it). It is this defiant wish that arouses God's indignation (here, vs. 33); to despair he responds with encouraging exhortation (33:10ff.; 37:12ff.).

serving wood and stone. Cf. Deut 4:28; 28:36, 64; 29:16. Evidently imputed to the people derisively.

33. *with strong hand . . . outstretched arm . . .* A Deuteronomic expression alluding to God's marvels worked against the Egyptians (Weinfeld, *Deuteronomy,* p. 329); here, however, it forms an *inclusio* around vss. 33–34, which are an oath (on *ḥay 'ani 'im lo* see comments to 3:6, "surely if I sent," and 5:11, "By my life!") complementing God's decisive "it shall never, never be!" of vs. 32. God swears

(vs. 33)	*with a strong hand,* etc.	I will be king over them
(vs. 34)	I will lead them out of exile and gather them	*with a strong hand,* etc.

The *inclusio* emphasizes by repetition the drastic measures to countervail Israel's plan of assimilating to the heathen; against whom are they to be taken? Medievals generally and some moderns say: against the captor nations; but this seems unlikely. God's enemy throughout the oracle has been Israel, and the opposition of the two reaches a kind of climax in vs.

32. Moreover, the unique coinage *ḥema šᵉpuka* "outpoured fury" echoes not only vss. 8, 13, and 21, in which it is said that in the past God desisted from pouring his fury upon Israel, but also the repeated predictions that God will pour out his fury on Jerusalem, found in 7:8; 9:8; 14:19; 22:22 (fulfilled according to 36:18 and Lam 2:4). Ezekiel never uses the expression in describing God's action against Israel's captors (30:15 is no exception, since Sin [Syene] is not a captor). We conclude that Ezekiel characteristically utilizes a traditional phrase with a shocking twist: in the new Exodus the ferocity that tradition asserted was unleashed upon Egypt in the old one will be turned against rebellious Israel in order to force it finally to accept what it never had before—God's kingship over it in the land he chose for it. Jeremiah partly anticipated Ezekiel in this skewed usage; see Jer 21:5: "I will battle you [Jerusalem] with an outstretched hand, with a strong arm, in anger, in fury, and in great wrath."

35. *wilderness of the peoples.* The Syro-Arabian desert, bounded by various peoples. "Face to face" occurs in Gen 32:31; Exod 33:11; Deut 5:4; 34:10, "on each occasion, of a personal contact between God and man in circumstances of peculiar awe" (Cooke). Here the absence of third parties to the judgment is also implied, "so that no gentiles witness your misfortune and gloat" (Kimḥi; cf. the sequence of vss. 8–11 and comment to vss. 8–9).

37. *pass under the staff.* An allusion to the manner of (arbitrarily) counting off animals for the tithe (Lev 27:32f.), described in detail in *Mishnah Bekhorot* 9.7. The phrase signifies not mere counting (for which cf. Jer 33:13) but selection—in Leviticus for dedication, here for destruction. "As when counting sheep, one holds a staff and counts one by one, setting the tenth apart as tithe, so shall I count you off so that the sinner shall be destroyed" (Kimḥi). Vs. 37a describes the sifting and selection of those who will be made to accept the obligation of the covenant in the second half of the verse.

lead you into the obligation of the covenant. This rendering of the hapax *msrt* follows Hayyuj (cited in B-Y): "As to *msrt* (*hbryt*), I take it as cognate with *w'srh 'sr* (Num 30:4, "she imposes an obligation"; lit. "binds a bond"), with *'alep* elided between the *mem* and the *samek* and unwritten; the primary form is *ma'soret* like *maḥgoret* ("girdle," Isa 3:24)." A parallel elision of ' occurs in the same root at Qoh 4:14, *ha(')surim* "the prisoners." Such an understanding underlies Aquila "bonds," Symmachus "collar"; Kimḥi; cf. tannaitic *msrt byd-* "be under obligation" (conventionally "to have a tradition") which alternates with *šbw'h byd-* "be bound by oath" in an anecdote about keeping temple-guild secrets (*Palestinian Talmud, Yoma* 3.9; *Tosefta Kippurim* 2.7; with this compare the combination of *šbw'h* and *'sr* in Num 30:11, 14). This rare usage in tannaitic Hebrew, recorded only in the speech of a scion of temple-guildsmen, appears to preserve a sense descended from biblical times and in a ritual context (as here); it was otherwise displaced by the sense "tradition," derived from *masar* "transmit"—a very common verb in postbiblical Hebrew. S *mrdwt'* elsewhere renders *mwsr* "discipline, chastisement"—in parallelism with *šbṭ* "rod" at Prov 13:24; 22:15; 23:13, and indicating an ominous interpretation of "causing to pass under the rod" (cf. Exod 21:20); Kara (second interpretation) and Eliezer of Beaugency also interpret *msrt* as from *ysr,* though the noun pattern would be anomalous from such a root (hence Cornill simply reads *mwsr*). Yet the overtones of *šbṭ mwsr* "rod of discipline" are indeed present, due to the context (cf. the preceding repeated, alliterative *nŠPṬ* "enter into judgment") and the quasi-parallelism of *šbṭ* and *msrt,* which cannot but evoke the commonplace word-pair connected with chastisement. G "in number" has been preferred by many critics to MT (*BHS, RSV:* "I will let you go in by number") as paralleling the counting image in the first part of the verse; accordingly, the hapax is emended to the supposed *Vorlage bmspr,* and the following *hbryt,* not represented in G, is judged a dittograph of *wbrwty* of the next verse and eliminated. Against this is the inappropriateness of *hby' bmspr* in our context; I Chron 9:28 shows that it means "to take the count of items as they come in" (or go out; cf. Isa 40:26) in order to check that all are present. But it is precisely for weeding out the wicked in judgment that the people are "passed under the staff"; hence *hby' bmspr* signifies the opposite of what the context calls for. Furthermore, it is not at all clear that G read *mspr* here—from which common word, as Cornill observed, the hapax *msrt* is not likely to have arisen; indeed, it is probable in the light of G's *exerithmēsan* "they counted out" for *wymsrw* at Num 31:5 that its *en arithmō* here reflects nothing else than *bmsrt,* understood as from dialectal Aramaic *msr* "count, number" (on which see Z. Ben-Ḥayyim, "Traditions in the Hebrew Language, with Special Reference to the Dead Sea Scrolls," *Aspects of the Dead Sea Scrolls,* ed. C. Rabin and Y. Yadin, Scripta Hierosolymitana 4 [Jerusalem: 1958], pp. 212f.). In view of the unsuitable meaning yielded by "number" here, it seems best to take G as both semantically inferior in its interpretation of *msrt* and textually inferior in not representing *hbryt* (by an error of haplography). The high incidence of repetition and alliteration in vss. 33–40 speaks for the originality of the sequence *hbryt wbrty.* The expression *hby' bmsrt hbryt* is patterned after *hby' bbryt* (I Sam 20:8) "bring into a covenant" and *hb'y b'lh* "impose an oath" (Ezek 17:13). The sense of vs. 37, then, is: after sifting the people, God will impose his covenant obligation on those who survive the selection; this is the future counterpart of the past imparting of laws and rules in the desert of Egypt (vss. 11f.).

38. *I will purge.* This verse returns to the topic of vs. 37a and elaborates it; its conclusion—just before the recognition formula—echoes the beginning of its subsection and thus closes it: "for I will take them out of the land of their sojourn" || "I will take you out from among the peoples

. . . from the lands" (vs. 34). The rebels against God (cf. 2:3) will be expelled from "the land of their sojourn" (what Canaan was to the patriarchs, Gen 17:8; Exod 6:4), where they preferred to remain and become like the nations. Their fate is that appointed in 13:9 for the false prophets of the exile. The cardinal point made in this subsection is that in the first, pre–land entry stage of the redemption, rebels will be purged; this point is stated in the selection figure of vs. 37a and enlarged upon in vs. 38; it will bring home to Israel the sovereignty of YHWH.

39. *Each of you go worship his idols.* Ironical, like "Come to Bethel and sin!" (Amos 4:4), "Very well, then, fulfil your vows [to the Queen of Heaven]; by all means perform them!" (Jer 44:25). In place of "go worship" G reads "remove," eliminating the irony.

and afterward, if you do not listen to me . . . This dubious rendering of a puzzling sequence takes it to be an incomplete conditional, like "But now, if you forgive their sin . . ." (Exod 32:32—supply "well and good" [see GKC § 159 dd]); here it is supposed that a threat is left unspoken, namely, "I will give you your due." With this and the preceding, medievals compared the ironic, threatening verse, "Rejoice, young man, in your youth . . . and follow the path of your heart and the sight of your eyes; but know that for all these things God will bring you to judgment" (Qoh 11:9); moderns regard the last clause ("but know," etc.) as from a different, orthodox glossator.

Some moderns understand *'m 'ynkm* ("if you do not") as an oath expression: "surely you will (obey me)" and connect it with what follows; but the oath particles are *'m l'* plus finite verb, not *'m 'yn* plus participle.

desecrate my holy name with your gifts . . . idols. The clear implication is that the rejected forms of worship were directed toward YHWH; cf. the "desecrations of the name" in Lev 18:21; 20:3 ("Molech" sacrifices of children; see Structure and Themes); 21:6 (priestly misconduct); 22:32 (impropriety in sacrificial procedure).

As here rendered the sentence predicts an end to the defiled worship of the people, started in the distant past by divine decree (vs. 26) and lasting into the present (vss. 30f.); this interpretation connects with the following verse. However, the verse is undeniably difficult, for which reason it may not be superfluous to adduce a medieval view that is philologically problematic (it takes *'ḥr 'm* in the unattested sense "since") but highly suggestive: "Each of you go worship his idols, since you won't listen to me but insist on being like the gentiles. Better that than desecrating my holy name with your [abominable] gifts. Better to forsake me altogether and worship idols than pretend to follow my laws but in fact forsake my ways!" (Kara)

40. *my holy mountain.* The contrast with "every high hill" (vs. 28) indicates that Zion's hill—the temple mount—is meant (as in Isa 27:13; 56:7; 65:11; 66:20; Joel 2:1; 4:17; Zeph 3:11; Zech 8:3; Dan 9:20) rather than the mountainous land of Israel in general (Isa 11:9; 57:13).

The appositional "high mountain of Israel" also means Jerusalem, as in 17:22f.; cf. 40:2—though in 34:14 (*hry* plural!) the similar phrase alludes to the whole land. That the site determines acceptable and unacceptable worship is underlined by the repeated *šam* "there" in both this verse and in the contrasting vs. 28. Less specific but still expressing the importance of location is the pun *b'rṣ . . . 'rṣm* "in the land . . . I will accept them," associating acceptable worship with the native country—an implicit rejection of any other site (see Structure and Themes). Finally, the stress on the integrity of the people—*kl . . . klh* "all . . . all of it"—appears to exclude a restoration of worship before the restoration of the whole people.

your choice offerings. When *rešit* occurs with another offering term it has the meaning of "the best, choice": "the choice portions of all the offerings" (*mnḥh;* I Sam 2:29); "the best of all firstfruits" (*bkwry,* Exod 23:19; 34:26; Ezek 44:30; cf. Num 18:12f. where *rešit* is in apposition to *ḥeleb* "fat," i.e., choice part); cf. H.-P. Müller, *THAT* I, p. 714. For a parallel, see *mbḥr ndrykm* "your choice votive offerings" (Deut 12:11); the explication in *Sifre Deut.* § 69 that votive and other offerings must be of choice (i.e., fattened) animals illumines our phrase as well. *maś'ot* "offerings" (Gen 43:34; II Sam 11:8; only here for sacred gifts) derives from *nś'* "bear, offer gift," as in *ś^e'u minḥa* (Ps 96:8). An older view takes *rešit* as "firstlings/fruits" (G S [double rendering]; T "first [yield] of your kneading trough" [*mš'rwtykm!* as Exod 12:34; cf. Ezek 44:30 and Num 15:21]) and is followed by some moderns (e.g., Fohrer, Zimmerli); the construction must then be inverted (i.e., for *maś'ot rešitkem* "your firstfruit offerings")—a common enough phenomenon (e.g., *'ene gabhut* for *gabhut 'ene,* Isa 2:11; *q^edoš hekaleka* for *hekal q^edoš^eka,* Ps 65:5; see H. Yalon, *Pirqe lašon* [Jerusalem: Bialik Institute, 1971], p. 158, fn. 26).

Sound play is prominent in this passage. Within vs. 40b there is much alliteration: ŠM 'DRŠ 'T TRMTkM w'T RŠT MŚ'TkM—like the repetition and alliteration in vs. 40a, designed to emphasize the thought; similarly between our verse and vs. 31, with phonetic and substantive variation pointing to contrast:

(vs. 31) *wbś't mtntykm lkl glwlykm 'drš*
(vs. 40) *'drš r'šyt mś'wtykm bkl qdšykm*

The choice of *rešit,* with its overtone of firstling offerings, also recalls the contrasting horror of firstborn sacrifice (vss. 26, 31).

41. *With a soothing savor.* That is, by means of the sacrificial offerings —properly made (contrast vs. 28)—you will win my favor; contrast "vexatious offerings" of vs. 28. For *raṣa b-* "(find) accept(able) through" cf. *hitraṣṣa b-* "make oneself acceptable by means of" in I Sam 29:4.

assert my sanctity. Sanctity here is the equivalent of majesty, sovereign authority, as in Isa 5:16 (|| *ygbh* "be exalted") or Lev 10:3 (|| *'kbd* "be glorified"). By not destroying Israel in the past God's name was not publicly desecrated (vss. 9, 14, etc.); by his marvelous restoration of them in the future his holy majesty will be affirmed before all men.

43. *remember . . . loathe*. The combination of emotions as in 6:9; but it will occur not, as there, in the exile but—conform to thought of the intervening 16:61, 63—only after the restoration.

44. *act on your behalf*. This is the sense of *'aśa 'itt-* (= *'im*) as in Exod 34:10; Deut 1:30, distinct from *'asa 'ot-* "deal hostilely with" (Ezek 17:17 and other passages cited in the comment there).

for my name's sake. Though evoking vss. 9, 14, 22, in this context the reference is rather to the affirmative sense alluded to in vs. 41.

corrupt deeds. *nišḥat* "corrupt" (nif'al) is found only here and in the Flood story, Gen 6:11f. (of the "earth"); *hišḥitu 'alila(-lotam)* "they have corrupted their deeds," only in Zeph 3:7 (of the Jerusalemites) and Ps 14:1 (of the base man).

STRUCTURE AND THEMES

The oracle begins with a date formula and its occasion—the arrival of some elders for an oracle of YHWH. A revelation formula (vs. 2) introduces God's refusal to respond, enforced by an oath (vs. 3) and followed by an exhortation to arraign the elders (vs. 4). A messenger formula ("thus said Lord YHWH") starts the recitation of Israel's vicious early history, set out in three stages: the slave generation; the slaves emancipated and in the wilderness; their descendants (vss. 5–26). These stages are framed by YHWH's making himself known to them as their God in Egypt (vs. 5) and his resolve, finally, to desolate them so that they might know he is YHWH (vs. 26). A fourth stage of sinning, after the settlement, sets in with *laken* (vs. 27), a renewed exhortation to speak, and the messenger formula (vss. 27–29). This stage concludes with a name-midrash on *bama* "high-place." A second *laken*, again followed by exhortation to speak and a messenger formula, introduces two consequences: (1) God's refusal to respond to the present continuers of past sins (vss. 30–31; vs. 31b echoes vs. 3b even to the oath—note the inversion!); and (2) his firm resolve to force his kingship on them and drive them from exile into a new judgment in the wilderness (vss. 32–38, ending with the recognition formula). A fresh address ("And you . . ."), followed yet again by a messenger formula, introduces the final reconciliation between Israel and God, beginning with an ironic invitation to continue idolatry and followed immediately by prediction of the ideal worship on God's holy mountain (vss. 39–42). The section ends (vss. 42–44) with a recognition formula extended by an evocation of God's oath—the oath with which the arraignment commenced (vs. 6). Emotion subsides in a coda, analogous to 16:61ff., foretelling Israel's shame over its misdeeds (vss. 43f.) and ending in another extended recognition formula.

For most critics the complexity of this oracle indicates the presence of secondary elements. The resumption of vs. 3b (*'m 'drš lkm*) in vs. 31 appears to round off the opening theme, and this appearance serves as the ground for declaring vss. 32–44 to be secondary. The assumption that the nation is in exile in vss. 34–38, 42, and the (alleged) despair expressed in vs. 32 (but see comments) are said to point to a post-fall date: "Addressing himself to the despairing exiles, the prophet resumes the theme of wilderness wandering and expands his earlier prophecy with words of hope for Israel's restoration" (Carley; Zimmerli speaks of supplementing by "a promise of salvation"). One may wonder, however, whether such terms do justice to the angry tone of most of vss. 32–44, whether the forecast of a compulsory exodus from exile, a purge in the "wilderness of the peoples," and the future self-loathing of the redeemed really depart from the condemnations of the first part of the oracle. Yet it must be admitted that there is disjointedness in the oracle that throws doubt on its unity. Our inquiry begins with structure: to what extent do the parts of the oracle cohere and exhibit an overall design?

A. Israel's past rebelliousness (vss. 5–29)

The historical survey unfolds in four stages, formally three graduated likes and a fourth unlike (for this pattern, see Y. Zakovitch, *"For Three . . . and for Four"* [Hebrew] [Jerusalem: Makor, 1979]). We note the variation within the repetitions.

1. In Egypt (vss. 5–10)
   - a. YHWH reveals himself as Israel's God
   - b. He swears to take them out and bring them to the promised land
   - c. He commands them to abandon Egypt's idols
   - d. The people refuse
   - e. God refrains from destroying them for his name's sake (no punishment)
   - f. He takes them out into the wilderness (bridge to next stage)
2. First wilderness generation (vss. 11–17)
   - a,c. God gives them good laws and sabbaths to consecrate them (= his self-revelation and his command to abandon idolatry in 1, as follows from the equivalence of vss. 5b, 7b, and 12b [with which cf. vs. 20b])
   - d. The people refuse
   - e. God refrains from destroying them for his name's sake, but
   - g. He swears they won't enter the promised land (vs. 15, a punishment partially countering vs. 6)
   - f. He spares their children (bridge to next stage)
3. Second wilderness generation (vss. 18–26)
   - c. God commands them to forsake conduct of the fathers and

a. Accept him as God
d. The people refuse
e. God refrains from destroying them for his name's sake, but
g. He swears he will scatter them among the nations (vs. 23, a punishment countering vs. 6) and
g′. He gives them bad laws and pollutes their cult (vs. 25, a punishment countering vss. 11f.)

4. In the land (vss. 27–29)

The fourth stage of rebellion (*bamot*) diverges formally from the preceding three. Moreover, despite opening with *laken,* it does not seem to be a consequence of the foregoing but rather to interfere with the argument that continues with *laken* of vs. 30. Hence many critics regard it as secondary ("a disciple wished to fill out the picture of Israel's sinfulness after the settlement," Stalker). However, since God's rejection of Israel has been completed by the end of the third stage, the pattern of God's address and the people's defiance cannot be repeated. After vss. 23–26 Israel can only act out its assigned role and defile itself through a perverse cult until it is desolated. Accordingly, vss. 27–29 show Israel practicing *bamot* worship, disdained by God. In that way *laken* (vs. 27) suggests that Israel's cultic misconduct in its land was but a consequence of God's punitive measures described at the end of the third stage.

B. Application and consequences (vss. 30–44)

B1. God's refusal to respond to inquiry (vss. 30–31)

With vs. 30 (*laken*) the lesson of the history is applied to the present audience (not merely the elders but, as in vs. 27, the entire "house of Israel"): since they continue in their fathers' way, they cannot expect a divine response to their inquiry (vss. 30f.). Instead of ending here—and leaving one puzzled over the elaborate grounding of God's refusal to respond (contrast the simple retort of 14:1–3)—the oracle turns abruptly to denounce the people's thoughts and to announce God's counter-plans.

B2. The new Exodus and God's plan realized (vss. 32–44)

This section is divisible in several ways. Closing recognition formulas delimit: (a) prior to the land entry: God's plan for a new Exodus and judgment in the wilderness (vss. 32–38); (b) in the land: the contrast of Israel's present defiled, and future purified, worship (vss. 39 [with its opening "And you, O house of Israel"]–42); (c) coda: Israel's future shame when realizing how undeserving it was of God's faithfulness (vss. 43–44).

Cutting athwart this sequential division are envelope structures formed by echoing passages (marking closures) of greater thematic and structural import. Thus the heart of B2 is embraced by the oath of vss. 33f. and its echo in vs. 41aβ. Its salient feature is correspondence in motifs with A—together with variation in terms and terseness and greater density. Vss. 35b–36 explicitly compare the future judgment in the "wilderness of the peoples" with that "in the wilderness of the land of Egypt" (A2g, where the verb *nšpṭ* does not occur). The verbal and ideational configuration of vss. 40–41aα closely parallels that of A4:

vss. 40–41a	*A4 (vs. 28)*
mountains, mountain heights	high hill
there (3 times)	there (4 times)
worship (*'bd*)	make sacrifices, offerings, libations
soothing savor	soothing savor
accept (*rṣh*)	vexation (*k's*)

Vs. 35a, "I will bring you into the wilderness of the peoples," corresponds to vs. 10b, "I brought them into the wilderness." Vss. 32–34 describe the people's intention to assimilate to the heathen and God's oath to be their king, lead them out of the lands, and gather them (to their land). This answers to God's oath to the ancestors in Egypt to be their God and lead them out of Egypt to the land he chose for them, and their refusal to give up Egyptian idolatry (A1). On the other hand, vss. 37f.—telling how God will make them pass under the rod, enter the obligation of the covenant, and purge them of rebels—relate tersely and in fresh terms the future equivalent of events in the wilderness told at length in A2, 3.

Vs. 41 closes the scene of the future with a succinct statement of the divine motive ("I will be sanctified in the sight of the nations"), echoing God's concern for his reputation referred to repeatedly in A's survey of the past. Two extended recognition clauses close the entire oracle, the first (vs. 42) recalling God's oath to give Israel a land, with which A's history started (vss. 6f.); the second (vs. 44) invoking for Israel's restoration the same motive as for its past survival, namely, YHWH's concern for his name. Due to these envelopes, formed by echoing passages, this oracle taken as a whole can be seen to display the "halving" pattern we have repeatedly noted, in which the second "half" of the oracle (B) concludes with iterations of the language and themes of the first (A).

It will be seen that B1 and B2 (vss. 30–44) draw two consequences from the historical survey of A: B1—the ground of God's refusal to respond to inquiry (vss. 30f.); B2—the paradigm of God's future dealings with Israel. As we noted, most critics consider only B1 original to this oracle. Whether the lengthy historical review of A is justified by the two verses of B1 has rightly been questioned (Eichrodt). Whether or not A requires B2, none can gainsay B2's dependence upon A (against Zimmerli's treatment of it as a wholly separate piece); this should be clear beyond cavil from the following parallel presentation of the narrative set forth in them:

past (A)	*future* (B2)
Since Israel would not obey YHWH's command to forsake Egypt's idols and accept him as	Thwarting Israel's intention to assimilate to the nations and worship idols, God will forcibly

God, he took them out into the wilderness, where he gave them distinctive, good laws to consecrate them to him.	be their king and take them out of exile into the wilderness of peoples, where he will lay upon them covenant obligations.
Since they defied him, he condemned them to death; only their children would enter the promised land.	He will enter into judgment with the wicked, condemning them to die, so that they shall not enter the land of Israel.
Once settled, the Israelites made offerings at *bamot*, which God disdained.	The entire people shall worship God at his holy mountain, where he will take pleasure in their offerings.
God refrained from destroying Israel in Egypt and the wilderness so as not to desecrate his name among the nations.	Thus he will assert his sanctity among his nations, and Israel will realize he has dealt with them for his name's sake.

Unlike the historical surveys of chs. 16 and 23, in which only past and future are depicted, this oracle addresses several verses to the present, including the citation of the people's intention to assimilate to the nations (vss. 30–32, 39). Though this introduces a complication in that the lesson of the past must serve two ends (present and future), it is just the present references that contain one theme that runs through the whole oracle—idolatrous cult offerings. The present generation continue the defiling worship of their fathers—who clung to Egypt's idols, were eventually punished with bad laws (notably the polluting sacrifice of firstborn), and practiced the contemptible cult of high-places. However, after a purge their restored remnant will in the future make acceptable offerings to God. The fact that this theme suffuses every part of the oracle argues for a unified composition.

The absence of references to God's laws, rules, and sabbaths in B would seem to indicate its separate provenience. Yet the divine laws are alluded to there; when the audience is said to be defiling itself "in the way of your fathers" (vs. 30), an echo is heard of the wilderness generation's adherence to "the laws of their fathers and their rules" (vs. 18). But the latter, in turn, are themselves but a travesty of God's laws, rules, and sabbaths. And the notice that the redeemed of the future would be brought into the obligation of the covenant serves as the future equivalent of the "laws, rules, and sabbaths" laid upon Israel in the past. So the issue of obedience to divine laws also connects past, present, and future.

Indeed, besides such thematic correspondences, there is an impressive congruence of terms and concepts (synonymous, antithetic) throughout this oracle (verse numbers in parentheses):

past	*present*	*future*
house of Israel (13)	27, 30	39, 40
each throw away the loathsome things before his eyes (7)	each go worship his idols (39)	all will worship me (40)
with idols (*glwlym*) do not defile yourselves (7)	31, cf. 30	defiled through misdeeds (43; note assonance of *'lylot* and *glwlym*)
loathsome things (7, 8)	30	
their heart goes after their idols (16)		
their eyes were after their fathers' idols (24) (cf. loathsome things of their eyes, 8)	after their loathsome things you go whoring (cf. Num 15:39, your heart . . . your eyes, after which you go whoring)	
(your) fathers (18, 24)	30	42
(your) offerings (gifts) (26)	31	39
deliver over (26)	31	
	shall I respond (*'drš*) (31)	I shall require (*'drš*) (40)
nations . . . lands (23)	32	peoples . . . lands (34, 41)
pour out wrath (8, 13, 21)		33, 34
to take out (of foreign land) (9, 10, 22)		34, 38, 41
scatter (23)		34, 41
bring into wilderness (10)		35
come/bring into the land (15, 28)		38, 42
obey me (8)		39
desecrate my name (9, 14, 22)		39
—in sight of nations (9, 14, 22)		I will be sanctified in the sight of the nations (41)
mountain height (40)		high hill (28)
there . . . there, etc. (28)		40
soothing savor (28)		41
I solemnly swore (about land) (6, 15, 28)		42
God acts for his name's sake (9, 14, 22)		44

Summing up the structure and design, the oracle falls into two main corresponding parts: A. a description of past, mainly cultic, guilt articulated in a series of three graduated episodes of like form capped by a fourth differently formulated (vss. 1–29); B2. a briefer description of the future as a new Exodus consummated by the acceptable worship of God on his holy hill (vss. 33–44). Connecting the two is B1, a short denunciation of the present "audience" (vss. 30–32) in which one circle is closed—the question of God's response to the elders' inquiry—and another is opened—the rectification of the present wrongdoing. Two matters are thus intertwined: onto the refusal to respond to inquiry is superimposed the cultic issue, whose past aspect serves to ground the refusal but then links up with present and future to provide a conspectus of the entire course of Israel's sacrificial worship.

The outcome of the first three stages of Israel's rebellion is a series of punitive decrees canceling the gifts made to Israel: exile instead of possession of the most desirable of lands; bad laws that deal out death instead of life-giving laws—in particular child sacrifice; and defilement of the cult in general. The effect of these decrees was immediately visible in the corrupt and vexing *bamot* cult. Before studying the elements of this construct, it is important to notice the intertwining of land, life-giving laws, and pure cult. At the outset Israel's election involved the gift of a choice land, subjection to vivifying laws and sanctifying sabbaths, and a worship of God enjoined by him. Balking at any one of these vitiated them all, as deprivation of one involved the rest as well. The indissoluble link among these three elements seems fundamental to the thought of this prophecy and may serve as an indicator of its central concern.

The structural complexity of the oracle is matched by the variety of its (often singular) themes, which do not lend themselves readily to integration. No other historical survey (chs. 16, 23) focuses so singlemindedly on cultic, to the exclusion of political, issues—defilement, idols, loathsome things, child (firstborn) sacrifice, (im)proper cult sites. No other survey makes so much of the promised land versus other lands (*ha'areṣ*—five times, *'admat yiśra^{e}el*—two times; *'ereṣ miṣrayim*—six times, *ha'araṣot*—six times, *'ereṣ m^{e}gurehem*—once). Here, for the first time, the main motive of history is God's concern for his name (only ch. 36:16ff. is comparable). Adjunct to this fresh motive is the extent of direct divine intervention in Israel's destiny: issuing bad laws, defiling Israel's cult, and forcing the people out of exile into a new covenant with him. Especially remarkable—when compared with the allegories of chs. 16 and 23—is the limited scope of the past surveyed in this oracle: from the Egyptian sojourn to the establishment of *bamot* in the land, and nothing later; even the exile is at bottom a pre-settlement event! One may well wonder whether all these features can be embraced in a single interpretation.

Yet one is not free to desist from trying, and a convenient starting point is the limited historical scope. The correspondence of past and future indicates that the boundaries of the retrospect have been determined by those of the prospect. As the prospect extends from the present exile to the future acceptable worship of the holy mountain, so the (antithetic) retrospect starts with the Egyptian sojourn—a kind of "exile"—and ends with the disdained *bamot* worship on every high hill. A peculiar passion pervades the two terminal stages, expressed in the repeated use of "there" (*šam*) that underscores their correspondence; we shall later inquire into the significance of this passion. The oracle as a whole shows how Israel, having aborted God's design, will be made to run the course again, this time agreeably to God's will. Only so much of the past as provides a key for understanding the stages of God's present and future dealings with Israel until their resettlement is surveyed. It follows that precisely the second part of the oracle, supposed by some to be secondary, determined the scope of the (putatively original) first part—otherwise inexplicably truncated.

The lesson of the past, according to this oracle, is that God's concern for his name determined Israel's destiny. God willed Israel to be his people; their refusal to comply resulted in calamity, but it was never final, so that God's name should not be desecrated. The present generation continues defiant, clinging to the polluted "way of its fathers" and thinking of assimilating to the nations. The primary stimulus of this oracle was evidently the saying imputed to the people, "We shall become like the nations . . ." Like ch. 18, this prophecy is a reaction to a subversive popular saying. Its core message is the assertion of God's sovereign control over Israel in spite of Israel's ceaseless rebellion. In the past God's will and ancient decrees shaped the fate of the people, and so they shall in the future; ultimately the disaffected will be doomed and God's design for Israel fulfilled.

The Pentateuchal traditions concerning the Exodus and the wilderness wanderings, especially as formulated in the priestly writings (see, e.g., comments to vss. 5–20), have been adapted to serve this message. Early Israel has been made over to mirror the prophet's conception of the present apostatizing generation. So the theme of rebellion during the wandering has been radically schematized and modernized. Even the late Ps 106 (which shows some striking contacts with Ezekiel) preserves in its litany of rebellions the nuances given in the Pentateuch; it distinguishes among lack of trust (vss. 7, 13, 24), defiance of delegated authority (vs. 16), apostasies (vss. 19, 36), and so forth; Ezekiel, however, generalizes all as violation of God's commandments. For the Pentateuch, the first divine commandment Israel defied concerned the manna (Exod 16); Ps 106 starts Israel's rebellions (lack of trust) at the Reed Sea (vs. 7); Ezekiel alone knows of a command to abandon idolatry already given in Egypt and straightway violated. Thus, for Ezekiel all phases of Israel's sin are alike and consist in defying God's laws and replacing them with man's. We may regard as modernizing Ezekiel's concern to meet a requirement of Deuteronomistic historiography: divine admonition to obedience, which precedes and justifies punishment (e.g., II Kings 17:13f.; Jer 7:13; 11:7, etc.)

Desecration of God's name (*nḥl šm YHWH*) acquires a new significance in our oracle. Heretofore it consisted in human violation of a divine norm, a show of contempt toward God (Amos 2:7; Lev 19:12; 20:3; Jer 34:16); this is its sense here, in vs. 39, and in 22:26. But in vss. 9, 14, and 22 a public act of God injurious to Israel can also desecrate his name (=bring him disrepute). God's self-interest, to which Moses appeals in Exod 32 (Deut 9) and Num 14, is given the rubric "for my name's same (*lm'n smy*)." While prayers often cite it as a motive for divine aid (Jer 14:7, 21; Ps 25:11; 79:9, etc.), here it is (for the first time? cf. Ps 106:8) a basis for interpreting past events and foretelling future events. Later it will provide solace (36:22f.), but here its menacing aspect is foremost. Thus, it explains the survival of rebellious Israel in the past and, implicitly, in the present. As in Egypt, so now, out of regard for his reputation, God postpones his reckoning with the wicked until he and they are "face to face" in the wilderness, no stranger's eye beholding. Accordingly, the historical Exodus acquires something of the character of an expulsion of a people redeemed against its will, a model and warning for Ezekiel's complacent audience, who (as he regards them) see themselves freed from subjection to God. Go worship your idols today, says God, but do not imagine your apostasy will forever go unpunished (vs. 39). All has happened, all will happen for the greater glory of my name; nothing you do can prevent the attainment of that glory.

This motive and its terminology are developed in 36:16–38—a post-586 B.C.E. restoration oracle based on the scheme of history first set out here. Here, notably, the exile is not counted among the threats to God's reputation—doubtless because prior to the disaster of 586 its full weight (and shame) were not yet felt; in 36:20ff., however, the exile is the prime cause of desecration of God's name. As to terminology, in 20:44 God's acting "for his name's sake" is given a fresh turn; whereas in vss. 9, 14, and 22 it meant forbearing to punish in order to avoid desecration; in vs. 44 it means to perform a marvel—the restoration of Israel—in order to gain glory. This positive nuance attaches to our phrase from the force of *wnqdsty bkm* "I will assert my sanctity through you" in vs. 41, which colors it. Only in 36:23 is a new, specific term for such affirmative action for the sake of God's name coined: *qiddeš šᵉmo* "sanctify (i.e., win glory for) his name"—a unique innovation, antithetic to *ḥillel/neḥal šᵉmo* as used in this oracle. Such a development of concepts original to this oracle in a piece clearly later than 586 suggests dating this oracle prior to the fall of Jerusalem (in line with its heading).

Ezekiel seems to have innovated the idea that even before Israel entered its land God had decreed both the exile and the sin that would justify it. Comparable is the condemnation of the Amorites in Gen 15:13–16: in Abraham's time the iniquity of the Amorites already justified predetermining them to expulsion after four hundred years—during which centuries their measure of iniquity would be filled, thus justifying the decree. More immediate antecedents of Ezekiel's idea are the conditional warnings of exile for breaching the rules of chastity in Lev 18:24–28; 20:23f.—where the fate of "the nations that I am expelling before you" is expressly compared—and for covenant breaking in Lev 26:33; Deut 4:25–27; 28:36, 64. Closer still is God's virtual prediction, based on his knowledge of Israel's nature, that eventually they would apostatize and suffer exile (Deut 31:16–18, 20f.). It is but a step from Moses' prediction of apostasy and exile to Ezekiel's portrayal of God's oath to exile Israel after ensuring they deserved it, already taken in the wilderness. Why did Ezekiel take that step? Perhaps because it was necessary, for saving God's sovereignty in the face of his people's collapse, to establish not only that the calamity was deserved but that God both foreknew and, indeed, predetermined it ages in advance. Not for a moment had events passed out of his firm control. So keened the author of Lam 2:17 after the fall of Jerusalem: "YHWH has done what he purposed, / Has carried out the decree / that he ordained long ago." This is neither hyperbole (Hillers, *Lamentations,* AB) nor allusion to prophetic forewarnings (traditional commentaries) but precisely Ezekiel's conception. Predetermined disaster is, of course, a basic feature of apocalyptic interpretation of history; apocalypses, however, forego theodicy, unlike Ezekiel, for whom justification of God's conduct and vindication of his honor is primary—and worth almost any cost in human freedom; cf. ch. 36.

Ezekiel's formulation of Israel's cultic offenses appears to derive from the law of centralized worship in Deut 12 (though in this oracle priestly terminology predominates). Deut 12 enjoins Israel from bringing their repertoire of offerings (vss. 6, 11; cf. the analogous listing in our vss. 28, 40) at every place they see (vs. 13; cf. "see" in our vs. 28), on high hills and under leafy trees (vs. 2; cf. our *'abot* [Lev 23:40] for Deuteronomy's *ra'anan*). Only where God approves may they come and bring them (vss. 5–7, 11, 14 with *šam*[*ma*] repeated as in our vs. 28; *ba*/*hebi šamma* comparable to our vs. 29). Worship at many sites is a heathen custom that Israel will be tempted to imitate (vss. 4, 29f.; cf. our vs. 32); they must not, for the gentiles typically burn their children for their gods, an abomination to YHWH (vs. 31; cf. our vs. 26).

Ezekiel's fusion of idolatry, *bamot,* and child sacrifice in such a way that each involves the others evidently reflects this Deuteronomic configuration—itself doubtless based on realities of the late Judahite monarchy. Ezekiel's model for the pure, acceptable worship of the future, described in 20:40f., is likewise the chosen site of the future whose worship is ordained in Deut 12. Characteristically—as in chs. 16 and 23—Ezekiel projects current sin back to the origins of the people. As he portrays it, throughout Israel's life in its land its cult was perverted, idolatrous, an affront to YHWH. His contemporaries only carry on the corrupt practices of their ancestors. We still have to consider why the topic of worship sites (improper and proper) climaxes both the retrospect and prospect of our prophecy.

The intention to apostatize is embodied, in vs. 32, in an echo of the defiant request for an earthly king in I Sam 8:20: "So that we too shall be like all the nations." That request was declared tantamount to apostasy (I Sam 8:8); just so its motive—to be "like the nations"—is here explicated by the equivalent "to serve wood and stone." (In Deut 4:28; 28:64 such inane worship is held over the people as a degrading punishment; here, in their degeneracy, they deliberately propose to embrace it.) That the story of the crisis of kingship in I Sam 8 underlies Ezekiel's formulation of the people's purpose is confirmed by God's angry retort, "By my life, I will be king over you!" (vs. 33). This unique self-assertion, with its sequel, in which God's might and fury—traditionally reserved for his enemies—are turned against Israel, once again reflects a crisis of authority. A tannaitic midrash on Num 15:37ff. (our oracle has several contacts with that passage, as we have seen) elaborates on this crisis dramatically:

> Why [in Num 15:41] is "I YHWH am your God" repeated after "I YHWH am your God who took you out of the land of Egypt to be your God"? To foreclose the possibility of Israel's saying, "God gave us commandments so that by obedience we might deserve to be rewarded; well, we will not obey and we forego the reward." This is what is reported of Ezekiel, when some elders came and sat before him. They said, "Ezekiel, if a man sold his slave, doesn't he lose jurisdiction over him?" Ezekiel replied, "He does." They said, "Well, then, since God has sold us to the nations, we've passed out of his jurisdiction!" He replied, "But what if the master sold his slave on condition that he be returned; has he then lost jurisdiction? 'That which you think shall never be, when you say, We shall be like the nations roundabout us [contamination with Deut 17:14], serving wood and stone. By my life, declares YHWH, with a strong hand and with an outstretched arm and with outpoured fury I will be king over you!' " A strong hand refers to pestilence (Exod 9:3), an outstretched arm refers to sword (I Chron 21:16), and outpoured fury refers to famine. After I inflict these three scourges on you one after the other, I will be king over you whether you like it or not. That is why "I YHWH am your God" is repeated (*Sifre Numbers* § 115).

This vehement assertion of the irrevocability of God's election is a high point of Ezekiel's theology. "Israel are bound to God with an eternal ironbound covenant . . . they will never be able to serve wood and stone . . . There is no reversing the fateful election, for it is not for the sake of Israel, but for the sake of God" (Kaufmann, *Religion,* p. 144). Medieval Jewish commentators appreciated its relevance: "This is a momentous utterance, a conclusive retort to all who would have us abandon our faith. For we see that of old God decreed—and made it known through Ezekiel—that once having entered into a covenant with him . . . we are not entitled to remove ourselves from his jurisdiction" (Ibn Caspi; cf. Kimḥi).

Can we determine what real situation is reflected in this oracle and who are the culprits being addressed? Medievals and moderns alike have had difficulty in crediting the prophet's accusation that his exile audience was "to this day" making idolatrous sacrifices, let alone offering up their children; Kimḥi, Cooke, and Zimmerli, for example, doubt it, the first two supposing that homelanders are meant. Yet vss. 39ff. ("Each of you go, worship his idols") evidently address a present audience—an audience of exiles, as is clear from the ending of vs. 41 ("when I take you out of the peoples"). Regrettably, there is no other evidence by which to control these assertions. Jer 44 attests that Judahite refugees in Egypt after the fall of Jerusalem practiced a cult of the queen of heaven; something similar may have occurred among Jehoiachin's exiles. However, considering the peculiar emphasis on proper and improper sites of worship (alongside the accusation of idolatry) and the iteration of the promise of land, it seems more likely to suppose that a *bama* had either been established or proposed by the exiles. Since, in concurrence with the view of Deuteronomy, Ezekiel does not distinguish between outright idolatry and disapproved modes of worshiping YHWH, he would have regarded this as a continuation of apostasy. Such a heathen practice, adopted as an accommodation to living on heathen soil, might well have stimulated this diatribe, with its singular stress on the indissoluble link between promised land, legitimate worship of YHWH at the proper site, and having YHWH as one's God. It would explain why both retrospect and prospect culminate in scenes of worship (proper and improper). It would also explain the coloration of Israel's rebellion as a preference for assimilating to, and living with, heathens. One might further speculate that this cultic issue came to a head on account of the conjunction of (a) the failure of Hananiah ben Azzur's prophecy of restoration, and (b) the arrival of Jeremiah's letter to the exiles urging them to reconcile themselves to a long exile and to seek YHWH and pray to him (Jer 29:12f.; see Introduction, Table of Dates, note 7). How better might this be carried out than by establishing a traditional altar to YHWH in Babylonia?

In 1888 M. Friedmann suggested that the elders planned to erect an altar to put a stop to uncontrolled private sacrifices, including child sacrifice; that, he submitted, was the issue about which they came to consult the prophet (*Ha-ṣiyyun, hu be'ur li-nvu'at yeḥezqel siman 20,* Vienna: n.p., 1888). Friedmann assumed that the object of the inquiry in vs. 1 might be inferred from the response (among others, M. Greenberg in *Oz le-David,* pp. 433–42, and Eichrodt followed him). Fohrer, employing the same logic, inferred that the inquiry was about making an idol of YHWH. Since the oracle does speak of idols and YHWH-worship and not of altars, there is some reason in Fohrer's otherwise bizarre notion that anyone would approach such a zealot as Ezekiel with this sort of a plan. But, in fact, any attempt to infer the object of inquiry from the oracle is misconceived; since God emphatically refuses to respond to the elders, we are not justified in looking for a response in the sequel (so Y. Hoffmann, *Beth Mikra* 63 [1975], 473ff., who supposes they came on some private errand). Properly speaking, everything after God's refusal (vs. 3b) is merely the ground for it. But instead of resting with the brief statement of vss. 30f.—in which case our passage would have resembled 14:1–3—the prophet spells out the ground in the detailed condemnatory retrospect, whose ulterior aim later proves to be to serve as an antitype for a new compulsory Exodus.

The elders' inquiry gave an occasion for the prophet to speak, but he spoke not to their inquiry but to the cause of God's refusal to answer it—an accommodation by the exiles to their surroundings that threatened the continuation of Israel as a people set apart for YHWH. What emerged in this polymorphous oracle was the "preliminary expectoration" (to use Kierkegaard's phrase) of the law of Israel's ineluctable destiny; in ch. 36 this law was to be restated in a sublime and awful prophecy of restoration.

Are there good grounds for questioning the date assigned to this oracle in its heading, or for limiting that date only to some part? We have argued for the coherence of the whole, structurally and thematically; it is denunciatory throughout—allusions to restoration being ancillary to rebuke. Do references to the exile and ingathering in vss. 33–44 indicate a date after 586 for the latter part of the oracle? Not unless the identical expressions in 11:16ff. indicate the same—and there is good reason to place that oracle well before 586 (see § VII, Structure and Themes, end). We have pointed to signs of the conceptual priority of our oracle to its complement in 36:16ff.; since the latter is definitely post-586, ours would have to be earlier—especially since it ignores the problem of the exile as an insult to God. It may be that this oracle comprises heterogeneous material, or that its composition proceeded in stages rather than from a single impulse; notwithstanding, no chronological or ideational considerations bar assigning any part or all of it to the time at or about the date given in the heading.